REVOLUTIONARY WORLDS

INDEPENDENCE, DECOLONIZATION, VIOLENCE AND WAR IN

INDONESIA

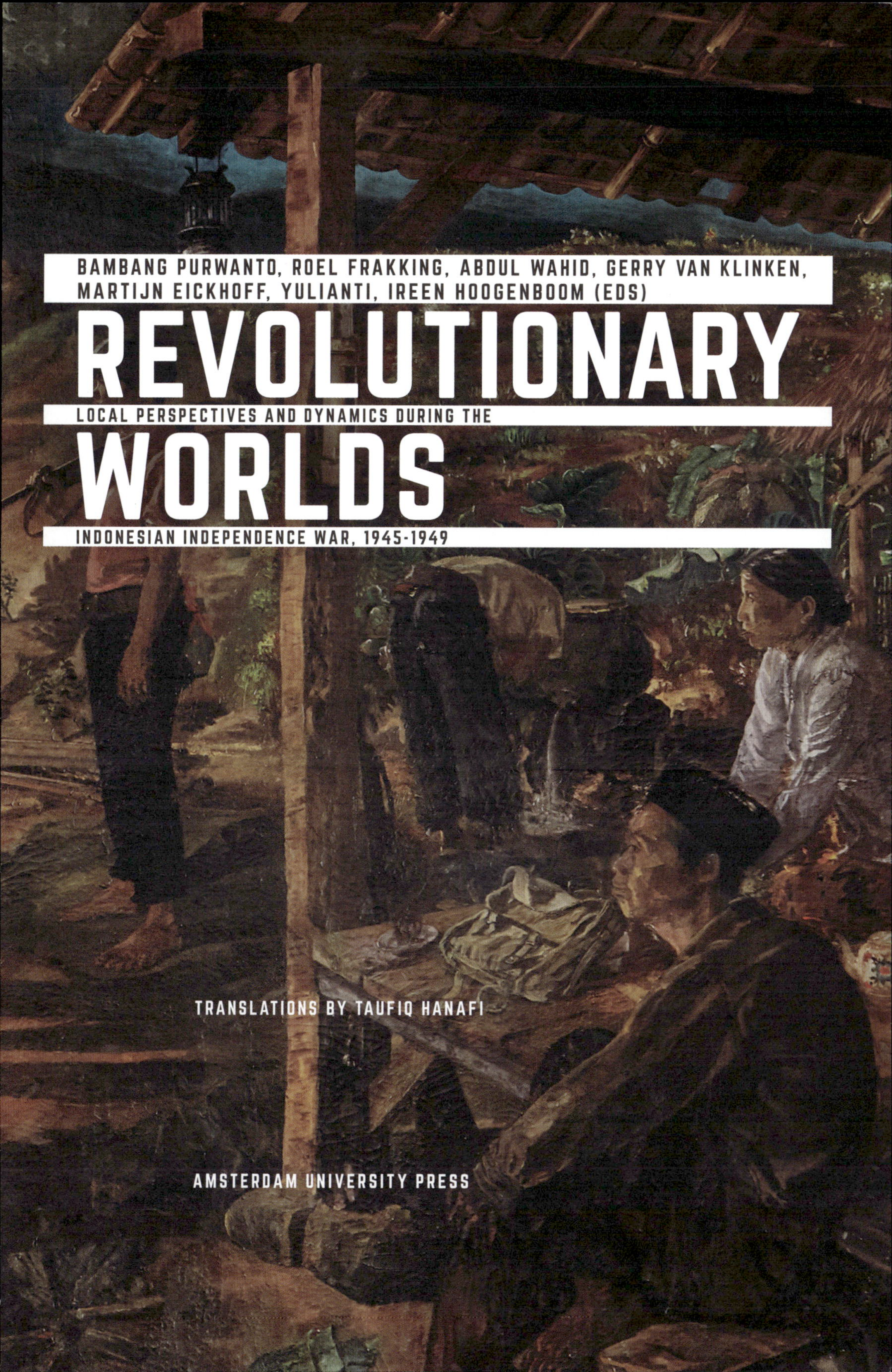

BAMBANG PURWANTO, ROEL FRAKKING, ABDUL WAHID, GERRY VAN KLINKEN, MARTIJN EICKHOFF, YULIANTI, IREEN HOOGENBOOM (EDS)

REVOLUTIONARY WORLDS

LOCAL PERSPECTIVES AND DYNAMICS DURING THE INDONESIAN INDEPENDENCE WAR, 1945-1949

TRANSLATIONS BY TAUFIQ HANAFI

AMSTERDAM UNIVERSITY PRESS

This publication is the result of the research programme *Independence, Decolonization, Violence and War in Indonesia, 1945-1950*. A complete overview of the programme's publications and the acknowledgements can be found at the back of this book.

The research programme was carried out by the Royal Netherlands Institute of Southeast Asian and Caribbean Studies (KITLV-KNAW), the Netherlands Institute for Military History (NIMH) and the NIOD Institute for War, Holocaust and Genocide Studies (NIOD-KNAW), in accordance with the guidelines on independent scholarly research set by the Royal Netherlands Academy of Arts and Sciences (KNAW). The programme was partly financed by the Dutch government.

The translations for this publication were made possible by an award from the Philippus Corts Fund (PCF), which is managed by the Members' Association of the Royal Netherlands Institute of Southeast Asian and Caribbean Studies (Koninklijk Instituut voor Taal-, Land- en Volkenkunde, KITLV). The PCF's mission is to preserve and make accessible original archival sources (in local languages and in Dutch) in Indonesia and the Netherlands relating to the shared history of these two territories in the period 1602 to 1949. Applying for a grant from PCF is open to students and researchers working in the Netherlands or to a joint Dutch and Indonesian team conducting and contributing scholarly research in collections in the Netherlands and/or Indonesia in line with the stated mission statement. For more information, see: https://www.verenigingkitlv.nl/philippus-corts-fonds/

Cover image: *Revolutionary graffiti in Yogyakarta 1948: 'Siapa toeroet N.I.C.A. pengchianat' (Who sides with NICA is a traitor) and Toedjoean Kita Merdeka' (Our goal is independence) 'Soekarno-Hatta YES, Van Mook-v.d. Plas NO'. Source: J. Zijlstra, Nationaal Archief, Dienst voor Legercontacten.*
Title page image: *'The guerrilla's are defining their tactics' (Gerilya Mengatur Siasat) 1964. Painting by S. Sudjojono, Presidential palace, Bogor.*

Cover design and interior: BVDT – Bart van den Tooren
Image editing: Harco Gijsbers, Ellen Klinkers, René Kok
Maps: Erik van Oosten
Index: Femke Jacobs

ISBN 978 94 6372 758 7
e-ISBN 978 90 4855 686 1
DOI 10.5117/ 9789463727587
NUR 680

Map 1

Overview Map of Indonesia
PACIFIC OCEAN
PALAU
PAPUA
THE PHILIPPINES
LEYTE
HALMAHERA
MOLUCCAS
SERAM
AMBON
BANDA
KEI ISLANDS
ARU ISLANDS
TANIMBAR ISLANDS
ARAFURA SEA
BABAR
TIMOR-LESTE
TIMOR
TIMOR SEA
Darwin
AUSTRALIA
Manado
MOLUCCA SEA
BANDA SEA
CELEBES SEA
SULAWESI
Kendari
Makassar
MAKASSAR STRAIT
FLORES SEA
FLORES
SUMBA
SUMBAWA
LOMBOK
Lombok Strait
BALI
P. KAGEAN
P. SAPUDI
MADURA
Surabaya
Yogyakarta
JAVA
Jakarta
JAVA SEA
INDIAN OCEAN
0 250 500 km
SOUTH CHINA SEA
Cam Ranh Bay
VIETNAM
CAMBODIA
BRUNEI
MALAYSIA
(SARAWAK)
KALIMANTAN
Balikpapan
Banjarmasin
Pontianak
BELITUNG
BANGKA
Palembang
Singapore
MALAYSIA
SUMATRA
Padang
Medan
Banda Aceh
SIMEULUE
NIAS
BATU ISLANDS
MENTAWAI ISLANDS
Cartography: Erik van Oosten - NIMH

Map 2

Dutch-occupied area on Java
J A V A   S E A
I N D I A N   O C E A N
S U M A T R A
SUNDA STRAIT
KRAKATAU
BAWEAN
M A D U R A
MADURA STRAIT
BALI
Tangerang
B A N T E N
JAKARTA
Bogor
Balongsari (Rawagede)
K R A W A N G
Bandung
P R I A N G A N
Linggarjati
Tasikmalaya
Cirebon
Tegal
Purwokerto
Cilacap
B A N Y U M A S
Pekalongan
Purworejo
K E D U
B A G E L E N
Magelang
Semarang
Jepara
Ambarawa
Yogyakarta
Klaten
Surakarta (Solo)
Rembang
Ngawi
Madiun
K E D I R I
Kediri
Surabaya
Bangkalan
Malang
Probolinggo
Pamekasan
Sumenep
Banyuwangi
0 50 100 km
Legend
Dutch-occupied area on Java before Operation Product
Dutch-occupied area on Java during Operation Product North Madura followed in November 1947
Dutch-occupied area on Java during Operation Kraai
Demarcation line 1947
Cartography: Erik van Oosten - NIMH

Map 3

West Java
JAVA SEA
INDIAN OCEAN
SUNDA STRAIT
KRAKATAU
BANTEN
KRAWANG
PRIANGAN
SALEM
BANYUMAS
NUSA KAMBANGAN
P. Kapal (Onrust Island)
JAKARTA
Tangerang
Cililitan
Balongsari (Rawagede)
Cikampek
Bogor
Puraseda
Ciawi
Sukabumi
Malebe
Ciharashas
Cimahi
Bandung
Baruhtunggul
Garut
Citabu
Tasikmalaya
Linggarjati
Kuningan
Cirebon
Tegal
Balapulang
Purwokerto
Kalibagor
Cilacap
0
25
50 km
Cartography: Erik van Oosten - NIMH

Map 4

Central Java
JAVA SEA
INDIAN OCEAN
Tuban
Rembang
Jepara
Demak
Dempet
Gubug
Semarang
Pekalongan
Tegal
Balapulang
Cirebon
Linggarjati
Kuningan
Citabu
Tasikmalaya
SALEM
BANYUMAS
NUSA KAMBANGAN
Cilacap
Purwokerto
Kalibagor
Karanganyar
Kebumen
BAGELEN
Purworejo
Bogowonto
Magelang
Progo
KEDU
Ambarawa
Banyubiru
Salatiga
M.MERAPI
Klaten
Yogyakarta
Surakarta
(Solo)
M.LAWU
Solo
Ngawi
Madiun
M.WILIS
Kediri
KEDIRI
Jombang
Brantas
0
25
50 km
Cartography: Erik van Oosten - NIMH

Map 5

East Java
JAVA SEA
INDIAN OCEAN
MADURA STRAIT
MADURA
BALI
KEDIRI
Semarang
Jepara
Demak
Dempet
Gubug
Rembang
Tuban
Ambarawa
Banyubiru
Salatiga
Surakarta
(Solo)
Klaten
Yogyakarta
M.MERAPI
M.LAWU
Ngawi
Madiun
M.WILIS
Kediri
Jombang
Mojokerto
Cerme
Gresik
Surabaya
Bangkalan
Pamekasan
Sumenep
Sidoarjo
Trawas
M.ARJUNO
Pakisaji
Malang
M.BROMO
Probolinggo
Lengang
Kadangjati
Kulon
Jember
Sempusari
Bondowoso
Pasir Putih
Banyuwangi
Solo
Brantas
0
25
50 km
Cartography: Erik van Oosten - NIMH

Map 6

Sumatra
BAY OF BENGAL
SOUTH
CHINA
SEA
PENANG
MALAYSIA
Banda Aceh
ACEH
Meulaboh
Medan
Tebing Tinggi
Lake Toba
Melaka
(Malacca)
MALACCA STRAIT
SIMEULUE
Singkel
Tapos
Barus
Rantau Prapat
Sibolga
SINGAPORE
SUMATRA
RIAU
ISLANDS
NIAS
Daludal
Natal
Air Bangis
Bonjol
BATU
ISLANDS
Bukittinggi
Payakumbuh
Padang
Panjang
Rengat
Reteh
Pariaman
Padang
SINGKEP
MENTAWAI
ISLANDS
Jambi
Muntok
Pangkal Pinang
BANGKA
Bangkakota
PAGAI
ISLANDS
INDIAN
Palembang
BELITUNG
Bengkulu
JAVA SEA
OCEAN
ENGGANO
JAKARTA
JAVA
0
100
200 km
Cartography: Erik van Oosten - NIMH

Map 7

South Sulawesi
LUWU
Barupu
Mamasa
TORAJA
Rante Pao
Palopo
Sepang
Makale
MASENREMPULU
LUWU
BINUANG
Balanipa
PINRANG
Majene
BAY OF MANDAR
Enrekang
SAWITTO
Pinrang
Rappang
Suppa
WAJO
Pare-Pare
BAY OF BONI
SIDENRENG
Sengkang
JAVA SEA
Pampanua
SOPPENG
Pasempa
Watampone (Bone)
BONE
TANETTE
Mara
Maros
MAKASSAR
Balangnipa
Sinjai
GOA
Limbung
Polombangkeng
Takalar
Bonthain
Bulukumba
Turatea
Jeneponto
Selayar
0
25
50 km
Cartography: Erik van Oosten - NIMH

Map 8

Bali
BALI SEA
Buleleng
Bungkulan
Singaraja
Jagaraga
BULELENG
G. SILANGJANA
G. BRATAN
G. BATUR
G. LESONG
BT. POHEN
G. ABANG
JEMBRANA
KARANG
BT. BATUKAU
BANGLI
G. AGUNG
TABANAN
ASEM
Blimbing
Karangasem
KLUNG-
KUNG
Klungkung
MENGWI
GIANYAR
LOMBOK STRAIT
BADUNG STRAIT
INDIAN
Sanur
Denpasar
NUSA PENIDA
BADUNG
OCEAN
0
10
20 km
Cartography: Erik van Oosten - NIMH

Content

I.

INTRODUCTION

FREEDOM is the GLORY OF ANY NATION.
INDONESIA for INDONESIANS!

1.

Revolutionary worlds: an introduction

Roel Frakking and Abdul Wahid[1]

The idea behind the book

This book is firmly grounded in the belief that much of what is assumed to constitute the Indonesian Revolution (1945-1949) is actually not understood all too well. There is still much ground to explore and explain. With that in mind, this edited volume begins with the question: 'What was the revolution like as a lived experience?' This is a rather broad and open approach, but that was exactly the point. First and foremost, the book breaks the revolution up into separate regions, which are studied by different researchers. Eight maps at the front illustrate Indonesia's sheer geographical complexity. This allowed them to devise their own research question along with primary and secondary research questions that, taken together, provide

Indonesian freedom slogan painted on a colonial-era office in Malang, early 1947. Similar slogans adorned many buildings in major towns and cities and were an integral part of the revolutionary landscape. *Source: Cas Oorthuys, Nederlands Fotomuseum.*

answers to the book's central question. This book's regional approach reflects the need to dismantle the idea that there was one revolution that looked the same everywhere and elicited similar responses from Dutch and Indonesian actors alike. Our approach reflects the multitude of vantage points and perspectives as well as – equally important – a coming together in dialogue of two historiographies that have remained separate for too long.

A cursory glance at Dutch historiography as it stands today proves this point. Most recently, scholars have homed in on the particularly violent nature of decolonization and its so-called 'extreme' properties. On the one hand, this has been occasioned by the demands put forth by survivors and their relatives that former colonial empires recognize and offer reparations for the horrible abuses committed.[2] On the other, this 'violent turn' was the logical endpoint of a question everyone knew the answer to but whose answer was difficult to put on paper, partially due to the staying power of veterans' narratives. This question was, quite simply: How pervasive and systematic was Dutch violence during the Indonesian War of Independence in particular and during centuries of the Dutch colonial occupation of Indonesia in general? The persistence of survivors and their relatives dovetailed with historians and cultural institutions who, in varying degrees, were finally ready to address their nation's sordid past – or at least bring it out into the open.[3]

The larger historical project (funded by the Dutch government) of which this book is a part is entitled *Independence, Decolonization, Violence and War in Indonesia 1945-1950*. It focused on precisely the problem of Dutch military violence during the last major colonial war the nation conducted – in Indonesia. In a series of substantial volumes totalling thousands of pages, it concluded that Dutch violence in that war had been both extreme systematic and structural. The Dutch cabinet immediately offered a 'deep apology to the people of Indonesia today (reinforcing earlier apologies including one by the king in 2020)'.[4] Unfortunately, although this 'violent turn' in Dutch colonial studies has finally led to the Netherlands owning up to the violence, it has again resulted in a neglect of the experiences of those who stood at the receiving end of colonial violence who sought to escape or combat it on their own terms. The present volume is one of a small number within that larger project to seek engagement with Indonesian historians. How the resulting dialogue progressed – haltingly at first, but in the end in an inspiring manner – is discussed at some length below. Here, we would simply note that the participating Dutch and Indonesian historians came to the project with their own background of a dominant national interpretive tradition.

Indonesian historiography, in turn, has had its own blind spots. For a long time, it was the state that determined what historical inquiries were allowed and what was frowned upon.[5] Whereas Dutch historians tended to focus on violence, Indonesian historians traditionally opted to present the revolution as something the entire nation stood behind monolithically, fighting for the Republic of Indonesia that Sukarno and Mohammad Hatta had famously proclaimed independent on 17 August 1945. The *periode perang kemerdekaan* (the independence period) or the *periode revolusi kemerdekaan* (the revolutionary war period) thus became a sacred period, a narrative very much pushed by the successive New Order governments under President Suharto. During this period, Indonesians – regardless of their ethnicity, class or political interests – united to defend their independence. Nationalistic and military themes became dominant, whereby the featuring of 'big men', such as Sukarno or Sudirman, and heroic stances – the Battle for Surabaya or the 'Convoy War' in Sukabumi come to mind – became the norm. At the same time, other stories were minimized – stories about regional differences, internal disputes and violence, the contributions of left-wing politicians and revolutionaries and the daily lives of ordinary people. They were branded as unnecessary and edged out of the frame. Either way, the Indonesian Revolution is often seen from distinct national perspectives.

Revolutionary Worlds aims to breach the boundaries between the Indonesian and Dutch historiographies. In doing so, it approaches literature *and* historical trends critically. It must be noted, however, that the book does not present a *unified* Indonesian-Dutch history, instead it critically engages and furthers the existing literature on various levels. On one level, this collection decentralizes the narrative in order to reduce Java's historical preponderance in general and the influence of the Republican government in Yogyakarta specifically. On another level, the collection breaks with teleological traditions. Too often, historical analyses pretend that the Republican interpretation of *merdeka* was shared across Indonesia's vast archipelago and that local revolutionaries acted in total accordance. Although this may have been unintentional on the part of the historians – for example due to a strong focus they may have put on Dutch violence (extreme or otherwise) that analytically displaced Indonesian experiences (depicting Indonesian as hapless victims of faceless opponents) or due to an approach that overemphasized the extent of unity among the Indonesians – the chapters in this volume seek to dispel this notion.[6]

Put differently, this edited volume aims to reinsert the complexity in an otherwise oversimplified interpretation of the 1945-1949 period that holds sway both in the Netherlands and Indonesia: the idea of one conflict wherein the Republic and its armed forces worked to keep the returning Dutch from reclaiming their erstwhile colony in Southeast Asia. We want to show that there were other insurgent groups, fighters and polities besides the Republic, their Dutch opponents and their respective armed forces that were actively involved in the conflict, and that the Indonesian Revolution was a highly multifaceted event constricted and shaped by actors representing different political, religious, social and regional entities. They displayed these differences sometimes through the medium of fire and sword, sometimes through words alone, sometimes parallel to the larger Dutch-Indonesian conflict, and sometimes as an integral part of it.

Taken together, these developments and the changes they wrought in Indonesia's social, political and economic landscapes can best be studied and dissected at the local and regional levels, which reveal the different perspectives of local communities and alternative social movements – all with their own ideals, motives and fears – acting in contexts and situations wherein strategic and sometimes existential choices were unavoidable and highly decisive. *Revolutionary Worlds*, then, brings out the plurality of experiences that spawned multiple revolutions. With this point of view firmly established, the concept of 'revolutionary worlds' attains greater meaning: it refers to the multivariance of experiential worlds, inhabited and animated by collectives and individuals chasing local and regional interests, seeking organization or disorganization to channel these interests in an attempt to mould their own futures in the context of rapid, major changes. To reveal the layered histories in question, including their intricate dynamics and their mutual dependencies, each of the chapters in this volume focuses on a specific region of the vast Indonesian archipelago. Without seeking exhaustive treatment of the revolution in each region or executing one-on-one comparisons, the chapters reveal – individually and taken together – elements of the revolutionary worlds situated in Bali, North and West Sumatra, South Sulawesi, and West, Central and East Java. Unfortunately, and this points to a weakness of this edited volume, we do not cover all Indonesian regions and two important ones, Kalimantan and Papua, are left out. The intention was there to include them, however due to practical reasons we did not succeed.

Naturally, there are other, ground-breaking scholars who have preceded us. Already in 1986, *Regional Dynamics of the Indonesian Revolution*, edited by Audrey Kahin, compiled studies on various regions during the revolution. It too sought to decentralize and thereby reduce Java's influence. Conceptually, however, this collection differs from *Revolutionary Worlds*, most notably in its treatment of each region in isolation and in the way the Republic's brand of revolution appeared to unfold rather similarly in each case. One critical historian later called this approach the 'franchise model'.[7] This edited volume, by contrast, breaks away from analyses that look back on the Indonesian war against re-colonization with the fixed outcome – the transfer of sovereignty in December 1949 – in mind.[8]

The notion, furthermore, that various Indonesian factions competed with each other (often violently) over the proper way to defend Indonesia's independence against the Dutch and over the political endpoint they had in mind – a unitary state, a federation, a communist Indonesia or an Islamic Indonesia – has also been argued elsewhere. One early example was Henri Alers, who already in 1956 addressed the notion that the independence movement was from its very inception deeply divided. This rift was caused by the fact that an older generation of nationalists – together with much of the traditional feudal aristocracy – favoured diplomacy over outright warfare. They faced off with younger firebrands (ex post facto dubbed the 'Generation of 1945') who would stop at nothing to formalize independence sooner rather than later.[9] A select number of Indonesian scholars have also addressed similar themes from the 1980s onwards.[10]

The title

Regardless, this volume breaks new ground by introducing the concept of 'revolutionary worlds'. The title illustrates the notion that when Hatta and Sukarno declared Indonesia's independence on 17 August 1945, even if the Republic of Indonesia's national anthem was being sung across Indonesia, the exact course of the revolution and development – the very notion of 'being' independent – was still largely up in the air. The idea of 'revolutionary worlds' recognizes this fact; it is a testimony to the various experiential worlds constructed by the people in Indonesia – Indonesians, Indians, Chinese, Dutch, etc. – while furthering or countering the revolution, either collectively or as individuals. These worlds existed both locally and nationally, were organized or disorganized, but were always populated by a myriad of groups and individuals.

The concept of 'revolutionary worlds' has various sub-concepts and themes attached to it. For one, the revolution must be understood as a clear break with pre-Second World War Indonesia. This volume has sought to capture that break by understanding the revolution as a time of 'people's sovereignty'. All layers of society, from *raja* to *tani*, understood that massive change was underway – a change that had been in the making for half a century at least – and that it was now possible to reify dreams of self-determination and, on a more personal level, advancement in various forms.[11] Despite the project's emphasis on revolutionary Indonesia, *Revolutionary Worlds* teases out continuations as well in order to recognize the long trajectories of violence, suppression, expropriation, expulsion and discrimination that the Dutch systematically subjected Indonesians in all walks of life to, linking the post-1945 situation to pre-revolution lives. Such a longer analytical perspective also allows the collected chapters to underline that the Indonesian revolutions did not just 'happen', thereby giving the lie to the assertion still made in some quarters that the Japanese occupation was what instilled political consciousness in Indonesians. Rather, our book aims to show how the need for – and ideas about – independence had been growing and thriving in local, regional and global contexts for decades.[12] Seen from this vantage point, the violence unleashed during the revolutionary period between 1945 and 1950 was not singular or 'excessive' at all. The peasants' revolt in Banten, West Java (1888), the Aceh War (1873-1913), or the communist uprisings (1926-1927), for example: all point to a continuum of resistance as well as violent Dutch repression – a continuum that this book illuminates.

Another common analytical point of departure is that revolution implies the overthrow of an unjust system or government or authority. In Indonesia's case, the Dutch government had collapsed as a result of the invasion by Japan, which proceeded to systematically dismantle the Dutch Colonial Civil Administration (*Binnenlands Bestuur*). The Japanese replaced it with their own naval and military authorities who, in turn, retained the dual governing system with its Indonesian rulers and administrators largely in place. The latter continued to govern after the Japanese surrender on 15 August 1945 and the proclamation of independence two days later. The returning Dutch attempted to destroy Indonesian centres of authority wherever they found them. Many studies in this volume therefore feature the violent competition between Indonesian-Republican and Dutch spheres of influence. The chapters reveal the seemingly endless local dynamic of state formation and collapse that made it difficult for locals to see the distinction between insurgent and counterinsurgent, just as Dutch and Indonesian forces could no longer differentiate between combatant and non-combatant.[13]

As a result of the local revolutionary and counter-revolutionary dynamics, the violence unleashed by Dutch and Indonesian civil and military authorities against local populations, whose support both Dutch and Indonesian authorities relied upon, became 'law-establishing' violence. Its goal was to communicate who was in charge and which party demanded fealty, compliance and support. Over time, it was argued, such violence would engender more robust forms of control from which proper governance could follow.[14] As the contestation between spheres of influence failed to result in a decisive triumph for one side or the other, and as borders between such spheres remained porous at best, both spatially and temporally, the violence that was meted out was immediately enormously intense and remained that way throughout the revolutionary years. As Indonesian and Dutch troops demanded cooperation from the local people, the violence they used to enforce it became more and more pervasive, entering the very homes of people in order to control their bodies.[15] A corollary to this nexus of violence and control was that it pushed communities exposed to it into various directions. Where Indonesian troops or paramilitaries held sway, communities tended to support them. Conversely, where Dutch authorities posed a credible threat, people provided them with intelligence and cooperation. Communities, in other words, lived in a state of liminality while at the same time seeking safety, security and access to resources such as food and shelter.[16] Most often, Indonesians and others ended up supporting more than one party.

This duality of allegiance can also be detected in the staunchly anti-Dutch, anti-colonialism camp. Although other works have pointed this out in passing, *Revolutionary Worlds* shows how, on many occasions, the revolution had less to do with Dutch activities and more with a systematic reconfiguration of specifically local power structures and relations, demeanours, habits, comportment and – above all – political futures, even beyond the narrower confines of revolutionary warfare. The importance of Dutch actions was relegated to the background. The attention given to Dutch activity was superseded by internal Indonesian discussions and actions focused on what being independent meant. *Revolutionary Worlds* gives countenances to these negotiations and inward dynamics to reveal tensions between the different interpretations given to how to achieve independence. The resultant tensions reared themselves in various ways – mentally, but also spatially and temporally.

There were many instances in which Republican-dominated statecraft emanating from Yogyakarta (Central Java) where the Republican government resided, clashed with different, local-regional interpretations of nationalism, statecraft and representation. Such tensions often involved the young firebrands of the Generation of '45, the often-militarized youths who, in their wish to die rather than lose independence, quarrelled with the older, cautious nationalists who advocated a mix of *diplomasi* and confrontation with the Dutch. Furthermore, the Republic and its official army, the Tentara Nasional Indonesia (TNI), constantly had to contend with other armed organizations that had different endgames in mind. The Negara Islam Indonesia (NII, Indonesian Islamic State), for example, not only combatted Dutch forces; they were equally keen to fight the TNI over ownership of the revolution. At yet another level, women grabbed the chance that the revolution offered them: their participation ensured that they could renegotiate age-old societal conventions regarding their conduct both at home and in public.

For heuristic purposes, the book is divided into two sections. Each highlights the term *Revolutionary Worlds* in a slightly different way – one emphasizing its overwhelmingly 'revolutionary' character, the other its manifold 'worlds' character. The first section is therefore entitled simply *Revolutionary...* The chapters in this section bring into focus the *revolutionary* energy that fired up many parts of the population in Indonesia. They underscore the assertion made above – that the revolutionary movement was by no means monolithic – by demonstrating just how widespread its radical spirit of renewal was. Revolution inflamed the hearts of a great many people in all walks of life. This section of the book offers a view that may come as more of a surprise to Dutch readers than to Indonesians. Its youthful, hopeful energy is worlds away from the colonial assertion that Indonesians wanted 'tranquillity and order', that colonial business-as-usual was the best of all possible worlds, and that the *pemuda* were mainly a security problem. It is also worlds away from the image of Indonesians as passive victims of Dutch military violence. Indeed, the Dutch military are not even that central to many of these chapters. Where counter-revolutionary violence does occur in them, it is seen in this section to be particularly ill-judged and illegitimate. But Indonesian readers, too, will find much in this section to challenge what they thought they knew about their revolution. The whole idea of revolution is itself being rediscovered by Indonesians who yearn to consult a bottom-up history of that momentous event.

The second section is entitled ... *Worlds*, as a reminder that there were many revolutionary worlds. Here the focus is on groups and places within Indonesia where the revolutionary energy, which inevitably reached them too, in some way looked problematic. It takes a particular interest in various minorities, some of whom saw the revolution in a difficult light. These chapters make it clear why they saw it that way – it was by no means always a case of dyed-in-the-wool colonial attitudes – and how attempts to relieve their anxieties were sometimes successfully accommodated within the Republic. While we would not want to say that this section contains more surprises for Indonesian readers than for Dutch ones, it is undoubtedly true that negative revolutionary experiences among minorities have until recently been a taboo subject within Indonesian historiography. Their discovery by young historians today is challenging and revitalizing history departments around Indonesia in ways we explore further below.

Revolutionary...

The great Indonesian historian Sartono Kartodirdjo suggested some time ago already that the focus of Indonesian history-writing should be society and not any particular institution within it such as the military or any big name such as the president. As a structural functionalist, Sartono wished to map it all out rather than focus only on one group. A revolution, too, is a sociological phenomenon involving many different groups. He wrote about this in the 1980s, at the height of the militaristic New Order.[17] The present book focuses on society. It is thus clearly not an innovation. Sartono (1921-2007) was a professor at Universitas Gadjah Mada (UGM). Avoiding the 'big name' approach to history-writing is the UGM approach. But narrowly nationalistic and frankly anti-intellectual impulses arising from the historical controversies immediately following the *Reformasi*[18] have ironically made this approach less self-evidently commendable than it once was. Research into the revolutionary period, so important to understanding Indonesia today, has been dominated by a state narrative, to the detriment of an academic approach. It is now necessary to revive Sartono's insight. One of the spin-offs of the present volume is another book, an anthology produced by UGM consisting of historical articles on the revolution in the spirit of Sartono that includes chapters on everything from vagrants (*gelandangan*) to women.[19]

There are those who fear that broadening the scope of writing on the revolution to include such disparate social groups will lead to a revisionist weakening of the national narrative. To them, the UGM historians among us say: 'No, that is not where we want to go'. One recent example of where they do want to go is a volume compiled by UGM historian Sri Margana and his colleagues on the revolutionary attack on Dutch-held Yogyakarta on 1 March 1949. It showed that this spectacular event could not have succeeded without the co-operation of many groups within society. Yet for a long time the government insisted it was all accomplished by Suharto, then a young officer who later became president.[20] Indeed, this insistence on individual heroism is part of a pattern. The revolution is today widely considered a time when everyone tries to get one of their own recognized as a national hero – someone from their region or their institution – because this is when Indonesia was formed. There is a veritable cottage industry of heroic narratives. A healthier approach in the present volume is demonstrated by the chapters by Galuh Ambar Sasi and Farabi Fakih. They show that this was the period when Indonesia *strengthened* its identity as a nation precisely by working together as a society.

Galuh Ambar Sasi's contribution to this book highlights the role of women in the Indonesian revolution centred in Yogyakarta. Her vivacious insights show that their meaning-making activities in this city in the heartland of the revolution went far beyond soup kitchens or even conference organizing. They were intellectually and culturally transformative, emancipatory personal experiences that were never inferior to those of men. Galuh's contribution is vital in showing why women's roles should be part of the standard histories.

Highlighting another facet of Yogyakarta, Farabi Fakih employs a rich examination of diaries, novels and films to describe the atmosphere in the revolutionary capital. Beyond being uniformly heroic, he shows how Yogyakarta life proved more ambivalent than commonly assumed. The specific sticking point is the identity of the ubiquitous pemuda, who were represented by the Dutch as barbaric and violent and by the educated Republican elites as the future-oriented moral backbone of the nation, but who were hardly able to represent themselves. Some subalterns, especially artists, criticized the 'life of luxury' lived by Republican elites in Yogyakarta.

Adopting a meta view of the archipelago, Yuanda Zara's pioneering study foregrounds how a Republican propaganda machine depicted the enemy as barbaric, arrogant and non-human through ad hoc posters and caricatures. Across this monstrous 'Other' stood Indonesians, who were either humiliated or, in the case of freedom fighters, cast as the agile and victorious hero. This iconography created as well as reflected negative images of the Dutch within the population. Its portrayal of the manipulative and cruel colonial administration and military remains salient today.

Martijn Eickhoff's chapter offers a view of the revolution from the Central Javanese harbour city of Semarang. By contrasting Indonesian accounts of the contested Dutch reoccupation of Semarang with Dutch ones, the chapter brings into sharp relief the problems the Dutch faced in terms of their legitimacy. In order to gain control over the administrative apparatus (for the sake of security and economic welfare), the Dutch had to trust a large body of Indonesian officialdom. The refusal on the part of hawkish Dutch officeholders (here represented by garrison commander Van Langen) to dispense such trust – and, indeed, the underestimation by all Dutch personnel of the depth of revolutionary commitment among ordinary Indonesians – was to cost them their entire project.

In the chapter 'East Java, 1949: The revolution that shaped Indonesia', Gerry van Klinken and Maarten van der Bent speak directly to the internal tensions within the thrust and direction of the revolution in 1949. By way of Commander Sungkono, this chapter traces the popular side to the revolution to show that the militancy of the 'red' revolutionaries of East Java resulted in Indonesia ultimately becoming a non-ethnic, centralized, democratic and sovereign republic. It was through their influences – more so than the Westernized moderate 'green' diplomats nominally in charge of the national revolution – that another path to independence was effectively blocked, one favouring an ethnicized, federal, aristocratically led nation within a Dutch sphere of influence.

Any military campaign is dependent on logistics. Between 1945 and 1950, both Republican and Dutch forces faced logistical problems. More specifically, as Julianto Ibrahim demonstrates for Central Java, shortages revolved mainly around access to food and weapons. Both Dutch and Indonesian forces tried to enforce blockades in order to control what and where food and weapons were available but also what access their opponents had to such provisions. Dutch restrictions on food circulation and availability harmed civilians and can be considered war crimes. Even if many considered controlling food availability a revolutionary activity, both Indonesian and Dutch forces engaged in criminal activities to seize weapons, provisions and other necessities. Participation in revolution, in other words, involved costs that devolved upon the local communities. Access to food was one element closed off at various times and in different places across the Indonesian archipelago .

In Bali, the region that Anne-Lot Hoek writes about, Dutch military action aimed to block political alternatives to the federal programme that would make Bali part of the State of East Indonesia (Negara Indonesia Timur, NIT) after 1945. The chapter argues that historians have often wrongfully disaggregated Dutch violence on the island from Dutch neo-colonial political designs for the incorporation of Bali into the federal state. The military suppression of a Republican resistance unit in Bali, the Dutch military campaign in South Sulawesi, and the attack on Palembang all serve to illustrate that the objective was as much to protect Dutch 'clients' as to eliminate anti-Dutch enemies.

Whether featuring men or women, subaltern youths or educated urbanites, soldiers or civil servants, the chapters in this section bring to light the sheer variety of ways in which the revolution energized people and made them feel ready to make the ultimate sacrifice. Those tasked with counter-revolutionary activities had to resort to repressive violence of a kind that was to win few friends among such a mobilized population.

… Worlds

A revolution always has a dark side. It is not all glory; it divides and pits communities against each other. The revolutionary experience of various ethnic and religious minorities, who, as suspects often too closely tied to the colonial system, were treated violently in many places, is a case in point. The topic is important because it touches on identities, shifting loyalties and international orientations that would otherwise rarely be considered.

We already knew a fair amount about the revolutionary experiences of the ethnic Chinese in Indonesia. Since the fall of Suharto, historical studies on the ethnic Chinese have flourished within Indonesia, including – or perhaps especially – concerning their experiences during this revolutionary period. Ravando Lie and Didi Kwartanada have written numerous papers about the ethnic Chinese during the revolution, and they have inspired other young historians in Yogyakarta and beyond, for example in Malang. The present volume adds to our knowledge with no less than three original chapters. We learn that as relatively recent migrants at the time, the ethnic Chinese were not considered – and often did not consider themselves – citizens of the Indonesian nation. The politically interested among them were instead engrossed by the revolution taking place at that very time in China. Chinese consulates all over the archipelago issued instructions on how to respond to the Indonesian revolution. In many places, the Republic of Indonesia did not really protect them from the local violence they faced. Aceh was an exception, and that was because the Republic there was relatively secure from Dutch military intervention. Other minorities have until now been altogether forgotten – the Belanda Depok just outside Jakarta, for example, or the Indians in and around Medan.

Even the term 'minority' is debatable. After all, everyone is a minority in some way. And wasn't the revolution precisely about eliminating ethnicity as a basis for discriminating against them? But the discussion does present us with questions we would otherwise not consider. What about people who lived in the archipelago but were not considered colonial subjects or were neither 'native' nor 'local'? These people did not belong to the categories of people who felt most abused by colonial exploitation and who were most enthusiastic about the promise of the revolution.

That the topic is sensitive is also understandable. Many members of ethnic minorities who experienced violence during the revolution have been reluctant to speak about it within Indonesia, not wanting to be seen as disloyal to the nation of which they are now inseparably a part. In the past, the topic has for this reason been left largely to foreign researchers such as Mary Somers Heidhues.[21] That is now changing. FX Harsono is an Indonesian artist who has combined research into anti-Chinese violence during the revolution with commemoration rituals.[22] This kind of work has opened up room for public discussion on social media. Suddenly many aspects of the revolution that had long been known by experts but never very openly discussed are generating a sense of discovery within the broader society. The popular history magazine *Historia* has made available much of the history that previously had been discussed only among specialists.

The Indonesian historians involved in the present volume understand that not all the material we are presenting here may be suitable for use in schools, where the intention is to strengthen the national spirit by placing exemplary heroes in the spotlight. We are academics, and we just want to know what actually happened. We feel we must learn to accept that no nation's history can be only about the good and glorious things. We can also learn something from the bad things in the past.

As a matter of fact, as the following chapters richly illustrate, heroism is by no means absent even in the midst of a logic of violence that otherwise has little to recommend it. A case in point are three chapters focusing largely on the revolution in South Sulawesi, a part of Indonesia where the Republic of Indonesia was unable to build much of a presence in the face of rival forces. Sarkawi Husain's chapter explores the State of East Indonesia (NIT) in South Sulawesi. The NIT should not be viewed as solely a Dutch construct. Beyond Dutch manipulations, Indonesian administrative elites were very much instrumental in building up the state as well as giving it administrative life. As long as overt statecraft was made impossible – partially due to the heavy-handed Dutch monitoring of the NIT – federalism was regarded as a valid form of governance to some Indonesian politicians. While operating within the confines of a federal state, these politicians continually and deliberately undermined associated Dutch symbolism, for example by using the Indonesian-Republican flag and the Indonesian national anthem as representations of the NIT. In a way, these elites could not do otherwise. A variety of non-elite revolutionary movements, meanwhile, engaged in demonstration, propaganda and violence in support of a unitary republic.

The title of Roel Frakking's chapter is a quote from a Sulawesian man whose son had gone off to fight the Dutch: 'The harsher they act, the more fuss there'll be'. This saying represents a kind of heroic refusal to surrender and submit to Dutch authority, even in the face of impossible odds. Staying within NIT territory generally and South Sulawesi specifically, Frakking shows the entrenched nature of Indonesian mobilization against the Dutch re-colonization attempt after August 1945. Moving the focus away from Captain Raymond Westerling's Special Troops Corps, Frakking brings back into the equation how resistance cells derailed all Dutch endeavours to govern but also how local anti-Dutch organizations dealt with Republican influences from Java. Without placing Dutch and Indonesian violence on an equal footing in terms of end-goals, the chapter illustrates how hyper-intense violence was the result of assumptions adopted by both sides that they could only win by denying the opposition the right to exist. Numerous examples of the senseless violence this assumption gave rise to are discussed. They largely impacted communities whose opinion was never asked.

Local intra-elite rivalry also played a role in perpetuating the violence in South Sulawesi, as Taufik Ahmad shows in his chapter on the former kingdom of Polombangkeng south of Makassar. It delves further into the inner working of Sulawesi's anti-colonial militia groups and their political affiliations. Local elites charted their own course between the two opposing pressures of the Dutch and the Republic. These elites made such decisions to satisfy their need to safeguard their positions of power vis-à-vis other local, rival elites. The instability of the revolution heightened inter-elite rivalries going back at least a hundred years. The contest for authority first became intense when the Dutch set up a powerful colonial administration over their heads in the mid-nineteenth century. The imperatives of complex and shifting local alliance-formation led to violent and damaging behaviour at moments when it was unclear who had the ultimate rule-making authority.

The tragic consequences for subaltern villagers of a revolutionary situation deadlocked between multiple militarized forces are also highlighted in Roel Frakking's chapter on West Java. The last years of the revolution in West Java saw no less than three political-military forces competing for control over the same territory: the TNI (and affiliated militant organizations), the Darul Islam and the Dutch (and their client state Pasundan). Each deployed the same logic of violence in their interactions with the local ethnic and village communities, namely that those who did not 'submit' were 'traitors' (*bugot*). This logic sent whole populations into evacuation camps, where they suffered disease and deprivation. It blurred the lines between 'revolutionary' and 'counter-revolutionary' warfare.

The first of the chapters on minorities is by Tri Wahyuning M. Irsyam and concerns an indigenous group living on the Depok 'private lands' for hundreds of years. They held a relatively privileged position within society before the Second World War, having already been emancipated in colonial times. The violence they experienced at the hands of revolutionaries was both criminal and ideological in nature. They had the added misfortune of living in militarily contested boundary territory. After the revolution, they faced new citizenship challenges with respect to the majority culture.

The next three chapters address the ethnic Chinese communities during the revolution, all of which play out in various parts of Sumatra. The first chapter breaks the stereotype of generally prevalent anti-Chinese revolutionary violence. Mawardi Umar shows that, while elsewhere in revolutionary Indonesia the Chinese minority often suffered violence for its supposedly pro-Dutch attitudes, in Aceh the transition was largely peaceful. The reason for this is that the Dutch never managed to re-occupy Aceh. A unified political elite in Aceh offered conciliatory leadership. The Kuomintang leadership in China, influential among the Chinese in Indonesia, also eventually supported the Republic.

The reasons behind the eruption of anti-Chinese violence in East Sumatra (around Medan) in the same period are explored in the chapter by Anne van der Veer. She shows that while tensions between ethnic Chinese and indigenous Indonesians predated the revolution, revolutionary violence exacerbated them. This can be seen in three developments. One was the establishment of the Chinese Security Corps (Pao An Tui), set up in the wake of the arrival of Allied forces. This was accompanied by the rise of conservative leaders within the Chinese community, after progressives were sidelined amidst the violence. Both these factors stimulated the growth of Chinese particularism, in which the Chinese community lost faith in both Dutch and Republican abilities to protect them and relied instead on their own means.

Erniwati has conducted a micro-historical study of the everyday life of the Chinese community in Padang. She shows that their situation was made more difficult early in the revolution by the efforts of Allied and Dutch occupying forces to keep them isolated from the Republican bumiputra community. Meanwhile, the Kuomintang leadership in China, influential within this community, initially advised adopting a 'neutral' stance towards the Republic. Attitudes changed when the leadership of a key Chinese community security organization (Pao An Tui) in Padang was replaced by a more conciliatory figure.

Last but not least, Apriani Harahap shows in her chapter that the Indian community in Medan and surrounding areas also suffered during the early revolution. This was attributed to the community's supposedly pro-Dutch attitudes but should also be linked to the arrival of troops from India brought in by British Allied forces when they arrived in Sumatra. These troops implicated the local Indian community in their own communal politics. It was not only ethnicity but also class that played a role in local Indian attitudes to the Republic. Youths tended to be Republican and wealthy merchants were usually more anti-Republican, while many others tried to stay out of trouble.

Taken together, the chapters in this section illustrate that the intentionality of the revolution as an emancipatory ideal for Indonesians, and as a security nuisance for the Dutch, was apt to get lost in unintended consequences the more the war came down to a complex interplay of available resources. That was particularly the case in areas outside Java, where the Dutch were able to mobilize their troops on the ground before the Republic was able to be truly organized. The problem for the Dutch was persuading people of the rightness of their cause. In these situations, rival forces looked for allies among this or that group, leading to more bitter polarization within society. Nevertheless, in every one of these cases, the ultimate outcome was a resolution in favour of the emancipatory ideals with which it all started, an outcome that appears to have been welcomed everywhere.

The collaboration

In this final section, we reflexively examine our own experiences in writing this book. We draw some generalizations about how the two groups of historians who collaborated on it dealt with the expectations laid upon them by their respective national traditions of history-writing. Rather than going over the diplomatic complications that formed the backdrop to the larger project – they are explained in the introductory volume *Beyond the Pale* – we allow ourselves some personal, almost intimate observations on our own experiences as they emerged from the collaboration.

When it became known that UGM would be involved in *Independence, Decolonization, Violence and War in Indonesia 1945-1950*, it immediately aroused criticism from various groups within Indonesian society, including some historians, as well as within the Netherlands. The Indonesians among us found themselves in a hostile media spotlight. The argument more or less went as follows: Accepting money from the foreign power that had once colonized the country, and that would no doubt seek to whitewash its own colonial past, was tantamount to 'prostituting oneself'. Even if the actual conclusions of the larger *Independence, Decolonization, Violence and War in Indonesia 1945-1950* project were, in fact, scathing of that colonial past, the Indonesian team stated right from the start that its participation would be on the basis of independence. The Indonesian researchers, for example, did not focus on violence per se, certainly not as much as the Dutch team did. In the same vein, the Indonesian team did not engage with any questions about Dutch war crimes, as this was (and is) a particularly Dutch discussion to begin with. Indonesian researchers simply upheld their own perspectives at every opportunity, which included a wide array of research questions, and sharing them freely with their Dutch colleagues and attempting to educate them. It was on this basis that the Indonesian and Dutch teams worked together.

The Indonesian team's participation in *Revolutionary Worlds* was never about obtaining a Dutch apology or about Dutch violence per se. Instead, they saw it as an opportunity to learn more about a crucial period in Indonesian history. The objective was always to conduct good research and to write some high-quality publications. If the present project could stimulate further research, that was all to the good. It brought together eleven Indonesian researchers who worked with Dutch researchers to produce this book. They came from different universities around Indonesia, with various academic qualifications. Five of them were post-doctoral researchers, two were PhDs, and four were Master's or pre-PhD researchers. Beyond that, it paid for a Bachelor's thesis and no fewer than nine Master's theses about the revolutionary period. It would not be too much to say that it has contributed to the birth of a new generation of Indonesian historians who are able to participate in international debates on this period in Indonesian history between the proclamation of independence in 1945 and the resolution of most of the contestation by 1950. It has, moreover, helped to build a significant research database about this period that can be beneficial for future researchers.

The present book came out of a long-standing partnership between Gadjah Mada University (UGM) and the Royal Netherlands Institute of Southeast Asian and Caribbean Studies (Koninklijk Instituut voor Taal-, Land- en Volkenkunde, KITLV) in conducting collaborative research about Indonesian history. The UGM team, like their Dutch counterparts, set up their own research independently, which included formulating the research theme, selecting a methodology and perspective, and recruiting researchers. The only stipulation was that the research be conducted with academic rigour, based on the principle of mutual respect and openness. The objective was to promote an academic dialogue between Indonesian and Dutch historians over this particular period.

Research collaboration of this nature had been fruitful in the 1980s. It evolved in the 1990s for both a good reason – Indonesia grew prosperous and needed foreign assistance less – and a bad one – the Indonesian government cut research links with the Netherlands in 1992 over the latter's human rights protests. A new, more independent generation of Indonesian historians reaffirmed links once the New Order ended: KITLV and UGM have worked together since 2003. They wanted to contribute something critical from their side. They wanted to teach their Dutch partners what an enlightened Indonesian perspective looks like. Indeed, they did this for their own country as well, in their own way.

Dutch researchers came to the collaboration with their own baggage. Like their Indonesian colleagues, they had to deal with an inward-looking historiography with a long history going back to the war of 1945-1949. They too experienced angry reactions to their attempts to breach the boundaries between the two perspectives. They still had to contend with the notion that the Dutch archives were enough to reconstruct historical processes and access truths of the revolution. The *Revolutionary Worlds* collaboration produced new sources. Where the older generation of Dutch historians may have relied primarily on the extensive National Archives in The Hague, the historians involved in this project looked to Indonesian sources to an extent not possible even a few years ago. The project involved a massive exchange of archives. We look forward to doing more of this. One example of future research could be to find more Indonesian and Dutch sources on the same revolutionary event, and thus to understand the reason behind the Dutch colonial myopia.[23]

Most researchers in the present project belonged to a new generation of historians, who no longer doubted that the Netherlands had been on the wrong side of history in 1945-1950. They had become used to thinking of the Netherlands as a perpetrator nation. But they were keenly aware that they were writing about a society that was very different to the one they lived in and that they were writing other people's history. Who were they, as former colonizers, to write about a history that was not their own? They were warned that Dutch and Indonesian researchers would not be able to get beyond their competing national perspectives. However, these warnings turned out to be well wide of the mark. Instead, we have tended to experience more pushback from adherents of inward-looking historiographies in our *own* countries.

The socially more prominent version of such a historiography enjoys what can only be described as an iconic status in the Netherlands. It originated within the 'community of memory' of (descendants of) Dutch civilians who had come to the Netherlands after experiencing extreme violence in the first months of the revolution. In the so-called 'Bersiap' memory (referring to a cry of the revolutionary pemuda), these people had been the victims of hate crimes committed by anarchistic youths inflamed by fascist Japanese propaganda. The painful memories of this community eventually became part of a veritable Dutch identity politics. Every time scholars or journalists made a fresh attempt to contextualize these crimes by engaging with Indonesian experiences of the same period, pointing for example to *their* suffering created by the Dutch decision to go to war, these politics reached new heights of intensity. The larger project of which the present book is a part evoked another storm of controversy in 2022. A major exhibition on the revolution in the national Rijksmuseum, and the official Dutch apology mentioned above, helped carry the controversy into the headlines, but also showed that more cosmopolitan alternatives were possible. Commenting on what they regarded as the insular Dutch Bersiap historiography, one Indonesian scholar in the project wrote that it constituted 'historical amnesia... which ensnares healthy intellectual thought and civility'.[24] A Dutch historian wrote pointedly that 'reducing revolutionary experiences to Dutch victimhood and Indonesian cruelty creates not only a hierarchy of suffering, but also one of culture ... In that sense, little has changed since 1945'.[25]

Revolutionary Worlds does address issues raised by the Dutch Bersiap controversy. No fewer than five chapters, most by Indonesian researchers, explore the experience of minorities widely considered pro-Dutch. One of them explicitly concludes the Bersiap narrative about this episode is 'lopsided' (Tri Wahyuning M. Irsyam's chapter on Depok). We could have added chapters on similar experiences among Ambonese, Timorese, and Menadonese communities. We *should* have had one on the one community that did not subsequently go on to become citizens of the Republic, namely those dispossessed people who left for the Netherlands. Unfortunately our research group did not manage the latter.[26] We may hope that Indonesian researchers in future will be able to help their Dutch colleagues to write about this too, in the contextual, bridge-crossing manner this book has advocated, just as Dutch scholars have done for and with Indonesians over the years.

A few more words about the collaboration will illustrate why we feel so positive about it. The first fruitful exchange took place right at the stage of formulating the project. The KITLV had put forward a budget for a series of 'regional studies on violence' as defined in the bigger project. Three Dutch researchers would work together with three Indonesians. This idea had not been designed together with the Indonesians, and it was clearly naïve. When told about it, the Indonesians felt they were capable of much more than a subsidiary role in a project of such importance. Thus, the exchange of perspectives started at the proposal stage. It ultimately yielded this much more ambitious work, one that moreover gave each side room to define the problem the way they saw fit. *Revolutionary Worlds* was conceived in all its complexity.

The discussions between the Dutch and the Indonesian historians felt a little stiff at first. Everyone seemed to be on their guard and reluctant to share their thoughts. The first spark came when a Dutch group came up with the term 'decolonization' to describe the dynamics of the period in question. This led to the first big clash of perspectives when the Indonesian researchers explained that they did not refer to this period as a process of 'decolonization' because their nation had already been sovereign from August 1945. (Other terminological discussions were left open. Indonesian authors do not use 'Japanese occupation' – suggesting a post-war return to the status quo ante bellum – but 'Japanese colonial rule'. The book consequently designates the period in different ways.) The 'decolonization' discussion was a good way to break the ice, and from then on, what to call things was at the forefront of everyone's mind. It made Dutch researchers realize they had something to say about this history because it was also a shared history.* The questions then became: How can we make those two historiographies, which have always been separate, into stories that can open up to each other? Can we as Dutch researchers let go of the absurd idea that 1945-1949 was essentially a question of diplomacy? Could Indonesian researchers, meanwhile, let go of the 'big men' perspective that dominates their school history textbooks?

By agreeing to look at the revolution from the bottom up and seeing it much more as a social revolution than as a security problem, the Dutch researchers at any rate felt they would never go back to history-writing the way it had been. As one of the Dutch historians said during a project retrospective, the exchange taught them to completely let go of those Dutch perspec-

* The discussion on the term decolonization eventually led to a change in the title of the larger programme. 'Independence' was added in 2018.

tives on how to write about history that had been involuntarily imprinted in them. They now traced their personal insecurities to the way history-writing had been done in a Dutch context. They chose to resolve them by adopting a much more clearly Indonesian historiographical context. The very act of finally being able, in a new study, to dispense with some entrenched popular preconceptions such as that Dutch soldiers had been sent to Indonesia to protect the people, made them feel they were doing good work.

For their part, the Indonesian researchers enjoyed meeting with these Dutch historians in their early careers, people who brought their own fresh, critical insights to the problem and were keen to produce something new. A language barrier arose as most Dutch researchers spoke little Indonesian. Likewise, having the discussions in English was initially somewhat daunting for those Indonesian participants from institutions with little international experience. More senior members of the Indonesian team kept telling younger colleagues to speak up, to be confident, to let others know their thoughts. They found their Dutch colleagues receptive to their ideas rather than patronizing. In the end, they spoke about sensitive and emotional topics openly. Before and after project meetings held in the Netherlands, Indonesian researchers also met with a non-specialist Social Resonance group that included representatives of military veterans, the war memorial committee, and the Indo-European community to interview some of these people for their own research.

The COVID-19 pandemic did lead to a serious interruption of this rhythm of exchange. The original plan involved much more travel between Indonesia and the Netherlands in order to contact eyewitnesses as well as to consult written archives. The book would have been quite different without the pandemic. Some of the Dutch researchers, among them Roel Frakking and Martijn Eickhoff, aspired to do more research on the spot and gather personal accounts from people who were there or their relatives. Unfortunately, this was simply made impossible by the travel restrictions caused by the pandemic.

Nonetheless, we do feel the spirit of open enquiry to which we aspired is apparent in the book as it is. We hope that you, the reader, will share the excitement that we experienced from our discoveries on the immensely important topic of the Indonesian Revolution of 1945 to 1949.

II.

REVOLUTIONARY...

BERDJOANGLAH ANAKKOE,
IBOE BERDO'A!

2.

The meaning of independence for women in Yogyakarta, 1945-1946

Galuh Ambar Sasi

INTRODUCTION

The Indonesian National Revolution created new ideas about equality and unity. The ancient word *merdeka* (freedom) acquired revolutionary meaning as the readiness to fight the Dutch elements that had tagged along with (*membonceng*)[1] British troops late in 1945. The Proclamation of Independence signified personal freedom and a new awareness for every Indonesian individual.[2] So why are women so rarely included in the Indonesian historiography of the period? Why do Indonesian school textbooks cover the overthrow of Dutch colonial rule and the Japanese colonial rule but leave

Pamphlet Mother's Support. *Source: NL-HaNA Algemene Secretarie van de Nederlands-Indische Regering (AS), 2.10.14 inv.no 3767.*

out the role of women in the revolution?[3] Many scholars have written about the need to include women's perspectives in the history of the revolution.[4] Yet even in scholarly writings, they are often depicted only in soup kitchens, in the Red Cross, in militias and women's organizations and as organizers of and participants in various political congresses.[5] There are many other aspects of women in the revolution.

Yogyakarta during this period was given numerous names. It was the Capital of the Republic of Indonesia; the Heart of the Republic (*Jantung Kiblik*); the City of Islamic Restoration (*Kota Hijrah*);[6] the Congress City (*Kota Kongres*);[7] the City of Hope, Dreams and the Future of Indonesia (*Kota harapan, impian,* and *masa depan Indonesia*);[8] the city of refugees[9] and even the place of pleasure (*kaum plesiran*).[10] But Yogyakarta was also the heart of the women's movement. The first women's national congress was organized there from 22 to 25 December 1928.[11] This chapter asks: how did female revolutionary actors create meaning out of the newly proclaimed independence? It examines archives and ego documents written by women in the first year after the Proclamation.

The euphoria of national freedom

The proclamation of independence in Jakarta on 17 August 1945 marked the beginning of the Indonesian National Revolution. In Yogyakarta, the proclamation was directly relayed by the Domei Kooti News Agency at 10 am. A couple of hours later, the news was delivered during the Friday prayer sermon in the Great Mosque of the sultanate of Yogyakarta and the princely state (*Kadipaten*) of Pakualaman. Later in the afternoon, students of the Taman Siswa school marched on the street in celebration.[12] Joining them were several groups of women, among whom was Suratmi Iman Sudiyat. She rode her bicycle, chanting *merdeka* and distributing flyers with information about the recent proclamation in Jakarta.[13] The Aisjijah, the women's wing of the Islamic non-governmental organization Muhammadiyah, also expressed its joy upon hearing the news. Members decorated their clothing with red and white pins.[14] Thus women participated in the collective euphoria of independence in Yogyakarta – a festivity that in many scholarly articles was celebrated only by men.

However, it may very well be that in those first few days, women did not yet have a concrete idea of the meaning of independence. The first week of independence in Yogyakarta is described today as a period of joy, gratitude and elation. The five-volume memoir of women activists in Indonesia depicted it as a blissful moment. At last they could reunite with comrades-in-arms and re-activate the organizations the Japanese had disbanded.[15] They marched; they gave political speeches. They put up Indonesian symbols. They then went in and out of nearby villages to teach reading and writing and to introduce the new Republic and all the attributes of a new Indonesia to the people. They believed rural communities would only understand independence when they could read. The women also introduced them to the Indonesian symbols: the national anthem and other songs, the red-and-white flag and the triumphant salute. During the first two weeks of the proclamation, that salute to the victorious moment was still the Japanese *banzai*. After 1 September, they replaced the shout of *banzai* with *merdeka*, while lifting their hand shoulder-height in salute. This at once removed a Japanese colonial element and infused independence with a new, more personal meaning.[16]

Emancipation

In the third week, the euphoria in Yogyakarta shifted. Independence acquired yet another meaning. Aisjijah chose this moment to reclaim assets that had been under Japanese control. The organization specifically demanded that Muhammadiyah's educational agency for women nurses and doctors, the Pertolongan Kesehatan Oemoem (PKO) be returned to them.[17] Despite this demand, Muhammadiyah made it a collective asset.[18]

Women in Yogyakarta now began to interpret the moment as one of organized emancipation. They established the Indonesian Women's Federation (Persatuan Wanita Indonesia, Perwani). It was intended to represent the women's spirit as an integral part of the Republic of Indonesia. Perwani went ahead and organized the fifth Indonesian Women's Congress, earlier planned for Semarang but cancelled due to World War II. The women wished to relive the 1928 national congress in an independent state.[19]

British air raids on Yogyakarta on 25 and 27 November 1945 forced them to relocate the congress to nearby Klaten.[20] The British intervention made them rethink the meaning of independence. No longer merely about liberation from the Japanese colonizers, it was now about defending it against British attacks and the Dutch attempts to restore its colonial rule. Independence also entailed gender equality. The women demanded equal wages for female and male workers,[21] a revision of the marriage law and better education for women. As the Perwani leadership put it, independence was about 'intellectual formation for women, because when they are intelligent, oppression shall be over'.[22]

The Battle of Kota Baru and other meanings of independence

For female students, *merdeka* also meant being absent from the classroom.[23] All school activities had been temporarily stopped. They began taking an active part in political meetings. They joined organizations and militias and took part in neighbourhood watches.[24] In the collective memory of the people of Yogyakarta, this period of hiatus is known as the 'time to get ready' (*mangsa siap-siapan*) or 'standby' (*bersiap*).[25] All those who were considered adults, particularly if they had received Japanese military training, were obliged to take part in military activities in the urban villages, such as training and patrols. Young girls were asked to help with the logistics and medical care.

In Yogyakarta, *bersiap* was not meant as a cue to launch attacks against the Dutch, against any Indonesian elites, or against certain ethnic groups that were thought to be sympathetic to the Dutch, known as *kemlondo*. Rather, *bersiap* was an attitude of preparedness or caution in anticipation of three possible events, namely, Japanese attacks from their base in the Yogyakarta suburb of Kota Baru to maintain the status quo; British military raids from the cities of Semarang, Ambarawa and Magelang which they had newly occupied (Map 4); or a bloodbath during a possible takeover of power within the Republic. *Bersiap* also meant being responsive to the order given by their Great Leaders (*Pimpinan Agung*) on 19 August 1945. Sultans Hamengkubuwono IX and Pakualam VIII on that day issued a joint decree instructing the population to 'maintain the safety of the people in villages, factories, and shops, as well as to avoid riots'.[26]

The presence of Allied forces, however, gave rise to angst amongst the people in Yogyakarta's villages. They began to join numerous local movements. One of these was a vigilante group in the urban village (*kampong*) of Pathuk. This group had been known for their active ambushes and kidnappings of Japanese troops. They were also the main actors in the parade of September 1945, in which the Japanese flag was removed from the Office of Sultanate Affairs (Kooti Zimu Kyoku Tyokan). This incident exacerbated the tension that was building between Indonesian youths in Yogyakarta and the Japanese army. Two female members who took part in the incident were Oemiyah and Ngaisyah.[27]

Tensions between Indonesian groups who now identified themselves as citizens of a free state and the defeated Japanese colonizers prompted the Republican government to issue a decree for a Censorship Agency on 10 October 1945.[28] Instead of reducing the friction, however, the agency ended up rousing anti-colonial feelings. Selo Sumardjan, the head of a sub-district in Yogyakarta and the right-hand man of Sultan Hamengkubuwono IX, later said the increased hostility was a popular expression of the psychological need for Indonesians to channel their feelings as free human beings.[29]

Young women demonstrated their enthusiasm by intensifying their social activities in the kampongs at this time. They provided medicines and treatment at two hospitals, Tjuo Boin (now Bethesda) and Panti Rapih.[30] They feared that a breakdown in negotiations with the Japanese at Kota Baru might lead to a bloodbath. Their fears were soon proven true, as a call of '*siap*' went out in the evening of 6 October 1945 for youth to prepare for an attack to disarm Japanese soldiers. Most youths were armed, but only with sharpened bamboos.[31]

The Battle of Kota Baru killed 21 men and injured 31 others. As many as 360 Japanese soldiers were disarmed and taken prisoner while 15 trucks of firearms were seized, together with submachine guns and grenades. However, the real outcome of this battle was an increased fighting spirit in the hearts of the people.[32] The event made a deep impression on ordinary youths. It filled them with joy and pride to have defended (*nglabuhi*) their sovereign state, just as the youths had done at the battlefronts to the north in Central Java.[33] As for the young women, the battle forced them to abandon their femininity. They cut their hair short, replaced their Javanese blouse (*kebaya*) and skirts with pantaloons made of rice sacks. These were dyed in green, lacked proper cutting and stitches, and were often oversized.[34] They also donned other martial attributes, such as leather boots, a tommy gun and hand grenades. The only feminine aspect that was left was the face powder made of rice flour.[35]

Fighting at the battlefront was not easy for these young women. They were not yet skilled in handling firearms.[36] They bore stigmas from their surroundings – they were supposed to be in school and to be concerned with puberty and menstruation. Not bothered by society's stigma, a female freedom fighter proved that she chose to focus on attending to injured soldiers or burying the dead. Many like her were overcome by the revolutionary spirit, which led them to disregard danger. They became enraged when their parents reprimanded them or when patronizing people undermined their spirit by advising them to be careful. They would talk back and tell their parents they were not mindless animals.[37]

For these young women, independence meant a new space for emancipation. One organization, The Women's Assistance for Struggle (Wanita Pembantu Perjuangan), withdrew its members if they were only tasked with 'domestic' jobs such as cooking, washing or taking care of logistics. It was not acceptable for them that the women who had gone to great lengths to train in the military were only given assignments limited to providing for men's needs.[38] However, they often came into conflict with male troops who considered them weak. Such conflicts mostly occurred in border areas. For them, the revolution in mentality often began with simple matters, such as refusing gifts from local officials loyal to the Dutch authorities (among them the Recombas, an abbreviation of the Dutch title *Regeringscommissaris voor Bestuursaangelegenheden*).

Mothers also created new meanings of independence. They began giving political speeches. One of these was heard at a large meeting to celebrate the first month since the proclamation. Mrs. Imam Moeghni had lost her son in the Battle of Kota Baru. In her speech she affirmed that she had not stopped her son from taking part in the revolutionary struggle. Instead, she had given her blessing. This had been her duty (*dharma*), that of a mother for the nation's independence.[39] That was how mothers in Yogyakarta gave meaning to Indonesia's independence.

A changing concept of mothers

Varying experiences of living under previous regimes also contributed to the way women made sense of independence. In general, they can be grouped into two categories: those women who had been activists under Dutch colonization before 1942, and those who had recently become active due to the mobilization forced upon them by Japanese rule. The former tended to interpret independence as a moment when women would gain political equality, a moment of national awareness, and the opportunity to fight at the battlefront. For the latter, independence entailed their participation at the home front by being good wives, wise mothers and supporters of the men. They argued that defending the home front was the only way to join the revolution and defend the nation's independence.

The idea that independence could only be achieved through revolution was demonstrated in Yogyakarta by Aisjijah and by Moeslimat, a women's organization associated with Nahdatul Ulama. Both left the Women's Organization Contact Agency (Badan Kontak Organisasi Wanita, BKOW) on the grounds that it was not revolutionary enough. The Indonesian Christian [Protestant] Women (Wanita Kristen Indonesia, WKI) and the Catholic Party of the Republic of Indonesia (Partai Katolik Republik Indonesia, PKRI) also distanced themselves from the organization.[40] Instead, they convened an emergency women's congress on 11 April 1946, where it was decided to elect a new chairperson and to move the 'capital' of the women's movement from Yogyakarta to Malang in East Java. By doing so, they wished to keep moderate political influences away from their organization.

The first group considered the relocation of the centre of the women's movement a victory for their generation of women activists. They were of the firm belief that revolution was the opportunity for women to use any means to defend independence, including by getting directly involved in politics. Holding on to their idealism, they later formed their own political organization, the Women's Party for the People (Partai Wanita Rakyat, PWR) on 22 September 1946, with a total of 3,050 members.[41]

Under the leadership of Sri Mangunsarkoro, they constructed a new concept of the Indonesian mother. Old concepts were no longer relevant for women in the new state. The proclamation had ordained them as new mothers – mothers of the Indonesian state. Moreover, they declared, revolution was a way of achieving a socialist society based on God and humanity. The mother of the state had to defend women, their rights and their dignity, in accordance with the Constitution of the Republic of Indonesia.[42]

A revolution in mentality

The Indonesian Revolution has been called a bourgeois revolution, a social revolution or a national revolution.[43] But in 1964 President Sukarno, in his opening speech to the tenth Indonesian Women's Congress, called it a revolution in the attitudes and mentality of women.[44] This was evident, he said, in their new attitudes and even their outward appearances, which were different from the previous period.[45] Another interpretation was given by Sarmidi Mangunsarkoro, a prominent figure in the Taman Siswa educational movement (and husband of Sri Mangunsarkoro, the leader of the Women's Party). Revolution, he argued, had remodelled the old, dilapidated home of the Indonesian people into a new, magnificent and harmonious building. The old house referred to the feudal-capitalistic society, with the power of its socio-economic establishments. The new building was the democratic society committed to equality and harmony.[46] All this could be achieved when women as the mother of the state gave birth to a new nation and raised a society that was different from the previous era.[47]

The women who supported Indonesia's first prime minister Sutan Sjahrir in Yogyakarta viewed revolution as he did, namely as an era of transition. Yet even they marched to the battlefronts shouting the Japanese-era slogan against Britain and the United States: *Inggris Kita Linggis, Amerika Kita Setrika* ('We shall bludgeon the British and iron out America'). They rejected Dutch cultural prestige by joining in a witty Javanese wordplay called *jarwa-dhosok*, whereby the word for the Netherlands, *Belanda* or *Landa* was said to be a contraction of *alon-alon nggone mbandha* ('slowly collecting fortunes').[48] They also adopted the slogan *rawe-rawe rantas, malang-malang putung,* which means everything that is in the way of revolution shall be destroyed. *Sekali merdeka tetap merdeka* meant freedom once and for all. Putting their trust in the short-lived Sjahrir cabinet, the women believed that revolution entailed a far-reaching independence for all Asian people, to be achieved through resistance against foreign powers by means of political and economic struggle.[49]

Meanwhile, leftist women in Yogyakarta argued that a revolution required rigorous discipline in order to avoid the kind of turmoil that had taken place in Russia.[50] They felt responsible not only for the independence of their homeland but also for its development and for the welfare of the state and its people. They fought against illiteracy, against unliveable housing, and against rags, cruelty and oppression. Democracy and total freedom would bring an end to all of that.[51] The meaning they created was of socialism. They supported 'the ideological pillars for achieving socialist revolution, which will be a house protecting proletarian society from capitalism'.[52] They believed that in such a society, women would be entirely liberated.[53]

Women workers belonged to this socialist group. They identified all working women as 'labourers' (*buruh*) and believed that the revolution should be both led and followed by women. They feared that many women were still using bourgeois norms in carrying out their struggle; they found it necessary for the struggle to be corrected. They organized meetings and gave training in bookkeeping, language skills, engineering, childcare and lodging. They believed the national revolution aimed not only to liberate the people from colonialism and imperialism but also to bring them social welfare, free from capitalism.[54]

Differences in the way they made sense of independence created disappointment and frustration among certain women groups too. This was particularly true among women who had migrated to Yogyakarta from North

Sulawesi and Maluku, many from families connected to the former colonial army, the Royal Netherlands East Indies Army (Koninklijk Nederlands-Indisch Leger, KNIL). For them, the revolution was unexpected. It brought them nothing but disillusionment. They felt their sacrifices for the KNIL had been in vain. And they believed Republican fighters were only concerned with the interests of the Javanese. Many Sulawesi women left Yogyakarta to join forces with Kahar Muzakar in Sulawesi. They brought with them all their students from Sulawesi in Yogyakarta and even former prisoners released from the Nusakambangan prison island. Believing that 'Sulawesi is for the people of Sulawesi', they centred their activities for Sulawesi in Sulawesi because they thought that they were the only ones who could help Sulawesi.

For the Chinese women in Yogyakarta, revolution entailed an even more complex situation. It swept them up in a state of euphoria, as evident in the action taken by Liem Gien Nio, the owner of restaurant Oen. She changed the uniforms of her waiters and waitresses into something resembling the one donned by President Sukarno: a white shirt, pants and a black cap called a *peci*. This was an expression of her identity as a citizen of the new Republic.[55] Despite her revolutionary spirit, she still faced negative stereotypes and heard the mocking slang *Cino loleng*. The nation's constitution stated that only 'original Indonesians' (*orang-orang bangsa Indonesia asli*) had automatic citizenship. This was often thought to exclude ethnic Chinese. Yet these Chinese women consistently rejected the use of the terms 'majority' and 'minority' because in their view everyone, especially women, should have an equal position in the new country.[56] Various other polemics befell Chinese women. They often felt socially isolated in the Chinese neighbourhood called Kampung Ketandan (near the Beringharjo markets). It was only after the first Dutch military aggression in 1947, in which they were able to prove their loyalty to the Republic, that they felt their life gradually regaining some normalcy.[57]

New moral values

Their dreams were of complete moral renewal, yet in reality the revolution created a paradox. At first, they had interpreted independence as the impetus for a renewal of all life values, for freedom, and for liberation from old values. But gradually that all became unclear. The original objectives of national sovereignty and economic sustainability progressively faded into the background.[58] The old feudal regime once more took control. Old officials who had thrived under colonialism returned to their positions in government offices. They brought with them their corrupt ideals, which the revolution had managed to abolish in the early days of independence. Corruption returned to the scene in 1946. It soon became one of the most acute social problems.[59] As corrupt practices worsened,[60] the ministry of defence formed a special body to investigate the worst cases.[61]

One of the more common practices in Yogyakarta was forgery of cover letters to lift one's social status by the revival of old titles, including aristocratic titles. A number of professionals and intellectuals as well as government officials who had already obtained the educational titles Mr. (*meester in de rechten*, law degree) or Ir. (engineer) bought new royal titles such as KRT, *Kanjeng Raden Tumenggung*. Furthermore, the comradely term of address *bung* ('bro!'), which had entailed camaraderie in the new Republic, was replaced with *Bapak*, meaning 'father'. The egalitarianism and solidarity of the revolution was disappearing and being replaced by the patron-client relation – a hierarchical status in which subordinates were obliged to show loyalty and service to their patrons. Higher government authorities were now addressed with the title *paduka* (Your Highness) or *paduka yang mulia* (Your Excellency).[62]

No records have yet been found revealing whether women protested against such practices. But several sources show that, amidst the turbulent situation on the borders of Yogyakarta and the Dutch-held areas, women held on to their ideals.[63] They acted against cross-border profiteering, which was rife during the revolution. They often faced male authorities who were involved in these bad practices.

Differences in the way they made sense of independence and the revolution also caused ruptures within the family. Many husbands left their wives on the premise of joining the national struggle at the battlefront, only to end up practising polygamy. Practices of free sex, due to increasing Westernization, led the women's organization Perwari (Persatuan Wanita Republik Indonesia, the successor to Perwani) to urge the legalization of prenuptial agreements.[64] All these meaning-making processes filled the socio-cultural spaces in Yogyakarta, a proud focal point of Indonesia that was loyal to the Proclamation of 17 August 1945.

Conclusion

The experience of women in Yogyakarta at the beginning of independence illustrates that they were not merely objects of the revolutionary process. It did not take long for them to play an active role in the revolution. They fought the Dutch re-colonization attempt, especially once their city, the centre of Javanese culture, also became the centre of the new Republic in January 1946. Far from simply conforming to the initiatives of men, they embarked on their own revolutionary steps. Nor was their activism confined to a particular social class. Women from all walks of life played revolutionary roles. They established unity and solidarity across social classes.

In responding to almost every revolutionary phenomenon, they transformed themselves from colonial subjects to citizens of a newly independent nation-state. They seized the liberty to move out of their private domestic realms in order to take part in public events. Such heightened awareness often triggered conflicts with fellow women as well as with men, within the family and beyond it. Independence changed their private and personal matters into collective, social and even state matters. It gave birth to a new mentality, a new women's morality, in regard to Indonesian state formation and nation-building.

The national revolution was for these women not simply a physical struggle to maintain independence but a response to the proclamation at an intellectual and a cultural level. Nor was making new meanings of independence simply an individual matter of self-modernization or emancipation. They saw independence as the soul and mentality of an entire society or nation. It was this mentality that distinguished theirs from the previous colonial society. All this proves that an Indonesian revolutionary historiographical narrative dominated by men is due for a revision.

Indeed, Indonesian women in Yogyakarta did interpret the revolution in various ways. They defended the new nation, but they also erected a firm new moral foundation for it. Their fight against old norms and feudal tradition was their way of serving the country. They did not all make the same sense of independence in Yogyakarta. Yet they remained in solidarity as each of their interpretations pushed them both personally and collectively to formulate new positions within the independent state. Culturally and intellectually, in their struggle for freedom and revolution, they were never inferior to men, nor to women of the West where imperialism and modern colonialism originated.

BERDJALAN

3.

The battle for the nation and pemuda subjectivity

Contradictions in a revolutionary capital

Farabi Fakih

Introduction

Yogyakarta became the revolutionary capital of the nascent Indonesian Republic in early 1946, after British troops entered Jakarta. That ended when the Dutch attacked and took over the city in late 1948. During this period of less than three years, Yogyakarta became the symbolic centre of the Republic – a city synonymous with the Republican state. Foreign relations and meetings were held in the city. The state invited people from outside

An everyday scene on the busy Malioboro Street in Yogyakarta, the heart of the Republik Indonesia, 1948. Source: Charles Breijer, Nederlands Fotomuseum.

to showcase the progress of the nation-state as testament to its legitimacy. Today, the spaces of the former capital – its hotels, streets and buildings – contain layered histories of the birth of the state and of the nation.

Yet one of the most perplexing aspects of the history of the revolutionary city is its lack of commemoration. The most significant monument to the revolution in Yogyakarta is a propaganda piece that celebrates the heroic deeds of Suharto, built in 1985 during the height of President Suharto's New Order government. After the end of the New Order and the enactment of the policy of decentralization, books on Yogyakarta's role as the revolutionary capital began to be published in the province, pushed by the need for Yogyakarta to legitimize its special status as a kingdom within the Republic. Yogyakarta's revolutionary credentials became defined within the Sultanate's role in the independence struggle,[1] and nothing more.

How can we understand this lack of memory of the city's *revolutionary* status? The chapter explores this question through a reading of the enunciations and performativities of its residents. It examines the cultural productions of the revolution as they related to the city and to how the state allocated functions to its spaces. It explores paintings, novels, plays and memoirs. It particularly aims to elucidate the potentiality of these imaginaries of Yogyakarta as a peephole into the problematic workings of the *pemuda* (the youth) in postcolonial Indonesian society. The capital city functioned as a space in which the Republic could enact the performative and enunciatory acts of the nation-state. It was the stage through which the nascent nation-state could be rendered real through repetition and a mode of citation that allowed people to become citizens.

When a Dutch leftist student who was associated with a Communist international youth group visited the city in 1947, he attended an artistic exhibition, proclaiming: 'I didn't know you people had time for this!'[2] The Republic had been boxed into a small space centred in Yogyakarta. Surrounding it were the pestilence and death of war. Social revolution had ravaged many parts of the country. Fighting had destroyed parts of Bandung and Surabaya. Yet they not only made time for art, they prioritized it as a way of performing the corporeal forms of an imagined society that had been non-existent just a couple of years prior. These acts did not merely proclaim the existence of the nation-state, they were essential to conjuring up its being. As Judith Butler has noted, the very act of performing and enunciating these acts made possible the thing it performed. The nation did not exist prior to these acts but appeared simultaneously and repetitiously in and through them.

If the revolutionary city provided such republican spaces to enact performances that were so vital to conjuring the nation-state into being, then why the ambivalence regarding its commemoration? Why has Jakarta never commissioned a celebratory historical book on the revolutionary capital? Why has there never been a monument to celebrate this fact in Jakarta or Yogyakarta? My principal argument is that the ambivalence to Yogyakarta represented a deeper ambivalence in the construction of the identity of the nation-state. That ambivalence was felt specifically in regard to the position of its prime mover during the revolution, the so-called *pemuda*.

The Indonesian revolution, like all twentieth-century revolutions, was framed within the modern enlightenment revolution of creating a new man.[3] The task of performing this new Republican man fell to a vague group of what later would be delineated simply as the *pemuda*. Their age and naiveté afforded them the ability to don the new enlightenment values as a new man. Yet their image has also been tied to notions of violence, depravity and lack of control.

The ambivalence in the history of Yogyakarta as revolutionary capital points to the deep unease that many have felt with the mode of being 'national' in the period. Analyzing the enunciatory and the performative within the revolutionary capital allows us to understand how an Indonesian identity was crafted in a particular historical situation, one that had path-dependent consequences for the further development of the Indonesian nation-state.

Theorizing the *Pemuda* Revolutionary Split Spirit

The so-called performative turn that occurred in various social studies in the 1990s and 2000s provides the major theoretical impetus for the analysis in this chapter. The work of Judith Butler is central. Her theory on gender and its relation to performativity was a critique of an essentialist reading of interior essences of gender identity.[4] She argued that pre-verbal gender identity did not exist outside of its repetitious performance, that gender was not a stable identity but that it was constituted through history, through a regimentation of a 'stylized repetition of acts'.[5] The control of the body through stylized repetition here is central to the conjuring of gendered identities.

This historicism regarding performativity points to the importance of the ways in which a society controls and disciplines how bodies move and act through space. 'The act that one does, the act that one performs, is, in a sense, an act that has been going on before one arrived on the scene. Hence, gender is an act which has been rehearsed, much as a script survives the particular actors who make use of it, but which requires individual actors in order to be actualized and reproduced as realities once again.'[6] Another important aspect is the relationship between performative identity and space, in particular the social production of space. Space is also constructed historically. Social space functions in conjunction with repetition to craft a social order for various identities. Henry Lefebvre's idea of the social construction of space is here central to the revolutionary character of such an approach.[7]

The interesting aspect for Butler and others in using this approach to understand gender production is its ability to understand when slippage occurs within this order. 'The argument that gendered, sexualized, racialized, or commodified spaces do not simply "exist", but are produced through the repetitious enactment of particular social norms, opens up the possibility that such spaces might be performed otherwise.'[8] The possibilities for redefining gender or racial identities through historic disruption to the normal order of repetition provided political scope for activism. We can widen this idea of slippage so that it embraces political revolution and its efficacy in defining national identity – or, in this case, the *pemuda* identity, which carried with it implications of Indonesian nationhood.

The revolution here is central to the ambivalence of the *pemuda* identity because it represented a time of disjunction, a slippage with respect to the normal repetition of acts that had constituted nationalist identity since the rise of the nationalist movement in the early twentieth century. The historicism of the *pemuda* identity was shaken as a result of war, the Japanese colonial rule and the subsequent revolution. The perlocutionary act of conjuring the Republican nation-state opened up new possibilities for connections and claim-making.[9] This ambivalence towards the *pemuda* identity is central to understanding how its differing performativities could be connected to Indonesian nationalism. The uncertainty of its definition was the result of slippage during the revolutionary period. Yet, as we shall see, it was not merely the result of the nationalist elite losing power to the *pemuda* conception of national identity.

At the height of the Suharto regime, the New Order commissioned a book on the history of the *pemuda*. It chronicled the rise and development of the *pemuda* as a distinct group of organization-wielding nationalists. *Pemuda* here were categorized and defined in a practical manner through their various party and non-party-based organizations.[10] This was an elitist view of the *pemuda* that depicted them as modern people with developmentalist aspirations. They came with a political programme and modernist notions rooted in European ideologies such as social democracy, liberalism or communism, or in the implementation of non-Western modernist goals such as modernist Islam. Takashi Shiraishi had similarly identified the *pemuda* or *kaoem moeda* as primary agents of the modern during the 'age in motion', the *zaman bergerak* of the early twentieth century.[11] These *pemuda* were elite children of the native upper-class colonial society. They deployed certain middle-class aspirations that equated modernity with a form of cultural citizenship. They were the product of what Henk Schulte Nordholt has described as an education of desire based on their middle-class culture of consumption.[12] They often exhibited a child-like innocence. Rudolf Mrázek called them dandies. They were worldly: they were the children of a cosmopolitan culture that was in tune with the latest Hollywood movies as well as with the social theories and political philosophies of Europe.[13]

The historian Ranajit Guha, in his book on the decolonization of India, points to the failure of the Indian liberal bourgeois elite to achieve hegemony, although they did achieve dominance. They thus failed to speak in the name of the nation. Their defeat of the subaltern, who was also prevented from establishing hegemony, made it impossible for the national project to fulfil its goal of enlightenment and a developmentalist modernity. Instead, to this day the subalterns cling steadfastly to a pre-modern logic that defies the expectations and aspirations of the liberal elite. This outcome was unlike the liberal revolution of the West, which did succeed in convincing the lower classes to take up modern aspirations and thus allow the new liberal elite to speak in their name. The reason for the failure of Indian liberalism lay in the different workings of capitalism in colonial India in comparison to its European counterpart. Indian colonial capitalism failed to undermine the feudal structure of traditional society, something that social scientists had 'universally' expected it to do. The new, liberal interpretation assumed that there was a totality to the diverging identities, as if they represented completely different beings.[14] Yet the division is often confusing and the boundaries fluid. The modern and the traditional are differing modes in which people, both middle class elites and subalterns, can switch back and forth in their enunciation. What's important is the strategic value of having these differing, alternative modes.

In writing about the *pemuda* revolution of 1944-1946, Benedict Anderson has stressed the rupture of *pemuda* identity as a result of the Japanese colonial rule. In his view, the militant *pemuda* of the revolutionary period arose not from the classrooms of the Europeanized dandies but rather from the traditional Javanese mode of youth, the transitory period in life between the mode of childhood and that of adulthood, a period in which the Javanese develop relations of apprenticeship with adults other than their parents. These apprenticeships are often highly personal. They may, for instance, develop relations with 'criminal' types such as local *jagos* (literally: 'roosters'), or they may be nurtured within traditional institutions such as the Islamic boarding school (*pesantren*). This mode of youth had been around in traditional Javanese society for a long time, yet the slippage of the Japanese period was an important occurrence. By using local schoolteachers, officials and Islamic notables, the Japanese formed an apprenticeship programme that coupled the Javanese mode of youth and the modern, Westernized youth of Indonesia's elite classes with the occupation-state project of mobilizing the population. Thus, the Japanese conjoined modern, Westernized elite youths with the subaltern youths of traditional society.[15]

This other youth – created through Japanese machination – was qualitatively different from the dandy. '[T]he "other youth" also presented itself by its distinctive fashion – its non-haircut worn loose, boots on bare feet, samurai swords worn like a stick, bamboo *roentjing*, sharpened bamboo stick, worn like a rifle, headbands worn bloody red, the ammunition belts worn crisscross around a naked chest.'[16] This was the youth romanticized as carrying forth the revolution. Yet William Frederick, in his essay on *pemuda* and fashion, found it difficult to pinpoint its origins.[17] He felt the image of the raggedy youth was as much Dutch propaganda designed to depict primitive, non-modern violence within the Republic, picturing it as a rabble of fanatic murderers, as it was a genuine expression of a new Javanese mode of youth. David Wehl, a public relations officer at the Southeast Asia Command of the British Army, said this of the *pemuda* in his 1948 book on the Indonesian revolution: 'Into this mass of turbulent Indonesian young men, agitated by many different passions and loyalties, many of their organisations rival to each other, fighting and quarrelling among themselves, and united only in the desire to do rather than to think, apt pupils of the Japanese lessons to the young idea on how to shoot, was thrown the hysterical intoxicant of a sex war.'[18]

This Dutch propagandistic image of the *pemuda* as un-modern or even anti-modern was sometimes shared by the dandy generation, tucked away inside the musings of their biographies. One of them, Ali Sastroamidjojo, recounted in his memoir his first visit to revolutionary Yogyakarta:

> There were many *pemuda* with long hair and weapons. They were generally in badly worn attire. Their attitude and manner were as if they were fighters who had won the war. Feeling victorious, strong and brave to oppose the enemy or anyone against their state and nation or… in fact against *them* and their groups. These long-haired *pemuda*, the armed fighters with no name, and their haphazard manner, are the center of our Revolutionary power. Without them, the history of the independence of our country might look very different.[19]

Note the distinction Sastroamidjojo made between the *pemuda* and himself. This was not unique to Sastroamidjojo, for the dandies were sometimes criticized when they proclaimed their right to be the voice of the *pemuda*. For example, the prominent *pemuda* Sukarni criticized Chaerul Saleh in the revolutionary parliament (Komite Nasional Indonesia, KNI) for claiming his was the voice of the *pemuda*.[20] This unease was always present beneath the speech acts of the modern *pemuda*.

To what extent did the distinction between these two modes of youth represent corporeal manifestations of particular socio-economic and cultural forms of identity? Are middle class aspirations truly rooted in class forms, or were they the continuation of strategic colonial differences? Bart Luttikhuis has pointed out that the defining difference of colonial class categories was not race but culture, in particular the degree of cultural *Europeanness* that an Indonesian elite internalized.[21] Yet as Ann Laura Stoler has shown, this porosity in colonial categories was itself strategic to the interest of the colonial state in maintaining discipline.[22] Partha Chatherjee's idea of colonial differences has a similar thrust.[23] Very few Indonesian youths were so thoroughly Westernized as to be completely detached from the worldview and rationale of their traditional brethren. Colonial differences worked under the threat of falling into colonial subalternity, the threat of what was referred to as 'going Indian' (*verindischen*).[24] Thus, the middle-class education of desire that was inculcated in colonial society was a form of violent subjugation that produced an existential angst about the conception of the self: that one's modern identity had to be re-inscribed constantly in order for it not to lapse under the threat of falling into the traditional category.

Our reading of the performativity of the *pemuda* in relation to the revolutionary capital is thus based on understanding the unease about the self that was inflicted upon the young, modern Indonesian elites. The so-called subaltern left very little discourse in the archives. Even if one were to interview members of these groups, the question would remain, as Gayatri Spivak says: can the subaltern speak? This is not to say that they lacked the faculty of speech but that 'there is no unrepresentable subaltern subject that can know and speak itself'.[25] The category of the non-modern itself is important only in regard to the violent threat it imposed on the national self. Perhaps there never were subalterns other than those conjured up as a result of the unease of the elite about failing to be modern. Thus, the new modern developmentalist elite had the duty to re-inscribe colonial differences in their constant efforts to achieve recognition from their white colonial fathers, only this time under a new, international diplomatic order. In their effort to re-inscribe, they ultimately revisited the same colonial logic and violence that was at the heart of the developmentalist project of colonialism. It is with this context in mind that I believe we should re-read the discourse of Yogyakarta as revolutionary capital.

Yogyakarta as performative space

The decision to move the capital to Yogyakarta was made in early January 1946. Prior to this, the Sultan and Pakualaman of Yogyakarta had sent a letter informing the Republic of their willingness to host the capital. The Sultan had successfully strengthened his position by restructuring the local government of Yogyakarta under his office. During the Dutch colonial period, Batavia had controlled Yogyakarta through the office of the Premier (*Patih*), who had run the executive branch of the native government under and alongside the Dutch Resident. In August 1942, however, the Japanese had appointed the Sultan as head (*koo*) of the Province (*Kooti*). This was a major coup for the Sultan, for it allowed him to bypass the Premier. He later became head of the Hokokai, an organization established by the Japanese to mobilize the Javanese population for the war. As head of the Hokokai, the Sultan used its mobilizational capacity to integrate Yogyakarta's traditional bureaucracy and thus to strengthen his feudal government. In 1944, a series of bureaucratic reforms was enacted within the provincial government that led to the introduction of neighbourhood-level government. When the last Premier, Danuredjo VII, retired in 1945, the office was abolished. In April 1945, another spate of reforms introduced village and upper-level elections and eliminated the *kawedanan*, streamlining the bureaucratic structure between the Sultan and the people. These measures instilled greater loyalty to the government among the population of Yogyakarta. At a time when many local governments were collapsing, Yogyakarta's government remained relatively solid and stable.[26]

In a speech to officiate the move of the capital, President Sukarno said that 'no national state can stand without centralism. Russia has Moscow, America has Washington, England has London, Majapahit had Wilwatikta. Central government, central power, central leadership – this "*Zentralgewalt*" is a most important element of the national state.'[27] Sukarno would later put to use his architectural and spatial ideas of nation-building in Jakarta, though not in Yogyakarta. His address to the nation was thus a perlocutionary act of state-building at a time when the Republican state was ephemeral and its corporeality patchy. He spoke of the need to ensure the conjuring of the nation-state itself. '[I]f our Indonesian nation makes it so that "everything is running well" and "running well" as in under the order of the central government leadership; if the Indonesian nation has obtained this element, then we can call the Republic of Indonesia an Indonesian national state.'[28] Sukarno was fond of enunciating this mantra. He inserted it into the performative pageantry of nationalist rallies, which were held in the squares of small, medium and large cities throughout Java. Sukarno's audiences were not only the Indonesian people who attended the rallies and were fixated and enthralled by the president's theatrical grandeur but also the coteries of local and international journalists that travelled with him.

This speech act of 'all is running well' was thus performed for both observers from outside Indonesia and for the people living inside the territory. The message for the observers was that the Republic was real and that the people were making it real. For the elite, it was the perlocutionary act of conjuring up their hegemonic aspirations by means of speech acts but also through a series of government programmes that were meant to discipline the *pemuda* and transform them from scary, long-haired fighters into the idealized embodiment of national youth. In both regards, Yogyakarta became the site, the spatial centre through which an imagined republic was performed, while a programme was enacted to discipline and integrate the unruly *pemuda*. It was an optical strategy to win the hearts and minds of observers, while at the same time a stage upon which the repetitious citational order of the nation-state could be enacted by the people, and in particular by the *pemuda*.

Clifford Geertz famously described the Balinese traditional state as one in which power was not effectuated through the institutions of the state but through pomp and ceremony. It was state through theatre.[29] Power was diffused into various hierarchies, kinship networks and sacred centres. His analysis represented an anthropological approach to understanding the form of the traditional Javanese state prior to the colonial period. In many ways, the modern revolutionary Republican state mimicked its pre-modern ideal type. Yogyakarta was a capital city lacking modern state power. Instead, its power was diffused inside and outside its fluid boundaries. Its fighters were drawn from various groups with allegiances to different ideologies and traditional institutional networks ranging from Muslim places of worship and criminal gangs to cultural groupings. The Indonesian army itself was based in two major centres – one in Bandung, West Java and the other in Central Java. The spiritual head of the army, General Sudirman, was constantly moving about in Republican territory and lacked a proper headquarters.

Central state institutions, so important to Sukarno's notion of normality, were here diffused. Sukarno's office, the centre of executive power, was located in that important stretch of Malioboro Road at the centre of Yogyakarta. Parliament was technically located at Purworejo (Map 4) but held moving parliamentary meetings, going from one Republican city to another. The Ministry of Foreign Affairs and the Prime Minister's office maintained their location in Jakarta. Various ministries occupied buildings in surrounding cities like Surakarta and Klaten. President Sukarno, Vice President Mohammad Hatta and the various prime ministers were also always on the move – attending rallies, meeting with their diplomatic counterparts in Jakarta, or traveling outside Indonesia. The Yogyakarta-based nationalist newspaper *Kedaulatan Rakjat* would often notify its readers of the arrival of the president in his own capital city, as if it was a special and rare occasion.

In terms of economic management, the formation of a Republican central bank and the issuance of the Republican currency looked as if normality had been achieved. Yet underneath this veneer, Yogyakarta maintained minimal control. Republican tender was issued diffusely through several bank 'branches', which also issued their own 'regional tender'.[30] Even cities and organizations began issuing their own tender, with the knowledge of the central bank. What looked like the proper attire of statehood – a central bank and its own sovereign currency – hid the fact that the state had little monetary control.[31]

It was the *pemuda* – as labourers, army units, artists, religious groups and so forth – who operated the trains, took over the sugar factories, ran the oil installations and managed the radio and publications that saturated the airwaves and hence the public discourse in Republican towns and cities. These modern *pemuda* organizations held massive rallies and created schools and educational institutions that invited leaders such as Sukarno and Sjahrir to teach. They worked with the government to create new business ventures and to develop new forms of cooperative organizations to express the possible future of an independent Indonesian economy. They held developmental conventions, art exhibitions, sporting events and beauty pageants besides the incessant political rallies.

The hollowness and diffuseness of the Indonesian state required an almost ceremonial movement through its Republican spaces, as noted by the movement of the president and the head of the army. These movements obviously differed for each profession. But for each of them, the capital was a node – important and symbolic – in the movements of government officials, diplomats, elite leftist *pemuda* leaders, ulamas and their followers, artists, professors and students on their way to their diplomatic meetings, religious rallies, theatre performances and art exhibitions, and youth, women and labour conferences.

These movements were not dictated by the circumstances of war itself. The war was incidental to an otherwise 'normal' engagement of citizens to fulfil their independence. Suwandi Tjitrowarsito's short story, *Journey* (*Perdjalanan*), tells of a young, modern Republican lady on the train meeting with an old *pemuda* acquaintance returning home from a conference he had attended in Yogyakarta.[32] The train was attacked by Dutch forces, and they both had to flee. Here, the heroics of these youngsters were tested. They experienced the attack almost as a surprise, as if it had befallen them out of nowhere. Instead, what transpired was the image of people going to and fro on nation-building business; to a conference in Yogyakarta, a rally in Madiun, a sport event in Surakarta or a gallery or play opening in some other city.

The hollowness of the capital city afforded it possibilities of symbolization. It was a place of stability and safety, where fighters came for rest and recreation. One newspaper article described Yogyakarta's euphoric atmosphere of unimpeded action: 'Elaborate theories are thrown away, instead, practical, fast, important and quantitative work is put up front. Perhaps it is because conditions in Jogja are safe and sound that we can discuss a lot of stuff for a long time.'[33] This site of intense activity contrasted with conditions at the front. Indonesian revolutionary artists often depicted the latter in non-descript forms: rice fields, jungles, villages (*desa*) and the occasional ruined urban landscape. These spaces lacked coordinates; they represented non-places.

Yogyakarta was different because it had definable places; in particular the two-kilometre-long stretch of Malioboro Road in the centre of town. At the northern end of the road were the major hotels Merdeka and Tugu, the most modern in town, where many officers, civil servants and diplomats stayed. One of them had one of the best halls in town and thus was used to hold national festivities for elite Republicans. Along the street were shops and restaurants mostly owned by Chinese-Indonesians. This was where many people in Yogya, including fighters from the front, civil servants, and the general population, liked to visit, to see and be seen, to window-shop or to have a bite to eat and drink. At the southern end of the road were located the major institutions of the Republic, including the presidential palace, the central bank and the entrance to the sultan's palace, the Kraton. Malioboro was also the road in which rallies and nationalist festivities were held. *Pemuda* strutted around its pavements for the evening's enjoyment. Not all government departments were located in Malioboro. The Ministry of Information had an office owned by the Catholic Diocese of Yogyakarta.

Thus, the way the streets and spaces of Yogyakarta were used reinforced the embodiment of the Indonesian state. It was a diplomatic offensive *par excellence*. While the Dutch argued that the Republic was a ragtag bunch of radical primitives, the Republic could show that it was the centre of an Eastern inculcation of Western enlightenment values. Dutch journalists invariably derided such performances and poked holes in it by naming the city itself a mirage. One called it Sukarno's model republic or dream city.[34] The famous Indonesian painter Sudjojono recounted the strategies artists used in making nationalist posters:

> None of the posters were violent. The posters must pluck the strings of the most refined cultural sense of the Western world. We reminded

them of the values of Kipling, Rousseau, Shakespeare and Washington. The slogans of the French Revolution, the American war for independence and the spirit of William of Orange were prominently displayed. We were in dialogue with them.[35]

The audience was Western and the posters, alongside banners, were a carefully choreographed pageantry of state pomp.

The performance began at the airport, where delegates were swarmed by paparazzi photographers often 'shooting' without film.[36] The delegates would wind their way down the major streets of the capital with the population lining the streets yelling '*merdeka*!'. The streets were clean and orderly. Banners and posters were strategically placed in perfect English to convey the wishes of the people to the Australian, American or Chinese delegations. In a report in the Dutch newspaper *Friesch Dagblad*, the journalist Willem Tausent reported his visit to the Republican capital with the Dutch delegation in October 1947. He was part of a large Dutch delegation to the city. From the airport, the delegation was treated to snacks at a halfway house at Terban. Each table was adorned with purple, velvety orchids while the waiter gave everyone cream cakes and a glass of ice-cold lemonade. At the Merdeka Hotel, his room was adorned with a large banner written in English calling for the end of Dutch colonialism. His image of a city under siege in the middle of a war – lacking earthly comforts, with a population under terror from fanatical Republicans – was shattered.

Tausent wrote:

> The term 'dining room' appears to be a euphemistic concept for the luxurious rooms in which, neatly covered, there are dozens of tables, all with red and white flags. It is a bustle of interest and the colourful scenes caused by the toiletries of foreign secretaries, the uniforms of foreign military attaches, and especially not to be forgotten by the 'brave' suits of the Republican officers of the army, sea and air force – it involuntarily brings to mind the thought of a chic dinner at an over-chic 'party'. The lunch is superbly lavish: fried potatoes, tender steak and fresh vegetables, with a full *rijsttafel* next to it, followed by a two-colour (ask what colours?) pudding and finally coffee with whipped cream, although the red-and-white flags in this context look very propagandistic: 'Look at how good we have it in

> the republic.' Add to this the life-size photo of Mr. Sukarno, who is adorned in full regalia above the entrance of the banquet hall, and it will be understood that I am not at all sad when this ceremony is finally over.[37]

Tausent also reported the scenes he saw in Malioboro Road just outside his hotel.

> We see barricades, children coming back from school, *merdeka*-calling kindergarteners, Dutch-women-married-with-Indonesians, well-fed but badly dressed Yogyakartans ('As a result of the Dutch blockade', people whisper in my ear). We see a parade. Dozens of young people, both girls and boys, march, stiffly in step, through Malioboro, Djokja's main street. A few drum butchers in front, flag carriers behind it, then some advertising runners ('Away with the Dutch') and finally the long, long line of lesser beneficiaries without a drum or flag or plate.[38]

The function of Yogyakarta as a moral optic for the Indonesian Revolution is apparent in the readings above. While the Republican state may have been devoid of real state power, the capital's symbolic spaces were stages in which the corporeality of the Republican state was performed. Yet, to an extent, people who were enacting them understood the limitations of this state pageantry; they understood the illusory nature of the performance. It was to the audience that such plays became real. The international, Western gaze was key to the performance because the success of the Republic was seen, through Republican eyes, in convincing the rest of the world of the normality of its nation-state and the fundamental similarity of its values, resting on the liberal foundations of enlightenment and modernity. But in order for the play to become real, it was also important for the state to convince the rest of the Indonesians to take on the same developmentalist values that had animated Republican nationalism. While the 'people' were the major location in which this transplantation of middle-class aspirations were to be conducted, its implementation during the revolution was much more limited to the *pemuda* as the embodiment of the fighting spirit of the nation. The performativity of Yogyakarta also functioned to discipline the *pemuda* in mind and body.

The developmentalist capital and *pemuda* identity

In his speech on the first anniversary of the Republic on 17 August 1946, Sukarno reiterated the importance of discipline and obedience to the leadership of the central government as a form of development. 'On this discipline-awakening front *pemuda* can become heroes, they can become *helden*!'[39] He reiterated that the Revolution, like a river that has burst forth from its banks, 'has awakened the energies of the people, some constructive while others destructive. The state constantly endeavours to nurture these useful energies, constantly the government invites: to construct and to develop! Aside from the nurturing and the invitations, the government also tries to shy away from the dangers of the minds and soul of the troublemakers.'[40]

This division between troublemakers and developers, heroes and destroyers formed the developmentalist logic underlying the aspirations of the Republican elite. It was a reinforcement of the differing modes of being that were thrust upon one another, between the moderns and the subalterns. The 'unleashing' of the *pemuda* from the bowels of traditional society was something that could potentially engulf the control of those modern dandies, with their liberal and enlightened worldviews. Fifty-thousand moderns moved from the cosmopolitan capital Jakarta to the feudal backwater of the new capital. There they confronted the contra-

Government posters concerning pemuda discipline. *Source: Republik Indonesia. Daerah Istimewa Yogyakarta (Jakarta 1953).*

dictions between their developmentalist logic and the traditional culture which the people retained. They were civil servants, professors, teachers, doctors, artists and others. Most carried with them their part of the national project. Many were visibly upset at the lack of understanding among the people of the programmes that they crafted. They read this lack of understanding as the lethargy of the traditionalists, as an unwillingness to appreciate their values. Selo Sumardjan, secretary to the Sultan, quoted with some annoyance their criticism of Yogyakartans: 'We came here to develop Yogyakarta, in order that Yogyakartans can work harder.' According to Sumardjan, these Jakarta Republicans lamented that 'outside of Yogyakarta, I can work efficiently in the field of developing education. but after entering Yogyakarta, everything becomes slow, everyone becomes easy-going, in no rush, without a care, because people are used to the philosophy of getting there by walking slowly.'[41]

Republican moderns were like fish out of water. Their ridiculous contrast with the wider traditional society, which they deemed themselves to be representing, resulted in almost caricatural self-renderings. John Coast said of them:

> The dignity of their position, they imagined, was secured by going into ties, shirts, trousers and shoes, and they were convinced that a man that sat in his steaming office wearing a suit with collar and tie was necessarily a correct and important person. Even the women oiled their hair into the curious plaits and pigtails of the Dutch *huisvrouw* [*housewife*] and wore ill-cut dresses in tasteless colours with very short skirts, which showed for the first time the unfortunate broadness of the Javanese female knees. Such costumes had the effect of making this already youthful people appear as overgrown children on the Dutch model.[42]

This generation of dandies maintained an absurd presence, asking the Dutch delegation strange questions pertaining to Benedetto Croce or how T.S. Elliot was doing, in the midst of a revolution.[43]

Yet this childlike gullibility hid a ruthlessness to the moderns' developmentalist goals. They had in mind nothing less than the creation of a nation-state, and central to this were strategies of control of the *pemuda* mind and body. Tied to independence was a programme to create a new man with a new body, one that would relinquish the colonial image of the Indonesian body as meek, weak and sickly.

Sports during the revolution. Source: Lukisan Revolusi Rakjat Indonesia, 1945-1949 (Yogyakarta 1949).

The prime minister's office issued a statement in October 1946 on the importance of sport for the 'regeneration of the nation and in the effort to lift up the Indonesian image in the international arena'.[44] In a speech at the congress of the Republic of Indonesia Sports Union (Persatuan Olah Raga Republik Indonesia, PORI) in January 1947, Sukarno lamented the physical weakness of the Indonesian but in particular of the 'wong Djowo' or Javanese. They had small bodies, he said, a median height of 155 cm, short noses and soft movements (*klemak-klemek*). He hoped that the Indonesian body would become strong like the knights of Gatotkotjo and Wrekoedoro from the fabled Hindu Mahabharata epos.[45] This concern for the body translated into a fixation with sport.

The head of PORI said in an interview in mid-March 1947 that 'pride in our self-worth has to be implanted first in the bosom of our youths, so that when they are outside the country they will not be inflicted by feelings of inferiority'.[46] PORI was the state organizer for sport at the national and international level. Sport was an effort to instil nation-building. 'And these exercises will be given to the whole of our people so that they become sports-minded,' the head of PORI went on. 'The people's sport will no longer be imposed upon them, as the Japanese had done, but will be a sport that is practised based on fun and willingness.'[47]

At the first PORI congress held in Surakarta on 18 and 19 January 1947, attended by the president, vice president, minister of defence and several other ministers, an Olympic vision of the new Indonesian was imagined. The Indonesian Olympic Committee was inaugurated.[48] Indonesia planned to send athletes to eight sporting events at the London Summer Olympics in 1948.[49] In mid-June, the head of the Working Body of the International Olympic Committee, J. Sigfrid Edström, sent a letter requesting all Indonesian national federations to join the international Olympic federation.[50] Although Indonesia ultimately failed to participate in the London Olympics, between 9 and 12 September 1948 it held its first national sports games (*pekan olahraga nasional*) in the neighbouring city of Surakarta.

Interest in sport and nation-building was widespread. Leftist youth groups within the Socialist Youth of Indonesia party (Pemuda Sosialis Indonesia, Pesindo) planned a series of sporting events as part of the socialist World Federation of Democratic Youth Conference they wanted to host in Madiun in November 1948. Indonesian youth would have played against their Indian, Burmese, Chinese and Filipino counterparts.[51] Clearly, the Republic was active in solving the nation's problem of people with small, frail bodies.

These performances of the new Indonesian man and woman took various forms. Indonesia's first airline, Indonesian Airways, started flying in April 1947, with Indonesian air hostesses and pilots. The first international route commenced in Yogyakarta. A five-hour journey on a Dakota took it to Singapore.[52] In the same month, the first national flight route was inaugurated connecting Yogyakarta with Malang in East Java. It carried 29 passengers and was crewed by British and Indonesian pilots.[53] The American pilot who flew the Dakota from the US to Yogyakarta said in answer to Indonesian reporters that Indonesians had capable bodies to fly airplanes, although they perhaps were of smaller size. A similar question was addressed to a Ms. Constantine, a foreign fashion designer, on whether Indonesian ladies had the right mindset to become air hostesses. She replied that Indonesian ladies were graced with intelligence and artistry. Indeed, an article in *Kedaulatan Rakjat* praised the young air hostess aboard the inaugural flight: 'The teenage lady looked fearless throughout the entire flight and with a beautiful smile attended to the drinks of the passengers, talking in fluent English with the foreign guests.'[54]

These evocative forms of nation-building, relying heavily on the 'foreign' if not 'Western,' gaze, represented a form of postcolonial haunting that evoked strategies of elimination. The very act of this search for a new man and woman conjoined the modern Indonesian mode of being with its colonial subjugation. The weakness of the Indonesian man, its body and behaviours, was constantly on display. Indonesian national subjectivity was intimately intertwined with the foreign gaze, within an ideological space of Republican modernity. The importance of the Lacanian gaze and performativity in the construction of Indonesian subjectivity is instructive here.[55] The mere presence of the subalterns, roaming the streets of Yogyakarta, was a constant reminder of the failure of the Indonesian to rise up to the challenge of modernity. It became a headache to the moderns and their developmental goals. The athletes, the artists, the air hostesses and so forth conducted their exemplary performances specifically as a contrast with the general failure of the Indonesian to rise to the occasion.

At one point, Suripno and Francisca Fanggidaej, heads of Pesindo, travelled around the Republican space after their own peregrinations in Europe and India. As they visited town after town to meet with the thronging masses, theirs was the gaze of the outsider, reflected back toward the nascent national audience. They told the crowd of the well-wishes from

Pemuda developmentalism in Madiun. Source: Lukisan Revolusi Rakjat Indonesia.

50,000 members of the Democratic Youth Federation and from two and a half million members of the International Union of Students. They talked of the solidarity exhibited at the Asian Relations Conference in India. Their discourse posited a new subjectivity based on a postcolonial, foreign gaze that diminished the position of the white colonial master. These sentiments would later echo in the Bandung Conference of 1955 and throughout the Third World Movement. Yet even there, the logic of the modern ultimately failed to achieve true postcolonial liberation.[56] While the audiences for these performativities were the Indonesian masses, who were shown what the nation aspired to be, their legitimacy rested in the end on the outside gaze. This need for foreign approval, it seems to me, was ultimately rooted in the failure by the middle-class elite of the Indonesian state to achieve hegemony. Instead, they were redeploying colonial forms of discipline by attaching the project to the authority of foreigners.

Moral criticism of the Republican state

The 1951 film directed by Kotot Sukardi, *The Cripple* (*Si Pintjang*), was one of the first Indonesian films produced after the transfer of sovereignty. It was showcased at the Prague Film Festival in 1952. Like many artists during the war, Sukardi stayed in Yogyakarta and wrote several plays whose thematic concerns mirrored *Si Pintjang*. In late 1946, he premiered a play at the Soboharso theatre titled *Yogya is not Hollywood* (*Djokja boekan Hollywood*). It was enacted by the group Pantjawarna. Although the script is lost, we know the play was a moral tale of how elites in the capital led a life of 'luxury' in the midst of suffering. *Si Pintjang* was the story of an orphaned boy named Giman who had to flee to the capital during the war. He fell in with a ragtag group of child beggars and hoodlums. With the assistance of a modern and naïve dandy, they were taught to become part of the nation. It was the Republican developmentalist dream: a depiction of how village children were made into Indonesian *pemuda*. The last scene ended triumphantly, with the children becoming a shabby militia (*laskar*). Yet the film can also be read as a criticism of this Republican nation-building. While hailed as a 'nationalist' film immediately after the revolution, the protagonists and antagonists of *Si Pintjang* were not the Indonesians versus the Dutch. The war was an important but almost irrelevant backdrop to the true conflict: the moral dilemma in the creation of the nation-state. Like the Dutch colonial state, the Republican state was also absent, except as an impediment to Giman's straining for a happy life. The police arrested his friend who had stolen medicine to treat Giman's illness. There were scenes of rich Indonesians in their cars (Republican officials?) shooing away beggars. While triumphant, the final scene was also melancholic: they were still poor and disfigured.

The moral question Sukardi pointed to occurred not at the battlefront but at the symbolic heart of the Republic: Malioboro, the Broadway of Yogyakarta. In an article in *Kedaulatan Rakyat*, he wrote about the street that people from fighters to foreign diplomats and journalists had visited: 'The revolution has forced the people to come to the city of Yogyakarta... and visiting Yogyakarta means coming to know Malioboro, whether one wants to or not.'[57] He wrote about the restaurants and shops thronging with people keen to buy; moneyed people who were able to purchase things available at inflated prices in the Chinese-owned shops without a care in the world; buying another pair of shoes, even if they had a mountain of shoes at home. Even the Dutch newspapers, a recent historian has noted, had recorded the act of *malioberen* or 'going to Malioboro' as part of popular *pemuda* culture.[58] Kotot Sukardi also wrote wryly about the so-called *extremisten*, the *pemuda* in their funky, revolutionary attire roaming the streets. And of course, there were the poor people, the beggars and 'coolies' who were themselves also sons of the revolution. He wrote about a mother-beggar waiting for people's alms with her five-year-old in tow. Her husband had disappeared as a *romusha* forced labourer. Kotot asked: 'Isn't she a hero? She deserves to be recognized, to be looked upon... this simple old lady. Her name will never be spoken by the masses, but she has made a sacrifice and we can now feel her sacrifice. Now what is the rank of this heroine? A beggar! And her fate depends on the kindness of Malioboro.'[59] The street, regularly shown to foreign visitors as the exemplary centre of an imagined Indonesia, was thus here seen with cynicism and disgust.

In the 1950 novel *Jogja under chaos (Djokja diduduki Chaos)* by Dimyati, the protagonist also went to Malioboro and, as in Kotot's account, saw the street as a symbol of the divide between rich and poor in revolutionary Indonesia.

> Malioboro was very crowded, with people going to and fro; especially near the Beringhardjo market, people were jostling in front of the market; on the sidewalks of Malioboro was a stream of humanity mimicking a rivulet; they walked in a hurry, as if haunted by a special need. The restaurants were full, the shops and stores were full of peo-

ple. I became jealous seeing so many people throwing away money and how fast money was circulating from one hand to another, like the circulation at a gambling table. I saw Sultan Bagindo sitting in front of a large shop, counting a stack of Republican money with a Chinese trader.[60]

The protagonist, while poor, is an honest and true Republican. The antagonist is the Sumatran Sultan Bagindo, a cunning and pragmatic businessman. When the Dutch invaded and took over Yogyakarta at the end of 1948, Bagindo proclaimed that the end of the Republic was certain. When the protagonist protested, Bagindo replied that 'little people' did not understand geopolitics. In a patriotic novel, the ending would show the protagonist's true faith in the Republic being rewarded, while Bagindo's pragmatism would be his undoing. Instead, Dimyati ended the novel in the opposite direction. While others in his neighbourhood left the city to find shelter, the protagonist's faith saw him remaining in the city. During this period, his wife met an untimely death. Eventually, Sukarno was returning to the city in full triumph, and everyone in the city came out to welcome him. They thronged the streets from the airport all the way to his palace at the southern end of Malioboro. Bagindo, returning from exile, met with the protagonist and told him to join in the procession, lest he be considered a Dutch sympathizer. Thus, in a period of sorrow following the death of his beloved wife, his true patriotism was betrayed by its public performance. It was unnecessary to believe in the Republic; it was only necessary to move to the rhythm of its motion.

Such moral unease with the Revolution was an important component of many stories produced during or in the years after it. This has been forgotten as the state's heroic version of events became paramount in the years after independence. The war that was raging in the minds of many was not so much the war for independence against the Dutch but the war for the creation of a moral Republic. The Dutch were a backdrop and mostly irrelevant, because their presence was incidental to the goings-on of people performing their nationalities, fulfilling their independence. This morality was inherently part of the enlightenment, developmentalist goals of the state. Yet, as seen through the eyes of its prominent artists, the state itself ultimately failed to enact them. Thus the 1954 film *After Curfew (Lewat Djam Malam)* discussed a traumatized *pemuda* who was unable to enter normal life after the killings he had committed in the name of the revolution. At the end of the film, he once more sees the state as having no answer to his pain.

Instead of the new, athletic Indonesian body, some stories depict imperfect, disabled ones. Imperfect bodies were visible in the title of *Si Pintjang*. The writer Djakasuria published a short story titled *Kasim the Shoemaker (Si Kasim Tukang Sepatu)* around this time. It was set in the home of a family whose boy, Kasim, had joined the fighting as a *pemuda*.

> One night Kasim appeared at the frame of the door – in front of everyone – big, fat, healthy, just a little bit darker. Everyone present held their breath – emotional. His sisters were the first to smile – running up to him to hug him. Kasiman himself stood still in his place. Kasim's father hunted for and held his son's hand, he groped... They all suddenly cried in surprise. Were they crying? Or were they laughing? The father stood silent, he had no power to do anything, except to look at Kasiman. His son, Kasiman, a shoemaker apprentice, no longer had fingers.[61]

Rusman Sutiasumarga's short story titled *Bekasi Maiden* (*Gadis Bekasi*) is about a woman who waits every day at Bekasi station, waiting endlessly for the trains. We learn that her story is one of tragedy: 'A body that was once strong and full, that had once been the desire of many bachelors, is now just bones wrapped in skin, blackened and dried with a nasty smell. Warsiah had become a living corpse.'[62]

The clothing and style of the *pemuda* can also be read as a moral protest against the presumption of the enlightenment values that the Republic itself enunciated. A pro-Republican Dutchman named Peter 't Hoen, after his visit to Yogyakarta, described the *pemuda* he saw at Malioboro:

> A comical moment arises when a soldier comes in from the [revolutionary militia] KRIS. He is a young man of about twenty years old. He has allowed black locks to grow to his shoulders, while a small goatee tries to give a masculine accent to his face. He wears a pair of high, yellow boots and light blue trousers with a shirt of the same colour, under which hangs a canary yellow jerkin. His waist is surrounded by a heavy belt, on which hangs a large holster, from which the grip of a powerful gun protrudes. His black locks are crowned by a giant yellow-brown hat with a wide brim. There is a wide, fire-red ribbon around the hat, hanging from behind as a sash. The young man is a happy person. He is self-aware and young, and his victorious gaze de-

> fies the whole environment. With a royal gesture, he places his right arm on his hip and strides in a stately fashion to a table, where a few acquaintances sit, who greet him with cheers. He sympathizes with their enthusiastic reception and with a wide gesture he takes a seat in a chair that has been put up for him. Where have I seen him before? In a Tom Mix movie? But that was less stately! In a Cyrano de Bergerac show? But he was not so youthful! At our BS [Binnenlandsche Strijdkrachten, anti-fascist underground in the Netherlands] just after the liberation? But we were not so badly done up! He has certain traits in common with the *hidalgo* from an old Spanish chivalrous tournament. With a graceful arm gesture, which he had apparently spent some time studying, he summons Brother Waiter. While I am still watching him carefully, the door opens and a whole procession of similar nobles enters. They are dressed in the same way and they have a few KRIS girls in their company, who look just as bright, but less agile than the boys. Words of concise and crisp greetings have been exchanged, a large hat flies several times through the air, and everyone watches with bated breath.[63]

Like Sukardi's criticism of Hollywood, the style of the *pemuda* here was not subaltern. Instead, it was contemporary and modern, a celebration of the cowboy culture that had been seen in imported Western movies. It represented not a form of traditional irrationality but a modern alternative to the stuffy developmentalism of enlightenment values. The performances of some *pemuda* – who were acting out their appropriation of Hollywood, or of something else like those wielding samurai swords or the mujahedeen in West Java – engendered a dislike in the Republican elite. They framed it as a moral panic that went to the heart of Indonesian identity. After independence, moral panic against what they saw as youth intransigence was conducted through such forms as banning popular Western music, which happened after Sukarno mocked the Beatles as just 'noise' (*ngak-ngik-ngok*).[64] In the New Order, it took the form of a genre of moral tales stressing the potential for moral degeneracy among the youth.

Unlike the state's project for the creation of the Indonesian body, the performative disruption conducted by the *pemuda* themselves was not delineated by the foreign gaze. Instead, it was determined by the failure of the state to live up to its vaunted moral principles. Sukarno's anti-Hollywood stance, particularly in the 1960s, was constructed within a geopolitical contest between imperial Hollywood against Third-Worldism.[65] Yet the co-optation of Hollywood performativities by so-called subaltern *pemuda* lay exactly in the attack on the moral unease and potential violence that his revolution had brought to the table. It shied away from foreign relationships and stressed the moral issue inherent within the national relationship. The co-optation of 'hybrid' cultural practices could be seen as a form of mimicry that, as Homy Bhabha has said, 'is at once resemblance and menace'.[66] In this way, some *pemuda* elevated their subversion to the level of the nation-building myth that had been crafted by Republican elites. By mimicking the Hollywood modern, the hegemonic claim of the elites became problematic.

One can argue that the end of the revolutionary capital was not so much the result of the Dutch invasion of December 1948 as it was of the destruction of the Communists and their youth leadership at Surakarta and Madiun three months earlier, following a struggle for power. That conflict cannot be read as a division between the dandies and the subalterns, as a fight between the elites against the traditionalists. Both Yogyakarta and Madiun contained dandies and subalterns, traditionalists and elites. Many Republican elites, especially Sukarno, often shifted their enunciations between differing modes. They were able to appropriate them within their speech acts. Yet the very act of moving between these modes actually strengthened the legitimacy of the subaltern and problematized the state's disciplinary project.

As we have seen, the so-called subalterns or traditionalists themselves coded their performance as mimicry of modern modes such as the Hollywood cowboy or the samurai. Instead of seeing these struggles as essentialized battles between defined modes of being, it may be more fruitful to see them as the result of a strategic tension engendered through the commitment to the effort of nation-building. The physical weakness of the theatre state opened up a channel for *pemuda* participation, one that subverted the developmentalist logic of elite Republicans. It created a space in which people could eke out an existence within the dominating yet weak 'hegemony' of the aspirational middle class. This space, so full of tension, would periodically erupt in violence that denigrated further the enlightenment moral claim of the Republican state while further crippling the notion of the Indonesian moral subject and amplifying the unease felt about the dandies' developmental project.

Conclusion: The strategic notion of *pemuda*

The ambivalence of the memory of the revolutionary capital is strikingly different from the heroic celebration of the revolution as we understand it today. This is, in part, the result of the military interpretation of the Indonesian Revolution that has emphasized the centrality of the armed struggle with the Dutch enemy. This grew to be the dominant interpretation during the New Order regime, especially through its principal historian, Nugroho Notosusanto. In many publications and movies, especially during the New Order, the Republic's idealized *pemuda* – as a rugged, selfless individual with a complete, muscular body – became a reality. It was the tale of a unified nation against a foreign enemy. Yet as we have seen, one of the major issues during the revolution was the struggle for the moral Republican subject, in which Yogyakarta, as its exemplary centre, became entwined. People in those days saw the revolution less as a fight against a foreign enemy and more as a fight within the nation to determine the moral relationship between the state and its people.

What the *pemuda* represented was itself difficult to determine. The *pemuda* as a political movement belonged very much to the modern Republican elites, many of them associated with the communist party. But this was subsequently destroyed during the Madiun Rebellion of September 1948. One of its members, Prime Minister Amir Sjarifuddin, said in *Kedaulatan Rakjat* in 1946 that the revolution must be in the hands of the *pemuda* and not the grandpas, by whom he meant the old bureaucratic elite accused of corruption and compromise, among other things.[67] Yet the *pemuda* obviously represented various groups from across the political spectrum in Indonesia. They were busy running much of the state and culture of the new republic and putting their stamp on the narrative of the revolution. Publications written from within the leftist *pemuda* movement in the early 1950s discussed mostly the organizational development of the movement and its relations with the state. Yet efforts by *pemuda* artists to develop a museum for revolutionary art also came to naught, even though they were made in the post-revolutionary period before the New Order. The tendency to forget about the complexity of the involvement of the *pemuda* in the building of the state and the nation was thus something that preceded the militarization of national history by the New Order.

Yogyakarta as a symbolic centre for Republican mythmaking allows us to interrogate this claim of the subalternity of the *pemuda*. The issue was already a battleground upon which various people put forward their interpretations of the moral issue of the future Republican state. Sukarno's notion of 'all is running well' ran up against this contested reality. Yet the counter-discourse was silenced exactly through the depiction of the *pemuda* as a subaltern, unmodern and scary force instead of the modern developmentalists that they were in their organizations. This depiction of the *pemuda* as unmodern, subaltern and barbaric – made by the Dutch – was inadvertently used by Republican elites so as to strengthen the legitimacy of their position and to stop what was seemingly a devastating moral critique of the Republic launched by leftist artists.

The use of a colonial disciplinary tool of 'difference' was effective exactly because no one claimed the position of the 'subaltern extremism' of the *pemuda*. No voice was there to counter the attack. This is not to argue that there was no violence, nor that human rights violations were never perpetrated by many so-called *pemuda* especially against Europeans, Eurasians, Chinese and other Indonesians. It is simply to say that, as a whole, the *pemuda* lacked a foundational coherence of identity to speak on behalf of itself. *Pemuda* performativity did not denote their subaltern identity because many of the elite *pemuda* looked upon themselves as proper agents of Republican developmentalism. Anderson's reification of the *pemuda*, ironically, played into one section of the moderns' effort to gain hegemony against their rival moderns. The continuation of this discourse on subaltern *pemuda* threatens to limit the broader, inclusive narration of the revolutionary period that is now needed. It represents a form of narrative violence that continues to this day in the national historiography of Indonesia.

Neen, hoor!
SELFDETERMINATION
FOR ALL NATIONS
PR 169

4.

Monsters and capitalists

Revolutionary posters demonize the Dutch [1]

Muhammad Yuanda Zara

Introduction

Complementing their armed campaign for independence, Indonesian nationalists deployed propaganda. They aimed to get the public to join the struggle against the Dutch. Studies on propaganda during the Indonesian War of Independence are relatively new. Recent analyses have elaborated the actors, themes, techniques and forms of propaganda, especially of a verbal kind.[2] Studies on a more limited scale have explored print caricatures[3] and the role of graphic artists in imagining, designing and creating wartime propaganda posters.[4] Why was anti-Dutch sentiment necessary in the strug-

Image 1. A poster depicting an Indonesian woman defending herself from the threatening grip of a Dutch monster hand, imitating the treachery of Nazi Germany. Source: NL-HaNA AS, 2.10.14 inv.no 5465.

gle to defend Indonesian independence? In war, one crucial aspect of offence is the construction of a bad image of the enemy. Without it, conflicts would not occur. The creation of such a bad image is entirely based on the identity perception of 'us' versus 'them', 'good' versus 'evil', which is continuously reproduced and distributed by means of various communication channels. Propaganda is a systematic effort to convince large groups of audiences to join one's particular cause.[5]

William Eckhardt writes in his study of enemy images that the word 'enemy' entails hostility, threat, harm and fear, all of which may manifest in violence.[6] It therefore provides a justification to defend oneself, to fight back or even to resort to similar violence when necessary. It also leads to solidarity, bonds and loyalty as one associates with patriots as opposed to associating with an enemy attempting to take away one's freedom. The practice of showing visual images in which the enemy is cruel while simultaneously glorifying the righteousness of one's own group is common in wartime. It is closely tied to the notion of Self and Other. The starting point of any politics of hate, according to Marja Vuorinen, is the definition of the self as good: 'Goodness, honesty, righteousness, purity, proper manners, hard work, right religion, high but not over-ripe culture and decency are the hallmarks of the Self, while the Other is accused of being evil, untruthful, crooked, impure, ill-mannered, lazy, superstitious, barbaric or decadent, and immoral'.[7]

Elsewhere, historians have long studied how enemies were visually mocked during wartime. In the First World War, the American propaganda poster 'Destroy This Mad Brute' depicted the German as a giant gorilla that had destroyed Europe and would soon annihilate the United States.[8] In the Second World War, Germany retaliated with similar propaganda posters. One of them was made by the artist Leest Storm and was entitled 'Kultur-Terror'. It depicted 'a beast who brings the American way of life to the European continent and leaves only destruction in his path'.[9] David Welch examined the depiction of Japan in American and Australian propaganda during the Second World War. He found that the Japanese were often portrayed as inferior to humans. Drawing on racial stereotypes and feelings of superiority, the Japanese were portrayed in American propaganda as menacing pests such as rats, snakes and monkeys. The idea, according to Welch, was to 'undermine the human dignity of the enemy'.[10] All this research underlines the importance of visual propaganda in dehumanizing the enemy during war.

This chapter looks at how the Dutch were demonized in Indonesian propaganda caricatures and posters, a topic that is rarely discussed by historians of the Indonesian-Dutch conflict. The images were used to convince the people that the existence of the Republic of Indonesia was under threat and to intensify popular resistance against the Dutch by portraying them as evil aliens. In this light, the chapter aims to answer three questions. Why did Indonesian propagandists ridicule the Dutch for their attempt to recolonize Indonesia? Who or what Dutch elements were targeted by this visual ridicule, and why did they target these specifically? What representational techniques were used to send this visual message demonizing the Dutch?

To answer these questions, the chapter draws on various sources. The main primary sources are Indonesian revolutionary newspapers collected in the National Library in Jakarta, the Jogja Library Centre in Yogyakarta, and the library of the NIOD Institute for War, Holocaust and Genocide studies in Amsterdam; as well as archives from the National Archives in The Hague. I checked the archives of the Ministry of Information of the Republic of Indonesia at the National Archives of the Republic of Indonesia in Jakarta but did not find any relevant visual propaganda material. The great number of posters in the National Archives in The Hague indicates how carefully the Dutch observed developments within Indonesian public opinion without looking away from negative images of the Dutch in their former colony.

To foreshadow the chapter's conclusions, it will be shown that the archives do not reveal a systematic or official Indonesian organization to produce visual mockery of the Dutch. Only a few posters were officially printed by government bodies to denigrate the Dutch. Anti-Dutch posters could be made by any individual or group, without requiring express permission from Republican authorities.

Indonesian visual propaganda: content, context and responses

Ideally, any analysis of propaganda caricatures and posters should situate them in the socio-political context of their times. The motivation for printing caricatures in a newspaper can often be explained by referring to the moment of its publication. It also helps to know the precise target and reach of a caricature. However, most separately printed posters were not equipped with additional information on the makers, time of production, place of distribution, target audience and their responses. This makes it difficult to measure their degree of effectiveness.

The fact that most Indonesian propaganda posters were anonymous was both intentional and understandable. They portrayed the Dutch in far more gruesome terms than did the caricatures in newspapers. The makers were certainly vulnerable to Dutch threats. In a small number of cases, the producers and distributors of posters were known. Some posters were stamped 'Penra', referring to Penerangan Rakyat, a local branch of the Republican Ministry of Information. But even these did not reveal the names of the artists. We know the artists for only very few posters. The Indonesian revolutionary poster that is best known today depicts an Indonesian man with a red-and-white flag behind him, breaking the chains that bind his hands while shouting, 'Join us, comrades!' ('*Boeng, ajo Boeng*'). It was made by the famous painter Affandi.[11] Due to the lack of documentation about the posters, their limited scope of distribution, and the anonymity of the artists, the analysis here will focus more on content than on context.

An investigation of the paper used for the posters reveals that most were distributed by pasting them on walls or trees in crowded areas. This would have allowed them to be seen by large numbers of ordinary Indonesians going about their daily activities. This made the posters unlike the caricatures printed in nationalist mass media, which were distributed with commercial purposes in mind and only reached a literate audience.

Judging from the scope of the audience, the main targets of the visual propaganda were urban Indonesians who were in need of a regular supply of information about the latest situation of the Dutch-Indonesian conflict and who were interested in public opinion. Meanwhile, the English-language magazine *The Voice of Free Indonesia,* affiliated with the Indonesian government, specifically targeted foreign correspondents, particularly from Allied countries with representatives stationed in Java.

Several cases allow us to reconstruct the Dutch response to the Indonesian propaganda posters. Indicators added to the posters specify that the Dutch recognized and examined Indonesian propaganda materials after they seized them. The texts printed on the posters were translated into Dutch in order for Dutch agencies to know the meanings behind them and, if necessary, to take immediate action.

The Dutch army submitted the seized posters – their copies, photos or negatives – to Dutch agencies tasked to suppress Indonesian propaganda, such as the Netherlands Forces Intelligence Service (NEFIS).[12] An army officer would write down where the poster was found or seized, including detailed coordinates. This was obviously part of their strategy of mapping the location of Republican troops who were thought to be behind the propaganda mission.

Dutch information agencies such as the Regerings Voorlichtingsdienst (RVD) and the Inlichtingen Dienst were also active in collecting Indonesian propaganda materials. They snatched posters pasted on trees in crowded places and distributed them to other Dutch agencies to be analyzed, with a view to eventually suppressing their makers. In the Dutch archives, Indonesian propaganda was classified as 'Anti Ned. Propaganda'. The term reveals that the Dutch thought of these materials as a form of attack on them that required an immediate response, among others by stopping them from being seen in Indonesian public places.

As for anti-Dutch caricatures in print media that were considered denigratory of the Dutch government, Dutch troops repeatedly raided the offices of the nationalist media. Even though the anti-Dutch caricatures were not cited as one of the specific reasons for the raid, it is safe to assume that such negative visual representations contributed to the increasing dislike among the Dutch towards the Indonesian print media.

Visualizing the Netherlands as an evil monster

The depiction of the enemy as a monster is a common way to expose the enemy's cruelty, as an entity beyond the limits of humanity. The enemy is identified as the Other with all the bad and non-human qualities attached thereto, such as extreme cruelty, brutality, greediness, gruesomeness. One way in which Indonesians could show the Dutch as the worst Other was to identify them with a creature that humans fear the most: the monster.

The portrayal began as the conflict between Indonesia and the Netherlands escalated to its climax. Immediately after Indonesian independence was proclaimed and the Dutch returned to Indonesia, skirmishes broke out between the Indonesians and their opponents, namely the remaining Japanese soldiers, British troops and the Dutch army which had come to reclaim its colony.

Besides responding with equal violence, Indonesians resorted to narratives that delegitimized their enemies' existence. This was done by means of posters that gave a visual construct to the imagination of the Indonesian people and framed the Dutch as the source of the mayhem in Indonesia. Below are two examples of propaganda posters depicting the Dutch as frightening, non-human creatures. The first (Image 1) is a hand-drawn image in grayscale of a giant right hand. It has thick hair and long, sharp, pointy nails, giving the impression of the deadly grip of a giant hand. Between the thumb and the wrist, a swastika is vividly printed. Synonymous with Nazi Germany in World War Two, the swastika in this poster, however, is left-facing or counterclockwise, also known as the sauwastika. This could have been due to ignorance or may have been done on purpose to mock the Dutch as bad imitators of the Nazis. Beneath the threatening hand, a young Indonesian woman is seen about to swing her long sword, which she wields in her right hand.[13]

The poster suggests a possible outcome: the woman falling victim to the dreaded giant hand. In the Indonesian imagination, this was the equivalent of the monstrous Dutch attempting to take over Indonesia and destroy its people. It was thus simultaneously an appeal to the youth to save Indonesian women from the cruel actions of the Dutch.

But this poster was also meant for the Dutch. The caption at the top reads: '*Neen, hoor! Selfdetermination for all nations*'. '*Neen, hoor*!' ('Oh no you don't!'), a Dutch phrase, could be interpreted as the Dutch rejecting the Indonesian nationalist goal of self-determination, a right for all nations. But it could also be saying the Dutch should immediately stop their attempts to recolonize Indonesia.

Accompanying this poster was another with a similar visual narrative, for which we also lack information on the makers and the context. This poster depicts almost the same monster hand but this time complete with its lower arm, painted black, signifying darkness and evil. It is holding a right-facing swastika, like that of Nazi Germany. The word 'Belanda' (the Indonesian word for the Netherlands) is written on its wrist. Standing in front of the hand, on top of a map of Indonesia, is a young Javanese woman. She is clearly the visual representation of the 'Self': Indonesia as a young nation, innocent but courageous in defending her rights. The emergence of the young woman looks like a volcanic eruption, an explosion that would destroy the Dutch offensive. At the bottom of the poster a caption reads: *Setapak pantang mundur* – 'not a step back' – reflecting determination.[14]

A more complete image of the Dutch as a monster appeared in the Jakarta-based newspaper *Merdeka* on 12 October 1945.[15] It shows half of a ghastly monster body. On its chest is written *Keboeasan NICA* – 'the savagery of NICA', referring to the Netherlands Indies Civil Administration. On its waist is the label *Bataljon 10*. This was the NICA battalion in Jakarta that engaged most frequently in armed contact with the Republican army in the early revolutionary period. It was greatly feared by Indonesian civilians in Jakarta.[16] This fearsome giant is about to devour a baby it is holding. A caption next to the baby reads: *anak-anak* (children), *pemoeda* (youths), *toekang betjak* (becak drivers), *dll* (etc.). The newspaper clearly intended the caricature to engender fear of Dutch cruelty, especially their Bataljon 10. The Dutch are depicted as they are about to eat not the professional Indonesian army but rather innocent and unarmed civilians in Jakarta. The clear message here is that they were a threat to everyone.

Through such negative portrayals, Indonesian nationalists reacted to NICA atrocities committed in October 1945, especially in Jakarta. The Jakarta-based magazine *The Voice of Free Indonesia* described the violence committed by the NICA in Jakarta and several other regions in Java as 'terroristic daily operations', which included 'deliberate murders, ill-treatments, insults, kidnapping, inciting disorder and confusion'.[17] This was the context in which Bataljon 10 NICA was imagined as a merciless, gruesome giant and a threat to the Indonesian people.

Early in 1946, an internal Republican conflict broke out between supporters of Prime Minister Sutan Sjahrir who opted for negotiations with the Dutch and the opposition led by Tan Malaka who insisted on 'complete freedom' (*100 % merdeka).* The conflict led to a new media campaign that intended to unite the two opposing groups by blaming the monstrous Dutch and their divide-and-conquer politics. Caricatures portrayed the Dutch as a provocative giant, stirring up turmoil and ruckus among Indonesians. One caricature in the newspaper *Lasjkar* on 9 May 1946 went further than others in its gruesomeness. It depicted the NICA as a combination of the satanic image commonly known in the Western tradition and the mean giant in Javanese folklore known as *buto ijo*. Its right hand, with the word 'NICA' written on it, has coarse hair and long and sharp fingernails. It is seen toying with much smaller human figures representing Indonesian community groups, both civilians and security apparatuses. At the bottom, a caption reads: *Siapakah jang roegi...kita. Dan siapakah jang oentoeng...moesoeh kita* - 'Who is suffering loss? We are. Who is profiting from it? Our enemies.'[18] This was clearly meant to be a reminder that the loyalty of the Indonesian people was supposed to be solely dedicated to the Republican authorities working for unity among community groups, instead of to the Dutch who were inciting division.

In 1947, the Dutch intensified their efforts to gain control over Indonesian occupied territory. The Linggarjati Agreement of November 1946 did nothing to stop the Dutch army from expanding its territory. To add insult to injury, they even resorted to extreme violence, as with the campaign led by Captain Raymond Westerling in South Sulawesi as well as during the establishment of federal states on the other islands. Republican concerns over this situation were evident in a coloured poster produced by the Army Information Office, Regiment I, Division Gajah II, Sumatera, in May 1947. As with the posters examined previously, this one shows an unusual non-human right hand wearing a blue sleeve, which is part of an official uniform. The hand has long and sharp fingernails, ready to grip the map of Indonesia. But before it does so, the hand is crushed, stepped on by the boot of the Indonesian army. At the top of the poster, a caption reads: *Djangan Oesik Indonesia*! – 'Do not disturb Indonesia!'.[19]

American propaganda during World War Two often depicted Japan as a monkey or a rat gnawing at America's territory. One US Navy poster, for example, shows a grey rat wearing a hat with the imperial Japanese war flag on it. The rat is about to bite into a piece of cheese placed on a mousetrap on a map of Alaska. The caption reads: 'Alaska, death-trap for the Jap.'[20] Mark Johnston argues that such depictions were meant to emphasize white supremacy and the inferiority of non-white nations and Asians.[21] But were the Dutch not depicted likewise in Indonesian propaganda?

A similar visualization did indeed appear in the pro-Republican magazine *Merdeka* in response to the establishment of the Soviet Republic of Indonesia led by Muso in Madiun in September 1948. Here, interestingly, the non-white artist has depicted some white people as animals. The caricature consists of three animals. It was placed as prominently as possible at the top of the front page of the newspaper, making it immediately visible to the reader.[22] On the left is Muso (sometimes also spelled Musso) represented by a bear. In the middle, a mighty Indonesian bull (*banteng*) is seen lifting its front legs, giving the impression that it is ready to stomp on the other animal in front of it, which is the Dutch lion. The lion's mouth is wide open, showing its fangs, while its sharp claws are ready to pierce the Republican bull. As the bull's front legs are raised to anticipate the lion's attack, however, its head looks back as its tail is bitten by the bear Muso.

Muso, the former leader of the Indonesian Communist Party (Partai Komunis Indonesia, PKI) in the 1920s, had returned to Indonesia in August 1948 under the strong influence of the Soviet Union. Muso and the PKI insisted that Indonesia should become more closely aligned with the Soviet Union. Then, in September 1948, they unilaterally established the Soviet Republic of Indonesia, followed by the communist rebellion in Madiun, East Java. Given this situation, the Republican armed forces TNI had to face two enemies at the same time, the Dutch and the communists. For the Re-

Image 2. A caricature representing the Dutch as a lion playing with the UN *Security Council in full view of the international community.* Source: Merdeka, 19 February 1949 (NIOD Collection).

publican government, Muso and his supporters were enemies within. They were backstabbers at the precise moment that Indonesia had to focus all its attention on fighting the external enemy, which was the lion preying on the Indonesian bull.

On 28 January 1949, the UN Security Council issued a resolution pressing Indonesia and the Netherlands to cease all military actions. It urged the Dutch to release imprisoned Indonesian leaders so they could restore their government, and it encouraged the two governments to return to the negotiating table. In direct defiance of this resolution, the Dutch launched further military action in early February 1949, with Dutch air and ground attacks in several regions in Central Java causing civilian casualties.[23]

One of the Indonesian responses to the Dutch violations of the resolution was to create a visual representation of the Dutch as a ferocious lion refusing to heed the international community's ultimatum to stop its malice. On the front page of its 19 February 1949 issue, *Merdeka* printed a black-and-white caricature depicting the Dutch as a lion in front of a human audience, in an amphitheatre resembling the UN Security Council Assembly (see Image 2). In the foreground, covering more than half the space, is an anthropomorphic lion standing on its two legs.[24] Roaring angrily, its rear left leg is lifted, showing that it has just kicked a globe bearing the words 'Security Council' (Dewan Keamanan). Around the globe are two olive branches, which are considered a symbol of peace in both Greek and modern European traditions. Here the Security Council is portrayed merely as a ball that the lion can play with as it pleases. The olive branches look withered from being kicked by the lion – a sign of waning peace due to Dutch savagery. In the background, dozens of spectators are watching the lion's action. Judging from their clothes, they represent various countries in the world including Burma, India, Britain, several other European countries, the United States, Arab countries, and possibly the Soviet Union and Turkey or Egypt.

This caricature highlights the abhorrence the Indonesian authorities felt for the atrocities of the Dutch, who had launched a massive attack on Indonesian-controlled territory on 18 December 1948 and refused to comply with the Security Council resolution at the end of January 1949. In December 1948 and January 1949, the United States and the UN Security Council alternated in exerting pressure on the Dutch. However, as the caricature shows, the Netherlands responded slowly and reluctantly. Indonesians saw this as evidence that the Dutch were deceiving the UN Security Council and the international community. It was not until April 1949 that the Netherlands began to soften its stance in response to the US and UN pressure.

Indonesian newspapers commonly depicted the Netherlands as a lion, which was, after all, its national emblem. However, in one Indonesian propaganda poster, it was depicted as a monkey (see Image 3).[25] More sensationally, the monkey represented Queen Wilhelmina of the Netherlands (r. 1890-1948). To heighten the extreme insult, the poster – which was naturally anonymous – is in colour. It depicts a chained monkey wearing a white European aristocratic-style women's dress with orange polka dots. Around its neck is a scarf with blue, orange and white patterns, directly reminding people of its association with the Netherlands. The monkey's face is sad and pitiful, as if in dire need of help. Its right hand is raised and opened, a sign of begging, while its left holds an empty tin cup. A large caption in red on the top, right and bottom of the poster reads: '*Wilhelmina sedang minta2*' – 'Wilhelmina is begging'.[26]

Image 3. A poster depicting a beggar monkey with a sad face, complete with the caption 'Wilhelmina sedang minta2' (Wilhelmina is begging). Source: NL-HaNA NEFIS/CMI, 2.10.62 inv.no 5411.

The chained monkey recalls an entertaining attraction often seen in colonial Javanese society known as the 'the dancing monkey' (*topeng monyet*, Dutch: *apenspel*). Originating from India, *topeng monyet* was run by a master dressed in an Indian outfit.[27] The monkey was trained to don human clothing and to perform attractions for the public, handing the tips to his master. The depiction of Wilhelmina, the head of state of the Netherlands, as a dancing monkey was an effort to degrade her socio-political status, to dehumanize her existence and to reduce her to a target for mockery, an unserious plaything. The empty cup and the hand gesture were possibly a satire on the desperate financial straits the Dutch were in, given that they depended heavily on aid from the United States to rebuild their country after World War Two.

The Dutch as the mean and egotistical master

Visuals were also used to portray the Dutch as harsh and greedy capitalists, taking the imagination back to the colonial era. One such visual was a poster produced by the Information Bureau of the Republic of Indonesia, Cirebon Residency Office (Image 4). Although the year of production is not known, the maker was clearly an official government agency. It is safe to assume that the poster represented an official view.

Its context is equally clear, namely Labour Day (1 May). The poster shows a man with a very formal appearance typical of men in Europe, particularly in the Netherlands. He is depicted as a factory owner, as suggested by the mechanical metal pressing machine that he is standing on. He is turning a wheel to apply pressure as the top plate moves downward and meets the lower plate. In between the two plates is a person, pinned down. Half his body is trapped in the machine, unable to escape. The man is clearly an Indonesian worker, as can be seen from his white shirt and black cap *(peci)*, as well as from the Indonesian language he is using. Both his hands are stretching out, asking for help from anyone who can see him. From the poster, it is obvious that the factory owner does not care about the man's suffering. With a face showing pain and sadness, the oppressed worker says: "Workers! Unite! So we can never be oppressed again!' (*Boeroeh! Bersatoelah! Agar djangan digentjet lagi!*).[28]

The pressing machine symbolizes capitalism and the height of Dutch manufacturing and at the same time the sufferings of Indonesian labourers forced to work hard for very low wages. The happy smile of the factory owner is in stark contrast to the pitiful face of the worker. However, we also have the impression that, though terribly oppressed, the Indonesian worker still has the courage to resist.

The image of the civilized, well-off but smug European man indeed became a frequent target of ridicule in Indonesian visual propaganda. Another poster is worth mentioning here. It is not known by whom or when the poster was produced. In it, a Dutch official or possibly a financier is seen running recklessly as he is chased by two sharpened bamboo stakes, a generic symbol of the resistance put up by Indonesian fighters.[29] Although the bamboo stakes miss their target, the image invokes the idea that the next one might strike the European man. At the bottom is a vivid call to fight such

Image 4. A poster depicting an Indonesian worker being pressed by a European (Dutch?) capitalist. *Source: NL-HaNA AS, 2.10.14 inv.no 5465.*

men: 'The sharpened bamboos are always ready to kick out the colonizers, comrades' (*Bamboe roentjing siaap mengoesir pendjadjah, kawan*). There are two 'a's in the word '*siap*' ('ready'), probably emphasizing the readiness to fight. Or perhaps it transcribes the long shout used by Indonesian fighters when confronting either an imminent Dutch attack or launching an attack of their own on the enemy. The word '*siap*' functioned as a kind of verbal intimidation toward the Dutch; it was the word they feared the most.

Meanwhile, another poster depicts a white man in a white coat, white pants and white pith helmet.[30] The helmet symbolizes colonial power, as it was often worn by Dutch foremen or plantation owners when making inspections or when punishing their native coolies whom they accused of underperforming. The white man in the poster is seen sitting on top of a Javanese noble (*priyayi*), who is on all fours. He is looking up while his hands are tucked into his pockets, giving the impression of a great master. The Javanese man is seen wearing glasses, a metaphor for his education. His face is turned downward, expressing weariness. One can immediately see the resemblance between him and a horse being ridden, mimicking a direct insult to an esteemed member of the bumiputra community.

Interestingly, another poster ridicules both the Indonesian and the Dutch. In the background is a steep ravine, on the edge of which two men in formal clothing are standing. The one on the left – half-bald, fat-bellied – appears to be laughing. His right hand is in his pants pocket, suggesting arrogance. A pocket watch chain hangs on his belly. It shines and signifies wealth. In addition, he dons a luxurious ornament on his chest. While his right foot stands firm on the ground, his left foot is depicted kicking two soldiers who appear to have fallen into the ravine.[31]

At the bottom of the ravine is a blazing fire waiting to engulf the two falling soldiers. Right under the falling soldiers is a caption in Dutch that reads: '*Koloniale oorlog*' or 'colonial war'. Clearly the two soldiers – one Indonesian, another Dutch – have been sacrificed in the colonial war by the Dutch capitalists. The other man standing next to the fat man is seen enjoying the scene. Next to the two men is the following message in Dutch: 'Dutch soldiers... You will not die for your country!! But you die only for these fat businessmen and money-eating wolves.' ('*Hollandsche soldaat...niet voor je land ga je dood!! Maar enkel en alleen voor die vette ondernemers en geldwolven*').[32] This illustration was intended to draw sympathy and build awareness among Dutch soldiers that the war they were waging against the Republic of Indonesia only benefited financiers while making their own nation miserable. The message was that the war was not aimed at defending the dignity of the Dutch state.

The greedy, cruel but weak Dutch soldier

Between 1945 and 1950, about 150,000 Dutch soldiers were deployed in Indonesia. Before being sent to Indonesia, they were indoctrinated with the message that their mission was to restore peace and build Indonesia with whatever means necessary, including war and violence.[33] A caricature in the English-language magazine *The Voice of Free Indonesia,* previously printed in *Merdeka*, shows Indonesian people mocking the Dutch soldiers who claimed they were on a mission to build Indonesia. Entitled 'Australia defends the rights of the Indonesian people', it portrays a Dutch soldier standing on a pile of boxes and cans of rations with the label 'Made in Australia'. Next to the Dutch soldier is an Australian soldier who taps his Dutch counterpart on the shoulder and reminds him in English: 'Not only your own nationals and your followers, but also the Indonesians…according to our former agreement'. In the left corner of the caricature, an Indonesian family is looking at the two expectantly. This caricature was an attack on the selfish attitude of the Dutch authorities who had been greatly helped by the Australians but who were only concerned about their fellow Dutchmen while ignoring the Indonesian people, who faced much bigger problems in their daily lives, including food shortages.[34]

Dutch soldiers were often depicted as being cruel to Indonesians. One black-and-white poster depicts the cruelty of the Dutch army on the Indonesian people, a cruelty that had not changed since the colonial period (see Image 5).[35] The consequences of the euphemistically named 'police action' – the Dutch military aggression of 27 July 1947 – are portrayed as the continuation of economically motivated acts of violence since colonial times that had taken the lives of many Indonesians, also in rural areas. There are two images in the one poster that draw parallels between Dutch colonial behaviour and their actions in 1948 after Indonesia had gained its independence. The first image has the caption 'The year 1923' (*Tahun 1923*), while the second is captioned '7-1-1948', both images showing the violence committed by the Dutch against the Indonesian population in rural areas. The poster then calls on Indonesian workers to resist Dutch occupation.

The first image portrays a Dutchman in the full uniform of the marshals (*marechaussee*) riding on the back of a very thin bumiputra man who is seen wearing worn-out shorts and is barefoot. In his left hand, the Dutchman holds the reins attached to the indigenous man's mouth. In Indonesia, reins were commonly used on cows or water buffalos only, so this action represents a deep insult towards the Indonesian. His right hand is seen holding a fishing rod, at the end of which hangs a coin on a string. It signifies the harsh economic situation of the population that had to live on only two and a half cents a day, a result of 350 years of colonization. The left hand of the Indonesian man is seen supporting his entire body upon which the Dutchman is riding, while his right hand is trying to take the coin at the end of the fishing rod held by the Dutchman.

On the back of the Dutchman is a bag with sugar, quinine, rubber and tea, signifying the natural resources that the Dutch had been exploiting in Indonesia. These commodities were sold in the global market by the Dutch and in no way contributed to the welfare of the Indonesians at large. The image is accompanied by a narration that reads: 'Indonesia was colonized by the Dutch. Our resources were sold in the global market. Only for the benefit of the Dutch capitalists. Remember workers!!! Your promise on 17-8-1945. That you will not work for the Dutch anymore.'[36] The final clause 'you will not work for the Dutch anymore' is underlined, stressing the importance of not cooperating with the Dutch. The key message that the image tries to get across is that any loyalty the Indonesian worker gives to the Dutch is denigrating to the dignity of the Indonesian people, who have suffered for so long under Dutch oppression.

The image at the bottom of the same poster shows a typical Indonesian village. In the foreground, a Dutch soldier is seen stabbing a skinny Indonesian man with his bayonet. The caption reads: 'Comrades!!! As a result of the Dutch Plosionil [sic] action, the purpose of which was said to be to secure and guarantee the safety of Indonesian people. But the reality is, as evident in Cilewo and other places within the district of Cikampek, farmers were stabbed to death with their bayonets. Comrades!!! We shall not let this continue.'[37] Clearly, the violence inflicted upon villagers in West Java by the Dutch during their first military aggression was the inspiration for the artist to display the atrocity and greed of the Dutch colonizers and the suffering of the Indonesian people.

Nonetheless, the Dutch army was not always visualized as powerful. They were only depicted as such when portrayed as oppressors of unarmed Indonesian civilians. When appearing together with the Indonesian army in a poster, their might was always absent. This type of visualization aimed to

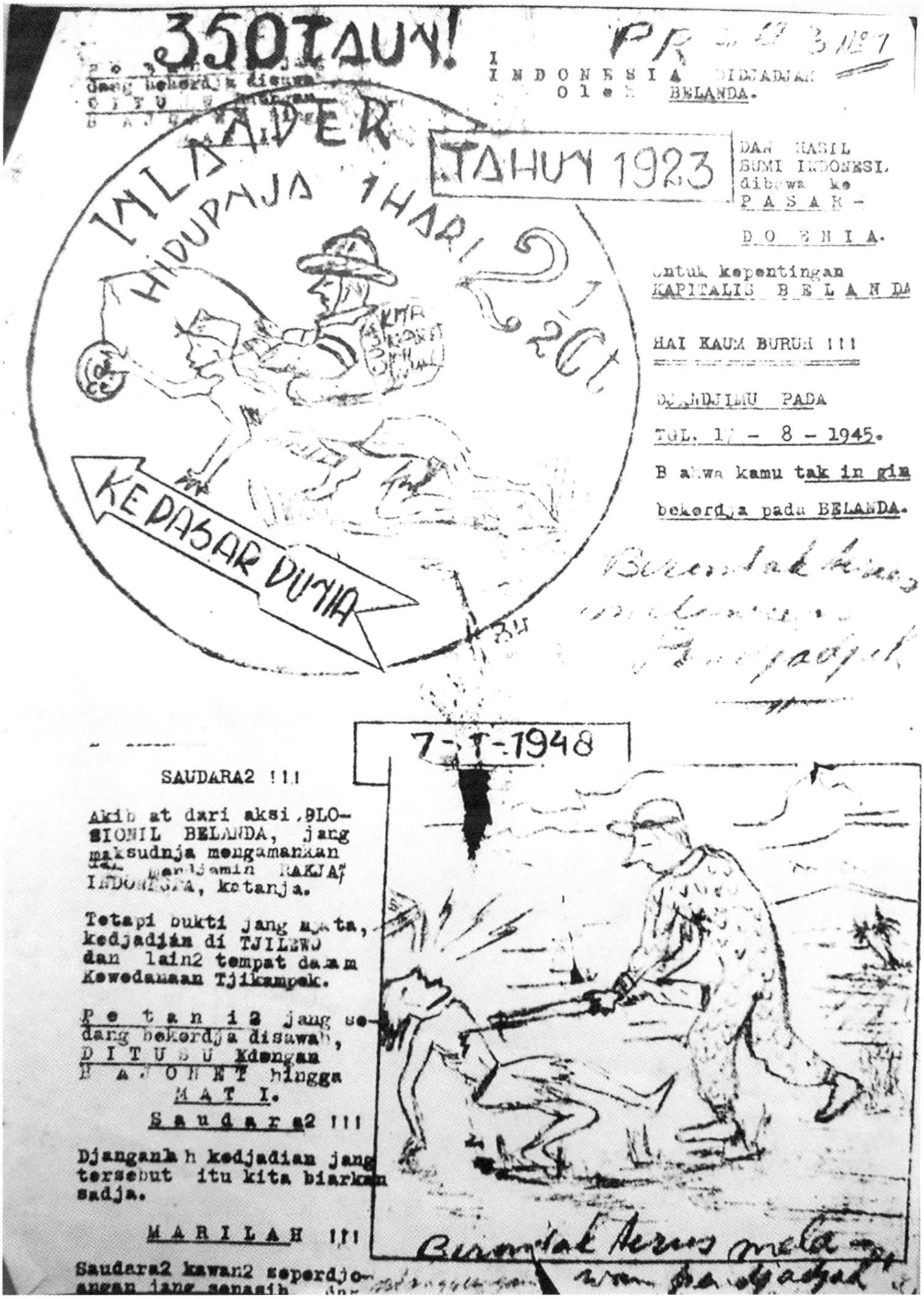

Image 5. A poster depicting the misfortune of Indonesian farmers under Dutch rule, both in the colonial period and in 1948. Source: NL-HaNA AS, 2.10.14 inv.no 5465.

emphasize a positive idea of 'Self' and simultaneously to boost the people's fighting spirit. Indonesian fighters were depicted as ideal soldiers: disciplined, strong, weapon-savvy, courageous, smart and, of course, victorious.

Such a depiction is evident, for example, in a comic-strip-like poster with six horizontally interrelated panels entitled "Watch out, the Dutch are looking for land to occupy!' (*Awas Belanda minta tanah! – Untuk Dijajah!*). It sent a message to the people that, even though Indonesian fighters were only armed with sharpened bamboo sticks, they could defeat well-armed Dutch soldiers. They could even manage to confiscate their modern weapons. A caption reads: 'As long as the Dutch colonizers remain in our land, there shall be chaos and misery! Therefore, with whatever means, we shall destroy them.'[38] At the bottom right is written 'Pepolit' (Pendidikan Politik Tentara, Political Education of the Armed Forces). This was a special body under the Ministry of Defence of the Republic of Indonesia tasked with ensuring that the political views between the state and military leaders were coordinated.[39] The production of anti-Dutch propaganda was part of Pepolit's mission.

Van der Plas: Invader and provocateur

Ch. O. van der Plas was governor of the State of East Java and before that one of the NICA administrators who had arrived early in Jakarta from Australia on 15 September 1945 to prepare the city for incoming Dutch troops. He was one of the Dutch officials most frequently mocked in Indonesian prop-

Image 6. A caricature depicting Van der Plas, first published in Merdeka and reprinted in The Voice of Free Indonesia magazine, first edition, 1945. The original caption reads: 'Modern Don Quixote of the 20th century'. *Source: The Voice of Free Indonesia, No. 1 (Collection of The National Library of Indonesia).*

aganda posters. The earliest visual that mocked Van der Plas was a caricature in the Jakarta-based *Merdeka,* later reproduced in the magazine *The Voice of Free Indonesia.* It depicts an old man, bearded just like Van der Plas, wearing a beret and military outfit (see Image 6). Set against a tropical landscape, the old man is seen riding a donkey. His left hand is holding the bridle, while his right is holding a banner emblazoned with the word 'NICA'. The donkey looks fatigued, with a wound patch on its rump, suggesting it is severely ill.[40]

The caricature is entitled 'Modern Don Quixote of the Twentieth Century'. It suggests that Van der Plas, an experienced figure in the bureaucratic world of the Dutch East Indies and very knowledgeable about Indonesia, was actually nothing more than a hapless Don Quixote. The main character in Miguel de Cervantes' novel *Don Quixote de la Mancha* (1605), Don Quixote was a madman who undertook daring adventures that were only figments of his imagination. It was as if, after several hundred years, Don Quixote had been reborn in the modern age in the form of an old Dutchman wanting to become the saviour knight for Indonesia. He was portrayed as a cavalryman, but he rode the wrong kind of animal, meaning he could not grasp reality and chose to live in his own false fantasy instead. That fantasy in the case of Van der Plas was the pre-war atmosphere, when Dutch colonial rule was still in place. Like Don Quixote, he misunderstood the changes that were occurring and kept resorting to brute force.

In another caricature, which appeared in *Merdeka* on 6 January 1946, Van der Plas is seen in the same room with Lieutenant Governor-General van Mook, together with Republican Prime Minister Sutan Sjahrir and three Dutch soldiers who have just entered the room. The soldiers are given the captions 'Dutch army landing and mobilization' ('*Mobilisasi pendaratan tentara Belanda*') and 'Terror by NICA gangsters' ('*Terreur gangster NICA*'). Before them is a desk, on top of which is a piece of paper. Van Mook is seen banging the table angrily. At the bottom of the poster a caption reads: 'the negotiation is surely doomed to fail because the Dutch prefer violence' ('*proendingan jang tentoe gagalnja…karena Belanda sebenarnja menghendaki kekerasan*').[41] The caricature's clear message is that the Dutch were acting as if they were willing to negotiate with the Indonesian authorities – represented by the anti-fascist Sjahrir – but it was all under pressure of terror and armed threats.

Van Mook: Provocateur and evil master

Just like Van der Plas, Lieutenant Governor-General H.J. van Mook was also the butt of Indonesian visual mockery. Van Mook was assigned the task of restoring Dutch colonial rule in Indonesia. He had already formed his ideas about the future of the Dutch East Indies in the 1930s, when he imagined a commonwealth between the colony and its mother country.[42] This vision of his made no room for independence for Indonesia. Van Mook's initial mission in Jakarta was to convince the British that administrative affairs in Indonesia were Dutch affairs and to insist that Sukarno and Hatta be arrested.[43]

In the imagination of Indonesian nationalists, Van Mook was perceived as basically similar to Van der Plas. Both had a desire to re-establish Dutch colonialism in Indonesia. Van Mook only differed from Van der Plas in his much more manipulative way of dealing with Indonesians. He used his power to pit Indonesians against each other. After failing to persuade the British to arrest Sukarno and Hatta and to disband the Republic of Indonesia, Van Mook looked for another way. He was responsible for the creation of numerous federal states in various regions of the archipelago. Van Mook felt that federalism was the way to accommodate the wishes of the local population. Indonesian authorities, however, saw it as a strategy of the Dutch to divide and conquer.

One of the earliest depictions of H.J. van Mook was featured in *Merdeka* on 8 November 1945. He was portrayed as a chicken farmer – the chicken being the obedient Indonesian population. Van Mook's right hand is seen holding a chicken coop labelled: 'Colonialism' ('*Pendjadjahan*'). The ground on which the coop is about to be placed has all sorts of chicken feed, which are labelled: 'promotion, big salary, commonwealth, removal of national differences, people's welfare, strong army, and other promises' ('*pangkat tinggi, gadji besar*, commonwealth, *penghapoesan perbedaan bangsa Belanda-Indonesia, kemakmoeran pendoedoek, tentera jang koeat, d.l.l. djanji*'). In the background is a pile of three big sacks; on one of them is written: 'supply of promises' ('*persediaan djandji*').[44]

Since mid-October 1945, Van Mook had been talking to Indonesians about the Dutch effort to build Indonesia's future, one of whose elements, he said, was to eliminate colonialism, as promised by Queen Wilhelmina herself in December 1942. But for Indonesians, as depicted in the caricature, the Dutch were only full of false promises and deceptions because it was clear they wanted to remain dominant in the promised new Indonesia. Another caricature in the *Kedaulatan Rakjat* newspaper of 12 December 1945 depicts an Indonesian bull goring a man made to look like Van der Plas while stepping on another man who resembles Van Mook.[45]

At the first official negotiations between the Republic of Indonesia and the Netherlands, which took place in the Hoge Veluwe in the Netherlands between 14 and 25 April 1946, the Dutch insisted that the Republic of Indonesia should have territorial authority only on Java and Madura islands, excluding the regions that had by then been occupied by the Dutch. The strong reaction to this in the Indonesian press is evident in the caricature published in *Lasjkar* on 8 May 1946. Van Mook, depicted with a disproportionate physique, is seen handing a miniature of Java Island over to an Indonesian standing before him. His right hand is hidden behind his back, carrying a miniature island of Sumatra, which he would offer to the Indonesian authority after Java. Next to Van Mook, a caption reads: 'commonwealth, Sulawesi, Kalimantan', indicating that the islands of Sulawesi and Kalimantan were to be made a Dutch commonwealth, denying Indonesian authority over the islands. The Indonesian man in the poster, however, firmly rejects the offer, saying: 'No! 100% freedom for Indonesia, all of it.' ('*Tidak! Hanja 100 % merdeka oentoek Indonesia seloeroehnja.*').[46] The caricature was a firm rejection of the Dutch offer at the Hoge Veluwe conference.

Van Mook reappeared in a caricature when Indonesian authorities faced internal turmoil. In the 4 October 1948 edition of *Merdeka*, he is depicted as a man seeking to gain something out of another man's difficulties (see Image 7).[47] Indonesia is faced with the communist rebellion in Madiun. The smiling man on the left is Muso. The protagonist in the middle, wearing a white shirt and black *peci* with the word 'nasionalisme' on it and sitting on a chair

Image 7. A caricature depicting 'Indonesia' being fought over by nationalists, communists and the Dutch, printed in Merdeka, 4 October 1948. Source: Merdeka, 4 October 1948 (Collection of The National Library of Indonesia).

labelled 'Indonesia' probably represents Sukarno. Meanwhile, another man who looks like Van Mook is attempting to take over the seat. Muso's right hand is seen pulling Sukarno's right hand, trying to keep him from his chair. Muso's left hand is holding a chair bearing the word 'communism' and a hammer-sickle symbol, conveying the message that Indonesian nationalism was to be replaced by communism with Muso as its top leader. Simultaneously, Van Mook is depicted partially seated, with a cane for additional support. He seems to be pondering how to occupy the Indonesian chair entirely.[48]

Van Mook's desire to gain control of Indonesia by any means necessary became a frequent theme in Indonesian visual propaganda. An anonymous and undated poster depicts Van Mook riding a seemingly fatigued Dutch military officer. His head appears to be disproportionately bigger than the rest of his body. This poster was probably produced to underline Van Mook's manipulative strategy to gain control of Indonesia. The caption reads: 'Don't ever become van Mook's dog!!!' ('*Djanganlah mendjadi andjing van Mook*!!!').[49]

Another poster with the English title 'The Man on the Right Please [Place]' is an attack on the Dutch and their federal states (see Image 8).[50] Van Mook is sitting on a wooden litter of the kind in which slaves traditionally conveyed royalty. Here, however, the litter is carried by two indigenous royal figures. The porter at the back is Suria Kartalegawa, a Sundanese noble who was against the Republic and leader of the Dutch-backed Sundanese People's Party (PRP).[51] In May 1947, the PRP established the State of Pasundan, which also became the target of mockery in propaganda posters. The front porter is seen wearing a Dutch-style outfit – long-sleeved white shirt, white pants and formal shoes. He is supposed to mimic Hilman Djajadiningrat, a supporter of the State of Pasundan.[52]

From the top right, a kris is thrown by Indonesian fighters. It is flying directly towards the pith helmet on Van Mook's head. Surprised and shaken, van Mook accidentally elbows Suria Kartalegawa in the face, making him stagger and eventually fall – and also causing his sandals to fall off. At the same time, Van Mook's right foot kicks Hilman Djajadiningrat in the head.[53] Suria Kartalegawa and Hilman Djajadiningrat are here portrayed as nothing more than Van Mook's slaves, persons who will moreover immediately be eliminated as soon as the Republic has defeated Van Mook. The poster conveys a very strong message, especially for the Sundanese, the largest ethnic group in West Java, not to follow – let alone be loyal to – those who are nothing more than errand boys for foreigners despite their high social status.

Image 8. A poster illustrating Van Mook being carried on a stretcher by two Sundanese nobles. Source: NL-HaNA AS, 2.10.14 inv.no 5465.

Another caricature attacking Van Mook and his project of establishing a federal state in West Java appeared in *Kedaulatan Rakjat* on 10 May 1947. It depicts Van Mook as the Sundanese wooden puppet master and Suria Kartalegawa as his puppet.[54] In many similar caricatures, the Dutch are almost always depicted as the great master, while the Indonesians are simply puppets without thoughts of their own. Another caricature in *Merdeka* on 11 January 1947 entitled 'The Denpasar Drama and Its Players!' ('*Sandiwara Denpasar dan pemain2nja!*'), again depicts Van Mook as the puppet master. It refers to the Denpasar Conference of December 1946, which established the large federal State of East Indonesia (*Negara Indonesia Timur*, NIT). Van Mook is engrossed in playing with his three puppets, which represent Indonesian nobles who played a prominent role in the NIT, namely Sukawati, Daeng Malewa and T. Noor. Van Mook is seen moving their mouths and hands, giving the impression that he is the mastermind behind these three known supporters of federalism.[55]

All these Republican visual presentations succeeded in building a sustained image of Van Mook as an evil man. Both Ch.O. van der Plas and H.J. van Mook were portrayed as the worst type of enemy for trying to re-establish Dutch colonial rule in 1945-1949. They had to be hated and held responsible for all the suffering experienced by the Indonesian people after proclaiming their independence on 17 August 1945.

Conclusion

Visual mockery was part of the effort by Indonesian propagandists to fight the Dutch, maintain their own newly gained independence and resist Dutch plans to re-establish colonial rule. Visual propaganda was carried out by means of two channels, namely separately printed posters and the print media. It targeted the powerful Dutch domination over Indonesian territories by depicting a hierarchical relationship between the master and his pet, the oppressor and the oppressed. The Dutch were almost always represented as arrogant and abusive, while Indonesians were often presented as humiliated, only able to move according to the wishes of their exploitative Dutch master. The Dutch were frequently portrayed with disproportionate or deformed physical features. This was meant to emphasize the abnormality or even the physical and mental illness of the Dutch. Two important Dutch figures, Van der Plas and Van Mook, became the main targets of Indonesia's visual demonization. Van der Plas, depicted as a symbol of Dutch colonial power, was ridiculed as a fragile old man whose insatiable ambitions for power made him lose his mind, leaving him living in his own fantasy, unaware of the rapidly changing realities. Van Mook was depicted as a most dangerous, threatening, manipulative, mind-controlling and provocative figure. He was typically portrayed as the mastermind behind the Dutch strategy of pitting Indonesians against each other in order for the Dutch to regain control over Indonesia. Van Mook's success in controlling the thoughts and attitudes of local rulers was evident in his idea of federalism, which received support from local figures.

In other representations, the Dutch were symbolized by animals. The lion, drawn from the Dutch national emblem, was repeatedly used to ridicule Dutch barbarism. The monkey was used to portray the miserable Queen of the Netherlands, who was reduced to begging. Elsewhere, the Dutch were portrayed as menacing monsters – large creatures with long hair, sharp fingernails, horns and very long canine teeth. They instilled fear in the hearts of the Indonesian population.

All these images gave the impression that the Dutch were not human – or if they were, they were not normal human beings. The sharp fingernails and long canine teeth were used to stress the non-human, threatening aspects of the Dutch. This was used to give rise to mixed feelings of fear, hatred, anger and disgust, which would in turn create a justification for fighting these ugly, barbaric, inhuman creatures with brute force if necessary. The same images were also meant to generate sympathy for and loyalty to the Republican government rather than the two previous colonial powers: Japan, which had just lost the war, and the Netherlands, which aimed to restore its colonial rule.

The visual propaganda proved to be effective throughout the Indonesian War of Independence. This was evident in the increasing support for the Republican government and in the correspondingly negative attitudes towards the Dutch. It also successfully created a consistent larger narrative – one that remains salient in Indonesian historiography to the present day – about the manipulation by the NICA politicians and the atrocities committed by the Dutch army in their failed attempt to re-establish colonial rule in the Indonesian archipelago.

5.

The violence of Dutch public security

Semarang and its Central Javanese hinterland, 1945-1949

Martijn Eickhoff

INTRODUCTION

On 17 August 1945, the day Indonesian independence was proclaimed, Semarang had a population of 225,000, of whom 40,000 were ethnic Chinese. It was an important centre of industry and trade. Its harbour on the north coast of Java between Jakarta and Surabaya, as well as its airport, its road and railway connections, made it a crucial logistical junction (see

During the Dutch-Indonesian conflict, troops constantly moved into the opposing forces' spheres of influence, despite official 'demarcation lines' separating Republican-controlled from Dutch-occupied areas. Civilians, too, moved across such lines, and often back, as well. Pictured here are Indonesians who in December 1947 were trekking across a stream into Republican territory at Salatiga, Central Java, assisted by TNI personnel. Source: *Nationaal Archief, Dienst voor Legercontacten.*

Maps 2 and 4). But it also depended on the hinterland for food, water and electricity. Its strategic position and its tradition of trade unionism made Semarang potentially an important stronghold for the new-born Republic. Its *pemuda* movement was robust. At the Villa Isola Youth Congress that took place between 16 and 18 May 1945 in Bandung, held under Japanese supervision, Semarang delegates had successfully pleaded for prioritizing independence above supporting Japan.[1]

News of the proclamation arrived at the Kantor Berita Domei Semarang news agency via wireless telegraphy. Due to Japanese censorship, it was not published in the local newspaper *Sinar Baroe* but it was somehow broadcast via the local radio station *Hoso Kyoku,* just before Friday prayers. The news also reached Assistant Resident Kanjeng Raden Tumenggung Wongsonegoro (1897-1978), who was chairing a pro-independence meeting in the Jawa Hokokai building. Wongsonegoro enjoyed aristocratic Javanese status, had colonial and Japanese-era administrative experience, and adhered to nationalist principles.[2] Nonetheless, the audience – made up of mostly *pemuda* – had to force him to read out the proclamation.[3] On Sunday 19 August – while still being pressed by the Semarang *pemuda* group – he told a public meeting at the city square (*alun-alun*) that Central Java was now under the authority of the Indonesian National Committee (Komite Nasional Indonesia, KNI). On 28 August, he was officially installed as the KNI representative.

The *pemuda* movement played an important role as the Republican administrative and military infrastructure began to take shape. The Youth Forces of the Republic of Indonesia (Angkatan Muda Republik Indonesia, AMRI) was founded in Semarang on 19 and 20 August. Bambang Suprapto was its leader. A special 'seizing unit' (Barisan Srobot) commandeered buildings in the city, marking them as 'Property of the Republic of Indonesia' ('Milik RI'). A colonial villa on the main street at Bodjong 89 – long a centre for popular gatherings – became their headquarters. They began disarming Japanese troops. On 28 August, a regional branch of the People's Security Agency (Badan Keamanan Rakyat, BKR) was formed from former members of the Semarang battalion of the PETA (Pembela Tanah Air, an Indonesian volunteer army established by the occupying Japanese), local *Heiho* (auxiliary Indonesian military units of the Imperial Japanese Army) and *pemuda*. In the week following 31 August, Raden Pandji Suroso was installed as governor of Central Java and Iman Sudjahari as mayor of the city of Semarang. Sumarsono became head of police, while Wongsonegoro became Resident.[4]

Tensions between different groups rose as Dutch and Indo-European internees were released from Japanese internment camps. While the Japanese caretaker troops forbade the flying of Dutch flags, Dutch B-25 Mitchell bombers dropped pamphlets on Semarang promoting the future cooperation between 'Indonesia and the Netherlands'.[5] The first anti-Dutch pamphlets appeared in the city on 10 September with the message that Indonesians should claim their rights and not take orders from the Dutch and that the colonies should vanish.[6] The scene seemed set for a clash, but the situation soon turned much more complex and violent; over the subsequent five years, Semarang and its hinterland would be the scene of a series of battles and attacks, military and inter-civilian violence, and changes in civilian administration and regimes.

This chapter explores these events through the eyes of different groups and individuals. Via a special focus on border areas – including demarcation lines – it aims to better understand the complex, layered nature of developments in the region, including in particular the social role that Indonesian subalterns were to play. Yet a Semarang-based perspective on the Indonesian War of Independence is strongly linked to a colonial gaze on Central Java, for the Dutch soon brought the city under their control and from there expanded into Central Java. The gradual Dutch expansion mimicked the older trajectories of colonial subjugation. It aimed to impose Dutch 'peace' and 'order' on the Central Javanese revolutionary space and to shape the trajectory of 'decolonization' under the self-appointed guidance of the Dutch and under conditions set by them.[7] If this research had been conducted on other large Central Javanese cities, it would have produced different perspectives. Solo, for example, is generally described as a centre of radical revolutionary nationalism in the international literature. And Yogyakarta became the capital of the Republican government in January 1946, so a focus on that city would reveal that it symbolized the centralist and diplomatic version of the revolution (see the chapters by Galuh Ambar Sasi and Farabi Fakih in the present volume).

The following three sections, taken together, help to deconstruct the colonial gaze by including multiple perspectives. The first section provides an overview of the main military events and their actors. It is primarily based on Indonesian, Japanese, British and Dutch historical sources. The next section zooms in on the diverging terminology these different sources deploy, illustrating their different perspectives and creating an initial awareness of the forms of colonial near-sightedness that were at play. The final section focuses on Dutch attempts to bring Semarang and its hinterland under their control and the reactions of people involved in it. But the political and military suppression they practised worked at cross-purposes with these attempts to build legitimacy among the population.

Military conflict in Semarang and its Central-Javanese hinterland during the Indonesian independence war

Semarang and its hinterland in this period were characterized by a series of violent clashes. First came the Battle of Semarang, known as the 'Five Days' Battle' (Pertempuran Lima Hari),[8] that took place between 14 and 19 October 1945 when *pemuda* fighters seized an estimated 30,000 weapons from Japanese garrison troops stationed in Semarang under the command of Major Kido Shinichirō.[9] Though defeated, Japan's troops had remained intact. The British-led South East Asia Command (SEAC) had ordered them to maintain the status quo while awaiting the arrival of Allied troops. But the Republic of Indonesia was determined to reject all foreign control.

After the arrival of the 3rd battalion of the 10th Gurkha Rifles under the command of Lieutenant Colonel H.G. Edwardes on 19 October 1945, Semarang became a British 'key area', along with Jakarta and Surabaya. More British troops arrived later.[10] By that time, fighting between the *pemuda* and Japanese troops had stopped. On 26 October, mosques in Semarang organized a commemoration – *sholat ghaib* – at which Islamic victims of the Five Days' Battle were declared martyrs. Wongsonegoro laid the first stone of a monument in their honour at the city square (*alun-alun*) on 28 October, Youth Pledge Day (Hari Sumpah Pemuda), the day in 1928 when Indonesian youths had sworn an oath at a congress in Batavia/Jakarta. After this battle, he said, Indonesia could no longer be underestimated as a nation. The colonial stereotype that Indonesians were the tamest people on earth had lost its meaning, he added.[11]

British troops now pushed into the interior to protect the Dutch and Indo-European internees in Central Java who were still in the Japanese internment camps, surrounded by *pemuda* fighters. An effort named 'Recovery of Allied Prisoners of War and Internees' (RAPWI) had parachuted men into Magelang as early as 18 September. This team had found six camps with over 14,000 people in Ambarawa and Banyubiru. Five camps in Semarang contained a similar number of internees, few of whom had left the camps.[12]

The team worked together with local Indonesian officials, who were prepared to cooperate as long as Republican sovereignty was respected. But when the first Dutch troops landed in Jakarta on 29 September, tensions began to rise.[13] When Gurkhas were sent to Magelang and Ambarawa soon after landing in Semarang to make contact with internees and start organizing their evacuation, Indonesian leaders were convinced it was a cloak for the reinstalment of Dutch authority. They pointed to representatives of the Netherlands Indies Civil Administration (NICA) who had accompanied SEAC officials.[14] When negotiations broke down between the British on the one hand and Sukarno and Wongsonegoro on the other, the Battle of Magelang started on 30 October (ending on 2 November).[15] A fortnight later, Semarang became the site of a battle between British and Japanese forces on the one hand and Indonesian forces on the other. Wongsonegoro had been arrested early in the morning of 18 October but managed to flee that same night. During this 'Second Battle of Semarang', which took place between 18 and 21 November, Indonesian forces tried unsuccessfully to conquer the British headquarters.[16]

Ambarawa, which was in a precarious state since the Second Battle of Semarang, witnessed violence in December. As the internees were steadily evacuated to Semarang, Indonesians blocked roads, sniped at British positions and shelled the camps. Edwardes asked a number of former KNIL (Koninklijk Nederlands-Indisch Leger, Royal Netherlands East Indies Army) soldiers who had just been released – Dutch and Moluccans – to form a small guard platoon. They were headed by the Dutch Captain Arnold Visser. This arming of prisoners fuelled anger and distrust on the Indonesian side. As the British pulled out of Ambarawa, Indonesian soldiers led by then-Colonel Sudirman attacked them in the Battle of Ambarawa, which lasted from 11 to 15 December. The Indonesian forces were able to capture Ambarawa and the Ambarawa-Semarang highway.[17] Amidst continuous skirmishes, British troops only just managed to hold Semarang, including the strategic Gombel Hill and the airfield Kali Banteng.[18] A British military report described the dramatic situation within the city:

> As a direct result of the unsettling conditions, which were marked by arson, murder and looting on a large scale, the inhabitants of the town had lost all confidence. Business was at a complete standstill, markets were non-existent, people kept to their houses and hardly dared to move about in the streets, and there was no civil administration.[19]

The Dutch T-Brigade – also known as Tiger Brigade – arrived in the city on 9 March 1946. British troops planned to leave on 17 May. The British had been fearful of the effects that the arrival of the Dutch would have – one report expected 'strikes' and 'outbreaks of violence from both inside and outside of town' – as well as on the position of their own troops. Therefore, the 'heads of the various communities' were told the Dutch would be under British command. Although the Dutch arrival was in reality the first step towards the British departure, this assurance proved effective. The Dutch landing passed without incident.[20] The repatriation of all Japanese – except war criminals – was started on the basis of Anglo-Indonesian co-operation. The first Japanese troops had already left Semarang on 24 October 1945.

The T-Brigade was led by Colonel Rein van Langen of the KNIL. Expanded expeditiously, the brigade now consisted of four battalions of war volunteers (*oorlogsvrijwilligers*, also known as OVWers). Many had had experience with military violence during the liberation of the Netherlands. Upon arrival in Semarang, they felt 'like a cat in a strange warehouse'.[21] They did not know the 'enemy', while the city was full of nationalist graffiti and Indonesian flags.[22] They replaced Japanese troops guarding the southern access roads to the city and took over the western parts of the city, at first in collaboration with the British. The Dutch sometimes compared their intervention in Semarang to the Dutch resistance during the German occupation of the Netherlands and thus gave their presence legitimacy. When communists held a protest strike in the harbour of Amsterdam on 24 September 1946 against the deployment of the first group of war conscripts sent off to the Indonesian archipelago, the soldier journal *De Tijger* published a letter from a war volunteer in Semarang. It invited the communist leader Henk Gortzak to visit the city and see with his own eyes that what the T-Brigade was doing was in line with the spirit of resistance against the German occupation.[23]

For Indonesian forces, meanwhile, reconquering the city had been their fervent wish ever since British troops had occupied it, and in the meantime they had been busy professionalizing themselves. BKR was first renamed the People's Security Army (Tentara Keamanan Rakyat, TKR) in October 1945, and in January 1946 it was once again renamed – first as the People's Safety Military Forces (Tentara Keselamatan Rakyat, TKR) and then as the Army of the Republic of Indonesia (Tentara Republik Indonesia, TRI). In June 1947, it was renamed once more as the Indonesian National Armed Forces (Tentara Nasional Indonesia, TNI). From December 1945, the Central Java Command II coordinated its confrontations along the 'Semarang front' from its Central Battle Headquarters (Markas Pusat Pertempuran, MPP) in Magelang. Its Division IV, headquartered in Salatiga, had five regiments based in Pekalongan, Kendal, Salatiga, Purwodadi and Pati and was in charge of the Semarang-Pati area. Attempting to surround and isolate the city, they organized four 'fronts': the East Front, the Southeast Front, the South Front and the West Front.[24] At the time, at least 17 more informal and paramilitary groups known as 'battle groups' (*badan perjuangan*) or militias (*laskar*), loosely connected with the TKR/TRI, were active in and around Semarang. Later incorporated into the TNI, they had diverse religious, social, geographical and political backgrounds. Some date back to the time of the Japanese occupation, while others emerged as a result of the revolution.[25] As Dutch troops took over Semarang, the TRI increased its attacks, leading to three months of clashes. In reaction, the Dutch built a defensive line around Semarang. From 1 to 5 August 1946, Indonesian forces launched a general attack, yet without lasting success. Offensive activities diminished later that month.[26]

In the second half of 1946, the Dutch managed to expand the area under their control and strengthen their position. The British diplomat Lord Killearn facilitated negotiations leading to a ceasefire on 14 October 1946, and this included a first demarcation line (*garis demarkasi*).[27] On 15 November 1946, the Linggarjati Agreement was initialled (it was formally signed on 25 March 1947). Yet despite all this negotiated agreement, the Dutch initiated more fighting in December 1946. Van Langen decided that quick military action was needed to secure the Dutch position. The TRI was well prepared, which meant that the Dutch military operation took three weeks. Finally, a new ceasefire was established on 15 February 1947.[28] This left no Indonesian positions within the demarcation area. Signs along the demarcation line marked a demilitarized zone that was two kilometres wide. The TRI now made this their defensive zone, with land mines, road blocks and checkpoints, while blocking roads and railways.[29] Thus ended the military action within the city of Semarang.

In the following years the city, with its harbour and airport, functioned as a base for Dutch attacks on the Republic. New, mainly conscript battalions arrived. On 21 July 1947, the Dutch abrogated the Linggarjati Agreement and launched their first military aggression, Operation Product.[30] By the end of this operation on 5 August 1947, the T-Brigade had conquered large parts of Central Java. The Dutch began by breaking through the demarcation line and occupying Ungaran, Ambarawa, Salatiga (where the TNI headquarters of the 'Semarang front' was based) and Jelok. As the TNI left Salatiga, it burned houses and abducted many Chinese inhabitants to Solo as part of their 'scorched earth' tactics (*bumi hangus*).[31] Air raids from the Kali Banteng airport targeted Yogyakarta, Madiun and Solo. Troops occupied Mranggen, Purwosari, Demak, Dempet and Gubug to the east; Kaliwungu, Kendal and Weleri to the west; and Banyubiru and Bandungan in the south.

From the Dutch perspective, Operation Product broke Semarang's isolation. An overland connection now ran to West Java. The city redeveloped as an economic and administrative centre for the region.[32] On 29 August 1947, the Dutch unilaterally proclaimed the Van Mook Line, enclosing the area they held at the end of Operation Product (Map 2). The Republic refused to acknowledge this line. It still had almost 30,000 troops in Dutch-controlled Central Java and now started a guerrilla war.[33] This included attacking Indonesians who were willing to collaborate with the Dutch. The Dutch strategy of controlling occupied areas via checkpoints and patrols soon turned out to be ineffective.[34]

On 17 January 1948, the two sides ratified the Renville Agreement, which turned the 700km-long Van Mook Line into the Status Quo Line. The Indonesians promised to withdraw their troops from the 'pockets' in Dutch-controlled areas. They called this the *Hijrah*, referring to the journey of Muhammad and his followers out of Mecca, where he would later return victoriously.[35]

Dutch military aggression caused economic and social conditions to worsen in Central Java in the course of 1948. A lack of food (also the result of heavy rains in late 1947), countless refugees and a commercial standstill exacerbated by the Dutch naval blockade caused social tensions to escalate.[36] The Dutch established many new states in the areas of the archipelago they had reoccupied. On 8 July 1948, the leaders of these states established the Federal Consultative Assembly (Bijeenkomst voor Federaal Overleg, BFO) to plan for the establishment of the federal United States of Indonesia.[37] The Madiun Affair broke out within the Republic in September 1948, pitting the Indonesian Communist Party (Partai Komunis Indonesia, PKI) against the government in Yogyakarta. It came to a close at the end of November when most leaders and many members of the PKI and the associated People's Democratic Front (Front Demokrasi Rakyat, FDR) were detained and executed by the Siliwangi Division.[38] What had initially been a struggle between hinterland military units determined to preserve populist support and a high command determined to bring the field units under greater central control quickly took on Cold War dimensions. The outcome strengthened the international position of the Republic.[39]

The Dutch Army Commander, General Simon Spoor, had started already in June 1948 to push the idea of a second military action, which he believed was needed in order to eliminate the Republic.[40] Abrogating the Renville Agreement,[41] he ordered the so-called Second Police Action to begin on 19 December 1948 under the name Operation Kraai. The offensive lasted until 31 December. Now the aim was to conquer the Republican capital Yogyakarta and arrest the government. Semarang's airport Kali Banteng played an essential logistical role. A military column from Semarang crossed the Status Quo Line and arrived in Yogyakarta on 21 December.[42] The demarcation line had now lost its (un)official function. But while the Republic had lost its capital, the Republic itself remained very much alive, contrary to Dutch expectations.

The Dutch did not turn Central Java into a federal state but did start preparations aimed at including it in a federal Indonesia. In March 1949 they installed the Temporary Representative Council of the People of Central Java (Dewan Perwakilan Rakyat Jawa-Tengah Sementara) in Semarang. Also known as the Midden-Javaraad, the council was chaired by Valentinus Sudjito (1905-1958), a locally trained doctor active in the Indonesian Catholic Political Party.[43] It was to propose new administrative structures for the area and was directed to participate in conferences of the Federal Consultative Assembly. Some say Sudjito more or less hindered Dutch attempts to create a federal Central Java state.[44] In any case, the situation soon changed. The Roem-van Roijen Agreement of 7 May 1949 stipulated the withdrawal of the Dutch from Yogyakarta and led to the ceasefire of 10 August 1949.[45]

At the same time, the TNI adapted to the changing situation. After the Dutch attack on Yogyakarta, the Siliwangi Division retreated westwards, sometimes with whole families. The so-called Long March lasted one to three months.[46] Other TNI troops managed to regroup in Central Java and engaged in guerrilla warfare based on the Wehrkreise strategy of Colonel Abdul Haris Nasution. General Sudirman had left Yogyakarta in time and went into hiding while wandering around in Central Java.[47] He continued to command military activities throughout Java, including the 'general attack' (Serangan Umum) on Yogyakarta on 1 March 1949.[48] Dutch problems multiplied in the occupied areas. Their position was vulnerable, local support decreased, and even the use of intensive military violence could not prevent them from being on the defensive.[49] On the north coast and around Semarang, Indonesian troops engaged in sabotage and agitated against collaborators. Internally, TNI troops also clashed with Darul Islam battalions.[50] After the Dutch withdrawal from Yogyakarta (on 29 June 1949), the bridge on Kali Krasak became the semi-official border crossing between the Republic and Dutch-controlled Central Java. The river was considered the new, 'natural' demarcation line.[51]

In 1949, Lieutenant Colonel S. Sudiarto (1925-1950) managed to merge a group of freedom fighters in the Semarang-Pati area into the so-called Brigade SS (Brigade Semarang Stoottroep). It was incorporated into the TNI as Brigade VI Division II in May that year. Sudiarto had joined the Republican army already in 1945 as leader of the 24th TKR regiment of Kendal. But in September 1948, the Republican government detained him at Yogyakarta's Wirogunan prison for involvement in the Madiun Affair. He escaped during the Dutch attack on Yogyakarta. In the small village of Garangan, east of Ambarawa, he met a military unit consisting largely of his former subordinates. They reorganized themselves into the Brigade Semarang Stoottroep. In June 1949, this brigade started preparing an attack on Semarang. Inspired by the motto 'Heading towards the City of Semarang' (*Menudju ke Kota Semarang*), they surrounded the city. The 10 August ceasefire pre-empted their attack.[52] But J.M.J. Morsink, the then-highest civil official in Semarang, said the security situation in the city deteriorated rapidly after this. He spoke of 'cold infiltration'. TNI units, freed of the need for guerrilla tactics, were marching openly along the roads leading to Semarang. He urgently advised the city to prepare for the evacuation of women and children and to build emergency food supplies.[53]

Finally, on 27 December 1949, the day dawned for the official transfer of sovereignty. Two ceremonies took place in Semarang, respectively transferring military and civilian authority to the Indonesians. At 5 pm, the Indonesian flag was raised at the former governor's office, known as Het Grote Huis. There was a speech by the outgoing Dutch officeholder J.H. Statius Muller, followed by a speech by the new Governor of Central Java, Raden Budiono, a man with impressive administrative credentials under the Dutch, the Japanese and the Republic. He later went on to become Minister of Foreign Affairs and Minister of Home Affairs.[54] Earlier that day, at 10 am at the railways building (NIS), Major General Frits Mollinger had transferred military authority to Colonel Gatot Subroto.[55] A few days later Gatot Subroto, accompanied by Sudiarto, inspected the Brigade Semarang Stoottroep in Semarang, which was by then housed in the Djoernatan military barracks.[56]

In the following months, Sudiarto helped initiate the commemoration of the Indonesian Independence War in Semarang. He was involved in the erection of the Monument of the Youngsters (Tugu Muda) in the former heart of the colonial administration. It memorialized the Five Days' Battle (Pertempuran Lima Hari). On 9 May 1950, he officially opened the Heroes Cemetery (Taman Makam Pahlawan), where Indonesian victims of the war were reburied. It contained 1,843 graves in 2011, 509 of them for the years 1945-1949.[57] Sudiarto was to be killed later in 1950 during the TNI operation against the Republic of South Maluku (Republik Maluku Selatan, RMS).[58]

Diverging terminology and multiperspectivity

In the international historiography on Semarang and its hinterland during the independence war, and in the archival sources, the ways in which these events are described diverge enormously. The various discursive practices reflect the different understandings of the conflict. Taking stock of these differences in terminology helps to create both multi-perspectivity and an awareness of the forms of colonial near-sightedness at play.

A classic example concerns the two military expeditions that the Dutch used to describe as police actions. Indonesian authors normally refer to this with the more realistic term *Agresi Militer Belanda*. In the historical parts of a 1953 official history of Central Java, the second expedition is even signified as *Mata gelap Belanda yang terakhir*, which means that the Dutch were blinded by rage for the last time.[59]

Yet, the spectrum of diverging terms and understandings is broader. The Japanese social historian Ken'ichi Goto speaks for example of the Five Days' Battle as the Semarang incident, which decreases its scale and importance.[60] In a comparable way, the Dutch and English literature ignore the Battle of Ambarawa or describe it as a 'withdrawal' of British troops. In 2005, the Dutch historian Herman Bussemaker added cynically that this withdrawal was then celebrated as a 'big Indonesian victory'.[61] In 1955, the Semarang-based civil servant Max Busselaar wrote, in an account of his 1946 stay in the city, of the 'ignominious, or should I say "strategic" retreat of the English army'.[62] Indonesian historiography meanwhile considers the

Battle of Ambarawa one of the eight main battles (*palagan*) fought in defence of Indonesia's independence.[63]

In British and Dutch sources, the *pemuda* are often described in a deprecating way as 'extremists', while their political and nationalistic motivation is ignored.[64] In 1955, Busselaar spoke of a city surrounded by rebellious gangs (*opstandige benden*), thus effectively criminalizing them.[65] In the Dutch literature, October and November 1945 are generally related to the phase of inter-civilian violence known as *bersiap*.[66] This primarily refers to the experience of Dutch and Eurasian victims of the *pemuda* while denying the wider spectrum of perpetrators and victims and ignoring the context that this was an era of revolutionary nationalism.

The term *bersiap* as used by the Dutch dates from the late 1940s. It can be illustrated by the ill-famed killing in Semarang on 19 October 1945 of four women and a small boy belonging to the pharmacist family Flohr. The murderer, Slamet Depok, was 22 years old and a member of Angkatan Muda. When Dutch security officials interrogated him in May 1946, the term *bersiap* was not used.[67] However, when in March 1948 the case was brought before the Temporary Court Martial (Temporaire Krijgsraad) and Slamet Depok and his leader Jatin were sentenced to death, Dutch-language newspapers spoke of the Bersiap Era (*bersiap-periode*) and of *bersiap* murderers (*bersiap-moordenaars*).[68]

In the same period, the Dutch side developed a specific vocabulary to talk in a heroic way about Semarang being saved from disorder by the Dutch. In a report of 2 February 1946 by the Netherlands Forces Intelligence Service (NEFIS), written as the Dutch were about to take over from the British, Semarang was dramatically described as 'a dead city' ('een doode stad').[69] A commemorative volume of the T-Brigade from 1948 spoke of 'the fortress Semarang' (*de vesting Semarang*).[70] The local Dutch-language newspaper nicknamed Colonel Van Langen 'the defender of Semarang' (*verdediger van Semarang*).[71]

As late as the 1990s, such vocabulary was still reflected in a Dutch series on the regional histories of various Indonesian cities called *Beeld van een Stad*. The book dedicated to Semarang mixes *tempo doeloe* nostalgia with precise descriptions of events during the years 1945 to 1949.[72] The protagonists are exclusively Dutch and Eurasian civilians and the Dutch military. The idea is prominent that the Dutch were defending 'law and order', albeit in vain. This makes the perspective a colonial one and gives the supposed Dutch heroism a tragic twist, all the more so given that Indonesian actors are not given a biography and Dutch war crimes are not mentioned. Especially this last feature is remarkable, as in the Netherlands, Dutch violations of the laws of war were known already since the late 1940s but certainly after the publication of the *Excessennota* in 1969.[73] It was clearly not one of the aims of the authors of *Beeld van een Stad* to develop a narrative that really questioned the way the supposed good intentions of the Dutch military clashed with the realities of warfare.[74]

Indonesian sources and literature referring to Semarang in the years 1945 to 1949 employ an entirely different vocabulary. The central themes covered are resistance, (brave) suffering and revolutionary spirit. The revolutionary orator and militia leader Sutomo, known as Bung Tomo, spoke in a radio speech in July 1946 of Semarang as symbol of the continuous Indonesian revolution. He predicted that, on the first birthday of the Revolution, Indonesian troops would have a glorious parade on Bodjong, the main street in the centre of Semarang. The speech was followed by large-scale Indonesian attacks on the city on 4 and 11 August 1946.[75] In his 1956 military history, Nasution referred to these events while discussing the so-called Semarang Front of 1946 and 1947.[76] The military historian Imam Sumardi used the more explicit term 'Terror Belanda' when describing the evacuation of the people of Semarang following the arrest of local Republican leaders in Semarang in 1946.[77] The Indonesian journalist Rosihan Anwar, who visited the city early in 1946, wrote about Semarang's suffering (*Penderitaan Semarang*) at that time. He wrote of misbehaving Ghurkas. He described inhabitants forced to work as harbour 'coolies' for the repatriating Japanese and Dutch but who silently kept alive their revolutionary spirit.[78] The Dutch had been dependent on these workers as a social group in colonial times but gave them no individual attention. To the present day, the subalterns remain practically unmentioned in the Japanese, British and Dutch literature on the main events of the years 1945 to 1949 in Semarang and Central Java. When they are featured, their lack of food and clothing is stressed, and they are often depicted as having no political agency.[79] This type of colonial myopia entirely obscures the central social role that Indonesian subalterns were to have in the revolution, as the next paragraph shows.

In the east of today's Semarang stands the *Bugen* monument, which best exemplifies how diverging vocabularies are connected with different stories and understandings of the conflict. The monument can best be described as a cluster site consisting of a mosque, a mass grave where martyrs (*pahla-*

wan-sjuhada) of the Hizbullah/Sabilillah group are buried, and a teak house with numerous bullet holes. It commemorates a Dutch attack that, according to local information, took place on Sunday (*Ahad*) 11 *Muharram* 1366 AH, which corresponds with 5 December 1946 in the Gregorian calendar,[80] in which 74 Islamic warriors were killed in and near this house and buried nearby. In the walls of the house, the bullet holes are still visible. In 1960, 46 warriors were reburied in Semarang's Heroes Cemetery.[81]

There are remarkable differences between the Dutch and Indonesian depictions of this event. The *Beeld van een Stad* volume dedicated to Semarang does not mention it, although a picture shows the surrender of some of the fighters.[82] The Dutch action report from 15 December 1946 makes clear that the 2-7 RI and 1 RS battalions aimed to 'clear' (*zuiveren*) a large area near Semarang, including the kampong Bugen. During the attack, the Dutch encountered a group who first fired from the trees and then fled into the house. The Dutch then surrounded this house and started negotiating with the Indonesian fighters, who refused to surrender. Then the Dutch started to fire on the house. This led to the death of 37 fighters inside and six outside the house. In combination with three soldiers who fell earlier, that makes a total of 46 casualties. After 15 minutes, the remaining fighters surrendered. The number of prisoners was 64.[83]

The Indonesian historian H. Supanto described this violent event in 1992 from a different perspective. The Bugen site is indicated as the house of the religious teacher Kyai Haji Mustofa. It served as the headquarters of the Hizbullah-Sabilillah laskar, whose struggle against the Dutch enemy had a clear, religious motivation. He described how during the attack on the house the *takbir* – the Arabic phrase *Allahu Akbar* – sounded from all sides. Inside the house, with its teak walls four cm thick, the warriors stayed faithful to their vow not to surrender to the enemy but to fight to the death. When the shower of bullets started, the heroes died and the sound of the *takbir* stopped. Only two young men survived because they had managed to hide themselves under a pile of rice.[84]

The violent character of the Dutch civil administration in Semarang

During the Indonesian War of Independence, the Dutch officials aiming to bring Semarang and its hinterland under their control faced manifold challenges. This section will show how their quest for legitimacy and their aim to acquire popular support by guaranteeing public security went hand in hand with their policies of political suppression and the use of (military) violence.

The first attempts to set up an administration were Republican, as described above. Building a governance structure was the priority – youth organizations, security, police, the Red Cross, relief for war victims, religion, political parties. But everything was seriously hampered by the military conflicts with the Japanese and British forces later in 1945.[85] The Republican administration left Semarang on 20 November 1945 after the Second Battle of Semarang. On 8 January 1946, the Republic appointed Raden Mas Mohammad Icksan as its representative in the city. Icksan had studied law in Leiden since 1924 and had been an active member there of Perhimpunan Indonesia, the anti-colonial and nationalist association for Indonesian students. Graduating in 1934, he became a civil servant in colonial Java. During the Japanese occupation, he was General Attorney.[86] His task was to establish Republican authority in Semarang. Based in the town hall (Balai Kota), he started building up control of public services such as the police, the railways and public health; technical services like urban cleaning and road repair; agriculture; the market sector; education and urban administration. The import of rice caused him many problems, as did the levying of taxes. The Allied Commander did not recognize his authority. But this was not a problem, Icksan wrote to the Republican government in Yogyakarta, since the Indonesian civilians in the city did.

The situation deteriorated for Icksan after 1 March 1946 with the establishment in Semarang of the Allied Military Administration Civil Affairs Branch (AMACAB). This was the successor organization to the Netherlands Indies Civil Administration, the NICA. After the departure of the British troops and the disbandment of SEAC, AMACAB became known as the Temporary Administrative Service (Tijdelijke Bestuursdienst).[87] AMACAB began by taking over the police and then increasingly took the initiative, to the detriment of Icksan.[88] On 16 May 1946, during a small ceremony, the British transferred the authority over their former bridgehead to Colonel van Langen.[89] The first head of AMACAB in Semarang was P.H. Angenent (1895-1958). From 19 July onwards, he was also *Recomba* (*Regeringscommissaris voor Bestuursaangelegenheden*) for the province of Central Java.[90] His office was in the former governor's office at the Bodjong. According to the British Brigadier General Sir Kenneth Darling, Angenent was 'broadminded', 'cooperative' and had 'considerable organising ability'.[91] He was born in the Indonesian archipelago and had studied law and mining in the Netherlands, where he wrote a PhD on colonial water management.[92]

While Angenent developed a pragmatic attitude towards nationalistic and revolutionary Indonesians, Van Langen was unbending, following a mix of military and Dutch nationalistic principles. In May 1946, when the repatriation of Dutch internees from Central Java via Semarang was in full swing, an incident occurred that exemplified the different attitudes of the two men. The evacuation was organized by the British in collaboration with the Indonesian forces of the TRI. Angenent advised Van Langen not to hoist the Dutch flag at the Kali Banteng airport during the evacuation. In this he was following the advice of Brigadier General Darling. He did not wish to give the TRI any pretext to stop the evacuation. Van Langen refused to lower the flag, saying he was willing to take responsibility for any eventualities, including cessation of the evacuation.[93] In military circles, Angenent's approach was described as 'lacking pride' (*weinig fiere houding*). Angenent, for his part, believed he had merely done his duty.[94]

Angenent's main task, next to the restoration of public works, was to ensure public security under Dutch guidance. For this, he needed the support of Van Langen. The city was besieged by Indonesian fighters. The supply of water, electricity and food was problematic. Angenent concentrated his efforts on establishing law enforcement, medical services and policing. As before 1942, colonial policing had a twofold function: to safeguard public order and to uphold the reputation of the administration.[95] In addition, functioning roads, railways, irrigation canals and communication structures such as post offices were crucial for legitimacy in any colony. They were also a stepping stone for re-establishing control over resources.[96] Yet for this, the Dutch were dependent on the loyalty of Indonesian staff, something that was difficult to enforce. The drawn-out process between July and September 1946 of appointing the Indonesian official M. Johannes to head the AMACAB post and telegraph office in Semarang illustrates this problem. His nomination confronted the Dutch with their vulnerability.[97] The post office was, after all, a place of potential Republican infiltration, espionage and sabotage. One member of the Dutch administration considered Johannes's appointment 'risky'.[98] Van Langen was also alarmed,[99] but informal inquiries soon confirmed that Johannes was 'reliable'.[100] Johannes himself announced he did not feel physically and mentally fit for the function. But after a special meeting of senior officials, at which Van Langen made it clear he remained suspicious, Johannes was nonetheless appointed on 28 August.[101] This incident highlights just how isolated the Dutch colonial apparatus was and demonstrates the diverging Dutch ways – from moderate to radical – of dealing with their own anxieties around re-establishing their rule. Was its legitimacy really carried by the loyalty of citizens, or were there just superficial forms of affiliation at play?

Given the sense of insecurity among the Dutch at this time, it was crucial that they organized their intelligence gathering. What social and political organizations were being established and when? Who was in charge of these organizations and what did they set out to accomplish? Who supported them? In one overview document dating from October 1945, the Komite Nasional Semarang was described as the city's most prominent nationalist organization.[102] Another from November 1945 mentioned the presence of 1,300 *pemuda* in the city, 1,000 of whom were armed. They functioned as auxiliary policemen, wore no uniforms, but could be recognized by a red-and-white armband. Their leaders were Pane and Sitoeroes, both ethnic Bataks and prominent in the Angkatan Muda. Colonial anxiety was further fuelled by the fact that Pane had a relationship with Marie Haighton-Van Gorcum, a Dutch woman who transgressed not only colonial ethnic-racial boundaries but also political divisions, as she was known to be anti-Dutch.[103] The reports generally considered all Indonesian political activities as threatening and potentially criminal.[104]

Semarang continued to be the scene of nationalist and revolutionary activities. *Pemuda* who had stayed in the city after the Second Battle of Semarang or who had been released from British captivity formed underground organizations and battle groups.[105] Their networks were first and foremost family-related but also drew on economic, social, religious and cultural relations. Transgressing the artificial border between Dutch-controlled areas and Republican-controlled areas, they were breeding grounds for political mobilization. Dutch authorities constantly feared 'infiltration', particularly into organizations for public works and security. Time and again, the police rounded up 'subversives'.

On 2 June 1946 they arrested Sutjipto, alias Saribun, a communist who had arrived in Semarang in February 1946 aiming to report on the situation in the city to the Republic. He wanted to connect with Icksan to discuss the police, among other things. He also wished to unite the different underground organizations in Semarang. On 28 May, he received a visit from

Prapto, who came from Salatiga, who informed him about a plan to attack the city. Saribun in turn informed Icksan about this on 30 May. During that meeting, Icksan gave Saribun a letter for the Minister of Defence in Yogyakarta. According to his interrogation report, Saribun had worked as an estate agent before 1942. During the Japanese occupation he had been imprisoned in Ambarawa for his communist activities, only to be released in June 1945. Afterwards he came to Semarang where he started working for the KNI (the Indonesian National Committee). When the KNI branch in Semarang was closed in November 1945, he went to Magelang, where he worked for the Republican Intelligence Office (Kantor Penyelidik). He had visited Semarang twice, in February and May 1946. During his visits he had taken a particular interest in the position of the police.[106] Papers he was carrying brought to light the underground organization City Struggle Headquarters (Markas Perjuangan Kota, MPK). Five leaders of this organization were immediately arrested. Further inquiries revealed that MKP collaborated with the 400-strong Black Bull Front (Barisan Banteng Hitam). There were also connections with the Girls Group (Pemudi) and the Indonesian (Indische) Civil Police and the Chinese Civil Police. In case of an attack, the Indonesian Civil Police was to join in by taking off their uniforms and attacking military positions within the city. The Chinese Civil Police was less involved. Following Saribun's arrest at the town hall, 118 more people were arrested, including Icksan, although soon afterwards 90 of them were released.[107]

According to Nasution, since this event 'the Dutch were in control' in Semarang.[108] He was ambivalent about the position of Icksan. Nasution stated that cooperation could indeed achieve some tactical results, namely getting a chance to defend local Indonesian interests, but it could also result in support for the enemy because it gave their troops the opportunity to consolidate their strength.[109]

The underground MKP had attempted to create one central organization out of a variety of militant groups in the city.[110] It had been critical of Icksan's Balai Kota administration for not providing sufficient information to the city's inhabitants.[111] The MKP was clearly competing with the Balai Kota group, presenting itself as more revolutionary. Icksan defended himself to interrogators by stating that his aim had always been to realize de facto recognition of the Republican government in Semarang. Keeping law and order had been his main objective, as was letting social life flourish again without any form of violence.[112] Icksan remained in prison until October

1946 and was then expelled from Dutch-controlled territory. He reunited with his family in Magelang.[113]

After Icksan's arrest, it became more pressing for Angenent and AMACAB officials in Semarang to reorganize the Indonesian administrators. The sweeping arrests made by the Dutch had widened the divide between the Dutch and those Indonesians willing to cooperate with the Dutch. Angenent acknowledged in a report that the arrests at Balai Kota of what he called 'semi-official representatives' (*semi-officieele vertegenwoordiging*) of the Republic had been necessary for 'military reasons'. But it left sub-district and urban village administrations unmanaged. Angenent now opened negotiations with a group of Indonesians who had been part of the colonial administration.[114] They refused because they felt that joining AMACAB would compromise them. Their relatives lived in Republican areas, and they feared retaliation. Angenent then approached some of the interned members of the Balai Kota group, all of whom were experienced administrators.[115] He said he would accept their political convictions – they were against violence but supported the Republic – and that their collaboration was important if only for the sake of law and order. They were to join a new organization called the Representative Body of the Indonesian People of Semarang (Badan Perwakilan Rakyat Indonesia Semarang, BAPRIS). Angenent was moderately optimistic. He had the impression that this administrative body had good intentions and was willing to expel 'extremist elements' (*extremistische elementen*).[116] The men involved could function as Republican civil servants, he said, while the Dutch 'occupying army' (*bezettingsleger*) gave them the opportunity to govern the Indonesian people of Semarang. In this position they collaborated with AMACAB without being part of it. The head of this administrative body was Raden Sukandar.[117] Born in Karanganyar in 1904, he had graduated from the colonial administrators school OSVIA (Opleidingsschool voor Inlandsche Ambtenaren) in 1923 and had had a career in the civil service.[118] Chris Abbenhuis, chief commanding officer of AMACAB, was less optimistic. He wrote to Angenent that he feared they would end up with a hybrid government with strong Republican connections. He wondered whether no other representatives of the city's 'settled middle class' (*gezeten burgerij*) were available.[119]

During this period, strong military support remained essential to the Dutch presence in Semarang. By enlarging the area they controlled and reinforcing their position behind a demarcation line, the T-Brigade aimed to create a 'no man's land' (*niemandsland*) outside the canals surrounding the city. Gombel Hill and the Tjandi quarter lay in this zone. This was rather successful, although the Indonesians had outposts from which artillery and mortar shelling took place regularly. Dutch soldiers in Semarang soon became used to bloodshed, as they enforced their authority using military firepower that indiscriminately hit men, women and children. One veteran later recalled 500 victims.[120] The Indonesian attack on the airport of Kali Banteng resulted in 'heaps of dead bodies'; some of which were 'hanging in the barbed wire barriers'.[121] The Dutch soldiers often felt pity for their lightly armed and untrained enemies, especially during the attacks of August 1946.

Yet killing Indonesians soon became a normality. One Dutch soldier, Bart Horsten, wrote in his diary that the Indonesian officers responsible for the bloody attacks 'did not know how to take their responsibility' (*niet met hun verantwoordelijkheid weten om te gaan*).[122] A similar mix of military logic, feelings of superiority and externalizing responsibility is present in the commemorative volume *Tussen Sawahs en Bergen: Het Leven van de Soldaat in de Tijger Brigade* (Between Rice Fields and Mountains: The Life of the Soldier in the Tiger Brigade):

> Despite the joy of the new victory, many could not suppress a feeling of despondency as they saw the young lads who had just been sent to their death with no chance of success...[123]

Their military commanders found such human considerations counterproductive. In a secret report of September 1946, Van Langen wrote that at the start of violent encounters his troops often had to get beyond a certain 'fear of shooting and being shot at' (*vuurschuwheid*). But he also noticed that soon afterwards they developed the needed 'dash'.[124]

A more aggressive Dutch approach fitted well with Van Langen's perception of the future of Semarang and Central Java, in which there was no place for the Republic. In a secret report from September 1946, written just after the Indonesian attacks on the city of early August, Van Langen made it clear that the city should never be given up. As the most important harbour in Java, it was a threat to the Republic. But the Dutch did need more hinterland, for economic reasons. For the supply of electricity, water and agrarian products, places like Tuntang, Ungaran and the areas near Demak were crucial.[125] He thought Semarang would be an excellent starting port for conquering the hinterland the city needed, and for that matter all of Central

Java. If this was the case, the newly occupied areas could be best governed by a military commander.[126] For Van Langen, making the British 'key area' into a Dutch 'fortress' was clearly not only an aim in itself. It was part of his aim to eliminate the Republic, which was best done using military violence and not diplomacy.

Nonetheless, negotiations did start between an Indonesian and a Dutch delegation, in a tent camp south of Semarang at Ngesrep on 1 and 6 December 1946. The ceasefire of 14 October 1946 implied that at the local level, demarcation lines should be drawn by the Dutch and Indonesian sides.[127] After the first round of negotiations failed, a second session – between Van Langen and Sunarto Kusumodirdjo in February 1947, again at Ngesrep – was successful.[128] However, for Van Langen this situation was far from ideal. In April that year, rumours reached him about an upcoming return of Icksan as mayor of Semarang. He wrote a protest letter to Spoor in which he spoke of an unacceptable attack on his authority.[129]

Meanwhile, the demarcation line surrounding Semarang had become a prominent feature of the conflict in Central Java. It appears in many contemporary and later Dutch military reports as well as in their letters and private photo albums. It recurs constantly in the daily reports of the OVW battalion 2-7 RI from Amsterdam, which had arrived in Semarang on 20 April 1946. A report from March 1947 mentions collaborating with the TNI to place signs along the demarcation line. The following month it was noted that Dutch and Indonesian troops often met along the line and waved at each other. But in that same year the reports describe how Indonesian troops trespassed the line and burned down a rice crop.[130] In the diary of Lieutenant A. Verhulst – of OVW battalion 2-6 RI – the demarcation line was omnipresent as a place of communication, negotiation, military violence and smuggling.[131] The commemorative volume of the T-Brigade from 1948 states that many Dutch soldiers realized the demarcation line was not the beginning of a reconciliation process but the completion of a separation.[132]

The conscript Jacques van Doorn, in Semarang from 16 July 1947 to 7 February 1950 with Battalion 4-6 RI, later became a sociologist. For him, the demarcation line became an object of academic reflection. In the Dutch sociological journal *Mensch en Maatschappij*, he concluded that by the time of Operation Kraai, the demarcation line had become an artificial military-strategic construct lacking any ethnic or political backing. A federal future for Central Java bounded by that line was therefore in his eyes far from realistic. The situation had been different before the start of the first 'police action' when Semarang – within the demarcation line – was primarily inhabited by 'Chinese, Indo-European and European people'. But after the first 'police action', the area within the line became more and more an economic entity, lacking political meaning. The population of the areas close to the line stayed politically aloof. Sometimes they simply removed the demarcation signs. They continued to cross the line, following their family ties, especially in hilly regions.[133]

For the Dutch soldier Johannes Cornelis Princen (1925-2002), better known as Poncke Princen, passing the demarcation line on 25 September 1948 east of Semarang – near Demak – was an irrevocable step towards desertion and towards joining the Siliwangi Division.[134] For Sayidiman Suryohadiprojo, on the other hand, who by that time was a freedom fighter in the same division, this line was first and foremost related to policies and diplomacy that he, as a soldier, rejected. In 2020, the retired Lieutenant General stated: 'for us, the *Garis Demarkasi* was irrelevant'.[135] It was thus with good reason that Van Langen not only feared an attack from the outside but also an inside attack, by infiltrators, as he stated in his secret report on the situation in Semarang of September 1946.[136] For the Dutch military, the enemy could potentially be everywhere.

At the start of 1948, Angenent had the impression that the group of Indonesians supporting a federal Indonesia was growing and that they felt more distant to the Republican government in Yogyakarta.[137] He decided that the cautiously formulated BAPRIS – the newly formed Representative Body of the Indonesian People of Semarang – was no longer necessary and therefore abolished it on 23 February 1948.[138] BAPRIS chairman Sukandar was now named Regent (*patih*) of Semarang.[139] At the end of February, a new organization was founded aiming to represent all Indonesian 'social groups' (*maatschappelijke groepen*). It was named the Indonesian Union of Groups (Persatuan Golongan Indonesia), soon renamed the Agency of Indonesian Social Associations (Badan Perhimpunan Masyarakat Indonesia).[140] The optimism of Angenent and his administrative circle is best illustrated by the publication in 1948 of the commemorative volume of the T-Brigade, *Tussen sawahs en bergen*. The initiative was supported by recommendations from 26 Semarang prominents, among them Angenent and Sukandar.[141]

Yet there were also other voices. In July 1948, the biweekly journal *Serodja* (Lotus), published by the newly founded Semarang-based cultural centre

Pusat Kebudayaan, roused the suspicions of the intelligence agency Inlichtingen en Veiligheidsgroep (IVG). Pusat Kebudayaan was headed by Brotokusumo, and the journal's editor was Mangunkawatja, who had worked as a teacher. Both were known as 'non-cooperators' and more specifically for refusing to work with the federal state the Dutch were building. According to the head of the IVG, *Serodja* made Republican propaganda. Its poetry and songs contained 'veiled allusions and parables' (*bedekte toespelingen en parabels*) that were potentially highly effective because they could be part of a 'whisper campaign'. The song *Pengisi Halaman* (Page Filler), the poems *Nur-Sari* (Light Essence), *Pelangi* (Rainbow), *Dahaga* (Thirst) and *Bimbang* (Worried), and the song of praise for the female battle corps *Barisan Srikandi*, all created a revolutionary and nationalist spirit that ran counter to the federal politics of the Dutch.[142]

Even organizations of the Dutch civil administration, which were crucial to public safety (or at least the safety of their members), could easily turn pro-Republican. Following the Saribun case of June 1946, in July 1948 it was discovered that the Semarang police had been infiltrated. Effendi and Wadjib, both working there, had come under suspicion of having Republican sympathies. Criminal investigations revealed that Effendi had created a pro-Republican circle around him consisting of 21 men, many working for the (traffic) police. Known as Barisan Pendem (Underground Corps) or sometimes as The Fifth Column (Barisan Kelima), the group reported to the Republic about the military situation in the city. They stole weapons and ammunition to be transported to Republican parts of Java.[143] In the same month, Semarang police were informed that some members of TNI Battalion 8 of Purwodadi, headed by Major Poernawi, intended to infiltrate the police, the KNIL, and the Army Organization Centre (Leger Organisatie Centrum, LOC). Their aim was espionage, sabotage and, again, stealing weapons and ammunition. Their orders came from General Sudirman. It turned out that Darham, a former KNIL soldier who lived in Semarang's Kampong Kaliwiru, was the central figure.[144] The Semarang-based newspaper *De Locomotief* reported that the group had prepared to take over the city during festivities at the end of the fasting month (*Lebaran*), or when the Third World War broke out. The latter intention was interpreted as 'the shadow of the Kremlin' (*de schaduw van het Kremlin*).[145]

The anti-Dutch underground had an unstoppable resilience. In February 1949 another resistance group was rounded up, now consisting of 17 men and 2 women. Information gathered by the Chief of Police (*Chef der Recherche*), Bambang Sumadi, revealed that the organization was controlled by the Republican Ministry of Defence. It was headed by Semarang-born TNI Sub-Lieutenant Sudianto.[146] The group aimed to gather firearms and medicines, plan sabotage, make propaganda, collect information about the situation in the city, and prepare the return of the Republic, whose army had been planning to attack the city on 1 January 1949. The group had existed for some months, making its plans during secret meetings at private homes.

Bambang Sumadi's interrogation reports, which today are stored at the National Archives in The Hague, are complicated historical sources. They served a specific legal purpose, and it cannot be ruled out that violence was used during the interrogation. Nonetheless, the biographical information of the 19 arrested members of this group reveals, if nothing else, the weakness of the Dutch administration, which depended on the support of Indonesians who were potential opponents. Sudianto had successfully infiltrated the Equipment Division (Divisie Materieel Park) as a supervisor (*mandoer*), giving him excellent access to information on Dutch troops and arms.[147] Bero, 17 years old when arrested, worked as a house boy (*djongos*) at the military barracks at the Kanarilaan.[148] Suwono, 20 years old, was a mechanic for the Semarang Motor Transport Service (Motor Transportdienst Semarang, MTD).[149] Murtisumarjo, 27 years old, also worked as a *mandoer* but at the Telegraph section of Semarang, a crucial communication hub.[150]

The 19 biographies also illustrate how frequently they had travelled across boundaries during the preceding years of Japanese and Dutch occupation, violence and war. Kasimin, for example, 23 years old, had been transported to Borneo as a forced labourer (*romusha*) during the Japanese occupation. He had lived in Banjarmasin, Batavia/Jakarta, Yogyakarta, Solo and finally Semarang.[151] Sungkowo, 20 years old, had been militarily trained in Semarang by the Japanese as a member of the Seinendan. In November 1945, after the battle against the British, he went to Ungaran, where he volunteered for the TKR. Later he served with a laskar of the TRI. During the first 'police action' he stayed in Solo, returning later to Semarang.[152] Sudianto, the leader of the group, just 19 when arrested, became a member of the Angkatan Muda in Semarang in October 1945. Later he joined the Student Army (Tentara Pelajar) in Salatiga. A few months before the first 'police action' he went to Tegal, where he attended the Maritime Academy to become a Republican

Navy officer. During the first 'police action' he took part in the defence of Tegal. After this city was occupied, he went to Yogyakarta, where he worked for the Ministry of Defence (Kementerian Pertahanan). In March 1948, he was sent on a mission to Semarang.[153]

A closer look at the biographies of the 19 men and women shows that the military interventions and conflicts in Central Java of 1945 to 1949 uprooted not only the members of the group but also their families. A good example is Benni, who was 18 years old when arrested. Born in Semarang, he evacuated to Salatiga with his parents in January 1946, following the fighting with the British. Six months later they returned to Semarang, where he went to the local primary school Sekolah Rakyat. In 1948, the family moved within the city to the house of Sudianto, who just before the second 'police action' recruited him for the secret resistance group.[154] Prawoto, 16 when arrested, was also a pupil. He and his parents had evacuated to Salatiga following the Five Days' Battle. When Salatiga was occupied by the Dutch during the first 'police action', the family went to Solo and later to Purwodadi. There, Prawoto was a pupil at the junior high school (Sekolah Menengah Pertama, SMP) and as such became a member of the Indonesian Students Association (Ikatan Pelajar Indonesia, IPI). In November 1948, following the Madiun Affair, he fled to Semarang. Like Benni, he was recruited by Sudianto, who told him this was no time for studying, as fighting would soon start in the city.[155] For the female members of the group, too, school had been a place of mobilization. Giartisumiati was born in Klaten and was 19 years old when she was arrested. She was studying at the Girls Teachers College (Sekolah Guru Puteri, or *kweekschool*) in Solo. She, too, joined the student association IPI. During the first 'police action' she was drafted by the Indonesian Girls Militia (Laskar Puteri Indonesia) to help casualties and evacuees. Afterwards she continued to work for this organization. During the second 'police action' she was still in Solo. When Solo was attacked, she decided to flee to Boyolali. There she met members of the resistance group and decided to join them.[156]

Concluding remarks

In contemporary Semarang, the military museum Mandala Bhakti gives a good impression of the local official military memory culture with regard to the Indonesian War of Independence. One room is dedicated to the main battles that took place in Central Java between 1945 and 1949.

It consists of four paintings, depicting the *Pertempuran Lima Hari Semarang* (15-19 October 1945), the *Pertempuran Tiga Hari Magelang* (19-21 October 1945), the *Palagan Ambarawa* (October-December 1945) and the *Pertempuran Empat Hari Surakarta* (7-10 August 1949).[157] Indonesian heroism and nationalism are central in the images of these battles won by the Indonesians.

By contrast, in Dutch contemporary memory culture about the Indonesian War of Independence, specific battles are remarkably absent. In the 2019 four-part documentary series 'Onze Jongens op Java' (Our boys on Java) for example, in which Dutch veterans share their experiences, the only battle that is described in some detail is the attack on Yogyakarta's Maguwo airport of 19 December 1948. The failed Republican attacks on Semarang of August 1946 are mentioned in passing.[158] The Dutch 'defence' of Semarang has become an untold story, while the 'heroism' of the soldiers involved – which at the time in the Netherlands was beyond doubt – is now forgotten. Obviously, with the passing of the decades, the story has become too complicated and sensitive for a Dutch public increasingly aware of broader perspectives. After all, it is in hindsight clear that the Dutch strategy to isolate the Republic using military aggression combined with political suppression, as implemented in Semarang and Central Java in these years, only contributed to Dutch isolation in the end. As a result, the federal structures the Dutch had been building within Central Java collapsed completely in 1949, like a house of cards.

Dutch attempts to establish a civil administration in Semarang and to guarantee public security were, as this chapter shows, from the start strongly connected to the aim of creating a Central Java in which there was no place for the Republic. That aim was enforced by military means. The security the Dutch tried to create might have brought a sense of social wellbeing to some, but it was still inherently violent. If the Sudianto interrogation reports of February 1949 make anything clear, it is that Republican nationalist ideas not only lived among an Indonesian intellectual elite that fulfilled leading administrative duties with mixed feelings, as the history of Icksan shows; they had a strong base in other strata of society as well. The Sudianto interrogation reports also show how individual war experiences in Central Java in the preceding years involved both spatial mobility and political and military mobilization. The Dutch mixed use of political suppression and military violence had created its own enemies. As the abolition of BAPRIS in 1948 shows, it created a divide with those Indonesians willing to function as intermediaries to the Republic. The civil and military authorities structurally underestimated the consequences of Dutch policies implemented with the intention of building a stable society according to their own ideas of law and order but without consulting the Indonesian population. These policies had their own intrinsic logic originating in colonial traditions of political patronization and military violence. The idea that the aggressive military reconquering of Central Java, in combination with the political suppression of Republican governmental structures, could create the federal future the Dutch envisioned, turned out to be nothing more than a fatal self-deception based on colonial myopia.

Acknowledgements

The author thanks Dhia Oktoriza Sativa and Maarten van der Bent for their research assistance and their valuable comments and support during the writing of this article. He is grateful for the critical reading of earlier drafts of the text by Eveline Buchheim, Roel Frakking, Peter Keppy and Tico Onderwater and for the subtle editing work by Gerry van Klinken.

6.

East Java, 1949: the revolution that shaped Indonesia

Gerry van Klinken and Maarten van der Bent[1]

Introduction

Bismillahirrohmanirrohim, Freedom!!! Brothers of the poor throughout Indonesia, especially brother residents of Surabaya... In past battles we have shown that the Indonesian people of Surabaya – youths who come from Maluku, youths who come from Sulawesi, youths who come from Bali, youths who come from Kalimantan, youths who come from all Sumatra, youths from Aceh, youths from Tapanuli, and all the Indonesian young people who are in this city of Surabaya; each with their own troops; together with the people's forces formed in the kampungs – we have demonstrated a defence that cannot be penetrated; have shown such strength that they are out-flanked everywhere. Only

Image 1. Colonel Sungkono (right) meets with Republican troops near Kediri, September 1949. Source: Nationaal Archief, Dienst voor Legercontacten.

> because of their own deceitful tactics, brothers, by bringing the president and other leaders here to Surabaya; so we agreed to stop fighting. But... This is our answer. This is the answer of the people of Surabaya. This is the answer of the Indonesian youth to you all.... As long as the blood of Indonesian bulls still runs red, so that it makes a white sheet red and white, so long will we refuse to surrender to anyone.
> *From a radio speech by Sutomo aka Bung Tomo in Surabaya, 10 November 1945*[2]

No icon in Indonesian history beats the revolution; nothing revolutionary beats the Battle for Surabaya; and nothing there beats this rhythmical, inflammatory radio speech. It is today used in Indonesian public speaking manuals. Youths in the tens of thousands streamed onto the streets in their rags, armed with whatever they could find, in ad hoc militias commanded by no one, to face the superior weaponry of British armed forces that had come to accept the Japanese surrender. They did not even heed their own President Sukarno, whom the British had asked to come over to calm them. They were defiantly local yet not parochial. Sutomo addressed as 'brothers' all those in the cosmopolitan harbour city who had come to join the struggle, each with their own group or organization, regardless of their ethnicity.

Images of the *arek Suroboyo*, as the Surabaya hooligan is still lovingly labeled in football circles – with his blazing eyes and his red headband and sharpened bamboo stake – decorate Independence Day parades throughout the country to the present day. Perhaps somewhat embarrassed by their flamboyance, though, many historians relegate these images to the background. In the somewhat stylized reality of such histories, it was the Americans who forced the Dutch to concede ... it was Sukarno who led the nation to independence ... it was the diplomats ... it was the armed forces. Until very recently, there was not even a book-length history of the revolution in East Java (the ground-breaking new study by Ari Sapto is discussed below).[3] There are good reasons to rethink that neglect. The book of which this chapter is a part wishes to shed historical commonplaces and revisit the messy events on the ground. We now know the death toll was nowhere higher than in East Java in 1949, the war's bloodiest phase. In that final year, between 50 and 200 people died in East Java alone nearly every day. These figures are conservative; they generally do not include those killed by aerial strafing, bombing and mortar attacks (see graph). The first question this chapter asks is therefore: Why was the death toll so high? The second follows from the first: Did these deaths materially affect the outcome of the war, and if so, how?

Daily deaths, recalculated from figures retrieved (and where necessary corrected) from Dutch military reports by Harinck et al.[4] These figures are considered conservative. The value for the period ending 31 December 1948 is only available as a total, not by region.

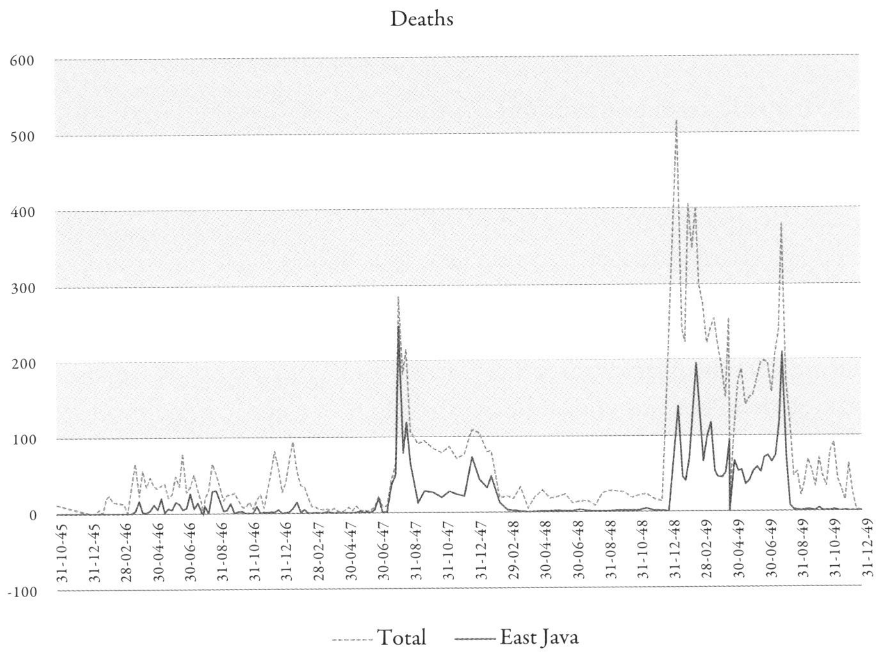

These questions lead us through the historical specificities of the struggle in Indonesia to the problem of interpreting them. The Dutch narrative at the time was that military action was necessary in the face of Indonesian anarchy. This idea of Indonesian chaos has proven tenacious – not so much in relation to Indonesian diplomacy or nationalism, which is now widely admired, but in relation to the violence, which is still often seen as anomic. Even the rush of recent Dutch historical studies have not seriously questioned this default position. In failing to match their interest in *Dutch* violence with an equal interest in Indonesian war-making, these studies have failed to challenge existing perceptions on that score. From their perspective, the outcome of the war – Indonesian independence – was mainly the result of clever diplomacy, while the violence was a regrettable side-effect.

In this chapter, we view the conflict in East Java as a revolutionary war. Charles Tilly defines a revolution as a contest among 'multiple sovereignties' in the same territory:

> A revolutionary situation begins when a government previously under the control of a single, sovereign polity becomes the object of effective, competing, mutually exclusive claims on the part of two or more distinct polities. It ends when a single sovereign polity regains control over the government.[5]

This dramatic arc nicely captures the clash of 1949 that this chapter focuses on. At the beginning of 1949, the government of Indonesia was effectively under the control of a single Dutch polity. It enjoyed international recognition, held all the towns and cities, controlled most of the economic resources, and had a large, modern armed force in place. Its acknowledged aim was a delayed, ethnicized and federal form of the future nation, to be led by local aristocracies and protective of Dutch interests, not unlike the kind of entity Malaysia became a decade later. By its end, however – or more properly by August 1950 – the government was under the control of an alternative Republican polity that had fought to achieve a non-ethnic, anti-feudal, independent and socialist-tinted nation-state led democratically by Indonesians. In between, the rival Dutch and Republican polities each exercised some control over some territories and populations. The Dutch and their indigenous allies had a colonial military and civil apparatus based out of Jakarta. Republican Indonesians had a president and cabinet – who were in detention for the first half of 1949 – and an improvised armed forces operating out of a continuously relocating headquarters in those months. They also had diplomats overseas.

Rather than viewing this as a simple clash of Dutch versus Indonesian polities, however, we can only answer our research questions by acknowledging that each rival polity was actually a coalition of allies. We need to make a particular effort to improve our clarity on the nature of the Indonesian coalition, which was complex and diverse. It will hardly do to dismiss this winning coalition as predominantly anarchic, as if it had achieved its incredible results *despite* being disorganized. A more promising approach is to inquire about the springs of revolutionary order that energized the coalition in a way that belied the outsider's impression of chaos.

Each of the rival polities had its moderates and its radicals. The actual outcome was determined by the relative abilities of each faction within those two coalitions to attract supporters to their side and to suppress the flow of support elsewhere. Each attempted to cajole, deceive or coerce not simply those within the opposing polity but also those within their own who saw things differently. An outcome can be called revolutionary when radicals within the challenging polity rise in influence and radicals within the governing polity decline in influence.

This is what happened in East Java in 1949. Without Dutch radicals (such as Simon Spoor and Louis Beel, respectively Chief of Staff of the Royal Netherlands East Indies Army and High Commissioner of the Crown), no new offensive would have been launched in December 1948. But late in January 1949, Beel made a *volte face*. Realizing he had lost his moderate allies in both countries, he offered the Indonesians an early transfer of sovereignty while still holding out for the possibility of a strong union with the Netherlands.[6] At the same time, without Indonesian radicals (such as the intransigent fighters inspired by Sutomo), moderates on both sides might have agreed to a Malaysian-style outcome.

How and why did this happen, and what did the violence have to do with it? A thorough account would require a book, but here we give an illustrative history by turning the spotlight on one of the key radical actors residing within the challenging polity: Colonel Sungkono (1911-1977). A serious-looking, slightly built man (see Image 1), this son of a provincial tailor played a leading role among the agitated young men on the streets of Surabaya in November 1945. In December 1948, he was commander of all Republican forces in East Java. On 17 March 1950, a Dutch photographer pictured him chatting with several tall Dutch officers who, amiable in defeat, had just given him the keys to their military wagon park (see Image 2). Moments earlier, watched by a jubilant crowd, these Dutch officers had saluted during the singing of the Indonesian national anthem.

Prologue: Republican radicals vs moderates

The Republican polity struggling toward a new future was in reality an alliance of groups representing a spectrum ranging from moderates to radicals. The moderates were headed by Western-educated figures in charge of the cabinet, the armed forces and diplomacy abroad. Their style was characterized by top-down, authoritative and legally binding decision-making, and realpolitik was their operating practice. The radicals consisted of the numerous revolution-minded, spontaneous and socially embedded local groups on the ground in Java. Their bottom-up demands had an imperious validity, arising at a special moment and a special place within an assemblage that somehow represented 'the people'. Indonesians themselves have long distinguished these two extremes as 'green' and 'red' respectively.[7]

Sungkono rose to leadership among the 'reds'. His first job was as a mechanic at the new seaplane base of the Dutch colonial navy in Surabaya. But in 1933, the navy jailed and sacked him for complicity in a labour protest that saw some Indonesian navy men take over a ship in Aceh. An interest in politics drew him into the scouting movement of the (moderate) nationalist political party Parindra. During the Pacific War, he joined a decentralized Japanese auxiliary force called PETA (Pembela Tanah Air, Fatherland Defence Corps), rising to company commander (*chūdanchō*). Formed to confront a possible Allied invasion, PETA's lightly armed soldiers were trained intensively in the Japanese *bushido* martial code. He learned there that bravura, the exercise of an iron will and a flaming spirit were more important to success than military skills or equipment. For the restless young men who joined PETA, these qualities resonated with the romantic image of the *jago*, a kind of Robin Hood social bandit who appears as a popular champion in oppressive times.[8] While in itself not political, the PETA spirit did have revolutionary overtones. It was opposed both to the ethic of rational order and expertise emphasized within the colonial Dutch bureaucracy and to that of moral refinement and harmony at the heart of the traditional Javanese aristocracy.

The many PETA officers who joined the revolution after 17 August 1945 stood in between the 'green' professionalism instilled in modern militaries such as the Dutch colonial armed forces (Koninklijk Nederlands-Indisch Leger or KNIL) and the 'red' anarchistic comradeship of the *arek Suroboyo*. Sungkono was to spend his best years trying to coordinate the numerous self-organized militia groups that had sprung up to defend their freedom, while at the same time satisfying the demands of the (mostly Dutch-educated) national Republican leaders. At the Battle of Surabaya, he was a commander in a coordinating body called the People's Security Agency (Badan Keamanan Rakyat or BKR), a forerunner of the Indonesian National Armed Forces, the TNI (Tentara Nasional Indonesia). His role involved corralling young men who had been in the Japanese auxiliary regiments, the police and navy. But he also offered leadership to groups formed out of post office, railway, public transport and market workers labelling themselves 'socialists'. There were self-styled 'rebels' who followed Sutomo, students from Islamic schools organized under the names Hizbullah or Sabilillah, and numerous neighbourhood gangs based in some urban *kampung* (neighbourhood) or ethnic association. All covered their own expenses – and having weapons helped with that, too. There was no planning or equipment from the state. Each group was led by a charismatic individual – a father (*bapak*) – who could, however, just as easily be dumped if he failed to provide for his men or do as they wished. A.H. Nasution, the Western-trained soldier who was Sungkono's superior in all these years, later wrote about them:

> The leadership of the central headquarters was not felt at all. ... the [armed forces] rose out of the revolution itself, from the lap of the people themselves.... The command no longer went from above below, but from bottom to top... Everything had to be done 'extraordinarily'. Military prowess was not a matter of skill but of courage.[9]

The Dutch military in Indonesia saw nothing but banditry in these Indonesian groups (*bendewezen*). Indeed, Nasution himself saw mainly military amateurishness in them. But in reality, they were not merely sources of disorder. Like today's tenacious rebel 'armies' in East Congo, they released new energies, some of which created order even while they did not belong to the state.[10] Amidst violent struggles over participation and over citizenship and over who could determine the rules of conduct, they created new forms of 'governance without government'. The colonial order had been based on strict control by agents of the bureaucratic state and by customary agents certified by that state. By contrast, these revolutionary bands moved towards a much more informal yet also more totalizing form of control. They made no distinction between social norms, economics or politics. The revolution was popular, militarized and covered all of life.

It was inevitable that tension arose between the 'green' realpolitik of the Republic of Indonesia's central leaders and the 'red' fervour of the socially embedded Republican armed forces. It became decisive in 1949, but the prologue to that climax was long. Up until December 1948, the top leaders operated out of Yogyakarta. They controlled much of Java but little outside of it. In July 1947, Dutch forces overran the richest areas of Java during their military campaign dubbed Operation Product. Republican forces failed to stop them. The Republican cabinet felt compelled to sign a ceasefire pact – the Renville Agreement of January 1948 – that drastically reduced its territory (see Map 2). Republican forces withdrew from the Dutch-held parts of Java and stayed behind what were called the Status Quo lines. Within the

Republic, however, the Renville Agreement severely damaged the authority of the moderates who had signed it while boosting that of the radicals who opposed it. Impeccably democratic, the cabinet in Yogyakarta resigned when political parties withdrew their support. The ex-prime minister, Amir Sjarifuddin, joined the radicals. The new cabinet could find no parliamentary party to support it. Prime Minister Mohammed Hatta, a Dutch-educated economist, reported only to President Sukarno. (He would later look back and declare that 'a revolution should not last too long, not more than a few weeks or a few months').[11] Arguing that he could not possibly pay for the estimated 463,000 revolutionaries now crammed into the much-reduced Republican territory, Hatta teamed up with his Armed Forces Chief of Staff Nasution to radically 'rationalize' the Republican army.

Sungkono was by this time commander of one of three divisions operating in the Republican-held parts of East Java. Many of his men had belonged to the rag-tag bands – known in Indonesian as *lasykar* (*laskar*) or *badan perjuangan* – that had fought in the Battle for Surabaya. He liked their spirit and treated them as comrades. As a senior commander, he knew that something along the lines of what Nasution was suggesting ought to be done, but as a revolutionary *bapak*, he had to act on the outrage boiling within the ranks.[12] The rationalization order was not simply a threat to their jobs, for they were not dependent on central state funding. When they heard of a newspaper report that their leaders might have been thinking of a Republican force only 50-60,000 in size, one that would eventually be incorporated into a Dutch-led federal armed forces mainly as administrative personnel, this was a grave insult to the flaming spirit within their breasts.[13] Sungkono organized protest meetings among his peers in East Java. One on 28 May 1948 claimed that the rationalization plan had been whispered to Nasution by Spoor and Beel; another on 30 May spoke out against Nasution for having sidelined their great commander Sudirman (who also opposed rationalization). In response, the authorities in Yogyakarta placed Sungkono on non-active duty, claiming he was uneducated and spoke no Dutch. An Honour Council led by Nasution condemned him for insubordination and degraded his rank from colonel to lieutenant-colonel.[14]

The struggle continued to escalate between the numerous units determined to preserve a mass populist army on the one hand (particularly in East Java), and on the other hand the top leadership represented by Hatta and Nasution who wished to assert their centralizing authority. The small Republican territory was awash with refugees. A Dutch economic blockade rendered its currency worthless. Gradually, the Yogyakarta leadership was able to gather more resources into its hands. It was helped by Nasution's powerful Siliwangi Division, which had withdrawn to this area from West Java under the Renville Agreement. Various Islamist groups were also increasingly ready to assist Yogyakarta against what they saw as dangerous left-wing radicals. Meanwhile, populist armed groups, initially based in Solo, withdrew in September to regroup in Madiun in East Java (see Map 5). Rationalization had seen all of these groups nominally incorporated into the Indonesian armed forces, but they retained their own leaders and ideologies. On 18 September, some of the socialist-oriented groups rashly decided to occupy the local government offices.[15] Yogyakarta chose to interpret this as a communist coup. It retaliated with what Hatta called an 'iron fist'. Growing Cold War rhetoric from the Republic's great ally – the United States – provided the basis for this interpretation.

Yet the radicals of the revolution were by no means down and out. Yogyakarta's leaders, short of manpower to suppress the radicals they didn't know, now made their peace with the radical they were acquainted with. They reinstated Sungkono, made him military governor of East Java with martial law powers, and told him to assist the Siliwangi Division in the bloody work against fellow Indonesians in Madiun. Although Sungkono assigned some troops to the operation, he did so less than wholeheartedly according to historian David Charles Anderson. He later re-absorbed a good number of the rebellious men into other units within his fold. Those who he had to forcibly demobilize he sustained using the proceeds of state-owned businesses under his control.

The communist firebrand Muso was killed by Republican troops near Madiun at the end of October. But within a month, Sungkono's forces were harbouring the even more incendiary revolutionary, Tan Malaka. Under pressure in the early Cold War years, the central government had jailed Malaka in 1946 for opposing its diplomatic strategy. But they released him in September 1948, hoping he would help them against the Indonesian communist party (Partai Komunis Indonesia, PKI), which he opposed. During his decades of clandestine wanderings all over late colonial Asia, he had written a brochure about where the revolution was going to start: the Solo River Valley in East Java.[16] Its industrial proletariat and immiserated peasantry would provide the basis for a new anti-capitalist, anti-imperialist movement. A special train now took him to Kediri, located in the next valley across from the Solo River and the base of one of Sungkono's battalions led by Sabarudin. Sungkono allowed him to tour the region for 'briefings' with soldiers and ordinary villagers. Tan Malaka fired up their militancy with warnings that the Dutch were likely to attack. He spoke disparagingly of the weak resistance that Sukarno and Hatta were putting up to the Dutch. His slogan '100% Freedom!' quickly became common currency. By the end of December 1948, with the Dutch attack Malaka had predicted now a reality following the start of Operation Kraai, about half the battalions in the region declared they were joining Tan Malaka's movement GPP (Gabungan Pembela Proklamasi, or Group in Defence of the Proclamation).[17] By the end of 1948, the radicals appear to have regained their prominence on the ground in Republican territory.

December 1948: Dutch radicals go to war again

The Dutch decision to go to war again in December 1948 was driven by right-wing radicals. They felt they had made both military and political gains up until that point, also in East Java. People on the island of Madura had responded enthusiastically to the offer of 'a state of their own' that the Dutch had made in a plebiscite on 23 January 1948 (which was conducted under martial law and was illegal under the terms of the Renville Agreement). A famine contributed to a desire for change among Madurese voters. Their aristocratic ruler Raden Adipati Ario Cakraningrat had urged them to vote in favour; what they did not know was that he had defected from the Republic (see Image 3). But elections for a Madurese legislative assembly a couple of months later brought many vociferous Republicans to power. The Dutch intelligence force promptly jailed half of them for subversion. A Dutch intelligence officer told a visiting American scholar in April 1949: 'It is not possible to maintain law and order here without the Netherlands army intelligence service.'[18] The State of East Java covered the eastern parts of the island held by the Dutch. It had cost the Dutch governor – the 'Machiavellian' Charles van der Plas – more trouble to set up than Madura. Republican sentiment was widespread, particularly in Surabaya and Malang. The State was only barely legalized when Operation Kraai was launched. It had no seat of government, no constitution, an unknown bureaucrat as governor and a parliament that never did meet.[19]

General Spoor and his ally Beel, who had been prime minister of the Netherlands from 1946 to 1948 and was now High Commissioner of the Crown in the Dutch East Indies, had long argued there was 'no alternative' to the complete military elimination of the Republic. Spoor's biggest fear was not a frontal battle with the Republicans but rather a determined, massive Republican infiltration into his tenuously held Javanese territory.

Depicting the situation as virtually ‘untenable’ (*onhoudbaar*) and Dutch military morale as in danger of decline due to inaction, he finally persuaded the hesitant left wing of the Dutch cabinet to ignore warnings issued by the United Nations and to approve an invasion across the Status Quo lines.

Spoor had, of course, read the warnings in the military textbook by Carl von Clausewitz against occupying territory without first destroying the enemy. He considered the Republic to be like a European state, led by a head that could be cut off. An airborne assault on Yogyakarta quickly managed to capture the Republican cabinet. Pamphlets showing a detained Sukarno were soon dropping out of Dutch planes, claiming the Republic was no more. Under pressure from the moderates at home and from the United Nations, General Spoor ended Operation Kraai on 5 January 1949. His correspondence at the time mentions the ‘former Republic’ and the ‘ex-TNI’ in order to emphasize the elimination of the Republican apparatus.[20] The Dutch Ministry of Overseas Territories ordered the press to no longer refer to organized resistance but only to ‘robbers’, ‘bandits’, ‘terrorists’ or ‘malignants’ (*rampokkers*, *benden*, *terroristen*, *kwaadwilligen*).[21]

But the Republic of Indonesia was not a European state made up of ‘greens’. Spoor had not reckoned with the ‘reds’ – i.e. the autonomous radicals on the ground. East Java was his biggest problem. A heavily armoured column of Dutch troops made an amphibious landing northwest of Tuban, then struggled for days through monsoon mud and past mined bridges to join other motorized columns crossing the Status Quo lines. By the time they reached their provincial destinations, Republican forces had long set fire to the towns and had decamped. The planned encirclement of Republicans in the Kediri Valley had failed. Spoor visited East Java from 17 to 19 January and learned that the situation was worrying and getting worse.[22] Dutch authorities at the end of January characterized East Java as ‘very precarious’.[23] Their statistics showed that by March, TNI activity was five times higher than it had been in the ‘untenable’ October before Operation Kraai.[24] Although Spoor was livid at the Marine Brigade commander for having been slow, it was in fact his own concept underlying Operation Kraai that had failed.[25]

In the Republicans’ rationalized military structure following the Madiun Affair, Sungkono was now both military governor and commander of the single military division (Division I) within East Java. Dutch intentions had been clear to the Republicans for some time before the start of Operation Kraai. Nasution had prepared an elaborate set of instructions for guerrilla warfare. He was determined not to be caught out again confronting superior Dutch force directly on the battlefield. But few of them had been implemented when the Dutch struck with a speed that only just allowed his troops to get away. The first few weeks were dreadful for the Republican troops. All the main roads and cities became no-go zones. The enemy easily intercepted radio traffic. Units lost contact with each other. Men wandered around in a daze. Many practised Javanese asceticism to regain their moral composure. Hundreds surrendered. Ammunition for Japanese-era weapons began to run short – only explosives were plentiful – as did medicines. The September 1948 civil war around Madiun had left armed forces in that area severely depleted. One of Sungkono's larger units, the Hayam Wuruk Command, which was attempting to reoccupy a township on the northern slopes of Mount Arjuno, was detected from the air by the washing its men had spread out to dry. A running series of Dutch attacks chopped them up so badly that the demoralized unit was eventually disbanded.[26]

But Republicans had escaped encirclement. Morale improved in March – as shown in the reduced number of surrenders.[27] The Dutch had thrown everything they had at them and were now fully stretched, while the Republicans could only improve, at least for a while. Simatupang, a highly astute assistant to Nasution, later recalled observing Dutch-occupied Yogyakarta from a small hillside village late in January 1949:

> ...for us, the most critical phase of the war was over. We had managed to preserve ourselves from *Vernichtung* [destruction]. However, we were not in a position to crush the Dutch military forces or drive them into the sea in the foreseeable future.

He wrote to his military superiors on 19 January that the future now lay in the hands of the people:

> At present, it is not possible to predict the outcome of such a struggle, for it will be determined by many factors – [including] the extent to which the Indonesian people are prepared to make the highest sacrifices for their independence...[28]

Spoor's failure to destroy the Republican forces had consequences beyond the military. By removing the moderates – Sukarno and Hatta and his cabinet – he had unwittingly strengthened the radicals of the Indonesian revolution who had risen from below. In his history of the revolution in East Java,

Ari Sapto describes how this happened.[29] He begins by citing a prediction from the early nationalist E.F.E. Douwes Dekker in 1913 of a coming 'war of liberation' if the colonialists did not yield to their 'long pent-up' desire for a nation of their own. In 1945, a charismatic national elite had voiced the revolutionary new values that seemed to fit the cataclysmic social changes around them, and people had followed them. But when the uncharismatic Hatta cabinet replaced that of Amir Sjarifuddin in 1948, people in East Java had turned to their own elites, figures who shared their cultural values born of suffering. Conventional Indonesian historiography of the revolution depicts a united population ready to sacrifice itself behind heroic military leadership. Sapto instead sees the energy of the revolution not in a military hierarchy but among the diverse perceptions of ordinary people in local settings. We might call this a citizenship perspective. Such a perspective is agenda-setting in its democratic spirit and its openness to contingency and internal conflict, while never letting go of the 'ordering' power of the revolution. Sapto's study has had an important influence on this chapter.

The most urgent question this now opens up for future historians is: How were people mobilized to keep supporting the armed struggle for four long years? Exactly as Simatupang hoped they would, ordinary Indonesians in sufficient numbers did provide the intelligence and logistical support a guerrilla army needs to survive. It is a remarkable thing they did not tire of it all before the Dutch public did. The 'rebels' of Surabaya not only killed foreign soldiers but also played their part in the deaths of more than 3,000 Dutch and Eurasian civilians throughout Java in the first eight months after August 1945.[30] The Republican 'scorched earth' strategy left thousands of urban government facilities and private shops in ruins.[31] Thousands of allegedly pro-Dutch ethnic Chinese were killed, mainly by irregular Republican forces retreating from advancing Dutch troops during their two military operations.[32] This led many of their compatriots to refuse Indonesian citizenship upon independence.

Republican military forces must have won compliance both by their prestige and by intimidation. Many of their leaders had won their spurs in Surabaya. They asked village heads to allow resident students and refugees to form local militias (*Pager Desa*). These ran errands, carried logistics, warned of Dutch patrols, guided fighters, dug holes and levelled trees to disrupt traffic. Villagers supplied troops with food, especially when there was fighting nearby. Policing and propaganda units were formed, taxes were collected, salaries were paid. Although partial, these practices did reveal a legitimate order.

Sungkono established himself in a tiny village on the rugged north-eastern slopes of the Mount Wilis volcanic complex, between Madiun and Kediri. A slow but reliable network of walking couriers kept information flowing. Air Force technicians heroically kept some radio transmitters going in the face of constant aerial bombardment. One on the Mount Lawu complex dividing Central from East Java communicated with Sumatra and abroad.[33]

He was a *bapak* (father) to his 'children' (*anak buah*). Historian Harry Poeze collected reminiscences about him from various subordinates:

> Officers under him called him 'reliable, cool, stubborn, a good soldier, a *bapak*' ... [but also] 'not clear, in fact stupid and lethargic'. [Others spoke of him as] 'silent', [a man] 'with a stern face' who never allowed himself to yell orders, who approached his men with respect and was therefore much loved among them.[34]

One wrote of him later:

> A simple human being, quiet. He had a calm character, he spoke calmly. He spoke in a refined way, calm even under pressure. He was the living figure of a warrior commander, unafraid to die no matter what the circumstances. That's why, a lot of the cowboys of war and the fighting cocks, when they faced Mr Kono, their gung-ho cowboy and cock attitude disappeared at once.[35]

Republicans in East Java were now free to fully realize Spoor's fear of mass infiltration. The day after the Dutch attack began on 18 December 1948, a column of 5,000 Republican civil officials, soldiers and their families set off from near Kediri for their homes in the far eastern part of Java, around Jember. They had abandoned the area a year earlier, and the Dutch considered it 'pacified'. Walking at night along a mountainous route, protected front and rear by the Damarwulan Command, they reached their destination a month later. Their fighters then began near-daily pin-prick guerrilla attacks against Dutch targets. Taken by surprise, the Dutch took a couple of months to start responding.[36]

As is typical of guerrilla warfare, Republican forces now controlled most villages all the time. Small towns and secondary roads were theirs at night, when Dutch security personnel withdrew to safe shelter. The Dutch controlled the larger towns and main connecting roads. But guerrillas had applied scorched-earth tactics to these as they withdrew. Kediri was completely deserted until February 1949, when the market started up again cautiously. No government civil servants turned up for work there. One assistant sub-district head (*wedana*) who did was murdered on 5 January. Republican forces continually carried out major attacks (one on 5 January) as well as minor ones on the town until at least June 1949.[37]

Sungkono's military controlled the economy, which was entirely black. They handed out coffee plantation land to peasants in exchange for a portion of the agricultural proceeds. Smugglers paid Sungkono's men for permission to lug bags of sugar into Dutch-held areas. Stores of opium in formerly government-owned depots he sold to ethnic Chinese traders in exchange for weapons from Singapore. Twenty grams of opium got him two carbines, 75 grams a Bren gun. The enterprising Tony Wen (Wen Kin To) was his operator in the most daring ventures.[38]

Rival claims to authority in 1949

Despite their dependence on the idealism of the people, Republican military authorities in Java made little effort to stimulate it. They were busy with their own survival. Dutch propaganda efforts, meanwhile, were clumsy. Their East Java territorial commander marked Operation Product in 1947 by building a monument in Malang honouring the Dutch military dead. As if to taunt Malang's citizens, he placed it in their most sacred space: directly opposite the mosque on the square. To mark the 'demise' of the Republic in Operation Kraai, he then destroyed a monument commemorating the independence declaration which the city's leading republicans had nearly completed in 1946.[39]

The violence that both Dutch and Republican fighters inflicted often also had an exemplary purpose in addition to a purely military one. An ability to reach targets in contested territory could both intimidate opponents and impress potential sympathizers and thus shift the tide of popular opinion towards the perpetrators. At times, these efforts worked and significantly affected the eventual outcome. But, as the monuments story illustrates, it was not always effective and could even have the opposite effect. Some more examples follow.

The summary execution of prisoners in the heat of battle appears to have been a common practice on both sides. In the midst of Operation Product, a Dutch colonel asked his Marine Brigade commander for permission to use 'the bullet' on 'rebels' because otherwise the 'restoration of peace and order' would be very difficult. The commander did not respond. The same year an officer in the Dutch Justice Department in East Java complained about the practice euphemistically referred to as 'taking a pee' (*effe pissen*), in which prisoners were told to turn around and take a pee before being shot in the back while allegedly trying to escape. Such practices were rarely if ever prosecuted.[40] Republican battle reports from East Java, meanwhile, occasionally mention the execution of a 'spy for the Dutch' after 'resisting arrest'. The aforementioned Damarwulan Command did this for example in the vicinity of Jember on 5 April and again on 8 May 1949.[41] Both sides reported the use by the opposing side of human shields. Republican troops saw the Dutch use a hundred villagers as living shields in a big operation on 17 March 1949 on the south-eastern slopes of Mount Bromo, east of Malang (near the village of Candipuro in the Lumajang district). This caused 'respect for the Dutch in the people's eyes to plummet,' wrote an Indonesian historian later.[42] Several Dutch soldiers recalled long after the war having been equally horrified by the Republican use of the human shield during engagements. One described firing into a group of women and children driven before an attacking line of Republican soldiers on 18 December 1947 at Mojoagung, near Jombang, southwest of Mojokerto.[43] Such battle tactics heightened emotions of revulsion among the fighters.

Other executions were specifically intended to demoralize a wider 'enemy' population by a display of cold-bloodedness. The execution by a Dutch military unit on 8 March 1949 of Rusdi Hamid in a hillside village not far outside Malang was one such shocking event. The charismatic commander of Battalion 30, a former PETA soldier, was known in his hometown as the Hero of Malang. Since early January he had been harassing Dutch troops, sabotaging trains and bridges, and seizing the identity cards the Dutch used to control movement into and out of the city. He was found in his bed at midnight, taken some distance away with five others, and shot.[44]

The execution by Dutch special troops (Korps Speciale Troepen, KST) of the civilian Republican Youth Minister Supeno on 24 February 1949 on the slopes of Mount Wilis was even more shocking. He was one of just three cabinet members to escape arrest in Yogyakarta on 18 December 1948, as he was touring the countryside in East Java. Ever since, he had been walking with a small bodyguard from village to village, meeting Republican officials who were themselves in hiding and who continued their work on tiny salaries and very little staff. The uselessness of the 'instructions' he issued during those meetings was balanced by the symbolism that a civilian Republican bureaucracy still existed. Dutch intelligence was aware that the Mount Wilis complex harboured many top Republican leaders. Sungkono had his headquarters there too, with many men. To compensate for the failure in January, the Dutch East Java commander Major General W.J.K. Baay brought in the notorious KST for a rolling series of fast and intensive actions in February and March. The KST had been created to respond to the revolutionary war with 'unconventional means', that is, with 'counter-terror'.[45] The plan was now to make one gigantic sweep through the mountains of East Java that had seen no Dutch patrolling for months. The first action was into the Mount Wilis complex and took place between 20 and 24 February. (It was also to be the most successful; subsequent actions saw Republican forces melt away only to regroup after KST left.) Tan Malaka was a particular target. In the jungle they came upon Minister Supeno returning from his morning bath with some young men. When he refused to say who he was and where the others were – in fact, Justice Minister Susanto Tirtoprojo was nearby – they put a pistol in his mouth and fired. The six youths with him died too.[46] The Dutch historian of the KST wrote that 'extrajudicial executions and liquidations of prisoners occurred regularly and belonged to the standard performance of KST'.[47] The Dutch patrol report for that day mentions neither Supeno nor this mass execution. It notes instead the killing of a 'Lieutenant Iskandar, whom the population regarded as invulnerable'.[48] Dutch and Indonesian reports agree the killing that day took place in the hamlet of Ganter in the Nganjuk district. We have found no Indonesian reports of the death of a field commander named Iskandar there that day. We suspect the KST may have taken Supeno, who was dressed in black and by then heavily bearded, for a fighter named Iskandar they had been chasing for days. The Dutch never investigated the incident, even after it became known that a cabinet minister had died. 'Public executions were a means... to intimidate the people,' wrote a Republican military report on Dutch tactics at the time.[49] 'After such a display of power, clothing and food would be distributed [by the Dutch].' The Mount Wilis operation resulted in the arrest of East Java's civilian governor, Murjani, the deaths of 93 'TNI' men (in contrast to zero Dutch fatalities) and a large haul of weaponry. Commander Sungkono escaped, but Nasution acknowledged that it had been a 'major blow'.[50]

Despite the gruesomeness of these scenes, however – and we know of many more that cannot be described in one short essay – they seemed to have stimulated further defiance rather than cowering among the target Indonesian public. This was also true of large-scale atrocities – mass deaths due to aerial strafing, bombing, mortaring or indiscriminate machine-gunning. Dutch troops rarely documented these atrocities, and Dutch memories since then have tended to explain them as the result of emotional lapses on the part of individual commanders. For example, a mortar barrage by the Dutch marines on the 'wrong' East Javanese village on 5 May 1949 was blamed on errors and on risk aversion. At other times, the problem was pinpointed as laziness or an unwillingness to carry the mortar shells home again at the end of a patrol.[51] Yet Indonesians saw all these attacks as a form of psychological warfare. Dutch historians have recently compared Dutch and Indonesian military archives of the same incidents. They discovered that when Dutch archives did record strafing and bombardments, they assessed them only in terms of their 'effectiveness', whereas the Indonesian records mentioned enormous civilian casualties. 'The effect of such attacks therefore lies more in the psychological than in the material damage they brought about,' they concluded.[52] Watching the columns of smoke rising from villages all around Yogyakarta, and then travelling east to see the damage with his own eyes, the Republican officer Simatupang observed: 'All along the way from Gelaran to Ngawen and on to Tjandiroto, that day, there were casualties among the people who had been strafed from the air.'[53] He thought these activities were part of a plan of 'breaking the people's spirit (bombing *kampung* and market places, burning down houses, and other atrocities).' The growing list of carnages should not be blamed on individual Dutch commanders, he felt, but on their having been instructed to break the people's resistance but not being given sufficient means to do so. Just as aerial bombing failed to 'break the will' of the German population during World War II, however, Dutch fire power did not have the desired effect on the Indonesians.[54]

There is a striking example of the effect of extreme violence on Indonesian morale in East Java during Operation Product in 1947. Roswita Djajadiningrat was a Republican nurse. She came from the prominent, highly educated Javanese aristocratic Djajadiningrat family, and kept a diary for several months that year. On 26 August – three weeks after the UN-brokered ceasefire – she was asked to bring a badly wounded patient to another Republican hospital at Turen, 30 kilometres south of Malang, as her own clinic was full of injured young fighters. The man was a farmer, about 40 years old, from Pakisaji, on the road south-southwest just outside of Malang. He told her that his village had been indiscriminately fired on with mortars and machine guns as revenge for Republican mine attacks on 'four' passing Dutch military vehicles, in which 'all' those inside had died. For that, the whole village had to pay. Everything was shot up. Three-quarters of the population had been killed. Already wounded in both arms, the farmer had taken his wife and four children to shelter under a bridge, but even there they were not safe. Only he survived. He was only taken to hospital the next day. With his head in her lap, he moaned continually in Javanese: 'My whole life I have never done anyone any wrong. Why do I now have to pay the price?'[55] When a week later she was asked to go back to Turen to identify the bodies of nine Republican policemen who had been shot in their sleep, their eyes, noses and tongues cut out by Dutch soldiers, she lashed out in her diary (4 September 1947): 'How can I still honour and respect the Dutch people… I hate them, I loathe them. They call themselves a civilized nation, Westerners with a higher civilization and culture than ours. Is this what they call being polite and civilized?'

The incident with the policemen was described in an action report of a Dutch special forces unit named '1 Para KNIL', which was later merged with the KST.[56] On 31 August 1947, this unit and two others were looking for the source of mortar fire coming from the hills to the east of Malang. Without mentioning mutilations or executions of sleeping men, the report spoke of shooting and killing 'ten … operators (*bediening*)' of a machine gun belonging to a police unit. The Pakisaji incident did cause an uproar in the Netherlands, but not because of that farmer's misery. It was because three of the Dutch soldiers had refused to take part in what they saw as a 'revenge' action, arguing that it was against their Christian principles. A court sentenced them to expulsion from the marines and many months of jail, declaring that 'strict obedience' was a *sine qua non* for the effectiveness of the armed forces. This uncomfortable reminder of the Nazi expression *Befehl ist Befehl* (orders are orders) ensured that the issue even reached the Dutch parliament. Yet in the official account, there was no machine-gun fire and only the barest hint of mortar fire that 'could' have claimed lives. The 'sparse' village population had been 'evacuated' before a 'part' of the village adjoining the road was burned down for 'tactical' reasons.[57]

A similar Dutch revenge action took place on 24 July 1949 in the village of Prambon Wetan on the banks of the Solo River, 20 kilometres south of Tuban. It too was discussed in the Netherlands afterwards but was not recognized as a revenge action, while in Indonesia the event generated outrage and further defiance. The village had been regularly mortared by Dutch troops from a distance for weeks before this day. When a Dutch marine patrol led by Lieutenant Teeken turned up in the village on 23 July, Republican fighters laid an ambush that killed or captured the entire patrol. The next day, more marines turned up and machine-gunned the village. Villagers recently showed Dutch researchers a document naming 64 victims. A monument commemorating the event is kept freshly painted. Every year since then, the village honours the dead there.[58]

Republicans also committed violence against civilians. Most shocking were the executions of civilian officials working for the Dutch puppet states of East Java and Madura. Raden Subroto, assistant district chief (*wedana*) of Woninongan near Pasuruan and a member of the (Dutch) East Java Council, disappeared with his family while out driving in May 1949. The jeep was found abandoned, and their decapitated bodies were found some weeks later.[59] By the end of July, 16 mid-level civil servants had been murdered in East Java, and 55 had disappeared. Village heads suffered even more – 184 died and 343 disappeared over the period 18 December 1948 till 31 July 1949.[60] The assassinations were official Republican policy. Chief of Staff Nasution on 5 January 1949 signed an instruction stating:

> All citizens of Indonesia who cooperate with the enemy will be considered traitors in time of war, and brought to justice as such in accordance with military law.... In order to facilitate the struggle it is necessary to draw dividing lines (demarcation) between patriots and traitors. Every Commander of a Military Region must list the names of traitors in his region to be dealt with accordingly.[61]

The order was applied selectively. Many Indonesian officials within the Dutch administration willingly supplied information to their Republican contacts out of town. But Republicans saw other such collaborators as 'adventurers' who had little organic connection with the area. These individuals had come in to take up posts vacated by Republicans after the Dutch invasion; many said they could not work without Dutch military protection. Some killings were carried out not by Sungkono's men but by local groups taking revenge for perceived cruelties by that individual. These resembled the late-1945 frenzied murder by villagers of aristocratic officials in Central Java who had oppressed them on behalf of the Japanese military, and the similarly bloody social revolution in East Sumatra in early 1946.

The assassinations were intended to make Dutch rule impossible, and they did. By June 1949, top Dutch decision-makers in East Java were no longer optimistic. The visiting Dutch Minister for Overseas Territories, J.H. van Maarseveen, heard that many officials within the puppet state of East Java were working for Republican 'shadow administrations'. According to his report, 'Militarily our troops are in control of the situation, but in policing terms not. Maintenance of order, peace and security is beyond the power of a purely military apparatus. Hence... a great measure of insecurity.' (Since 'policing' had been precisely the reason for both Dutch military operations, which they had even called 'police actions', this confession was laden with irony.) Indonesians were abandoning the Dutch, he acknowledged, because they (the Dutch) were only protecting themselves and not the Indonesians.[62]

Doubts had set in months earlier. In March 1949, a meeting of Indonesian leaders of the many small proto-federal states insisted on consulting with the detained President Sukarno. This 'betrayal' came as a shock to the Dutch. Added to the military quagmire, it produced 'a sense of moral and military defeat in the archipelago'.[63] George Kahin, an American scholar in Indonesia at the time, heard from a dispirited Cakraningrat of Madura in April 1949 that no powers had actually been devolved to him. The state leaders felt they were mere puppets in a project that was under complete foreign control.[64]

The Dutch radicals were thus quickly losing their moderate allies. The defection to the Republic by Indonesian moderates who had till then sided with the Dutch side was mirrored in the Netherlands by a loss of faith in the Dutch radicals' agenda. When the moderate diplomat J.H. van Roijen arrived in Jakarta in mid-April to negotiate with the Republicans, he ignored Spoor's protests. Spoor's own senior officers even hosted a reception for Van Roijen without inviting their commander.[65] On 7 May 1949, Van Roijen and his Republican counterpart Mohamad Roem announced an accord in the Hotel des Indes in Jakarta, where it was decided that the Republican central leadership would return to Yogyakarta, military hostilities would end, and a diplomatic conference would be held in The Hague. The radicals Spoor and Beel were outraged by this betrayal of their mission. During the weeks it took to work out the detailed final agreement in June, the Dutch military successfully re-introduced their favourite Status Quo lines. This strategically meaningless stubbornness led to the bloodiest fighting of the entire war as Dutch forces strove to grab Republican-held territory (see graph).

By the time local military commanders from each side began working out the practicalities of a ceasefire early in August, morale within the Dutch armed forces had sunk to new lows. The Dutch East Java commander Baay lent Sungkono a jeep plus a UN escort so that Sungkono could inform his troops about the ceasefire – on the condition that he refrained from discussing 'politics' with them. Figuring that the UN representative did not understand Indonesian and that the Dutch could not stop him, Sungkono used the opportunity to encourage his troops not to rest until

Image 2. Colonel Sungkono (centre), East Java territorial commander, receives a large number of military vehicles from the Dutch commanders, represented by Major General J.A. Scheffelaar (left) and Lieutenant Colonel A.L. Nouwens (right), 17 March 1950. Source: *Nationaal Archief, Dienst voor Legercontacten.*

all the Dutch were gone.[66] Dirk Cornelis Buurman van Vreeden, who had taken over command of Dutch troops in Indonesia following Spoor's sudden death in May 1949, confirmed in a note written on 2 September 1949 that the Republican infiltration that Spoor had feared so much was now an inexorable reality. All Dutch government offices were being 'noiselessly' taken over by Republican military personnel. The Dutch military now faced a total paralysis of both their incoming intelligence and their ability to conduct propaganda. Whereas 18 months earlier, Republican forces had complied with the Status Quo lines of the Renville Agreement, this time, Buurman van Vreeden wrote, they simply infiltrated every nominally Dutch-held area openly on the street, knowing that Dutch troops would not shoot at them. They themselves fired not a single shot. Every district in Central and East Java came under a Republican military command office (Komando Distrik Militair, KDM, and Komando Onderdistrik Militair, KODM). These organized the replacement of disloyal village heads and other state functionaries. Months before the Dutch flag was lowered for the

Image 3. Raden Adipati Ario Cakraningrat (in front), head of the State of Madura, inspects his Madurese militia, May 1949. On his left is Major General W.J.K. Baay, commander of Dutch troops in East Java. Source: Nationaal Archief, Dienst voor Legercontacten.

last time at the palace in Jakarta on 27 December 1949, Dutch authority on the ground had collapsed.[67]

The erosion of the pro-Dutch federal states of East Java and Madura began before they had even been officially recognized by the establishment of the Republic of the United States of Indonesia. Already in December 1949, men under Sungkono's command were seizing weapons held by security personnel belonging to these puppet states. They were 'borrowing' vehicles owned by their functionaries and running them into the ground. On 1 December 1949, the Surabaya branch of the Indonesian National Party (Partai Nasional Indonesia, PNI) was the first to issue a 'motion' to dissolve the State of East Java to which they belonged. Many more motions were to follow. Street demonstrations ensued in January. The American scholar Kahin watched the campaign to eliminate the federal states completely overshadow all other issues in the first seven months of 1950. Sungkono's troops had a hand in stimulating this (an 'intelligence operation', wrote Sapto).[68] As they had done before, moderate Indonesian political leaders in the capital (now Jakarta) were concerned that these East Javanese tactics would erode international confidence in the Republic's faithfulness to its diplomatic promises. They called in Sungkono and his colleague Suwondo for a talking-to but did not punish them. By March 1950, both the Madura and East Java federal states had dissolved themselves and joined the unitary state of the Republic of Indonesia.

1950: ROUTINIZATION

Every revolution comes to an end. Every charismatic moment fades or becomes routinized. With the Dutch gone and the federal states being dismantled, the outcome that the Indonesian radicals had envisaged in 1945 was a reality by early 1950.

The process of dousing the flaming spirit of the *arek Suroboyo* within the state had actually begun long before 1950. Republican troops had first rejected Nasution's 'rationalization', then carried it through with some qualifications. They at first welcomed the communist agitator Muso, then executed him. One of Sungkono's battalions had at first harboured the militant populist Tan Malaka, but he, too, was executed, on 21 February 1949, with Sungkono's permission. The reason was not that Sungkono disliked his ideology of '100% Freedom'; rather, it was because Tan Malaka had begun to openly criticize his military hosts. The story is complicated – Harry Poeze takes 1,500 pages to tell it – but it can be condensed as follows. After Sungkono welcomed him to his fold following the capture of the Republican cabinet in Yogyakarta, Tan Malaka began to speak as if he himself was president of the Republic. He then turned to attack other Republican commanders in East Java. He called Lieutenant Colonel Surachmad, who had a long history of conflict with Sabarudin, a 'fascist,' alleging that he had abandoned Kediri to the Dutch without a fight.[69] He then criticized Sungkono himself:

> Where is he, and is he still alive, who was once the 'lion' of the front in Surabaya, Colonel Sungkono, commander of East Java, who gave the order to take up arms for the second colonial war. Has the 'lion' also fled to Mount Wilis with the officers of the national army, who according to [Tan Malaka's political party] Murba People Youth fled as quickly as the Dutch aeroplanes flew!

Moreover, the battalion led by Sabarudin that protected him took no notice of Sungkono's orders to position itself elsewhere in East Java. In the midst of the chaos of that February Dutch commando attack on the Wilis complex, Tan

Malaka and Sabarudin were both arrested by Surachmad's men. Tan Malaka was secretly executed (although the mystique lived on), but Sabarudin escaped. He was recaptured in November 1949 and executed. A reputation for extreme violence and sexual predation had long made him a loathed and feared figure.

In mid-1950, it was Sungkono's own turn to be made redundant. With the revolution a complete success, and with the elimination of the popular mass movements represented by the PKI and Tan Malaka, his military enjoyed almost total political domination. But dissatisfaction with the dominance of the military began to be heard in East Java between April and June 1950.[70] The press described Sungkono as a 'warlord', and in May there were demonstrations against martial law. The Defence Ministry in Jakarta, keen to improve its image in East Java as well as rein in overly independent commanders, accused senior officers in East Java of living it up while their troops suffered. The military was meanwhile heavily involved in the black market and the protection of gambling rackets. Some profits ended up in private pockets. Trouble had first erupted late in February, when a dispute between two units over control of some coffee plantations led to a fatal shooting match across Blitar's town square.[71] Newspapers complained of violence by armed gangs. In June 1950, they blamed the demobilization of Sungkono's troops for it, the men having taken their guns with them. Jakarta felt that some of the commercial licences that Sungkono had issued were not his to issue. The reality was a little more complex. Not all armed gangs were linked to the military. The gambling racket was intended to help demobbed men who might otherwise have turned to highway robbery. But Sungkono took the blame. On 6 June 1950, he was moved to a Jakarta desk job. The ministry denied that the transfer had been related to his smuggling activities. The routinization of the armed revolution had been carried to its logical conclusion.

Conclusion

The outcome was revolutionary because by September 1950, the displacement of personnel in the state was complete (though this was not quite the case in the business world). Almost all the feudal aristocracies were gone, as were all Dutch officials beyond technical advisors. Trajectories that start from a revolutionary situation and end in a revolutionary outcome can properly be called revolutions. Indonesia and certainly East Java followed just such a trajectory from 1945 to 1950.

The first question this chapter asked was: Why was the death toll so high in East Java? The answer is that this was a confrontation of revolutionary proportions. During a revolution, people will accept much higher death tolls than normal. In his book on revolutions, Charles Tilly quotes Ted Gurr, who argued that violence arises when coercive forces are in balance: 'The likelihood of internal war increases as the ratio of dissident to regime coercive control approaches equality. [For 'equality', read 'one'].'[72] Both sides in Indonesia had in fact realized this by the beginning of the decisive year of 1949.

A bloody revolution was by no means inevitable. It was triggered in the first place by radicals on the Dutch side, who repeatedly declared that there was 'no alternative' to military action. But the resources at their disposal did not match their bravado. The political public at home was divided, the new United Nations were anti-colonially minded and to top it off the Dutch had insufficient troops to eliminate Republican resistance. Nonetheless, in December 1948, they did throw themselves into a second war with gusto. Historical work in the Netherlands is only now bringing to light how brutal Dutch military tactics were. However, that brutality does not by itself explain the high death toll nor why it was so high in East Java specifically. If all Indonesians had complied with the humiliating terms dictated in the various agreements with the Dutch leading up to December 1948, no further war would have occurred. It was the refusal of the Indonesian radicals particularly in East Java to keep within the Status Quo lines that prompted the Dutch radicals to up the ante. The Indonesian radicals had been born out of the eruption of popular outrage during the Battle of Surabaya in November 1945. In ways that still need further clarification, they then managed to sustain that mobilizational success for four years.

The prominence of these radicals within the Republic was also not inevitable. Nowhere were the internal difficulties the Republic of Indonesia faced in establishing a single sovereignty as great as in East Java. Even while battling Dutch military pressure, its moderate top leaders first suppressed a populist movement in Madiun in September 1948, then continued to confront Tan Malaka's nationalist communists and other populist militias well into 1949 as well as popular protests against their federation into 1950. The locally rooted revolutionary alliance was more insistent than the Yogyakarta moderates that there would be no surrender without full independence. Indonesia eventually became more or less what these revolutionaries envisaged. It did not become the ethnicized federation within the Dutch sphere of influence that Yogyakarta moderates were prepared to accept (the Malaysian scenario). This revolutionary outcome could not have been achieved without the provincial radicals. Despite their setback in Madiun in September 1948, they managed to bend the narrative towards the radical end of the spectrum. Nasution, an arch-moderate of the Republic, later included great sections of Tan Malaka text in his history of the armed forces, no doubt to defend himself against suggestions of treachery from the radicals.[73] The mobilization that the radicals conducted in East Java drove more people towards them in the course of 1949 than deserted them. This conclusion appears to fly in the face of the tremendous violence committed against so many.

For the remainder of 1949, members of both contending parties – Dutch and Republican – were roaming over the same terrain, addressing the same population, attempting to win them over to their side. They did so using persuasion, deception and coercion, directed at both potential supporters and perceived enemies. The subsequent course of the conflict was shaped by the relative abilities of the Dutch government and the Republican contenders to win support among the population on the ground, particularly in East Java. As violence escalated throughout 1949, people were forced to choose sides. The Republic was the beneficiary of these choices. The defection of the two federal states within East Java proved to the Dutch how widespread radical nationalist feelings were. By contrast, the Dutch regime lacked either the will or the means to repress the opposition sufficiently, and it failed to offer the kinds of services expected from a ruling government. War finally ebbed not because Indonesian moderates had won the day within the Republic but because the Dutch radicals lost support within Indonesia, within the Netherlands, and within the United Nations.

The second question we asked at the beginning of this chapter is a follow-up on the first: Did these deaths materially affect the outcome of the war, and if so, how? This is not quite the same as asking whether the same result could have been achieved without all this mayhem. That question implies yet another question, one that is in fact imponderable: What if the Dutch radicals had been brought to heel *before* they rushed into the fray? Nor is it the same as asking whether the violence was worth it. That is a question that only Indonesians can answer (though we might note that a revisionist history of the revolution has yet to emerge there even now). Nonetheless, the conclusion is inescapable that the revolutionary outcome of a non-ethnic, democratic Republic of Indonesia depended, under the existing circumstances, on a prominent role for the 'red' Indonesian radicals. They were willing to accept the ultimate consequences for their actions and were able to persuade – in ways that further study should bring to light – large numbers of Indonesians in East Java to do the same.

7.

War logistics in revolutionary Central Java

Julianto Ibrahim

Introduction

This chapter examines the war of logistics between the Indonesian armed forces and the Dutch troops. What strategies did the two belligerents employ to fulfil their needs and simultaneously destroy the enemy's logistics in Central Java? Why did the Indonesian armed forces engage in banditry to seize Dutch logistics? And why did Dutch troops similarly carry out criminal acts during patrols to seize Republican logistics?

The United States Department of Defence defines logistics broadly as war supplies that include medical services, communications, engineering, transportation, training of troops, and weaponry.[1] Defined more narrowly, logistics are supplies for combat troops at the front line.[2] In this sense, they are supplies needed to maintain the troops' 'stamina' to fight the enemy and

Two TNI soldiers inform themselves by reading posted pamphlets and newspapers in a street in Yogyakarta, 1948. Charles Breijer, Nederlands Fotomuseum.

win the war.[3] The ability to manage logistics in battles is decisive to the outcome of a war.[4]

The newly independent Republic of Indonesia faced difficulties in providing logistics for the frontline due to the unstable and poor economy.[5] Plantations and factories had been ravaged during the Japanese occupation.[6] People's food sources had run low after having been commandeered by the Japanese military.[7] The state treasury was empty, and Republican authorities found it difficult to fund the struggle.[8] Inflation was soaring due to the use of three different currencies.[9] This degree of austerity made it impossible to achieve the prosperity that people had hoped for from independence.[10]

The extreme economic condition was worsened by a Dutch naval blockade imposed since early 1946 and intensified in 1947.[11] This halted the export of Indonesian natural resources and the import of numerous important goods such as medicines, automotive spare parts and textiles.[12] Mohammad Natsir, the Information Minister in the Hatta Cabinet, said in 1948 that the economic blockade had destroyed the Indonesian people and made them suffer even more.[13] Brian Walsh has argued that a total economic blockade inevitably targets civilians and is therefore incompatible with the doctrine of a just war.[14] This argument is applicable to the Dutch embargo during Indonesia's war of independence. It was a direct manifestation of violence against the population. In his study of Indonesian military logistics in Central Java during the revolution, the historian Nazaruddin Zainun concluded that the root cause of the Indonesian government's inability to provide adequate logistics for its military was this embargo.[15]

Under these severe conditions, Indonesian armed groups resorted to banditry in order to meet their logistical needs. This was especially true in Central Java, which until late 1948 was divided into a western part under Dutch control and an eastern part under Republican authority (see Map 2).[16] It was sometimes difficult to tell the difference between freedom fighters and bandits.[17] Indonesian freedom fighters often joined with bandits to commit robbery and looting within Dutch-controlled territory.[18] They targeted civilian homes – especially those belonging to the Chinese – as well as Dutch military bases. Coalitions of bandits and young nationalists helped shape the course of the revolution, as Robert Cribb has shown.[19] Indeed, Henk Schulte Nordholt has demonstrated that the revolutionary relationship between criminals and nationalists reflects a long colonial history of relations between rulers and gangsters. Bandits who worked for regents as heads of districts (*wedana*) would order their men not to rob anything in the area and were even asked to maintain security. In return, the bandits were exempt from taxes, given shares in the opium trade, and even given protection when in trouble. The local rulers benefited from reduced crime in their area and from stolen goods from other areas.[20] For the criminals, the instability and euphoria of the revolution provided the perfect opportunity for personal gain in the midst of chaos.

Dutch troops also faced logistical difficulties in Central Java, especially food provisioning. Although they imported food from Burma and the US, the population and the military in Dutch-occupied territory faced food shortages.[21] This was exacerbated in 1948 when imports experienced delays and when the US cancelled its Marshall Plan support for the Dutch administration in Indonesia (the Netherlands Indies Civil Administration, NICA) on 22 December.[22] To meet their logistical demands, Dutch troops also committed criminal acts by seizing rice from the population.[23] During patrols after the second Dutch military aggression in December 1948, Dutch troops also confiscated valuables such as gold jewellery and diamonds.[24]

This chapter is divided into four sections. An initial section on the agrarian and military context is followed by a comparative analysis of Dutch and Republican logistics strategies. The third section focuses specifically on criminality practised by both sides in the war of logistics. The final section outlines my conclusions.

Central Java: A stage

Central Java is a fertile region, with lowland shores in the north, active volcanoes in the middle, and limestone hills in the south. Most of its land was at this time designated for agriculture, both wet paddy and dry fields. In 1935, out of a total of 13,217,400 hectares of land in Java, 7,885,000 hectares or 59.7 per cent was designated to the smallholder agriculture sector (see Table 1).

Rice, cassava and corn dominated agricultural production in Central Java (see Table 2). Rice was the largest agricultural product in Central Java. As the product most in demand by the Republican army, it was crucial to the course of the revolution.[25] Rice was also favoured by the non-European Dutch troops who came from various regions in the archipelago. Tuong Vu states in his study on rice and revolution in Java that farmers in occupied areas were often deprived of their staple, as their rice was forcibly taken by the Dutch army.[26]

The Dutch-controlled territory had been managed by Allied forces before they 'gave' it to the Dutch in mid-July 1946. After the first military aggression launched by the Dutch on 21 July 1947, better known as Operation Product, the Dutch army expanded its territory 80 km into Central Java

*Table 1. Land Use in Java in 1935**

Land Use	Size (ha)	Percentage (%)
People's Agriculture:		59.7
Rice fields	3,370,000	
Dry fields	4,515,000	
Total size	7,885,000	
Fish farms	69,300	0.5
Plantations (*Onderneming*)	1,010,900	7.6
State-owned forests	3,090,900	23.4
Miscellaneous	1,161,300	8.8
Total area	13,217,400	100

Source: Reksopustoko archives (Arsip Reksopustoko) MN viii/709, Report from the Persatoean Kaoem Technik 17 August 1946, Pembangoenan dan Indoestrialisasi.
* Persatoean Kaoem Technik 17 August 1946, 'Pembangoenan dan Indoestrialisasi' Arsip Reksopustoko Mangkunegaran Surakarta/709.

*Table 2. Agricultural products in Central Java and Yogyakarta in 1950***

Plant Type	Central Java (in 100 kg)	Yogyakarta (in 100 kg)
Rice (Irrigated rice fields and dry fields)	21,890,840	1,349,543
Corn	3,729,497	155,509
Cassava	24,269,234	2,018,520
Sweet Potatoes	2,510,165	129,031
Peanuts	640,411	155,940
Soybean	467,149	85,634

Source: Kementerian Penerangan, *Republik Indonesia: Provinsi Djawa Tengah* (Jakarta 1953) 256 and Kementerian Penerangan, *Republik Indonesia: Daerah Istimewa Jogjakarta* (Jakarta 1953) 467.
** Kementerian Penerangan, *Republik Indonesia: Provinsi Djawa Tengah*, (Jakarta 1953) 256 and Kementerian Penerangan, *Republik Indonesia: Daerah Istimewa Jogjakarta* (Jakarta 1953) 467.

(see Maps 2 and 4).[27] It included Cilacap, Purwokerto, Tegal, Pekalongan, Kendal, Weleri, Ambarawa, Salatiga, Semarang and partly Demak.

As for the Republic of Indonesia, it controlled most regions in the east, which comprised Magelang, Kedu, Yogyakarta, Surakarta and several other towns on the north shore such as Rembang, Kudus and Pati.[28] After the second military aggression by the Dutch, all cities in Central Java, including the Republican capital Yogyakarta, came under Dutch control. The Republican army moved its bases to the mountains, hiding in small villages as they resorted to guerrilla warfare to tackle the well-armed Dutch military.

Republican authorities used rice as a means of negotiation against the Dutch,[29] despite a gradual decline in production since the beginning of the

1940s.[30] Dutch-occupied territory faced a rice shortage caused by mismanagement in its distribution, rampant illegal trade and looting by Dutch soldiers.[31] Republican newspapers reported that the total number of Dutch soldiers in Indonesia reached a peak of 220,000. As many as 138,000 to 140,000 were of Dutch origin, while 75,000 to 80,000 were Indonesians belonging to the colonial army (Koninklijk Nederlands-Indisch Leger, KNIL).[32] The Dutch soldiers consisted of 120,000 personnel of the Royal Army (Koninklijke Landmacht) and 20,000 of the Royal Marines (Koninklijke Marine). Of that number, 100,000 were conscripts, 30,000 volunteers, and only 1,000 were professional soldiers.[33] The Indonesian Department of Defence had the number of Dutch soldiers in Java and Sumatra per 14 December 1946 at a total of 96,150. The number decreased to 89,178 by 1 May 1947. The number of troops in Central Java was 5,500 by 14 December 1946, which had increased to 7,180 by 1 May 1947 (see Table 3). In addition, as many as 14,819 KNIL soldiers were deployed in Sumatra, while 55,810 were in Java, 6,284 of whom were stationed in Central Java (see Table 4).

Indonesia's military strength consisted of the army and militias (*laskar*). At first, the two belonged to different factions and were sometimes at each other's throats while also being connected in a complicated relation. The term People's Militia (*laskar rakyat*) did not refer to one particular armed group but was adopted by diverse armed groups, most of which were unconnected. A *laskar rakyat* was self-sufficient, fluid and obedient only to its own leader. It lacked military discipline and tactics. While the national army had to submit to the ruling government, the *laskar rakyat* could just as well be the armed wing of a political party, perhaps even one ideologically opposed to the government.[34]

The many people's militia groups in Central Java included, to name but a few, the Indonesian People's Revolutionary Front (Barisan Pemberontak Republik Indonesia, BPRI), the Youth Forces of the Republic of Indonesia (Angkatan Muda Republik Indonesia, AMRI), the Student Army (Tentara Pelajar, TP), the Socialist Youth of Indonesia (Pemuda Sosialis Indonesia, Pesindo) and the Islamic groups Hisbullah and Sabilillah. Armed groups in Yogyakarta included the Mataram People's Army (Tentara Rakyat Mataram, TRM), the Falcon Force (Pasukan Alap-Alap), the Oembaran Extremist Militia (Laskar Ekstremis Oembaran, LEO), the Sabil Army (Askar Perang Sabil, APS), the Student Army, the Women's Legion (Laskar Wanita, LASWI), the P-Brigade (Barisan 'P') and the Pathuk Youths (Pemuda

Table 3. Number of Netherlands armed forces soldiers (army, marines) in Java and Sumatra

Region	14 Dec 1946	1 May 1947
West Java	58,000	52,350
Central Java	5,500	7,180
East Java	13,000	13,195
North Sumatra (Medan)	10,600	6,392
Central Sumatra (Padang)	4,200	3,953
South Sumatra (Palembang)	4,850	6,148
Total	96,150	89,178

Source: Arsip Disjarahad Bandung, Kementerian Pertahanan, 10 July 1947

Table 4. Number of KNIL soldiers in Java and Sumatra

Region	Number
West Java	37,940
Central Java	6,284
East Java	11,586
North Sumatra (Medan)	5,722
Central Sumatra (Padang)	3,398
South Sumatra (Palembang)	5,699
Total	70,629

Source: Kementerian Pertahanan, 10 July 1947.

Pathuk).[35] In Solo, there were the Young Generation Army (Angkatan Muda Tentara, AMT), the Indonesian Labour Militia (Laskar Buruh Indonesia), the Red Militia (Laskar Merah), the Gajah Mada Militia (Laskar Gajah Mada), the Indonesian Women's Militia (Laskar Putri Indonesia), the Buffalo Front (Barisan Banteng), the Laskar Janget, the Leftist Militia (Laskar Kere), the Lamp Militia (Laskar Pelita), the Falcon Militia (Laskar Alap-Alap), the Arab Indonesia Young Generation (Angkatan Muda Arab Indonesia, AMAI), among others.[36] In Semarang, there were the Young Railroad Workers (Angkatan Muda Kereta Api, AMKA), the Young Post and Telegraph Workers (Angkatan Muda PTT), the Union of Semarang High School Students (Gabungan Pelajar Sekolah Menengah Semarang), the Union of Pati High Schools (Gabungan Sekolah Menengah Pati, GASEMPA) and so on.[37]

The army, meanwhile, was formed progressively by the fusion of various armed groups. Initially named the People's Security Army (Tentara Keamanan Rakyat, TKR), it was later renamed Army of the Republic of Indonesia (Tentara Republik Indonesia, TRI). On 3 June 1947, this merged with other people's militias to form a new official Indonesian National Armed Forces (Tentara Nasional Indonesia, TNI).[38] Within the TNI, there were three major groups: soldiers trained in the KNIL, those professionally trained by the Japanese mainly through its auxiliary force PETA (Pembela Tanah Air, Fatherland Defence Corps), and the people's militia groups without any military training.[39] TNI chief of staff Abdul Haris Nasution later wrote that the TNI had an estimated 300,000 to 400,000 personnel, 37,600 of whom were former PETA soldiers and another small portion of whom were former KNIL. The remainder were former members of militia groups with little military knowledge.[40]

Indonesian and Dutch logistics strategies

The Indonesian strategy to obtain armaments had begun early in the revolution by confiscating Japanese weapons and ammunitions. They became the property of the Republic of Indonesia (Milik Republik Indonesia). This was how the youth militias obtained their weapons.[41] During their occupation, the Japanese had built Indonesian auxiliary forces consisting of 25,000 soldiers equipped with 15,000 revolvers, 10,000 rifles and 80 machine guns.[42] However, when PETA and the Heiho were dissolved on 19 August 1945, their members were forced to hand over their arms to the Japanese officers, who had been charged by the Allies to maintain the peace. This led to a dramatic decrease in the number of weapons held by Indonesian armed forces.[43] Supreme Allied Commander Louis Mountbatten and wartime Japanese officer Shizuo Miyamoto agreed that, until 19 September 1945, Indonesian military personnel would remain without firearms.[44]

Youths and fighters in Central Java therefore began raiding Japanese armouries in October 1945. On 4 October 1945, Semarang youths belonging to AMRI found and confiscated Japanese gunpowder supplies in the Kembangan Cave.[45] More weapons were seized in Semarang on 7 October 1945 after youths and fighters attacked the Japanese military base Kido Butai in Jatingaleh. The Japanese initially handed over 160 pieces after negotiations, and another 500 the second day. The total number is not known.[46] On 5 October 1945, Indonesian fighters in Solo (Surakarta) attacked the military base of Butai Masse and the Kenpeitai military police headquarters on Slamet Riyadi Road a few days later. The attacks forced

Commanders T. Masse and Sato to surrender their armouries located in the Tampir Camp in Boyolali.[47]

On 7 October 1945, freedom fighters in Yogyakarta attacked the Butai Masse headquarters in Kotabaru and seized 15 military trucks and hundreds of boxes of firearms, grenades and ammunition. This raid led to the deaths of 21 fighters. Their names were later given to several streets in Kotabaru.[48] Meanwhile, from Banyumas, a forerunner of the TKR called the People's Security Agency (Badan Keamanan Rakyat, BKR), led by former PETA officer *(daidancho)* Sudirman, managed to pressure the Japanese Division based in Magelang to hand over a huge cache of weapons belonging to the Keibitai Naval Special Force, without bloodshed:[49]

> There were 5,000 rifles, 700 pistols, 500 Sten guns, 150 light machine guns, 80 machine guns M 23, 4 heavy machine guns, 2 7.5 cm field cannons, 2 7.5 cm mountain guns, 5 naval cannons, 4 armouries of ammunition, 1 storage of military tools, 1 storage of transportation means, 13 sedans, 60 trucks, 4 Bren carriers, and small military equipment such as binoculars, swords, and motorcycles.[50]

According to Nasution, Republican forces obtained at least 70,000 firearms in Central and East Java alone. Others mentioned figures around half that.[51] This control of Japanese weapons by the Republican army made Allied and Dutch forces anxious. After they had discovered that youths in Surabaya had seized as many as 21,826 weapons from the Japanese army and 3,000 more from the navy, the British gave them an ultimatum to surrender their weapons before 10 November 1945. Refusing to do so, the youths then used these weapons to fight the British in the Battle of Surabaya on the day the ultimatum expired.[52] Immediately after landing on 2 October 1945, the returning Dutch East Indies bureaucracy – known now as the Netherlands Indies Civil Administration (NICA) – imposed a trade embargo in order to inhibit the entry of firearms into Indonesia. Simultaneously, the Dutch prohibited the export of plantation products and did their best to prevent 'foreign influences' on the Indonesian people whether economic, ideological, or military.[53] The economic blockade worsened Indonesia's socio-economic conditions, as the country could not generate export revenue and it was deprived of much-needed imported goods.[54] The blockade also directly affected logistics for the Indonesian armed forces and freedom fighters.[55] Especially in Republican-controlled areas, the economic distress reduced popular trust in the Republic.[56]

Due to the Dutch blockade, the Indonesian government maximized its main potential, namely rice, to fulfil its logistical needs. Rice was not only used for consumption by the population and soldiers at war but also as a diplomatic means to suppress the enemy.[57] During skirmishes between British troops and Indonesian youth in Semarang in October and November 1945, rice supplies dwindled as Indonesian fighters blockaded Semarang.[58] The Dutch retaliated with a trade blockade to prevent goods from coming in and out of Republican areas, to which the Indonesians responded with a complete rice blockade into areas occupied by the British and the Dutch. This enraged the population in the occupied regions, as evident in the following report from the newspaper *Berjuang*:

> The food situation is chaotic. It causes the people to suffer. Looting is becoming widespread. The British do not care about food for the people, while they are responsible for this situation. The people would definitely embrace the Republican government. But first, they have to make sure that rice is distributed fairly to the people in the city.[59]

After the Dutch took over from the British in the occupied territory, the demarcation line that separated the Dutch-occupied territories from Republican-controlled areas became even sharper. Some areas such as Maos and Kroya (both near Cilacap on the south coast) suffered from starvation due to the decline in rice production and the interruption of supplies from other areas.[60] The Dutch took advantage of this situation to garner sympathy from the population by distributing food and medicine, and by organizing people's festivals.[61] As a result, in Kebumen, for example, 50 kilometres east of Kroya, youths formed several anti-Republican organizations. One named itself the Movement Against Indonesian Independence (Gerakan Anti Merdeka Indonesia, GAMI), another simply Anti Republic (Anti Republik or Ranti).[62]

To provide logistical services for the population in their territory and their troops, the Dutch imported food from Burma and the US.[63] According to the Trade Commissioner of the Netherlands East Indies, E.C. Zimmerman, the Dutch imported 145,000 tons of food to Indonesia in 1947 and 292,000 tons in 1948.[64] Dutch soldiers, however, complained about the poor quality of the food, which they deemed unsuitable for human consumption. Two of them wrote in the left-wing and anti-colonial newspaper *De Waarheid*:

...What would you think if you were offered food that even dogs or cats in the Netherlands would not eat? The hospital has no milk. The meals that we get daily are five slices of bread with fish or jam in the morning, white rice in the afternoon, inedible because it was too dry. In the evening, the same.[65]

The costs of the imported food and other necessities for the NICA government were partly covered by the Marshall Plan scheme. This US-funded aid to the Netherlands was to have totalled 1,324.3 million US dollars. By April 1948, however, the Netherlands government had received less than half of this, i.e. 599 million dollars.[66] On 8 June 1948, a spokesperson stated that the government would seek a loan of 400 million dollars to help support the Dutch East Indies government. However, according to the Dutch historian Lou de Jong, the first Dutch military aggression had lessened the chances of the Dutch government receiving financial aid from the United States.[67] Eventually, the Dutch government provided credit assistance to the Dutch East Indies government amounting to 100 million guilders.[68] When US Senator George W. Malone came to Indonesia in September 1948 to investigate the use of Marshall Plan funds, he found that Dutch authorities there had not spent the money to feed the population:

The American people initially thought that the money was spent on food for the starving Indonesian population, to rebuild industry, and to curb communist movement. Reports, however, show that the Netherlands spent an estimate of three-quarters of a million dollars daily on its military in Indonesia. It is not a small amount, and it is impossible for the Netherlands to provide it alone.[69]

It is not known for certain whether it was Senator Malone's report that caused Marshall Plan aid earmarked for the NICA to stop on 22 December 1948. But this threw Dutch logistical services into disarray.[70] This explains why Dutch troops changed their behaviour in 1949 and began resorting to looting the people's food supplies and valuables. Senator Malone also made a report on the situation of the population living in the Republican-controlled territory:

The Republican area suffered from a shortage of clothing, medicines, engines and cultivating tools. Only a small portion of the goods was

> allowed by the Dutch to enter the Republican-controlled territory. As for food, it is not a concern at all.[71]

From the report above, it is evident that despite the adversity caused by the Dutch blockade, the Indonesian population in the Republican-controlled area had enough food supplies for both the population and the fighters at the battlefront. To facilitate distribution of rice and other food supplies, the State Minister for Food Affairs Sudarsono formed a Centre for Food Collection (Persediaan dan Pembagian Bahan Makanan, PPBM). It set rice collection quotas and coordinated with local officials. PPBM was assisted by another agency called the Supervision of People's Food (Pengawasan Makanan Rakyat, PMR), which was tasked to collect and distribute rice from the farmers to villagers within the Central Java region. Rice that had been collected could be immediately distributed to the people upon approval from PPBM.[72] Complexity emerged only when Indonesian fighters from West Java arrived in Central Java and required a large amount of food. The TNI then instructed food supplies to be organized by local authorities in collaboration with the local population.[73] Republican authorities affirmed this strategy with a decree:

> In every sub-district, citizens must pay dues in order to accommodate at least 50 soldiers. The soldiers shall stay in people's homes. Small groups of soldiers that are on patrol or pass by the sub-district should be allowed to stay overnight and be given food without charge. On feast days locals should slaughter cows, goats, and so on. If soldiers are involved in a skirmish in that sub-district, locals should automatically set up a communal kitchen *(Dapur Umum)* so that our soldiers can eat wherever they fight.[74]

There was a marked difference in food accessibility between Republican-controlled and Dutch-occupied areas. Sukardi, a guerrilla fighter who fought in Sleman, Yogyakarta, later testified that in the Republican eastern part of Central Java, food supplies were relatively sufficient: 'When I was in the guerrilla, I patrolled around Yogyakarta. I found that we never had any logistical issues when we were in Sleman.'[75] This was confirmed by Djiyo, who said that during the struggle in Yogyakarta he could regularly eat a 'delicious' meal: 'As for food, I liked it best when we were in Si (around Kalasan) where the land was fertile and we could eat rice and our staple food.'[76] However, conditions in the Dutch-occupied western part of Central Java were less favourable. During this period of guerrilla warfare, the Republican fighters were given insufficient food supplies. This was confirmed by one of the locals, who testified that:

> Rice, chickens, livestock, fruits were confiscated by passing [Republican] soldiers. Cassava, sweet potatoes, taro, and maize that grew in dry fields were also consumed by the soldiers who would eat them raw because there was no time to cook. The people also made containers, gave lodgings to the soldiers, and warned them when the enemy was coming.'[77]

Besides food, TNI troops stationed near the Dutch-occupied territory also needed an allowance. The Ministry of Defence allocated every soldier an allowance for side-dishes worth 0.75 in Dutch guilders and a 0.50 daily allowance. The money was to be spent on salt, sugar, rice and kerosene.[78] More fortunate soldiers were also provided with gold, diamonds and opium. To obtain opium, fighting units could send a request to the Ministry of Finance or even to the Office of the Vice President to issue an order for the Central Office of Opium and Salt to release the requested amount.[79] Gold and diamond came from people's donations. The people of the town of Pati once handed in valuables worth 2,165 guilders to the Pati branch of the Fighting Fund (Fonds Perjuangan).[80]

Banditry and patrols: The Dutch-Indonesian war on logistics

Banditry was one of the methods adopted by Republican fighters to arrange logistics. After the first Dutch military aggression launched on 21 July 1947, there was a drastic increase in banditry by Indonesian armed groups in Dutch-controlled territory. The deep Dutch penetration led to numerous armed contacts with freedom fighters.[81] This was confirmed by the Dutch authorities, who reported that the TNI became more brutal. Robberies and lootings were widespread, the population was terrorized, and armed contacts became more frequent.[82] Another Dutch report stated that in less than one month (between 29 September and 26 October 1948), occupied Java had had 280 robberies, 193 shootings, 45 acts of arson, and several other cases such as phone tampering and sabotage.[83] Newspapers wrote that the population in Central Java was terrorized by gangs of robbers that created chaos in cities like Tegal, where they demolished a tapioca factory.[84] Robberies took place in Purwokerto,[85] robberies and murders of several Chinese people in Purworejo,[86] murders in Banyumas,[87] murders and robberies in Wedono in Gombong,[88] terror in Pekalongan,[89] a dramatic increase in the number of robberies in Bumiayu,[90] robberies against medical workers in Salatiga[91] and robberies in Demak.[92]

Robberies, murders and other acts of chaos committed by the Indonesian army in Dutch-occupied territory were part of its strategy to weaken the Dutch and seize Dutch logistics. Smuggling, robbery and theft were considered the most effective methods. Unsurprisingly, therefore, Indonesian authorities formed units of thieves *(pasukan maling)*, tasked to steal valuables belonging to the enemy. One of these units was formed in Wangon, Purwokerto. It was known as the Thieves' Front (Barisan Maling-Maling) or also as the Five Tasks (Panca Koa), namely: 1) to love the motherland, 2) to sacrifice, 3) to eliminate enemies, 4) to support the TNI, and 5) to provide information to the TNI. At the end of 1948, the Panca Koa troops were led by Supomo. Disguised in black outfits, they committed crimes while also helping the TNI soldiers to navigate during the guerrilla warfare. They managed to seize firearms, ammunition, clothing, money, gold, food and medicines. Working in groups of ten, they looted a Dutch armoury in Ajibarang and obtained food supplies, gold and money from Chinese shops and tax offices. All proceeds were handed over to the TNI.[93] How much they looted was never known exactly. The TNI also worked with a group in Dutch-occupied Pasir calling itself The People's Movement in Occupied Areas (Gerakan Rakyat Daerah Pendudukan, GERDAK). GERDAK troops looted Dutch and Chinese homes for the TNI and passed on information. Both GERDAK and Panca Koa thus helped the TNI to influence Dutch-occupied areas without the TNI having to enter the enemy's territory.[94]

At the end of 1947, two armed groups called Barisan Gobed and Barisan Golok, from the joint Adimulyo and Kewarasan District of Karanganyar, Kebumen Regency, similarly looted people's homes.[95] With the full support of the TNI, they operated in marketplaces and roads, on the premise that they were looking for Dutch soldiers. They looted cooked and raw food at the markets and raided civilians, confiscating whatever they had with them such as cows, buffalos, goats and chickens. They even took the clothes their victims were wearing, giving them hessian in return. Several wealthy people in Tambakrejo village in Adimulyo were robbed of their money, clothing, cattle and horses in this way.[96]

In May 1948 in Banjarnegara, a series of robberies took place. They were perpetrated by groups of rogues formed by a political organization in Banyumas.[97] Each group consisted of between five and twenty personnel. They entered people's homes and took whatever they could find, such as goats, cows, clothing, food and jewellery. They looted no less than 31 homes, inflicting losses in the amount of 139,000 rupiahs. They also frequently harassed Dutch posts in Banjarnegara. Afterwards, they would immediately flee in the direction of the Republican-controlled village of Punggelan.[98]

In another such incident, on 9 March 1947 a militia group from Semarang broke into the home of Oe Tiong An in Salatiga and looted all his possessions.[99] In mid-1948, Batallion 171 in Kebumen ravaged a cigarette factory called Dau Tiga, taking five cans of kerosene and a ream of paper worth 4,000 rupiahs. The same battalion also destroyed the homes of several Chinese people, taking wooden pillars from their houses as firewood for the Republican communal kitchen.[100] On 18 September 1948, an armed group of 100 rode the train from Telawah station in Grobogan Regency to rob houses in Semarang. They seized property in the suburbs of Perakan, Gedangan, Soneng and Ngenden, loaded their proceeds onto the train, and returned to Grobogan.[101]

The main targets were food and guns. Chief of Staff Nasution had said that firearms were the most important component in war. The armed groups therefore looked for and attacked Dutch convoys and bivouacs to seize weapons and ammunition.[102] They also made their own firearms. Sugar factories in Cilacap, Slawi and Tegal were transformed into weapons factories.[103] According to a participant named Atmosugondo (quoted in Nazaruddin Zainun), they simply used whatever tools were available:

> Before the second [Dutch] military action, we had to have weapons. And here we had a factory to make them, in Slawi, Tegal. The weapons were made from water pipes, called Dutch pipes (*pipa londo*). They were of varying lengths. Grenades were made from milk cans, filled with gunpowder from fireworks, and named Bearded Grenades (*granat jenggot*) because they were ornamented by feathers resembling beards. The cans were tied to a fuse made from hessian ropes. Probably 70 per cent of them never actually exploded. There was also a blacksmith called Empu Janil from West Purwokerto (Karang Luwes) who crafted machetes, arrows, bayonets, and other sharp objects.[104]

Another way to obtain weapons was through smuggling from Singapore to Central Java via Tegal, to evade the Dutch blockade. Suryono Darusman was the pioneer in this action.[105] Darusman was a member of the Indonesian military mission in Singapore and ran a contraband operation called 'Operation Meriam Bee'. He left for Singapore a few days before Christmas in 1945 on a 150-ton wooden barge called San Giang. With help from Joe Loh, Darusman and his three friends Izak, Mahdi and Bagdja managed to obtain weaponry from the Allied forces armoury in Changi Naval Base. The haul consisted of 1,800 Lee Enfield rifles, six Oerlikon anti-aircraft cannons, kitchen equipment and military uniforms. All of this arrived safely in Tegal on 5 October 1946.[106]

The unstable prices of key agricultural products left government finances vulnerable. From July 1947, the Republican government under Amir Sjarifuddin began resorting to the opium trade to support Indonesian logistics.[107] A special team to smuggle the contraband was set up by the Ministry of Finance, consisting of the nationalists Tony Wen, Karkono Kamajaya, Mukarto Notowidagdo and Subeno Sosrosaputro.[108] Of the 22 tons stored in the opium warehouse in Salemba, Jakarta, more than 8.5 tons were smuggled abroad, mainly to Singapore. It was transported by means of barges, speedboats and Catalina amphibious aircraft. [109]

The smuggling did not always go as planned. The Dutch army intercepted several barges and aircraft and confiscated their cargo. On 18 September 1948, the Dutch daily newspaper *Het Dagblad* wrote:

> After months of preparation by the Singapore police, in close cooperation with the Netherlands Indies police, a Dutch police inspector in the bay of the island of Aier Aboe (Riau Archipelago) together with the Royal Dutch Navy seized a Philippine Catalina, an English speedboat, and forty chests of weapons and ammunition.[110]

The arms were sourced from factories in the Philippines and had been traded for opium from Java.[111] The loss put the Republican government in a logistical predicament, despite sufficient supplies of food.

The reverse was experienced by Dutch troops, who were short of food but not arms. A Dutch correspondent in Dutch-occupied Jakarta and other areas reported that food shortages were an issue for Europeans in Indonesia. Potatoes became increasingly expensive, while the Dutch could not get used to eating local food. Newly arrived Dutch soldiers immediately began complaining about the food. This was exacerbated by an outbreak of the plague.[112] Logistical supplies became even more delicate once food imports from Burma and the US were halted in 1948.[113] This caused a food crisis in the Dutch-occupied area, linked to a dramatic increase in food prices, especially rice.[114] Republican newspapers reported that the Dutch looted and seized rice from the population in both Dutch-controlled and Republican territory, especially behind the demarcation line.

Jusuf and Saifudin, who fled with their families from Bumiayu to Yogyakarta after the first military aggression, testified that Dutch patrols looking for suspects often terrorized their village after Republican fighters fled to the mountains.[115] It was very common for Dutch patrols in Bumiayu to snatch food and rice from the farmers. This caused the population to flee to Republican-controlled territory, especially in Yogyakarta.[116]

Massive looting of rice by Dutch troops in Dutch-occupied areas took place in November 1948. The distribution of more than 120,000 tons of rice to Dutch troops stationed in Jakarta, Bandung and Bogor depleted food supplies elsewhere. The rice was milled in mills owned by Chinese businessmen, namely Tang Yon Swan, Oei Liang Tjan and Thung. Rice was still available to the general population but cost much more.[117]

Dutch patrols also seized other property and valuables, often accompanied by harassment and even murder. On 2 February 1948, Tjokopawiro, a village official *(Bekel)* from Kalipucang near Cilacap, reported that his water buffalo and valuables had been confiscated by 'a Dutchman who was carrying a gun' (*Tiyangipun kados ndoro* [*Belanda*] *lan ugi mbekta senjata*). The same Dutchman also harassed the villagers Rudi and Samsudi from Genting village, in nearby Jambu sub-district, witnessed by 13 other Dutch soldiers.[118] On 9 May 1948, Dutch troops deployed in the Karimunjawa Islands robbed villagers there. More than 130 Dutch soldiers entered people's homes, forced open their cupboards, and took valuables. A Chinese man, Tjang Hong Tik, was robbed of 500 guilders from his shop, another 500 guilders belonging to a cooperative, and 31 guilders he kept for school fees. The soldiers also confiscated clothing, store goods and even a wooden rifle toy that belonged to his nephew.[119]

After the second military aggression, Dutch troops became even more creative in carrying out their acts. The end to Marshall Plan aid on 22 December 1948 created a food shortage for both the population and the Dutch soldiers.[120] Now operating throughout Central Java, their looting became more intensive to meet their logistical needs. Seizures by Dutch patrols for the period August and September 1949 were recorded by the Republican Defence Ministry (see Table 5).

Table 5. Looting and robberies by Dutch troops in August-September 1949

Date	Time	Acts	Victims
10 August 1949	-	Dutch soldiers seized two wooden logs worth 500 rupiahs, four teak logs worth 400 rupiahs, four wooden planks worth 100 rupiahs, and one chandelier worth 400 rupiahs.	Residents in Kadibolo Juwiring Klaten
15 August 1949	-	13 Dutch soldiers seized 80 litres of rice.	Residents of Tegalrejo
17 August 1949	10.00	Eight green beret soldiers stole money in the amount of 250 rupiahs.	Martosudarmo
18 August 1949	08.00	Eight armed Dutch soldiers arrested a civilian and took three of his chickens.	Unknown
	13.30	Three armed Dutchmen arrested Sastropawiro. But Sastropawiro was eventually able to escape.	Sastropawiro
	19.30	Three fully armed Dutchmen rounded up several villagers and instructed them to look for firewood and bring them to the military base.	Karanglo Village, Juwiring, Klaten
2 September 1949	10.00	Four Dutch soldiers took 25 eggs and eight young coconuts *(degan)*.	Hardjosumarto
4 September 1949	12.30	Nine Dutch soldiers forced locals to destroy four wooden houses, to be used as firewood at the Dutch military base.	Karanglo Village
9 September 1949	-	Dutch patrol cars roamed around Solo and Yogyakarta, taking electronics belonging to the locals.	Juwiring Klaten Village
12 September 1949	14.00	Thirty Dutch soldiers patrolled and seized coconuts.	The villages of Delanggu, Karangmojo, Gaden, Ngadisari, Juron

Source: Kementerian Pertahanan, 1 October 1949

In April 1949, around 100 Dutchmen and 50 colonial civilian police members searched people's homes in the Batur and Dieng villages in Wonosobo and took valuables. They even confiscated valuables from Chinese worshippers at the local temple.[121] On 13 July 1949, a Dutch patrol shot at the TNI and the locals in Ngargoyoso village in Karanganyar, killing four TNI soldiers. They disarmed the remaining TNI soldiers and seized five cows, three goats and five buffalos and burned down five houses.[122] On 23 July 1949, a Dutch patrol confiscated property in Krasak near Wonosobo. They seized clothing worth 7,000 rupiahs, shirt buttons worth 3,000 rupiahs, large bags worth 2,000 rupiahs, gold fountain pens worth 6,000 rupiahs and money in the amount of 11,393.40 rupiahs. On 30 July 1949, Dutch soldiers returned to Krasak and seized more of the people's possessions, namely kerosene lamps, matches, axes, pincers, hammers, shields, ceremonial knives (*kris*) and money in the amount of 6,300 rupiahs.[123] On 10 September 1949, Dutch soldiers riding three military trucks entered Muktisari village in Gombong and seized people's possessions and 3,500 rupiahs in cash.[124]

The war of logistics also took place during skirmishes between the TNI and Dutch troops. Armed contacts in Banyumas throughout March 1949 resulted in both casualties and the seizure of military equipment and cash. During at least 143 armed contacts, 820 Indonesian and 78 Dutch soldiers were killed. The TNI managed to seize 145 firearms and to destroy 43 Dutch military vehicles. Dutch soldiers seized 47 firearms and 14,100 rupiahs in cash.[125]

In the General Offensive of 1 March 1949 in Yogyakarta, the Wehrkreise III unit attacked the Dutch base in Vredeburg Fort and seized logistical provisions and weapons. Widodo Company, part of Subwehrkreise 102, marched from Mangkuyudan to Sentul, then moved westward to Pakualaman before eventually attacking Dutch positions in Watson Factory and Kotabaru.[126] The attack on Watson was a big victory since the Widodo Company managed to seize five tons of ammunition stored in the factory. Pierre Heijboer wrote in his book:

> [...] in the east, the troops under Captain Rakido's command surrounded Watson factory where ammunition was stored [...][127]

Company 2-B in January 1949 managed to seize weapons, food and clothing in Dutch-occupied Bobotsari in Purbalingga Regency in Central Java.[128] At the end of January 1949, TNI guerrilla fighters in the Wonosobo-Banjarnegara region intercepted a Dutch patrol and demolished two lorries, confiscating ammunition and heavy weaponry. On 16 April 1949, TNI guerrillas in Tegalrejo (east of Magelang) seized a Bren gun, three carbines, a machine gun and four bullet holders.[129] They also cut off the transportation lines used by Dutch troops and destroyed enemy vehicles. In Sambung, Pekalongan, the TNI blew up jeeps carrying provisions for the Dutch troops in Pekalongan.[130] They destroyed transportation facilities and blew up buildings so the Dutch military could not use them. Sugar factories in Tegal, Cilacap and Slawi were burned down after important manufacturing tools were removed.[131] Buildings along Wates Road were torn down and bridges destroyed to hinder the advance of Dutch troops.[132] Among the bridges demolished were those at Kali Progo in Sentolo, at Madukoro and at Kali Bogowonto, to name but a few. Railroads were also sabotaged, such as the one between Purwokerto and Tegal, which caused the train to derail into the adjacent river. A train carrying food and clothing for the Dutch military was sabotaged and seized in Tonjong near Brebes by Republican forces based at Cilacap (Sub Pertahanan III).[133]

Some Republican fighters also committed robbery against the population in Republican-controlled territory. In February 1948, soldiers led by Lieutenant Colonel Junus from the Central Java Armed Forces, Majors Hidayat and Mulyono from the mobile 'Sambernyawa' unit, and Lieutenant Mulya from 'TNI T.B.' based in Yogyakarta looted rice belonging to a man named Oeneb that was supposed to have been bartered for sugar at the Gesikan sugar factory.[134] Oeneb suffered a loss of 70,000 rupiahs.[135] At the end of August 1948, rice silos in Solo, Klaten, Sragen, Boyolali and Wonogiri were looted and sealed by TNI soldiers belonging to a 'student' company from Solo (P.P. IV B) and to a unit named 'MKB'. From 23 August to the end of August 1948, TNI soldiers looted 14,764 kg of rice from the warehouses of Pasar Legi Solo; 250 kg of rice, 983 kg of sticky rice, and 88,196 kg of fermented cassava *(gaplek)* from Widuran warehouse; and 2,500 kg of rice from Warung Pelem warehouse.

On 25 August 1948, TNI soldiers looted 30,000 kg of rice from the Kaonderan Juwiring warehouse in Klaten. On 27 August 1948, TNI soldiers forcibly took 4,150 kg of rice from the Kasdadi mill in Sragen. Later, on 30 August 1948, they took another 70,000 kg of rice. On 27 August 1948, TNI looted 605 kg of rice, 1,775 kg of husked rice, 21 kg of soybeans and 280 kg of red beans from Mojongso warehouse in Boyolali; they took 5,825 kg of rice and 3,621 kg of sugar from Banyudono warehouse; and 5,871 kg of rice, 5,221 kg of sugar, 65 kg of peanuts, 60 kg of coffee beans and 49 kg of salt from Sawit warehouse in Boyolali. On 26 August 1948, TNI looted 5,500 kg of rice from a warehouse in Sukoharjo and 1,510 kg of rice from the Jatisrono warehouse in Wonogiri.[136]

Looting and robbery (*penggedoran*) by non-ideological bandits drastically increased towards the end of the revolution and even beyond. Bandits led by Suradi Bledeg from the slopes of the Merapi Merbabu volcanic complex, Sastro Jenggot from Sragen, and Karto Lawu from the slopes of Mount Lawu at Karanganyar were responsible for a tenfold increase in crime (see Table 6).[137]

Table 6. Number of crimes around Merapi and Merbabu late 1950 - early 1951

Regency	Region	November 1950	December 1950	January 1951	February 1951
Boyolali	Throughout the regency	473	249	709	Not available
Klaten	Throughout the regency	-	376	244	148
Semarang	Ungaran	20	-	-	-
	Ambarawa	31	-	-	-
	Salatiga	159	-	-	-
	Tengaran	70	-	-	-

Source: Disbintal Angkatan Darat Bandung, *Suara Merdeka,* 2 October 1950, and *Kedaulatan Rakjat*, 3 April 1951.

The table shows that the intensity of actions by the Suradi Bledeg group of thugs began to increase in Klaten and Boyolali from early November 1950, especially compared to Semarang. This was because the group focused its criminal acts in these two regencies, notably in January 1951 with 709 cases. The lowest number took place in Klaten in February 1951 with 144 cases. The crime rate in Boyolali was higher than in Klaten and Semarang, averaging 477 cases per month, whereas the monthly average in Klaten was 256 cases. Boyolali was an easy target. It was a plantation area where people owned a great number of cows. Cows were prized by Suradi Bledek due to their high value and the ease with which they could trade them for firearms. Farmers in Boyolali and Jemawa also voluntarily donated cows to the security forces – 37 of them in April 1951.[138] Thus the war of logistics between Dutch and Indonesian forces during the revolution affected almost all levels of society in Central Java.

Conclusion

Success or failure in war is largely determined by the extent to which the belligerents manage to meet their logistical needs. Dutch and Indonesian authorities each had their own strategies to ensure that their logistics ran smoothly while simultaneously disrupting the other's supplies. The Dutch had superior logistics in regard to weapons and ammunition, while the Indonesians had the advantage in rice supply.

In the face of serious limitations, the newly independent Indonesian government fulfilled its logistical needs by seizing them from other parties. Shortly after the proclamation of independence, Indonesian youths confiscated weapons and ammunition from Japanese armouries in various areas in Central Java. Worried about the circulation of weapons in the hands of Republican fighters, the Dutch responded by imposing an economic blockade. This inhibited Republican authorities from obtaining funds for their struggle and eventually created an economic predicament for the entire population.

Central Java was central to the nation's food production. It provided outstanding benefits to the Republican government. The eastern part under Republican authority was more productive than the Dutch-controlled western part. The Republican government took advantage of this situation to prevent the supply of rice to Dutch-controlled areas. Worried that they were losing the sympathy of the Indonesian population, the Dutch began importing food from Burma and the US to feed Indonesian colonial employees and the general population in the occupied area as well as to guarantee rations for their army. When imports were halted in late 1948, the Dutch resorted to confiscating people's food supplies in both the Dutch-controlled area and Republican territory.

After the first Dutch military aggression, the war of logistics between Dutch and Indonesian fighters took place throughout Central Java. While the Dutch focused on seizing food, Indonesian fighters seized practically anything that could be used for war, including weapons, ammunition, food and valuables. Indonesian political leaders and the army worked with bandits – men who often claimed magical invulnerability to metal weapons (*duk deng*) – to ravage and loot Dutch military bases as well as homes in the Dutch-occupied area.

After the second military aggression, the war of logistics spread throughout Central Java, since the Dutch were now everywhere, including the Republican capital Yogyakarta. During patrols or after skirmishes, Dutch troops looted people's food, gold, money and other valuables. After the US suspended Marshall aid to the Netherlands, the looting and violent acts including murder became even more prevalent. Meanwhile, banditry from the Republican side was equally rife. They seized Dutch weapons, food supplies and other necessities.

All in all, both sides engaged in a war of logistics by resorting to theft, looting and robbery. This often led to both military and civilian casualties. Against this backdrop, the Dutch attempt to rebuild its colonial power in Indonesia imprinted many episodes of suffering on the collective memory of the Indonesian people in Central Java.

8.

State-making is war-making

Military violence and the establishment of the State of East Indonesia in 1946

Anne-Lot Hoek

Introduction

This chapter analyzes the establishment of the State of East Indonesia (Negara Indonesia Timur, NIT) in December 1946 during the Denpasar Conference and the simultaneous deployment of Dutch military violence. It focuses in particular on the quashing of the leadership of the Republican forces in Bali (the People's Security Army or Tentara Keamanan Rakyat, TKR), the military campaign in South Sulawesi, and the full-out attack on the Sumatran city of Palembang. I argue that these military actions were strongly related to the establishment of the State of East Indonesia, which

Prime minister Najamuddin Daeng Malewa delivers his first speech as the Prime minister of the Negara Indonesia Timur (NIT), 13 January 1947. The NIT was the first federal state of the Republik Indonesia Serikat. Source: Collection Fotoafdrukken Koninklijke Landmacht, NIMH.

was part of a federal construction to counter the Republic of Indonesia. In response to the Indonesian Proclamation of Independence on 17 August 1945, acting Lieutenant Governor-General Huib van Mook focused on the 'Great East' – as the islands east of Java were called in colonial times – because the occupation of Java was not feasible on a short-term basis.[1] In order to set up the new state of East Indonesia, the Dutch sought to establish 'law and order' in that region. This counterinsurgency strategy strongly opposed the political motivations of large groups of Indonesians. But failure was not an option for Van Mook: the success of the Dutch federal policy depended on the successful establishment of the NIT.

The 23-year-old Balinese freedom fighter I Made Widja Kusuma plotted an attack that was to take place prior to the Denpasar Conference, which was held in the Balinese capital between 17 and 25 December 1946. The conference's intended outcome was the establishment of the State of East Indonesia, and the conference itself was a result of the previously held Malino Conference of representatives from the outlying regions, and of the Linggarjati Agreement that had been concluded between the Netherlands and the Republic of Indonesia just prior to it. Before the conference, Kusuma walked around Denpasar dressed in religious clothing. As the former fighter later indicated, the objective of the attack was not so much to attack Governor van Mook as to cause a disturbance. 'We wanted to show the world that the Balinese resistance meant business.'[2] According to Kusuma, Van Mook's delayed arrival put a stop to his plans. Later, another militant did manage to throw a hand grenade at the Dutch-built Bali Hotel, the building in which the conference took place.

Such acts of resistance were of no avail. Much to the indignation of the Republican movement in Bali, the new State of East Indonesia was founded just before the end of the year, with the Balinese monarch Tjokorda Gede Raka Sukawati installed as head of state. Looking back on the establishment of the state, Balinese veteran Rai Susandi (1926-2019) later said that the Dutch did not accept Indonesia as a united entity but wanted to divide it into a federal nation, which the militants opposed. 'That's why Van Mook called us terrorists.'[3] The Dutch policy of promoting an Indonesian federation, which took shape from 1946 onwards, has been presented by some historians as part of a gradual process of decolonization and by others as a 'divide and conquer' strategy.[4] But it is remarkable that the dynamics of the establishment of the NIT in relation to political violence in the outer territories has received so little historiographical attention, particularly given the importance of East

Indonesia to the Dutch federal policy. In the Indonesian literature, General A.H. Nasution made a connection between military violence in Bali and the setting up of the State of East Indonesia, and so did the Balinese author and veteran N.S. Pendit. In the Dutch literature, by contrast, W. van den Doel, J.J.P. de Jong and T. Bouma have focused mainly on the political process. R. Limpach in his study on Dutch military violence repeats an argument previously made by H. Alers and B. Harvey, namely that Van Mook likely took a firm approach to the outlying regions in order to support his policy of creating an Indonesian federation, but Limpach only focused on military violence and didn't connect what happened on the ground to the federal policy and the chronology of political and military events.[5]

The American sociologist, political scientist and historian C. Tilly, who studied the formation of nation-states in Europe, argued that there is a mutual dependency between state-making and warfare. States undertake a variety of steps in the process of state-making, the most important of which is warfare. This could involve the elimination or suppression of enemies within the territory of the new state-in-the-making as well as the provision of protection for the state-makers' own 'clients'. In the case of the state that the Dutch wished to create in post-war Indonesia, this meant protecting the monarchs who were cooperating with the Netherlands and who were becoming part of the new state, and eliminating or suppressing *their* enemies. States consistently use the concept of 'security' to legitimize the use of violence, and they do so from a position of authority that they claim is legitimate.[6] Anything contrary was deemed subversive, as the Balinese veteran Rai Susandi recently put it in an interview. Indonesian political motives were thus suppressed at the time, but they were also not taken sufficiently seriously in later Dutch historiography.[7] The silence around freedom fighters or anti-colonial resistance movements even had its strong effect on Western history writing, as the Haitian-American anthropologist M.R. Trouillot argues.[8]

Re-occupation of East Indonesia

Early in the twentieth century, most of the areas that were part of the so-called Great East at the time – such as Bali, Sulawesi, Lombok and Borneo – were completely occupied by the Dutch East Indies government for economic and political reasons. By the end of the 1930s, Bali, South Sulawesi and the Bornean sultanate of Pontianak were given so-called self-government. This meant that the rulers were given more power than they had had immediately after the conquest.[9] The strengthening of self-government, and with it of feudal power, was mainly motivated by the rise of Indonesian nationalism in Java. Especially in Bali and Borneo, the growing discontent about colonial society, which was based on racism and oppression, had led to the emergence of a host of nationalist-inspired organizations.

In 1942, Japan put an end to Dutch rule in the East Indies. A year later, the Japanese began training many local youths in Bali, as in Java, within Japanese paramilitary organizations. The PETA (Pembela Tanah Air), the Heiho and other such units were intended to help repel an expected Allied landing. This process of training youths started later in South Sulawesi.[10] Two days after Japan's capitulation, these trained military groups stood ready to defend the Indonesian independence that had been proclaimed by Sukarno and Mohammad Hatta on 17 August 1945. Republican governors were soon installed in both Bali and Sulawesi, which put significant pressure on the feudal-colonial system. In Lombok, by contrast, the Republican movement was relatively small.

Most of the islands in East Indonesia were occupied by Allied forces quite soon after the Japanese capitulation. Borneo and Sulawesi were occupied in September. However, South Sulawesi soon proved to have a strong pro-Republican following. It was led by Sam Ratulangi, the Republican governor of Sulawesi, and supported by the lawyer Tadjuddin Noor and the nationalist Najamuddin Daeng Malewa. The Republican political party PNI (Partai Nasional Indonesia) was established before long, as was the Sulawesi People's Welfare Centre PKRS (Pusat Keselamatan Rakyat Sulawesi) and various armed groups such as the Lipan Bajeng.[11] The armed groups in South Sulawesi were placed under the command of LAPRIS, the Indonesian People's Rebel Army in Sulawesi.

It was not until 2 March 1946 that some 2,000 soldiers of the Royal Netherlands East Indies Army (Koninklijk Nederlands-Indisch Leger, KNIL) landed in Bali, operating under the name of Gajah Merah (Red Elephant). There they had to contend with an estimated 6,000 fighters hiding in the mountains and jungle under the leadership of I Gusti Ngurah Rai, leader of the Republican armed forces TKR (Tentara Keamanan Rakyat, later renamed Tentara Republik Indonesia, TRI). The Gajah Merah soon imprisoned Ketut Pudja, the governor of Bali who had been appointed by Sukarno. In May 1946, Rai united all the armed groups in Bali under his command in the MBO DPRI SK organization

(General Headquarters of the Republic of Indonesia Struggle Council in Lesser Sunda, or Markas Besar Oemoem, Dewan Perjoeangan Republik Indonesia Sunda Kecil). Rai had accepted orders from Sukarno to defend independence on the island. The Balinese historian Anak Agung Bagus Wirawan has not labelled the Dutch re-occupation of these islands part of a *de*colonization process, as is done in the Netherlands to mark the period 1945-1949, but a *re*colonization.[12] This reflects the fact that it was a military occupation of a territory where a Republican government was already in place.

By contrast, the Dutch viewed their own presence in the archipelago as legitimate. They considered the resistance in East Indonesia to be unlawful violence and labelled the perpetrators 'terrorists'. This was clearly a one-sided and criminalizing perspective. The resistance movement in Bali aspired to an equal, free and just society and was politically diverse, just as the Dutch resistance to Nazi occupation had been during the Second World War. Various armed and unarmed resistance groups sprang up. One of the few progressive politicians in The Hague at the time did try to correct this one-sided image being portrayed. As early as 1946, Frans Goedhart, a former anti-Nazi resistance fighter and journalist who became a Labour Party member (PvdA), visited Bali and gave his insights into the motivation of the resistance movement there. Painting a different picture than that suggested by the term 'terrorists' commonly used in the Dutch press, he depicted the armed groups as politically motivated and fighting re-occupation. In Bali, he spoke with the imprisoned Republican governor Ketut Pudja and others. On 12 August, Goedhart wrote in the Dutch newspaper *Het Parool* that the Balinese resistance headed by I Gusti Ngurah Rai was continuing its fight in a smart and brave manner. He referred to the Balinese fighters as 'partisans'. (The same term was later used in the English translation of the memoirs of a veteran of the Balinese resistance.[13]) Rai was not just anybody, Goedhart explained to the Dutch public. He was a man who enjoyed the deep respect of many and who was also a former resistance fighter against the Japanese. Rai had outwitted the Dutch with his guerrilla tactics, Goedhart said. He had maintained contact with Java and enjoyed widespread support among the population.[14]

Anti-Malino resistance

It became apparent soon after the Dutch arrived that there was significant support in East Indonesia for the Indonesian Republic. But this became even clearer after the Malino Conference, which took place between 16 and 25 July 1946 in a small town in South Sulawesi of the same name.[15] It was the first conference that included Indonesian representatives from regions where the Republic had not yet been established. Conceived mostly in Jakarta and The Hague, it was to be part of a series of conferences with a clear agenda aiming to bring about a new political reality: a federal structure for Indonesia and the establishment of its first federal state, East Indonesia.

Moves to federalize the archipelago had already started before the war. Some Indonesian nationalists supported such moves at the time, including Sam Ratulangi, who would become the Republican governor of Sulawesi, and Najamuddin Daeng Malewa, a member of the pre-war People's Council (Volksraad) in the Netherlands East Indies. At the end of the 1930s, such people viewed federalism as a means of achieving independence. However, Emilia Pangalila-Ratulangi (1922), the daughter of the former governor, recently recalled that after the war, many Indonesians saw the form of administration proposed by the Dutch as a ruse, a *siasat*. They believed the Dutch intended to retain their power. Her father, she said, had drawn a sharp line after the return of the Dutch: either you fought against the Dutch or you agreed with their return. He opted for the former.[16]

At the Malino Conference, the representatives from the outlying regions, most of them appointed by the Dutch, decided that the new form of government for Indonesia should entail a federal construction. From the perspective of the Dutch, this new state would at best be led by the old traditional aristocracy. The conference participants did not, however, have in mind a puppet state. They mostly had their own agendas, and many wanted to get rid of the Dutch as soon as possible.[17] The two most important representatives to play a role in the establishment of East Indonesia were the Balinese monarch Tjokorda Raka Sukawati and the previously mentioned Sulawesian nationalist Najamuddin Daeng Malewa. Both had been members of the People's Council. Some of the Indonesian representatives from East Indonesia accepted the Malino agenda as a necessary step towards further political reform. However, many Republican-minded Indonesians saw it as a Dutch ploy to weaken the Republic. Later that year, the State of East Indonesia was to be established at the Denpasar Conference. But the resistance to the establishment of such a federal state, which was strengthening in Bali and also in South Sulawesi, became increasingly problematic to the Dutch, for it tarnished the image they presented to the outside world of an area loyal to

View of the conference room in the Bali Hotel where the Denpasar Conference was held from 7 until 24 December 1946. During this conference representatives of various projected federal states discussed the composition of the United States of Indonesia. It resulted in the founding of the Negara Indonesia Timur (NIT). Source: Nationaal Archief/Anefo.

the Netherlands. The Denpasar Conference was supposed to function as the perfect model of a democratic decolonization process.

Initially, the Malino Conference seemed to cause hardly a stir in Bali. L.C. van Oldenborgh, head of the Netherlands Forces Intelligence Service (NEFIS) in Bali, observed in his weekly report on 15 August 1946 that there was little interest in the Malino Conference. According to him, this was because the masses were not in the slightest politically interested, as demonstrated by the meagre 40 Indonesians attending an important lecture about Malino in the Malay language.[18] His interpretation was typical of the inability of the

Dutch authorities to understand that the low level of interest might reflect the lack of popularity of the Malino agenda. It was also a view that reflected the pre-war colonialists' image of the apolitical Balinese.[19]

Van Oldenborgh suddenly changed his tune in the last week of August. The resistance was conducting a widespread underground campaign, he reported, with pamphlets containing fierce anti-Malino agitation. The actions mainly targeted the monarchs, who were presented as 'NICA accomplices' (referring to the Netherlands Indies Civil Administration) and not true representatives of the people. Van Oldenborgh wrote about 'anti-Malino elements' that returned to the villages to exert their influence there.[20] Astonishment can frequently be read between the lines of the intelligence reports about the capability of members of the resistance, including the fact that the propaganda came from intellectuals who spoke Dutch. In the first week of September, it was reported that the 'widespread' and 'very well organized' underground movement was much larger than had been stated in the previous report. With an extensive pamphlet campaign, the resistance movement was strongly opposing the conference.[21] Rumours persisted about an underground operation that was anti-Dutch, anti-Malino and pro-Republican.

In southern Borneo, the Resident also reported that prominent Republican figures were absent from a meeting about the Malino meeting and that 'part of the radical group' was fiercely against Malino. A political report written up in August mentioned open expressions of sympathy for the Republic and 'antipathy against Malino and the Malino spirit'.[22] There was underground activity taking place to procure armaments and prepare for combat. The main building of a night market (*pasar malam)* in the town of Kandangan – due to be opened on 31 August on the occasion of Queen Wilhelmina's birthday – was set on fire. In Banjarmasin, a government official wrote that southern Borneo had been under constant Republican influence. Large groups of young Indonesians opposed the upcoming conference in Denpasar. They were dismissing Malino and sabotaging the Denpasar elections. According to the official, at the core of the 'extreme anti-Malino standpoint' and the 'anti-Denpasar movement' was a long-cherished desire for freedom that had its roots in the pre-war political movements of the independent schooling movement Taman Siswa and the political parties PNI and Parindra.[23]

In Lombok, local leaders went so far as to openly oppose the establishment of the federal state. They had previously refused to select delegates for Malino, and they made it clear that they wished to serve neither under Java nor under Bali. A Dutch former government official in Lombok later wrote in a retrospective: 'When the NIT was set up, we had to talk them into it, they were unwilling… We brought all these leaders together in the cinema to have a big forum, and we laid matters out there.'[24] Unrest arose on the island concerning imminent pro-Republican activity around the Queen's birthday. An informant for the Dutch found out that Republicans had drawn up a plan to turn off all the lights in the Europeans' social club and to launch a large-scale attack against official buildings in the towns of Ampenan and Mataram. The plan was foiled just in time.

In South Sulawesi, too, unrest grew in the months following the Malino conference. Large-scale attacks were staged around Makassar, Gowa and Pare-Pare by resistance organizations and gangs. They targeted the residences of colonial inspectors (*controleurs*) and local officials as well as other symbols of colonial power. The People's Sovereignty Party (Partai Kedaulatan Rakyat) held a conference in Makassar at the end of November, where it demanded that Sulawesi be affiliated with the Republic and Sulawesi representatives to the Denpasar Conference be delegitimized.[25] The historian Willem IJzereef has written that the period from July until the end of December 1946 – following the Dutch takeover from the British, which took place at the same time as Malino – was characterized by an increase in the number of violent incidents in Sulawesi.[26] Various causes could be identified, such as the lifting of the state of war. But conversations with local people led one Dutch colonial observer to surmise that there was a 'connection between the course of the negotiations between our Government and the Republic and the growing resistance activity here, and, according to the reports that reached me, also elsewhere, such as in S. and W. Borneo'. According to the observer, the fighters believed that the strongest possible resistance against the Dutch would result in the fastest possible inclusion into the 'free territory', i.e. the Republic.[27]

During a congress in Yogyakarta in the second week of October organized by the Kebaktian Rakyat Indonesia Sulawesi (KRIS) – a pro-Republican group from Sulawesi – it was stated that 'popular defence movements against the Dutch' were widespread in East Indonesia. Both Republican and Dutch sources showed that such movements existed in Sulawesi, Bali, Borneo, the Lesser Sunda Islands and even the Moluccas, which were long known as being loyal to the Netherlands. These movements were able to challenge the authority of the Dutch in those areas.[28] While Republican authorities could not obtain accurate information from outlying areas occupied by the Dutch, it was becoming increasingly clear that the situation was significantly less rosy than the picture the Dutch authorities and their propaganda were painting. In September, the PNI was prohibited in South Sulawesi. Its schools and offices were closed and its leaders arrested. This led to a demonstration in Makassar with the slogan 'Once free, forever free!'.[29] All this politically motivated resistance could be viewed as a response to the negotiations in Malino, which were intended to result in the establishment of a new state later that year.

The business of selling protection

The Dutch also had their hands full in Bali with the work of eliminating enemies of the new federal state. In the run-up to the Denpasar Conference in December 1946, the Dutch military intensified its campaign of violence against the Balinese population and the Republican forces headed by I Gusti Ngurah Rai.[30]

The Linggarjati Agreement between the Netherlands and Indonesia had just been concluded a few weeks earlier, on 15 November. The most important part of this agreement was the de facto recognition of the Republic as the authority in Java, Sumatra and Madura. In return, the Republic agreed to the establishment of the NIT, or the State of East Indonesia, which was an important breakthrough for the Netherlands. On 20 November 1946, right after Linggarjati and shortly before the December conference in Denpasar, the Balinese TKR commander I Gusti Ngurah Rai was killed together with an estimated 95 of his men during a battle at Marga called the Puputan Margarana. Under the banner of 'peace and order' and security, the Dutch had violently eliminated the most significant opponents to the Denpasar Conference, denying their status as official Republican troops and referring to them as 'gangs' in their reports.[31] In reality, Rai symbolized the existence of a persistent and well-organized Republican resistance movement in Bali. It had been directed against the Dutch occupation of the island in a straightforward conflict with the Dutch 'decolonization' agenda dictating a voluntary union.

That a political reality was being promulgated through violence became even more obvious as the planned opening of the Denpasar Conference on 14 December approached. The opening was repeatedly postponed because the Dutch architect of the federal agenda, Van Mook, had not yet arrived. This was in turn because the Dutch government in The Hague had not yet approved the constitutional amendment required for the foundation of the new federal state of NIT. The proposal of establishing a State of East Indonesia caused great consternation among reactionary forces in both the Netherlands and the East Indies wanting to preserve the unity of the Netherlands East Indies state. They moreover opposed the Linggarjati Agreement because it recognized the Republic of Indonesia. Van Mook, still waiting for the go-ahead from The Hague, found himself having to act according to his own judgement in response to the worsening situation in the outlying areas. 'In four areas of South Sulawesi, I had to declare a state of war today,' he reported.[32] In Van Mook's perception, it was due to a lack of clear action and clear statements from the Dutch side regarding the new form of government that Republican influences were gaining ground. Without a clear signal that the new State of East Indonesia would have a status equal to that of the Republic, Van Mook considered himself powerless to bring real stability in the area.

On 10 December, the Dutch Minister of Colonial Affairs, Jan Jonkman, finally issued a statement adopting a unilateral Dutch interpretation of the Linggarjati Agreement. This allowed him to order the Denpasar Conference to proceed. A day later, the special forces known as the DST (Depot Speciale Troepen) and the notorious Captain Raymond Westerling, started their advance in South Sulawesi. All 'remnants of discord, degradation and terror' must be eliminated from East Indonesia with the utmost speed, Van Mook contended in his opening address at the Denpasar Conference.[33]

Dr Onvlee, a well-informed missionary from Timor who was present at the Denpasar Conference, wrote in a letter to the mission consul in Jakarta that in his view the turmoil in South Sulawesi was a reflection of the opposition to the Malino agenda.[34] A member of the temporary court martial (Temporaire Krijgsraad) similarly wrote that Malino had resulted in more organized violence: 'After Malino 1946, the organization of resistance in South Sulawesi became ever stronger. In the final months of 1946, it led to such serious terror (the victims of which were Indonesians in more than 90 percent of cases) that strong military countermeasures had to be taken.'[35] Both witnesses reported a clear connection between the political negotiations and the increase in violence, resulting in Van Mook's deployment of the special forces. In South Sulawesi, special forces, KNIL, KL (Koninklijke Landmacht) and – local – police forces killed at least an estimated 5,182 Indonesians, for which no political responsibility was taken.[36] The Indonesian widows and other surviving relatives of the victims have recently filed lawsuits against the Dutch government. In cases brought to court by the Committee of Dutch Debts of Honour (Yayasan Komite Utang Kehormatan Belanda, KUKB), ten widows from South Sulawesi were awarded compensation and apologies.

An important reason for the use of force in Bali and South Sulawesi was to provide protection to the partners of the Dutch with the aim of forming a successful federal state. As Tilly states: the formation of a state also involves protecting that state's so-called 'loyalists'. Van Mook had to offer security to his Indonesian partners, those who were working with the Dutch in East Indonesia. At a meeting in Jakarta on 13 November, Sukawati had expressed his concern about the unrest in outlying areas. Former prime minister Willem Schermerhorn, who was part of a negotiating committee appointed by the Dutch government in The Hague, replied that in order to form the federal states, the Netherlands would bring the situation under control by enforcing the rule of law.[37] The Indonesian leaders who came to power not long thereafter within the NIT appear to have approved of the military violence employed in South Sulawesi. Onvlee even wrote that one of the prominent leaders had mentioned the necessity of forceful measures.[38] The NIT leaders Najamuddin and Sukawati could only establish their position as reactionary cornerstones of the new Indonesia if opposition against the new state was eliminated. An important reason for the use of force in Bali and South Sulawesi was therefore to provide protection to the partners of the Dutch with the aim of forming a successful federal state, as Schermerhorn himself had already indicated.

Violence played a crucial role in the attempt by the Dutch East Indies and the Netherlands, supported by a number of Indonesian politicians, to create a political reality for the benefit of a new state. The chronology of events demonstrates this very clearly. The military necessity that Van Mook invoked in South Sulawesi was, in fact, a political necessity. Moreover, the command given by the Dutch authorities in Indonesia – backed by The Hague – to Captain Westerling and his special troops was to 'restore order', which resulted in the committing of crimes.[39]

State security

The Dutch policy of using force to create a political reality became even more clear during the Denpasar Conference that started on 17 December 1946. The discussions focused on providing the new state with security, one of the key aspects of state-making as explained by Charles Tilly. The Republican objections to this conference were naturally also directed against the Indonesians who gathered at the conference and who were viewed as lackeys of the Dutch.

It is important to emphasize the political agency of the group of Indonesian representatives at Denpasar. The political orientation within the group of NIT representatives was diverse, and the accepted idea of an exclusively pro-Dutch elite is contestable. There were also pro-Republican Indonesians attending the conference, such as the Balinese education official Made Mendra and the lawyer Tadjuddin Noor from South Sulawesi. In a later interview, Widja Kusuma, the Balinese freedom fighter mentioned earlier, characterized all the conference members from Bali – 'maybe except for Anak Agung Gede Agung (who was at that time still *raja* and later on minister and prime minister in NIT)' – as pro-*merdeka*. They only differed in how they thought it was best to achieve independence: one group of representatives felt supporting the guerrillas was the way to go, while another group preferred the diplomatic path. But Kusuma viewed almost all the Balinese attendants at the Denpasar Conference as part of the opposition against the Dutch.[40]

Yet those who eventually led the new state – first and foremost the first president of the State of East Indonesia, the Balinese Sukawati – belonged to the conservative, feudal group that supported the Netherlands in its strategy to retain power. While Anak Agung Gede Agung, who later became prime minister, seemed to be pro-Dutch, he was actually a brilliant opportunist who also used grave violence against political opponents on Bali.[41] The extent to which the Netherlands was bent on retaining power and was prepared to use force under the pretext of maintaining security is illustrated by the notes taken by an official of the Dutch government information service (Regeringsvoorlichtingsdienst, RVD) on 13 December 1946. This document is an important source because it was not an official report but rather the official's own observations and interpretations. He wrote that the importance of the establishment of the federal state centred exclusively on security. The establishment of the NIT was mainly intended to counterbalance the *desire* of Indonesians to join the Republic. He remarked that in the 'areas of resistance' near Java – such as Bali and South Sulawesi – such resistance was therefore directed against the NIT itself. The 'psychological value' of the new NIT was, in his view, that freedom fighters in the Malino areas now had to be crushed by their own Indonesian government.[42]

Sukawati, who was elected president during the conference, already hinted at that violent message during the conference: 'We will now have to take the reins ourselves throughout the Negara Indonesia Timur region, and with a stronger hand, and there will have to be peace and order, law and security; and where this is not yet understood, effective measures will have to be taken.'[43] From the Dutch perspective, as suggested by the Dutch official, the major advantage of equality between the Republic and the Malino areas was that the international community would now bear witness as the Republic and the Malino areas devastated each other, thus proving to the world that both parties were not ready for true *kemerdekaan* (independence). Dutch authorities emphasized a struggle was going on between 'East' and 'West' Indonesia, between 'federalist' and 'unitary', but according to the Indonesian general A.H. Nasution it was a actually struggle between colonialism and independence.[44]

Violence flared up again in Bali during the Denpasar Conference. According to Dutch reports, 'exasperating acts of terror' took place, including arson, plunder and murder. Various militia groups murdered Balinese people considered 'loyal' to the Netherlands. In addition, a solid underground system was devised under the leadership of the aforementioned Widja Kusuma. Propaganda was distributed, and data about informers was gathered for the Republican leadership in Bali. 'Our people do not wish to be governed by another race,' reads a propaganda document from the first week of the conference and seized by NEFIS from the resistance.[45] The establishment of the NIT seems to have strengthened the opposition in both Bali and South Sulawesi.[46]

Echoes of violence

The extent to which Van Mook was committed to achieving security is evident from his expressed wish that 'everything be done to pacify the Great East and Borneo, including Bali and Lombok, as soon as possible, and to take military action in such a way that no setbacks are suffered'. He made this known immediately upon conclusion of the Denpasar Conference, where a new state had just been founded, on 24 December.[47] At that time, it was already known that Dutch troops in South Sulawesi were brutally dealing with any – alleged – opposition. But for Van Mook, only one thing mattered: establishing a successful state that could counterbalance the Republic and could protect the Indonesian partners of the Netherlands.

Before the State of East Indonesia had even seen the light of day, its chances of survival were already under pressure from the resistance in that region. The problem was not restricted to East Indonesia. Sumatra and parts of Java also saw a great deal of violence during this period. In addition, discord arose both in the Netherlands and in Indonesia over the as-yet-unsigned Linggarjati Agreement. Signing it was crucial to the continuation of the federation policy. During that politically unstable phase, concurrent military operations were undertaken against the 'bridgeheads' or 'key areas', as the British called the cities of strategic importance in Java and Sumatra: Surabaya, Semarang, Buitenzorg (Bogor), Palembang, Padang and Medan (Map 1). These actions have rarely been discussed in the historical literature, and when they are, they have been considered largely in isolation from the political decision-making process. Yet they cannot be separated from that process surrounding the establishment of the State of East Indonesia. As Charles Tilly contends, state-making requires the elimination or neutralization of both the enemies of the state's clients, such as in Bali and South Sulawesi, and the enemies of the state itself – that is, the Republic.

The Dutch government always reserved the option of using military action to force the Republic into making concessions at the negotiating table. The chief of staff of the Dutch military in the Indies, Buurman van Vreeden, set out his military vision as early as March 1946. If a political solution with the Republic could not be reached, West Java would need to be occupied. The Dutch government was prepared to carry out this plan; it was the British who did not give their consent.[48]

Lieutenant Governor-General Van Mook preferred a political solution. Military plans for a full-scale occupation were not raised again until February 1947, when Linggarjati was finally signed.[49] The operations conducted between November 1946 and February 1947 were viewed on the Dutch side as unavoidable clashes resulting from ambiguous demarcation lines. With the departure of the last British troops at the end of November 1946, Dutch military activity against the Republic's armed forces was no longer hampered by British restrictions and as a result increased significantly in the course of December 1946. The Dutch military occupied an area outside Surabaya, while in Buitenzorg near Jakarta, the local commander refused to accept the Republican form of administration agreed upon at Linggarjati and chose instead to use force against it.[50] These types of actions led to angry responses by Republican representatives, including a furious radio speech by the Indonesian supreme commander, General Sudirman. They considered the Dutch military initiatives to be a blatant violation of the truce agreed upon at Linggarjati.

In Sumatra, Dutch control was minimal and Republican morale was strong. On 8 December 1946, just two days before Dutch military operations kicked off in South Sulawesi, Van Mook notified Jonkman that the situation in Medan had deteriorated to such an extent that he had to take forceful action there as well. Unrest also arose in Palembang in southern Sumatra, which was strategically important due to the nearby oil fields. A political overturn in Palembang was unlikely, though. A Dutch official of the temporary civil service there wrote that Dr Isa, the Republican representative in Palembang, had accepted news of the Malino agenda with 'a friendly yet sceptical smile'. He and Isa had agreed to exchange their newspapers (the Dutch-language newspaper *Juliana Bode* and the Indonesian nationalist paper *Obor Ra'jat*) so they could keep abreast of the other side's views.[51] According to the official, the people of Palembang were not anti-Dutch but rather 'anti-colonial': they were against a political system in which the Netherlands did not recognize the Republic.

To the displeasure of the Dutch, however, Sumatra's pro-Republican stance strengthened the position of the Republic. This became clear during a meeting late in October 1946 of the General Commission for the Dutch East Indies (Commissie-Generaal voor Nederlandsch-Indië), a delegation sent to Jakarta by The Hague to assist in finding a solution – of which Schermerhorn was the chairman. The General Government Commissioner for Borneo and the Greater East – who was also attending the meeting – Willem Hoven and Van Mook both indicated that they feared that an imbalance might arise between Borneo and East Indonesia on the one hand and a unified Java and Sumatra on the other. They therefore came up with a plan for Sumatra. Hoven expressed the wish that Sumatra would stay apart from the Republic, which according to Van Mook would be a logical consequence of the establishment of the federation.[52] Their perception was that, although Sumatra was part of the Republic, it would want the same economic advantages and development as Borneo and East Indonesia and would moreover choose its own independence over dependence on Java.

As long as the Linggarjati agreement remained unsigned, the political situation resulted in a conceptual vagueness that in turn created room for the Dutch military on the ground to enforce the demarcation lines in favour of the Netherlands. In Palembang, this resulted in one of the biggest air-sea-ground attacks to take place prior to what the Dutch refer to as the First 'Police' Action (known as Agresi Militer Belanda in Indonesia) of July 1947. The attack caused a large number of civilian casualties and is known locally as the Battle of Five Days and Five Nights (Pertempuran Lima Hari Lima Malam).[53] The Y-Brigade – a brigade under the command of Frits Mollinger composed of Dutch war volunteers and troops of the Gajah Merah previously stationed in Bali – launched the attack on 1 January 1947. Part of the city was reduced to smoking ruins after the assault by the Dutch air force and navy. Indonesian and Chinese sources and Dutch veterans later reported deaths varying in number from several hundred up to 2,000 to 3,500 deaths, but the official number remains unknown. The population, which included many Chinese, was taken completely by surprise, because the airstrikes had not been announced beforehand.[54] The Republican Minister of Economic Affairs, Dr A. Gani, described the situation in Palembang as the most serious since the truce of Linggarjati.[55] A Dutch medic at the scene confirmed that the city had been 'destroyed' and that there were 'dead bodies everywhere'. The medic spent days nursing badly injured people, including children, in the city and the surrounding villages.[56] Dr Isa reported 'piles of dead bodies' and 'injured women and children'.

The Dutch immediately tried to shift the blame onto the Indonesians, but several sources indicate that the assault had been part of a clear plan to enforce Dutch control of Palembang. On 7 January, Van Mook explained to the Minister of Overseas Territories that the Dutch military action had been triggered by aggression on the part of Indonesians trying to prevent the implementation of the Linggarjati agreement – not only in Palembang but also in Bogor (Buitenzorg) and Medan. But there are records showing that Van Mook sent a code telegram to the local government official in Palembang on 9 January asking for proof of this allegation. The reply that Van Mook received was that hard evidence was still lacking.[57] Documents at the Netherlands Institute for Military History instead show that the Y-Brigade's Chief of Staff, F. van der Veen, drew up a detailed plan for the capture of Palembang and the surrounding oil fields.[58] That Dutch troops were expecting such an attack to take place in the very near future is evidenced by the fact that in the days leading up to it, war volunteer Ch. Destrée saw preparations being made for an attack with the arrival of quartermasters and a landing boat full of small armoured cars called Bren carriers. On 31 December 1946 – a week after the Denpasar Conference – Commander F. Mollinger sent Batavia a code telegraph requesting 'permission to change the status quo'.[59] The attack on Palembang was part of a deliberate political decision to attack several bridgeheads simultaneously, as the minutes of the 15 January 1947 meeting of the General Commission reveal. Operations of this magnitude could only have been launched 'after consultation with the government'. It was expressed during the meeting that the Dutch military position could be strengthened through 'judicious timing' of the operations in not only Palembang but also Medan.[60] General Commissioner Schermerhorn even used Palembang as an example during a General Commission meeting to show that 'good results' could be achieved by taking military measures against the Republic. Van Mook wrote in 1950 that 'peace' was only possible if the Republic 'transferred its sovereignty to the sovereign United States of Indonesia on its own [that is, Dutch] terms'. The signing of the Linggarjati Agreement was an important part of this Dutch insistence on imposing its own terms[61] – terms that were enforced by military means. On 25 March 1947, the Republic signed the Linggarjati Agreement, which established the State of East Indonesia. One month later, the East Indonesian parliament, under the presidency of the Balinese Sukawati, took office in Makassar, South Sulawesi.

Conclusion: The establishment of the State of East Indonesia led to widespread violence

The Dutch response to the proclamation of independence on 17 August 1945 by Sukarno and Mohammad Hatta was not the recognition of the Indonesian Republic but the pursuit of an Indonesian federation so that a 'decolonization' process would take place on Dutch terms. In order to establish the first state of this federation – the State of East Indonesia – Dutch Indies/ Dutch authorities not only tried to enforce the loyalty of a civil population and eliminated the state's enemies in order to serve their cooperating partners, they also used force to coerce the Republic into signing the Linggarjati Agreement, all the while citing 'peace and order' and security. As far as Van Mook and the Committee General were concerned, a successful State of East Indonesia facilitated that 'peace and order'. C. Tilly has argued that appealing to security is a cover that states often use during state formation in order to be able to eliminate political opponents. The aim throughout the conflict was to retain Dutch political and economic control in Indonesia. The military actions discussed in this chapter resulted in the deaths of thousands of Indonesians in Bali, South Sulawesi and in Palembang alone. A state's obsession with security inevitably leads to large numbers of victims, including civilians, who are often unjustly viewed by governments as a kind of 'collateral damage' on the road to military and political success.[62] This is precisely why it remains so important for historians to establish the connection between the political decision-making process and the military force employed. In the case of Indonesia, this connection reveals that the Dutch East Indies government and the Dutch government in The Hague were prepared to accept the deaths of thousands of Indonesians and to allow crimes to be committed against a civilian population in order to establish a state on Dutch terms within the framework of 'decolonization'.

Shortly before his death, the Balinese veteran I Nyoman Nita explained in plain terms why so many Balinese chose to fight against the mightier Dutch military in 1946, even at the cost of so many lives. He quoted his prewar teacher, a nationalist and freedom fighter who died during the Dutch occupation, who had told him: 'It's better to die than to be colonized.'[63] It is this message and conviction that has remained unrecognized and misunderstood by the Dutch, long after they agreed to transfer sovereignty to Indonesia in 1949.

III.

...WORLDS

PARLEMEN(T)

9.

From the parliament to the streets

The State of East Indonesia, 1946-1950

Sarkawi B. Husain

Introduction

This chapter aims to provide a new understanding of the practice of federalism, specifically in the State of East Indonesia (NIT). Historians have tended to regard the NIT as merely a Dutch initiative to re-establish their position and influence in Indonesia after the proclamation of independence. This chapter, by contrast, highlights the role of those Indonesian elites – NIT officials and parliamentarians – who principally had one ultimate goal, namely the unitary state of the Republic of Indonesia. Far from seeing federalism as inherently anti-nationalist, they saw it merely as an initial form of

Entrance gate to the parliament building of the Federal State of East Indonesia in Makassar (1948). Source: Collection Tropenmuseum, National Museum of World Cultures.

statehood. It was not surprising, therefore, that at various state events they insisted on singing the *Indonesia Raya* as their national anthem and flying the red-and-white flag as their state flag.

Despite its significance, there have been few studies on the history of the NIT. One was written by its former prime minister, Ide Anak Agung Gde Agung. He recorded the historical journey of this federal state from its conception in the Malino Conference to the rise and fall of its three cabinets, from that of Najamuddin Daeng Malewa to the last one of J. Putuhena.[1] His work did not include the conflicts, debates and intrigues that characterized the history of the state. Another was written by the Indonesian historian J.R. Chaniago. It limited its examination to comparing and contrasting the dynamics of local leaders in two regions, namely South Sulawesi and East Sumatra.[2] Other historians have given the NIT little attention, regarding it merely as a puppet state of the Netherlands and providing no analysis of the active involvement of Indonesian elites in its formation.[3]

Some of the other federal states had small geographical areas and homogenous political orientations. This was true of the States of Pasundan and of East Java, for example. The NIT, by contrast, brought together several vast geographical regions, each with diverse and complex political orientations. Nonetheless, despite the disputes, frictions and intrigues within the state, the NIT was committed to a free and sovereign state of Indonesia. This was reflected, for example, in several parliamentary sessions where some of its members demanded the recognition of the red-and-white flag as the state flag, the obligation to sing the national anthem and so on. It cannot be denied that there were also groups who wanted to make the NIT a base for their own political interests. But along the way, these groups were forced to eventually recognize the determination of the majority of the people in Eastern Indonesia, including those in parliament, to make the Republic of Indonesia their ultimate political goal.

Dutch authorities used both military pressure and diplomacy to reclaim their power. Lieutenant Governor-General Hubertus van Mook was the master of the latter. He focused first on the outer islands, where Republican influence was at its weakest and where he could find a number of local leaders willing to side with the Dutch in exchange for autonomy.[4] He approached a number of moderate as well as liberal-minded Indonesian leaders, and he negotiated with the heads of the traditional local governments known as *hadat*, among them kings whose forebears had been politically bound by colonial contracts (the 'Lange Contracten' and 'Korte-Verklaringen'), long before the Japanese occupation.

Van Mook organized the Malino Conference, which took place between 16 and 25 July 1946, in which the Dutch government hosted local rulers from Kalimantan, the Great East (all islands east of Java beginning with Borneo, including West New Guinea), Bangka-Belitung and Riau (Map 1). These 'outer' islands beyond Java and Madura had long been known as the Outlying Districts (*Buitengewesten*). He then succeeded in organizing subsequent conferences at Pangkal Pinang on 1 October 1946, at Linggarjati in November 1946, and in Denpasar in December 1946. These led to the formation of as many as 16 new federal states. Among them were the State of Pasundan,[5] the State of East Sumatra (1947),[6] the State of East Java (1948)[7] and the State of Madura (1949). The latter was interesting because its people had always been considered to be privileged by colonial rule. This led some of them, especially those affiliated with the anti-Republican militia Pasukan Cakra, to support the Dutch.[8] In this way, Van Mook tried to reshape Indonesia's political landscape against the Republic by means of federalization, aiming at the same time to keep Indonesia firmly within the Kingdom of the Netherlands.[9]

The Indonesian National Revolution and the formation of the State of East Indonesia

Indonesia's proclamation of independence on 17 August 1945 immediately triggered a positive response from numerous societal elements that were committed to defending it. The Outlying Districts turned out to have a stronger sense of nationalism than Van Mook had anticipated. Resistance by the people of Sulawesi against the Dutch in the second half of 1946 left most of Sulawesi beyond Dutch control. This prompted Dutch authorities in Jakarta to deploy commandos led by Captain Raymond Westerling as well as auxiliary troops to Sulawesi in early December 1946 in order to suppress the 'terror' of the Republic of Indonesia there.[10]

Prior to the atrocities committed there by Westerling, Sulawesi had been under the control of Allied forces under the command of Britain and Australia. After the Japanese capitulation on 15 August 1945, Allied forces began landing all over the archipelago. Australian troops were assigned to Kupang (11 September), Makassar (21 September), Ambon (22 September) and Manado (2 October). They were headquartered in Morotai island. In the third quarter of 1945, Australian troops moved from Kalimantan to occupy Sulawesi. The campaign received the full support of the Netherlands Indies

Civil Administration (NICA) which, despite its name, had a semi-military character. The Allies gave the NICA, reinforced by Dutch colonial troops (Koninklijk Nederlands-Indisch Leger, KNIL), permission to deal with social disturbances, while Australian troops remained on guard.[11]

The Australian soldiers serving in Makassar were given the name the 'Macassar Force'. Before their landing, a former prisoner of war, Major Gibson, was appointed as liaison for the Allied forces in Makassar. The government of the Republic of Indonesia in Makassar and the Governor of Sulawesi, Sam Ratulangi, warmly welcomed the Australian troops because they seemed unpretentious and were only concerned with the repatriation of the Japanese. Nonetheless, rumours began to spread that there were several Dutch officers within the Australian army unit. This caused some Indonesian youths to suspect all Allied soldiers. The Australian force consisted of only one battalion, but it turned out that this force included, as feared, one NICA unit with a strength of 150 personnel.[12] At the end of October, about 400 former prisoners of war were brought in to reinforce the KNIL garrison in Makassar. When they were on patrol, they were immediately confronted by militant Republican youths, known as *pemuda*, most of whom had been trained by the Japanese army.[13]

According to Anthony Reid, the resistance in Sulawesi was inspired by the Battles of Surabaya and Semarang in October and November 1945. Hundreds of *pemuda* attacked Makassar on the evening of 25 October until the early hours of 29 October 1945. However, the attacks were quickly quashed by Dutch and Australian military forces.[14] In December, militias led by the dominant group named Lipan Bajeng rolled out another attack in Makassar, which was immediately suppressed by KNIL soldiers. Despite the defeats, the situation remained unstable, which forced KNIL soldiers to start patrolling in early January 1946 to keep Makassar and surrounding areas under Dutch control.[15] In 1946, various underground resistance attacks by Republican armed forces worsened the situation, and this led the Dutch to arrest Governor Ratulangi and six other Republican leaders.[16]

Meanwhile, Sutan Sjahrir's appointment as the new prime minister of the Republic of Indonesia gave him the power and authority to negotiate with the British and the Dutch, who had been refusing to talk, especially with Sukarno, whom they regarded as a Japanese collaborator. The negotiations between Sjahrir and Van Mook, however, did not show satisfactory results. This made Van Mook turn his attention to arranging state affairs outside the effective territory of the Republic of Indonesia. This was the context of the Malino Conference.[17]

Several months later, on 15 November 1946, in Linggarjati, the Dutch recognized the de facto authority of the Republic of Indonesia over Java, Madura and Sumatra. The Linggarjati Agreement also opened the constitutional door to the formation of the State of East Indonesia.[18] The Dutch then organized the Denpasar Conference, which took place between 7 and 24 December 1946. This conference was also attended by representatives of the Dutch government and delegates from the Great East, with the aim of establishing a sovereign and independent state within Indonesian territory in accordance with Articles 2 and 4 of the Linggarjati Agreement.

The Great East consisted of 115 little administrative territories known as *landschappen*, out of a total of 298 *landschappen* in Indonesia. A total of 70 delegates attended the Denpasar Conference, coming from 13 regions: South Sulawesi, Central Sulawesi, North Sulawesi, Minahasa, Sangihe-Talaud, North Maluku, South Maluku, Timor, Flores, Sumba, Sumbawa, Lombok and Bali. Of these, 55 had been appointed – and not elected! – as regional delegates, while 15 others had been appointed directly by the Dutch. The Denpasar Conference was a continuation of the Malino and Pangkal Pinang Conferences and was designed to follow up on the Linggarjati Agreement. It resulted in the formation of the NIT, with its capital in Makassar, on 24 December 1946.[19]

Fighting for Indonesia through the NIT

As previously mentioned, the NIT spanned a vast territory consisting of many social groups, each with their own respective interests. Dutch endeavours to tame these groups through the formation of the State of East Indonesia were ultimately in vain. Instead, the state's formation prompted Republican politicians to use it as a medium to achieve their ideals. For evidence of this, we can follow the story of G.R. Pantouw. Together with Ratulangi, Najamuddin Daeng Malewa and other Republicans, he had been active in various organizations in Sulawesi such as Source of the People's Blood (Sumber Darah Rakyat, Sudara)[20] and the Party of Popular Sovereignty (Partai Kedaulatan Rakyat, PKR). But eventually he came to the conclusion that nothing could be achieved through such organizations. He therefore joined the NIT together with Malewa, cooperated with the Dutch, and became minister of information in the first cabinet of the NIT. His main concern was to tackle the many social problems confronting the Indonesian people due to the Japanese colonial rule and the Allied bombings. Pantouw was fully aware that the NIT was widely regarded as a Dutch puppet. But he was determined to turn it into a tool to push the Dutch into ending their colonialism. Pantouw argued that it was impossible for the Republic of Indonesia – which had no power, no army and no weapons in this part of Indonesia – to fight the Dutch effectively.[21]

For pro-Republican activists like Pantouw, joining the NIT was a necessary step given the tempestuous political conditions. Tadjuddin Noor, former head of the Makassar branch of the Indonesian National Party (Partai Nasional Indonesia, PNI) and once treasurer of the nationalist student organization Perhimpunan Indonesia in the Netherlands, initially refused to accept his appointment as South Sulawesi delegate to the Denpasar Conference. But after being persuaded that a federation was the most realistic system of governance during this period, he did finally join the NIT.[22] Tadjuddin Noor's political stance was evident in the statement he made after the Denpasar Conference: '...the resolution agreed in Den Pasar is the greatest possible achievable result for East Indonesia in the current political condition'.[23]

The number of pro-Republican activists who wished to use the NIT as a bridge to realize their ideals grew stronger. On the first day of the Denpasar Conference, Abdullah Daeng Mappuji, a delegate from South Sulawesi, made a statement highlighting the need for a unitary state and urging the acceptance of the red-and-white flag. This was echoed by Ajuba Wartabone, a delegate from North Sulawesi.[24] They also expressed their objection to the formation of the NIT as a state in a federation.

The Dutch designed the NIT as a model for other federal states. They gave it more power to govern itself due to its rather unique condition. The nationalist movements the Dutch faced in the eastern regions differed from those they confronted in Java and Sumatra. According to an American observer who was in Indonesia at the time, George Kahin, this was due to the different approaches taken by the Japanese during their three and a half years of occupation. Eastern Indonesia had been ruled by the Japanese navy, which sought to suppress the Indonesian nationalist movement, thus limiting its growth. By contrast, the Japanese army in Java and Sumatra had encouraged the movement with the aim of mobilizing its energy for the war effort. Accordingly, once the Japanese were defeated, the nationalist movement in Sulawesi and other parts of eastern Indonesia was weak and soon went awry. Its leaders expressed their allegiance to the newly declared Republic and its leaders in Java, but due to their limited armaments and lack of organization, they were completely powerless in fighting the Dutch forces, which were moreover assisted by Australian troops.[25] When the Dutch arrested and imprisoned the Republican Governor Ratulangi and his staff on 5 April 1946, the Republican government in Sulawesi came to an end. Any kings and local rulers in Sulawesi who supported the Republic were also rounded up and imprisoned or exiled. However, even without their leaders, the people of Sulawesi, especially in the densely populated southwest region, continued to show fierce resistance.[26]

Facing resistance from armed groups, the Dutch used military force and eventually resorted to extreme violence from December 1946 to March 1947. In areas where the resistance was most difficult to quell, Captain Raymond Westerling, nicknamed the 'Turk', was given the authority to do whatever was necessary to crush it.[27] Simultaneously, the Dutch maintained a diplomatic approach, one of which was to organize the Malino Conference that led to the establishment of the NIT. These approaches were expected to suppress all elements of resistance in Sulawesi and other regions in eastern Indonesia. However, the Dutch decision to appoint Haji Muchtar Luthfi and Mohammad Akib as delegates to the Denpasar Conference proved how futile their strategy really was. Luthfi and Akib were among the conference participants and members of parliament who voiced support for a return to the unitary state.

Strengthening the Indonesian symbols: The national anthem and the flag

The deep desires and aspirations of members of the NIT apparatus for a unitary state of Indonesia were reflected in their persistence in arguing for the NIT's adoption of the Indonesian national anthem and flag. The issue was already a hot one at Malino. The conference decided that:

> Regarding the matter of national anthem and flag, it is decided that Indonesia Raya can be accepted as the national anthem. It is left to each region to determine the time when the national anthem will be allowed to be sung in the area concerned. As for the Red and White, several regions, such as the Great East and Kalimantan, have not been able to accept it as a national symbol. Similarly, South Maluku will wait until this is decided by the people's representative body of the area concerned.[28]

Besides economic and political affairs, this issue became a major point of discussion in the NIT parliament and during every visit that the NIT president, Tjokorde Gde Rake Sukawati, made to various regions in the NIT. During the general assembly of the first NIT parliamentary session on 22 April 1947, in front of President Sukawati, a number of members of parliament insisted that the Indonesian national anthem be sung and the red-and-white flag raised throughout the territory of the State of East Indonesia. They believed that the acts of singing the anthem and raising the flag would encourage peace throughout the archipelago.[29]

Van Mook himself never expressed any objection to the demand. He merely appealed to the parliamentary delegates to exercise proper and careful policies regarding the matter in order not to create tension in the community.[30] His appeal was based on the fact that some regions within the NIT still could not accept the red-and-white flag as the flag of the State of East Indonesia. He also warned against possible internal rifts, which might endanger the existence of the NIT. Therefore, he requested that members of parliament have patience in dealing with the ongoing realities and advised against making decisions on this matter until national peace was achieved and conflicts among groups were solved.

During the first session of the Provisional Representative Body of the NIT, the issue of the anthem and the flag continued to be discussed. As agreed at Malino, every region in East Indonesia was free to choose whether or not to adopt the national anthem. The progressive faction insisted that the national flag was red and white and that it should immediately be mandated in all regions within the NIT.[31] According to Muchtar Luthfi – a member of the progressive faction – the Red and White was the national flag that united the Indonesian nation.[32]

However, the NIT prime minister, Najamuddin Daeng Malewa, in his speech during the parliamentary session on 22 April 1947, responded to the ongoing debate by asserting that:

> We shall be prudent in making decisions about the flag in order to avoid disputes or clashes. Since the question of the flag concerns the entire nation, it should be decided later when the independent and sovereign United States of Indonesia is formed. If there is one group who wishes that NIT shall have its own flag, it should be noted that it must be approved through a negotiation which considers its relation to the national flag.[33]

Prime Minister Najamuddin Daeng Malewa giving a speech in Bali concerning the formation of the Negara Indonesia Timor (NIT), 18 December, 1946. Source: Collection Fotoafdrukken *Koninklijke Landmacht,* NIMH.

Van Mook approved of Malewa's statement, adding that the use of the Red and White should be delayed, as it could become a source of conflict. Representatives from North Maluku and East Borneo agreed with this. Van Mook also wanted the Provisional House of Representatives to be notified regarding this postponement.[34] Several other representatives wanted to adopt the Red and White with the addition of a vertical yellow stripe running across or parallel to the flagpole. According to Andi Massarappi, this was meant to represent each self-governing territory (*zelfbestuur*). However, Balinese parliamentarian I Gde Panetje rejected this design, insisting that 'the flag should be red and white. There shall be no other colour'. Abdurradjab Daeng Massikki, a member from Sulawesi, supported Panetje, urging that the Red and White should immediately be raised in every corner of the state. He concluded his statement by saying: 'Once to Djokdja, always to Djokdja; Once independent, always independent.' Mohammad Akib from South Sulawesi echoed this demand.[35]

While debates at the Malino Conference and during the NIT parliamentary sessions centred on the flag, the discussions that took place on every visit by President Sukawati to the many regions in the NIT focused on the Dutch national anthem, the Wilhelmus, and the Indonesian national anthem, the Indonesia Raya, which were sung one after the other. When the president arrived in Makassar, for instance, he was welcomed warmly by a Chinese choir who sang both the Wilhelmus and the Indonesia Raya.[36] This was also the case in Tanete, Pare-Pare, Pinrang, Sidenreng, Soppeng, Sengkang, Toraja and several other regions that the president visited (Map 7). When he visited Lombok accompanied by a large delegation on 20 March 1947 to plant the NIT Tree of Freedom (Pohon Kemerdekaan NIT), he was again greeted by the singing of the Wilhelmus and the Indonesia Raya, followed by other national songs accompanied by traditional *gamelan* music.[37]

The national anthem and the flag had extreme importance in the minds of the east Indonesian people. People were willing to fight for them, in and outside parliament. A political report of *Residentie Zuid Celebes* in May 1947 stated that on 17 May 1947, a social organization calling itself the Agency to Support War Victims and Family of the Indonesian War of Independence (Badan Penolong Korban Keluarga Perjuangan (BPKKP) Kemerdekaan Indonesia) was established in Makassar. Joined by approximately 400 former prisoners of war released from Japanese detention, the organization put forward a motion for the recognition of the Red and White and the Indonesia Raya as the official flag and anthem.[38] Adnaal Beoma Adilolo, chair of the council of kings of Tanah Toraja, Central Sulawesi, added to his demand for recognition of the Red and White and the national anthem another demand: that the Great East be at the same level as the Republic of Indonesia. Haji Muchtar Luthfi from South Sulawesi expressed his concern upon learning that the Indonesia Raya had not been allowed to be sung since the Denpasar Conference.[39]

Nonetheless, several regions in the Great East and Kalimantan still could not accept the Red and White. The King of Bone in South Sulawesi, Andi Pabenteng, who was also the head of Hadat Tinggi and a local customary leader in South Sulawesi, refused to recognize the Red and White until an agreement was achieved in the Inter-Indonesian Conferences held in Yogyakarta and Jakarta.[40] These conferences, in Yogyakarta between 20 and 22 July and in Jakarta from 31 July to 2 August 1949, did indeed eventually end the debate. Among the decisions made was one to recognize the red-and-white flag, the Indonesia Raya and the Indonesian language (Bahasa Indonesia) as the official symbols of the United States of Indonesia.[41] This was further officiated by the NIT Ministry of Information with the publication of a book entitled *Sovereignty* (Kedaulatan). With a red-and-white cover, it contained elaborations on issues that had been debated in the NIT parliament, with chapters on the flag, the anthem and the language.[42] After the publication of this book, the anthem and the flag were never a source of dispute in NIT parliamentary sessions again. Furthermore, signs of an imminent return to a unitary state were becoming ever clearer.

The return to a unitary state: The people's movement

Until the early 1950s, objections to the formation of the NIT were barely audible among the political elite. The only objection in the early formative period of the NIT had been expressed by the religious organization Muhammadiyah. During the Malino Conference, the South Sulawesi branch of Muhammadiyah organized a congress in Mamajang (Makassar) and issued a statement that it supported the Republic of Indonesia.[43] Although detailed information regarding the statement is not available, this protest reveals Muhammadiyah's political stance against the developing political conditions.

The general lack of protest in South Sulawesi against the formation of the NIT was in contrast to the spirit of nationalism among the people, as seen in the various struggles by political organizations and militias. There are at least two hypotheses to explain this strange paradox, and both may be correct. First, pro-Republican politicians decided to join the NIT as a political means to fight for a unitary state of Indonesia. Second, the people of Sulawesi who had fought for the Republic of Indonesia in various militant groups chose to leave Sulawesi for Java to receive military training.[44]

In any case, the transfer of sovereignty on 27 December 1949 created new momentum for Republicans to achieve their goal of disbanding the NIT and returning to a unitary state. The atmosphere can be gauged from a political report of the traditional rulers council (Majelis Harian Hadat Tinggi) of South Sulawesi in February 1949:

> This is a period of trial in the sense of confirming and filling in the independence and sovereignty fully fulfilled at the end of the year. Generally, it can be said that this start was successful: public order and security are maintained, dangerous incidents can be avoided...[45]

It helped that several jailed or exiled Republican supporters had now been liberated. Andi Jemma (Datu Luwu), Sultan Daeng Raja (Karaeng Gantarang) and Pojanga Daeng Ngalla (Karaeng Bulukumba), leaders of the struggle in South Sulawesi against the NICA in 1946, were warmly welcomed and greeted with joy by the people.[46]

The political atmosphere in the early period after the transfer of sovereignty was stable for only a brief interval. Around the end of January 1950, various movements and mass protests began taking place calling for the dissolution of the NIT. They pressed the cabinet led by J.E. Tatengkeng (27 December 1949 to 14 March 1950), the first cabinet of the NIT under the United States of Indonesia (Republik Indonesia Serikat, RIS), and the cabinet of D.P. Diapari (14 March to 10 May 1950) to take immediate action. Between January and May 1950, pro-Republicans took to the streets to demand the dissolution of the NIT, using demonstrations, public meetings and pamphlets. I have found no less than 12 pamphlets containing the demand for the dissolution of the NIT; perhaps there were more.[47] Between 5 and 7 February 1950, the freedom fighters who had just been released from Dutch prisons organized a conference in Polombangkeng, approximately 30 km from Makassar. One outcome was the establishment of the Supporters of Indonesian Freedom Fighters (Pengikut Pejuang Republik Indonesia, PPRI). Another was a resolution demanding the dissolution of the NIT and the RIS and the incorporation of the federal state into the Republic of Indonesia.[48] Later, on 16 March 1950, another new republican organization calling itself the Association of the Struggle for Indonesian Independence (Gabungan Perjuangan Kemerdekaan Indonesia, GAPKI) held a large meeting in Makassar attended by 12 political parties and mass organizations. This resulted in a motion urging the RIS to immediately disband the NIT and to merge it into the Republic of Indonesia. On the following day, as many as 200,000 people marched in a street demonstration in Makassar. Its organizer A.N.

Hadjarati went into the NIT parliamentary building and handed over the motion to the head of parliament, Husain Puang Limboro, to be forwarded to the RIS government in Jakarta.[49] A month later, on 17 April 1950, another street action urged the people to break away from the authority, law and the government of NIT. Its proclamation stated that the people would defend the NIT only as part of the Republic of Indonesia.[50]

Yet opposition to the mass protests was equally intense. Many pro-Dutch Christian Ambonese were against the dissolution of the NIT and the unification of the archipelago. They argued that the Republic of Indonesia was exclusively dominated by Javanese, Muslims and leftist politicians.[51] On 5 April 1950, a skirmish broke out between Captain Andi Azis with his company of 300 Ambonese KNIL soldiers and the National Military Forces of the Republic of the United States of Indonesia (Angkatan Perang Republik Indonesia Serikat, APRIS). This later became known as the Andi Azis Incident or the Makassar Uprising. It was the beginning of the end for the NIT.[52] The defeat of Andi Azis forced Soumokil,[53] the initiator of the resistance against APRIS, to leave Makassar for Ambon. In Maluku, he continued his activism against the unitary state and proclaimed the establishment of the Republic of South Maluku in Ambon on 25 April 1950.[54]

The Makassar Uprising also led to the disbandment of the Diapari Cabinet in April 1950.[55] This tragically ended Diapari's political career. He was the sole head of the Progressive National Faction. His faction was in coalition with the Socialist Faction and the People's Faction led by E.U. Pupella, all three of which supported the federal government. A motion by the people's faction of Pupella,[56] supported by the government coalition, now alleged that Diapari had been involved in the Makassar Uprising. This forced Diapari and several of his cabinet members, as well as supporters of the federation, to be detained on the orders of the RIS attorney general.[57] On 10 May 1950, Martinus Putuhena was inaugurated as his replacement by the acting president of the NIT, Husain Puang Limboro, and was given the authority to form his own cabinet.

The change led to talks about reunification among delegates from the federal government led by Mohammad Hatta, from the NIT led by Sukawati, and from the State of East Sumatra led by T. Mansur on 4 and 5 May 1950. Afterwards, President Sukawati did not return to Makassar but remained in Jakarta.[58] The Putuhena Cabinet was tasked with making preparations for the 'integration of NIT into the unitary Republic of Indonesia in accordance with the mandate of the Proclamation of Independence 17 August 1945.'

His cabinet included prominent pro-Republican politicians such as Lanto Daeng Pasewang as minister of internal affairs and Andi Burhanuddin as minister of information.[59]

Even though the Putuhena Cabinet was fully committed to the Republic of Indonesia, the youth grew impatient. This led to increasing tensions. Moreover, Ambonese KNIL soldiers were still seen in Makassar even after the proclamation of the Republic of South Maluku. This provoked some youth groups to attempt to seize weapons from KNIL bases. As a result, between 14 and 16 May 1950,[60] a clash broke out between the youths and KNIL soldiers. A similar clash occurred on 5 August 1950, causing a great number of casualties, including Muchtar Luthfi. He had been a member of the Provisional House of Representatives of the NIT and was known as an Islamic leader and initiator of the Great Mosque of Makassar.[61] That tragic incident is now known as the 5 August Incident (Peristiwa 5 Agustus).

In the meantime, intensive negotiations towards unification were taking place in Jakarta between Mohammad Hatta, the prime minister of the United States of Indonesia (RIS), and Abdul Halim, the prime minister of the Republic of Indonesia.[62] Eventually, on 15 August 1950, before the Provisional House of Representative (DPRS) and the Senate in Jakarta, President Sukarno proclaimed the Unitary State of the Republic of Indonesia and announced the resignation of Prime Minister Hatta of the RIS, together with his cabinet.[63] This was followed by the resignation of Prime Minister Putuhena of the NIT on 16 August 1950 and the disbandment of the NIT House of Representatives (Badan Perwakilan Rakyat, BPR).[64] Thus, after three and a half years in existence, the NIT came to the end of its journey.

Conclusion

The formation of the NIT as one of the federal states highlights the complexity of Indonesian history. The NIT became the foundation of the postwar Dutch colonial government and simultaneously an experiment for the Kingdom of the Netherlands, led in particular by Van Mook, in a Dutch attempt to re-establish their colonial power in the Indonesian archipelago. However, it is not entirely correct to see the State of East Indonesia as merely a Dutch initiative to exercise political power after Indonesia's proclamation of independence. The political elites of east Indonesia played a major role in its formation, and many of them used the NIT as an effective means – given the limited ability of the Republicans to resist Dutch efforts – of re-establishing their rule.

For the educated elites and politicians, the establishment of the NIT went beyond nationalist or federalist concerns; for them, it was merely a system of governance. Through the NIT, they fought for the unitary state of the Republic of Indonesia. In this regard, their demand for the incorporation of the Republican red-and-white flag and the national anthem Indonesia Raya can be easily understood. These were important symbols for the formation of the unitary state. However, it is undeniable that there were also groups who took advantage of the NIT for their own personal gain, and this led them to express strong objections to these symbols and to the goal of a unitary state. These differences gave rise to debates and prolonged political intrigues, which only ended when the Inter-Indonesian Conference reached the decision to incorporate the Indonesia Raya, the Red and White, and the Indonesian language as the official anthem, flag and language of the NIT.

While the elites and politicians fought for a unitary state within the structure of the NIT, other groups who could not fight in the parliament building took their struggles to the street. They self-organized into various mass organizations or militant groups. They held public conferences, large meetings and demonstrations; they formulated resolutions and motions; and they printed and distributed pamphlets that demanded the immediate dissolution of the NIT and the return to the unitary state of the Republic of Indonesia. These actions, led by Indonesian freedom fighters, finally paid off when President Sukarno announced the dissolution of the RIS and a return to the unitary state of the Republic of Indonesia in his speech on 17 August 1950. Thus, the NIT as a federal state was disbanded, bringing to an end a chapter in Indonesian history, one that was filled with dramatic episodes. This dissolution of the NIT allowed those who had struggled against the Dutch attempt to re-establish their colonial power in the eastern part of the Indonesian archipelago to finally put their suffering and trauma behind them.

10.

The harsher they act, the more fuss there'll be

Dynamics of violence in South Sulawesi, 1945-1950

Roel Frakking

'The harsher they act, the more fuss there'll be,' Andi Jalanti wrote to his son, away fighting the Dutch in South Sulawesi. These words capture the essence of the revolution there: endless violence.[1] But also that violence was reciprocal and that Indonesian and Dutch violence were inextricably linked. Despite this link, the Indonesian and Dutch historiographies of the Indonesian

The harbour of Makassar in 1947. After the calamitous crack-down by the Dutch Special Forces, the Sulawesi struggle organizations proved resilient. The sea-faring routes to Java proved instrumental in re-invigorating the fight against the Dutch, as did routes to for example Kalimantan for acquiring arms. Source: Nationaal Archief, Dienst voor Legercontacten.

struggle against Dutch re-occupation between 1945 and 1950 are very different and are rarely connected. Many of the studies that have emerged out of both countries have shown reductionist tendencies. One strand of Dutch literature, for example, foregrounds political-diplomatic manoeuvrings to the detriment of the more local complexities of revolutionary warfare. Such approaches focus on attempts by Dutch policymakers, aided by specific Indonesian elites, to keep Indonesia under Dutch tutelage in a federal United States of Indonesia.[2] Another strand of Dutch literature has firmly embraced the recent 'violent turn' within decolonization studies, with its focus on the structural but above all 'excessive' or 'extreme' violence meted out by European army and police forces in Indonesia after 1945 and elsewhere.[3]

Aside from some of its murkier terminologies, this violent turn in the context of the revolutionary war in Indonesia disproportionately foregrounds the application of Dutch violence and seeks out its causes in the colonial mindsets of that period, the lawlessness of security forces, discriminatory judiciary systems, or the very fog of war itself. This dominance of Dutch violence, however, diminishes the role of Indonesian revolutionaries themselves as well as that of ordinary people who ultimately shaped the dynamics of Indonesia's independence movements, refashioning them into extras instead of proper actors. In the case of South Sulawesi, the violent turn has often meant that scholars have analyzed how Dutch policymakers instigated and afterwards whitewashed the massacres of circa 4,950 Indonesians between roughly December 1946 and March 1947.[4]

What happened after March to the peoples of Sulawesi or their resistance movements is often neglected, as is a theorization of mass violence and its dynamics that depend on Indonesian input. Indonesian studies of revolutionary South Sulawesi, by contrast, tend to focus on revolutionaries and on specific, so-called 'struggle organizations'.[5] Concentrating on these latter groups leads to narratives that tend to inventory the various groups in a region and to lionize their exploits. This results in teleological readings of the revolution that portray these groups as having one goal in mind: the destruction of the Dutch in the name of the Republic. In such studies, everyone battled for Indonesia's independence in equal measure, as if driven by one singular logic of resistance.[6]

In an attempt to move away from such flat interpretations of Sulawesi's struggle to maintain independence, this chapter deploys a more comprehensive approach that aims to connect the often-disparate Dutch and Indonesian historiographies. As argued above, the Indonesian and Dutch experiences of this period in history were in fact intricately linked. Amplifying these linkages shows the complexities of how Buginese, Makassar, Toraja, Javanese and Dutch actors in South Sulawesi shaped the events that together constituted a revolutionary period. This more comprehensive approach places events and actors within the same analytical framework to try and make sense of the large-scale violence meted out by both Indonesians and the Dutch in this period.

In what follows, this framework is conceptualized as the pursuit of 'permanent security' by both the forces working for the restoration of Dutch power and those that sought to kick out the returning Dutch. The pursuit of permanent security describes best how the often paranoid Dutch and Republican quests to achieve their respective end-goals necessitated the aggressive destruction of all immediate and future threats to those goals, which led to security-enhancing activities such as the so-called 'pacification' of areas, programmes that devolved into wholesale and sustained destruction.[7] The objective of such activity was not only to assert one's authority but also to attack and destroy the opponents' legitimacy. And in the process, both sides were transformed. Affirming their fantasies of being liberators, the Dutch tried to transform themselves into the rightful owners of Indonesia, returning to protect Indonesia from itself. In turn, Indonesians fighting for independence became powerbrokers in their own right, destroying in the name of independence. They began to believe that all things colonial needed to be violently encountered, including suspect or disloyal Indonesians.[8]

Naturally, the discussion here is informed – implicitly or explicitly – by very common causes of violence during a period of revolution. Among them are, indeed, the elements mentioned above such as lawlessness. But the overall notion of 'permanent security' allows the analysis to also include shifting alliances, the consequences at the local level of Dutch-Indonesian political and military agreements such as Linggarjati (1947) or Renville (1948), and the need for security forces to work towards an end-goal that had to be enforced by violence in contexts where possibilities for de-escalation or cooperation had radically dwindled. Lastly, the impossibility of separating foe from friend – and, indeed, the unwillingness within the armed forces to do so – strongly influenced the intensity of violence. Apart from these elements, this chapter focuses on a larger common driver: the need shared by both sides of the (highly artificial) colonial divide to eliminate the choices available to the *other* side of that divide.

Overall, force became a means to deal with the high levels of insecurity that informed the context of revolutionary war. This insecurity stemmed from the constant threats that each side perceived were being posed to its legitimacy and authority. Political and/or military resistance – both real and perceived – had to be eradicated to allow for the authority and legitimacy of one or the other side to take hold. Dutch and Republican authority and legitimacy could not co-exist in any given location.

Given that the elimination of insecurity and the establishment of one's authority at the cost of another's were paramount in the war-fighting mentalities in Indonesia, it makes sense that 'Republican' and 'Dutch' behaviours and the rationales they used closely resembled each other. General Abdul Harris Nasution's assertion that '[a]ll civilians of Indonesia who cooperate with the enemy shall be considered traitors' mirrored the Dutch way of thinking.[9] This transformed the 'locals' into potential traitors. Where enemies could not be distinguished from supporters and 'fake identities' abounded, 'producing "real" [...] enemies out of the uncertainty posed by thousands of possible secret agents seems to call forth a special order of rage, brutality, and systematicity'. Torture, killing and incarceration 'restore[d] the validity of somatic markers of "otherness"' upon which the empire rested.[10] Violence served to scrub out 'uncertainty [and] treachery' in favour of 'purity': rigor mortis fixed bodies *and* their identities into place, either as vanquished enemies or as martyred comrades-in-arms. One step below the totality of killing was the threat of the transformative powers of 'pain and demoralization' that villagers faced, which '[inscribed] state [or insurgent] power into the body'. Violence, then, forced communities to declare their support for either the Indonesian or the Dutch cause.[11] Permanent security fostered a 'culture of violence' and 'societies of enmity', wherein violent humiliations supposedly separated good from bad.[12]

The notion that Republican and Dutch policymakers and fighters strove to enforce certainty in highly ambiguous contexts and used violence to do so explains key characteristics of the South Sulawesi revolution that this chapter will touch upon. First and foremost, it explains the Dutch and Indonesian forays into the interior as attempts to claim ownership over communities. Second, the search for absolutes shows why attempts at co-operation between Indonesian and Dutch leaders – initiated by people such as the Republican moderate Dr Gerungan Saul Samuel Jacob Ratulangi or local kings (raja) – quickly collapsed due to mutual distrust. Third, this distrust affected local communities as well. Nationalist and Dutch forces therefore subjected these people to high levels of violence to enforce compliance and to ensure that local communities were no longer able to divide their support between the two sides. Violence, in other words, was a means to win the support of local communities: they had nowhere to turn for shelter, security or food. Where one authority held sway convincingly, villagers chose that authority – at least in terms of their outward behaviour.[13]

As a final introductory remark, it must be noted that the analysis below does not equate Dutch violence with Republican violence. Indonesian fighters tried to overthrow an unjust and unwanted racist and predatory regime, after all. Far from delegitimizing revolution, the analysis is based on the idea that historians have not taken the revulsion of violence as their starting point often enough, including violence's own internal, bloody logic. To the Dutch, violence was the means to a restoration of their power; for their Indonesian opponents, the desire for what they considered a just peace was often stronger than the desire for life itself.

Requesting recognition of the Republic

For Sukarno and other long-time nationalists, their conviction of the need to fight for independence had reached a pinnacle decades before the proclamation of independence on 17 August 1945. Three years earlier, the Japanese conquest of Indonesia had fatally exposed 'the weakness and hollowness' of Dutch rule. In the midst of sustained cruelty during the Japanese colonial rule, the old roots of Indonesian nationalism kept growing.[14] When 'vigorous nationalistic speeches' and the 'appointment of nationalists' were finally allowed by the Japanese in 1944, Sukarno and others raised the 'national consciousness... to the highest level'.[15] In April 1945, Sukarno visited Makassar, South Sulawesi. With the Indonesian red-and-white flag fluttering everywhere, he spoke of independence.[16] His words resonated widely. As one commentator later wrote, the people had grown tired of false promises of prosperity under Dutch tutelage.[17] As the 1946 Republican Political Manifesto stated, the *proklamasi* constituted the apogee of Indonesian national consciousness. The Dutch did not have the 'moral right' to return as if they had not been ousted in 1942.[18]

Dutch policymakers thought differently. Under the wing of Australian, British and Commonwealth troops, Dutch administrators and troops returned to what they still considered to be the Netherlands East Indies. In fanning out into the archipelago, reuniting with soldiers of the Royal Netherlands East Indies Army (Koninklijk Nederlands-Indisch Leger, KNIL), they were dismissing the Republican Ministry of Foreign Affairs' exhortation that a 'Dutch military [invasion] in Indonesia means a violation of the sovereignty of the Republic'. In Makassar, officials of the Netherlands Indies Civil Administration (NICA) soon shed their military uniforms to resume their duties as civil servants, after having been reinstated for all intents and purposes by Australian troops in 1945.[19]

Compared to Java or Sumatra, the nationalist movement in South Sulawesi got off to a slower start, although it was never absent.[20] The Japanese Naval Administration did not allow the nationalists to organize anything substantial, although the movement certainly did constitute more than what one Dutch commentator disdainfully described as a group of 'epileptic old women'. In the 1940s, older nationalist leaders such as Najamuddin Daeng Malewa joined younger ones like Manai Sophiaan. It was only in 1945, however, with the Japanese war effort faltering, that the nationalist movement was able to truly grow, helped along to some extent by the *Pewarta Selebes* newspaper (later *Suara Selebes*) where Sophiaan worked.

The emergence of the nationalist organization known as Source of the People's Blood (Sumber Darah Rakyat, or Sudara) in Makassar in June 1945 had more of an effect. Its chairman, Andi Mappanjukki, the influential Raja of Bone, leaned on his nationalist credentials born from his heroic last stand against the Dutch in 1905. Daeng Malewa joined him and was appointed mayor of Makassar in May 1945. In addition, two nationalists from outside South Sulawesi, with some 40 followers in tow, had already been promoting the nationalist message as advisors to the Japanese naval authorities. They were Tadjuddin Noor, who was from South Borneo, and Sam Ratulangi, a Minahassan mathematician who soon came to dominate Sudara.[21] In August, just days after independence, the Jakarta-based Indonesian Independence Preparatory Committee (Panitia Persiapan Kemerdekaan Indonesia) appointed Ratulangi as the Republican governor of Sulawesi.[22]

Important local nationalists, among them Daeng Malewa, Sophiaan, Noor and various aristocrats, welcomed Ratulangi upon his return from Java to Sulawesi. His delegation delivered a declaration that it would 'defend every inch of Indonesia against the greed of our enemies who want to re-colonize our country'. Despite his strong words, Ratulangi proceeded with caution. He was unsure of support from aristocrats and local nationalists, and he also feared that the incoming Allied Forces would take revenge on him for having worked with the Japanese, a fear he shared with Sophiaan. Moreover, he felt Sulawesi could not be defended against the Allies. As Ratulangi prevaricated, Sudara took the initiative, increasingly acting like a government. Its members established a Bureau of General Affairs and, with Tadjuddin Noor at its helm, a Bureau of Economic Affairs. Sudara reconstituted itself as the Partai Nasional Indonesia (PNI) in February 1946 under Noor, fully embracing the idea of *merdeka* (freedom). Sophiaan's associate Andi Mattalatta, meanwhile, gathered together some 3,000 revolutionized youths (*pemuda*) from various Japanese-sponsored militias. Against Japanese orders, they disseminated news of the proclamation of independence deep into the interior of South Sulawesi.

By September, some 25 *pemuda* groups were operating in Makassar.[23] The next month, the PNI received support from another Sudara heir: the Centre for People's Security (Badan Pusat Keselamatan Rakyat, BPKR; renamed Pusat Keselamatan Rakyat Sulawesi, PKRS, in February 1946). This umbrella organization acted as a kind of 'brain trust' for Ratulangi's gubernatorial office.[24] Two months to the day after independence, a petition to the United Nations was signed by 391 rajas, higher officials and those heading religious, political and social groups from Makassar, Palopo, Watampone, Rappang, Sidenreng and elsewhere (Map 7). They appealed to the United Nations to respect the people's wish for independence and to 'acknowledge' the Republic of Indonesia. The Dutch had deprived the Indonesian people of 'sovereignty and selfgovernment [sic]' for long enough, they argued, and the Republic's functioning administration assured proper governance.[25]

Bonthain high jinks: The race from Makassar

The Dutch civil servant H.J. Koerts and his associates were shocked upon their return to Makassar by the extent of these nationalist activities. They discovered that actual power lay with an 'independent Indonesian Government'.[26] Denying the sincerity of the *proklamasi* and acting on the basis of ingrained feelings of paternalism and racial superiority, the returning Dutch civil servants tried to counter the increasing influence of the PKRS and PNI offices.[27] In October 1945, Australian troops paved the way for this by occupying Pare-Pare, Sungguminassa, Maros, Bonthain and Watampone.[28] Koerts, a colonial reactionary, made it his mission to undo the 'rotten' anti-Dutch atmosphere in Makassar.[29] Aided by his Indonesian subordinates – old 'friends', as he called them – he retook the radio station, cancelled the Japanese-sponsored *Suara Selebes* newspaper in favour of two pro-Dutch newspapers, and operationalized the Residential Office. A list of 'collaborators and spies' was drafted (but ultimately unused), and the Japanese-installed Muslim organization Jamiyah Islamiyah was approached for potential collaboration. Koerts also oversaw the dissemination of pamphlets that informed people that Makassar was once more under Dutch rule.[30]

Dutch civil servants fanned out from their posts to re-establish Dutch rule, casting themselves as heroic ruffians. Assistant Resident Maarten Peddemors had his Australian protectors beat up Japanese soldiers in the crowded centre of Pare-Pare. Translating the Australian commander's speech, Peddemors told onlookers that the Australians would protect them until the 'Dutch army' could return. Elsewhere, he publicly burned stacks of Japanese currency. By his own account, this approach ensured that a semblance of 'order' was soon re-established.[31] In the meantime, Koerts was actively garnering support everywhere. With three Indonesian officials, including a local senior *hadat* law litigator, he visited the septuagenarian Mangi Mangi Karaeng Bontonompo of Gowa. In his report, Koerts boasted how the karaeng, an erstwhile advisor of Sudara, had changed his tune. The karaeng was even willing, Koerts averred, to trek north to 'talk sense' into his cousin the Arumpone of Bone so that he, too, would cooperate with the Dutch.[32] Koerts then travelled to Bonthain, as the karaeng there, Andi Manappiang, had told him over the phone earlier that he now supported the Republic.[33] He called upon the Australians in Makassar for help. From Makassar, the Australian command sent armed KNIL soldiers and two administrators who scared off the local nationalists the next day. Koerts looked back on these 'high jinks' with more than a small measure of pride.[34]

Controller J.J. Wesseling and Assistant-Resident L.A. Emanuel travelled with the Australian 16th Battalion to Watampone, the capital of the Bone District, to bring the Autonomous Councils (*Zelfbesturen*) of Bone, Wajo and Soppeng back under Dutch control. Wesseling and Emanuel too placed little stock in nationalist aspirations, claiming that in a mere month they had succeeded in changing the local population's aloofness into 'an official declaration [of cooperation] by the entire autonomous council of Bone'. And yet, everywhere they went, they were confronted by the emergent spirit of the Republic. Royal rulers refused to show their faces. Dutch officials encountered *pemuda* sporting red-and-white insignias, their *badik* (a type of Buginese dagger) drawn. Other onlookers displayed red-and-white flags, shouting 'Long live the Republic!'. One local district head dryly remarked that matters had been running quite smoothly without Dutch interference. Although local officials everywhere seemed cooperative, mostly without repercussions, in Watampone, nationalists killed two local workers for offering their services to the Australians. Watampone's rulers received threatening letters. As Ratulangi and the PKRS's nimble propagandist Lanto Daeng Pasewang followed the Dutch-Australian team closely, anti-Dutch propaganda found its way into many Sulawesi hands.

Regardless, Emanuel, Wesseling and the Australians doubled down. They told Bone's entire Autonomous Council on 17 November that the Allies did not recognize the Republic. They forbade the flying of red-and-white flags, and the 'unreliable' Ratulangi was to be ostracized. Bone's Arumpone, the same Andi Mappanjukki who had chaired Sudara, initially said that only a direct order could sway him to cooperate with the Dutch. His mind was changed after intensive pressure from the Australians. Early in December, Andi Mappanjuki publicly delivered a formal statement of cooperation, as did the Datu of Luwu (north of the Bone district), the Datu of Soppeng and several district heads.[35]

In those last months of 1945, in other words, nationalists and Dutch administrators alike raced into the interior soliciting compliance. The Dutch sought a restoration of power, while the fledgling nationalist organization needed support to 'defend its sovereignty', as there was, in their own words, 'no central government'.[36] The nationalists had the advantage, for they found people very willing and had had a head start before the arrival of Allied troops and Dutch administrators. People started whispering 'independence' within days after the Japanese surrender.[37] Across South Sulawesi, communities met to discuss how to position themselves, and aristocratic envoys travelled widely to circulate the *proklamasi*.[38] In May 1945, Watampone had seen Andi Mappanjukki with the Datu of Luwu, Andi Jemma, declare war on the Allies – an entirely different meeting from the one Emanuel and Wesseling convened later. In Luwu itself, a highly ranked Japanese police official named Sakata had already in August 1945 motivated the sons of local rulers, including Jemma's son Andi Makulua, to start a militarized youth organization for the national cause.

Before long, Andi Makulua controlled the movement and contacted Ratulangi in Makassar. With the latter's permission, Makulua and his compatriots opened a PNI chapter in Palopo.[39] Mappanjuki's sons, Andi Pangeran and Abdullah Bau Massepe, the Datu of Suppa, had already been installed by the Japanese as high-echelon administrators in Bone and Pare-Pare, respectively, and were rallying people behind the nationalist movement.[40] When Dutch administrators summoned the Datu of Suppa after the Japanese defeat, the latter refused to show up, claiming to be sick, and bluntly relaying the message that he had opted for the Republic.[41] On 23 November, Karaeng Daeng Ngalle asked the heads of Polombangkeng and four surrounding districts to oppose the Dutch restoration of power and to hide the rice supplies.[42]

Anti-Dutch stances were spreading, also among the heads of the most powerful Autonomous Councils in South Sulawesi.[43] On 30 December, a conference of rajas, political leaders and local customary leaders decided on a temporary administration that included power-sharing between Sulawesi leaders and the Commanding Officers of the NICA (CONICA).[44] Three months later, however, South Sulawesi's branch of the Republic's Central Indonesian National Committee (Komite Nasional Indonesia Daerah Sulawesi) went against that decision, calling on people to evade Dutch taxes, which, they argued, were 'unlawful'.[45] Wesseling and Emanuel, meanwhile, began to feel increasingly outwitted by Ratulangi and nationalist propagandists.[46] *Pemuda* from Makassar had presented Ratulangi's message of resistance to the Karaeng Pajonga Daeng Ngalle. This message meshed neatly with Ngalle's own thoughts. He and his brothers already nursed older grievances against the Dutch.[47] In Enrekang, Ratulangi himself spoke to *pemuda* gatherings in December 1945 that operated under Ratulangi's PKRS. Meanwhile, the Police Chief of Enrekang, Abdurrachman, responded to revolutionary exhortations from Pare-Pare by founding yet another struggle group. Allied to Ratulangi, they swore to lay down their lives fighting the NICA. Others travelled to Makassar to see Ratulangi, such as Haji Saidde from Palopo. On his return, Saidde established PNI offices and helped set up the Pemuda Republik Indonesia (PRI, Youth of the Republic of Indonesia). Around Mandar, Aje Mea acted as Ratulangi's spokesperson. Inside Makassar, Ratulangi's position was now solid.[48]

As the proliferation of *pemuda* groups and the increasing number of individual organizers cooperating with Ratulangi suggests, the nationalist movement also took hold among 'ordinary' people. Not for nothing did the elite PKRS and the Komite Nasional – as well as, later, Republican troops – focus their activities on them.[49] The PKRS's February 1946 resolution underlined people's growing hatred of the NICA as a destructive and destabilizing force.[50] In South Sulawesi and beyond, even sports clubs became anti-NICA.[51] The XV Infantry Battalion of the KNIL received a lukewarm reception in Pare-Pare. They had to contend with active anti-Dutch attitudes, as local elites' mentalities of resistance had crossed class barriers to take hold among their followers.[52] Clearly, this went far beyond the opportunism of ordinary criminals that Dutch officials often claimed was the root of the nationalist movement.[53] In 1946, the PNI had tens of thousands of members across South Sulawesi. Other revolutionary parties boasted nearly 50,000 additional members.[54] In Sulawesi, as elsewhere in Indonesia, the combination of careful planning, spontaneity and passion made for a powerful force indeed.[55]

Swimming in a 'sea of blood': War against the people of South Sulawesi

South Sulawesi was being carved up into Dutch and nationalist spheres of influence that often overlapped. Ratulangi's group argued that the nationalist movement governed with the people's mandate and that the Dutch were mistaken if they thought they could restore their pre-1942 rule.[56] Koerts, in turn, belittled nationalists for denying that '1905', when Dutch rule over Sulawesi had supposedly been finalized, had happened.[57] Such thinking, Koerts claimed, ran counter to reality: according to him, no less than 90 percent of traders, old-guard Indonesian civil servants and farmers both in Sulawesi and beyond viewed 'the movement' with passivity or even outright hostility'.[58]

How could both camps entertain similar yet mutually exclusive ideas about local support? Thinking in terms of zero-sum solutions and fantasies of permanent security dictated that controlling the common people was indispensable in any attempt to beat the enemy in protracted warfare. Mao Tse Tung's dictum that '[m]obilization of the common people throughout the country will create a vast sea in which to drown the enemy' applied to both the Dutch and Indonesian endeavours in South Sulawesi as well.[59] Within the spaces of claimed governance that were thus created, locals from all stations in life were forced to orient and reorient themselves.

Both nationalist and Dutch troops tried to achieve control through the application of violence. Violence was remarkably suited to the objective of controlling populations: its systematic application transformed those subjected to violence into supporters who provided everything from intelligence and food to manpower and acquiescence. Those killed were forever the enemy. The ability of violence to make people fall in line and declare themselves supporters, in other words, solved the conundrum of having to operate based on incomplete information. Violence mobilized people into action and support, regardless of their actual wishes.[60] The next sections of this chapter contend that, through the application of mass violence, the war-

'Radio Indonesië' housed in Studio Makassar was among the buildings hotly contested during the early revolution in South Sulawesi. Source: Nationaal Archief, Dienst voor Legercontacten.

ring parties deliberately diminished the room for manoeuvre available to opponents and supporters alike so as to enforce cooperation.

Commentators often claim that the violence intensified as the revolutionary war in Indonesia developed.[61] For those subjected to this violence, such debates about the intensity of violence often were purely academic. To the victims – and, perhaps, the perpetrators as well – differences between 'moderate' or 'intense' or 'extreme' violence did not matter much. Dutch soldiers were quick to resort to shooting prisoners on the roadside and torturing others with electricity.[62] Mutually exclusive and unaltering points of view drove this dynamic. Lahade, one of Sulawesi's premier fighters, confirmed this in one of his radio broadcasts. He called on his 'brothers and sisters' to rid themselves of 'the slave spirit that the Dutch and the Japanese delicately nurtured'. '[D]estruction', Lahade exhorted, was preferable over 'slavery'.[63] Dutch points of view were similarly emphatic, as evinced by the following note by Koerts from 1945: '*Sukarno movement* = prohibit'.[64]

On 2 October 1945, members of the reconstituted KNIL in Makassar, some 500 in number, indiscriminately fired on Indonesians displaying the red-and-white flag. This sparked off a spiral of tit-for-tat violence that went on for years. *Pemuda* soon began to commit reprisal killings of Ambonese and Dutch troops they encountered in the city. On 13 October, Ambonese soldiers again shot 'haphazardly' into Indonesian crowds, callously killing or wounding Chinese and Australian onlookers. Two days later, another incident resulted in 32 people killed or wounded.[65] At dawn on 28 October, high schoolers and members of the 'Barisan Berani Mati ('Dare to Die') group had had enough of Ratulangi's passivity and tried to rid themselves of him while also taking over Makassar's police station, two radio studios, the Hotel Empress hosting NICA officials, and the CONICA office. Ratulangi escaped, and Makassar's *pemuda* dispersed. Still, violence had spread beyond Makassar.[66] In October, revolutionary violence, said Dutch reports, had claimed some 50 to 60 Ambonese men, women and children. In retaliation, Am-

Makassar in turmoil, December 1946, like so many other cities across Indonesia. Source: Nationaal Archief, Dienst voor Legercontacten.

bonese soldiers 'dispatched' several nationalists.[67] Without a trace of irony, Dutch reports blamed the Japanese for having fomented hatred between the Ambonese, Indonesians and other communities.[68]

Invariably, the immediate and systematic Dutch modus operandi of violence, including its disdain for people and their wishes, drove people to move beyond merely founding various organizations and towards actual resistance.[69] In Bua in Luwu Regency, at least one KNIL soldier and two Indonesians working for the NICA were killed by local youths in December 1945.[70] Incensed, KNIL units with local 'accomplices' frequently visited Bua looking for their attackers. When KNIL soldiers entered a mosque and abused its guard who prevented them from tearing up a Quran, their brazenness galvanized Bua's incensed villagers. The local *pemuda* issued an ultimatum to the KNIL, which in turn countered with its own. Within days, heavy clashes ensued.[71] Elsewhere in Luwu, Kasim, the head of the Republican local offices, also reacted to the NICA's intrusion. Together with ex-KNIL soldiers, he barred the NICA and Australians from entering the town of Barru in November 1945, claiming that it was a Republican area now. Some 1,500 people then attacked Lieutenant Boom and his 'bodyguards', killing two of his party and capturing another two and taking their weapons. After negotiations with the Allies on 1 December, Kasim and another Republican leader, Andi Map-

A photographer of the 'Netherlands Indies Government Information Service' (NIGIS) fetishizes an Indonesian girl after having given her a sten gun and having placed her on the hood of a car in 1945, not long after the Japanese surrender in the Pacific. Source: *Collection Losse Fotografische Objecten,* NIMH.

panjompa, agreed to hand Lieutenant Boom over. Afterwards, the Allies did not dare bring up further disarmament of the local *pemuda* again.[72]

With the need for protection and defence against roving Dutch teams glaringly obvious, ad hoc groups of *pemuda* known collectively as Pemuda Republik Indonesia (PRI) started coordinating their activities.[73] Local standing or familial ties were used to form veritable resistance networks, often with Makassar as the central hub.[74] Insurgent groups consolidated themselves more robustly, and increased their striking power.[75] They armed themselves by hoarding and stealing weapons,[76] and they inserted themselves into black markets to barter rice that was often ill-gotten– destined for general distribution and in short supply – for guns.[77] A PNI-funded cooperative assumed the dual function of sailing to Kalimantan for weapons procurement and, in Sulawesi, building up rice supplies to feed the underground.[78]

Locally, these networks of resistance functioned as governments. Andi Pawilloi, the Pabicara (customary office-bearer) of Pinrang, joined Mapanjukki and his son Abdul Baoe Masepe to allocate resistance tasks across Pare-Pare, Suppa, Pinrang and Sidenreng. They called themselves the 'Three Stars'. Ngalle, his four brothers and their sons operated the Bajeng Centipede militia (Lipan Bajeng, LB) based in Polombangkeng.[79] In a notice issued to the people, LB declared its goal to be independence, defending the Indonesian unitary state – thereby opposing the Dutch federal plan – and 'showing the international world that we, the Indonesian people of Celebes [Sulawesi], do not recognize Dutch authority'.[80] In December 1946, three LB executives decided that the LB in Bajeng would operate as the 'Preparatory Committee for the Establishment of the Republican Government in Celebes [sic]'.[81]

Another struggle group, the Secret Islamic Youth Service (Kebaktian Rahasia Islam Muda, KRIS-M) from West Sulawesi, joined the fray in October 1945. It was based in Balanipa and was led by a female leader named Maradia Tobaine Depu. Emissaries of KRIS-M soon reached Makassar, Mandalle, Bonthain and Maros. Their aim was to raise 7,500 fighters.[82] From Suppa, fighters left for Balanipa to support the KRIS-M.[83] The Indonesian People's Service Sulawesi (Kebaktian Rakyat Indonesia Sulawesi, KRIS), an organization first set up in Jakarta by Ratulangi's daughter, began streamlining the resistance around Suppa in July 1945. At the same time, the KRIS maintained ties to its Yogyakarta headquarters through Manai Sophiaan. Mappanjuki's cousin, Tahir Daeng Tompo, led the KRIS-Suppa; its influence soon reached Majene and Soppeng. He furthermore brought another Sophiaan-inspired group, the

Indonesian National Youth Centre (Pusat Pemuda Nasional Indonesia, PPNI) into the Lipan Bajeng's fold. The KRIS, too, acted as a government: its Makassar 'resistance headquarters' operated as an information and intelligence service. Around the city, at least five kampongs (villages) aligned with the KRIS. Internal correspondence spoke of 12,000 members and a budget to match.[84]

The revolutionary leaders understood that despite their interconnectedness, groups operating horizontally needed vertical integration.[85] Convening in Polombangkeng in July 1946, the leaders of the LB, the KRIS-M, the PPNI and other groups therefore decided to unite some 14 South Sulawesi resistance organizations under the People's Rebel Army Sulawesi (Laskar Pemberontak Rakyat Indonesia Sulawesi, LAPRIS). With half the LAPRIS subsidiaries existing largely on paper alone, the conveners decided to quickly recruit some 1,000 fighters and train them in scorched-earth tactics, in unmasking enemy spies, and in sabotage.[86] The actions taken by LAPRIS to frustrate Dutch governance bore fruit almost immediately. A February 1946 attack on Pare-Pare City, for instance, had already cemented the revolutionary pedigree of the leader of the KRIS-Suppa, Tompo.[87] Andi Tjammi, under the influence of the 'Three Stars' and connected to LAPRIS by way of Andi Selle's Indonesian People's Rebel Front (Barisan Pemberontak Rakyat Indonesia, BPRI), directed his own group, the Ganggawa Rebel Front (Barisan Pemberontak Ganggawa). It attacked Rappang to the north of Pare-Pare on three consecutive nights in August. Crowds of between 800 and 3,000 people provided support during the raid.[88] Already on 22 January 1946, the city of Palopo had come under sustained attack when a core of 50 well-trained fighters from Kolaka held the 'entire city' together with at least 400 additional participants. Out 'hunting', the Dutch-appointed autonomous ruler of Palopo had fled the scene. Bonthain buzzed with rumours about looming attacks as well.[89] By October, roving LB groups, partially in uniform and brandishing automatic weapons, graduated to attacking Dutch military convoys. Around that time, fighters slowly encircled the centre of Dutch power, Makassar, while spies operated within governmental services.[90]

At this juncture, struggle organizations began violently separating those who supported the revolution from those who did not. The January attack on Palopo left 40 'pro-Ned. Indonesiers' dead. One of Palopo's autonomous rulers was killed for non-participation.[91] Villagers in Rappang, Pinrang and Sidenreng were targeted for not being PNI members. Survivors questioned by Dutch officials either refused to divulge information about their attackers or fled.[92] Those who had witnessed and lived through the attacks thought twice before cooperating with the Dutch. The Lipan killed village heads, police and government officials they believed were disloyal. The Laskar Pemberontak Turatea (LAPTUR), a combat group based in Turatea consisting of *pemuda* from around Bangkala, Binamu and Arungkeke, also set its sights on villagers. Well into 1947, Said Daeng Sila and other leaders directed mass killings of so-called NICA sympathisers or 'spies'. The reports drawn up by LAPTUR after such actions claimed that villagers had given its fighters consent to kill the traitors; elsewhere, fighters encouraged villagers to do so themselves.[93] While the Dutch considered these acts unjustified murder, LAPTUR viewed them as deeds that furthered the revolution by weeding out its enemies.

Meanwhile, increases in Dutch troop numbers exacerbated their own tendency to undertake violent zero-sum solutions. The Dutch continued to adamantly dismiss the 'latent longing for liberation from foreign rule [...] present among the masses'.[94] Consequently, the PNI chapters that the Dutch troops and administrators encountered did not in their view constitute a legitimate expression of nationalism. Dutch officials explained away the fact that PNI membership numbers had soared by claiming that people only signed on to safeguard themselves from robbery and murder.[95] In September 1946, Dutch officials banned the PNI and its subsidiaries, driving nationalists further underground.[96] By doing so, they drove moderates into the arms of the more militant-minded. Simultaneously talking to *and* organizing against the Dutch, as for example the ruler of Gowa had attempted in 1945, became increasingly difficult.[97] Well before the PNI's ban, however, the chief officers of the NICA had burned their bridges to all moderate voices, having already petitioned the Australians in November 1945 for Ratulangi's removal. They did so despite Ratulangi's willingness to assert his influence against 'lawlessness' in conjunction with the Dutch. Five months later, when they were in charge, the Dutch forcefully removed Ratulangi and exiled him to New Guinea. He had continued to rally rajas and armed *pemuda* while promoting a non-NICA government. It must be noted here that it was the Australians who had suggested that Ratulangi pursue the establishment of a non-NICA government.[98]

Dutch policies not only turned moderates away, their one-dimensional focus on obtaining a position of authority and power also transformed ordinary people into active participants in the revolution. When 250 locals stormed a Dutch post shouting 'merdeka', they deliberately targeted the large quantities of 'foodstuff [and] textile blankets' the Dutch had kept stored there. Facing only spears, lances and Buginese daggers, the Dutch nonetheless shot dead 15 protesters.[99] Mass arrests, often without actionable evidence, taught many Sulawesians to hate the Dutch. Once freed, they immediately 'joined the resistance fighters'.[100] Survivors of direct Dutch military action equally nursed feelings of revenge.[101] Undoubtedly, revolutionaries such as Andi Selle made use of such feelings of resentment to build up the BPRI after the PNI had been banned. Likewise, Wolter Mongisidi was able to establish the LAPRIS around the same time.[102]

Although Dutch reports dismissed the Republican killing of civilians as 'terrorist activity', they recognized its purpose all the same. Across Indonesia, fighters chose highly visual methods to instil fear and compliance.[103] In response, Dutch civil-military authorities unleashed 'counter-terror' measures of their own that were often directed at civilians.[104] Australian troops had done the same, and according to Indonesian sources, they detained, kidnapped and murdered 'in the dark'.[105] Brigadier Frederick Oliver Chilton forbade demonstrations and unofficial uniforms; suspected saboteurs or those carrying arms could be shot where they stood.[106] The Dutch adopted the same practices. The State of War and Siege declared for Bonthain, Makassar, Mandar and Pare-Pare on 11 December 1946 did not cover executions without due process, but semantic finessing soon ensured that any act of resistance was simply categorized as combat, whereby anyone could be shot 'unless they could be made prisoner of war without risk'.[107]

Under such lawless circumstances, life in Sulawesi became 'hell'. Writing to his son, Andi Jalanti blamed the violence on 'the Dutch [S]atans and [...] our own countrymen, who commit betrayal' by aiding the Dutch. Still, Jalanti went on, people would keep struggling until Sulawesi 'had become such a mess, that the Dutch with their henchmen finally can no longer keep order'.[108] He was right, and when this 'mess' had made South Sulawesi ungovernable in Dutch eyes, the latter sent for Captain R. Westerling and his Special Troops Corps (Korps Speciale Troepen, KST). They arrived in December 1946 supposedly to 'pacify the environs of Makassar and break the reign of terror' that the insurgent groups had unleashed. He and a limited number of KST officers – and later some KNIL and police troops – were given the right to dispense summary justice (*standrecht*), by which 'persons, guilty of grave terror crimes [sic] could be executed on the spot by way of [a] sped-up procedure'. Dutch high officials maintained that local intelligence, spies and the help of the public would ensure that the summary justice was precise and that only the guilty would be punished.[109] Officers brandishing lists of the supposedly guilty, play-acting orderliness and standardization, reinforced such fantasies and transformed ordinary people into killable enemies.[110]

As local struggle groups dispersed due to the KST's activities and governance was supposedly restored, the Dutch concocted a narrative about its success in subduing the terror with 'a minimum of casualties'.[111] Statements by eminent members of society were used to reinforce these narratives. After a round of executions in Maewa District, customary leader La Itjin was quoted as saying that 'the people at the moment feel [at ease]'. He recalled how in Kampong Maroangin, 31 people had been executed, some having been pointed out by an informer. La Itjin himself had been ordered by KNIL Captain Bertold Rijborz to address the surviving villagers, saying the spectacle 'should be a lesson to them, [and] that those who [are] in cahoots with [the executed robbers], will end like that', too. No more food, shelter or clothing was to be given to resistance fighters. New policemen were installed as well as a new village head, his predecessor having been executed.[112]

By KST's departure from Sulawesi in early March 1947, close to 3,500 adult and juvenile males lay dead. The majority of those had been killed *en masse* and publicly.[113] Many more had suffered from sexual abuse, theft or arson. Dutch newspapers quickly produced narratives about the KST's precision, and reports stressed how villagers around Makassar had lauded KST's 'bravery [...] and their humane and benevolent [treatment of] well-meaning' people.[114] Within a year, the Dutch bureaucracy had whitewashed what had transpired in Sulawesi. The Enthoven Commission, established in April 1947 by the Lieutenant Governor-General in Jakarta to investigate alleged Dutch 'excesses' in South Sulawesi between December 1946 and February 1947, wrote off the deaths of 'hangers-on' as the price to be paid for restoring Dutch power. Besides, the commission concluded, 'only men, so no women and children were shot by soldiers'. Again, local opinion was used, this time in the form of a 'peoples' judgement' that stipulated that not executing those whom informers had accused would only have allowed the guilty to remain alive and exact revenge on the informers. In all, the commission wrote, the results spoke for themselves. With the people 'liberated', they returned to their residences, free to farm and trade, the report stated.[115]

Survivors of the 'sea of blood' that had washed over South Sulawesi – as one Indonesian commentator phrased it – produced altogether different accounts.[116] On 14 December 1946, 40-year-old medical professional Bagala

Daeng Tuda was taken by Dutch forces to a far-away holding area, along with about 7,000 others from six kampongs. When they were unable to divulge the whereabouts of two fighters, the soldiers opened fire. They then forced a teenager to point out more people for execution. 'So it went on until about one hundred persons had been shot down before our eyes'.[117] In Maroangin, La Itjin had no idea whether the dead had been guilty or not. In Majene, the supposedly orderly and effective method of recognizing enemies from the assembled villagers – which was to separate the men from the women, and then select and kill the men – failed spectacularly. An attack on the KST in a nearby village triggered soldiers to open fire on the men and women from that same village that they had corralled before them, resulting in close to 400 deaths.[118] In another account, two locals testified that soldiers had forced duos to fight to the death and that non-combatant PNI members had been shot without trial. In December, women from various villages wrote to Makassar's civil-military authorities detailing how 'us women and small children, including babies [...] were exposed to the sun' while soldiers ransacked their houses.[119]

Do civilians melt? Shifting alliances in the face of shifting power

Even outside the clutches of the KST or LAPRIS, the situation for villagers remained dire.[120] Positive reporting in newspapers could not wish away the 1948 drought that endangered the traditional rice surplus in South Sulawesi; as a result, corn had to be imported from elsewhere. The Dutch made a bad situation worse. Their aggressive military occupation (in mid-1947 and late 1948) of more and more territory in Java and Sumatra that had been declared *de facto* Republican territory in the March 1947 Linggarjati Agreement put massive additional stress on already limited Dutch economic reserves and capabilities. In protest against Dutch expansionism, the United States froze the dollar reserves that the Dutch authorities had allocated for Indonesia. With access to food becoming precarious and food prices and political insecurities rising in tandem, people started hoarding.[121]

Economic improvement, furthermore, hinged on the systematic reduction of violence.[122] This proved difficult, as anti-Dutch forces naturally refused to stop defending Indonesia's independence. In South Sulawesi, they eventually had to do exactly that, however, when Dutch repression proved too much to bear. Before that critical moment was reached, people like Daeng Tompo and Andi Selle tried to persevere. One way of postponing the collapse of the resistance was to cultivate Sulawesi-Javanese connections. Despite their meagre beginnings, these connections acquired grand proportions, not in the least in post-revolutionary retellings of these connections.[123] After crossing Dutch-infested waters, Saleh Lahade, Andi Mattalatta and others in January 1946 met President Sukarno himself in Yogyakarta. He famously asked them 'What do you need?'[124] In March, Republican leaders in Yogyakarta officially declared their official support for Sulawesi's struggle. The high command of the Indonesian National Army (Tentara Nasional Indonesia, TNI) tasked Lieutenant Colonel Kahar Muzakkar from Palopo with building up the TNI in Sulawesi under his command.[125] By 19 March, a Regional Sulawesi Commissariat in Jakarta was supporting Sulawesi financially, along with about 10,000 people who had fled Sulawesi to Java. Lahade travelled to Makassar as Chief of Staff to Lieutenant Colonel Muzakkar and to vice-commander Andi Mattalatta.[126] Meanwhile, Daeng Tompo and Hassan bin Tahir had returned from Java to start recruiting for the KRIS.[127] Mattalatta, with 100 TNI members, landed on Barru's coast in December; Lahade and others sailed on to Suppa. Lieutenant Latif landed there, too, where he met Andi Selle and Sjamsul Bachri, ready to commence organizing the Sulawesi TNI, which for the moment was called the Preparatory Army of the Republic of Indonesia, Sulawesi (Tentara Republik Indonesia Persiapan Sulawesi, TRIPS).[128]

To actually build up TRIPS as an operating force, envoys from the KRIS-M, the BPRI, the Ganggawa, the KRIS and other organizations met from 20 to 25 January 1947 around Paccekke. Mattalatta and Lahade explained to 41 delegates that a division, to be named 'Hasanuddin' and commanded by Massepe, would be formed. Makassar, Pare-Pare, Palopo and Kolaka would function as regimental headquarters.[129] In tandem with the emerging TRIPS army, Lahade ordered 7,500 pamphlets for Sulawesi to be printed in Cirebon in Java with slogans such as 'No More Legal Power for the Netherlands in Indonesia'.[130] The Hasanuddin Division immediately claimed responsibility for several attacks. North of Paccekke, near Malino and elsewhere, troops chalked up several enemies killed and wounded.[131] With new elan, the LAPTUR around Jeneponto targeted army patrols and ten kampong heads still in function.[132] Fresh KRIS arrivals from Java boasted having killed 30 enemies, including one 'full-blood "Hollander"'.[133] LB and fighters of the Tiger Army commanded by Mongisidi near Makassar attacked the Dutch relentlessly, refusing to fall back, wanting 'to kill as many Dutch as possible'.[134] Dutch army reports soon recognized the influence of the TRIP/TNI, noting that better-led guerrilla activity had substituted 'large-scale actions'.[135]

The rejuvenation inspired by the TNI landings between late 1946 and early 1947 proved short-lived.[136] Commander Latif was captured by the Dutch; others were killed or captured upon landing. Despite successfully landing with his men, Captain Andi Sarifin died later on his way to Paccekke, heroically attacking a KNIL patrol with a knife. Chasing infiltrators, the KNIL burned down 60 homes in kampong Salossu.[137] On 13 March, Captain Andi Bakar Lambogo's party was ambushed in Salo Wajo while bathing. '[C]ontrary to the Geneva Conventions', KNIL troops decapitated the wounded captain and paraded his head around a market in nearby Enrekang the next day. After forcing Lambogo's troops to kiss the head, the KNIL soldiers placed it on a pole to scare the townspeople.[138] Lahade and Mattalatta themselves had hefty prices placed on their heads.[139]

Local anti-Dutch organizations collapsed around the same time, even if others fought on.[140] What undoubtedly played a part in this collapse was the failure of efforts to centralize the revolutionary leadership. Some local leaders felt that Republican power emanating from Java was overbearing.[141] By 1948, infighting had weakened the Divisi Hasanuddin, with Muzakkar defending himself against the jealousy of what he called opportunists, whereby he possibly meant Andi Selle.[142] In addition to combating the Dutch, Depu used her brother's KRIS-M *pemuda* to fight her ex-husband Andi Baso for control over Mandar.[143] Polombangkeng's Karaeng fled into the mountains with his fighters, but in February he disavowed the KRIS-M before Dutch interrogators. If he had not supported the struggle organizations, he stated, *pemuda* would have murdered him 'as a traitor'.[144] The Tiger Army around Pangkajene collapsed soon after KNIL soldiers 'put down' one of its influential leaders, Andi Mappe. His sons capitulated.[145] LAPTUR suffered from a lack of food as the organization haemorrhaged members until its demise 'as an organized resistance organization'. Furthermore, Dutch killing zones – small military posts in areas forcibly emptied of people and food – proved fatal to local groups. The morale in struggle groups plummeted further as women and children decamped.[146] In Luwu, troops became inactive and desertion ensued.[147] In Kolaka, the dispersed resisters held out until the fall of 1948, despite local leaders having been imprisoned or exiled by the courts, as was the case with Kasim.[148] The Datu of Luwu and the Arumpone of Bone, Mappanjuki, languished in exile as well.[149]

Others disappeared permanently. A court-mandated firing squad executed the elusive Mongisidi on 5 September 1949.[150] KST soldiers 'cravenly' liquidated Arumpone's son Massepe, the Datu of Suppa.[151] Dutch authorities were pleased: his demise, they reasoned, loosened people from his grip.[152] Before Massepe's killing, his father Mappanjuki had already been sidelined when the Dutch installed rival Andi Pabenteng as police commissioner in Watampone. This move undercut Bone's resistance movement because Pabenteng, native to Bone, had more influence in Bone than Mappanjuki ever could, having come from Gowa.[153]

Mappanjuki's removal was no exception. To a large extent, the Republican-Dutch conflict in South Sulawesi involved the systematic remodelling of systems of governance and power. First and foremost, this affected the position of the various royal houses. The traditional position of the rajas as leaders of the local Autonomous Councils was threatened from multiple sides. On one level, the Dutch authorities did not hesitate to remove local kings and religious leaders (violently or otherwise) who supported resistance movements. It was in this way that royalty such as the Kings of Bone, Luwu and Suppa and the Karaengs of Pangkajene, Polombangkeng, Binamu and Gantarang lost power. Their places were taken by royals 'more amenable to cooperation [with the Dutch]'.[154] On another level, the Indonesian war for independence in Sulawesi, as elsewhere, ran parallel to a social revolution. This social revolution entailed the forceful removal by *pemuda* of those royals who declined to use their influence to support the independence movement. That *pemuda* dared make – and execute – such threats against royals and the Autonomous Councils was a striking reversal of traditional hierarchies that was made possible by the revolutionary worlds of Sulawesi.[155]

The position of local rulers – both individually and within the Autonomous Councils – was no longer secure.[156] A third threat came from the federalists attempting to establish the State of East Indonesia (Negara Indonesia Timur, NIT) as part of the federal United States of Indonesia. In Sulawesi, the federal programme meant that the Autonomous Rulers and Councils had to be fitted into the structure of the NIT. The NIT's foundations, resting on political parties functioning within a representative parliament, were not in line with the traditional hierarchical structures from which the rulers derived their power. During the revolution, power stemmed from keeping the Dutch at arm's length and working towards self-rule. As a consequence, progressive elements in the NIT determined that the rajas' roles needed to be diminished: the rulers had been linked too closely with the Dutch.[157] The rulers, in turn, took issue with the notion that the NIT offered opportunities to those operating outside of traditional networks of influence. Rulers looked down upon those seizing such opportunities. Dismissing one such nationa-

The President of the Negara Indonesia Timur (NIT), His Excellency Sukawati, welcomes the aristocratic traditional rulers of the Autonomous Council of South Sulawesi to the Government House in the NIT's capital Makassar in April 1947. Relationships between the traditional rulers and the functionaries of the NIT were often strained due to the precarious balance of power between the council and the NIT. Source: Collection Fotoafdrukken Koninklijke Landmacht, NIMH.

list political climber, Najamuddin, one ruler concluded that Najamuddin 'could not even be considered for election as village head'. According to the rulers themselves, they were '[t]he sole representatives of South, yes of [Sulawesi's] entirety'.[158]

The rulers were not the only ones who needed to negotiate and re-negotiate their positions. The revolution forced all layers of society to make similar choices. Local communities did so in relation to the shifts in power relations that took place where they lived. Whoever dominated the area could count on a modicum of support. This praxis remained in place throughout the entire revolutionary period. Even if large-scale resistance ceased to exist in a given area (in the course of 1948, for example), the revolutionary spirit survived. Struggle organizations did not disappear completely but reconstituted themselves. Makassar, in that respect, remained a centre for systematic underground organizing. Fighters could always count on support in various places, the more so as high-standing members of society still proved willing to support them.[159] Although the Dutch had banned the PNI and hunted down its members, the organization resurfaced in the course of 1948 as the Partai Kebangsaan (The National Party) in various places. Fighters who had temporarily decamped found each other again in different constellations, as part of local women's labour unions or youth organizations, for example.[160]

Unsurprisingly, such organizing continued to elicit violent Dutch counterreactions. Equally unsurprising was the fact that the people again found themselves caught between opposing forces. Individuals, communities or entire villages reorientated their direction of support. In kampongs where anti-Dutch cells killed suspect or non-revolutionary teachers or local leaders, village heads fled and police detachments were intimidated into acquiescence. Having waited for the opportunity to distance themselves from Dutch authority, entire villages rallied to the revolutionary flag, choosing to openly support and participate in the continued struggle against the Dutch.[161] Conversely, Dutch dominance of a given area dampened nationalist fervour, with the Dutch often making use of the fact that the heavy-handed revolutionary practices of Republican and nationalist soldiers had caused enmity 'between public and soldiers'.[162] The Gelarang of Borongloe and his auxiliaries, for example, aided Dutch troops. His example drew the support of 'sometimes thousands', and this impetus soon carried over into neighbouring areas.[163] As resistance fighters surrendered, kampong heads returned, followed by the villagers themselves.[164] The threat of Dutch violence trumped revolutionary fervour, forcing people into supporting the Dutch. Earlier oaths by locals that 'I would melt away should the Dutch capture me' became too dangerous to sustain.[165] People had little choice: signalling support for the strongest party of the moment proved a life-saving strategy.

Endgame in South Sulawesi

Unlike labourers and farmers, revolutionary leaders had the luxury of not being tied to a certain locale. While villagers faced the dangerous choice of supporting the incoming Dutch or Republican troops, Andi Selle, Mattalatte, Lahade and others had already departed for Java, bereft of the 'ammunition, medicine and reinforcements' promised by Muzakkar. In Java, Sulawesi's troops continued the fight for the Republic. To its members, this was no defeat – in stark contrast with Dutch commentators who saw cowardice in such relocations.[166]

The Republic, however, saw the revolution as an Indonesia-wide struggle. From this viewpoint, a setback on South Sulawesi was not detrimental to developments in the overall war against the Dutch. By the time men like Lahada relocated to Java from Sulawesi, the Republican victory had become tantalizingly close. Indeed, by early 1949 the Dutch had squandered all international support by having undertaken a second large-scale military attack in December 1948. One of the key goals of the attack entailed the occupation of Yogyakarta. The Republican government, refusing to abandon the Republican capital, allowed themselves to be arrested. The international community, with the United States and Australia in the lead, strongly condemned this Dutch act of aggression and demanded the release of the Republican officials. With international support thus dwindling, the Netherlands realized that the formal recognition of Indonesia's independence had become inevitable. The Round Table Conference (RTC) of December 1949 in The Hague finally transferred sovereignty over Indonesia to the United States of Indonesia.[167]

In Sulawesi circles, the inexorable end to Dutch rule caused consternation. Another round of reorientations commenced. As Indonesia was to become independent as the United States of Indonesia, Sulawesi would be governed as part of the Negara Indonesia Timur, together with the islands of Bali, Nusa Tenggara and the Moluccan Islands. Makassar would function as the NIT's capital. For the various Autonomous Councils, this meant that they had to re-negotiate their relations with the NIT government. They did not even know whether the Autonomous Regions would be included in the delegation the NIT would send to the Round Table Conference.[168] More troubling, however, was that the NIT's political cohesion – and, indeed, the federated United States of Indonesia itself – was threatened by unitarist Republican policies. As both Dutch and NIT officials admitted, throughout the NIT, Republican influence was on the rise, an influence that few dared to counter. The Autonomous Councils feared a Javanese administrative takeover of key posts.[169] Locally, communities living in Dutch-controlled areas were mortally afraid of being 'marked as "traitor"'.[170] Such fears were not wholly unfounded, as pro-Republicans forces could build upon the revolutionary networks that they had organized quite effectively. Through these networks, Republicans became increasingly vocal.[171]

They had every opportunity to do so, as the Dutch could not touch them anymore. The Royal Netherlands Army (Koninklijke Landmacht, KL) was preparing itself for its return to the Netherlands. The Dutch colonial army, the KNIL, was to be disbanded. This left local police forces without protection, a problem compounded by the fact that many policemen had nationalist leanings themselves. Many KNIL troops refused to be transferred to a federated Indonesian army that was so heavily dominated by their former enemy, the TNI.[172] Instead, some 30,000 wanted to return to the Moluccan islands or elsewhere; half that number opted to travel to the Netherlands. Until then, many were to be housed in 'Transit Camps'.[173]

Throughout 1949, well before the disbandment of the KNIL, South Sulawesi's stability hung in the balance. As we have seen, Republican forces scrambled to return to Sulawesi to finish what local struggle organizations had started: to 'conquer Celebes [Sulawesi] for the Unitary Republic of Indonesia' at the expense of the NIT.[174] In October, while NIT functionaries deliberated whether pardoning political prisoners would induce local score-settling or not, youth organizations including boy scout chapters began militarizing once more.[175] Together with incoming TNI soldiers, they planned to claim territory for the Republic, as Dutch troops were frozen in place due to another cease-fire. A vital stratagem in this process was boosting the number of TNI soldiers that were to form the backbone of the Federal Army of the United States of Indonesia. The NIT was further destabilized when it was revealed that the NIT's Minister of Justice had worked together closely with TNI Captain Sutikno, who had recently entered Sulawesi.[176] Nationalists such as Sophiaan ensured that pro-Republican propaganda continued to circulate among the people to have them understand that the Republic and not the NIT was taking charge.[177]

In the months after the transfer of sovereignty to Indonesia, the powerlessness of the NIT became clear for all to see. New rounds of fighting broke out as Republican troops, aided by local organizations, attacked the remaining Dutch-controlled enclaves in Makassar. Dutch officials appealed to both United Nations observers and Republican army liaisons for cease-fires.[178] When Ambonese KNIL Captain Aziz and his men in April 1950 struck back at Republican troops, neither the government of the NIT nor the Federal Army intervened. Between 15 and 18 May 1950, 12 KNIL soldiers and 11 Republican soldiers were killed. In a bid to show that it wanted to find a solution to the continued fighting, the Republic offered Aziz clemency and invited him to the Republican seat of government in Yogyakarta. Aziz accepted, but upon arrival, he was arrested; in Makassar, his men faced the same fate.[179] Earlier, several members of the NIT parliament who were sceptical of the Indonesian federation had wondered 'whether [they] should come to a unitary state through merging with the [United States of Indonesia] or by joining the [Republic]'. Within months, the Republic had decided for them: only the Republic of Indonesia would remain, as President Sukarno and Vice President Mohammad Hatta had intended all along.[180]

Conclusion

This chapter has attempted to address the gap that exists between Dutch and Indonesian retellings of the Indonesian revolutionary war between 1945 and 1950. In an attempt to bring both into the same analytical framework, this chapter has looked at the violent episodes in South Sulawesi and why they were perpetrated.

The analysis has done so with 'permanent security' in mind which, in the context of Indonesia's revolutionary war, was the idea that the mutually exclusive strategic end-goals held by the two sides (the Dutch restoration of power versus a unitary, independent Indonesia under the Republic) required Republican and Dutch policymakers and troops alike to forcefully remove any and all possible threats to those end-goals sooner rather than later. In terms of the violent turn and its focus on the heavy-handed repression and mass violence perpetrated by European troops, the chapter has de-emphasized the dominant role of Dutch violence and brought into the analytical fold the Republican/nationalist rationales for meting out violence. The resultant approach is more comprehensive and inclusive. This was important not to put Dutch and Indonesian violence on the same level but because this more comprehensive approach reconstitutes the TNI, the local struggle organizations and their leaders from merely fixed variables in retellings of Dutch violence into autonomous actors with their own rationales and objectives that, unsurprisingly, often existed separate from the Dutch activities. In that sense, the war in South Sulawesi revolved around Indonesian postwar considerations as much as it revolved around removing the Dutch from the island.

By looking at Dutch and Republican activities from this security-centred perspective wherein Republican nationalists, Dutch enforcers and, it must be noted, ordinary Indonesians operated, several key elements of the war in Sulawesi can be laid bare. Crucially, violence in the context of permanent security fantasies did not constitute random mass destruction. Violence, often highly visible, had very specific functions. As Dutch and Republican civil administrators and their soldiers – together with local fighters – tried to claim ownership over local communities, they often encountered people who were afraid to declare their support or simply did not want to give it. In the face of such reluctance, the soldiers and freedom fighters used violence as a tool to coerce people to accept their authority.

Given that these authority-seeking powerbrokers approached local communities with such hostility and suspicion, it became increasingly difficult for the Dutch or nationalists on the one hand and the people of South Sulawesi on the other to cooperate. At the level of governance, this meant that the Dutch eliminated those rulers who refused to declare and act out their support for colonial rule unequivocally. Similarly, nationalist groups intimidated or removed traditional rulers who were not on their side. At the more local level, ordinary people and their communities suffered as room for working together with either Dutch or Republican representatives, depending on who happened to pass by, diminished sharply. For local communities, the need to choose sides became enormously perilous. As we have seen, Dutch and nationalist forces killed locals in large numbers. The slightest suspicion of double-crossing or non-cooperation often had fatal consequences.

This violent dynamic between powerbrokers and ordinary communities remained in place throughout the entire revolutionary period in South Sulawesi, even if the number of confrontations between the Dutch and the nationalists dwindled in the course of 1948. Anti-Dutch resistance cells continued to strike, and they made sure that the communities they could still reach fell in line with them. What this chapter has also shown, then, is that while violence was able to enforce compliance, it did not trump actual political or ideological preferences. Indonesians who did not want to be governed by the Republic from far-away Yogyakarta, for example, such as Aziz, were forced to eventually accept a Republican takeover. The Dutch, in turn, had to concede that, despite their attempts at coercion, they could not stem the revolutionary tide in South Sulawesi or elsewhere. Whether in support of the Republic or the federation, anti-Dutch sentiments were far more deeply ingrained than was portrayed in the belief held by many Dutch that although 'the blood of the youth was still boiling' (*Darah pemuda masih mendidih*), under Dutch tutelage it would soon cool.[181]

11.

Polombangkeng, South Sulawesi

The contest for authority, 1945-1949

Taufik Ahmad

Introduction

> It is correct that the police and soldiers now carry out their duty and arrest people who have committed crimes. However, robberies continue. This situation has taken us back to the old era where a chief bandit once said: 'As long as the King is not from Polombangkeng, to rule this land, I will continue to enjoy myself and slaughter stolen buffalos before the eye of that King.'[1]

The above quote is excerpted from a letter written in March 1948 by Mangulung, a community leader in the South Sulawesi district of Polombangkeng, south of Makassar. It was addressed to the prime minister of the State of East

Image 1. Mourners carrying floral arrangements while attending the funeral ceremony of Wolter Mongisidi who was shot dead in Makassar on 5 September 1949. Source: ANRI/IPPHOS – 1367.

Indonesia (Negara Indonesia Timur, NIT). In it, he links the prevalence of robbery and theft to the decision to replace the king (*karaeng*) of Polombangkeng. A man named Lemo Daeng Lira had just been appointed *karaeng* of Polombangkeng to replace Pajonga Daeng Ngalle. As a direct descendant of the original Bajeng nobility, Pajong Daeng Ngalle had had a strong influence in the area. Lemo Daeng Lira, by contrast, was the *gallarang* of Lassang, an area recently added to Polombangkeng. Geographically and genealogically, Lassang was closer to the nearby kingdom of Gowa. A *gallarang* was a traditional functionary inferior to the *pajonga,* administering a territory also known as *gallarang*. The letter suggested that this replacement of the *pajonga* had been ill-advised and was one of the triggers for the rise of violence in the area.

The issue of violence in Polombangkeng during the revolution is an interesting one. Was the issue perhaps related to political choices for or against the Republic of Indonesia? Or was this a wider question of identity playing itself out on the revolutionary stage of power? Was the revolution perhaps a new arena for a contest over authority with a much longer history?

Polombangkeng lies in the Regency of Takalar, towards the southern tip of South Sulawesi. It was initially known as Bajeng, which was a sovereign kingdom in the sixteenth century.[2] However, Bajeng only enjoyed a short period of independence before it was conquered by the Gowa Kingdom lying to its northeast. Gowa's ruler changed the name of the region, but people continued to narrate their past identity as Bajeng people. The Dutch East India Company (Vereenigde Oostindische Compagnie, VOC) and the Dutch East Indies government took over the Gowa name of Polombangkeng. In the colonial period, the area became known for its organized robbers.[3] During the revolution, it was the headquarters of Lipan Bajeng, a leading organization within the Indonesian People's Rebel Army in Sulawesi (Laskar Pemberontak Rakyat Indonesia Sulawesi, LAPRIS). For an extended period of time, the fight against the Dutch was fierce here.

For the people of Polombangkeng, the revolution created a dichotomy between Indonesia as a newly independent state on the one hand and the Dutch government attempting to re-install its power on the other. It led to a complex scramble for authority as various social groups attempted to define new roles. The present study focuses on one of these groups in Polombangkeng known as the *toloq*. In the Bugis-Makassar language, *toloq* connotes bravery that wins respect even if it means breaking the law to achieve its goals. It also refers to the figure of the most astute and devoted leader of thieves. *Toloq* is thus like the *jago* in Java and Bali, often revered as the intelligent leader of thieves.[4] Like the term *jago*, *toloq* has both negative connotations (as the criminal) and positive ones (as the strong, violent protector of the weak). In the Dutch colonial period, such champions were used by the upper colonial and/or indigenous elites as personal and plantation guards.[5] During the revolution, the *toloq* faced a choice: either join a pro-Republican alliance or become an elite supporter of the Netherlands Indies Civil Administration (NICA). They could also remain unattached and still commit robberies. The different choices mirrored the heterogeneity of the *toloq* identity itself. How could the *toloq* build new alliances, or perhaps strengthen old alliances with the aristocrats *(karaeng)*, when all these local officials were themselves constantly in opposition to each other? This is the question that underlies this study.

Polombangkeng in the revolutionary period became a new arena for competition between aristocrats. This led to the emergence of violence in society. Various actors often quickly changed their political attitudes, oscillating between a pro-revolution stance and a counter-revolutionary one. This reflected the struggle for authority among the elites. The revolutionary era opened up space for new alliances and shifting alliances as well as opportunities to strengthen old alliances. The political geography of these alliances often reflected a history of aristocratic struggle going back to the Dutch colonial period.

Banditry and its relation to revolution and rebellion has received much attention from historians and other social scientists. Eric J. Hobsbawm introduced the concept of the social bandit. Social banditry had something to do with revolution because it was a social phenomenon of protest, if not a pioneer or incubator of rebellion.[6] Anton Blok rejected the concept of the social bandit. In a sharp critique, he argued that social bandits were merely figures of the imagination created in the farmer's world and did not reflect objective reality.[7] In line with Blok, the historian Richard W. Slatta showed in his pioneering study on Latin America that banditry was not part of some social protest arising from solidarity between farmers. Instead, it more nearly reflected the personal interests of the bandits themselves, who indeed often acted as accomplices of the elite or the ruling class.[8] Rosalie Schwartz's study of the Cuban independence revolution revealed that bandits used revolutionary organizations to legitimize their criminal actions.[9]

Historians of Indonesia have also paid attention to the complex relation between banditry and rebellion. Sartono Kartodirdjo, the pioneer of Indonesian social history, has described the social unrest in the mid-nineteenth century that prompted the emergence of robbers and bandits (*rampokkers*). Many were landowners or members of the old aristocracy who took an illegal route after losing their possessions. Bandits were often forced to cooperate with rebels against the authorities. The rebels then tended quickly to become members of the band of robbers. This led Banten to experience both open rebellion and highly developed rural crime.[10] Political changes in Banten from 1808 to 1890 increased the number of bandits.[11] Similarly, Suhartono W. Pranoto has traced the emergence of social movements to unrest in rural Surakarta.[12] He saw the phenomenon of the petty criminal known as *kecu* as a form of social banditry that emerged from protests against the penetration of plantations, which undermined the autonomous order of rural life. Farmers became dependent on the plantations backed by the colonial government. Social banditry marked the transition from an agrarian to a capitalist society, as the owners of capital established plantations and sugar factories and changed the rules of land tenure.[13]

The revolutionary period was also a stage for bandits. Anton Lucas showed that the bloody case of the 'Three Regions Affair' (Peristiwa Tiga Daerah) in Central Java cannot be simply explained as a social protest by bandits against Dutch exploitation. The social revolution of the Three Regions must be viewed in terms of leadership, ideology and the cultural context – and we must ask ourselves what revolution meant for the perpetrators themselves. Bandits, or in local terms *lenggoang,* interpreted revolution as an opportunity for revenge. They then emerged as leaders attacking former colonial officials, killing and looting their property.[14] Bandits were prominent in the formation of revolutionary militias (*laskar*) in Jakarta. Robert Cribb's study shows that one of the people's militias there consisted of gangsters from marginal groups in the suburbs of Jakarta. It eventually suffered destruction at the hands of the Indonesian army in the late 1940s.[15]

The study of banditry in Makassar by Edward Poelinggomang links the emergence of robbery and theft to political changes under the Dutch East Indies government. He describes robbery as part of a social movement protesting against the colonial government. Using Dutch archives, the study brings to light many acts of robbery in the Makassar area, including several in Polombangkeng.[16] However, the study does not use many local sources such as oral traditions, collective memory, myths or historical ethnography.

These could help us understand the subjective views of bandits as they interpret themselves. Napsar Palallo's study specifically considers I Toloq Daeng Magassing, a well-known bandit leader in Makassar during the Dutch East Indies period and explicitly categorizes the I Toloq movement as a case of social banditry.[17] Yet in the historical reality, I Toloq cooperated with local elites to seize power. Rather than social banditry, this looks more like the transformation of banditry into a political movement against the rulers. Both studies provide essential information about banditry practices in Polombangkeng before the revolutionary period.

During the war of independence, Polombangkeng became the centre of attention in South Sulawesi. The study by Mustari Bosra takes the case of Laskar Lipan Bajeng as demonstrating a connection between religion and nationalism in Polombangkeng.[18] Wilhelmus Theodorus IJzereef analyzes the hierarchy and autonomy of Polombangkeng from the colonial period to the national revolution. The aristocratic hierarchy was strong, determining the nature of the resistance by Polombangkeng fighters during the revolution.[19] However, neither of these two studies seem to see the position of bandits in a context of a local contest over authority with a history long predating the revolution.

The present chapter therefore traces the narrative of the 'black world' in Polombangkeng to a reality rooted in South Sulawesi's past. After the introduction sets the scene, the first section traces the emergence of banditry in largely agrarian Polombangkeng to the imposition in the nineteenth century of Dutch colonial government. The next takes the story up to the years leading up to the Second World War. This is followed by a political account of the revolution in Polombangkeng. The next three sections focus specifically on the strategies pursued by the *toloq*, examining their rise, suppression and aftermath into early independence. The chapter closes with conclusions.

Entering Polombangkeng and the formation of the bandit world

A first-time visitor to Polombangkeng will see agricultural activity going on as usual. To the left and right of the road are vast rice fields with people working in them. This has been going on for centuries. When the area was occupied by Gowa in the sixteenth century, it was a food estate with abundant natural resources. Polombangkeng became the main supplier of rice for the Kingdom of Gowa-Tallo before 1669.[20] In the east, there was and still is a dense forest surrounded by hills running to the foot of Mount Lompobattang. The western part is a vast expanse of gardens and rice fields, the primary source of livelihood for the community. Before the Gowa annexation, Bajeng was a small kingdom consisting of three *gallarang*, namely Bajeng (Moncongkomba), Malewang and Bontokadatto. After its conquest by Gowa, Bajeng turned into Polombangkeng with the addition of Lassang and Lantang.[21] During the Dutch administration, Polombangkeng was designated a district, with its area extended to include Patalassang.

Territorial mergers over time frequently led to competition between aristocrats. Three social groups emerged, each of which tried to maintain its identity. First were the aristocrats from the former Kingdom of Bajeng (Moncongkomba, Bontokadatto and Malewang). They called themselves sons of Bajeng (*ana' Bajeng*). They had the most powerful political position and were most entitled to become kings in Polombangkeng.[22] Second, aristocrats from the added areas Lassang and Lattang were genealogically closer to Gowa and did not have the right to become king of Polombangkeng. The third social group included the aristocrats from autonomous regions, such as Pappa, Manuju and Ballo. Even though they belonged to the administrative area of Polombangkeng, they did not recognize the power of the Polombangkeng king.[23]

Most of the population lived in the fertile lowlands in the west, while most *kampongs* were built along the main road running south from Makassar. The east was hilly and the southwest sparsely populated. In the eastern part of the hinterland, there were less dense settlements, with people's houses following the highway. In the first decade of the twentieth century, the population of Polombangkeng was about 25,000 people.[24] The 1930 census revealed it had grown to 31,494 indigenous people and 61 ethnic Chinese.[25] This number grew further to a total of around 40,000 people by 1940.[26] After the formation of the Takalar Regency in 1960, Polombangkeng was divided into two sub-districts, North Polombangkeng and South Polombangkeng, while Pattallassang was separated into a separate sub-district (see map below, and Map 7).

Robbery and theft with violence already began to occur during the Dutch colonial period and was linked to the colonial government reforms. On 17 July 1824, the governor-general issued a regulation reordering the administration of government and justice.[27] The traditional government hierarchy was placed under the colonial government hierarchy. The king (or *karaeng*),

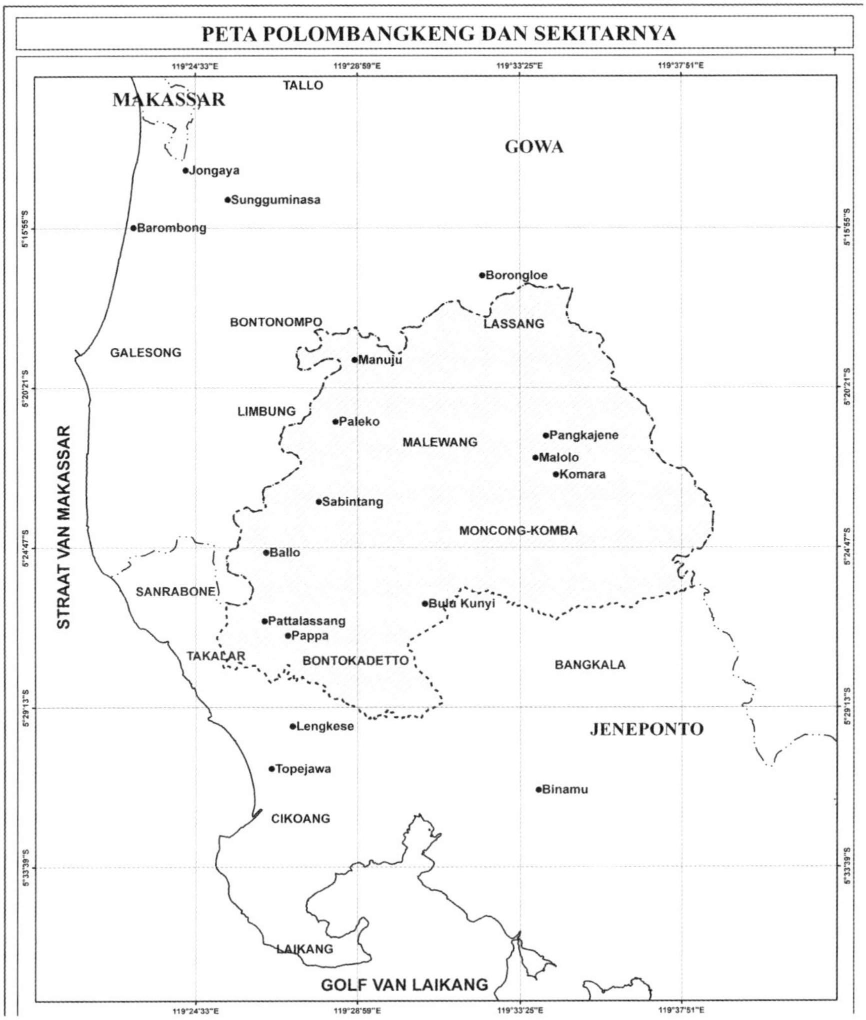

Polombangkeng and environs, around 1850 (IJzereef, De wind en de bladeren, 75).

appointed as regent, no longer acted as the ruler of his territory but only as the colonial government's executor. He functioned as a liaison officer between the colonial government and the people.[28] Above the regent was the *controleur*, the colonial official authorized to supervise, regulate and assign the regent.[29]

The colonial system weakened the authority of the *gallarang*, which caused the loss of their privileges and most of their income.[30] The *gallarang* of Moncongkomba and Bontokadatto had once had significant influence, but neither was included in the colonial government hierarchy. Disputes between the *gallarang* and the regent became common, even though they were related. A case in point was the rebellion of the *gallarang* of Moncongkomba against the regent of Polombangkeng in 1851.[31] The two *gallarangs* also did not like to be placed on the same level as other indigenous officials. If there were not enough seats in a meeting, they chose to stand until the meeting was over rather than sit on the floor next to other indigenous officials.[32] This was a subtle protest against the colonial government and, at the same time, an attempt to demonstrate their self-respect. These two *gallarangs* encouraged attitudes of defiance to show their power, leading to a refusal to pay taxes. They protected and were even behind cases of theft and robbery.

The situation was triggered by a colonial government structure that only accommodated a small subset of the existing nobility. Those who did not hold positions ended up organizing robberies and thefts. They had a large number of followers who were either paid or who shared in the profits.[33] Sometimes the poor, beyond the robbers themselves, also got a share. Regents chose to work with the robbers instead of fighting them, and some of them were close relatives.

Meanwhile, every indigenous official needed the support of the leader of the robbers. Thus, he had to both protect the robbers from the strictures of the law and welcome them when they entered his territory. The robbers in return ensured the safety and honour of the families of indigenous officials. The cycle of crime and the transfer of ownership of goods was thus based on loyalty and the distribution of power. As a result, theft and robbery became part of the economic activity of the Polombangkeng community. They were destructive products of the Dutch colonial imposition of new political relations at the local level. Similar to these robbers, the *jago* were correctly understood by Henk Schulte Nordholt to be not remnants of an old tradition but the product of new colonial relations.[34]

While the government had been lax in law enforcement before, in the twentieth century the determination to run a modern government led to changes throughout the Dutch East Indies.[35] This manifested itself in the so-called *pacificatiepolitiek* involving extensive military operations. In South Sulawesi, the government focused more on defence and control than on improving administration.[36] The Dutch East Indies government eroded the socio-political role of the high aristocrats and encouraged the emergence of a new, more educated aristocratic class. In Polombangkeng, this was initiated by the arrest in 1905 of the regent Hajina Daeng Masaung for his support of rebellion, robbery, theft and tax evasion. The government then allowed a new aristocratic class to emerge by forming sixteen new sub-districts in Polombangkeng. Each had a new leader whose position aligned with the *gallarang*. All these changes intensified social and political competition.

Governor H.N.A. Swart (1906-1908) viewed the increased robberies that resulted from these changes as merely an attempt to make ends meet.[37] This view was based on the decline in the community's economy due to the pacification war. Swart failed to see them as a complex response to dissatisfaction with the Dutch East Indies government, with the potential to develop into a rebellious movement.

In 1908, Tikolla Daeng Maleo was appointed the new regent of Polombangkeng. He was the eldest son of Hajina Daeng Masaung.[38] In the same year, a group of 40 robbers (*paggora patampuloa*) appeared, led by I Toloq Daeng Magassing. This group became legendary in Makassar society and was still being connected to robberies committed in the 1980s and 1990s. Its story is narrated in oral tradition, often accompanied by traditional music called *sinrilik*.[39] The I Toloq robbery movement succeeded in attracting the support of high-ranking aristocrats from Polombangkeng, Gowa and Maros. The number of robbery cases increased drastically.[40] Dutch officials concluded that robbery had become part of a political movement and that a military approach was necessary to quell it.[41] Among the aristocrats involved in the movement were Karaeng Batupute and Karaeng Barombong. They were detained on 3 May 1915 and exiled to Magelang in Java. The regent of Binamu, Lompo Daeng Raja, was removed from office in July 1915 and also exiled,[42] and the regents of Tanralili and Camba were likewise arrested on 25 September 1915.[43]

W.J. Coenen, the former governor of Celebes (Sulawesi) tasked with solving the I Toloq problem, encouraged the formation of civil groups to hunt him down, taking advantage of the tradition of conflict among aristocrats. He offered promotions to figures formerly considered troublemakers and promised a reward of 500 guilders for information leading to I Toloq's arrest.[44] Regent Tetebau and the head of the village of Pallangga openly formed a Residence patrol to track down I Toloq, which managed to kill Abasa Daeng Romo, one of I Toloq's followers, and to arrest 39 of his members. Police patrols together with hundreds of locals went into the forest searching for their bivouacs.[45] Police and civilian militias succeeded in immobilizing I Toloq's main followers, such as the karaeng Matika, Basareng, Paciro Daeng Matappa and Japa.[46] On 17 November 1915, I Toloq found himself in the village of Kalanipa, surrounded by police and civilian militia formed by the Kalukuang karaeng. I Toloq and several of his followers died in the attack.[47] His body was paraded around the village and then displayed in the market for a time.[48] This was done to prevent the reappearance of magical I Toloq stories, which could encourage the emergence of new gangs.[49]

After the crackdown on I Toloq's gang, the Dutch government carried out large-scale arrests of indigenous officials who had supported him. Tikolla daeng Maleo, the regent of Polombangkeng, and his nephew, Daeng Manajengka, were exiled to Aceh. Cincin Daeng Tompo, the brother of the regent, was exiled to Bondowoso in Java.[50] Those officials who had supported the government in crushing I Toloq received important government positions. One of them was I Makkarawa Daeng Ngalle, the former head of the village of Sastar, who was appointed Gallarang Moncongkomba. In contrast, the position of regent of Polombangkeng was left vacant for eight years. It was not until 1924 that Majadi Daeng Sisila, the younger brother of Tikollah Daen Maleo, was appointed as regent. However, he was arrested again in 1928 on charges of embezzlement and refusal to pay taxes.[51] He was later replaced by Pajonga Daeng Ngalle, who became the leader of the revolution in Polombangkeng. By the time Japan ended Dutch colonial rule in the Indonesian archipelago in early 1942, the Dutch East Indies government's policy of collaborating with various local interest groups had created an atmosphere of intrigue and violence.

Prior to the revolution

During his leadership, Pajonga slowly got rid of his political rivals, especially those who had cooperated with the Dutch government in eradicating the I Toloq gang. He began by appointing his relatives: Magulabbu Daeng Makkio as Gallarang Moncongkomba, his brother Baco Daeng Siantang as Gallarang Malewang, and his cousin Tarasi Daeng Bantang as Gallarang Bontokadatto.[52] All *gallarangs* of the former Bajeng kingdom territory were now under his family's influence. The network of aristocrats he formed within this strong circle of relatives was remarkable for its harmony. This solid political capital underlay Pajonga's political steps in the revolutionary period after the proclamation of independence in Takalar.

Those steps significantly aggravated the political dichotomy in Polombangkeng. Descendants from the former Bajeng kingdom occupied important positions. In contrast, descendants from Lassang did not have the right to become *karaeng* of Polombangkeng because the status of their area, which had been added later, was below that of Bajeng. Meanwhile, Pappa, Ballo and Manuju were autonomous villages that still refused to recognize the power of the Polombangkeng *karaeng*. Meanwhile, Patalassang in the south-east, historically also not part of Polombangkeng and economically oriented to Takalar, continued to try to escape from the influence of the Polombangkeng *karaeng*.

Polombangkeng was a fragile construction that continually produced competition among aristocrats. A new educated elite emerged from the modern schools. Some of them built networks with Indonesian nationalists in Makassar and cities in Java. However, a new generation was also carrying on the *toloq* tradition, and they remained connected with the patron aristocrats.

The Japanese colonial rule was a critical period in the history of Polombangkeng. Some youth leaders cooperated with the Japanese military government. A youth education corps established by the Japanese called Boei Teisintai (Barisan Pelopor Pertahanan Negara in Indonesian) was led by Manai Sophiaan. He had been raised in Takalar and had close contacts with youth leaders from Polombangkeng. Village heads also had to recruit people to join Heiho and Seinendan, the auxiliary forces raised for the Imperial Japanese Army. The same occurred in Bajeng: youths were recruited to join Heiho, Seinendan, Boei Teisentai and Keibodan – all military or paramilitary organizations formed by the Japanese occupiers.[53] They received rigorous military training and were then mobilized to join the fight against the Allies.[54] Several political prisoners who had been imprisoned during the Dutch colonial period were released and returned to Polombangkeng. Tikolla Daeng Malleio, Cincing Deng Tompo, Majadi Daeng Sisila and Baco Daeng Siantang were Polombangkeng aristocrats who had fought against the Dutch from 1905 to 1917. After spending many years in exile, they were now released.[55] Despite their long absence, they still had a strong network with the more elderly *toloq*. However, a new generation of *toloq* also came to mark this era. They worked on the black market for rice once the Japanese government began to control rice production. They had a strong network with robbers and had adequate knowledge of the Polombangkeng area. As a group that worked in crime, they controlled a network of forest trails connecting one region with another. While Polombangkeng had developed in various ways, it still maintained its long tradition of resistance, robbery and theft.

The tradition of opposition and the alliance of the revolution

A tradition of opposition had become part of Polombangkeng's political history. The revolutionary period offered a new political choice: to strengthen old alliances or build new ones. Anthony Reid has argued that the revolution destroyed the legitimacy of local dynasties and created a new myth of collective sacrifice in which a new 'imagined community' replaced the identity of a discredited past.[56] But in Polombangkeng, there were negotiations between this new 'imagined community' and those identities of the past. For the old aristocrats especially, revolution opened a door to restore the identity of Polombangkeng, which they felt had been marginalized for more than a century.

When the proclamation of independence became known in South Sulawesi, Sam Ratulangi was appointed governor of Sulawesi Province, based in Makassar. But this did not bring significant change. His position was unstable, and he lacked the confidence to run the government. When he arrived in Makassar between 20 and 23 August 1945, the Japanese were still in charge under the terms of the surrender. He did not announce himself as the governor appointed by the government of the Republic of Indonesia in Jakarta. Several prominent figures and youths urged him to do this, but he argued that the conditions to support his power had not been met. Ratulangi believed the new Republican government was fragile and did not have armed forces. He felt Sulawesi could not be equated with Java, where the conditions did support the Republican government.[57] When Allied troops arrived in South Sulawesi on 24 September 1945 – and with them the Dutch – no government of the Republic of Indonesia had been realized in South Sulawesi.[58] Ratulangi only had the support of a limited number of middle-class groups, had no military power base, and lacked the support of local authorities or the nobility. While he did succeed in establishing the Sulawesi People's Welfare Centre (Pusat Keselamatan Rakyat Sulawesi, PKRS), this had an associational rather than a political character. Ratulangi from then on only relied on the policies of the Allied authorities, who brought the NICA along with them.[59] He thus faced two significant challenges: the NICA's presence and the lack of support from local authorities.

When the NICA moved quickly to restore civilian rule and began approaching aristocrats, the situation grew more complicated. Ratulangi's indecisiveness and the entry of the NICA accelerated the development of alliances at the elite level, both for and against the revolution, which then spread to the community level. Power struggles appeared as soon as news of the Proclamation reached Polombangkeng. Nationalist youths Mukdan and Saleh Lahade founded the nationalist organization Support for the Republic of Indonesia (Penunjang Republik Indonesia, PRI) to represent Takalar. The PRI was intended to replace a youth organization established at the end of the Japanese colonial period called Sudara (Source of the People's Blood, *Sumber Darah Rakyat*).[60] It was to serve as a preparatory organization for the civilian government.[61] Initially, it received support from influential aristocrats in the Takalar region such as Pajonga Daeng Ngalle, Lemo Daeng Lira, karaeng Galesong, karaeng Lakatong, karaeng Lengkese, karaeng Pappa and karaeng Topejawa. However, problems began to arise when Lemo Daeng Lira was appointed chairman of the PRI and Pajonga Daeng Ngalle became his deputy. Six days after its founding, Pajonga Daeng Ngalle withdrew from the PRI on the grounds that he was not given a good position because he was under Lemo Daeng Lira. As explained earlier, Pajonga Daeng Ngalle was a high-level aristocrat with the most significant influence and the largest territory, while Lemo Daeng Lira was merely *gallarang* of Lassang, an area that had been added later to the Polombangkeng confederation. This competition for authority weakened the revolutionary alliance. After the first visit of NICA officials in Takalar, most aristocrats decided to renew their cooperation with the Dutch.[62]

Dissatisfied with the PRI, Makaraeng Daeng Manjarungi, Syamsuddin Daeng Ngerang and Madina Daeng Ngitung initiated a new organization. This did have the support of Pajonga Daeng Ngalle and the elderly aristocrats. On 2 September 1945, a meeting was held in Palleko, attended by all high aristocrats and youth representatives from various villages in Polombangkeng. A total of 150 people attended. This meeting resulted in a decision to establish a forum for the Polombangkeng youth to engage in resistance against the Dutch.

In developing the organization, the older and younger generations had different standpoints. Tikolla Daeng Malleio, Cincing Daeng Tompo, Majadi Daeng Sisila and Baco Daeng Siantang belonged to the older generation who still remembered their resistance to the Dutch from 1905 to 1917 and had spent long years in exile. They believed the purpose of the alliance was the independence of the Bajeng people, who had been marginalized for centuries. According to them, the Republic of Indonesia was only an ally to achieve the independence of Polombangkeng. They called themselves 'Bajeng Warriors' and considered it important to respect the traditions, identity and history of Bajeng through ceremonies of worshipping the royal regalia.[63] They also wanted a name for the organization that represented the identity of the Bajeng people.

Meanwhile, the young people were divided into two groups. The first included the nationalist youth, educated and involved in the Indonesian nationalist movement. Many had enjoyed formal education and were part of established networks with the Indonesian nationalist movement in Makassar and several cities in Java. The second were the militant youth, consisting of *jago* or *toloq*. This group was led by Ranggong Daeng Romo, who believed that only armed force could repel colonialism. The name chosen for the organization was Young Bajeng Movement (Gerakan Muda Bajeng), reflecting the desire to restore the greatness of the sixteenth-century Bajeng kingdom.

Ideological differences grew more apparent when the older generation prioritized traditional ceremonies, such as presenting the ancient flag of the Bajeng kingdom. Made of white silk with a picture of a centipede (*lipan),* the flag's name was *Jule' julea.* [64] The ritual had long been practised when about to face war. Younger aristocrats and members of the Islamic organization Muhammadiyah opposed this ceremony.[65] Differences were smoothed over by moving the old guard into the powerless role of protector, while the young held executive power. The oldest *karaeng*, Tikolla Daeng Malleio, was given the position of protector.[66] Pajonga Daeng Ngalle became chairman, with Makkaraeng daeng Manjarungi as deputy. The armed youths were led by Syamsuddin Daeng Ngerang and Ranggong Daeng Romo. All these active leaders were close relatives of Pajonga Daeng Ngalle.

In the first months, the different points of view determined the organization's strategy. Makaraeng Daeng Manjarungi, Syamsuddin Daeng Ngerang, Madina Daeng Ngitung and Fachruddin Daeng Romo tried to align their policies with Ratulangi's understanding of the situation and his political network. Meanwhile, Ranggong Daeng Romo and other youth groups engaged in physical resistance. The latter did not follow national political developments. 'Most of their members came from *toloq* who were known as bandits during the Dutch East Indies period.'[67]

Aristocratic status now became an issue. Hardline supporters of the aristocracy considered Syamsuddin and Makaraeng to have a relatively low status. Although Syamsuddin was the son of Cincing Daeng Tompo, his mother had no aristocrat title, and therefore he was not qualified to occupy a high position in Polombangkeng. The same was true of Makaraeng Daeng Manjarungi, the son of the village head Manongkoki. Both had spent most of their time in Makassar. In Bugis-Makassar society, those who cannot manifest themselves based on their status must compensate by obtaining higher education. Young people without formal education, among them the *toloq*, put forward courage and physical agility as their assets. Thus, most of the combat members of Gerakan Muda Bajeng were from the *toloq*.

The fragility of the structure of Gerakan Muda Bajeng became obvious as soon as it was formed. The organization accommodated all sub-district heads and village heads in Polombangkeng in its structure. But some of them were opposed to Pajonga Daeng Ngalle, especially in areas not included in the former Bajeng kingdom. This opposition dated back to the colonial period and was further intensified in the revolutionary period. Polarization grew between Bajeng aristocrats and aristocrats of non-Bajeng descent on the one hand and the old group with their local identity, the militant youth and the nationalist youth on the other. These rivalries characterized the early journey of the Bajeng Muda Movement as an organization with a strong local flavour. It affirmed its local identity and, at the same time, declared itself part of the unifying Republic of Indonesia.

The NICA was aware of these rivalries and exploited them. Its officials attempted to approach the Polombangkeng aristocrats. Around December 1945, Australian and Dutch officials tried to contact Pajonga Daeng Ngalle, but Pajonga did not respond. NICA officials then offered to cooperate with members of the nobility who opposed Pajonga Daeng Ngalle. This turned out to be a successful tactic. Lemo Daeng Lira, *gallarang* Lassang, expressed his willingness to cooperate with the NICA, and he was followed by other village heads, such as those of Ballo, Manuju and Pappa.[68] Likewise, the sons of *gallarang* Pattallassang and Makkarawa Daeng Ngalle, the head of the village of Sastar, chose to cooperate with the NICA. These choices seemed to echo the way their parents cooperated with the Dutch government to suppress I Toloq Daeng Magassing in the period between 1908 and 1915. Most of the aristocrats who accepted the invitation to cooperate with the NICA were motivated by the desire to regain their old positions seized by Pajonga Daeng Ngalle's relatives.

Lemo Daeng Lira's choice to side with the NICA was motivated by his desire for the position of *karaeng* Polombangkeng. His wish was later achieved when Pajonga Daeng Ngalle decided to escape into the forest to join Lipan Bajeng in 1947. The replacement of indigenous officials was the NICA's political strategy to eliminate the significant role of Pajonga Daeng Ngalle's close relatives in the local government structure. This put an end to the dominance of Pajonga Daeng Ngalle's relatives in the government hierarchy in Polombangkeng. However, these difficulties merely strengthened the internal solidarity within the Pajonga extended family. Almost all his close relatives strongly supported his opposition to the NICA.

Nonetheless, the children did not always follow their parents' choices. Oftentimes when parents sided with the Dutch, their children assisted Bajeng fighters on the opposite side. They asked shepherds to deliver food to the forest where the Bajeng fighters were hiding.[69] This complicated the NICA's strategy against Pajonga Daeng Ngalle. The NICA recruited spies among the nationalists, giving them special treatment. If any of these spies did something to displease the Dutch, the NICA delayed a response until after Polombangkeng was deemed safe.[70]

These shifting alliances gave rise to a competition for positions and roles that could not be separated from the aristocrats' power relations and traditions of opposition. Past relationships have always been a reference in determining present attitudes and choices. Lemo Daeng Lira and some aristocrats outside of Bajeng's lineage opposed Pajonga Daeng Ngalle by choosing to side with the NICA. Karaeng Pappa's support for the NICA could not be separated from Takalar's close cooperation with the Dutch government before the Japanese colonial period.[71] During the Dutch East Indies period, Takalar, as a sub-regency (*onderafdeling*), had the same rights as Polombangkeng. Likewise, Ballo and Manuju, located in Bontonompo, were also considered part of Polombangkeng. The Dutch government took advantage of this situation to gain the support of the local elite against the interests of Republicans. The council of kings was the main body used by the Dutch to exercise their power in South Sulawesi.[72]

The complicity of the *toloq*

In the revolutionary period, decisions made by the *toloq* to support or oppose the Republic were greatly influenced by the role of the aristocratic elite, who had been their long-standing allies. Whether they made such decisions or not, the *toloq* still committed robberies, for which the revolution gave them plenty of opportunity.

Ranggong Daeng Romo was one of the elites who associated with the *toloq* in Polombangkeng. He secretly established communication with strong and brave people from various regions – intelligent people with knowledge of the forest terrain – with the end goal of forming a fighting body. He initiated a meeting in Paggentungan in late September 1945 that was attended by representatives of *toloq* from Moncongkomba, Lantang, Cakura, Bulukunyi, Bontokadatto, Barana, Pattallassang, Bone-Bone, Sompu and Bajeng. They were assigned seats according to their respective regions. Representatives from Pattallassang and Sompu facing from west to east; those from Cakura and Bulukunyi facing from east to west; those from Bonto Kadatto, Bone-Bone and Barana facing from south to north; and those from Moncongkomba and Lantang facing from north to south.

Ranggong Daeng Romo spoke first and asked those present if they were willing to become executioners *(algojo)*. No one was willing at first. However, the representative from Moncongkomba, Basullu Daeng Lawa, then raised his hand, followed by Mangaweang Daeng Nuhung from Bontokadatto. In the end, all the *toloq* present agreed to become executioners. This meeting was where the term 'Moncongkomba with a firm stand' originated (*Moncongkomba Gassing Gau*) as well as the expressions 'Bontokadatto's twin' (*Bontokadatto kambara'na*), and 'State of Bajeng that holds a spear' (*Butta Bajeng to mappaenteng poke'na*). It resulted in a *toloq* organization named the Algojo Polombangkeng (Polombangkeng Executioners). The organization was placed at the forefront and was tasked with executing those who were considered traitors. An increase in violence in the community was the result. Ranggong Daeng Romo ordered the leader of Algojo Polombangkeng, Basullu Daeng Lawa, to execute those who were suspected of being spies for the Dutch. At first, the group simply guarded the river crossing that served as the border of Moncongkomba. They interrogated anyone who passed, and if they were suspected of being a Dutch spy, they were robbed and killed. They later began to terrorize all residents suspected of collaborating with the NICA. Threats of torture against spies were distributed in the form of pamphlets.[73]

The violence escalated when the Dutch army built military posts in Palleko and Pappa in January 1946. All those who came from these two areas were now suspected of being spies. Algojo Polombangkeng's violence also extended to villages beyond Polombangkeng when they forced young people to join the Gerakan Muda Bajeng.[74] They then started seizing livestock and property from ordinary citizens. A resident with four animals would have two of them confiscated. Hundreds of cows secured during the last months of 1945 were assembled in a field in the village of Jannang. Some of the loot was then handed over to the guerrilla fighters in the forest.[75]

The first serious challenge to Algojo Polombangkeng came when Siratu Daeng Manompo, the *gallarang* Moncongkomba appointed by the NICA, withdrew his brother Hamanja Daeng Leila and his followers from the Gerakan Muda Bajeng.[76] Among them were *toloq* who went on to cause friction at lower levels of society as pro-NICA Bajeng fighters. These men, too, were referred to as *algojo* or executioners. They did not hesitate to kill people they regarded as supporters of the pro-Republican Bajeng fighters. Among them were famous names such as Saelalla Daeng Naba, Batoto Daeng Tutu and Nongko, who guarded the post at Sungguminasa. Another was Hamzah Daeng Tompo, leader (*paccalaya*) of a union of villages in the Kingdom of Gowa. The special pro-NICA forces he led in Borongloe had many followers.[77] Hamzah Daeng Tompo's *toloq* meted out the same treatment to Ranggong Daeng Romo's Algojo Polombangkeng as the latter had dealt out to others.

Some individuals chose to play both sides. They cooperated with Dutch supporters but secretly supplied food and shelter to the resistance groups. They could be informants for the Dutch army as well as spies for the Gerakan Muda Bajeng. Others preferred not to get involved at all. People from Lassang later stated that they had agreed to join the Bajeng fighters but never took part in resistance activities. Their joining was a way of saving themselves and of avoiding becoming a target for robbery. For at the slightest indication that they were siding with the NICA, they would be added to the kill list.[78] The same thing happened when NICA supporters found people who were helping Bajeng fighters.

From January to March 1946, Gerakan Muda Bajeng and Dutch troops made physical contact 18 times. The Dutch army responded to an ambush by the Bajeng fighters with an invasion of the Gerakan Muda Bajeng's headquarters and the arrest of many of its fighters.[79] As mutual suspicions rose, the violence intensified. Basullu Daeng Lawa ordered Algojo Polombangkeng to investigate villages considered to be in favour of the NICA, such as Sapaya, Manuju and Pappa. They then arrested and killed anyone they thought was collaborating with the NICA. The exact number of casualties from these actions, which included house burning and murder, is unknown. Basullu Daeng Lawa was dubbed a mass murderer in newspaper reports.[80] He tended to terrorize villagers after a Dutch attack on his headquarters, as he suspected pro-Dutch spies.[81] Several times he threatened village heads that he would kill half the villagers if they did not give a signal when Dutch troops arrived.[82]

Atrocities committed by Algojo Polombangkeng reached both the lower classes of society and those aristocrats thought to be siding with the Dutch. Among them was Manrupai Daeng Nyau, recently appointed *gallarang* Bontokadatto,[83] who was murdered and his house burned down. The murder of Karaeng Manuju and several other aristocrats created internal problems for the Gerakan Muda Bajeng. Karaeng Manuju had many followers, whose subsequent rage weakened the position of the Gerakan Muda Bajeng. Some members of Lipan Bajeng, especially his kin, could not accept the death of Karaeng Manuju. His death caused an uproar in Polombangkeng. The feud between the Polombangkeng Executioners and Kareng Manuju's relatives continued long after the revolution ended.

In the midst of these multidimensional conflicts, there were attempts to expand the Gerakan Muda Bajeng network and connect it to the national struggle. On 14 January 1946, Gerakan Muda Bajeng sent a delegation to Yogyakarta to gain legitimacy for the struggle in Polombangkeng as part of the Republic, and at the same time to ask for weapons. However, the ship was stranded in Sumbawa and finally sailed back to Jeneponto Port on 7 March 1946 without having achieved its mission.[84] The Dutch, moreover, imposed strict isolation on the northern and southern regions of Polombangkeng which they had occupied. This meant that Gerakan Muda Bajeng fighters could only move about in the forests and mountains in the east. On 23 and 24 March 1946, the Dutch bombarded the headquarters of the Gerakan Muda Bajeng in Bulukunyi with cannons. This seriously degraded the movement's defences.[85]

Gerakan Muda Bajeng's resistance weakened further when the Dutch arrested several leaders, including Madina Daeng Ngitung, Syamsuddin Daeng Ngerang and Fachrudding Daeng Romo. These arrests greatly affected the organization. It collapsed almost entirely when the top leaders – Gassing (Ponggawa Paleko), Hamandha Daeng Lala, Siratu Daeng Nompo and Lemo Daeng Lira, all of nobility – defected to the NICA and withdrew their followers from Gerakan Muda Bajeng.[86] After this, Gerakan Muda Bajeng was no longer considered an effective insurgent group. According to Makaraeng daeng Manjarungi, the betrayal of the nobility was the main reason behind the failure of the movement, proving that Polombangkeng was indeed a den of robbers and rogues.[87]

On 2 April 1946, Ranggong Daeng Romo, Pajonga Daeng Ngalle and Makaraeng Daeng Manjarungi held a meeting with the Gerakan Muda Bajeng and decided that the organization was to be changed into an armed movement with a new name, Lipan Bajeng Militia (Laskar Lipan Bajeng). Pajonga Daeng Ngalle acted as patron, Makaraeng became chairman, and Ranggong Daeng Romo was commander of the troops. Renamed and under new leadership, the armed group grew in terms of both members and the area it covered. It spread beyond Polombangkeng to Gowa, Jeneponto and the southern part of Makassar. It had 17,257 members in total.[88] Campa Daeng Lawa was tasked with logistics, especially rice. He was assisted by cow herders who delivered supplies to the forests,[89] but the militiamen continued to forcibly confiscate livestock, all the way to the Jeneponto region. These *toloq* controlled the forest. Its secret passages enabled them to move easily from one headquarters to another.

Under Ranggong Daeng Romo's command, the Pasukan Lipan Bajeng expanded to 30 executioners. In addition, smaller units were formed, each with its own area of operation, consisting of *toloq* with strong local knowledge of the forest. These units became important liaisons between the resistance groups. The main transit route for the militias stretched from Polombangkeng through Manangkoki to Limbung, along the Barombong coast to Makassar. The other route was a secret path through the forest and foothills of Lombo Battang, Bulukunyi to the north to Moncongloe and Maros. In the past, the people dubbed this secret path the route of the bandits. Using this route, the militiamen of Lipan Bajeng communicated with leaders of other resistance groups, such as the Indonesian Tigers (Harimau Indonesia), the PPNI (Pusat Pemuda Nasional Indonesia, Indonesian National Youth Centre) and the KRIS (Kebaktian Rakyat Indonesia Sulawesi, Indonesian People's Service Sulawesi) to draft new strategies to deal with the police, spies and KNIL (Koninklijk Nederlands-Indisch Leger, Royal Netherlands East Indies Army) soldiers. They launched sporadic attacks in small groups with different compositions. When faced with immediate danger, they could quickly disperse and return to Polombangkeng.[90]

The end of resistance: Isolation, sabotage and arrests

Pressure from Dutch troops against the resistance in Makassar had a major impact on the situation in Polombangkeng. It actually led to the drastic growth of the Laskar Lipan Bajeng. One group of youths from Makassar wanted to go to Java, but since the Dutch had blocked their transportation routes, their journey ended in Polombangkeng. The group included the famous fighter Wolter Mongisidi.[91] In response, Makaraeng Daeng Manjarungi initiated a forum that united all militia groups under the Indonesian People's Rebel Army in Sulawesi, which came to be known as LAPRIS.[92]

The participation of Lipan Bajeng in LAPRIS helped expand the Lipan Bajeng network. The arrival of youths who had previously received Japanese military training in Makassar led to better war tactics. Lipan Bajeng was soon connected to the resistance movement in Java, which recognized it as part of the national struggle.

Unfortunately, LAPRIS also helped increase competition among the *karaeng* elites. The Dutch appointed Lemo Daeng Lira as head of the sub-regency Takalar and simultaneously gave him the noble status of Karaeng Polombangkeng. Meanwhile, Pajonga Daeng Ngalle, the leader of Lipan Bajeng, chose to go into the interior, moving from one place to another, from house to house. This gave him considerable territorial power. From here, conflicts of authority over territory and resources began to emerge, leading to increased violence. In mid-1946, Polombangkeng was considered an area afflicted with very serious crime and a lack of security. The Bajeng militias were known as 'gangs of terror' who operated out of the mountains under the leadership of Pajonga Daeng Ngalle while opposing the leadership of Lemo Daeng Lira.[93]

As the Dutch began to patrol the area more intensively, many Lipan Bajeng members were captured. In June 1946 alone, 24 were arrested.[94] On 10 October 1946, the notoriously violent *toloq* Hasamuddin alias Bakeri was captured together with two bodyguards.[95] Lipan Bajeng blamed the arrests on spies from the *karaeng* group supporting the NICA, who portrayed Lipan Bajeng of Polombangkeng as merely a group of criminals. They responded to the arrests with sabotage. Small groups within Lipan Bajeng cut off telephone lines in Gowa and blocked the main roads with logs. Other groups went covertly to Malino and elsewhere in Gowa, raiding the homes of Dutch police officers or spies. On 29 October 1946, *toloq* loyal to Pajonga

Daeng Ngalle and Ranggong Daeng Romo burned down the indigenous congregation house in Limbung.

The formation of the State of East Indonesia (Negara Indonesia Timur, NIT) on 27 December 1946 further sharpened divisions between the *karaeng* elites. Those who had been behind the NICA generally supported the new state NIT, while those opposed remained in the interior. In the view of Makaraeng Daeng Manjarungi, the NIT was basically sustained by an older generation who could not keep up with the ways of the young.[96] Mutual suspicion, murder and house burnings continued.

In response to the burning of the congregation house, around December 1946 Lemo Daeng Lira helped the KNIL and the Dutch Special Forces (Depot Speciale Troepen, DST) isolate Lipan Bajeng. The villages on the outskirts of Makassar were forced to cooperate with the Dutch, diminishing supply lines for Lipan Bajeng in Barombong and West and South Gowa. Many villagers even began to oppose Lipan Bajeng, attacking them with spears. The people of Borongloe in South Gowa took part in the KNIL operation. Hamzah Daeng Tompo ordered his *toloq* to take part too. The houses of those accused of sympathy for Lipan Bajeng were burned down and their food stores looted.[97] The operation resulted in the deaths of several hundred Lipan Bajeng members. The nobles who had led the resistance group fled to the south. On 25 January 1947, military pamphlets were circulated urging the population to find and arrest Pajonga Daeng Ngalle. Those who refused to take part were accused of belonging to the 'extremists'.[98]

Wolter Mongisidi and most Makassar youths were caught. Ranggong Daeng Romo was killed in a skirmish with the KNIL in Komara. In the three months between December 1946 and February 1947, he had led Lipan Bajeng in no fewer than 57 battles and LAPRIS in 51 battles.[99] After his death, only some small units remained. They were led by Mappa Daeng Temba, Makatang Daeng Sibali, Basullu Daeng Lawa, Makaraeng Daeng Jarot and Daeng Leo. In conjunction with the Linggarjati Agreement reached in March 1947 between the Republic of Indonesia and the Netherlands, armed resistance ceased. Nonetheless, acts of violence continued in Polombangkeng. To prevent Lipan Bajeng from coming into contact with the population, the Dutch evacuated villagers or guarded them with special troops. KNIL troops routinely conducted patrols in the eastern part of Polombangkeng.[100]

On 11 April 1947, the NIT government issued an ultimatum to the resistance groups hiding in the interior, urging them to surrender.[101] Some of the Lipan Bajeng militia complied, while others continued to deploy terror against those who worked for the KNIL. Around June 1947, police arrested more followers of Pajonga Daeng Ngalle. Among them was Muhammad Arief, who was also a member of the Republic of Indonesia Army (Tentara Republik Indonesia, TRI). They were handed over to military patrols.[102] More skirmishes took place between the police and Lipan Bajeng fighters in the first week of August 1947.[103]

In early January 1948, the NIT government opened negotiations with Lipan Bajeng. The group demanded recognition as a militia of the Republic of Indonesia and not as a criminal group, which would have given them immunity from prosecution by the NIT government.[104] When the NIT agreed to these terms, as many as 160 Lipan Bajeng fighters handed themselves in.[105] On 8 January 1948, another 45 surrendered (see Image 2). Among them were Makaraeng Daeng Jarot, Macang Daeng Leo and the most wanted executioner, Basullu Daeng Lawa.[106] The NIT government, however, did not keep its word. All the Lipan Bajeng fighters were handed over to the KNIL,

Image 2. Lipan Bajeng fighters who were arrested on 8 January 1945. *Source: Nationaal Archief, The Hague.*

who took them to Makassar. The leaders were imprisoned in Hoogepad jail in Makassar, along with 800 militiamen. Others were sent to several regional prisons.[107]

Violence after the revolution

Although the war between the Netherlands and the Republic of Indonesia officially ended when the Dutch recognized Indonesian sovereignty with the formation of the United States of Indonesia, the conflict between federalists and republicans continued. The notion of a federal state was not simply taken as a form of state administration. Supporters of the republic saw it as a political action to undermine the authority of the Republic of Indonesia based in Yogyakarta. Lipan Bajeng, too, viewed the federal NIT as a construction favoured by older generations who wanted to maintain the status quo. Their distaste for the NIT increased after the Dutch military detained its fighters in violation of the agreement that the NIT had negotiated.

After the Dutch–Indonesian Round Table Conference in The Hague from 23 August to 2 November 1949 had recognized Indonesian sovereignty and led to the liberation of political prisoners in South Sulawesi, Makaraeng Daeng Manjarungi formed a new organization aiming to disband the NIT and return to the Republic of Indonesia as proclaimed in 1945. The Bureau of Supporters of the Republic of Indonesia (Biro Pejuang Pengikut Republik Indonesia, BPPRI) was ratified during the Conference of Freedom Fighters in Polombangkeng on 7 February 1950, attended by 50 militias from throughout East Indonesia. Interestingly, even though the event was aimed at disbanding the NIT, the president of the NIT, Sukawati, gave a speech at the conference.[108]

However, the end of the Lipan Bajeng resistance, the formation of the NIT and the establishment of the BPPRI did not necessarily bring peace and order. Looting and theft remained rampant, motivated by economic and political incentives as well as revenge. The targets of the looting varied from local officials and foreigners to the ordinary population. The looters were armed and usually carried out their actions in groups of tens. Even though KNIL soldiers still routinely patrolled, robberies were unstoppable.

Politically motivated robberies were carried out against local officials who worked for the NICA and the NIT. Pajonga Daeng Ngalle had not been the *karaeng* of Polombangkeng since 1946, having been replaced by Lemo Daeng Lira. Many traced the root of the chaos in Polombangkeng to this replacement, as illustrated in the letter by Mangulung with which this chapter started. The NICA had replaced all those closely connected to him in the local government. In March 1947, people in Polombangkeng demanded the reinstatement of several relatives of Pajonga Daeng Ngalle, namely his nephew Samsuddin Daeng Ngerang and Tanggo Daeng Simpung, nephew of Karaeng Ilanga ri Mangkura. Local authorities ignored the demand. Although some Pajonga Daeng Ngalle relatives did hold NIT positions, they were not in positions where they could give cultural leadership within Polombangkeng.

On 9 April 1950, a robbery occurred in Cikoang-Topejawa, a well-off region and the centre of government during Dutch rule in Takalar. Five armed criminals robbed a Chinese home and took away valuables, jewellery and bonds.[109] This was soon followed by another robbery at the house of Karaeng Gallarang Lengkese, a well-respected nobleman and local official in South Polombangkeng. The robbers, 20 of them, were armed and extremely skilled. While ten of them were looting the house, the other ten were on the lookout in the front yard of the house.[110] This modus operandi demonstrated that it was not simply a robbery but a message to other noblemen and officials who might become their targets.

Widespread terror and shootings targeted the homes of local officials and motorists passing through Jeneponto and Takalar.[111] Shootings took place continually along the road between Gowa and Polombangkeng. Throughout the mid-1950s, the military patrolled the border zone between Gowa and Polombangkeng. Whenever soldiers increased patrols in urban areas, robberies became more rampant in rural areas, targeting the population's livestock. The robbers did not take all the livestock but only some or a few, similar to the modus operandi of the Lipan Bajeng group.

After the release of the Bajeng freedom fighters in 1950, internal conflicts began to grow. Each group within Lipan Bajeng was loyal to its own patron and royal elites. These grew into separate armed groups and controlled the interior of Polombangkeng. They were often involved in skirmishes among themselves. Some later joined the Darul Islam/ Tentara Islam Indonesia rebellion led by Kahar Muzakkar. Others became village heads or remained as *toloq*, forming criminal networks. All continued to be rebels as they had been accustomed to be for more than a century, constantly disrupting the socio-cultural and political balance in Polombangkeng. Only a small number of them were integrated into the national armed forces (TNI).

Conclusion

Polombangkeng, originally part of the Dutch colonial confederation, was basically a fragile governmental structure. Competition among the nobles was endemic. The aristocrats of the former Bajeng Kingdom often saw themselves as the rightful rulers of Polombangkeng, while noblemen from outside Bajeng were considered outcasts to be sidelined and kept away from the stage of local power. Similarly, the autonomous *kampongs* never officially recognized the rule of the Karaeng Polombangkeng but were trapped within their own authority.

The contest for authority began when the colonial government reduced the authority of the local leaders. The local *gallarang* responded with negligence or lawlessness. Meanwhile, those from outside Bajeng took advantage of the situation by opposing existing local powerholders in order to gain power. The contest was the product of the new, fluctuating system of colonial power relations, all heavily influenced by assertive identity representations and always accompanied by violence.

This historical pattern became even sharper and more dynamic during the revolutionary period. The Proclamation of Independence offered a new nation-state. The NICA, with its armed forces, aimed to re-establish Dutch colonial power and offered new positions and promises to reinstate the local elites. In the midst of this, the local identity of Bajeng grew stronger. For the people of Bajeng, what mattered most in the Indonesian revolution was their own freedom.

Having to choose between the Republic or the NICA caused deep splits among the Polombangkeng elites. Former Bajeng aristocrats declared themselves supporters of the Republic of Indonesia. Aristocrats from outside Bajeng, in their attempt to gain power, associated themselves with the NICA. These choices reflected a long history of contestation among the elites. In the midst of this crisis, the formation of the State of East Indonesia (NIT) was interpreted politically as yet another Dutch effort to maintain power. In reality, however, the NIT was an alternative meeting ground that served to bring the supporters of the Republic and of the NICA together.

Alliances – new, shifting or strengthened old ones – were shaped by each individual's interest in obtaining new positions and roles. Historical identities and power relations became important references in determining political choices, including those adopted by the *toloq*. They were inseparable from the struggle for authority among the Polombangkeng elites. Some *toloq* joined Lipan Bajeng, while others joined the NICA, depending on their political patrons. Each manifested their support in the form of criminal acts. Looting, theft, burning and executions became widespread as a consequence.

The historical reality in Polombangkeng demonstrates that the revolution and the Dutch attempt at recolonization created a new arena for ongoing contestation among elites. These conflicts in turn permeated to the lower societal levels. Conflicting parties took advantage of the unstable situation and the fragile elite relations that went back a hundred years into the colonial era. All this resulted in untold suffering for the people of Polombangkeng.

12.

Association with the people must be friendly

War against the people and the political partitioning of West Java, 1948

Roel Frakking[1]

By 1949, after more than three years of fighting, West Java had become crowded. When the Divisi Siliwangi of the Indonesian Armed Forces (Tentara Nasional Indonesia, TNI) slowly returned to its 'pockets' at the end of its famed 'Long March' from the vicinity of Yogyakarta, they encountered no less than two authorities vying for the people's attention. To begin with, the

Image 1. As stipulated by the Renville Agreement of January 1948, tens of thousands of TNI troops would evacuate West Java. In Tasikmalaya, TNI General A.H. Nasution sees to it that weapon and troop registration takes place in a disciplined fashion. Source: Nationaal Archief, Dienst voor Legercontacten.

still-active Dutch army was propping up a quasi-autonomous statelet called the Pasundan State, which was an outpost of the Dutch 1946 federalization project. There was also Darul Islam (DI), an armed Islamist movement, which had turned against the Republic, thereby '[betraying] the common struggle against the colonial army' according to the Republic. The Darul Islam had made inroads in West Java after the TNI had been forced to leave the province as part of the Renville Agreement signed in January 1948.

It was into this fray that the Siliwangi stepped to reclaim its eminent position as the Republic's representatives and foremost freedom fighters. Effectively, Siliwangi soldiers had to combat not only the Dutch-Pasundan axis but also the Darul Islam movement. Due to the presence of these groups, West Java had become home to 'three kinds of sovereign states, each with three kinds of armies', without counting the many so-called struggle organizations that were roaming the countryside.[2] The Siliwangi Division, then, helped unleash a three-way competition for legitimacy and authority in West Java.

Local communities were stuck in the midst of this three-way fight among possible powerbrokers and suffered severely as a result. According to the Republic's official history of West Java during the revolution, they bore '[a] ll the consequences of the colonial war and civil war'. The reason was that the Republic, through its Divisi Siliwangi, came 'in the form of a military force, not yet a civilian force'.[3] In their quest to cement the Republic's authority, Republican troops were not ill-disposed to the use of violence – and in this approach they were not alone. DI troops, who also needed to bind local communities to their cause, were apt to make an example out of those who failed to comply with their demands. The Dutch, in turn, proved equally aggressive in their operations, as the statistics in Dutch military reports show.[4]

As local communities could not find 'personal security' anywhere and the lines between the violent actions of one authority and those of another became increasingly blurred, villagers were forced to 'serve all three [authorities] for [their] own safety'. This, too, was a tactic that was full of risk.[5] As Republican sources stated, '[w]hoever helps one party will be suspected or punished by the other'.[6] It is this complex dynamic that existed between the establishment of authority and legitimacy on the one hand and the violence that forced communities into serving multiple powerbrokers on the other that forms the substance of the present chapter.

In a departure from most studies on the subject, the analysis that follows approaches the revolution in West Java in such a way that it includes local individuals and communities placed in mortal danger by powerbrokers trying to actualize political agendas that lay *beyond* the looming date of Indonesia's actual independence – which by everyone's account was fast approaching in 1948. The argument made here is that to understand the nature of revolutionary war, an analysis must include and elevate peoples' experiences, i.e. their attempts to survive, attempts that existed beyond the realm of whether or not they supported the independence movement (which they often did). The purpose is to home in on the dynamics of the revolutionary war in Indonesia, dynamics that are intrinsic to many revolutionary wars. In doing so, this chapter will provide more analytical intricacies than do studies that still use the violence of European armies as their point of departure, whereby they overemphasize European over Indonesian experiences, particularly when colonial sources form the dominant basis of their analyses.[7]

This approach involves decentring elements of the revolutionary war in West Java that still dominate scholarship, including major events such as the 'Bandung Fire Sea' (*Bandung Lautan Api*) or the 'Convoy War' in Sukabumi – both early events of the revolution – but also the dominant role of the Republican Army (TNI) that it has claimed for itself since 1945.[8] Related to this is the fact that other major works on the violence in West Java have analysed its dynamics more from a particular vantage point connected to one mass movement, for example Darul Islam and its spiritual leader Kartosuwiryo, or one political entity in the region such as the Pasundan People's Party (Partai Rakyat Pasundan, PRP).[9] The analysis below will consider how these groups interacted with each other, and with local communities. This chapter's shift in emphasis towards the violence directed at – and its effect upon – communities reduces the dominance of still-prevalent top-down perspectives that foreground 'big names' and their supposed political-military prowess – such as Lieutenant Governor-General H.J. van Mook and his federal plan for Indonesia, or General A.H. Nasution.[10] To a lesser extent, this chapter also decentres the primacy of the revolutionized youth, collectively known as *pemuda* and *pemudi*.[11]

Focusing on big events, big men or big mass movements tends to make specific leaders, specific organizations or singular events into analytical hubs to which other related events are then linked. This chapter instead allows room for the complexities associated with retellings of Indonesia's revolutionary period. Without ignoring the actions of the Darul Islam, for example, or the *pemuda*, it seeks to also chart the experiences of those who faced the consequences of, say, *pemuda* violence. Doing so will reveal the cost of war for communities and individuals who merely sought to survive the violence. Teasing out some of the ways in which they tried to maximize their chances of survival allows for the analysis of key yet often neglected characteristics of the Indonesian war of independence in West Java. In terms of the war's complexities: individuals and communities faced difficult choices, brought on by multiple, heavily armed and violent legitimacy-seekers who sought to control people by limiting the population's ability to remain neutral.[12] The choices made by communities caught in the crosshairs were often based on safety and insecurity. Such complexities existed at the crossroads where political shifts at the supra-local level intersected with local dynamics.

To gain insight into such complexities brought on by powerbrokers, their violence and the resultant survival choices for the victims of violence, the chapter foregrounds and probes the utility of violence in revolutionary warfare. Instead of treating mass violence as a phenomenon devoid of agency and as a by-product of (in particular) European colonial warfare conducted by tired, overextended European armies operating in unfamiliar, massive terrain without clear objectives, this chapter sees violence as a handy tool for powerbrokers operating on all sides of the conflict to enhance their legitimacy by enforcing peoples' compliance.[13] By thinking about violence in terms of its uses, the current chapter restores agency to violence (moving beyond the reasoning that 'it happened in colonial warfare'), a twist that yields several analytical advantages.

For one, the analysis is able to critically engage with interpretations of colonial violence that tend to reduce the very conscious choice to unleash it to merely a *reaction* flowing from anxieties and fears borne out of the 'vulnerability' or 'angst' of European officials and communities in uncontrollable colonial contexts.[14] Instead of seeing violence as a reaction, this chapter shows that with the Republic adamant to defend its independence and the Dutch equally adamant to reoccupy Indonesia, in the words of Hilmar Farid, 'violence was not unexpected'.[15] With that in mind, Republican-nationalist violence can enter the analytical frame next to Dutch violence, even if Republican-nationalist and Dutch violence had very different motivations and end-goals.[16] With useful violence as a leading concept, this chapter can begin to address the fact that Republican-nationalist violence remains an under-investigated component of the period under consideration according to Farid, certainly within the Indonesian historiography.[17]

By considering the violence committed by all parties – Dutch, Republican-nationalist and others – simultaneously, it becomes clear that specific (and often local) powerbrokers actively and deliberately chose to immediately resort to violence. As argued above, this was because communities responded by letting go of their neutrality: violence forced peoples' hand and made them support the violent powerbroker they had in front of them. This mechanism of revolutionary and counterrevolutionary violence in particular cannot be understood properly until one grasps the utility of violence to Dutch and Republican enforcers alike. To show this facet of violence, the analysis that follows must also highlight the consequences of violence and the multivarious ways that ordinary people sought to shield themselves as much as possible from violence. Such ways, as shall become clear, included placating multiple authorities, supporting various highly ideological political and military end-goals simultaneously and, in many cases, simply evacuating in a bid to escape food shortages, violence and disease. Lastly, this approach also illustrates how revolutionary fervour and ideologies were subsumed to the need for survival in the face of naked power projection, another key advantage of the use of violence. Taken together, violence's agency and the complexities of revolutionary conflict show yet another 'revolutionary world': the social and societal cost of the war, an element that is often relegated to the background.

West Java before the Renville Agreement, 1945-1948

For many policymakers, the first weeks of January 1948 were dominated by yet another spate of negotiations between the Republicans and the Dutch. Under the watchful eye of the United Nations Good Offices Committee (GOC) and after months of talking, Dutch and Indonesian diplomats signed yet another agreement. The Renville Agreement took its name from the troop carrier anchored in Jakarta Bay where the final rounds of talks had taken place.[18] The signatories agreed to a military 'stand fast and cease fire' and recognized 'status quo lines' within demilitarized zones to separate their respective spheres of influence. As both parties were to maintain 'law and order', 'trade and intercourse between all areas' would continue.[19]

It was clear that the Republic had been treated poorly, its representatives having signed under the twin pressures of a Dutch ultimatum and GOC insistence.[20] Instead of an earlier GOC proposal that called for Dutch troops to withdraw from those areas they had taken from the Republic during their large-scale military attack of July 1947, the Renville Agreement stipulated that Republican forces retreat from the now-enlarged Dutch-occupied territories.[21] Again, the Republic had to contend with a political status that relegated it to just one of the states 'within a sovereign, federal United States of Indonesia' (Republik Indonesia Serikat, RIS), which would in turn form a permanent union with the Kingdom of the Netherlands.[22] Moreover, the Netherlands would retain sovereignty over Indonesia until it was transferred to the RIS. Between six and twelve months after the signing of Renville, a plebiscite would determine whether the people of 'the various territories of Java, Madura, and Sumatra wished their territories to be part of the Republic of Indonesia or of another state within the [RIS]'.[23] With a further division of the Republic on Java now greenlighted, a unitary state under the Republic seemed further away than ever.

While Queen Wilhelmina audaciously claimed in February that '[c]olonialism is dead', Renville caused pessimism in various quarters in Indonesia. Siliwangi officer A.E. Kawilarang and his men were appalled. 'After we had conducted a guerrilla war for so long, we suddenly heard about the "Renville-accord" that forced us to leave West Java. It was a terrible message.'[24] One GOC member presciently noted that 'if [the] Republic accepts, violations [are] inevitable under [the] circumstances [which] will also give Dutch excuse [to] take Djocja'.[25]

By January 1948, the resistance in West Java, including the TNI, stood to lose much. Realistically, the Republic had constantly been on the back foot, as its primacy in West Java and elsewhere was being challenged continually. But its supporters had proven tenacious. Between August 1945 and January 1948, they had worked hard to uphold the notion that '[t]he "sovereignty" of the Netherlands is not a legitimate and absolute right, but a usurping right'.[26] They had built up and consolidated both an official army presence and struggle organizations, which involved droves of revolutionized youths, the *pemuda*.

Both had grown from humble beginnings in October and November 1945, according to the historical record on army and youth organizations.[27] The TNI attracted former soldiers of the Royal Netherlands East Indies Army (Koninklijk Nederlands-Indische Leger, KNIL) as well as former members of the military and auxiliary organizations formed by the Japanese. Men like Lieutenant-General Urip Sumoharjo placed these troops and other volunteers in three divisions that commanded Banten-Bogor, Jakarta-Cirebon and the Parahyangan area (Bandung, Sumedang, Tasikmalaya, Ciamis and Garut), even if mostly on paper.[28] Separate from the TNI, struggle organizations – the distinction between the two was sometimes hard to make – organized themselves in a similar manner. Attracting youths from various social strata – students, labourers, technicians – and from various settings, such as local shops, they adopted different names while being generally known as people's militia (laskar rakyat). In Krawang, Cirebon, Bogor and elsewhere, these groups included the Buffalo Front (Barisan Banteng), the Sharpened Spear Front (Barisan Bambu Runcing) and the Islamist Hizbullah and Sabillilah.[29] The 'Younger Generation' – some five million on Java and Madura alone – that founded and operated in such groups was imbued with a 'new mode of political life that [...] implied a radical critique of the values and political ideas Dutch rule had instilled'.[30]

But it proved difficult to repel the encroaching Dutch who, by 'piggy-backing on' the British Commonwealth troops that had occupied key areas across Java, had '[smuggled] back [their] troops' into various places in West Java.[31] Autonomy and chaos, an integral part of the revolutionary world of the militias, complicated the systematic organization of struggle groups. Movie-like bravado and '[c]owboy-ism' or the narrow personal objectives of a dominant 'respected elder' could easily undercut the cohesion of anti-Dutch organizations.[32] Nonetheless, *pemuda* groups amalgamated into larger coordinating bodies to make their mark, often with the TNI taking control, even though the Allies had managed to quickly throw the militias out of West Java's major cities and the Republican government had been forced to move from Jakarta to Yogyakarta in Central Java.[33]

Many heroes of the revolution emerged in the midst of the most dramatic episodes connected to rear-guard battles in West Java's cities. In March 1946, departing fighters turned Bandung into a 'Sea of Fire' (Map 3). During the 'Convoy Battle' between Sukabumi and Cianjur from December 1945 to March 1946, Indonesian Army Commander Eddie Sukardi and his troops claimed to have killed 50 British soldiers.[34] By the first quarter of 1947, TNI formations of 300 or 500 troops were not uncommon, and spies and saboteurs were sent out everywhere from TNI outposts.[35] Villagers came to expect such resistance. When in May 1946, Dutch and British troops chased out Republican administrators and the army from Tangerang, people were livid. 'Why did the army not protect us?', they asked.[36]

West Java in pieces: Competing for legitimacy, 1948-1950

So why did the TNI not defend cities such as Tangerang? The simple answer was that neither the TNI nor the *pemuda* could stem the Dutch expansionist tide.[37] Basically, Dutch soldiers in sufficient numbers could attack with relative impunity. In South Bogor, Dutch troops harassed the 'ranks of the people' in December 1946 with 'mortars and poison gas which caused people to vomit', the *Antara* news agency reported. Elsewhere, soldiers burnt houses.[38] 'Dutch terrorists' kidnapped Bogor's Republican officials, including the mayor, after they had killed his deputy.[39] As the Republic refused to give up its sovereignty, however, the Dutch proceeded to large-scale military action, which commenced in the night of 20 July 1947,[40] causing West Java to end up as Dutch-occupied territory.[41] Through some 457 infractions of the cease-fire agreement – including reconnaissance flights, shootings, general 'Area Expansion' and the taking of Tasikmalaya and Garut – the Dutch consolidated their positions further.[42]

Despite the adversity, struggle groups reorganized and fought on between August 1947 and January 1948. Many troops had survived the Dutch attacks: General A.H. Nasution had ordered the Siliwangi Division out of Tasikmalaya, for example.[43] Governor Sewake, who was in charge of West Java's Republican government, also left the city. He subsequently 'ran the government from place to place'.[44] Others 'intend[ed] to "undress" and continue' as guerrillas.[45] All had gained valuable experience fighting 'young children [fresh] from villages in the Netherlands'.[46] Resistance groups everywhere frustrated Dutch attempts at reconstruction. Around Sukabumi, isolated Dutch plantations became favoured targets for insurgents, who often set fire to buildings and killed or kidnapped Dutch and Indonesian plantation managers. In November and December 1947 alone, plantations around Purwakarta suffered 19 attacks.[47]

These were the circumstances under which the Republic and the Dutch government signed the Renville Agreement. As said, it proved disadvantageous to the Republic. Until the RIS was established, sovereignty over Indonesia remained in Dutch hands. In practical terms, this meant that Dutch policymakers could continue to link up with regional polities that desired autonomy and have them proclaim autonomous states (*negara*) or areas (*daerah*) in territory that the Republic considered its own. Moreover, the TNI had pledged to withdraw its troops from East and West Java, relinquishing territory that the Republic had lost due to Dutch military aggression. Ultimately, some 35,000 troops vacated these areas.[48]

Even though it was removed from the western third of Java, the Republic continued to lay claim to being the legitimate authority in West Java. Its method was to slowly but systematically reinsert both civilian and military power – operating in tandem – into West Java to make Dutch governance impossible. By the time such reinsertions gathered steam, however, several competitors had taken the Republic's place. It is here at this juncture that violence against civilians became the tool for Republican civil and military authorities to reclaim ownership over the people that the various other authorities crowding West Java also sought to govern. War amongst the people became war *against* the people, with differences between the actions of (revolutionary) insurgents and (reactionary) counterinsurgents blurring for those in the crosshairs.

Image 2. The Partai Rakyat Pasundan proclaims the Pasundan State in West Java, May 1947. The Pasundan State would never gain mass support and was constantly pressured by Dutch meddling on the one hand, and disruptions by TNI *forces and local struggle organizations on the other.* Source: Nationaal Archief, Rijksvoorlichtingsdienst.

One competitor encountered by the returning Republican-nationalist forces was the Pasundan State (Image 2). A direct outgrowth of Van Mook's pursuit of federalism, the rationale behind it was that it formed an ethno-state that, according to its founders, would finally provide a home for the more than eight million Sundanese who yearned for a separate status from the Javanese.[49] Pasundan's proponents argued that autonomy within the RIS would save the Sundanese 'culture', whereas incorporation into 'a revolutionary polity' – i.e. the Republic – would result in 'dissolution'.[50] The state that was proclaimed in May 1947 could not, however, count on the support of an actual popular movement, even if some of its political parties claimed thousands upon thousands of members. Infighting among Pasundan's politicians caused the state itself to be chaotically run, which tainted its reputation.[51] The state was never able to steer a proper administrative course. In reaction to Dutch meddling with Pasundan state affairs, opposition member Suyoso opined 'that "the Pasundan-cabinet is an imposed cabinet, formed in a hurry, [just to] be able to participate in discussions on the [RIS]"'. Others understood that the Dutch could not indefinitely support the Pasundan State, and they therefore increasingly looked towards the Republic.[52]

The TNI, meanwhile, had pleasantly surprised the Dutch with its orderly, timely withdrawal from its guerrilla bases and military posts (Image 1).[53] Where Dr Leimena, a Republican evacuation official, thus invested in goodwill with the Dutch, rival powerbrokers saw opportunity.[54] The Darul Islam developed as one more '[disruptor] of the [Republican] state' that, according to Republicans in Cirebon, added to the 'disturbances that swarmed as termites'.[55] The spiritual leader of Darul Islam, Imam S.M. Kartosuwiryo, proclaimed the establishment of the Indonesian Islamic State (Negera Islam Indonesia, NII) for Indonesia's entirety in August 1949. This state had long been in the making, with roots dating back to the early twentieth century.[56] Within a month after the signing of Renville, Kartosuwiryo sat at the helm of an Islamic Council that represented various Islamic organizations from across West Java, of which the most prominent was the Council of Indonesian Muslim Associations (Majelis Syuro Muslimin Indonesia, known as Masyumi).[57] The NII declared that it would not take the Republic's place. The declaration of the Negara Pasundan had, however, forced the NII's hand, its representatives said. As such, they aimed to take territory from the Dutch, although they did urge the Republic to reconfigure itself on an Islamic basis.[58]

Still, the timing of the NII's proclamation was inextricably linked to the eclipse of the Republicans in West Java. To Kartosuwiryo and his followers, the Republic had forfeited its revolutionary vanguard role by concluding the Renville Agreement with the Dutch. Independence, Kartosuwiryo reasoned, required more than words and meetings. He aimed to keep his revolutionary word, expressed as early as 1929: he would 'stand in front of our ranks' and fight.[59] The NII's claim to authority in West Java (and soon elsewhere) pushed aside the Republic. After all, 'since the signing of Renville, we Muslims of West Java demand a firm stance', a stance that the NII, not the Republic, now represented.[60] Contravening what was agreed on at Renville, the NII announced that 'it is practically out of the question that an agreement could be reached by peaceful means'.[61] And so, in December 1948, the NII and its Indonesian Islamic Army (Tentara Islam Indonesia, TII) – complete with an Advisory Council, ministries, parliament, and state police – declared a holy war.[62]

As a grass-roots organization, the Darul Islam movement rapidly attracted supporters and enforcers.[63] Members from other struggle organizations such as the Barisan Banteng and the communist-leaning Bambu Runcing Army also joined. Within these organizations, some felt that Renville had further diminished the already slim chances of successfully defending Indonesia's independence, which had been premised on a unified revolutionary front. They concluded that '[o]ur Government [...] has too little faith in the power of the revolution', a conclusion that put them in the orbit of the Hizbullah and Sabillilah.[64] In March 1948, revolutionary leaders in Tasikmalaya, Garut, Kuningan, Majalengka and Ciamis proclaimed their areas Islamic territory.[65]

Republican forces now faced pressure from two sides: the Dutch forces and the TII. Despite a slight dip in morale caused by the post-Renville setbacks, they nonetheless forged on to once more create space for Republican authority.[66] Their task was facilitated by the resilience of the pre-1948 *Wehrkreise* system – the community-based civil-military networks that harnessed the power of the people.[67] These networks enabled the appointment of pro-Republican village heads and the reactivation of Republican civil servants still in Dutch service, often with Yogyakarta's permission. Thus emboldened, new organizations emerged that swore to 'defend and uphold the Prestige of the Negara Republiek [sic] Indonesia' through sabotage, infiltration or espionage.[68]

Returning from Yogyakarta, TNI fighters slipped back into such networks, too. These troops were highly motivated, or so one eyewitness said. Despite the food shortages and 'cruelty' they had suffered at the hands of

Dutch and KNIL soldiers, they were determined to '[give] up their bodies and souls for the State'.[69] They rekindled the fervour within the various struggle networks, which grew as a consequence with each passing month. Colonel Hamzah, West Java's military governor, sought to integrate civil and military organizations, while youths were again called up to take part in village defence units.[70] Yet another umbrella organization known as the Field Preparation, provided intelligence, food, weapons and so on. Its branches soon littered West Java, including in Tasikmalaya and Garut where DI/TII units held sway.[71] Before long, TNI forces violently confronted the TII, especially where both tried to control the same areas where both sides assessed the Dutch troops' presence to be vulnerable.[72]

The target of savagery: The people and the Indonesian revolution

Local communities had faced similar predicaments before 1948, but that year, the situation in West Java's political landscape was particularly tense. The TNI's Divisi Siliwangi returned to those places where the Dutch/Pasundan forces and the Darul Islam were already vying for territory and influence. In its quest to assert their authority, the Siliwangi acted very aggressively. In the words of some of its targets, the Siliwangi used 'Dutch methods' that were devoid of 'humanity'. Siliwangi men, for example, had no qualms with attacking those groups they deemed to be communist.[73] The fighting between the Dutch, the TNI and the TII had dire consequences for local communities, whose fate and reactions are the subject of the sections that follow.

Above all, violence and the threat of violence became a major component of people's experiences during the Indonesian revolution. In February 1949, representatives of several villages around Sukabumi wrote to the Pasundan's head of state, arguing that Sukabumi's people were being subjected to the 'savagery' of Dutch soldiers, thereby joining the ranks of Sulawesi martyrs who had fallen before them. A total of 116 civilians had been killed not because they had attacked Dutch troops but because these 'villagers embraced a political trend the Dutch did not appreciate'.[74] Elsewhere, the TNI had already killed scores of villagers who supported the Pasundan.[75] Chinese communities were attacked as well. Due to the elevated social-economic status the Chinese had enjoyed within the Dutch colonial system, they were particularly suspect in the eyes of Republicans and their supporters.[76] Often seen as spies for the Dutch, many Chinese were subjected to mass murder, especially when large numbers of Dutch troops were approaching.[77] DI troops, who were given far-reaching mandates by their commanders to force the population to support their cause, turned against the people by 'roasting and burning and killing' them, as one Siliwangi report stated.[78] Many lives and houses were lost as a result.[79]

Although its victims may have considered this to be a wanton application of violence, it did possess an internal logic: to enforce compliance by making resistance costly. NII representatives declared that anyone 'who does not submit [is punishable as] *bugot* (traitor)', a logic equally employed by the Dutch and the Republicans.[80] *Pemuda* threatened death to anyone who sold rice to the Dutch. Those enlisted in the KNIL could expect to be kidnapped by Republican forces.[81] Such threats worked: near Bogor, women and children of several villages in NII territory refused to tell inquiring Dutch planters where the male labourers had gone.[82] The Republican State Police reported in June 1948 that many people had joined Darul Islam, estimating that it had some 500,000 to one million followers.[83] At the end of that year, the Islamic State declared Cirebon, Indramayu, Majalengka, Ciamis, Tasikmalaya, Garut and Sumedang to be within its sphere of influence.[84]

With people's compliance, some governance could begin to be provided. Villagers everywhere fell in line with the powerbroker that presented itself as being most believable as the local authority, a feat that these would-be powerbrokers were able to achieve by violence. Only after an initial show of power could they offer a measure of protection in the form of safety or food, the resumption of local trade, or the security needed by individuals and communities to finally espouse certain views about the future. Thinking in terms of their longer-term safety, organizations, in the name of the communities they represented, had clear motives to choose one side over the other. For example, the Bandung Chinese Unitary Front community organization (Persatuan Tionghoa Cu Kiat Kun), foreseeing that Chinese communities would soon be without Dutch protection, denounced the '"colonial" system' and declared its support for the 'development of the Indonesian community [towards] the sovereign [RIS]'. Other Chinese supported the Republic outright and laid down their work.[85]

Where no single powerbroker was able to prove that it was fully in charge and its authority remained contested, people were caught between opposing forces. Violence meted out by Darul Islam troops, for instance, caused communities in West Java to seek protection from Dutch authorities.[86] Where the Negara Islam Indonesia (NII, Indonesian Islamic State) was able to get a foothold and co-opt several village heads, for example by operating specific NII schools, various kampongs seemed to fall into the NII's orbit.[87] Incoming 'taxes' filled NII coffers.[88] The TNI *Wehrkreise*, for their part, took over civilian administrations to facilitate the mobilization of all available resources into the struggle.[89] Around Tasikmalaya, an area where DI forces were also present, the strong TNI presence drove villagers to declare themselves for the Republic. Republican attacks on Dutch-controlled police, military forces, and plantations preceded many such takeovers. Those who felt their protectors' power ebbing away, especially those who had earlier cast their lot with the Dutch, found themselves falling into a 'fear psychosis'.[90]

The Pasundan State drew special attention from the TNI-*pemuda* axis. Apparently aided by Republican officials in Pasundan's employ, by October 1949, the TNI military districts had usurped 'real governance over' the territories from the Pasundan, one well-positioned commentator stated. It was only in the presence of Dutch troops that Pasundan officials could govern.[91] From 1947 onwards, anti-Pasundan movements had sprung up, with village heads canvassing inhabitants' signatures in support of the Republic by the thousands. This trend continued into 1948. In March, the 'Anti Daerah Pasundan Commission' wrote to Yogyakarta to reiterate how 'the Sundanese people's [wish] to remain with the Republic [...] cannot be "stifled" any longer'. In response, TNI General Sudirman ordered soldiers to surreptitiously participate in the commission's planned 'mass demonstration'.[92] Elsewhere, petitions denouncing the breakaway Pasundan State in favour of the Republic circulated. The petition's organizers netted some 20,000 signatories around Jakarta.[93]

Even if this happened by sheer force, all parties involved tried to curry favour with the people, as each of the three contesting powers understood that taking care of the needs of the people could, in turn, evolve into legitimacy. The TNI wanted its soldiers to protect people 'pouring into the cities everyday' to escape the Darul Islam, whose troops scoured the countryside by the thousands.[94] In the Ciwai area, representatives of the Republican defence ministry tried to organize 'material assistance' to counter the violent measures employed by the Dutch to collect rice, which, according to the report, deprived the people of 80% of their rice surplus.[95] In line with earlier public and internal announcements, in 1949 TNI Commander Bambang Supeno ordered that, to 'protect the good name of the Republic', troops should avoid violently driving off Chinese communities, although anti-Chinese practices by Republicans did still occur frequently.[96] The Dutch, meanwhile, allowed ex-TNI Major Suhardi – now on Pasundan's payroll – to operate a 'Community Support Body' in Bandung which provided food to local families of TNI soldiers evacuated as a result of Renville as well as demobilized TNI units.[97]

The people's needs, however, were too large and multifaceted for anyone to address during a conflict dominated by destruction and disruption. Safety remained elusive, and none of the powerbrokers truly wanted to protect the people, it seemed. In September 1948, the Chinese Chung Hua Chung Hui organization in Kadipaten, Cirebon informed the Chinese Consul that the Dutch arrival a year previously had not prevented the subdistrict from plunging into chaos. When Tan Bian Kwi's property was ransacked, for example, no Dutch troops or police appeared.[98] At the same time, revolutionary aggression in Sukabumi soared in September, with 20 actions carried out against plantations alone. Clearly, the massive influx of TNI troops reinserting themselves back into West Java following Renville to link up with in situ guerrilla and regular troops was beginning to have an effect.[99]

Planters concluded that the Dutch government's 'weak behaviour sort of invited the Republic to continue its methods of sabotage[,] terror, robbery and murder'. The police and military were powerless as long as they 'traipsed through the country with the lawbook in hand'.[100] The behaviour of the colonial troops, however, had little to do with any laws. One soldier recalled how at one point, a villa between Bandung and Lembang named Isola functioned as a torture site for those with uncalloused hands. As most people that the Dutch soldiers had encountered worked as manual labourers, soft hands indicated to them that these people had spent time away from work perpetrating acts that undermined Dutch authority. According to this veteran, the infantry stationed at Villa Isola functioned as a 'murder squad'.[101] In early 1949, the Sukabumi Regency was once again targeted, this time by KNIL paratroopers. Internal military reports stated that, in the aftermath of heavy fighting, they had perpetrated 'all kinds of misdeeds' that by law are counted among the 'severest of crimes [such as] rape and dishonouring underaged girls'. In addition, 'innocent persons' supping, working or merely on the road had been shot dead, and hundreds of others had been robbed during searches. Elsewhere, Dutch soldiers molested village heads or beat prisoners to death.[102]

Navigating West Java: Oedema, malaria and scabies

Economically speaking, Indonesia was in dire straits. In the colonial parlance of the time, revolutionized youths were 'lost to productive labour', whereas others were too afraid to work or physically unable to. Even if labourers did want to work for Dutch planters, they often could not: many plantations were destroyed and abandoned.[103] Moreover, nationalists hunted down labourers, who were often killed as collaborators and their houses targeted for burning.[104]

In the first half of 1948, food was particularly scarce in areas between Republican-controlled and Dutch-controlled territories.[105] Already at the end of the previous year, food availability had become threatened. In Cirebon, harbour workers stayed away, rice husking stations were destroyed, and even if 34 tonnes of rice did manage to reach Bandung, flooding around Cirebon and Krawang and the intimidation of farmers severely diminished the chances of a rice surplus.[106]

As a result, to gain access to the means to continue fighting, struggle organizations quickly turned to predation upon local communities. Near Garut, the Sabillilah built a well-hidden forest village and extorted money from forestry personnel. Local trade networks went dark as 'dessa cooperatives' were intimidated out of business. Where they continued to function, around Bandung or Indramayu, for example, it was the large European firms that were the major buyers, not the locals needing goods. When plantations could not sell their produce, massive lay-offs loomed.[107] Republican-appointed village heads pressured villagers to hand over rice, money and clothing, which they then passed on to Republican fighters. Thus affected, 'agitated labourers' threatened to strike, demanding more rice and protection.[108]

Displaced by violence and destitution, people fled en masse from rural villages and hamlets into the urban 'periphery' in search of shelter, sustenance and safety.[109] Slowly, they ended up in evacuation centres. In November 1948, Pasundan representatives exhorted villagers to evacuate areas that 'now and in the future are economically of little importance'. Some 5,000 souls had to abandon 23 hamlets in the subdistricts of Majalengka and in the Sumedang Regency.[110] Many Chinese became displaced as well, as they had been in the past.[111] In June 1948, 721 Chinese had fled to evacuation camps. Evacuation Centre Malabarlaan 12 in Bandung received 269 evacuees; and an additional 105 Europeans and 27 Indonesians – KNIL families from Central Java – arrived on 1 June. In the first half of 1948, the Malabarlaan centre

Image 3. In Sukabumi in 1947, nationalist forces set fire to a rubber factory before Dutch troops arrived. A logical consequence of asymmetrical warfare is that retreating troops will deny their enemies the access to resources those enemies may use to restart local economies, distribute food, or, more generally speaking, protect the local population. At the same time, however, such measures caused great suffering among local communities. *Source: Nationaal Archief, Dienst voor Legercontacten.*

held 1,471 people, among them 344 Europeans. Flare-ups in fighting around Tasikmalaya and Garut caused another influx of displaced persons.[112]

The convergence of people in evacuation camps caused further shortages in food, clothing and medicine; a situation that was further exacerbated by the 'disruption of the health services'. Soon, the displaced were inflicted with 'the trio of "hunger oedema, malaria and scabies"'. In West Bandung, 178 people received treatment for 'food diseases' and 793 for scabies, while many more received medication to combat other maladies. Between January and March 1948, medical personnel detected 7,087 new cases of malaria.[113] By the second quarter of that year, people in the north-eastern parts of Cianjur Regency were 'completely undermined by malnourishment and malaria' and could only be treated and fed under Dutch military protection. A malaria epidemic spread over parts of Sukabumi Regency, too, threatening the city itself.[114] Wherever they landed, refugees were given rice, porridge or green beans as well as clothing. Meanwhile, 'Emergency areas' kept requesting rice for the malaria sufferers unable to work. In the first six months of 1948, more than a million portions of food were prepared for the destitute around Bandung.[115] All the while, the TNI continued to restrict food circulation: selling food 'which [benefits] the Netherl. soldiers and the Government' was punishable by death.[116]

A year later, people were still on the move. Tens of thousands of Sundanese streamed into West Java from Republican-controlled areas, for instance.[117] By April 1949, West Java's political landscape had splintered into three spheres of influence, a situation that had been formally agreed upon by Republican, Dutch and United Nations officials.[118] From across porous borders, the Dutch and Sundanese authorities warily eyed those representing the Republic or the NII. Incursions continued to take lives. Administrative posts reactivated by the Dutch one day were often abandoned the next when Darul Islam attacks made areas around those posts 'ungovernable'. The 'lack of safety[,] untilled sawahs, insufficient food, insufficient immunity, malaria, exhaustion' continued to result in people vacating areas to escape predation.[119]

Solidarity between the army and citizens: The TNI consolidates, 1949

While the plight of the people largely remained the same, 1949 brought radical changes for the Republic and the Dutch as well as the Darul Islam. The Roem-van Roijen Agreement of May 1949 compelled the Netherlands to finally recognize officially that Indonesian independence was real. The Dutch agreed to depart the archipelago by December 1949, thinking the RIS would still remain part of the Kingdom of the Netherlands. In many offices, army billets and guerrilla cells, this knowledge caused consternation. With West Java still divided, the TNI, DI and the Dutch all felt that, at the very minimum, they needed to consolidate their positions to the detriment of the others.

For the Dutch, their looming departure spurred them on to try to create a security situation that would allow the Pasundan State to hang on. As Dutch soldiers had to yield territory around Tasikmalaya, Ciamis, Garut and Sumedang ahead of their repatriation to the Netherlands, fresh troops were needed to defend the fledgling state.[120] Military authorities therefore undertook to raise a new KNIL battalion specifically for West Java. Moreover, they drew up plans for incorporating TNI troops into the federal RIS army and discussed finding an additional 18,000 federal recruits.[121] The Pasundan State, however, drifted closer and closer to the Republic in the course of 1949. Its officials understood that with the Dutch gone as its major guarantor, the Republic (within the RIS) would be the Pasundan's next best bet, also in terms of combating the Negara Islam Indonesia, which continued to disrupt Pasundan governance.[122]

As the Dutch and the Republicans shared a common enemy, namely the Darul Islam, the Dutch and Republican commands decided to start working together, a process facilitated by the fact that Dutch authorities needed to accelerate the build-up of the RIS Army. The general impetus behind this cooperation was the so-called s' Jacob Plan. Named after its initiator, Dutch diplomat H.L. s' Jacob, the plan mapped out the withdrawal of Dutch forces to specific regions, particularly in Central Java, while also allocating (shared) patrol areas to TNI and Dutch troops. Although the plan offended Republican guerrilla commanders in East Java who feared it would deprive them of territory, Dutch and Republican representatives accepted the plan, the former after stating that TNI forces would not evacuate 'federal areas'.[123] Subsequently, the Dutch government paid the TNI across Java and Sumatra the sum of 667,500 guilders per diem (almost 3.2 million euros today) for food and clothing. Part of this money flowed to the 40,000 troops that the High Command had stationed in West Java, provided they would finally adhere to the cease-fire agreement that was supposedly in effect.[124]

This deal was not an unmitigated success for the TNI in West Java. While high-level negotiations about cooperation took place, the Negara Pasundan convinced some Sundanese elements of the Republican Siliwangi Division to break away and start engaging DI troops in a bid to protect the Pasundan. At one level, this deal hinged on familial ties between Siliwangi Commander Achmad and Pasundan's head of state. At another, it was based on the longstanding disillusionment within elements of the division and the general feeling that they had been neglected and insufficiently recognized by the Republican government.[125] Pasundan parliamentarians were shocked to learn, however, that the co-opted Siliwangi units proved unable to dislodge DI troops.[126]

General Nasution's Siliwangi troops, meanwhile, did claim to have successfully 'carried out a purge' in May 1949 in Cirebon and the Parahyangan area against DI troops, even if in Central Java the Republican police and civil servants still suffered greatly from DI activity.[127] Java's army headquarters was in great spirits by September. Over the preceding three months, the Republican High Command had observed that their Dutch opponents had been rather inactive. Dutch documents captured by the TNI showed a drop in Dutch morale, both in political and military circles. Apparently, the military experienced trouble replacing the tens of thousands of troops setting sail to the Netherlands. While the Dutch had thus overreached, the Indonesian struggle had not yet tapped its full potential.[128]

As 1949 drew to a close, and with Dutch troops and administrators receding – as per the s' Jacob Plan – the way lay open for a final Republican advance. Now was the time, in Siliwangi discourse, for the Republic to transform itself into a 'civilian force' as opposed to its earlier ruthless form that would do everything to maintain independence.[129] Mere days before the Dutch officially recognized Indonesia as independent, the Republican 'City Army Command' (Komando Ketentaraan Kota) in Garut announced that '[s]eeing the surrender of Sovereignty[,] it should be understood by all people from all walks of life[,] that the power of the state and government has shifted from the hands of the Dutch' into Republican hands. 'This means that all responsibility for public security and peace is transferred to the government of our own nation.' As the TNI had entered the city 'to prepare for the maintenance of security and order', the City Command said, people must 'help by heeding this call'.[130] The Republican Regent, meanwhile, wrote to the manager of the Garut's Odeon Cinema. Surely, in the spirit of 'solidarity between the Army and Citizens', the TNI troops could catch a free show every Friday, he asked.[131] Wherever troops entered cities, their commanders exhorted them to act as disciplined representatives of an independent nation. Indonesians and foreign onlookers alike could not be disappointed: '[a] ssociation with the people must be friendly'.[132]

Behind such facades lay a more sinister purpose. Those in West Java who had worked with the Dutch and the Pasundan or had associated with the Darul Islam greeted the emergence of the Republic with trepidation. Desertion rates among security personnel under the employ of the Dutch rose dramatically. Lists circulated with the names of those who had worked with the Dutch intelligence services. Republicans jotted down the names of Darul Islam adherents, too. To counter reprisals, police and civil servants scrambled to offer their services to the Republic after Dutch civil and military authorities had vacated specific areas.[133] Across Java, Indonesian civil servants who had worked with the colonial administration were threatened with lay-offs and destitution – or worse, violence.[134]

For city dwellers, plantation workers and villagers, the period leading up to the final transfer of power remained fraught with danger. Even though the Republic's West Java Army Command succeeded in proscribing such avowedly revolutionary organizations as the Sharpened Spear Division (Divisi Bambu Runcing), the Citarum Brigade, the Indonesian People's Army (Tentara Rakyat Indonesia, TRI) and the Bambu Runcing-affiliated Rebellion Unit 88 (Satuan Pemberontakan 88, SP88) within a year, they were still operating at the end of 1949.[135] Violence was everywhere. Darul Islam and TNI forces continued to clash; Dutch troops still raided villages. KNIL and TNI units together attacked Bambu Runcing fighters who flew the Darul Islam flag.[136] Many, like Saad Doging, Samian or Ilyas were robbed of clothing, jewellery and cash in Pasir Angin; Masudin, an inhabitant of Citeko, was kidnapped by some 40 uniformed and armed men; 'His fate is unknown'. In August 1949, the independence fighters Haji Samsu and Pa Awang decided that several hamlets around Leuwiliang, Bogor had to donate large quantities of rice to struggle organizations that were still operating. At the end of September, forestry manager Saleh disappeared, taken by a group presumably belonging to the feared Bambu Runcing. At the same time, in Sukabumi, the notorious Hizbullah leader Palar Sofyan escaped TNI 'supervision', bringing along with him 150 followers. In all probability, they set out to link up once again with like-minded 'TNI apostates'.[137]

The official end of the revolutionary war in December 1949 brought very little change to the situation for many people across the archipelago. Besides continuing violence, local economies needed rebuilding, yet Indonesia's textile industry, for example, which was so important to West Java, was wracked by massive losses and strikes.[138] Scores of people remained displaced. In 1950, 'hundreds of thousands of refugees' continued to roam across West Java.[139] Chinese evacuees were afraid to return to the Indonesian communities that had thrown them out.[140] The RIS government's relief fund – worth six million Dutch guilders – could not begin to cover the cost needed to take care of these displaced persons. The money, moreover, could not be spent effectively, social affairs minister Kosasih admitted, as long as 'in certain places safety and order could not be guaranteed'. Thousands of refugees arrived in Bogor daily, bereft of food and clothing, as they had fled from Tasikmalaya, Ciamis or Sumedang where the Darul Islam and TNI continued to fight.[141]

With no regular life to turn to and weapons everywhere, behaviours associated with revolutionary worlds were hard to unlearn. In this context, some TNI veterans switched their allegiance to the Darul Islam.[142] Indonesian plantation managers and European planters were still fair game.[143] During

1949, 1950 and beyond, newspapers continually reported armed robberies perpetrated by apparently both experienced groups and ordinary farmers.[144] Apart from individuals, entire villages were sometimes affected. In one hamlet near Sumedang, 20 people were killed and 1,000 houses razed during a cattle raid. Between July and August 1951, District Indramayu near Cirebon was gripped by a spate of six murders and 11 kidnappings of Islamic religious leaders.[145]

More than a year earlier, in the darkness of their own impending defeat, Dutch commentators had already claimed that any and all 'authority was missing' in Indonesia and that civil war was imminent. The Republic's focus lay with the creation of a unitary state rather than ensuring the welfare of their citizens, they grumbled.[146] Regardless of the veracity of this view, it was true that the Republic sought to rule over a unitary state. When Captain Raymond Westerling, known for his murderously violent tactics with the Special Forces Corps during the war of independence, mounted a short-lived coup around Bandung and Bogor meant to save the Pasundan State, the Republic – or rather the RIS – stepped in to take over authority. By February 1950, the Negara Pasundan had virtually ceased to exist.

Conclusion

A central thrust of this chapter has been to try and illuminate the human experiences and activities of individuals and communities in West Java during the Indonesian war against Dutch re-occupation. It has argued that to understand the key dynamics of the revolutionary period in West Java, these experiences – and not just big events or big men – should be the main focus of the analysis. The latter have often dominated both Dutch and Indonesian historiographies, pushing away ordinary people's experiences in favour of ideologically laden memories and histories. First and foremost, the chapter has brought out of the shadows the activities of ordinary Sundanese, Chinese and other Indonesian people in West Java. In their search for safety, food and protection, and in order to realize specific political-ideological outcomes, they fled, became displaced, were subjected to violence, or supported various powerbrokers.

These behaviours have been illuminated by teasing out the internal logic that animated revolutionary and counter-revolutionary warfare. To begin with, this chapter has highlighted the sheer complexity that dominated life in West Java, in particular between 1948 and 1950. No less than three parties vied for authority there. Such entanglements were compounded by the fact that shifts in supra-regional power relations reverberated among the local communities. The Renville Agreement signed in January 1948 resulted in people who tacitly supported the Pasundan having to face forces that coerced them into joining a TNI-dominated network of village militias, for instance. When the TNI heeded the call to evacuate West Java, the same people were suddenly forced to pay Darul Islam taxes or perish.

For all would-be authorities, violence became a means to browbeat the people into cooperation, whereupon the aggressors could claim authority and legitimacy. Faced with the threat or application of force, locals were perennially expressing their support for one authority or the other. This particular dynamic continued well after Republican troops and administrators officially took over West Java's cities in December 1949. The reason was that Western Java's communities continued to be plagued by war, famine and displacement as the consequence of the ongoing battles between the Darul Islam and the TNI, coupled with ordinary criminality.

Crucially, then, this chapter has shown how the logic of violence was heedless of any ideological leanings of their own that the communities may have had. In that sense, all parties were responsible for blurring the lines between revolutionary and counter-revolutionary warfare. Certainly, communities fleeing from the violent actions of the Darul Islam, the TNI and the Dutch into camps where disease, hunger and overall destitution waited could not tell the difference. Studies that focus on violence as a mere force, together with those that concentrate solely on Dutch or Republican violence, risk ignoring the consequences of that violence for its victims and their reactions to that violence. In other words, such studies tell only half the story.

13.

Fighting over Depok

From colonial privilege to Indonesian citizenship, 1942-1949

Tri Wahyuning M. Irsyam

Introduction

The Depok private estate – known as *particuliere landerij* – is situated between Jakarta and Bogor. These two cities, approximately 50 km apart, accommodated the two official residences and offices of the colonial governor general, and today still accommodate those of the president of the Republic of Indonesia. During the Dutch colonial period, Depok was a sub-district (*onderdistrict*) – part of the Parung District – with 32 villages and eight estates (*landerijen*). The centre of government during the colonial period is thought to have been located around Old Depok Station.[1] Since 1999, De-

The Cornelis Chastelein Monument in Depok (circa. 1930). Chastelein (1657-1714) was a Dutch slave holder and land owner in Depok. *Source: University Library Leiden, Southeast Asian and Carribean collections (KITLV).*

pok has been a city-level administrative government unit in the province of West Java.

For a long a time, the area had been the home of distinctive groups of people, known by various names including the Dutch of Depok (*Belanda Depok*), free-men of Depok (*Mardijkers van Depok*), Old Depok (*Depok Lama*) or simply Depok folk (*Depokkers*) or Real Citizens of Depok (*Orang Depok Asli*). According to data from 1975, around 2,500 to 3,000 Real Citizens of Depok (Orang Depok Asli) lived in Pancoran Mas village, particularly in Rukun Kampung II.[2]

The area witnessed extreme violence between 1945 and 1949 during the national revolution due to the fact that its various communities were closely associated with Dutch colonial rule. Among them were the Depok Christian Congregation (*Djamaat Mesehi Depok*), the Europeans, and the Eurasian community. The latter was an ethnically mixed group also often referred to as Indisch, Indo-European, Indo or even Mestizo.

The historiography of this episode of extreme violence has been somewhat fraught. Dutch historiography depicts the Depok communities as victims of the so-called *bersiap* period, which was a time of political uncertainty, social panic and chaos.[3] In the standard Dutch perspective, the events are framed in a lopsided narrative of 'civilians killed in a horrific manner... almost none managed to escape...except for those who were evacuated by the British and Dutch military operation'.[4] Indonesian researchers, too, have described the murder, robbery, looting, arrest and various other crimes allegedly committed by the indigenous Indonesians (or bumiputra) who were consumed by nationalist radicalism.[5] In reality, however, violence was committed by both sides. Rémy Limpach has recently concluded that 'violence during the Bersiap period was not unilaterally exerted. The [colonial army] KNIL troops sporadically butchered Indonesians who were accused of being involved in the killings'.[6]

It is rare to find studies that seek to understand the complexity of the problems that occurred and that place them in the context of the end of Dutch colonial rule, the Japanese capitulation and the Dutch attempt to rebuild their colonial power. The present chapter seeks to reconstruct the Depok tragedy by placing it in its proper historical context. These events did not occur immediately after the Indonesian people proclaimed their independence but rather a couple of months after, in October 1945. There are, however, very few scholars who chronologically link the tragedy that occurred in Depok with the landing of the British troops as part of the Allied forces, accompanied by Dutch administrators and soldiers who were immediately suspected by Indonesians of re-establishing colonial rule. One

Dutch historian even erroneously claimed that 'the attacks [on civilians] began before Dutch troops landed on the island [Java]'.[7] It is now clear that Dutch elements were present in Jakarta during the incident and that they 'triggered the escalation of violence especially due to their unauthorized acts, without discipline, and full of provocation'.[8]

Privileged slaves on the outskirts of Jakarta

At the time of the attacks, the Djamaat Mesehi Depok was one of the main groups living in the Depok area. Their existence can be traced back to the end of the seventeenth century when Depok was first established as a *particuliere landerij*, as part of a system of land tenure that was inseparable from the long history of Dutch colonization in the archipelago. Most Depok residents were non-Europeans. According to the 1867 census, out of an estimated 1,492 residents of Depok, only eight were Europeans while 1,463 were indigenes known as bumiputra, and the remainder were ethnic Chinese.[9] The Djamaat Mesehi Depok's centuries-long loyalty to the Dutch amplified their differences with other communities, particularly those (non-Christian) bumiputra who lived within and beyond Depok, and therefore kept them socially separate.

Long before it was transformed into a private estate, Depok had been the original territory of indigenous groups of Malay-Betawi lineage later known as the Orang Kampung. Their identity had been shaped by a long process of migration of numerous ethnic groups to Batavia/Jakarta and its surrounding areas. These Orang Kampung shared political and religious identities as well as socio-cultural markers that were different from the Djamaat Mesehi Depok group.[10]

The Djamaat Mesehi Depok began as a group of people that were deliberately settled there by a rich Dutchman named Cornelis Chastelein (1657-1714). He controlled a vast area of land in Depok and its surroundings from purchases made between 1696 and 1712.[11] As the sole rightful owner of the Depok *particuliere landerij* and a former employee of the Dutch East India Company (Vereenigde Oostindische Compagnie, or VOC), Chastelein owned slaves who worked on his plantation belt. They came from various places within the Indonesian archipelago, especially Bali, Sulawesi and Nusa Tenggara, as well as from elsewhere in Asia, particularly South Asia. Several months prior to his death in June 1714, Chastelein wrote a will allowing for the release of his slaves. He also bequeathed the land he controlled with communal ownership rights to those who were willing to embrace Christianity. Those who did not convert were excluded. The area he granted to his former slaves was located in the sub-district known at the end of the twentieth century as Pancoran Mas. This is somewhat smaller than today's Depok city.

The former slaves later became the forefathers of the community widely known as the Belanda Depok by the communities surrounding it. Chastelein gave his slaves names based on their place of origin, such as Jarong van Bali, Louys van Makasar, or Lambert van Bali. Young slaves were socialized in the Western and Christian traditions of life. But not all were willing to become Christians, and these people were thought to have mingled with the bumiputra, who lived in the private estate, after Chastelein's death. Since being released from slavery, the Belanda Depok were protected by legal and social boundaries set up by the Dutch colonial state. Their economic privileges separated them from other communities.[12] In the 1930 census, they were given equal ethnic status within the bumiputra category, alongside the Javanese, the Bataknese, the Malays and so on.

In the centuries that followed, the Depok *particuliere landerij* grew into a special residence on the outskirts of Jakarta, mostly preferred by the Indisch community, full-blooded Europeans, the Chinese and Christian bumiputra communities. The latter group was made up of those who worked for the colonial government, either in civil offices or the military. This was the makeup of the people of Depok at the time of Indonesia's declaration of independence.

Passed on from generation to generation as the only spiritual guidance, Christianity made the Djamaat Mesehi Depok the first Christian indigenous group to ever live in the interior of Batavia and its Environs (Ommelanden).[13] Depok was often called the Christian municipality of Depok *(Christengemeente te Depok)*. To pay homage to Chastelein, the Djamaat Mesehi Depok built a prominent monument on the 200th anniversary of his death in 1914.[14] Beginning as a private estate, Depok became an autonomous municipality (*gemeente*) in the second half of the nineteenth century. It had an elected president whose responsibilities included the distribution of crops, housing and welfare for widows.[15] The communal owners, heirs of the freed slaves, became *primus inter pares*, the main societal group that owned and controlled land in Depok. As in other private estates within the colonial agrarian structure, they enjoyed absolute property rights (*eigendom verponding*).[16] They were also entitled to determine the spatial layout that they wished to control, resulting in interconnected establishments such as churches, schools, cemeteries, a housing complex and other public facilities.[17] The control of land rights made the Djamaat Mesehi Depok more economically dominant than the Muslim bumiputra and the former slaves who had refused to convert to Christianity.

This eventually turned the relationship between the Djamaat Mesehi Depok and the latter groups into one of master and servant, as many of the latter worked at the plantation belts owned by members of the Djamaat Mesehi Depok or in their households.[18] Some scholars even argue that bumiputra villages were designed in such a way as to provide labour for the plantation belts and homes of the Djamaat Mesehi Depok.[19]

Social memories on both sides are of fruitful relationships. Bumiputra could occupy strategic positions in the local government, such as foreman, skipper and even police chief. The latter occupation was responsible for the security of all of the Depok private estate.[20] However, religious differences and the colonial social status gap kept the Djamaat Mesehi Depok socially distant from the bumiputra. Where other ethnic groups chose to 'become Betawi' in order to win the right to live in the interior of Jakarta – and Islam is the 'official' Betawi religion – the Djamaat Mesehi Depok never did so. Consequently, to a certain extent, due to their privileges, the majority of the Djamaat Mesehi Depok were more easily integrated with the European community and the Indisch group, although formally they shared traits with the bumiputra. In terms of marriage, the Djamaat Mesehi Depok enjoined its members to marry within its own group. Transgressing endogamous restrictions – by marrying Orang Kampung, for example – was considered a status-reducing act.[21] While the majority of the bumiputra population was on the lowest rung of colonial social stratification, the position of the Djamaat Mesehi Depok was superior. Discrimination, segregation and impoverishment of the bumiputra were structural and systemic under the Dutch colonial rule. This exacerbated the inequality, especially when patronage relations were exercised without sincerity. A split grew between the South Group (Kelompok Wetan) and the West Group (Kelompok Kulon).[22] The Kelompok Wetan, living near the central station and very urban, distanced themselves even further from the Orang Kampung while maintaining a closer relationship with the European, Indisch and other communities that had strong affinities with the Dutch colonial government. The close interaction made it difficult later to clearly distinguish the Djamaat Mesehi Depok, who were bumiputra, from the Indisch. This can be seen in newspaper reports about the incident of October 1945, which stated that the main victims of the incident were Indo-Europeans.[23] Meanwhile, the Kelompok Kulon, who lived around the plantation belts and remained rural, continued to maintain close relations with the Orang Kampung, even after Japan took over from the Dutch.[24]

The Japanese occupation and the demise of colonial privileges

W.F. Wertheim once stated that, under the Japanese, white skin, Christianity and the Dutch language were the new markers of pariah groups.[25] This was in line with the policy of the Emperor of Japan issued on 20 November 1941, which stressed the implementation of Asian values as the new dominant standard and which required that all Western colonial traces be obliterated or replaced by a new system and structure of life.[26] In an attempt to seek the support of the bumiputra, who were mostly Muslims, the Japanese rulers allowed Islamic leaders without a Western education to take part in public administration.[27]

Japanese authorities garnered the support of bumiputra youth by offering them defence and security training, equipping them with communication and policing resources as well as organizing semi-military drills in several security branches such as the Fatherland Defence Corps (Pembela Tanah Air, PETA), the Heiho, the Seinendan and the Keibodan. They encouraged Indonesian elites to make preparations for an independent nation-state. It was during the period of Japanese rule that the ideal of independence matured; it was even felt at the grassroots level.[28] By the time Japanese rule ended, the bumiputra had developed the skills, networks and attitudes that allowed them to confront the European and Indisch communities and other groups that had been privileged by Dutch colonialism. When Abdul Kadir, an officer in the Netherlands Indies Civil Administration (NICA), interviewed President Sukarno immediately after Allied troops landed in Jakarta in September 1945, Sukarno said that the Indonesian people felt more united during the three-and-a-half years under Japanese rule than during the three-and-a-half centuries under Dutch colonial rule.[29]

By contrast, communities that had been privileged during the Dutch colonial period felt threatened under the Japanese colonial rule. In Java alone, there were no fewer than 200,000 Indisch people living under Japanese colonization.[30] Most Christian bumiputra and members of the Indisch communities were registered as soldiers of the Royal Netherlands East Indies Army (Koninklijk Nederlands-Indisch Leger, or KNIL). These were briefly detained when the Japanese landed, then kept under surveillance.[31] In general, the Japanese treated the Dutch and other Europeans differently from the Indisch and Chinese. While the full-blooded Europeans were strictly isolated in Japanese prison camps, most of the Indisch community – together with the Djamaat Mesehi Depok – enjoyed the same conditions as the bumiputra.[32] The Japanese colonial government did try to pit the Indisch community against full-blooded Europeans. Upon detention, members of the Indisch community, whether civilian or former military, were placed in separate sections of the camp from the Europeans, in order to create tension between the two.[33] The Chinese, meanwhile, who had previously been discriminated by the Dutch and had been victims of the chaos during the regime change, now received protection from the Japanese military. Some, however, were also detained and isolated in internment camps.[34]

Situated between Jakarta and Bogor, the fate of Depok was greatly dependent on developments in the two cities. When the Japanese invaded the archipelago, the Dutch military carried out a scorched earth policy in Jakarta. This also affected public services such as electricity supply in Depok.[35] As early as 20 March 1942, Japanese military authorities ordered the arrest and detention of all Dutch citizens. Later in the same year, on 30 November, all other Europeans, including children and women, were rounded up and sent to imprisonment camps.[36] The Japanese built two temporary transit camps around Depok for European civilian detainees.[37] One of the detainees was the Reverend A.A. van Daalen, the church leader in Depok, who died during imprisonment.[38] Although this had a deep impact on the Djamaat Mesehi Depok, in general they were not affected much by the Japanese authorities in the area. Infrastructures for Christian worship were not touched, except that seminary activities were prohibited after the Europeans priests and administrators were arrested. Church services and funerals and the like were still allowed to take place.

Identity and authority contestations at the beginning of Indonesian independence

Life in Depok grew more perilous when Indonesian independence was proclaimed on 17 August 1945. The one and a half months after the Japanese surrender were tense for Depok as revolutionary activity broke out in many places throughout the country. Despite the smell of revolution in the air, hopes grew among those who were once privileged by the Dutch, including the community groups in Depok, that Dutch colonial power would be restored. The new Indonesian government was unable to control the situation, including in Jakarta and its surroundings. The only legitimate means it had of enforcing security and order – through the People's Security Agency (Badan Keamanan Rakyat, BKR) – was only truly effective at the centre of power. As a result, various interest groups began acting on their own initiative, which made the situation even more precarious. This was further exacerbated by the arrival of the Allied forces, who were accompanied by Dutch soldiers and civil administrators in many parts of the country.

The Allied forces arriving in late September and early October 1945 were not able to restore order in Jakarta and surrounding areas, which were plagued by uncertainties on a number of different dimensions.[39] One decision was to have dire repercussions: the Allied forces released former KNIL soldiers from Japanese prison camps in and around Jakarta and allowed them to re-organize. Together with Dutch soldiers in Allied uniforms, KNIL troops soon became involved in stirring up armed conflicts with Indonesian supporters. Jakarta became a dangerous place, both for criminals and for supporters of the Republic. In late September and early October 1945, Republican supporters and other groups started to leave Jakarta, a number of them ending up in Depok. On 4 January 1946, following an assassination attempt on Prime Minister Sutan Sjahrir by armed supporters of the Dutch government, the central government of the Republic relocated from Jakarta to Yogyakarta.

Prior to the arrival of the Allied forces in Jakarta, there had been very few violent exchanges between the bumiputra on the one hand and the Europeans, the Indisch communities and Christian groups on the other. Various personal accounts reveal that Europeans were able to go to the marketplace undisturbed during the early weeks after Indonesian independence had been proclaimed. This began to change around mid-September and quickly worsened from the end of that month as Allied and Dutch forces increased their presence.[40] It was at that time that the incident known as *gedoran Depok* or *rampokan Depok* broke out. *Gedor* means to batter down a door; *rampok* means robbery.

Having benefited from Dutch colonialism, the Djamaat Mesehi Depok had rejoiced in the defeat of Japan, the arrival of the Allied forces, and the return of the Dutch civil servants and KNIL troops. While most bumiputra celebrated after 17 August with the ubiquitous red-and-white symbols of the Republic, the Djamaat Mesehi Depok kept aloof from such enthusiasm. In a personal interview with a descendant of the Djamaat Mesehi Depok, the author was told that Depok residents never heard the order to raise the red-and-white flag because they did not even know that Indonesia had become independent: the Dutch-language Radio Hilversum broadcast they listened to every day had not reported it.[41] In the collective memory of the Djamaat Mesehi Depok, they had gained independence from the Dutch long before the Indonesian people proclaimed theirs in August 1945. They understood the period after Japan's capitulation simply as a power vacuum and the absence of law and order.[42] When faced with the enthusiastic response of the Orang Kampung and other bumiputra groups to the proclamation of independence, therefore, members of the Djamaat Mesehi Depok became uneasy.

In contrast to the terrible economic hardship endured by the majority of the bumiputra population towards the end of the Pacific war, members of the Djamaat Mesehi Depok remained well off despite several years of tight controls by the Japanese government. One member recalled that 'In Depok, we lived a lavish life. We had rice fields and large gardens. Once harvested, the produce could feed us for two years. Imagine the abundance. We would normally give plentifully to our relatives, and employees. We lived a good life, luxuriously.'[43] Such social inequality, together with the hesitation and political apathy shown by the Djamaat Mesehi Depok, engendered much resentment among Republicans.

At the end of the first week of October 1945, armed Republican groups barricaded roads connecting Jakarta and Depok. This created a tense situation in the Depok *particuliere landerij*. The Indonesian people's heightened fighting spirit was directed against the threat of Dutch recolonization. Religious voices calling for war against the Dutch and their infidel allies were heard.[44] This was followed by a trade boycott on 7 October 1945 on all Europeans and community groups suspected of being Dutch accomplices. Armed groups even briefly occupied Depok railway station in order to deter the mobility of suspicious individuals. The next day, however, life in the private estate returned to normal.

The situation became tense again on 9 October, when several armed groups carrying red-and-white symbols marched on Depok. Five houses owned by members of the Djamaat Mesehi Depok were looted and the owners forced to leave. Local security forces were unable to stop the havoc. Dutch reports, which were later incorporated into the Dutch historiography of this period, interpreted this condition as an act of negligence by Republican police.[45] Later in the afternoon, after a police investigation, the owners returned home, only to find that their belongings had gone missing or been thrown away.[46] On the following day, the same armed groups looted food stores in the same location.

No victims of violence had been reported. That changed drastically on the morning of 11 October. Shortly after being looted, the houses were burned down. For several days, members of the Djamaat Mesehi Depok, the Europeans, the Indisch community, the Chinese and the Christian bumiputra suffered mass violence. This looting and a series of acts of violence with varying intensities lasted for several days in Depok *particuliere landerij*. This marked the beginning of the terror that came to be known as the *gedoran Depok*.[47]

The havoc was caused by armed groups coming from outside Depok, who suspected that the Djamaat Mesehi Depok, the European residents and other community groups in Depok would be used to restore Dutch colonial rule.[48] Although the looting and violence were carried out collectively, they were not structurally coordinated. They were based on the initiative of individuals or groups. This was evident in the conflicting opinions and actions among the armed groups once they had entered Depok private estate. Dutch intelligence reports and foreign correspondents at the time, however, declared uniformly that the actions had been carried out in an organized manner by 'radical' or 'extremist' thugs, whom they labelled 'nationalists', 'militia' or 'Muslim groups'. In addition, such reports also used the term 'Sukarno's security police'.[49] One Dutch report explicitly espoused the opinion that '[t]he government and police of the Republic of Indonesia were behind these incidents'.[50] As evidence, it cited the organized arrival of the looters, who were transported by train, trucks and carts. The report further alleged that 'local government officials, BKR, and members of the Japanese-era militia *Pelopor* were actively involved by not actually performing their duty to restore public order and even by leading the attacks'.[51]

Supporters of the Republic had a different narrative. The siege of the Depok private estate, which ended in riots, was carried out by various groups with different interests, such as the militia, troops within the BKR, and other community groups. Most of the literature claims that more than 4,000 rioters marched into Depok on 11 October, while some mention fewer than 2,000 rioters.[52] They came from all directions and moved without one formal command.[53] The day before the incident, Margonda, the leader of the Youth Forces of the Republic of Indonesia (Angkatan Muda Republik Indonesia, AMRI) which was closely tied to the BKR, had tried to mediate between supporters of the Republic and the Djamaat Mesehi Depok in order to avoid attacks.[54] But it all came to no avail. The contestation over identity and authority within Depok as either Indonesian or Dutch grew stronger and became unbridgeable. Thousands of people with varying interests invaded Depok for several days.

Everything considered to represent Dutch colonial symbols became a target for destruction.[55] Starting on 11 October, looters invaded the homes of those identified as Dutch supporters. Most of the looting occurred during the day, but some victims reported break-ins at night. They took valuables and ransacked and disposed of other items they did not find valuable. The roads into the estate were strewn with people's belongings.[56]

The looters also arrested and harassed residents who did not have time to flee Depok or because they decided to fight back. Some of the latter ended up dead.[57] An official report by the Dutch and Allied forces stated that at least 10 people were killed between 11 and 13 October. Other mass media stated that a total of 15 people died, either killed directly or succumbing to serious injuries.[58] Other targets of vandalism were the Immanuel Church – which was the centre of religious activities for the Christian population of Depok – the seminary, the district (*gemeente*) office, the Chastelein memorial and various other public facilities including cemeteries.[59]

Depok residents fled, but not very far. Many hid in the forest and plantation belt. On the first night, the men took their families into hiding and returned home in the afternoon or evening, only to find their property had been looted.[60] Those who still could find food left in their homes had time to prepare a meal to bring to their hiding place. Others fled to safer places of refuge, such as camps inhabited by Europeans and Indisch groups. Some unlucky ones were caught in their hiding places or during their escape to Jakarta.[61]

Of those detained, the women and children were separated from the men. Around 1,050 women and children were isolated in two intact buildings in the *gemeente* building complex, without proper clothing or food supplies. No resting place was made available, which meant they were only able to sit or sleep side by side in a cramped room. Dutch narratives particularly highlighted the severity of these privations. Dutch official reports equated the rioters with 'apes' and 'Hitlerjugend'.[62] The women and children were forced to stay there for several days as if in prison camps. Despite the inadequate facilities, they were still given the opportunity to cook daily, making meals from limited amounts of rice or cassava. Some families were even able to eat meat and milk after a few days.[63]

The fact that the isolation building was surrounded by armed Republican groups such as Laskar 21, under the leadership of Tole Iskandar, reduced to some extent the chance of further harassment by rioters. (Laskar 21 were former Heiho and PETA members who helped establish Depok BKR in September 1945). It thus created a somewhat safer atmosphere for the women and children. In addition, some families and individuals even received good treatment and were spared harassment due to help from their Orang Kampung friends. Johanna Laurentia Laurens, a former teacher in the Depok private estate, was among the few people who escaped violence and captivity. The 80-year old was saved by her former students, who were personnel of the Indonesian Security Army. They took her to Bogor and then to Jakarta, where she finally found freedom.[64]

Among the groups that attacked Depok, there were indeed differences in what they wanted to do with the women and children. Some wanted to release the prisoners, while others opposed the idea for fear that the women and children would be attacked if they were not guarded. Still others saw the prisoners as hostages; some even went further and threatened to burn down the buildings where the women and children were isolated. The worst scenarios were not realized. Local elites, together with Laskar 21, held several negotiations with the rioters, persuading them not to burn down the buildings. An agreement was achieved that the women and children would not be murdered but instead guarded and given enough food.[65] The Indonesian Red Cross (Palang Merah Indonesia, PMI) also helped to ease the burdens of the prisoners.[66]

The men, however, received different treatment. The rioters caught some of them when they were with their women and children. Others who escaped to the forest or plantation belt were caught when they returned to their homes. They had thought it was safe to return home early in the morning of 12 October after the attack had taken place. But they did not anticipate that the attackers would raid again. It was then that they were rounded up and taken to Depok station, where they were transported to Bogor and subsequently to Paledang prison. There are different perspectives on the detention of the 300 men of the Djamaat Mesehi Depok in Paledang prison. One Republican report described the 300 men as prisoners; another said they were evacuating them to safety.[67] On their trip to the prison and during their imprisonment, many were treated violently.[68] Several men who had hidden in the forest before fleeing to Jakarta managed to establish contact with the Allied units that had just arrived in Pasar Minggu.

For several days, neither the Allied forces nor the Dutch responded to the riots at Depok private estate. They claimed they only learned about what was going on in Depok from a war correspondent who had spoken to a Depok refugee who managed to reach Jakarta on foot.[69] (In actual fact, the Dutch media had reported the rioting before that.[70]) On 17 October, the Allied authorities in Bogor deployed their Gurkha troops of the Queen Alexandra Rifles battalion to secure the Depok private estate. Dutch soldiers also came along.[71] They freed the women and children in the two buildings near the municipal office, rescued the men in hiding and took them to Jakarta and Bogor,[72] and even managed to catch some of the rioters. Skirmishes led to casualties on both sides, including some of the women and children. The Allied forces seized the weapons used by the attackers, most of which were empty. The weapons were allegedly obtained from a warehouse belonging to the Japanese army, but the ammunition boxes had been missing.

The men held captive in Paledang were also released by Allied forces in collaboration with the Dutch military, which was becoming increasingly active and openly demonstrating its authority in its former colony. Most of the prisoners were then reunited with their families, who had been kept in isolation in Depok. But instead of returning immediately to Depok, they stayed in temporary settlements provided by the Allied forces and the NICA outside Depok. Some members of the Djamaat Mesehi Depok and other affected groups chose to remain there for several years. Around 2,000 residents of Depok, including members of the Dutch and Indisch communities, ventured back to their homes in the Depok private estate but left again almost immediately after they found their houses destroyed. After considering the availability of security and means of transportation,[73] they then decided to settle in Allied-NICA occupied regions or to leave for cities such as Jakarta and Bogor. Some even went back into hiding in the forest around Depok.

Once again, the Djamaat Mesehi Depok had to live in uncertainty. The Depok private estate was contested territory: on one side were supporters of the new Republic, bolstered by a surge of national awareness and pride in their newly independent and sovereign nation, and on the other stood the Dutch, eager to reassert their authority in their former colony.

Fighting over Depok's strategic position

The presence of Allied forces together with Dutch troops in the Depok private estate in the second half of October 1945 did not necessarily make the region safe. The setback that Republican supporters had experienced did not diminish their desire to control the 'fruit gardens of West Java' (*Ooftuin van West-Java*) laid out by Chastelein.[74] Both the Republicans and the Dutch saw the private estate as a strategic space between Jakarta and Bogor. Both stationed their troops in strategic locations close to each other. One of these was Mampang, close to the Bogor-Depok-Jakarta railway line. Another was the road from Bogor to Jakarta through Cilebut, Bojonggede, Pondok Terong and Ratujaya. As military tensions increased, the Depok area became part of a frontline that ran through Ciputat, Parung, Sawangan and Cisalak out to Tangerang in the west and Bekasi in the east.

The Allied authorities – who were short of staff and under significant pressure – stationed KNIL troops in the southern area of Jakarta near Depok until the end of 1945. In early January 1946, these troops were replaced by Dutch soldiers who had been freshly trained in Singapore. The Dutch presence increased further when more Dutch troops were deployed directly from Europe to replace the British soldiers after March 1946. These young volunteers had left the Netherlands with the conviction that '[t]hey could not let go of their responsibility towards the Indonesian people, and [that] it is their duty to help the country grow'.[75] In Jakarta and Bogor, this replacement process was carried out in phases from May 1946, with the British handing over all their powers in Indonesia to the Dutch by October 1946. The Dutch troops had never coordinated with Allied authorities when carrying out military operations. All this merely increased Indonesian suspicions of Dutch intentions.

The *gedoran* incident had, meanwhile, made it clear to the Republicans that not all armed groups around them had the same goals and interests. Some were genuinely criminal gangs who were participating in military operations for their own purposes. Republican collective memories today are of groups who carried out armed operations 'like wild gangs', consisting of 'recidivists who were really good at fighting' and even had the heart to kill their own comrades.[76] This naturally created a huge dilemma for the official Indonesian army and for true supporters of the Republic because such gangs often used the same Indonesian symbols. A.H. Nasution, Chief of Staff of the People's Security Army (Tentara Keamanan Rakyat, TKR, which was the new name of the BKR), visited Depok in November 1945, accompanied by Major Effendi, in order to investigate and find a solution. However, a lack of resources meant that control of the deviant armed groups remained largely ineffective.

The increasing Allied and Dutch presence in Depok led Republicans to begin intensive preparations to reclaim the area. On 16 November 1945, they launched a 'lightning attack' (*serangan kilat*) against Allied and Dutch troops in Depok. During fierce fighting that lasted approximately 24 hours,[77] Margonda and several of his comrades died. The Allied forces held onto the territory, but fighting continued. Under the command of Ibrahim Adjie, TKR troops (a precursor to the Tentara Nasional Indonesia, the Indonesian National Army) stationed in areas around Depok such as Citayam and Sawangan launched repeated attacks against Dutch positions. According to some information, Ibrahim Adjie's soldiers even managed to establish a headquarters in the Depok city centre.[78]

The Dutch became particularly concerned with their loss of control over the Jakarta-Bogor railway line through Depok. They ordered a fully equipped battalion to occupy the Depok private estate and its surrounding areas on 24 March 1946.[79] Although they managed to take control of the Depok train station, power plant, logistics and other strategic places, they continued to face resistance. Skirmishes took place in nearby Pasar Minggu and Lenteng Agung that same day.[80] Indonesian newspapers stated that three railway workers were killed and two injured. The chief at Depok station reportedly continued to carry out his duty of organizing traffic even though he was covered in blood from a head injury.[81] In the days that followed, Dutch forces continued their clearing operations around Depok, resulting in more casualties on both sides.[82] This led the Dutch to build a permanent army headquarters in Depok in an attempt to guard the railway and to protect residents of the Depok private estate. To limit the mobility of people entering Depok, in early October 1946 the Dutch declared the private estate closed to visitors, except for those working in the area.[83]

Incidents continued to erupt now and again. Less than a month after the Dutch occupied the Depok private estate in March 1946, a gun battle took place in the south of Depok between Dutch troops and about 100 Indonesian support forces. Newspapers reported that 30 Indonesian supporters died and 18 were injured, while the Dutch did not lose a single soldier. Prior to that, 300 Indonesian supporters clashed with Dutch troops around the bivouac near Depok, also resulting in casualties. Indonesian supporters continued to disrupt the Bogor-Jakarta railway line. At the end of April, railway workers were forced to stop a train at Depok station after a shootout between Indonesian supporters and the Dutch army resulted in six fatalities.[84]

Under these unstable conditions, the presence of Dutch troops had a significant impact on the life of Depok residents. Some members of the Djamaat Mesehi Depok, especially government officials, began returning to Depok in June 1946.[85] After that, more and more of them returned to their homes, together with Europeans, Indisch groups and Christian bumiputra. But most remained in refugee camps outside Depok. On 23 January 1947, refugees living in the Kedung Halang camp were told to return to their homes in Depok. They had to leave the camp by no later than 7 February 1947.[86] This forced most of the Djamaat Mesehi Depok to return home, although their preparations were limited and security conditions had not been fully restored to what they had been before October 1945. By mid-1947, daily life in the Depok private estate had begun to return to normal. Although not all residents had returned, the marketplace that had been abandoned for more than a year was trading again. Farmers began cultivating crops; most rice fields and gardens were planted.[87] Two Dutch-language schools and a Malay-language school were re-opened. A completely renovated church recommenced regular worship and other religious activities. More than 100 children attended Sunday school there. Residents returned to the tradition of celebrating Chastelein's festival on 18 June 1947.[88]

Nevertheless, the region remained restless. In mid-December 1947, Cilebut railway station, only two stations away from Depok, was attacked twice in one week by armed groups of 30 and 40 people.[89] This resulted in the deaths of 11 people and damage to the station building and houses in the vicinity. After this incident, the Dutch established a permanent army post at Cilebut station guarded by several fully armed soldiers.

Despite continued reports of armed incidents and robberies carried out by criminal gangs, daily life in the Depok private estate continued to improve throughout 1948 and into 1949. Together with Jatinegara, Tanjung Priok, Tangerang and Jakarta, the Depok private estate was now one of the most important military bases in the Jakarta region.[90] This led more Djamaat Mesehi Depok members to return home from exile. Some only had the courage to do this as late as 1949.[91] At the same time, newcomers were migrating to Depok in increasing numbers, so much so that in April 1949 the governor of Batavia and Ommelanden decreed Depok a closed city.[92] When the Dutch formally recognized Indonesian sovereignty with the establishment of the United States of Indonesia (Republik Indonesia Serikat, RIS) on 27 December 1949, the residents of the Depok private estate returned to their usual activities. The Djamaat Mesehi Depok and other Christian residents celebrated Christmas peacefully again, even though it did not feel the same as the last Christmas celebration during the Dutch colonial period in December 1941. The regime change in the mid-twentieth century that separated the Djamaat Mesehi Depok from its main patron had structurally altered the position of the community, which had been founded by Chastelein more than 200 years earlier.

Conclusion

The history of the Depok *particuliere landerij* and the Djamaat Mesehi Depok from 1942 to 1949 reflects the long history of Dutch imperialism and colonialism in the Indonesian archipelago. On the one hand, Cornelis Chastelein can be commended for having abolished slavery in Depok even when it was still upheld elsewhere in the archipelago and beyond. He thereby did his part to foster political equality in the midst of an exploitative, discriminatory and authoritarian colonial system. The Djamaat Mesehi Depok existed as a distinct community formed out of diversity, united by the same faith, and living together in harmony and privilege. On the other hand, Chastelein left a legacy that became a ticking time bomb, as the Djamaat Mesehi Depok emerged with an identity that set them apart from the communities that surrounded it. This easily led to alienation when the tide of revolutionary change excluded everything that was associated with Dutch colonialism. The social ties they had built could not prevent the change from happening, especially when strong external political forces intervened. Depok became a contested strategic space, as a result of which its people suffered from uncertainty, harassment and violence.

From one perspective, the entire process that took place in the private estate from the beginning of the Japanese colonial rule to the transfer of sovereignty to the Republic of Indonesia can be seen as a tragedy. From another point of view, the same events can be interpreted as justice served and a liberation from foreign hegemony. October 1945 and the incidents that followed left a deep divide between the respective views of members of the Depok private estate and supporters of the Indonesian Republic. Each group produced its own historiographical memory in accordance with their own logic and egocentric emotions in making meaning and writing history. Each side could claim to be the victim and argue that they were not to blame. As a result, one-sided accounts are presented as historical truth.

The historical journey of the Djamaat Mesehi Depok arrived at a point where its members were faced with a new challenge, namely, to choose a new identity either as Indonesians or as Dutch. The challenge became even greater in 1952 when the formal status of the right of control and ownership of the Depok private estate was changed. This was the year that marked the end of the Depok private estate. A government regulation in 1958 ended the special agrarian rights that had been attached to the Djamaat Mesehi Depok for hundreds of years.[93]

The loss of this agrarian land had a huge impact on those Djamaat Mesehi Depok members who had chosen to pursue the agricultural way of life. Those who had chosen the professional path as Western bumiputra (*Bumiputra Barat*) found that their response to the new challenges presented by modernity had been the more useful one. After the regime change to the Republic of Indonesia, they were no longer tied to the Depok land. Some of them decided to start a new life outside Depok. They spread far beyond Java and even abroad, many of them moving to the Netherlands, although they never forgot their homeland in Indonesia. Other Djamaat Mesehi Depok members decided to settle in their ancestral land as Indonesians, with all the consequences thereof. The Depok private estate lives on in memory, both sweet and bitter. To remain in unity, those who stayed and those who left keep in mind a brief inscription on the front door of Depok Immanuel Church, excerpted from the Bible by Chastelein: 'That they may all be one.'

INDONESIAN REPUBLIC HAS BETRAYED CHINESE
REPOEBLIEK INDONESIA MENGHIANAT BANGSA CHUNGHUA
THE INDONESIAN REPUBLIC AND ITS NURSE
REPOEBLIEK INDONESIA DIGENDONG BABOENJA
法西斯保姆襁褓中的印尼共和國

14.

A successful transition

The Chinese in revolutionary Aceh, 1945-1949

Mawardi Umar

Introduction

After the Japanese defeat in the Pacific War and the Proclamation of Indonesian Independence, the Dutch reoccupied most of the territory of the Republic of Indonesia – but not Aceh. Most Indonesian Chinese were confused about which side to choose. They had suffered during the Japanese colonial period and looked forward to the arrival of the Allied forces.[1] The Chinese Nationalist Government led by the Kuomintang wavered over whether to give diplomatic recognition to Indonesia in the early days of independence. China still considered the Dutch, American and British powers – their Allies in World War II – to be protectors of their citizens outside China, and it

Protest march by Chinese in Medan, who demand safety and protection, 4 September 1947. Source: Collection Rups, NIMH.

also distrusted the Republic. The Kuomintang Government encouraged the Chinese in Indonesia to adopt a neutral attitude in the Indonesian-Dutch conflict. This in turn caused pro-Republican indigenous Indonesians (known as *bumiputra*) to distrust the Chinese community. Open conflicts broke out between Republican fighters and ethnic Chinese in several places reoccupied by the Dutch, such as Tangerang, Bagan Siapi-Api and Medan, resulting in casualties and property losses. Bai Chongxi, a special staff of the Chinese Nationalist Government who served as intermediary between the Republic and the Chinese community in Indonesia, wrote that the Indonesian government had inherited a suspicious attitude towards the Chinese from the Dutch, although it was trying hard to eradicate it.[2]

Aceh presents a somewhat different reality. The Dutch failed to reoccupy any part of the province except the port island of Sabang. Although Aceh did not experience any direct confrontation between Republicans and the Dutch, it did endure social upheaval: ulamas (Islamic religious leaders) of the All-Aceh Ulama Association (Persatuan Ulama Seluruh Aceh, PUSA) opposed those who had been close to Dutch colonial rule. Horizontal social tensions and communal violence such as the Cumbok War were the result, in which PUSA's youth wing, the People's Struggle Army (Tentara Perjuangan Rakyat, TPR) went on a killing spree.

The Chinese community in Aceh was certainly susceptible to anti-Dutch sentiment. This chapter therefore asks: Why did they not fall victim to this in Aceh during the revolution? What survival strategies did they deploy, and what were the implications of these strategies? Who was involved in them, and what roles did they have? What factors influenced the process?

Until now, there has been no comprehensive academic study discussing the ethnic Chinese in Aceh during the revolution. Most studies on the revolutionary period in Aceh have focused either on the role of Islamic groups in supporting the Republic of Indonesia in its struggle for independence or on the conflict between the ulama and the nobility *(uleebalang)*.[3] While there are numerous studies on the ethnic Chinese in Indonesia at a national level, few have examined Aceh. Daniel S. Lev wrote a biography of the human rights lawyer Yap Tiam Hien that briefly discusses his family background and childhood in Kutaraja, known today as Banda Aceh.[4] Another biography of Yap Tiam Hien printed by Kompas in pocket book size also only briefly mentions his childhood in Peunayong, Kutaraja.[5] Emilysus E. Ismail, in his study on the opening of Sabang as a free port in 1962, discusses the economic opportunities enjoyed by Chinese traders, who engaged in smuggling between Sabang and the mainland (*ekonomi jenggo* or *jengek*) to avoid levies at Ulee Lheue Kutaraja port.[6] Irchamni Sulaiman wrote about the interaction between Acehnese and Chinese businessmen in Banda Aceh City.[7] A. Rani Usman examined cross-cultural communication between the Chinese community and the bumiputra community in Banda Aceh city.[8] There is a linguistic study on the Chinese community in Aceh by Wildan et al,[9] and a comparative project that incorporates the Chinese community in a village in Banda Aceh, including its archaeology.[10] Fachriza Murti and Triyanto's study on the Chinese community in Meulaboh is a contemporary sociological study.[11] However, none of these pursue the colonial and revolutionary history of the Chinese in Aceh.

Ethnic Chinese in Aceh before the revolution

The emergence of ethnic Chinese in Aceh

Unlike the Indians and Arabs, for example, the Chinese in Indonesia are still politically and sociologically considered immigrants, even though they have lived in the Indonesian archipelago for many generations. This is the background to the historical question about the reality of the Chinese community in Aceh, especially during the turbulent period of the Indonesian war of independence.

As elsewhere in Indonesia, the Chinese community in Aceh is largely urban. They are generally traders.[12] Most lived – and live still – in vertical duplex shop-houses called ruko (*rumah toko*), built in long rows adjacent to each other. The top floor is for domestic use by a nuclear family, while the ground floor is for retail. This enables inter-generational socialization between parents – and sometimes grandparents – and the young.[13] Culturally, the Chinese community in Indonesia was and is very much tied to the ancestral land in China, despite having lived overseas for so long.

Most of the Chinese community in Aceh come from the Khek (Hakka) ethnic region in Kwantung Province. Speaking Chinese with the Khek dialect created a strong bond. It remains openly the mother tongue today.[14] Their second language after Chinese was market Malay, the origin of Bahasa Indonesia, and other local languages acquired through school or interaction with the locals.[15] Chinese was commonly used within the family or the community, whereas Malay or other local languages were used when interacting with locals.[16]

The Chinese community was first established in Aceh along with the growth of trading posts along the coast. They came in small groups and settled in harbour kingdoms such as Pasai, Pedir and Lamuri. This created a bilateral relationship between Aceh and China. A benevolent visit by Admiral Zheng He to the Samudra Pasai Kingdom in 1415 is one proof of this relationship.[17] The relationship grew stronger after the establishment of the Sultanate of Aceh Darussalam in the sixteenth century. The advance of trade led more ethnic Chinese to settle in Aceh. In the royal capital, they built settlements concentrated in the Peunayong area, not far from the port of the Sultanate of Bandar Aceh Darussalam and not far from the centre of the kingdom.

However, large numbers only began migrating to Aceh in the colonial period, not long after the Dutch invasion in 1873. At first, they were brought in as labourers to build colonial facilities and as porters for military expeditions. The first group of Chinese brought in by the Dutch East Indies government included 190 people from Hong Kong. They arrived in Aceh in 1875, where the government built an exclusive settlement for them and appointed a Chinese captain and two lieutenants in October 1875 to look after the community. This policy led to an increase in the Chinese population in Aceh. Two years later, their number had grown to 3,200.[18]

The next even greater migration wave occurred as Aceh opened up to Western private capital. Most were again labourers working in the ports and plantations and in mining. Chaos, poverty and overpopulation in mainland China drove many to leave their ancestral land. Moreover, Western colonization of the Indonesian archipelago was leading to large investments that required a lot of manpower. The Chinese immigrants blended naturally with the locals through marriage with indigenous women. But the colonial government soon imposed a policy of segregation and inter-ethnic discrimination out of a fear that the Chinese would unite with the bumiputra and oppose the colonial government.[19] According to the 1930 population census, there were 21,649 Chinese in Aceh, which represented 2.16% of the population. By the end of the nineteenth century, this number had doubled.[20]

Not all the Chinese came directly from China. Many were brought in or came on their own initiative from other areas in the Dutch East Indies. One of them was Yap Tiam Hien's great-grandfather, Yap A Sin, who migrated from Bangka Island, a tin mining centre where many Chinese migrants of the Hakka ethnicity worked.[21] The Chinese brought in as labourers for Western private companies first came in 1896 and were employed by the

Sabang Maatschappij. They were Hakka- or Khek-speaking Chinese from Kwantung province. They were tasked with moving coal from its stockpile in port to docked ships. They were also employed as carpenters and blacksmiths at several port facilities.[22]

The colonial government policy of opening Aceh to foreign investment from the early twentieth century meant that more and more Chinese workers were needed, especially in plantations and mining companies. The Dutch East Indies government played an active recruitment role.[23] They hired the Chinese as indentured workers or casual labourers for private companies such as forestry companies in Simeuleu and tobacco plantations and oil drilling companies in East Aceh.[24]

After completing their contract period, most Chinese workers stayed in Aceh. (Some were repatriated by the companies they worked for because they were involved in riots and/or they were members of the secret society 'Sam Tiam Hwee', as happened in 1928.[25]) Known for their resilience and frugality, they became successful in business. With the money they had saved, they started their own businesses, which almost always generated more money than businesses operated by the bumiputra. They could even purchase a plot of land and shops. They moved from being employers to becoming their own bosses. Towards the end of the Dutch colonial period, they controlled most trades and services in Aceh. They even penetrated the small business world as vendors in the marketplace; owners of snack stalls, restaurants, coffee shops, laundries, barbershops and grocery stalls; produce middlemen and pig farmers. They were also active in large-scale businesses in construction, inter-island or inter-regional trade, shops, photo studios, export-import businesses and transportation.[26]

In Kutaraja, the Chinese business centre was Peunayong, which was also their place of residence. The Chinatown in Peunayong had been established since the time of the Sultanate of Aceh Darussalam, long before the Dutch occupied Kutaraja. According to local history, the name Peunayong comes from the Acehnese word 'Peu Payong', which means to cover, to protect or to serve. Peunayong was where the Sultan Iskandar Muda gave protection to or entertained royal guests from Europe or China.[27] During the colonial period, the Dutch rulers felt that it was more suitable for the Chinese to live in a separate part of the city as an exclusive community, especially with the aim of making them easier to monitor and exploit through taxes or levies.[28] Living in a separate settlement, the Chinese community could manage their own interests under the leadership of their own officers or *wijkmeester* (quarter leader) appointed by the Dutch East Indies government.[29] The *wijkmeester* in the early 1900s was Yap Thiam Hien's grandfather, Yap Joen Khoy.[30]

In the 1930s, Peunayong became more and more crowded as Chinese moved from the interior to the cities. The economic depression caused plantation and mining companies to lay off their workers. Those who did not wish to be repatriated to China moved to nearby cities. Urbanization continued during the Japanese colonial period and after Indonesia proclaimed its independence. Many Chinese previously living in the countryside sought security in the cities, including in Kutaraja.[31]

The government of the Dutch East Indies categorized the Chinese as foreign easterners (*vreemde oosterlingen*), along with the Arabs and Indians. All were given a higher social status than the bumiputra population.[32] Certain Chinese were positioned as intermediaries between the colonial government and the bumiputra, such as tax collectors. This gave some a better socio-economic life than bumiputra.[33] Even so, labouring Chinese people were socio-economically not much different from most of the bumiputra. The Chinese lost their privileged position during the Japanese colonial period, as the new Japanese rulers considered them part of the Dutch colonial system.

The treatment of the ethnic Chinese under Japanese occupation

When Japan came to Aceh in 1942, different feelings emerged among the Acehnese and the Chinese community. For the Acehnese bumiputra, the arrival of Japanese troops revived their hopes of being freed from Dutch colonial rule. Acehnese envoys to the Malay Peninsula had urged the Japanese to enter Aceh immediately. The Chinese, however, were overwhelmed by anxiety, especially those who had been enjoying power by virtue of the Dutch colonial government, such as wealthy merchants. Their concern was well-founded given Japan's anti-Western stance and its intention to eliminate Western influence in the Indonesian archipelago. Under the Japanese colonial rule, the Chinese were targeted. In Java, for example, more than 500 Chinese leaders were imprisoned in Japanese detention camps, and some were even executed. The Japanese occupiers also tried to strip the Chinese of their economic power and give it to the bumiputra. The Chinese community in Aceh, however, had its own way of surviving.[34]

Fear led some Chinese officials and merchants to flee Aceh before the Japanese invaded. They generally fled to Penang, an island on the west coast of the Malay Peninsula, bordering Siam. According to Aceh's last colonial vice-resident, A.J. Piekaar, many Chinese businessmen left their possessions in Aceh when they fled.[35] Teuku M. Hasan, the Republican governor of Sumatra, and S.M. Amin, the junior governor of North Sumatra, said in 1947 that there was a considerable number of Chinese refugees from Aceh and East Sumatra in Penang. Among them were Liong Yaw Hiong, Ci Kim Kew and Kho Hok Kian, who continued their businesses and became successful merchants in Penang.[36]

The fears of the Chinese community in Aceh were proven true. Shortly after Japanese troops landed, the first thing they did was eliminate all groups associated with the Dutch. Many Chinese were accused of having cooperated with the Dutch, and so they were arrested and imprisoned along with the Dutch.[37] The Chinese lieutenant in Sigli, Tjong Tjhi Tjhay, was among them. In a letter he sent from Penang to the queen of the Netherlands on 6 May 1946, he wrote that he and his wife and five children had tried to flee Aceh and hide in Medan, East Sumatra, because they did not want to work for the Japanese. But they failed. They were captured in Medan and sent back to Aceh to be imprisoned in Kutaraja for three months and 13 days. After Japan capitulated, he returned to Medan. Not long after, he fled to Penang. He was worried about the unfavourable conditions in Medan and its surroundings, which were fully occupied by armed militias.[38]

Japan also stripped the Chinese community of all the privileges they had enjoyed during the Dutch colonial period, such as their status as intermediaries. However, this Japanese policy – so detrimental to the Chinese community – was short-lived. Needing to operationalize their power in Aceh, Japan began using members of the Chinese community as translators, for example. One of them was Goh Moh Wan, secretary of the Chinese Trade Association (De Chinese Handelsvereniging) in Kutaraja, of whom more will be written below.[39]

In order to separate the functions of government institutions from one another, the Japanese authorities – in pursuance of directive Number 7 by the Resident of Aceh (*Syu Cokan*) dated 17 November 1943 – formed the People's Representative Body, or Aceh Syu Sangi Kai, as an advisory body for the Aceh Syu Cokan. At the time of its establishment, the Aceh Syu Sangi Kai had 30 members, all of them ethnic Indonesians. However, from 1 February 1945, in accordance with directive Number 2 of Aceh Syu Cokan, the members of the advisory body grew to 40. One of the new members was Thio Kie San, a prominent leader of the Chinese community in Aceh.[40] This reflected a change in the Japanese occupiers' policy towards the Chinese and a burgeoning recognition of the important role the Chinese could play in supporting Japanese rule in Aceh.

Confusion in the early period of the revolution, 1945-1946

The political attitude of the Chinese community in Aceh during the revolution was influenced by two main factors: first, the fact that Aceh was never directly occupied by the Dutch military, and second, the official political stance of the government in their ancestral land, China.

Transition period after Japanese capitulation

Acehnese only learned of the Japanese defeat of 15 August 1945 and the proclamation of independence of 17 August in the last week of August. In order to anticipate undesirable events, Japanese troops were immediately but secretly ordered not to leave their barracks unarmed. Meanwhile, the *Atjeh Sinbun* newspaper, the Domei news agency and the Hosokyoku radio station stopped operating.[41] The announcement about the surrender of Japan was only published in *Atjeh Sinbun* on 22 August 1945. The day before, all Indonesian auxiliary Giyugun and Heiho troops had been disarmed and returned to their respective villages.[42]

The Acehnese people became convinced that Japan had surrendered when an aeroplane of the Netherlands Indies Civil Administration (NICA) dropped a propaganda leaflet entitled 'To the Indonesian People' in several regions of Aceh, especially around Kutaraja. It informed people about Japan's surrender to the Allied forces and called on the Acehnese not to take any action against the Japanese.[43] Nonetheless, it was inevitable the situation would turn tense. The Japanese, who had remained silent about their defeat, became worried that the Acehnese would not obey the Allied call. In anticipation, they invited Acehnese leaders – among them T. Nyak Arief, Tgk. Daud Beureuh and T.M.A. Panglima Polem – to a meeting at which the Japanese Resident in Aceh (*Cokan,*) convinced them that Japan had 'made peace' with the Allied forces.[44]

Some Indonesians who worked for the Japanese media managed to spread news about the proclamation of independence and the formation of the state and government of the Republic of Indonesia in Jakarta. Teuku Muhammad Hasan was appointed Republican Governor of Sumatra. When he returned from Jakarta to Medan on 29 August 1945, the news became even more pervasive throughout Aceh, and more people began to believe it.[45] At the same time, news about the arrival of Dutch troops in Sabang gave rise to anxiety among Acehnese leaders who supported Indonesian independence. On 3 October 1945, the governor of Sumatra issued decree No. 1/X of 1945 appointing Teuku Nyak Arief as Resident of Aceh. He was assisted by Deputy Resident Teuku Muhammad Ali Panglima Polem and the Executive Board of the Aceh branch of the Indonesian National Committee (Komite Nasional Indonesia, KNI), chaired by Tuanku Mahmud. His executive staff included M. Husen, Teuku Hanafiah, S.M. Geudong, Hasan Basri and M. Mochtar. Soon, the new legitimate administration was supported by freshly appointed heads of offices, assistant residents and regional heads (*controleur*) throughout the Aceh region.[46]

The proclamation of independence also received full support from Acehnese clerics. On 15 October 1945, four prominent ulama – H. Hasan Krueng Kale, M. Daud Beureuh, H. Jakfar Sidik Lamjabat and H. Ahmad Hasballah Indrapuri, representing all Acehnese Islamic scholars – issued a call to fight a holy war (*perang sabil*) to defend the country's newly gained independence, which would be a continuation of the earlier struggle in Aceh led by Tengku Chik di Tiro and his guerrilla fighters. To mobilize Acehnese people into an organized 'sabil' or 'mujahideen' front (*barisan sabil* or *barisan mujahidin*), Tengku Hasan Krueng Kale called on Acehnese from all walks of life to support Indonesian independence and decreed that this fight was a religious obligation.[47]

Numerous Acehnese people immediately joined several insurgent groups and people's militias. One of them was the Indonesian Youth Force (Angkatan Pemuda Indonesia, API) in Kutaraja, led by Syamaun Gaharu. In a very short time, API branches were formed throughout Aceh. The API was transformed into an official government force and was ratified by the Aceh Resident on 12 October 1945. It became integrated into the People's Security Agency (Badan Keamanan Rakyat, BKR), which later became successively the People's Security Army (Tentara Keamanan Rakyat) on 1 December 1945, the Sumatra Division of the Republic of Indonesia Army (Tentara Republik Indonesia, TRI) on 24 January 1946, and the Indonesian National Army (Tentara Nasional Indonesia, TNI) in June 1947.[48]

Other militant groups began sprouting up exponentially. The Indonesian Youth Front (Barisan Pemuda Indonesia, BPI), led by Hasjmy, was formed on 6 October 1945 and was renamed a few days later the Youth of Republic of Indonesia (Pemuda Republik Indonesia). There was also the Mujahidin Front led by Tengku M. Daud Beureuh, the Paya Bakong Front led by Tengku A Husin Al Mujahid, the Indonesian Republican Student Army (Tentara Pelajar Republik Indonesia) and the Indonesian Islamic Student Army Regiment (Regimen Tentara Pelajar Islam Indonesia), all fighting for the newly gained independence and to prevent the Dutch from reinstating its colonial power in Aceh.[49]

The fighters also guarded the border with East Sumatra. The Allied forces' control over Medan, together with the Netherlands Indies Civil Administration, heightened Acehnese concerns that they would also gain control of Aceh. There were rumours that the Dutch were trying to re-enter Aceh and had begun controlling the roads and railways connecting Aceh with East Sumatra. The Dutch were reportedly trying to reclaim Japanese firearms that had fallen into the hands of Acehnese fighters, and they were allegedly planning to use Aceh as a basis for food logistics.[50] The Dutch did use Sabang as their military airbase, stationing warplanes and launching air raids from there. Acehnese fighters also went to Medan to help the people of East Sumatra take back Medan from the Allied forces and the Dutch. They failed in this but did successfully defend the border. And until the Round Table Conference was concluded at the end of 1949, the Dutch never made an entry into Aceh, except for Sabang. Once Yogyakarta in Java and Bukit Tinggi in West Sumatra were finally under Dutch control, Aceh became the last defence for the Republic of Indonesia. Many TNI troops fled to Aceh after most of Sumatra's territory fell into Dutch hands during the second military aggression in December 1948. Rumour also had it that, in addition to West Sumatra, Aceh provided a safe haven for the Emergency Government of the Republic of Indonesia (Pemerintah Darurat Republik Indonesia) led by Sjafrudin Prawiranegara.[51] According to a report from the CIA in August 1948, the TNI in Aceh had about 25,000 personnel, 10,000 of whom were equipped with light infantry weapons smuggled in from abroad. In addition, there were 350 Ambonese and Menadonese, former soldiers of the Koninklijk Nederlands-Indisch Leger (KNIL, Royal Netherlands East Indies Army), who had joined the Republican army to guard artillery weapons on the beach.[52]

Several Japanese military officers who refused to be disarmed by the Allied forces joined the struggle with the Acehnese. These well-trained Japanese officers could use cannons to deter Dutch air raids and were competent in espionage. Among them were Kuroiwa, Rusli Higuchi, Maida

Chui and dozens of soldiers who fought in the battlefronts in Medan.[53] A Dutch intelligence report by the Netherlands Forces Intelligence Service (NEFIS) stated that the operation and maintenance of Republican aircraft at Lhok Nga airbase – which today is the airport of Banda Aceh – was supervised by a Japanese defector. It was also reported that Japanese defectors repaired tanks and cannons, using spare parts imported from other parts of Sumatra.[54]

This did not mean that all societal elements in Aceh rejected the Dutch desire to restore colonial power. Several members of the nobility, *uleebalangs*, believed the return of the Dutch would restore their important role in society. This led to the Cumbok affair, in which Republican ulama together with several militias engaged in an armed conflict with them, causing much damage and many casualties. The conflict began in mid-October 1945 and reached a peak in mid-January 1946. The conflict posed a potential harm to the Chinese, as they had often been associated with Dutch colonial rule.

Welcoming the Kuomintang army

In contrast to the pro-Republican majority, some Chinese in Aceh did not immediately show their support for Indonesian independence amidst the fast-changing situation. This was due to their historical experience under Dutch colonial rule, the connection with their ancestral land, and the situation in other parts of Indonesia. They had also suffered under Japanese colonial rule and therefore looked forward to the arrival of the Allied forces.[55]

Even though they had been away from the Chinese mainland for decades, their ties to China influenced the strategy that the Chinese community took during the revolution. When Sun Yat Sen, the first leader of the Kuomintang nationalist government, died on 12 March 1939, they flew their flags at half-mast. When the Chinese revolution broke out on 10 October 1939, Chinese flags were raised throughout Aceh, shops were closed, and meetings were organized to collect donations to help China, which was suffering under Japanese colonial rule.[56] When Sukarno proclaimed the independence of Indonesia, the Chinese Kuomintang government was hesitant to give diplomatic recognition to Indonesia. In conflict areas, many Chinese families put up the Nationalist Chinese government flag to show neutrality, as advocated by the Kuomintang government. However, this turned out to be counterproductive, as it resulted in a growing distrust of the Chinese community among the bumiputra and to mounting tension in some areas.[57]

In early October 1945, news circulated in Kutaraja and surrounding areas that Allied troops would land at several ports, including the Ulee Lheue port of Kutaraja, on 13 October. They were to occupy Aceh as representatives of the winning coalition, of which China was a part. Chinese youths in Kutaraja were overwhelmed with joy. They gathered in several places dressed for a celebration. When the day arrived, they marched from Peunayong, Pasar Aceh, Seutui and several other places in Kutaraja towards Ulee Lheue to welcome the Kuomintang army. The youths were convinced the Chinese army would land on the beach. Despite waiting for a long time, nothing happened.

In reaction, Acehnese youths and fighters rushed to the Ulee Lheue beach to prevent the Kuomintang army from landing. Excitement on one side and displeasure on the other caused tensions to grow. Eventually the two groups left, without physical conflict.

Very likely, the tension was the result of agitation by Maarten Knottenbelt, a Dutch military leader who infiltrated Aceh with a team in December 1945.[58] It is quite possible that the news about the landing had been deliberately disseminated to create clashes between the Chinese and the Acehnese. Knottenbelt was on a covert operation to prepare for the arrival of Dutch troops in Aceh and simultaneously to assemble former KNIL soldiers. But his attempt failed, as the Acehnese soon found out about it.

A similar incident took place in Langsa, on the east coast of Aceh. According to the former chief of Langsa police, in the early days of the revolution, as Allied forces marched from Medan to Kutaraja, passing through Langsa, rumour had it that Chiang Kai-shek's soldiers were also participating in the march. The Chinese in Langsa made Chinese flags to welcome the Chinese army, with Chinese schoolchildren lining the streets waiting for the march. Bumiputra youths immediately reacted to this by preventing the Chinese from welcoming the troops. There was no open conflict between the two sides, as the Chinese youths soon found out there were no Kuomintang fighters among the Allied troops.[59]

To avoid further conflict with the bumiputra that might end in casualties, the Chinese community in Aceh began to take a different approach. Community leaders in Kutaraja held a friendly meeting at the office of the Overseas Chinese Young Men's Association (OCYMA) on 20 April 1946. The Aceh Resident, prominent community leaders and military officials were invited. One leader explained that the OCYMA did not intend to replicate the armed self-defence force of the Chinese-Indonesian community, the Pao An Tui militia, that was active in other parts of the archipelago. The Chinese community in Aceh wanted to live in peace with the local community. They had suffered as much as the Acehnese during the Japanese colonial rule. In order to prevent conflict, a joint organization called the Indonesian Chinese and Arab Joint Institute (Lembaga Gabungan Indonesia Tionghoa dan Arab, LEGITIA) was established on 24 May 1946.[60]

Goh Moh Wan: A controversial Chinese figure

One of the more ambivalent attitudes towards the Indonesian revolution was shown by a Chinese community leader in Kutaraja named Goh Moh Wan. Indonesian historiography remembers him as playing a double role in the early days of the revolution. Before World War II, he had been secretary of the Chinese Trade Association in Kutaraja and a prominent community figure. The Japanese then employed him as translator for their intelligence agency, the Kenpeitai.

After Teuku Nyak Arief was appointed Resident of Aceh, Goh Moh Wan became his interpreter and confidant. When the Allied representative for Aceh, Maarten Knottenbelt, arrived in Aceh, Goh Moh Wan's role became more important. He was the one responsible for bringing Knottenbelt together with the Resident – a significant task considering Teuku Nyak Arief's anti-Dutch stance. Before the Pacific War, the last Dutch Resident of Aceh, J. Pauw, had rejected Nyak Arief's request for an autonomous Acehnese government. When Maarten Knottenbelt withdrew to Medan, he appointed Goh Moh Wan the Allied liaison officer in Aceh.[61] In this position, Teuku Nyak Arief gave him a letter of acknowledgement.

A few days after the meeting between Teuku Nyak Arief and Maarten Knottenbelt, Goh Moh Wan visited Medan to confer with some Allied officials. This made the Acehnese youths suspicious of him. As a result, when Goh Moh Wan left Medan, he was kidnapped and killed by Pesindo youths. They found the letter on him from Teuku Nyak Arief, which they immediately delivered to the leftist leader Sarwono and his friends in Aceh, such as Husain Almujahid. The Goh Moh Wan case thus not only gave rise to suspicions about the Chinese community but also resulted in increased distrust among the supporters of the Republic of Indonesia in Aceh. Consequently, the PUSA and PRI found themselves unable to trust Teuku Nyak Arief and Syamaun Gaharu.[62]

It seems that Goh Moh Wan not only worked for Teuku Nyak Arief – as the interpreter and confidant who connected him with the Allied representative Knottenbelt – but also for Knottenbelt as an informant before being appointed Allied liaison officer for Aceh.[63] Suspicion towards Goh Moh Wan was not unfounded. The Dutch official A.J. Piekaar, who had experience with Aceh, later wrote in his memoirs that Goh Moh Wan was a financially slick man who should not be taken lightly. He had long opposed and undermined the Dutch-appointed Chinese Lieutenant Thio Kie San. Goh Moh Wan was one of the few to know every nook and cranny of Acehnese society.[64]

Supporting the revolution, 1946-1949

The Acehnese people became even more revolutionary after several prominent clerics issued a *fatwa* decreeing that fighting to defend Indonesia's independence was a religious obligation and that death during the struggle would make them martyrs. These feelings were heightened by the victory of the ulamas (PUSA) against the *uleebalang* of Cumbok in the so-called Cumbok War, which lasted from December 1945 to early February 1946. This was followed by a purge of the followers and sympathizers of the Cumbok *uleebalang*, which led to a more solid revolutionary struggle in Aceh. Previously under several commands, all now united under the command of the PUSA's Tengku Muhammad Daud Beureuh. Soon he was appointed Military Governor of Aceh, Langkat and Tanah Karo. The process of mobilizing fighters to strengthen defences in Aceh and on the borders with East Sumatra intensified. This made it increasingly difficult for the Dutch to enter Aceh.

The Chinese community now began reconsidering its attitude towards the proclamation of independence. After the episode about the rumoured arrival of the Kuomintang army, relations between the ethnic Chinese and the bumiputra gradually improved. The consolidation of leadership among the Republicans following the Cumbok affair further stimulated an improvement in relations.

Chinese community leaders from outside Aceh furthermore encouraged the Chinese to begin taking part in the Indonesian revolution. On 17 September 1945, a Chinese organization in Medan distributed pamphlets to Aceh 'clarifying' the incidents that had taken place between the Chinese and the bumiputra in East Sumatra, Simalungun and Tanah Karo, emphasizing that these had simply been due to a misunderstanding. China was a country that loved peace and had no intention of occupying Indonesia or interfering in its politics. The Chinese immigrants expressed their willingness to participate in building the nation, especially in the economic field.[65]

On 23 October 1945, young people distributed leaflets among the Chinese community in Kutaraja and its surroundings containing an open letter from Injo Beng Goat, the editor-in-chief of *Keng Po,* an important Jakarta-based newspaper. He had been imprisoned by the Japanese military. He wrote that it was completely wrong for the Chinese population only to focus on trade and to consider Indonesian current events through the eyes of the trader, i.e. simply as a matter of profit or loss. Instead, the Chinese should help the Indonesian people.[66]

Other historians have pointed to the characteristics of militancy, persistence and resilience among the Chinese in Aceh.[67] These had been forged from their affiliation with the brave and militant Acehnese people during their struggle against imperialism and Dutch colonialism since the Aceh War in 1873. This had contributed to the attitude of the Chinese in Aceh, who eventually actively participated in the Indonesian revolution.

On 30 October 1945, the Chinese community in Sigli, a city in Pidie Regency, expressed their willingness to help in the struggle to defend Indonesian independence.[68] Their counterparts in Kutaraja soon followed. On 17 January 1946, to celebrate five months of Indonesian independence, the Chinese community participated in organizing a large parade and public meeting. An estimated 45,000 people marched, forming a line two kilometres long. There were no fewer than 42 rows of participants including those from the Socialist Youth of Indonesia (Pemuda Sosialis Indonesia or Pesindo), the Mujahidin, the Police, the Special Police, students, foreigners and the general public, each carrying banners reading 'Freedom or Martyrdom' (*Merdeka atau Syahid*), but also 'Indonesian and Chinese Youth Have United' (*Pemuda Indonesia dan Tionghoa telah bersatu*).[69]

Another attempt to assemble the Chinese in Aceh to help the Acehnese struggle during the revolution was the establishment of the umbrella Overseas Chinese Association (Hua Chiau Chung Hui) in Kutaraja on 3 February 1946. It was led by Liong Jaw Hiong. Speaking at the opening ceremony were the Deputy Resident and Chairman of the Regional National Committee as well as A. Djalil Amin representing the Regional Headquarters of

Pesindo, Amir Husin Al-Mujahid, the leader of the Regional People's Army, Major Husin Yusuf representing the Indonesian Republican Army (TRI), and local dignitaries Said Abubakar and Sutikno Padmo. All spoke about the good historical relationship between China and Indonesia and hoped that this would be maintained for years to come. Portraits of Sun Yat Sen, Chiang Kai-shek and President Sukarno were pasted on the wall.[70]

In response to the upcoming Pangkal Pinang Conference planned by Dutch authorities for 1 October 1946, the foreign community in Kutaraja organized an even bigger meeting to oppose the conference. Indonesian military leaders and civilian officials attended the meeting. Liong Yaw Hiong, the All-Aceh Chinese community leader, accused the Pangkal Pinang Conference of being the 'twin' of the Malino Conference that had been much maligned by Republicans. He said that foreigners residing in Aceh had a connection to the Republic of Indonesia and were determined to support it, and they should oppose any movement not consistent with the struggle of the Indonesian people. Another representative of the Chinese community in Aceh, Pek Gim Tom, called the Dutch conference the 'Drama of Pangkal Pinang'.[71]

To help support the logistics of the struggle, on 8 February 1947 the Aceh Residency Defence Council recommended that the population donate money and other supplies. Indonesian, Chinese and Indian parties and women's organizations in Kutaraja joined together in a single Union of Indonesian Youth Parties, which aimed to coordinate forces supporting the home front. It provided first aid, outsourced replacement personnel and coordinated military training. The organization was led by a young bumiputra, Nurliah, and a Chinese woman, Tjun Ngo.[72]

The Chinese also supported the struggle financially. On 16 August 1947, the Association of Overseas Chinese (GPTP, Gabungan Perkumpulan Tionghoa Perantauan) in Sigli donated 50,000 guilders to the People's Struggle Council of Pidie Regency. This was soon followed by the Association of Overseas Chinese in Bireun, which donated 75,000 guilders to the Army Auxiliary Council there on 17 August 1947. The chairman of GPTP in Bireun, Tio Moh Lam, said the Chinese population sympathized with the struggle of the Indonesian people; he denounced those in East Sumatra whose actions were detrimental to the Republic. Shortly afterwards, Hua Chiau Chung Hui from Kutacane contributed 50,000 guilders to the local fund supporting the Indonesian independence struggle. On the same date, the GPTP in Meureudu stated that the Chinese there were ready to sacrifice their wealth and lives in order to support the Republic.[73] Several Chinese merchants from Aceh – among them Liong Yaw Hiong, the agent for Straits Steamship & Co. Ltd., along with his son Chi Kim Kew, chairman of the Chinese trade association in Langsa, and Kho Hok Kiat, a merchant from Lhokseumawe – gave such a large sum as to be 'unforgettable', according to a report from Penang on 16 September 1947.[74]

The Acehnese reaction to the Chinese political alliance

Suspected but never disturbed, 1945-1946

Dutch colonial restrictions meant that most of the Chinese community was forbidden to travel without a special permit (*surat pas*).[75] This resulted in a social distance and planted the seeds of disputes between the Chinese and the bumiputra communities. At the beginning of the revolution and even before, some Chinese were accused of being Dutch accomplices. When some of the Chinese and Dutch left Aceh ahead of the Japanese arrival, people looted and destroyed some of their properties.[76] However, this was not widespread. After the Goh Moh Wan case and that of the illusory Kuomintang Army, there was almost no news of open conflict between the Chinese community and the people of Aceh.

Those Chinese from Aceh who moved to Penang at the beginning of the revolution built up economic networks to facilitate trade relations with Aceh.[77] A report from March 1949 stated that 1,200 tonnes of copra were exported from Aceh through this network. Commodities such as patchouli aromatic oil, rubber and coffee were shipped from Aceh using the same network.[78]

The chair of the Central National Committee for Aceh Region issued a brief on 15 October 1945 to encourage the population to respect all societal groups, namely the Japanese, Chinese, Arabs and Indians, all of whom were in Indonesia as guests, and to cause them no harm. The Indonesian people were urged to maintain the safety and properties of these people so that they could live in peace under the Republic of Indonesia, which was in accordance with international regulation.[79] In 1947, another brief was issued by the Commander of TNI in Sumatra and Aceh instructing the population to maintain good relations with the Chinese community and to avoid conflict, since the Chinese government had promised support for the Republic of Indonesia. The brief assured the safety of the Chinese community in Indonesia.[80]

The fact that Acehnese leaders took steps to ensure the safety of the Chinese people to live and do business in Indonesia during the revolution made the Chinese community accommodative towards the situation in Aceh. They supported the struggle directly, participated in numerous meetings to address various problems faced by the people, and mobilized financial assistance from the Chinese community throughout Aceh. Seeing this, Acehnese suspicions of the Chinese community gradually diminished. A new opinion developed that the Chinese were also an important part of the struggle to defend Indonesia's independence. Aceh thus saw no significant violence against the Chinese throughout the revolutionary period.

A relatively safe Peunayong, 1946-1949

One of the barometers of the safety and peace the Chinese community experienced in Aceh during the revolution was Kutaraja's Chinatown, Peunayong. It was a safe haven for living and doing business. Most Chinese in Kutaraja practiced Buddhism and Confucianism, while a small proportion were Christian. In Peunayong, there were several houses of worship. The monastery or pagoda was originally built at Cermin Beach in Ulee Lheue in 1878 but was moved to Peunayong in 1936.[81] A Catholic church was founded in Peunayong in 1926.[82] None of these places of worship were ever vandalized.

In 1947, with the Indonesian revolution at its peak in Aceh, a festive Chinese wedding reception was organized in Peunayong on 26 June without the slightest disturbance. The marriage was between Tjia Sioe Lien, a carpenter, and Liong Sioe Lien, a *keroepoek* maker – quite ordinary folk.[83] A large number of Chinese families in Kutaraja registered the birth of children. In the first six months of 1947, the average was five babies per month.[84] This doubled in 1949 – for the period of 7 January to 15 May, there were 51 registrations; and for the period 12 August to 31 December 1949, there were 49 registrations.[85] The Chinese community in Kutaraja lived without fear, never feeling compelled to leave Aceh.

Streets in Peunayong continued to carry Chinese names, in accordance with urban culture and the earlier colonial naming system. Tapekong Street, Amoy Street, Sjanghai Street, Peking Steet and Nanking Street all retained their names – none were changed by the revolutionary spirit.[86]

The ethnic Chinese were given the opportunity to run for office in elections for the Kutaraja City Council on 24 March 1948. Two of the eight people elected were Chinese, Loe Foek Soen and Tan Jan Boen, despite the citizenship issue. They were also entrusted with various public activity committees, sanctioned by the government and the community. When President Sukarno visited Aceh, the regional government formed a welcoming committee chaired by the Resident of Aceh, and one of its members was a representative of the Chinese community, Han Tjauw Goan.[87]

The chairman of the Association of Overseas Chinese GPTP Aceh, Liong Jau Hiong, told two English-language newspapers – *The Straits Echo* and *The Times of Malaya* published in Penang, Malaya – on 9 June 1947 that the situation in Aceh was peaceful and safe. People ran their businesses in a respectful manner. '[W]hile there were price hikes in several other places,' he wrote, 'everything remains abundant and affordable in Aceh. The government of Aceh has been very effective since it joined the State of the Republic of Indonesia (Negara Republik Indonesia, NRI) almost two years ago. There are no disputes or incidents between the Acehnese and the Chinese living in the area. Trade is normal, not difficult.'[88]

This did not mean that disturbances were completely absent. A Chinese home belonging to the owner of a cigarette factory in Keudah village in Kutaraja was robbed on 9 September 1947 by a group of armed robbers dressed as Indonesian fighters. They managed to steal cash in the amount of 50,000 rupiahs. But they were arrested on the same day by the city's security forces in Kutaraja. The police investigation revealed that they were not from Kutaraja and had only lived there for a short time.[89] In another case, a Chinese student in Langsa was evicted from Aceh. He was suspected of being a Japanese spy and also for working for the Dutch.[90] These two cases indicate that the problems faced by the Chinese community were personal rather than communal. All in all, despite the revolution, Aceh provided a safe place for the Chinese community throughout the revolutionary period.

Conclusion

The Dutch failure to pierce the defences of the Acehnese people who supported Indonesian independence was one of the factors that kept Aceh a safe place for the Chinese community during the revolution. Although the Dutch did manage to occupy Sabang in the north and East Sumatra in the south, they were never able to conquer Aceh even though they used various methods, both direct military operations and intelligence operations. The absence of the Dutch gave a huge boost to the social, political and economic stability of Acehnese society.

In almost all Dutch-occupied areas after the Proclamation of Independence, social and political conflicts similar to those that took place under

Dutch colonial rule regularly arose. The Dutch presence sparked suspicion and tension, leading to open conflicts between the bumiputra and the Chinese communities. But in Aceh, it was a different story. Precisely because the Dutch were not around, the Chinese community was given room to adapt to the rapid changes taking place there on the path towards the establishment of the Indonesian state and government. The Dutch absence also encouraged the Acehnese people and elites to help alleviate tensions so that violence against the Chinese did not take place. Almost all the conflicts that involved or were directed against the Chinese community were personal or purely criminal acts. They were not communal or latent in nature.

This shows that the socio-cultural and religious differences between the Chinese community and the Acehnese were not a problem during the revolution. The political elites in Aceh at that time managed to find a way out, both sociologically and politically, together with the elites of the Chinese community. They were able to create conditions conducive to avoiding open conflict between the two, even though they were still overshadowed by the legacy of the Chinese community during the Dutch colonial period, which placed the ethnic Chinese apart from the bumiputra community and positioned the two groups in a hostile relationship. Almost all tensions at the beginning of the revolution centred on political issues. They arose directly from the Dutch effort to rebuild their colonial power and indirectly from the hesitant attitude shown towards Indonesian independence by the Kuomintang government in China, which remained a major point of reference for the Chinese community in Aceh. The Acehnese political and military elites demonstrated that they were able to give protection to the Chinese community amidst various internal upheavals and threats from the Dutch who wanted to return to power in Aceh.

The decision of the Chinese community both inside and outside Aceh to participate directly in revolutionary activities in Aceh, and the awareness of the Acehnese people that their struggle to maintain Indonesian Independence also required support from the Chinese community, ensured that the ethnic Chinese in Aceh led normal and safe lives during the revolutionary period, especially compared to other areas in Indonesia. Both in Kutaraja and other cities throughout Aceh, the Chinese were able to perform their daily routines and take part in their usual economic, social, cultural, religious and even political activities. Aceh's safe condition for the Chinese community reached its zenith a few months before the Dutch carried out their second military aggression in which they successfully took over Yogyakarta. It was during that time that two members of the Chinese community were democratically elected to the Kutaraja City Council. Most Chinese also preferred to stay in Aceh, unlike the exodus that had taken place when Japan was about to invade. Aceh, never fully occupied by the Dutch, provided a safe place for the Chinese community to continue to live their lives in the midst of the struggle for Indonesian independence.

蘇
華僑遊行
大會

15.

Navigating contested middle ground

Ethnic Chinese in revolutionary East Sumatra, 1945-1950

Anne van der Veer

Introduction

> At present, although it is still difficult to infer how the local situation will develop, we know one thing for certain: in the end the development will not be as before.[1]

Chang Kee Nan, Lee Djin Gun (Chinese Consul at Medan) and Lim Seng (Head of the Chinese Security Corps Pao An Tui, East Sumatra) address a Chinese crowd that demands protection from violence. Medan, Sumatra, 4 September 1947. Source: Collection Rups, NIMH.

On 9 December 1945, the Chinese General Association in Medan held its first general meeting. Four months earlier, on 15 August, Japan had surrendered to the Allied forces, marking the end of the Second World War in Asia, the end of Japanese occupation in Indonesia, and the victory of the Republic of China as one of the Allies. On 17 August, Sukarno and Mohammad Hatta had proclaimed the independence of the Indonesian people. These momentous changes put the relations between Chinese, Indonesian and European people in Indonesia on an entirely new footing.

The Chinese General Association (CGA) was the first organized answer to these changing relations by Chinese residents in Medan. As the 'supreme representative organ of the overseas Chinese in Medan', the CGA abolished and replaced the pre-war institution of Dutch-appointed Chinese officers serving as 'heads' of the local Chinese community.[2] Instead, the CGA was founded on the principles of democratic representation, independence and self-determination.

The population of East Sumatra was at this time highly heterogeneous, consisting of a mix of indigenous ethnic groups, colonizers and immigrants. The Chinese comprised 10% of the population of the Residency of East Sumatra and 35% of the population of major towns such as Medan and Pematang Siantar. Chinese migration to East Sumatra had coincided with the rise of pan-Chinese nationalism from 1870 to 1945. This resulted in a different kind of Chinese community there than those found in Java, Kalimantan and other parts of Sumatra, which had longer historical roots.

During the Indonesian Revolution, the Chinese in East Sumatra generally identified themselves as Chinese nationals residing abroad temporarily. They referred to themselves as overseas Chinese or sojourners (Mandarin: *huaqiao*; Indonesian: *perantau Tionghoa*). The year 1945 witnessed the defeat of Japan and the inclusion of China as a permanent member of the United Nations Security Council. It marked the culmination of a decade-long pan-nationalist struggle for emancipation by the Chinese people. That struggle had been framed in opposition to Japanese, British and French imperial incursions into China. Now, China was finally victorious. Her sovereignty had been restored. Chinese people residing in colonized countries abroad saw themselves in a new light. Watching Allied forces arriving to repatriate Japanese forces and to recover Allied war internees, they felt they now stood on an equal footing with the former colonizers.

The Chinese in East Sumatra soon felt the pull of no less than three authorities: Indonesian authority represented by the new Republic of Indonesia; Dutch authority which attempted to reclaim its lost colonial powers; and Chinese authority represented locally by consuls. Where Indonesians felt the only chronology that mattered was that of the revolution, the Chinese were equally absorbed by the civil war that erupted in China at the same time.

At the local level, this resulted in parallel chronologies seen from different perspectives. The disconnect between them can still be seen today in the historiography of the revolution in East Sumatra. Anthony Reid's magnificent book focuses on the competition between the Indonesian independence movement (Indonesian: *pergerakan*) and the indigenous aristocracy (*kerajaan*).[3] Local Indonesian veterans wrote histories of the struggle for independence in which they themselves had participated. The Dutch wrote histories and memoirs from their own perspective of loss. Chinese Indonesians also wrote and continue to write histories and memoirs, informed by the perspectives this chapter will explore.

Chinese-Indonesian perspectives on the revolution have a number of distinctive characteristics. In the first place, they see this as a formative period that reshaped relations between Chinese and Indonesians. It was the moment that overseas Chinese became Chinese-Indonesians, people who contributed to nation-building and who at the same time played (or at least were preparing to play) an active part as members of the new nation.[4] They also see this as a difficult period. The Chinese in East Sumatra found themselves caught in a complicated situation of political upheaval and public disorder. Opportunists were able to 'loot a burning house' or take advantage of people's misfortunes in other ways. There was talk of 'fake soldiers'.[5] In 2011, the Chinese-language newspaper *Guo Ji Ri Bao* (International Daily News), a major newspaper read in Chinatowns throughout Indonesia and North America, devoted a series of retrospective articles to the early days of Indonesian independence. The role of a self-defence guard called the Chinese Security Corps (CSC), initially established by the CGA, was a central topic in the series. It referred to the persecution of Chinese in East Sumatra as a 'dark page in the history of the Republic'.[6] The state of integration between Chinese and Indonesians was poor, making communication and mutual understanding between them difficult. In moments of crisis, it was impossible to 'quickly communicate through existing channels to explain or avoid the issue' and to get 'protection for the local society'. Instead, further alienation and escalation took place.[7]

Calling for unity

In East Sumatra, the period immediately following the capitulation of Japan on 15 August 1945 was marked by uncertainty over who was to rule Indonesia. Although the Republic of Indonesia had been proclaimed in Jakarta on 17 August, and Indonesian officials of the Province of Sumatra were officially appointed, little headway was made in the concrete establishment of the newly independent state in Sumatra.[8] In this period of uncertainty, tensions arose between Chinese and Indonesians. Confrontations occurred in several towns in East Sumatra in mid-September 1945. Indonesian commentators located the source of the tension in the widespread attitude of unabashed arrogance and condescension among the Chinese towards Indonesians and the Indonesian independence movement. China had emerged from World War II as one of the victorious Allies, thereby putting itself on the same level as the United States, Great Britain and the Soviet Union, while Indonesia had barely begun to prepare itself to maintain and defend its newly won independence in the face of Allied occupation.

The historians at the local publisher Biro Sejarah PRIMA in 1976 gave a telling account of the situation:

> At this very disquieting moment, at a time when it was still uncertain who was to rule Indonesia after the Japanese surrender, as if only to increase the worries in the hearts of the Indonesian people, the Chinese population, especially the Kuomintang group that ruled China at the time, hailed the new situation as its own victory.[9]

This was indeed reasonable, the PRIMA historians agreed, as China was one of the Big Five countries that came out of the Second World War as a winner. And it was only a part of the Chinese population in East Sumatra who had 'lost the ground under their feet' in exultation. But it had led some of them to become 'arrogant' and 'conceited'.[10]

Another eyewitness, Haji Abdul Malik Karim Amrullah, better known as Hamka, described how he encountered such an attitude on the day that the Japanese Governor publicly announced Japan's surrender to the Allied forces on 22 August 1945. Hamka was a member of the advisory council to the Japanese Military Administration. He was in Medan and was one of the first to hear the news that day. On his way home, overjoyed by the news, Hamka entered a shop for something to drink. Outside, the radios were still blaring the announcement. Inside, the Chinese shop owner and customers were greeting each other and cheering. 'Unbelievable how happy the Chinese people are,' Hamka recounted. But to him the Chinese looked 'as if they were mocking. Yes, really mocking – not as if.' He quickly paid for his drink and went home.[11]

During the following weeks, Chinese and Indonesians drew further apart in their respective – divergent – exultations about the new situation. While Chinese celebrated the victory of China and the end of imperialist violations of Chinese sovereignty, Indonesians celebrated the independence of the Indonesian people from Dutch colonial rule. Their joy only partially overlapped and only partially sprang from the same source. Both peoples had liberated themselves from foreign rule and shared a larger history of national aspirations and struggle. But whereas China had reached the pinnacle, the immediate future of Indonesia remained shrouded in uncertainty. The Indonesian state had been proclaimed in Jakarta, but in Sumatra little headway was being made with the installation of the new state, its institutions and officials. Allied forces were supposed to arrive soon to disarm and repatriate the defeated Japanese forces, but exactly which of the Allied forces these would be – American, Russian, British or Chinese – remained unclear. The Allies ordered the defeated Japanese forces to maintain law and order until Allied occupation forces could arrive. In this context, the idea caught on that it might well be the Chinese army that would be among the Allied occupation forces coming to Indonesia.[12] All this time, Chinese people were mostly rejoicing among themselves. To Indonesian observers, Chinese residents in Medan showed very little appreciation of the fact that Indonesia, the country where they were living, had achieved independence as well.[13]

Two weeks later, around 15 September, the first clashes occurred between Chinese and Indonesians in Pematang Siantar and several other towns in East Sumatra. Chinese organizations in Medan issued a pamphlet in response to these sad events, in an attempt to defuse the explosive atmosphere and reconcile the clashing groups.[14] It called for unity between Chinese and Indonesians. It conceded that there were indeed Chinese who behaved arrogantly and condescendingly toward Indonesians and indeed 'feared' Indonesian independence but added that they only constituted a minority. Instead, the pamphlet tried to clear up misunderstandings by stating that the majority of the Chinese sympathized with the independence of Indonesia, that both nations were founded on the right of self-determination, and that they, the Chinese, offered to help Indonesia to maintain independence.

Organizing self-protection

After the first skirmishes between Chinese and Indonesians were reconciled in September 1945, a new cycle of confrontation began around 15 October 1945. This reaffirmed the need to take action to ensure their self-protection.

Renewed tensions had arisen after the arrival of the Allied occupation forces, which consisted primarily of British troops and two parties led by Dutch commandos. Led by Lieutenants C.A.M Brondgeest and Raymond Westerling, these two Dutch-led parties clashed with Indonesian youth brigades in Pematang Siantar and Medan on 13 and 15 October. This was the start of what would come to be known as the Battle of Medan in Indonesian historiography. A rash of burglaries meanwhile occurred over the ensuing months, with Chinese residents in Medan targeted in particular.[15]

On 9 December, Chinese organizations and leaders convened a mass meeting and established the Overseas Chinese General Association with which this chapter started (Mandarin: *Huaqiao Zonghui* (Hanyu Pinyin); *Hua Chiao Chung Hui* (Wade-Giles)). Its purpose was to deal with the difficulties of the situation together. A total of 48 public organizations and 46 individuals were represented in the umbrella organization. The CGA was thus a federation of organizations. It presented itself as the 'supreme representative organ' of the overseas Chinese in Medan, thereby disavowing the pre-war institution of Dutch-appointed Chinese officers serving as 'heads' of the Chinese community.[16] This implied a fundamental break with colonial times. The representatives elected by the general meeting constituted a new generation of community leaders. Some of them had played key roles in helping the Chinese through the difficult period of Japanese occupation, while others had been active in the underground anti-Japanese movement.[17]

In order to address the lack of protection of their lives and property, the members of the CGA collectively decided to make appeals for protection to the local Indonesian and Allied authorities as well as to President Chiang Kai-shek of the Chinese national government.[18] However, as indicated in the manifesto of the CGA, there was little to expect from these appeals, as neither local nor homeland authorities were able to provide all-round security to the Chinese in Medan.[19] Therefore, on 13 December, the CGA opened a call for recruits for a self-defence guard named the Chinese Security Corps (CSC, Mandarin: *Bao'andui* (Hanyu Pinyin); *Pao An Tui* (Wade-Giles)), which would be raised under its responsibility to provide protection to Chinese residents in Medan.[20] Lim Seng, one of the individual representatives or special members elected by the CGA, was assigned to lead the CSC.

At the very beginning, the CSC unambiguously lent assistance to existing authorities in upholding public order. Its focus was to protect its own community against robbers. It made its first appearance in Medan at the start of January 1946. About 100 recruits had been enlisted and provided with uniforms consisting of peaked caps, armbands and personal number identity discs. A gong alarm system was set up and adopted by Chinese households. Potential looters were to be scared away by the mere beating of the numerous gongs in the area.[21] In the event of a robbery, CSC members would be called in. At night, CSC members made night watch rounds through Medan's Chinese neighbourhood, together with the Indonesian police.[22]

The local Indonesian-language newspaper *Soeloeh Merdeka* described how the newly formed Chinese 'guard brigade' marched through several streets on 3 January to introduce themselves to the public before lining up in front of the governor's residence to call upon the governor of Sumatra, Mohammad Hasan. The Chinese brigade were to work together with the Republican police, the People's Security Army (Tentara Keamanan Rakyat, TKR) and Indonesian youth organizations, *Soeloeh Merdeka* reported. It would be dissolved as soon as safety in the city could be restored.[23]

Neutrality put to the test

Yet the position of the Chinese Security Corps was marked by ambiguity from the start. Although established to protect Chinese residents against lawlessness and robbery, the corps was immediately caught up in the rapidly escalating conflict between Indonesian youth brigades and Allied occupation forces. Officially, both the CGA and the CSC explicitly declared neutrality in the conflict, following the policy of the Chinese national government. It cooperated with both Republican and Allied authorities. However, to many Indonesians the attitude of many Chinese people in Medan was ambiguous, and so were the actions of the CSC, which appeared to cooperate more closely with the Allied forces than with the Republican police. *Soeloeh Merdeka* reported that the CSC had seized five Indonesian youths on the evening of its first public appearance. But instead of handing them over to the Indonesian authorities, the Chinese guards on duty had taken the captives to an Allied car right away. This raised suspicions about whether there might be some sort of secret agreement between the CSC and the Allied forces. 'Where are the Chinese guards heading?' asked *Soeloeh Merdeka*.[24]

Indonesian youth groups retaliated the following evening. According to a Dutch periodical report, Indonesian youth groups took revenge by staging an attack on a Chinese house and ambushing the arriving CSC members, wounding 15 men. A few days later, the same tactic was repeated, during which two Chinese were killed and three kidnapped. The following day, a prominent Chinese man was kidnapped from his home.[25]

On 7 January, a funeral was held for the two victims of the staged attack. Approximately 6,000 Chinese residents joined the funeral procession, according to a Dutch report. They marched to the headquarters of the Allied forces to ask for extra protection. They asked for increased patrolling in the part of the city where they lived but also for permission to strengthen and arm the Chinese Security Corps. Until then, CSC members had only been armed with sticks and were only allowed to assist Indonesian and Allied authorities. The British refused to supply arms to the CSC, however, foreseeing a further deterioration of relations between Chinese and Indonesians if they were to allow them to carry arms.[26]

Soeloeh Merdeka that day published an open letter from CSC President Lim Seng. He explained that his men had not handed over the five youths to the English forces as reported by several newspapers in the city: 'when they were brought to our building on Hong Kong Street no. 11 for further investigation, before handing them over to the Indonesian police, then suddenly some 40 fully armed English soldiers, following us from behind, came to our building and took the five persons, paying no heed to our protests.' In order to prevent misunderstanding between the two sides, Lim Seng stated that they had never intended to hand them over to the English. They were trying to negotiate with the English to release 'our five brothers' and to express 'our regret and anger'. The English had already promised that the incident would be investigated together with a representative from the Indonesian government, and if the five had done nothing wrong, they would be released to the CSC to hand them back to the Indonesian police.[27]

A meeting was held on 9 January between Indonesian authorities, including the chairman of the National Committee for East Sumatra, the Resident of East Sumatra, the mayor of Medan, the deputy governor of Sumatra, and the directors of the CGA and the CSC. Aiming to clear up the misunderstandings that had arisen between the Chinese and Indonesian people, both sides expressed their wish to maintain friendly relations. Each gave their view on the situation and pledged to improve cooperation to protect peace and order. President Lim Seng of the CSC was willing to discuss the possibilities of dissolving the CSC once the Indonesian police had been raised to full strength to maintain public order.[28]

Cooperation between the CSC and the Indonesian police was plagued by difficulties, however. Mutual distrust arose almost immediately – from within the ranks of the two organizations but especially from commentators on both sides. While many Indonesians suspected the CSC of secretly cooperating with the Allied forces, many Chinese did not consider the Indonesian police to be up to the task of controlling the various armed groups operating in Medan. One of those groups was the Guard Brigade (Barisan Pengawal) of the Indonesian Socialist Youth (Pemuda Sosialis Indonesia, Pesindo), one of the major political parties in Indonesia. According to Anthony Reid, the Guard Brigade of Pesindo 'became the strongest single force within [Pesindo] in the strategic Medan area. During December, Sarwono [S. Soetardjo] became the chairman of Pesindo Sumatra and succeeded in dividing Medan into eight sectors'.[29]

From late November 1945 onward, the headquarters of the Pesindo Guard Brigade were located at the corner of Hong Kong Street and Lieutenant Street, right in the middle of the Chinese quarter. It functioned as a regular police office and the guard brigade as a regular police force. Its criminal investigation department, headed by a strong-bodied boxer named Sibarani, had built a reputation for rounding up the pickpockets, thieves, robbers, looters and other criminals in the area. Their aim was to stop them from damaging the reputation of the Republic. They were put to work on some community service or directly for Pesindo. It was not easy, however, to keep all criminals under control. Sometimes it required the use of force or some sort of trial of strength to force criminals into submission to Pesindo. It was well-known that Pesindo had co-opted the notorious Amat Boyan, 'king of the pickpockets' and his gang this way, with the intention of using him to head a special unit to plunder Japanese, Dutch and Allied warehouses.[30] But Amat Boyan and his unit got out of hand. Instead of targeting unguarded Dutch warehouses, they were also robbing private companies and people, especially the Chinese. Operating under the name Ax Brand Troops (Pasukan Cap Kampak), this unit was responsible for much of the violent crime spiralling out of control in Medan from December 1945 to March 1946.[31]

The situation was now that Chinese residents in Medan were supposed to be protected by the same organization (the Pesindo Guard Brigade) that incorporated the very criminal gang that the Chinese needed to be protected against (the Amat Boyan and Pasukan Cap Kampak). The regular police, being still in its formative stage, was in turn assisted by Pesindo in the maintenance of public order and was thus equally paralyzed with respect to Amat Boyan. The situation was further complicated when the Chinese Guard Brigade (known in Indonesian as Barisan Pengawal Tionghoa) entered the fray, aiming to assist the police (and Pesindo) in upholding public order – but in practice helping Pesindo to keep its unruly underlings in check.

This mix-up of roles was thorny enough in itself, but what complicated matters further was that the Pesindo youth were at the forefront of a revolutionary struggle. That struggle was taking place in an increasingly polarized climate with two mutually exclusive sides: one was either wholeheartedly for the Republic or against it. In December, Pesindo and other youth organizations and people's militias made efforts to coordinate their activities in a Supreme Headquarters (Markas Agung). This was in turn soon placed under the banner of the United Struggle (Persatuan Perjuangan, or 'Volksfront') launched in Java.[32] The United Struggle – with its powerful slogan of '100% Freedom', its 'minimum programme' and its rejection of diplomatic negotiations with the Dutch unless for total independence – presented a radically clear alternative to the difficult and moderate efforts of the National Committee. The United Struggle and its binary view set the terms for the continuing struggle on the streets. Any action by the Allied forces was interpreted as open support for the Dutch and their plans to recolonize Indonesia, or as a 'provocation' to thwart Republican authority. Unwelcome actions by unidentified Indonesian actors were now declared to be covert operations by the Dutch through collaborators. In this context, any open cooperation with the Allies was interpreted as plainly taking sides with the enemy. For the CGA and the CSC, which pursued a policy of neutrality and of keeping connections open with both sides, the polarizing climate produced an unworkable situation.

On 3 March, a bloodbath took place in East Sumatra that would come to be known as the 'social revolution'. All the royal families of East Sumatra's Malay sultanates were targeted. Acting Republican governor Amir himself fled to an Allied camp for protection. The journalist Mohammad Said used the words 'Butchery and seizure of property'.[33]

In such an atmosphere, the gap between political intentions and realities on the ground became wide indeed. In theory, at the diplomatic or political level, representatives from the Chinese community were able to maintain relations with Indonesian authorities, including Pesindo leaders. At this level too, it was possible to distinguish between revolutionaries and criminals. On the streets, however, in the dynamics of the struggle, that distinction was blurred. Criminals operated under the good name of the revolution; revolutionaries coercively demanded contributions and sacrifice to that same revolution. Agreements made by leaders at their headquarters and announced in the newspapers were easily lost in the dynamics on the streets. These dynamics grew more complex now that Chinese 'guards' had joined the competition for control of the streets. It did not help that leaders of the

CSC and CGA appeared to contradict each other. Conciliatory talks could not prevent further escalation. A series of clashes between the CSC and Indonesian youth brigades came to a head on the night of 30 March. A group of 30 Indonesian youths armed with hand grenades attacked the CSC post in Sumatra Street, which was also the house of CSC President Lim Seng. According to a British intelligence report, 'Two hand grenades were thrown which resulted in one Chinese being seriously injured, and the post was set on fire. Five members of the Chinese Security Corps were kidnapped.'[34]

After this incident, British authorities finally agreed to allow the CSC to carry firearms. They provided them with 50 rifles and 10 pistols on 31 March. Rumours that the CSC carried arms supplied by the British had been prevalent since its establishment.[35] Indeed, CSC leaders had made several requests along those lines, but the British command had always refused, citing fears of deteriorating relations between the Chinese and Indonesians. The British command now informed the Medan city council about its decision to supply arms to the CSC.[36] The command also supplied the CSC with a set of instructions, delineating the part of Medan put under the 'protection' of the CSC, and telling them how to carry out patrol duties and how to occupy static posts within the area assigned to it.[37]

It should be noted that, until then, the protection of Medan had been the sole responsibility of the Indonesian police. Allied forces were only responsible for the Recovery of Allied Prisoners of War and ex-Internees (RAPWI) and for the restricted area housing the RAPWI camp located in Polonia. The part of Medan often referred to as the 'Chinese quarter' was located in the eastern part of the city. Although the population living in the area was predominantly Chinese, there were also Indonesians (and Indians) living in the area or working there or running a business or shop. As the commercial heart of the city, the eastern part of Medan was not a closed area. At the same time, Chinese people also lived in other parts of the city as well as on the outskirts of Medan, in predominantly Indonesian neighbourhoods, such as in the vicinity of Petisah market.[38]

Many Indonesians found the British supply of weapons to the CSC unacceptable. They saw it as a 'provocation' by the British aimed at driving Chinese and Indonesians apart. How could the CSC still be neutral if it carried British arms? Journalist Mohammad Said blamed the British for unfair treatment: 'while the Indonesian people were being disarmed and searched in a humiliating way (as a result of "incidents"), except for several dozens of policemen, the Chinese people were allowed to raise their own fully armed brigade'.[39] Their level of armament had given the 'private' Chinese guard the same status as the regular Indonesian police. The arming of the CSC also sparked an intense debate among the Chinese themselves, between those who wished to arm the CSC with firearms supplied by the Allies and those who staunchly opposed the acceptance of Allied arms.[40]

The neutrality of the Chinese Security Corps was put to the test in April and May 1946, when Indonesian youth brigades issued a set of ultimatums to demand the incorporation of the CSC into the Republican police or else the dissolution of the CSC. The ultimatums came after an escalating series of clashes between the CSC and Indonesian youth brigades, and after the CSC obtained firearms from the Allied forces.[41] The ultimatums led the overarching CGA to convene a series of meetings in order to discuss how to respond to them. The discussions exposed underlying divisions within the Chinese community over three major issues, namely the use of firearms by the CSC, the degree of cooperation with Indonesian authorities on the one hand and with Allied forces on the other, and, ultimately, the effectiveness of the CSC in providing protection to Chinese residents. The result was a split vote. Part of the membership wanted to reject the ultimatum and maintain the CSC as an independent corps, whereas others wished to comply with the ultimatum and align the CSC with the Indonesian independence movement.[42]

Repositioning

Hereafter, the Chinese community was effectively divided in two. Having gone their separate ways, the CGA and CSC no longer needed to maintain unity between the two groups. Each faction was now free to pursue its own preferred strategy of self-protection, while at the same time repositioning itself in relation to Indonesian Republicans on the one hand and Allied and Dutch forces on the other. The CSC and its supporters continued their strategy of armed self-defence and cooperation with Allied forces. The CGA, on the contrary, withdrew from its responsibility for the CSC altogether and strengthened its relations with Indonesians.

The CGA strategy centred on promoting friendly relations between Chinese and Indonesians and on mobilizing support for Indonesian independence. It was in part inspired by anticolonial and internationalist socialist solidarity, and in part by the basic idea that their future lay in the Republic of Indonesia. The CGA requested and received official recognition from the provincial Republican authorities to serve as the representative organ of the Chinese community in East Sumatra and set up branches throughout East Sumatra.[43] The

CGA and its members sought to give shape to a new position for overseas Chinese in newly independent Indonesia. It explicitly severed its relations with Allied forces as well as with the CSC, pointing to the damage the CSC had done to the safety of Chinese people in East Sumatra.[44]

The strategy of the CSC, meanwhile, was to protect Chinese victims of crime and violence by means of armed self-defence. The CSC was financed by the local Chinese business community. It was trained by former soldiers of the Chinese National Army and staffed by local Chinese youths. Weapons were supplied by the Allied forces and also purchased independently. Cooperation with the Allied forces was formalized in a set of instructions.[45] Relations with Republican authorities were at a low point for most of the following year but never completely severed. Neutrality was thus maintained in principle. However, the CSC fiercely denounced radical Indonesian struggle groups as 'extremists' and mere criminals.

The Linggarjati Agreement of November 1946 introduced a new period of relative peace. Ways of restoring relations opened up. The CGA welcomed the official Dutch recognition of the Indonesian republic and was now able to reopen relations with Dutch officials without harming its relations with Indonesians. The CSC, by contrast, started to rebuild relations with Indonesian (military) leaders and authorities. At the same time, relations between the CSC and the Dutch became increasingly ambivalent as the CSC increasingly asserted its autonomy and defied the Dutch.[46]

Strategies of self-protection

The two opposing strategies of self-protection pursued by the CGA and CSC were put to the test in July and August 1947, when Dutch forces launched a large-scale military offensive to reoccupy Republican territory. Indonesian forces responded with scorched earth tactics to deprive the Dutch of the economic assets they aimed to recapture during Operation Product, as the Dutch offensive was called. Thousands of Chinese residents living in towns and villages throughout East Sumatra fell victim to Indonesian scorched earth tactics.

The threat of war had already loomed large in the weeks preceding the outbreak of hostilities between Dutch and Indonesian forces. Chinese commentators noted mounting tensions between the Dutch and Indonesian governments over (each other's) violations of the Linggarjati Agreement, foreseeing grave consequences for the Chinese if war were to break out. Other problems, including a naval blockade imposed by the Dutch and a food blockade imposed by Indonesians, remained unresolved and continuously caused friction between

Chinese and Indonesians. However, up until the launch of the Dutch offensive on 21 July, Chinese and Indonesians were able to maintain a delicate balance through careful negotiation and mediation.[47]

This balance was shattered in the vortex of the Dutch offensive and the Indonesian counterstrategy of scorched earth tactics. Chinese possessions, shops and houses were targets of theft, looting and arson. Chinese residents themselves were ordered by Indonesian authorities to evacuate shortly before the implementation of the scorched earth tactics or forcefully driven out of their homes upon refusal, leaving thousands of residents homeless and dislocated.[48]

The systematic employment of scorched earth tactics against ethnic Chinese by the Indonesian forces, sanctioned by General Sudirman and the highest Indonesian military command yet downplayed by Indonesian commentators, utterly disillusioned Chinese throughout East Sumatra. The loss of confidence in the Indonesian government was matched by urgent appeals to the Dutch army to provide protection to threatened rural communities. However, rural Chinese communities were acutely aware that the Dutch could not fully protect the Chinese either, as Dutch forces were severely underequipped, understaffed and altogether unable to effectively guard newly occupied territory.[49] The Dutch themselves, nonetheless, turned the tragic events to propaganda purposes in an attempt to win Chinese hearts and minds, thereby deflecting their own culpability.[50]

Protected by no-one, the Chinese in East Sumatra again had to rely on their own devices. The Chinese Security Corps quickly mobilized support among the Chinese population as well as from Dutch authorities. They stepped up to provide the necessary protection to rural Chinese. By the end of the Dutch offensive, the CSC was officially deployed by the Dutch army in 14 towns and villages across Dutch-occupied East Sumatra to guard and protect Chinese residents.[51]

At the same time, the CGA was severely weakened during the Dutch offensive after several prominent leaders residing in Republican territory were arrested by the Dutch. The conciliatory strategy of promoting friendly relations with Indonesian Republicans was severely discredited and indeed was seen to have utterly failed in the face of the scorched earth destruction.[52] Instead, conservative leaders and organizations, having previously withdrawn from the CGA, now formed a Chinese General Association of their own, the United Organization of Chinese Public Associations East Sumatra (Mandarin: *Sudong Zhong Hua Qiao Tuan Lianhehui* (Pinyin); *Sutung Chung Hua Chiao Tuan Lien Ho Hui* (Wade-Giles). This rival conservative CGA, taking the lead in voicing outrage over the scorched earth brutality, was able to gain influence at the expense of the existing progressive CGA for several months, until peaceful conditions were restored and room for reconciliation gradually opened up again.[53]

Conclusions

This chapter has demonstrated that violence exacerbated existing tensions and divisions between Chinese and Indonesians in East Sumatra. The sharpest divisions were those of an ethnic kind, and it was these that were brought to the fore by the violence. Three developments in this period point to that conclusion.

The first is the increased role of the Chinese Security Corps. Indonesian commentators seized on the strong presence of the CSC in Dutch-occupied areas in East Sumatra as confirmation of their suspicions that the CSC was acting as an accomplice to the Dutch. Moreover, that presence fuelled suspicions among Indonesians that rural Chinese had refused to evacuate despite being ordered to do so by Indonesian forces because the Chinese were preparing the ground for the Dutch and the CSC. The very presence of the CSC appearing in the wake of the Dutch forces confirmed Indonesian suspicions of collaboration – suspicions that had motivated violence against Chinese in the first place.

The second development is the increased prominence of Chinese conservatives. Violence was also the occasion for conservative Chinese leaders to gain influence at the expense of progressives. The latter's strategy of peaceful cooperation had proved to be a failure in the face of extensive violence. Where the progressives had sought to temper political polarization, the conservative Chinese viewpoint tended towards radicalization.

The third development underlining the ethnic divisions is the strengthening of Chinese particularism – the tendency to rely on their own devices rather than on building relations with Indonesians. Particularism was reinforced when the Chinese were left unprotected and forced to rely on their own self-defence organization. The Dutch failure to protect the Chinese thus to some extent contributed to further alienation of the ethnic Chinese within Indonesia.

However, there is a strange silver lining to these dark conclusions. When it was all over, no-one really took responsibility for the violence the Chinese had suffered. If Indonesians had blamed the Chinese for collaborating and thus bringing revolutionary wrath upon themselves, it would have been difficult to defuse the situation. However, they did not do this. Instead, they blamed anonymous 'collaborators'. As painful as it was for the Chinese victims, this did at least create some space for reconciliation once the situation had de-escalated.

16.

Everyday life of the Chinese in revolutionary Padang, 1945-1948

ERNIWATI

INTRODUCTION

This chapter examines the daily life of the Chinese community during the revolution amidst the extreme identity transformations and uncertainties of people's lives in urban Padang. It reconstructs and explains the interconnectedness between individual actions and experiences on the one hand, and institutions on the other. As a community group that was exposed to difficult circumstances after the arrival of Allied troops and the Dutch in Padang, the Chinese community was the perfect archetype of a marginalized group.

Image 1. The Cap Go Meh festival in Padang, 4 January 1948. Source: Nationaal Archief, Dienst voor Legercontacten.

Much research has been done on the history of the Chinese community in Indonesia, but only a few studies focus on the revolution and even fewer on daily life. Of these few, Noviati Mariyatul Hakim elaborates how the Chinese community became targets of racial violence in Surabaya.[1] They were constantly in a state of fear, exposed to food shortages, and socially displaced in spite of their active participation in the struggle for Indonesian independence.

Jumhari shows the dilemma the Chinese faced in Palembang during the revolution. They were trapped in an ambivalent position between political choice and economic interests that involved not only the warring parties – Indonesia and the Netherlands – but also the government of China.[2] Mary Somers Heidhues, a historian who has written extensively on the Chinese community in Indonesia, notes that the Chinese community in Java was faced with an increasingly tense political situation and put in a difficult position after Indonesia gained its independence.[3] Ravando, in his master's thesis at Leiden University, discusses the suffering of the Chinese community in revolutionary Tangerang.[4] Two other contributions in the present volume also consider the Chinese community in the revolution – in East Sumatra (Anne van der Veer) and in Aceh (Mawardi Umar).

In pro-Republican West Sumatra, the Chinese community went through the same ordeal. Many scholars have already written about the revolution in West Sumatra,[5] but few have touched on the daily life of the Chinese community, and then only briefly. They have discussed the West Sumatran Chinese community's efforts to build economic and communication networks with regions outside Sumatra, their participation in various historical events, and the violence that befell them, but never specifically their daily life. In my 2016 study, for example, I limit my examination to the activity of the Chinese organization Heng Beng Tong in Padang during the revolution.[6] Laila Kholid Alfirdaus delves into the impact of national political instability on social relations among ethnic groups in Padang since the beginning of Indonesian independence but focuses on the late 1950s and mid-1960s.[7]

On the whole, the historiography of West Sumatra and Minangkabau tends to exclude the Chinese community. They are one of the few groups that do not have the right to history. They are often portrayed as the antagonist and a source of complication and conflict in West Sumatran society, which strongly supported the Republic of Indonesia. The Chinese community was never considered significant in the process of Indonesia coming into being, in spite of historical evidence that the Chinese had been building social affinity with the people of Minangkabau since their settlement in the region.[8] Therefore, another perspective is needed in order to give a proportionate depiction of the Chinese community during the revolution, one that leads to a historical construction not founded only on the dichotomy of the Chinese on the one side versus the Indonesian on the other.

The history of daily life became popular in the 1970s. Alf Lüdtke's *The History of Everyday Life* is central to the present research. Instead of narrating big historical figures, it focuses on the survival of average people who often fall victim and yet are never named in history.[9] Indonesian historiography has never paid adequate attention to the history of everyday life, even though the tradition of social history writing has developed since it was pioneered by Sartono Kartodirdjo in the 1960s. Kartodirdjo placed the 'common people', especially peasants, at the centre of historical processes and removed the dominant role of the elites.[10] Kartodirdjo's social history has, for example, inspired A. Muttalib and Sudjarwo to write about vagabonds in times of revolution.[11] However, social history writing often focuses only on protest movements or on groups with direct connections to state power, overlooking the social dimension of ordinary people and their ordinary lives. A study on the everyday life of the Chinese community during the revolutionary period is important. It will give a voice to a historically marginalized group and bring in a new perspective on the Chinese in revolutionary Indonesia.

This chapter uses primary sources from all kinds of categories. I had access to the statutes and bylaws as well as meeting minutes from two Chinese social organizations, the Himpunan Tjinta Teman or Hok Tek Tong (HTT), and the Himpunan Bersatu Teguh or Heng Beng Tong (HBT), which can be translated as respectively the Society of Affectionate Friends and the Society of Firm Unity. At the National Archives in The Hague, I viewed documents from the Netherlands Forces Intelligence Service (NEFIS) and from the colonial civil administration (*Memorie van Overgave*, *Algemene Secretarie)*. Digitized newspapers, maps and other literature were obtained from Leiden University Library, the National Archive in The Hague (NA) and the National Library of the Republic of Indonesia (ANRI) in Jakarta as well as from the Library of DHD 45 of West Sumatra. The chapter also makes use of interviews with several informants from within the Chinese community and veterans as well as several other witnesses who lived through the revolution.

The Chinese Community in Minangkabau

The Chinese community in West Sumatra, especially in the city of Padang, has been present since before the arrival of the Western occupier in the Indonesian archipelago. They arrived in the sixteenth century, first in the context of trade relations between China and the Indonesian Kingdoms, and then in the context of expanding Western influence.[12] Chinese men came to Indonesia and later married local women. The third phase of arrival took place during the Dutch colonial era. From this perspective, it can safely be assumed that the Chinese community in Padang was shaped through long migration processes and stages. Minangkabau oral tradition speaks of relations between Minangkabau and China over a very long time.[13] One story has a Chinese king proposing marriage to a local noblewoman (*Bundo Kanduang*).[14] Some basic motifs and colours of Minangkabau's embroidery resemble those used in China, such as arcs, dragons, clouds and *hong*.[15] Chinese bowls, plates and jars were used by Minangkabau aristocratic families in the past.[16] Of the 40,158 people living in Padang in 1852, 1,140 were Chinese, 662 were Europeans and 953 were 'foreign Easterners', a designation used by the Dutch colonial government.[17]

In 1835, the colonial government implemented a segregation policy when they divided the settlement areas in Padang into nine regions. Being grouped with the Foreign Easterners (*Vreemde Oosterlingen*) and led by a government-appointed official, the Chinese were placed in a location separate from other community groups, along the Batang Arau River, close to Pasar Mudik, a marketplace and trading centre for the people of Minangkabau. The location was strategic, for it was close to river and sea transportation, making it easier to conduct business in exports and imports. The Chinese lived and did business in two- or three-storey buildings that were lined up facing the Batang Arau River, Gado-gado Hill and Mount Padang. The buildings were decorated with Chinese and European ornaments.[18] The neighbourhood also had its own marketplace (called Tanah Kongsi), the See Hien Kong temple, a meeting hall, a cemetery and other buildings to hold social functions. The government-imposed segregation was reinforced by various regulations specified by the government to make it easy for them to collect taxes and limit cooperation between the Chinese and other community groups.

The Chinese community in Padang engaged in international import and export to China, India and Persia.[19] They also traded into the interior of Minangkabau. Through these economic activities, they built social relations with the local community despite the restrictive government regulations, including marriage. Therefore, it is not surprising that they controlled the strategic economic sector, also in other areas of West Sumatra. This led to the growth of the Chinese population in Padang. In 1878, 2,630 lived in the Chinese settlement. This grew to 5,000 in 1905 and 7,263 according to the 1930 census.[20]

The life of the Chinese Community after the Arrival of the Allied Forces

During the transition from the Japanese military government to an independent Indonesia, the Chinese took advantage of the situation to serve their own interests but at the same time were impacted by hardships such as they had never faced before.[21] News of the proclamation of independence on 17 August 1945 arrived via radio broadcast and telegraph in nearby Bukittinggi and quickly reverberated in Padang. The arrival in Padang of several Minangkabau nationalists shortly afterwards boosted public enthusiasm. Flags were waved euphorically amid merry celebrations and chants. But the elation did not last long.

The arrival of Allied troops immediately changed the atmosphere. Allied forces under the command of Major General H.M. Chambers landed with Gurkha troops from the 26th Indian Division in Teluk Bayur Harbour on 10 October 1945. City residents initially welcomed them, but the mood quickly changed when people discovered that the Dutch army and soldiers of the Royal Netherlands East Indies Army (Koninklijk Nederlands-Indisch Leger, KNIL) hadjoined the Allied forces under the command of Major General A.I. Spits.[22] News about this caused unrest among the public, especially among the youths – disguised as day labourers (*kuli*) – who were assigned by the Indonesian Youth Information Agency (Badan Penerangan Pemuda Indonesi, BPPI) to spy on the Allied troops at the harbour. Although it was difficult to distinguish the Dutch from the British, some youths spoke Dutch and quickly knew they were there. Major General Spits had once been a European administrator (*controleur*) in Pariaman and Resident of Sumatra's West Coast.[23]

From Teluk Bayur, the Allied troops and militarized personnel of the Netherlands Indies Civil Administration (NICA) marched towards the city centre and took over Japanese assets. Later, they evacuated prisoners who had been detained by the Japanese, most of them Dutch soldiers, Dutch officials, Europeans and Indo-Europeans. Some sources mention that the Dutch officials who had just been released from Japanese internment camps seized assets, houses and business places that belonged to European owners before they were confiscated by the Japanese. For these Dutchmen, the arrival of the NICA signified freedom and Dutch victory. Other former prisoners could not return to their former houses and were given permission to stay in the Yamato Hotel (Hotel Oranje) together with other Dutch soldiers. Still others remained in former Japanese detainment camps in the Catholic

Church compound. Allied forces obtained the agreement of the mayor of Padang, Abubakar Djaar (1945-1946), to use these facilities.[24] Soon, Padang was entirely occupied by the Dutch.

The Allied troops and the Dutch began to approach businessmen, particularly the Chinese, to help them reorganize Dutch companies that had been abandoned or controlled by the Japanese. Some sources say that Europeans at the Yamoto Hotel received many visits from both Chinese and Minangkabau entrepreneurs who had once enjoyed relations with the Dutch.[25]

Nonetheless, not all Chinese in Padang were willing to cooperate with the Dutch in the city. Some Chinese became anxious when Allied forces and NICA troops tried to persuade them to support the return of Dutch rule. The location of the Chinese settlement – in the city centre and therefore under Dutch occupation – made them worried that the population would suspect them of complicity in the Dutch occupation.

Some tried to protect themselves by writing the words 'Chinese House' with red and white paint on the walls of their houses.[26] They wished to show that the Chinese people in Padang were not part of the Allied forces or the NICA, thereby avoiding being targeted by the masses. However, this did little to prevent attacks.[27] Chinese houses outside the Chinese settlement, such as in Pasar Jawa, were frequently attacked and looted by gangs such as the so-called Kambuik Army (Tentara Kambuik). These were clandestine groups from outside Padang using *kambuik* – little baskets made of dried leaves of the perennial mensiang plant, with a shoulder strap – to carry looted goods. Violence also broke out among the Chinese people themselves, creating intense fear within the Chinese settlement. The Chinese community in Padang called this period of constant alertness *zaman siap*, a reference to the fact that they always had to stand ready to save their most basic posessions.

Allied forces and the NICA took advantage of this constant fear by creating propaganda to instil antipathy towards the Republic of Indonesia among the Chinese community. They spread the rumour in both the settlement and in the outskirts that it was not safe for the Chinese to live and do business in Indonesian-occupied areas.[28] Their aim was to gain full support and to concentrate the Chinese people in areas favoured by the occupier. This strategy proved to be successful. Fearful Chinese immediately fled their homes under the escort of Allied and NICA troops, bringing only as much as they could carry from their homes.[29]

Shortly afterwards, Allied forces and NICA organized an open meeting in the courtyard of Yamoto Hotel. It was attended by Europeans, Indo-Europeans and Indonesians who supported the Dutch, who were briefed on how to support the Dutch returning to power in Padang. They provided logistics for the refugees, including those who fled to the Chinese settlement from Lubuk Alung, Pariaman, Tiku, Padang Panjang, Painan and other neighbouring areas (Map 6.).[30]

The situation in the Chinese settlement grew tense as theft, looting and vandalism became rampant. As a response, in early January 1946 the Chinese community created two security forces. One was called Pao An Tui, led by Yan Lim. It assisted Allied forces and NICA soldiers in maintaining security in the Chinese settlement. The other was the Association of Yellow Dragon (Perkumpulan Naga Kuning). Tasked with overseeing possible infiltration by Indonesian freedom fighters into the Chinese settlement, it also often harassed the population within the settlement. Its members seized valuables and even murdered those they accused of being sympathetic towards the Republic of Indonesia.[31]

Vigilant Indonesian youths in the city began distributing anti-NICA propaganda in the form of pamphlets, mass media and radio broadcasts. They printed flyers at two publishing houses in Pasar Batipuh, Padang Nippo and Gazaira.[32] Posters carried slogans such as 'Freedom or Death' (*Merdeka atau Mati*), 'Down with Imperialism', 'Beware of NICA dogs' (*Awas Anjing-anjing NICA*), 'Away with Colonialism', 'Indonesia for Indonesia', 'Holy War!' (*Tegakkan Perang Sabil*) and many more. They were pasted on the walls of office buildings and on road fences, vehicles, trees and electricity poles throughout the city centre (see Image 2). Small groups of armed militia also carried out numerous sporadic attacks on Dutch bases, guard posts and armoury. A group of 40 Indonesian youths led by Mohammad Kamal conducted surveillance on people commuting from one village to another.[33]

The (Republican) Padang Police Intelligence, meanwhile, were able to monitor the situation in the city, which was heavily guarded by Allied forces and NICA troops. They took reports from citizens in Palinggam and Kampung Jawo, who had often obtained the information from their own children. Aged between 7 and 12 years, these children 'patrolled' the streets while playing ball, flying kites and playing other games during the day, while at night, they spied on Allied and NICA soldiers. They were popularly known as 'child soldiers' (*Tentara Cilik* or *Tentara Samuik*).[34] Padang Police Intelligence reported that the Chinese were cooperating with the Dutch. On 21 October 1945, they noticed that Yan Lim, the Pao An Tui commander, helped three Dutch youths who had been ganged up on by residents of

Image 2. Anti-NICA propaganda pamphlets in Padang. Source: NL-HaNA 2.10.62 inv.no 3132; NL-HaNA 2.10.62 inv.no 6286.

Kampung Jawo.[35] They also reported that a group of angry youths burned down a house on 18 November 1945. The Dutch owner of the house had been ill-mannered and often threw large parties with some Chinese guests, which angered the locals. As many as 21 terrified guests ran out of the burning house, but there were no casualties. Later, however, other youths murdered several Chinese people in the settlement near Sungai Bong for allegedly siding with the Allied forces and the NICA.[36]

Violence was also triggered by displeasure with the condescending attitudes shown by some Chinese youths. They were considered arrogant for openly demonstrating their closeness to the Allied forces and NICA. What began as personal dislike later grew into a collective action with a broad social impact. In one incident, a Republican supporter passed through the Chinese settlement on his way home. He heard two Chinese men cheer and shout, 'Japan has lost, so have the Malays'. Offended by these words, he approached the two young men and slapped them.[37] News of the incident spread quickly and immediately fuelled the locals' antipathy towards the Chinese community. They began spurring Chinese people to 'leave this place' by destroying buildings, looting, kidnapping and throwing rocks at houses in the Chinese settlement.

The Allied and NICA forces suspected that the perpetrators were members of the Indonesian Youth Information Agency, the BPPI. This Republican organization had its headquarters in Pasar Mudik, near the Chinese settlement and within Allied territory. They immediately searched and vandalized the BPPI headquarters. Finding no suspicious persons or weapons, they arrested an administrative worker. This further enraged the youths, who by then had spread out and joined insurgent groups outside Padang.[38]

The incident made the situation worse and had a huge impact on the life of the Chinese community in Padang and more generally in West Sumatra. Acts of terror forced many to close their offices and shops, making them unable to run their businesses as usual. They had to sever trade with the Minangkabau merchants who lived in the interior of West Sumatra. Farmers could no longer grow their crops and even had to abandon their fields. This resulted in a shortage of rice amid high prices.[39]

To add insult to injury, internal conflicts began to arise. Members of the Chinese community grew suspicious of each other. Some sided with the Allied and NICA forces, others supported the Republic of Indonesia, while still others decided not to get involved with either side. In such an increasingly uncertain situation, an initiative emerged from both the residents of the

Chinese settlement and the locals to defuse the tension. Sho Boen Seng was a Canton-born socialist and influential man in Padang as a Chinese school teacher. He was a confidant of Major Kemal Mustafa, the commander of the Republican Singa Pasar Oesang (SPO) troop. Sho Boen Seng often provided Mustafa with information on NICA activities in Padang. On 22 November 1945, he held a meeting with one of the influential bumiputra leaders, Nasrun A.S., at a police precinct near the Chinese settlement.[40] Sho Boen Seng requested that Nasrun A.S. communicate with BPPI and suggest a mass gathering to bring together the Chinese community and the youths of Padang. Sometime later, a large meeting was held at the Rex Cinema near the Chinese settlement.

The meeting resulted in two agreements, one regarding the supporters of the Republic of Indonesia, and one having to do with the attitudes of the Chinese population. It was decided that Republican youths should continue their struggle to defend Indonesian independence, and the Chinese community should refrain from doing anything detrimental or obstructive to the Republic, doing instead everything they could to support the struggle. Nasrun A.S. said he understood that the Chinese community in Padang was divided into five groups. There were the 'carpenters' (*incek tukang kayu*), the Western-educated group, the Indonesia-born group (*peranakan)*, the full-blooded Chinese and the school teachers (intellectuals). Each had a different approach to the newly gained Indonesian independence. Responding to Nasrun A.S., Liem Giang Tjiang, a Chinese doctor, suggested that these groups should unite under one organization in order to facilitate coordination and find solutions for the Chinese people in Padang who had been hoping to return to a normal life. Despite protection from the Allied forces, the Chinese population felt their safety and belongings were constantly at risk. It is not clear how much response Liem Giang Tjiang's suggestion received.[41]

The understanding agreed to in principle at the meeting did not prevent further incidents targeting the Chinese community. Those that occurred at the end of 1945 were triggered by provocation from the Allied forces and NICA soldiers. The Indonesian youths, militia and freedom fighters as well as the locals were enraged by Yan Lim's open support for the NICA. Incidents in several locations – some in broad daylight – included the theft of bicycles, carriages and cars belonging to foreigners and Chinese residents.

Life in the Chinese community became more difficult after the murder of Brigadier General Major Anderson and a female member of the Red Cross from Britain, Allingham, at Beremas River in Padang city on 3 December

1945. Allied forces and NICA troops retaliated with attacks on villages near the crime scene along Teluk Bayur. Almost all houses in Mata Air village were burned down. Attacks on several other settlements resulted in significant loss of life and property.

In response, Indonesian fighters carried out retaliatory attacks against Allied and NICA guard posts on the outskirts of the city as well as in Tabing, Teluk Bayur, Simpang Haru, the southern block of the camp for RAPWI (Recovery of Allied Prisoners of War and Internees), the Muara Hotel, the Catholic Church Compound, Belantung Street around the Central Hotel near the present-day military command on Jalan Sudirman, the Ganting Military Hospital and the International Federation of Trade Unions camp (IFTU) at Simpang Haru. Attacks were also launched against Dutch patrols. Indian Allied troops thwarted the attack on the IFTU camp, but the logistics warehouse in Rimbo Kaluang was looted and demolished by a group of unidentified youths.[42] An atmosphere of war soon enveloped everyday life in Padang and its surroundings.

As a result, many citizens of Padang fled to neighbouring towns such as Lubuk Alung, Sicincin, Kayu Tanam, Pariaman, Padang Panjang, Batusangkar, Bukittinggi, Sawahlunto, Solok and Painan, leaving their possessions behind. Some people, mostly menial workers, then took advantage of this to loot empty houses, cut down trees, uproot plants and pick fruit.[43] News ofthe looting spread quickly. It was rumoured that Chinese men were among the looters. This heightened anxiety within the Chinese community, which feared further anti-Chinese sentiment.[44]

Allied and NICA troops tightened security on the outskirts of Padang, but inside the city the situation was chaotic. Interrupted food supplies from the hinterland produced scarcities.

Shops were closed due to rampant looting, or they were burned down, as happened to the convenience store owned by Eng Joe Bie on 14 December 1945. The youths who did this said the owner had helped the NICA by supplying them with food.[45]

To restore order, the Allies and the NICA imposed a curfew and arrested people they found suspicious. They carried out patrols and searched houses in the city, including those belonging to the Chinese, looking for weapons, food hoards or Republican spies. Some Chinese homeowners were forced to surrender valuable possessions, on threat of immediate torture. Some sources say Allied troops brutally raped Chinese girls while their families were at gunpoint.[46]

The measures implemented by Allied and NICA troops together with the Pao An Tui militia isolated the city, severing connections between the Chinese community and the outside world. The implications of this are described in numerous ego documents and personal testimonies of locals who lived in the Chinese settlements and had friendly relations with Chinese neighbours. One of them was the Indonesian freedom fighter Idrian Idroes. As a member of Tentara Cilik, little Idroes often had to conduct reconnaissance and then report whatever they had seen to the youths waiting for him in hiding near Palinggam, be it commotion among the Chinese or skirmishes involving Republican troops.[47] As Allied and NICA troops increased the frequency of their patrols and searches in the Chinese settlements, Idroes lost contact with his Chinese childhood friend, Lim Tek An, the son of a treasurer at the Padang Municipal Office.[48]

The worsening conditions prompted the Chinese community in Padang to send a letter to the Chinese Consulate in Singapore seeking protection. In response, the Kuomintang Government in China suggested to their fellow Allies in Padang that Allied troops and NICA searches should be accompanied by the Indonesian Civil Police, the latter under the command of Ismael Lengah.[49] Nonetheless, life in the Chinese settlement remained tense in the midst of thefts, vandalism and mutual suspicion among the Chinese population.

Amidst this situation, there was a change in leadership in the security organization Pao An Tui. The controversial Yan Lim was replaced by Sho Boen Seng, who was more sympathetic toward the Republic of Indonesia. Seng now proposed that the Allied forces hand over security matters in the Chinese settlement to Pao An Tui. Both the Chinese community and the Allied and NICA troops agreed that the latter would not enter without permission from Pao An Tui.[50]

From then on, it was Pao An Tui that conducted investigations and even arrests of suspicious members of the Chinese population. While this caused some unrest, it also created a sense of certainty, as it helped to overcome the rifts within the Chinese community. For example, Pao An Tui detained Leo 'Jap' Soei Hok, a Chinese man who once worked as a spy for the Japanese Military Police when it was headquartered in the shop Toko Betsuhan. He had been the cause of torture and even death inflicted on many Chinese and Indonesian victims.[51] Also, Leo Soei Hok was constantly creating commotion with other Chinese. He once threatened to kill his parents-in-law for refusing to give permission to their daughter to move with him out of the

Chinese settlement. This behaviour resulted in people in the Chinese settlement ganging up on him.[52]

Pao An Tui also arrested Chinese people who were too involved with the struggle of the Indonesian people. On 6 March 1946, Lie A Kang, a Chinese man who lived in Tanah Kongsi, was arrested for selling portraits of prominent Indonesian figures.[53] On 27 March 1946, Sho Ting Kang, who lived in Nias Village, was arrested on suspicion of being a spy for the Republic. Sho Ting Kang worked at the local Chinese Office (Tiong Hoa Hwee Koan, THHK). He was known as someone who had frequent contact with Indonesian people and the Republican government. During the interrogation, Sho Ting Kang claimed he maintained contact with the Republican government because of his work and in order to obtain political information that would be useful to the Chinese community. They could at least be ready when skirmishes between Republican fighters and Allied troops were about to take place. Good relations with the Republicans might allow him to know about bombs exploding at Allied or Dutch guard posts on the city outskirts, which might indicate follow-up attacks in the city. With this information, the Chinese community could seek immediate protection prior to the attacks. After this explanation, Sho Ting Kang was released.[54]

Chinese people living outside the settlement, within camps controlled by Allied forces for example, also faced adversity. One report mentions that the troops meant to protect them often targeted their valuables, such as gold, silver and money. Rumour had it that several Chinese women were constantly being harassed by the same perpetrators, without the chance of escape. Those Chinese who wanted to leave the camps had to pay a large sum of money. Only a few wealthy Chinese and Indian refugees were able to pay and flee to Singapore.[55]

In other reports, Chinese people themselves perpetrated violent acts, especially the Chinese 'security' group Perkumpulan Naga Kuning. They harassed anyone they encountered, whether Chinese or Indonesian. Members of this organization murdered several locals selling steamed peanuts and ice around the Muara Padang area. They also targeted and killed those they accused of being Indonesian freedom fighters, especially those who entered the Chinese settlement. No fewer than 30 people fell victim to the Perkumpulan Naga Kuning. All were buried in the open field behind the military camp.[56] However, none of these incidents were ever properly confirmed by representatives of the Kuomintang government or by the Chinese association Chung Hua Chung Hui in Padang.[57]

Pao An Tui and the Perkumpulan Naga Kuning were able to reduce crime within the Chinese settlement but not much outside it.[58] On 4 June 1946, five young Chinese men opened fire as they were strolling around the city, hitting a blind Indian woman. Indignant Republican youths began to claim the shooting was directed at them. The situation only calmed down after the five were arrested by Pao An Tui.

Another incident occurred on 15 June 1946 when a bumiputra who was riding a bicycle at Nias Village was attacked and his bike stolen by a Chinese man. Several days later, it happened again – another bumiputra was kidnapped while on his way to Kampung Pondok. His bicycle was also gone. These incidents led to more unrest. However, both Chinese and Indonesians suspected the perpetrators had been accomplices of the Allied and NICA forces who had been ordered to create an uproar in order to pit the people against each other.

As a follow-up, Pao An Tui collaborated with the Indonesian Civilian Police to handle the security issue. This helped improve Pao An Tui's relationship with the Republicans. Red-and-white flags were now raised at the Pao An Tui office in Padang. This gave the Chinese community hope that they would eventually be able to live a safe life.

Further cooperation between Chung Hua Chung Hui, a post-war umbrella organization for the Chinese population throughout Indonesia, and supporters of the Republic of Indonesia followed. The Chinese community in Painan, 78 kilometres south of Padang, had asked the Chinese Government Consulate to help them evacuate from the local settlements of Bandar X, Tarusan, Painan and Kambang. These settlements were plagued with smallpox as well as frequent robberies and harassment from local gangs and criminals.[59] Since Padang was already jammed with refugees, it was agreed with the Republican government that 20 Chinese from Padang and 258 others from Painan would be evacuated instead to Sungai Penuh in the hill country to the Southeast, and to Bayang north of Painan. That the two Painan signatories Tjoa Sin Soe and Tan Po Gwan agreed to this change suggested by the Republicans was taken as proof of their loyalty to the government of the Republic of Indonesia.[60]

The Chinese-Republican cooperation helped revive the economy in the city. Pao An Tui encouraged traders to sell cigars and cigarettes at a fixed, reduced price. A consideration for this was the high demand from workers, who were already heavily addicted to smoking. Meanwhile, Sho Boen Sheng, the chief of Pao An Tui, received a shipment of opium from outside

Padang, which he sold in Padang. He used the profits to purchase weapons and other logistics for war, which were then smuggled to Abdul Halim who was leading the fight for Indonesian independence in the interior.[61]

The cooperation between Chinese and Republicans grew even stronger when the Chinese consulate in Palembang attended the celebration of the first anniversary of Indonesia's independence. In his speech, the consul stated that the Chinese government sympathized with and would show their support for the Indonesian nation in the new United Nations. The presence and support of the Chinese consulate directly changed the political orientation of the Chinese community in Padang and in West Sumatra in general. The two sides now resorted to reciprocity and mutual agreement and tried to overcome their suspicions of each other.

Chinese cultural and spiritual life continued in the midst of these uncertainties. People remained active in the two major social organizations, Hok Tek Tong and Heng Beng Tong. The former had been founded in 1863 under its first chairman Lie Kauw Keng. Its members – mostly adult men – organized funerals as well as cultural and religious activities in honour of its patron deity Ho Tek Tjeng Sin.[62] Heng Beng Tong was begun in 1876, under its first chairman Oei A King Dewa, and held Kwan Tee Koen as its patron deity. Heng means eternity, Beng light, and Tong association, thus Heng Beng Tong was literally the Association of Eternal Light.[63] Prior to an event, they would request permission from Pao An Tui and the Indonesian Civil Police. Both organizations routinely held social gatherings, Cap Go Meh festivals and funeral ceremonies (Image 1).

Despite all the limitations imposed on them, they recruited new members each year.[64] In 1945, Heng Beng Tong gained 50 new members. A drastic increase in membership took place a year later, in 1946, with 350 new members.[65] A wave of refugees from throughout West Sumatra and beyond had arrived in Padang. Hok Tek Tong and Heng Beng Tong gained almost as many new members that year. Chinese from outside Padang who had lost their homes to vandalism and arson sought refuge in the organization and were automatically granted membership.[66] The organization provided houses for them. In order to maintain cleanliness, ensure public health, and avoid clashes, every member who lived in one of these houses had to join in cleaning according to a schedule coordinated by its leader, Ko Tjik Tjoan.[67] The organization's leader, known as *Toako*, greatly influenced the wellbeing of the organization, guaranteed the protection of its members and arranged the logistics.

Economic hardship did not reduce the enthusiasm with which the Chinese community made donations. Even though the festivals were not as merry as those in the years before, people understood the importance of togetherness, especially as manifested in the celebration of Cap Go Meh.[68] Festivities were also evident in the ritual offerings on the 15th day of every month, known as *Tjia Gwee,* to honour a Chinese deity named *Lauw Tjo,* and *Sintjoe* which were carried out during the day. However, it was considered unsafe to hold the evening ritual *Tjiak Tjiu* and some parades.[69] All of this shows that in their everyday life, Chinese people in Padang were able to adapt to their situation without having to leave out the spiritual aspect of their lives.

Chinese efforts to maintain solidarity with the bumiputra and to overcome the social issues they were facing were disrupted when Allied forces began to withdraw from Padang. This left more room for dominance by the NICA (which had changed its name in June to Temporary Administrative Service [*Tijdelijke Bestuursdienst*] but which local people continued to call NICA). The withdrawal started on 24 October 1946 and lasted until 30 November 1946. As the Allied forces left, the NICA brought in more troops to strengthen its existing defences.[70] This increased concerns, also among the Chinese in Padang. They feared that Dutch interference would once more have the effect of labelling them Dutch accomplices just as they were beginning to prove their new support for the Republic of Indonesia.

Elites from the Chinese community sought assurances from the Allied forces that their safety would be guaranteed. However, the Allied forces' commander, Colonel E.N. Marston, stated that he could not guarantee what the Chinese community needed, as the current situation did not allow him to remain in Padang. (Republicans attributed the British withdrawal to losses the British had suffered in Surabaya and elsewhere and to the unceasing spirit of the Indonesian freedom fighters. In reality, the Southeast Asia Command [SEAC] covering all of Southeast Asia was disbanded in November 1946.)[71]

More Dutch troops began arriving in Padang. Among them was the U-Brigade under the command of Colonel Sluyter, a former KNIL soldier from Suriname. His KNIL background made the Chinese fear the worst. They asked for help from the Chinese Consulate in Singapore[72] and from the Republican authorities.

With more troops at their disposal, the NICA aggressively increased its control over Padang. The Chinese settlement was heavily guarded, isolating its residents from the outer world. Even so, they were able to follow political developments through newspapers and radio broadcasts. They warmly welcomed the Linggarjati Agreement of 15 November 1946 and even sent a congratulatory letter to the Indonesian government via the Governor of West Sumatra in Bukittinggi.[73] One Chinese man even bravely shouted 'Indonesia merdeka' after reading the news about the agreement. Upon hearing this, four Dutch soldiers became aggravated and immediately battered the Chinese man. Responding to the violence, the Chinese community in Padang sent a letter of protest to the Chinese Consulate General in Singapore, urging them to help find justice and security for the Chinese community in Padang.[74]

On 30 November 1946, NICA officials and the Republic of Indonesia held their first negotiations about the demarcation line. This resulted in tightened NICA control over Padang, the disappearance of local citizens, and isolation of the city. After gaining full control of the borders by setting up defence posts near the demarcation line, the Dutch began launching attacks on Republican territory. Skirmishes ensued, and people who lived at the border were not allowed to leave their homes. The Dutch became more aggressive in attacking residential areas and other Indonesian territory using bombs and air raids. To avoid casualties, the Indonesian Police Chief instructed residents to immediately evacuate to the interior.[75]

Civilian casualties, however, were still inevitable as the attacks became more intense. Conditions improved only slightly after Republicans opened negotiations with the NICA in West Sumatra on 7 December 1946. The Republican delegation was led by Anwar St. Saidi, leader of a local ad hoc humanitarian organization called the Frontline Supporting Forces (Badan Pembantu Garis Depan, BPGD), which was supported by all the local Republican political parties. St. Saidi was also a member of the Executive Board of the West Sumatra branch of the proto-parliamentary Indonesian National Committee (Komite Nasional Indonesia, KNI). He was an entrepreneur, founder of the National Bank in Bukittinggi, and a close friend of Mohammad Hatta, who later became prime minister. He supported the Indonesian struggle by means of financial donations to advance education and the struggle for freedom in West Sumatra.[76] The two sides agreed on a truce once Cabinet Minister Sjafruddin Prawiranegara met the Dutch delegation in Padang. On 11 December 1946, another negotiation took place to determine the demarcation line, but this was only truly realized after the negotiation was resumed on 3 May 1947. The demarcation line separating

Republican from Dutch-held areas ran from South to North, from the Beremas River, through Lubuk Begalung and Kalawi Village to Tabing. The Netherlands and Indonesia each set up six posts.[77]

The new demarcation line meant that Teluk Bayur Harbour and the economy of Padang now fell almost entirely under the control of the NICA. This certainly had a great impact on the Chinese community. They became even more isolated and found it exceptionally difficult to carry out trading activities as their only source of income. Furthermore, they were faced with a shortage of food and stricken by poverty and hunger for months due to a Republican economic blockade and the disappearance of rice. The author and freedom fighter Hamka noted during his trip around West Sumatra that the areas most severely stricken by famine were Solok and Alahan Panjang. Some even died of hunger.[78] As had happened before, this predicament led to suspicions of each other and upset the relationship between the Chinese community in Padang and the Indonesians at large.

Attempts to restore good relations were hindered when the mayor of Padang, Bagindo Aziz Chan was assassinated in the Padang suburb of Lapai Nanggalo on 18 July 1947. This was followed by the launch of the first Dutch military aggression three days later. Padang was now completely under Dutch control, as all elements of the Republic of Indonesia were removed from the city.[79] Security problems and new tensions in social relations between community groups ensued. Chinese weapon depots, food warehouses, camps and settlements were attacked. As the representative of the Chinese government, the Kuomintang instructed the Chinese community in Padang not to show excessive sympathy towards the Dutch.[80] At the same time, the Indonesian authorities stated that they would protect the Chinese community as long as they did not show support for the NICA.[81] This slightly reduced anxiety among the Chinese in Padang, who were constantly worried that they would become victims if the situation continued to deteriorate.

To overcome the precarious situation of food shortages among the Padang Chinese, Chung Hua Chung Hui – chaired by Tjoa Teng Kiat and Sho Boen Seng[82] – urged the (Republican) Staple Food Committee (Komite Pengurus Bahan Makanan) to regulate food prices. For this, they created a slogan, 'If we have no more food, we shall die together with history on our side. The rich should start listening to their conscience'.[83] The demand from Chung Hua Chung Hui was met by the Indonesian authority, who agreed that:

1) The Resident of West Sumatra will maintain the safety of the lives and property of the Chinese population, on conditions that:
2) The Chung Hua Chung Hui promise to rid the Chinese community of NICA's accomplices;
3) Organize night watches;
4) Register every Chinese resident and have them sign a registration card that states the holder of the card will not harm the Indonesian independence movement;
5) Clear the settlement of NICA elements;
6) Conduct trade activities; and
7) Maintain good conduct.[84]

From here, Chung Hua Chung Hui together with Pao An Tui began searching the Chinese settlement for NICA accomplices and forging closer ties with supporters of the Republic. Chung Hua Chung Hui urged the Chinese population to raise red-and-white flags at their homes, shops and offices and helped them to contribute to the Indonesian struggle.[85] The organization worked together with Pao An Tui, Partai Pemuda Tionghoa Baru, and Kuomintang to collect rice and other staple foods and sell them to the people at affordable prices.[86]

Amidst the Dutch attacks, the Chinese community overcame Indonesian suspicions by continuously campaigning that it was a mistake to assume the Chinese community in Padang received protection from Dutch authorities. Instead, they were actually victims, as they could not run their economic activities. They lived under constant supervision by the Dutch military, to whom all activities had to be reported. In addition, the Chinese Consulate, represented by Chung Hua Chung Hui, requested permission from Mohammad Rasjid, the Republican Military Governor of Central Sumatra, to discuss economic and citizenship issues. In the discussion, Chung Hua Chung Hui was represented by Go Soe Tong and Lie Sin Cho.[87]

At the initiative of Chung Hua Chung Hui, a conference of Chinese organizations was held in Pangkal Pinang to find a way out of the uncertain situation caused by the dispute between Indonesia and the Netherlands.[88] The Indonesian government together with Chung Hua Chung Hui set up barbed wire fences around the Chinese settlement and only allowed those with special permits to enter.[89] When a riot broke out on 31 March 1948, which killed four Chinese youths, two of whom were mutilated, Indonesian authorities responded by taking preventive measures to avoid further casualties. Together with all Chinese organizations in Padang, the Government of the Republic of Indonesia in West Sumatra gave commitments to ensure the safety of all people, especially the Chinese, and to punish those who endangered that safety. In return, the Chinese population agreed to cooperate with the supporters of the Republic in defence of Indonesia's independence.[90]

On one occasion, the Resident of West Sumatra stated that the Chinese population in Padang and local traders maintained good relations. Oei Ho Tjeng, the holder of export rights to Singapore, cooperated with Minangkabau merchants in the interior.[91] Another Chinese merchant, Sho Ting Kang, also maintained an outstanding trade relationship with the Government of the Republic of Indonesia via intermediaries from the Indonesian military, one of whom was Major Kemal Mustafa.[92] Oei Ho Tjeng also maintained good relations with the Dutch, especially in mediating crops trade between the Dutch and Minangkabau traders. He was one of the few merchants who held a pass from the NICA that allowed him to make business trips from Pariaman to Teluk Bayur Harbour. Oei Ho Tjeng transported agricultural products such as gambier, clove and copra by ship.[93] This trading pass, however, was often misused by the holders, who threatened farmers to sell their crops only to them because they were the only ones who could sell the products at the marketplace. One of these unruly pass-holders was Lim Beng Gie who once forced Indonesian fishermen to sell their catch only to him.[94]

Although the Dutch continued to tighten their control over the city and at the same time aggressively expanded their territory outside Padang, security conditions in Padang began to improve. The agreement between the Chinese community and the Indonesians in time improved the lives of the Chinese population in Padang. They were now able to carry out economic activities and fulfil their needs without obstacles. Chinese and Indonesians worked together to establish order by rounding up former militia members of the Perkumpulan Naga Kuning (the organization itself had long been disbanded). Sho Boen Seng, who replaced Yan Lim, transformed Pao An Tui into an organization that maintained close relations with the Republicans and that simultaneously reduced disputes between the Chinese community and non-Chinese citizens. The result was evident in the re-establishment of trading activities between Chinese merchants and Minangkabau traders.[95]

Pao An Tui now had more freedom to carry out its organizational tasks, such as member meetings, regular management meetings, religious ceremonies as well as more open and festive celebrations of cultural holidays.[96]

Similarly, Heng Beng Tong was able to recruit more members: 53 new members in 1947, 39 in 1948, and 124 in 1949 (though one could argue that this new membership was due to limited mobility and economic hardship resulting from the Dutch military aggression).[97] New members of Heng Beng Tong and Hok Tek Tong participated in a simple procession that included a collective prayer to the ancestors. Both organizations also openly organized funeral processions, coordinated by the See Hien Kiong temple. Heng Beng Tong asked Hok Tek Tong to make the land located at Simpang Pulau Karam/Nipah available as the burial ground Bukit Sin Tiong, to be equally divided among both organizations for their common good.[98]

Entering 1948, the Chinese community in Padang was able to celebrate the Chinese New Year. Heng Beng Tong and Hok Tek Tong even threw a drinking party (*ciak ciui*) despite the economic blockade imposed by both the Dutch authorities and the Indonesian government as a retaliatory response to Dutch attacks in the interior of Central Sumatra.[99] The celebration was limited and internal but still merry, including parades. To share the joy with the children, Heng Beng Tong, Hok Tek Tong and Chung Hua Chung Hui organized a *Sipasan* performance which had been banned since the Japanese colonial period. It was performed from Saturday to Monday, starting on the fifteenth day of the twelfth month, called *Tjiaghwee*, starting at 4 in the afternoon.[100]

As a group caught between two conflicting parties, the Chinese community in Padang remained dependent on the Dutch. Even though the Dutch recognized Sumatra, Central Java and Yogyakarta as Indonesian territory according to the Renville Agreement of January 1948, they refused to cede control over Padang. Despite the growing cooperation between the Chinese community and the Indonesian people, the Chinese population could not avoid participating in the celebration of the fiftieth anniversary of Queen Wilhelmina's reign in 1948. For the celebration, Hok Tek Tong, Heng Beng Tong and Chung Hua Law Tung Hui – now all under the coordination of Chung Hua Chung Hui – collected donations from all Chinese organizations in Padang.[101] One of the organizations gave as much as 500 guilders.[102]

As expected, their participation made the supporters of the Republic of Indonesia suspicious, especially since the Dutch had occupied the capital of the new Republic, Yogyakarta, on 19 December 1948, as well as the West Sumatra region and Aceh, which had been temporarily used as the centre of the Emergency Government of the Republic of Indonesia (Pemerintah Darurat Republik Indonesia, PDRI) under the leadership of Sjafruddin

Prawiranegara. As the second Dutch military aggression spawned new tensions that could lead to new conflicts between the communities in Padang, the Chinese found themselves once again living in fear and in need of regaining the trust of the Indonesians.

Conclusion

The political strategy of the Allied forces and the NICA in approaching the Chinese community in West Sumatra had placed the Chinese population in a difficult situation. Tensions reached a new level when Allied and NICA troops provided protection and logistics to refugees in the Dutch-run camps and Chinese settlements while other populations were left to face extreme hardship. Furthermore, the arrogant and demeaning attitudes of some Chinese people in Padang and their support for the Allied forces and the NICA enraged the locals, who overwhelmingly supported the Republic. As a result, the Chinese population became a target of violence, which in turn meant that the Chinese lived in a state of anxiety. This fear of being the victim of violence, looting, arson or murder forced them to always be on the alert and even to become suspicious of each other. Conditions worsened when a new demarcation line isolated them from the outside world, and even more so when the Dutch military became the sole occupying power after Allied troops left Padang in late 1946.

The presence of the NICA supported by Dutch troops did not give a sense of security to the Chinese community in Padang. They knew the importance of establishing good relations with the Indonesians and of adjusting to the changing situation amidst the Indonesian struggle for independence. They relied more on the Indonesian people than on the Dutch. The Chinese community in Padang was well aware that they were not only faced with the ruling Dutch power at the time but also confronted with division within the Chinese community itself. This situation sometimes forced the Chinese population to have double attitudes towards the Dutch authorities that would actually put them in a predicament especially when they had to deal with Indonesian interests.

With support from Chinese organizations such as Hok Tek Tong, Heng Beng Tong, Pao An Tui, Chung Hua Chung Hui and the Chinese government, the Chinese community in Padang continued to try to restore its long-established, close and mutual relationship with the Minangkabau community. However, these efforts were thwarted by the Dutch attempt to restore its colonial power in Indonesia. The community was eventually able to build trade relations with Minangkabau merchants in the interior as well as with other elements of the Republic. This shows that the Chinese community in Padang consciously and rationally made its own choices about the future, despite the turmoil of the revolution.

Consolidation within the Chinese community and solidarity between the Chinese and Indonesian populations led to greater safety in the everyday lives of Chinese in Padang. To a certain extent, this also made both sides consider the Dutch their common enemy, which de-escalated conflicts that might otherwise have afflicted both the Chinese community and the Minangkabau people. Indeed, Padang remained a less than ideal place to live, especially once the Dutch launched their second military aggression. Anxiety was still part of everyday life, and the Chinese remained a target of various crimes. But by choosing the path of solidarity with Indonesians, the Chinese community was able to re-establish relations with the citizens of Padang when the Dutch eventually failed in their efforts to restore their colonial power and were forced to recognize the independence that Indonesia had proclaimed on 17 August 1945. That independence was to be a meaningful foundation for the life of the Chinese community in Padang in the years to come.

17.

Playing it safe

Survival strategies of the Indian community in East Sumatran cities, 1945-1946

Apriani Harahap

Introduction

The early days of Indonesian independence were marked not only by the struggle against the Dutch but also by intergroup conflicts.[1] Class struggle and ideological and ethnic tension often triggered such troubles. An absence of strong state authority, the presence of foreign elements, and personal interests exacerbated them. East Sumatra, with its large-scale plantations, was heavily affected by intergroup tensions. In March 1946, armed groups, mostly composed of migrants led by radical political actors, launched brutal attacks against the monarchs of the Malays, Simalungun and Karo on the suspicion that they were enabling the restoration of Dutch power in the region. Casualties among local elites and the East Sumatra aristocracy were high.[2]

One of the many ethnic communities in East Sumatra at this febrile moment of its history were the Indians. Largely overlooked in the Indonesian

Troops of the 26th Indian Division man mortars just outside Medan in Sumatra, probably. 1946. Source: photograph SE 7516 from the collections of the Imperial War Museum

historiography, they have been seen mainly as the source of the recruits that the British drew on for their occupation of Java and Sumatra at this time.[3] The present chapter broadens the focus and examines the impact the regime transitions had on the Indian community in East Sumatran cities as a whole. It asks the question: What was their strategy for survival amidst the social unrest that lasted from August 1945 to November 1946?

Upon Japan's surrender in August 1945, Indonesians declared independence in Jakarta and attempted to establish a Republican government throughout the archipelago. But Allied forces – composed mostly of British soldiers but including some Dutch units – soon attempted to control the same territory, with the result that rival authorities competed over the same spaces. This was also the case in the economically strategic region of East Sumatra. The new Republican government apparatuses in East Sumatra were not yet equipped to gain full control over the region. They were under constant pressure from armed groups, who fought not only against the British and the Dutch but also among themselves for territorial control and economic resources. The British and Dutch presence, meanwhile, kept the Republican government from functioning effectively. In such an extreme predicament, small conflicts could and did easily escalate into major violence.

For the Indian community in Medan and surrounding areas, as with most migrant communities, the early period of Indonesian independence was not a pleasant one. Many of them had earlier been contract workers in plantation belts and belonged to the lower classes. Their colonial status as foreign easterners (*Vreemde Oosterlingen*), however, had placed them above the continuously marginalized indigenous people. Accordingly, the presence of Indian soldiers in the British army made all civilian Indians in East Sumatra look like colonial stooges in the eyes of indigenous Indonesians. What was the experience of the Indian community during the post-war British occupation of Medan? In what ways did the presence of the British troops affect the Indian community? Why did the Indian communities in East Sumatra face the threat of communal violence? Who among them were most vulnerable to such violence? What was their strategy to survive during the British occupation? These are the questions this chapter will address.

The Indian community before the revolution

East Sumatra has long been inhabited by a great variety of ethnic groups. The population of 1.5 million recorded in the 1930 census consisted of local inhabitants such as Malays, Karo and Simalungun; *bumiputra* (indigenous) immigrants from Mandailing, Toba, Minangkabau and Java; as well as foreign immigrants from Europe, China, Arabia and India.[4] The flow of Indian migrants to East Sumatra began in the late nineteenth century, when European entrepreneurs were establishing tobacco plantations. A shortage of local manpower forced them to bring in contract workers from elsewhere – first from China and later from India and Java. The local population of Malays and Karos was too small to supply the required labour. Moreover, these groups had farming land and were not interested in plantation work.[5]

Contract workers from India were mostly ethnic Tamils.[6] Their numbers were not large: only 1,071 workers in 1881 and 4,140 in 1901. The small number of Tamil workers was due to the fact that plantation owners could not bring them directly from India. Colonial regulations prohibited the transfer of manpower from or to the colonies without the agreement of the British-Indian government. East Sumatra plantation owners consequently recruited Tamil workers from the Straits Settlements.[7] The Indian workers were mostly tasked to build roads and canals as well as to ride oxcarts to transport tobacco crops.[8]

When some of the tobacco plantations switched to rubber and oil palm, the number of Tamil workers gradually declined.[9] In 1930, there were only 1,021 of them.[10] Many were now unemployed and known as former contract workers (*bekas buruh kontrak*). But they did not immediately return to their country of origin. Instead, they moved to nearby urban neighbourhoods (*kampongs*). Meanwhile, new economic migrants arrived from India – mostly Sikhs, Chettiars and Sindhis – boosting the Indian population in East Sumatra.[11] The 1930 census recorded 13,912 Indians, 67 percent of whom resided in villages near plantation concessions. The remaining 33 per-

Table 1. Composition of urban population in East Sumatra, 1930

City	Bumiputra	European	Chinese	Indian and Arab	Total
Medan	41,270	4,293	27,287	3,734	76,584
Binjai	4,740	115	3,860	461	9,176
Pematangsiantar	9,711	163	4,964	490	15,328
Tebing Tinggi	8,377	315	4,844	490	14,026
Tanjung Balai	3,299	153	3,162	209	6,823
Total	67,397	5,039	44,117	5,384	121,937

Source: *Volkstelling 1930, Deel IV: Inheemsche Bevolking van Sumatra* (Batavia 1935) 142.

cent were spread across the five main cities in East Sumatra. In the capital Medan alone, there were 3,067 Indians.[12]

The Dutch divided the Indians in East Sumatra into four categories: Keling, Chetti, Bengali and Bombay.[13] Keling, a name often attributed to the ancient kingdom Kalinga on India's east coast, referred to the Tamils from South India.[14] The Tamils themselves considered the term Keling demeaning. Therefore, in 1927, Keling was changed to Voor-Indiër.[15] As for Chetti or Chettiar, this category was meant to designate Hindu traders from Tamil Nadu in South India.[16] Meanwhile, Bengali was used to refer to the Sikhs from Punjab and the Bengalis from Benggala. The last category, Bombay, referred to the Sindhis who came from the Sindh region in North India.[17]

Most Tamils in urban areas worked as menial labourers, helpers in trading companies or shops, housemaids, oxcart drivers, or small street vendors. Some of them also worked as dairy farmers, filling a local demand for milk.[18] Most Sindhis ran textile businesses, importing the commodity from their trading partners in Singapore.[19] They also supplied textiles to small-scale Sikh merchants who ran clothing shops in several marketplaces or worked as traveling vendors.[20] Sikhs also ran dairy farms or worked as security guards in various Western companies.[21]

Only a handful of Sikhs emerged as big businessmen. The brothers Hakkam and Gurdit Singh emerged as successful property entrepreneurs in Medan.[22] Some others stood out in the money lending business, competing with Chettiar loan sharks who had more capital. A 1922 report estimated the total capital of the 70 Chettiar-owned firms in Medan at between ten and twelve million guilders.[23]

Together with the Chinese and Arabs, many Indians enjoyed the privilege of being middle class in the colonial social stratification. As foreign easterners, their social status was higher than the average bumiputra. While subject to the same public laws as the bumiputra and tried in the same courts for criminal cases, their civil cases were mostly settled using their customary law.[24] Their social status reduced their interaction with other social groups. A zoning system (*wijkenstelsel*), first imposed in 1866, forced foreign easterners to live in special residential locations.[25] In Medan, Indians were instructed to live in a neighbourhood cluster known as Kampung Keling, separate from the bumiputra as well as from the Europeans and Chinese. Europeans resided in the Polonia area and the Chinese in Kesawan, while the bumiputra were spread out in villages on the outskirts of the city.[26] The zoning system was abolished in 1918, but most Indians remained in Kampung

Keling.[27] In 1927, they successfully urged the colonial government to rename Kampung Keling as Kampung Madras.[28] The new name began to appear in the local newspaper, *De Sumatra Post*, from the beginning of 1928.[29]

The politics of segregation turned the Indian community into an autonomous political entity, run by their own administrators. The colonial government appointed respected Indian individuals to the post of 'lieutenants' in cities with large Indian populations. These collected taxes, handled administrative tasks, maintained public order and appeared in court as staff or interpreters, to name but a few of their tasks. The best-known Indian lieutenant was Mohamad Ali, a Muslim Indian, who served in Medan for 40 years (1884-1924).[30] Due to his religion and ethnicity, however, Mohamad Ali was not considered able to represent the Sikh community in the city. In 1917, the Sikhs demanded that the colonial government appoint a lieutenant from their ethnic group.[31] The Hindu Chettiar and the Tamils made a similar request in 1920.[32] In 1924, Mohamad Ali was dismissed from his position due to tax embezzlement.[33] As a replacement, the government appointed two lieutenants for the Indian communities in Medan. Gulan Mohamad was appointed for the Tamil and Chettiar communities, and Ranjit Singh for the Bengali and Bombay.[34] This decision met the demand of the Sikhs but did not seem to please the Hindu Chettiar or the Tamils.

The discriminatory colonial politics of segregation were fundamentally racist. Various community groups internalized the racism and found it impossible to imagine that differences could ever be overcome in favour of unity. Even the new national awareness across the archipelago, growing from the beginning of the twentieth century as a reaction to Dutch colonialism, was considered exclusive because it only accommodated and was monopolized by the bumiputra.[35] Indeed, it did exclude the Indians because they had for the longest time been considered 'foreigners' who enjoyed a special social status provided by Dutch colonial authority. At the same time, Indian communities in East Sumatra did not actively engage in the Indonesian nationalist movement. Instead, they built their own community organizations that focused on developing the cultural, social and spiritual aspects of their communal life. One of their biggest religious organizations was the Deli Hindu Sabha. It was founded by the Hindu community in East Sumatra in 1937.[36] The Sikhs founded the Gurdwara Prabandhak Committee in 1925, while Indian Muslims founded the Indian Muslim Association in 1941.[37]

When it came to politics, Indians in East Sumatra oriented themselves towards their place of origin, India. On 6 May 1930, for example, they went on a massive strike, shutting down their businesses, as a form of protest against the detention of Mahatma Gandhi by the British Raj in India. He had been arrested in early May 1930 for leading a movement against taxes and against the monopoly of the British Raj on salt production. Later known as the Salt March, the protests grew into a large nonviolent civil disobedience movement against the British Raj.[38] East Sumatran Indians sent a telegram condemning Gandhi's arrest to the Viceroy of India and the Indian National Congress.[39]

Such attitudes essentially entailed the awareness of Indian communities in East Sumatra as a nation. This feeling only grew stronger under the Japanese colonial rule. Although generally considered harsher than the Dutch, the Japanese provided new opportunities that enabled an increasing national awareness among both the bumiputra and the Indians. Even though political parties were suppressed, the Japanese colonial government gave political roles to Indonesian nationalists in local government and propaganda bodies. It formed the propaganda agency Sendenhan as well as the Body for Assisting in the Defence of Asia (Badan Untuk Membantu Pertahanan Asia, BOMPA) to propagate anti-Western sentiment and garner support from the bumiputra for war purposes. Nationalist politicians later took advantage of these agencies to evoke a strong sense of Indonesian nationalism. The meetings and events they organized served as platforms for anti-Western speeches that induced patriotism while subtly evading loyalty to Japanese rule.[40]

At the same time, the Japanese built up their cooperation with the Indian traders and supported the establishment of the Indian Independence League (ILL) in Medan.[41] They sponsored the ILL in order to garner Indian support for the war against the British. The Indian traders saw this as an opportunity to liberate India.[42] In September 1942, the chair of ILL Medan, L.H. Mathani, a wealthy Sindhi merchant, received instruction from the central ILL based in Singapore to establish branch offices in several cities. By 1943, seven ILL branch offices had been set up in neighbouring cities. Chaired mostly by traders, these branch offices mobilized Indian communities in their cities to take part in the Indian independence movement with the help of Japan.[43]

Funding for ILL came from membership fees and fundraising.[44] Deploying both persuasion and coercion, the organization obtained major donations from Indian traders. ILL organizers often used Japanese authority to leverage contributions from the traders. Those who refused would immediately be reported to the Japanese military police, the Kenpeitai.[45]

Indian views on the ILL varied widely. Most chose to join the ILL but not always for the same reasons. Some dedicated themselves to the organization purely for the liberation of India. Others joined simply to get rice, sugar and clothing at a discount. The Japanese military government gave basic supplies to the ILL as a form of support.[46] The ILL's stark reliance on Japan discouraged other Indians from joining. They saw ILL as a 'Japanese puppet'.[47]

In mid-1943, the ILL began recruiting young Indians to serve in the Indian National Army (INA). In seven waves of recruitment, the ILL managed to enlist a great number of young Tamils and Sikhs. They were motivated not only by growing Indian nationalism but also by the fear of detention by the Japanese military government. They received military training from the Indian National Army's instructors, flown in directly from Singapore. In late 1943, the first four batches of new recruits totalling 150 personnel were deployed to Burma to fight the British. The fifth to seventh batches, however, were never dispatched. By 1944, many had left the INA.[48] After the war, those who had been sent to Burma chose to stay in Malaya and Singapore.[49] Only one-tenth of the total number of troops decided to return to East Sumatra.[50]

The Japanese replaced the various identity categories for Indians that had been specifically created by the Dutch with new categories. They distinguished pure-blood Indians (*bangsa* India) from descendants (*peranakan*). The term peranakan referred to the mixed Indian-bumiputra group, while bangsa India referred to the pure or non-mixed Indians.[51] Japan also changed the social system that had been imposed by the Dutch. The Indians, Chinese, Arabs and bumiputra were positioned below the Japanese but higher than Europeans and Indo-Europeans.[52] Under this new system, however, the Indians were considered non-citizens. They had to register as foreigners and pay fees of 100 or 50 guilders, for men or women respectively. Those not financially well off were given permission to pay in instalments over five to ten months.[53]

Taking sides in the revolution

The consolidation of Indonesian national awareness under the Japanese occupation reached its culmination when Sukarno and Hatta proclaimed Indonesia's independence on behalf of the Indonesian people in Jakarta on 17 August 1945, just two days after Japan surrendered. The proclamation was immediately followed by the formation of the government of the Republic of Indonesia and the establishment of the Preparatory Committee for Indonesian Independence (Panitia Persiapan Kemerdekaan Indonesia, PPKI).[54] All of Sumatra was designated a single province, with Medan as its capital. Two senior politicians from Medan, T.M. Hasan and M. Amir, were appointed governor and deputy governor of Sumatra.[55]

This series of important events, which took place in Jakarta, were beyond the knowledge of the people of East Sumatra, however. The two Sumatran representatives who attended the PPKI meeting, Hasan and Amir, did not return to Medan until 28 August 1945.[56] They carried a mandate to convey the news of the newly gained independence and to immediately form the instruments of the Republican government in Medan. In early September 1945, they held a meeting with senior politicians and the Malay royal elite to convey the PPKI's instructions. However, they were met with reluctance, as the Malay monarchs bluntly declined to cooperate.[57]

In mid-September 1945, news of the proclamation of independence finally became known to Indonesian youths housed at various Japanese military bases. They belonged to the now-obsolete Heiho and Giyugun, auxiliary forces formed by the Japanese in 1943 against expected Allied attacks in East Sumatra. They urged Governor Hasan to immediately announce the proclamation of independence. On 23 September 1945, they formed the Indonesian Youth Agency (Badan Pemuda Indonesia, BPI). Seven days later, the BPI organized a general meeting attended by at least 1,000 participants, before whom Hasan read the text of the proclamation and called for support for the Republican government. After the meeting, copies of the proclamation text were distributed, and several more BPI branches were formed in and outside Medan.[58]

The euphoria of independence soon began to overwhelm East Sumatra. On 3 October 1945, Hasan officially announced his appointment as governor. He appointed ten Residents for East Sumatra. The next day saw the establishment of the Indonesian National Committee (Komite Nasional Indonesia, KNI) with legislative powers.[59] Government offices formerly under Japanese control were taken over. On 6 October 1945, the red-and-white flag was officially hoisted during a general meeting on Medan's main square. Three days later, more than 100,000 people marched on the main streets of Medan in support of the new Republic. Similar mass demonstrations to celebrate the establishment of the Republic of Indonesia were held in cities across East Sumatra.[60]

The situation began to change when British troops landed in Medan on 10 October 1945. Consisting mostly of Indian soldiers, they were tasked with disarming and repatriating Japanese troops, freeing prisoners of war and other internees, and maintaining security and public order until the Dutch colonial government could return to its normal function.[61] The British handed over the tasks of civilian affairs to Dutch officials of the Netherlands Indies Civil Administration (NICA), which aimed to restore colonial rule. However, the British only had a limited number of troops, and their authority was confined to Medan. Outside Medan, therefore, the British cooperated with local authorities of the Republic of Indonesia to maintain security and order.[62]

Indonesian youths who had belonged to the Heiho and the Giyugun soon took advantage of this leeway to form Republican militia units, which they named the People's Security Army (Tentara Keamanan Rakyat, TKR). However, the TKR was quickly left behind by the rapid emergence of several new insurgent groups founded on common ethnic ties or on residential location. Each of these groups tried to control various parts of the city of Medan, financing themselves from irregular sources. Although TKR troops displayed more discipline and obedience to the chain of command as a result of their training, and they enjoyed more regular financial support, TKR soldiers also often operated according to the same modus operandi as the irregular armed groups. Both TKR and militia fighters confiscated weapons and ammunition from the Japanese soldiers. At the extreme level, various criminal groups took part in the activities on behalf of the revolution, which gave them justification to loot. In mid-November, anti-British sentiment flared up among the youth, fuelled by news of the Battle of Surabaya. This sentiment manifested itself in a series of skirmishes with the British-Indian Army in late November.[63]

Nationalist politicians in India, notably Pandit Jawaharlal Nehru, a prominent figure in India's independence movement, strongly protested against the deployment of the Indian army for the 'British occupation' of Indonesia.[64] Nehru urged the British not to use Indian troops against the government of the Republic of Indonesia and not to send military equipment from India to assist the Dutch.[65] Nehru's protest received much attention in the Indonesian mass media. The Medan-based newspaper *Mimbar Oemoem* published an article entitled 'Protes Nehru' on 14 November 1945. After quoting Nehru's statement against the British use of Indian troops to suppress Indonesian independence, the article insisted that Indian communities in Indonesia should persuade Indian soldiers to sympathize with the struggle of the Indonesian people.[66] Two days later, on 16 November 1945, the Indonesian newspaper *Soeloeh Merdeka* reported that politicians in India belonging to the All India Congress Committee had protested against the use of Indian soldiers to fight Indonesian youth.[67] News about Indian nationalists' protests against the British policy in Indonesia kept appearing in Indonesian newspapers. It became an effective means of propaganda for the Republic of Indonesia, serving to delegitimize British military actions in Indonesia. Whether it actually influenced British soldiers to support the Indonesian cause remains uncertain. Richard McMillan's study of the British occupation in Indonesia suggests that news coverage of the Indian protests had little effect on Indian troops in Indonesia. Their morale was more influenced by news about the social and political situation in India.[68]

Amidst Republican efforts to attract the sympathy of Indian troops, the Indian communities in East Sumatra were more concerned about the arrest of ILL leaders by the British army. The men were detained on charges of being Japanese collaborators and hence war criminals. It was only when these leaders were arrested that many former members of the Indian National Army joined the Indonesian militias, motivated by both anti-British sentiments and sympathy for the struggles of Indonesian youth.[69]

Gradually, the Indonesian revolution began to have a wider appeal to the Indian community in East Sumatra. Some of them joined the cause and personally approached Indian soldiers to support the Indonesian struggle. One Indian figure who played an important role in garnering Indian sympathy for the Republic was Hamzah Abdullah, a Muslim Indian merchant and member of the Indonesian National Pioneers (Napindo). This was a militia wing of the Indonesian National Party (Partai Nasional Indonesia, PNI). Abdullah was owner of the Fajar Asia restaurant, located near the Grand Hotel where the British-India Army barracks were situated. The restaurant served lamb curry favoured greatly by Muslim Indian soldiers. Together with two of his friends, Ajad Husin and Tabib Ansari, Abdullah approached his loyal Indian soldier customers and eventually succeeded in getting some to defect to the Republic of Indonesia. The Indian soldiers who fled from their units took their weapons and ammunition with them.[70] McMillan argued that these Indian soldiers deserted for various reasons. First, they were moved by religious sentiment. Aware of the significance of religious feeling, Republican propagandists made use of identity issues to appeal to their Muslim brothers to join the struggle. Second, Republican propagandists promised the Indian soldiers beautiful women if they would defect to the Republic together with their guns and ammunition. This lure proved the most effective, as evident in the increase of desertions in Medan in early March 1946. Third, the Republic also promised the soldiers their own land, which was also an effective incentive, especially for soldiers who had never owned land in their country of origin. And fourth, the Indian soldiers were also galvanized by their political sympathy with the Indonesians. Even though this was the least effective method, gaining sympathy by highlighting a common Asian sentiment also encouraged some Indian soldiers to defect.[71]

There were at least 71 deserters in Medan alone, most of them Muslim Indian soldiers. These were later enlisted in the Putera Asia battalion, a fighting unit of the TKR-B under the command of Captain Nip Xarim. The battalion itself was led by Abdul Sattar, a Muslim Indian, who had successfully influenced several Indian soldiers to desert. One of them was Nur Mohammad, who took with him 16 rifles and six crates of grenades when he defected. He later became the leader of the *Volksfront*, a militant armed organization, and at the same time served as propagandist to persuade his comrades in the British-Indian Army to defect to the Republican side.[72]

Sumatran Indian solidarity for the Indonesian cause became more apparent as various resistance groups emerged from mid-1946 onwards. On 28 April 1946, Indian youths in Medan formed the India-Indonesia Union (Persatuan India-Indonesia). This served as a bridge between the Indian and Indonesian youths in support of the struggle to strengthen the sovereignty of the Republic.[73] On 19 May 1946, Indian, Indonesian and Chinese youths in Medan initiated the Sumatran Youth Institute for New Democracy (Lembaga Demokrasi Baru Pemuda Sumatera). The goal of this organization was to fight for Indonesia's right to self-determination, reject capitalism and imperialism, and build democracy.[74] At the end of June, this institute established a representative branch in the town of Binjai.[75]

These facts indicate that Indians in East Sumatra, especially their youth, took an active role in the effort to defend Indonesia's independence. However, wealthier and more established Indian merchants tended to be less sympathetic to the Indonesian revolution. *Soeloeh Merdeka* depicted these merchants as opportunists who cooperated with the NICA for their own economic gain.[76] Even amidst the chaos, they made huge profits by smuggling basic needs. Boet Singh, a Sikh lawyer, painted a clear picture of the Indians who, he declared, were on the side of the Dutch:

> I will just mention them here, I mean those who are self-absorbed, who pay little attention to the development of the period, and decided to return to the previous Dutch East Indies era where they spent thousands of rupiahs to win the rank of captain, for example. At the time of the Japanese occupation, they supported the regime by establishing a puppet organization that was said to help liberate India. From that time on, they were extremely favoured by the regime and given unlimited power to run the black market, without the slightest control from the *Kenpeitai*. After Japan surrendered, they still collaborated with the

> regime, and continued to thrive, living by *where there is a will, there is a way*: trucks transported eggs, chicken, and shoes to and from [the Japanese base at] Rantau Perapat. They were successful.[77]

Other Indians in East Sumatra were not interested in the conflict between Indonesia and the Dutch and chose to remain neutral, minding their own business.[78] This group was represented by the All-Indian Representative Committee, which dealt with the political authorities of the Republic of Indonesia as well as with the British and the Dutch. Founded and chaired by D. Kumarasamy, this group also aimed to maintain social order for all Indians in East Sumatra. The group later changed its name to Sumatra Indian Union.[79]

Looking for a safe way

Towards the end of 1945, acts of violence began to flare up in Medan. According to historian Ann Laura Stoler, 'much of the violence was directed against the person and property of those perceived to be Dutch sympathizers (with ethnic Chinese and Indian merchants both easy targets and easy to blame'.[80] The perpetrators were criminal gangs who took advantage of the revolutionary label.[81] In mid-December 1945, J.J. van de Velde, a Dutch official of the humanitarian Recovery of Allied Prisoners of War and Internees (RAPWI), revealed that Indian and Chinese traders were being intimidated by 'extremists' – the biased Dutch term for armed youths – not to sell their commodities to Europeans:

> In Medan, things were calm; only, the extremists were so vicious in their terror that the Chinese and Indians no longer dared to sell us goods. They were spied on, threatened, and sometimes abducted, and what really happened to them afterward we could only speculate.[82]

Indian traders who sold goods to the Dutch were accused of not supporting the struggle for Indonesian independence. This in time became the justification for attacking and looting shops owned by Indians. Some of the shops' owners were even targeted for kidnapping and murder.[83] On 6 February 1946, the Dutch-language newspaper *Het Dagblad* covered the murder of two Sikhs, four Chinese and one European. All seven victims, found buried on the outskirts of Medan, were killed in early January by criminal gangs led by Timur Pane, who were also suspected of committing numerous other robberies, kidnappings and murders in Medan for several months. Except for Timur Pane, who managed to flee, his members were rounded up by the British troops.[84]

As conflicts between the British army and Indonesian fighters escalated, acts of violence against Indians extended beyond Medan from the early months of 1946. Terror, threats and robberies were directed against Indians, not only business owners but also Indian commoners living outside Medan. This resulted in a mass evacuation. They fled to Medan and looked to the British and Indian troops for protection, many of whom helped the evacuation process.[85] In late July 1946, British Indian troops evacuated at least 70 Indian civilians from Sunggal and Galang. During the evacuation, they were shot at by Indonesian militia groups and one Indian soldier was killed as a result. In retaliation, they captured 18 members of the armed groups.[86]

It is not known how many Indians fell victim to the violence and raids. However, the number of those who fled to Medan reached almost 2,000 people.[87] Ironically, the more the British Indian troops helped the Sumatran Indian civilians, the more often acts of violence took place. This was due to a growing suspicion of the Indian Army's complicity in the British and Dutch military campaigns against the Republic. The Indian troops were considered colonial accomplices. The Indian civilians were moreover suspected of supporting the return of Dutch rule. Such lurking prejudice easily rose to the surface because the Indians were almost always considered 'foreigners'. The residential segregation by the Dutch, which was later sustained by the Japanese, contributed to their constant alienation.

Acts of violence against East Sumatran Indians were not only perpetrated by the Indonesian youths and militias. Indian soldiers, especially Muslim soldiers who deserted from the British-Indian Army, were also involved in robberies and attacks on Indian civilians.[88] Their violence was fuelled by political conflicts between Hindu and Muslim groups in India. The India Muslim League's demand to partition India into two nations, Pakistan and India, had been rejected by the Hindu politicians from the Indian National Congress, and the resulting tension sparked major clashes between Hindu and Muslim groups in 1946, which in turn led to the anti-Hindu sentiment among the Muslim British soldiers from India who had joined Indonesian militias.[89] This prompted acts of violence by these deserters against the Hindu and Sikhs communities in East Sumatra.[90]

On 6 February 1946, *Het Dagblad* reported that the Medan-based Indian Relief Committee had sent a message to New Delhi to ask the British Raj to intervene in East Sumatra and repatriate Indian civilians to avoid further acts of violence against them.[91] Responding to the request, the British Raj assigned its delegate in Malaya, S.K. Chettur, to monitor first-hand the condition of Indian civilians in Indonesia.[92] Chettur arrived in Medan on 17 July. After seeing the condition of the Indians in refugee camps, Chettur set up a meeting with Luat Siregar, the Resident of East Sumatra, and expressed his concern about the ongoing kidnappings and killings of Indian civilians by Indonesian militants.[93] Responding to Chettur, Luat explained that:

> The Indonesian people are not hostile to other nations. We are very willing to live in peace with all nations. We are aware that there have been killings of Indians, who were probably very absorbed with themselves. Nonetheless, the Indonesian Republican government will take harsh action against those who commit radical violence and will try them in public Republican courts.[94]

Luat Siregar also stressed that in Republican-controlled territory, social relations between ethnic groups were healthy. To prove the truth of this statement, he offered to show Chettur the condition of Indian communities in various other cities in Sumatra and Java.[95] From his visit to Medan, Chettur reported that the conditions of the Indians in the refugee camps were relatively good despite their pressing demand for repatriation to India. The Dutch policy on repatriation, moreover, became an obstacle. They charged a very high fee of 250 guilders for individuals and 500 guilders for families. This made it prohibitive for the Indians who wished to return to India and settle there.[96]

Chettur's visit received a response from a journalist for the English-language newspaper in India, *Free Press of India.* In his piece entitled 'Indonesia's call to Pt Nehru', the journalist commented on Chettur's visit with a cynical tone. He noted that

> [T]he Indian Representative in Singapore leave for Sumatra on July 17. In a few days after that, '10,000 Indians persecuted by the Indonesians in Medan' will be in the news! He will report to Government of India who will be satisfied and agree to the use and retention of Indian troops! As a result, Indian troops will be hated to an increasing degree just as the Jap troops who are reported to be used by the British to fight the Indonesians in Sumatra.... It is understood that the Indian Representative in Singapore is touring only allied occupied areas in Indonesia in a Dutch plane as a fully accredited ad hoc diplomatic representative to the NEI Government.[97]

Concerning acts of violence against Indians, the journalist wrote:

> Now, the militarists come to the rescue of politicians by inventing 'incidents'. So, it is likely, they will prepare an 'atrocity story' describing Indonesian excesses against large numbers of Indians in Sumatra which would necessitate the use and retention of Indian troops. In reality, there has been no such excesses against Indians in any part of Indonesia except where the persons concerned were guilty of spying or acting against the interests of the Indonesian state.[98]

Despite an impression of leaning towards the Republic, the article accurately described a discourse of violence in which the British Raj tried to find justification for deploying Indian soldiers to Indonesia – a subject that had also been heavily criticized by nationalist politicians in India itself.

Indians who felt threatened and sought protection from the British-India authorities in Medan were housed in camps together with ethnic Chinese, European, Indo-European and Ambonese refugees. The Red Cross supplied them with food, clothing and other basic needs. Dalip Singh, a Sikh merchant, helped mobilize wealthy Indians in East Sumatra, who contributed 105,497 guilders towards the operational costs of the Red Cross. Assisted by 68 Indian volunteers, the Red Cross provided care for refugees in Medan as well as those in camps in Binjai, Tebing Tinggi and Tanjung Balai.[99]

The inter-regime transition was marked by constant skirmishes. It was not an easy period for most people in East Sumatra. Over time, Indian civilians, especially the youth, attempted to reduce the stigma, distrust and hostility that the community experienced by building commitment and loyalty to the Republic of Indonesia. On 27 June 1946, *Mimbar Oemoem* reported that Indians in Binjai had formed the Institute of Indian Union (Lembaga Gabungan Bangsa India), which sought to support the Republic of Indonesia through various forms of cooperation.[100] A similar organization was formed in Langkat Hulu, named the Committee of Indonesian-Chinese-Indian Union (Komite Gabungan Indonesia-Tionghoa-India), whose objective was to strengthen social solidarity among the various nationalities in support of the Indonesian revolution. On 17 July, the committee issued a strong condemnation of the Dutch, who were deemed to have damaged social relations between the Indians, Chinese and Indonesians:

> We, the Indonesian-Chinese-Indian group, hereby express our strong protest against the provocation and divisive politics of the Dutch government. Furthermore, we demand that the Indian soldiers should be immediately withdrawn from Indonesia and must not be given orders to kill the Indonesian people. Similarly, the Chinese must not be taken advantage of by the NICA. We, the Indonesian-Chinese-Indians, have joined hands for not only years but centuries.[101]

In November 1946, the interim Indian government sent two ships to transport 3,000 Indians seeking repatriation.[102] They had been waiting for at least two months since Chettur visited Medan in July 1946.[103] The Indian government set a travel fare of 240 guilders per person. However, since almost all of the money they had was spent during the two-month waiting period, the passengers were only requested to sign a statement letter that they would pay 42 guilders upon arrival in India.[104] Despite the distance and hardship, they chose to return to the homeland to set themselves free from turbulent times and multidimensional conflicts in East Sumatra, the land that had blessed them for the last few decades.

Conclusion

This chapter shows that the Indian community in East Sumatra was heavily affected by the conflicts and uncertainty that overwhelmed Indonesia in the early days of its independence. On the one hand, they were victims; on the other, they were also perpetrators. The multidimensional character of this history forced the Indian community to create their own strategies to set themselves free from the entanglement of revolutionary complexity.

The Indian community in East Sumatra responded to the revolutionary situation in three ways. The youth played an active role in Indonesia's struggle to maintain independence. Wealthy merchants, by contrast, supported the British and Dutch efforts to re-establish colonial rule. Others deemed this group to be opportunists who took sides only for their own economic gain. A significant number of Indians civilians, meanwhile, refused to be engaged in the political conflicts and chose to stay neutral. Each response was influenced by that group or individual's social status and historical experience. It is certain, however, as this research has shown, that more than one factor motivated the Indian community's response to historical events in East Sumatra.

Similarly, there were significant variations in both the temporal and spatial contexts of the hardship that the community faced. Violent acts against the

Indian community in Medan and surrounding urban areas began in late 1945, especially after the arrival of the British Army, many of whom were Indian soldiers. The situation worsened as Indonesian militias engaged in more frequent skirmishes with the British troops. This resulted in a high number of casualties among Indian traders and civilians. The presence of British troops in East Sumatra contributed to an escalation of threats to the Indian community; at the same time these troops were unable to provide sufficient protection for that community. In contrast, Indian civilians living within areas under Republican control beyond Medan were free from such threats and violence.

Acts of violence can also be traced to the lasting Indonesian perception of the Indians in East Sumatra as 'foreigners'. The residential segregation based on race, first imposed by the Dutch and continued by the Japanese military government, exacerbated the social separation between Indonesians and ethnic Indians.

Violence experienced by Indians in East Sumatra also had an international dimension. It partly originated from the internal political constellation in India. The presence of the British-Indian Army was seen by the Republican fighters as an integral part of Dutch efforts to re-establish colonial rule, eventually leading to threats against the Indian community in East Sumatra. The communal political tensions in India itself that led to demands for partition contributed to an escalation of public violence in East Sumatran cities. The perpetrators were not only Indonesian armed groups and criminals but also Muslim Indian soldiers who defected from the British-Indian army.

The violence, coming on top of earlier Japanese repression, made life more miserable for many Indians in East Sumatra. It forced them to flee to Medan in the hope of getting protection from the British-Indian troops. This did not always turn out to be a good decision. Internal problems within the British forces and the distortion that originated from the involvement of Dutch elements actually increased the threats towards Indians and exacerbated their problem of a lack of protection. Other Indians resorted to different strategies to avoid stigmatization, distrust and hostility. They demonstrated their commitment and loyalty to the Republic of Indonesia and fought together with Indonesian freedom fighters. They did this especially by utilizing socio-political organizations that supported Indonesian independence and thwarted Dutch plans to re-establish their colonial power in Indonesia.

In the centre of Republican power, Yogyakarta, a man changes the tire of an official car that flies the red-and-white Republican flag, 1948. Source: Charles Breijer, Nederlands Fotomuseum.

Notes

1. **Revolutionary Worlds: an introduction**

1 We are grateful for the discussions we had about this chapter with Gerry van Klinken, Bambang Purwanto, Yulianti, Martijn Eickhoff and Ireen Hoogenboom.

2 This happened for example in Kenya ('Mau Mau Rebellion Victims claim Parliament was Misled over Torture. Compensation Claim Brought by 44,000 Kenyans Alleges Widespread Atrocities of British Colonists in 1950s Were Covered Up', *The Guardian*, 23 May 2016.

3 See: Jeffry Pondaag and his Yayasan Komite Utang Kehormatan Belanda (KUKB, Committee of Dutch Debts of Honour), https://kukb.nl/ (accessed on 15 April 2022); 'German Colonialism, Fragments Past and Present', *German Historical Museum*, Berlin, October 2016-May 2017; A. Wightwick, 'Welsh Historian reveals Key Role in Securing £20m Payout for Mau Mau Torture Victims', *Wales Online*, June 2013, https://www.walesonline.co.uk/news/wales-news/mau-mau-torture-welsh-historians-4073034 (accessed 15 April 2022); 'Academic Sleuthing Uncovered British Torture of Mau Mau Fighters', *The Conversation*, June 2013, https://theconversation.com/academic-sleuthing-uncovered-british-torture-of-mau-mau-fighters-15010 (accessed 15 April 2022).

4 G. Oostindie, B. Schoenmaker and F. van Vree (eds) *Beyond the Pale: Dutch Extreme Violence in the Indonesian War of Independence, 1945-1949* (Amsterdam 2022), and associated volumes. (https://www.aup.nl/en/series/onafhankelijkheid-dekolonisatie-geweld-en-oorlog-in-indonesie-1945-1950).

5 M.W. Poesponegoro and N. Notosusanto (eds.), *Sejarah Nasional Indonesia* I-VI (Jakarta 2010); K. McGregor, *History in Uniform: Military Ideology and the Construction of Indonesia's Past* (Honolulu 2007).

6 D. van Reybrouck, *Revolusi: Indonesië en het Ontstaan van de Moderne Wereld* (Amsterdam 2020); R. Gunawan et al., *Sejarah Berita Proklamasi Kemerdekaan Indonesia* (Jakarta 2015).

7 A. Kahin (ed.), *Regional Dynamics of the Indonesian Revolution* (Honolulu 1985); the regions are addressed separately here, not in an integrated analysis. Others have also addressed regions separately: A. Reid, *The Blood of the People: Revolution and The End of Traditional Rule in Northern Sumatra* (Kuala Lumpur 1979); T. Abdullah (ed.), *The Heartbeat of the Indonesian Revolution* (Jakarta 1997).

8 Such an approach is in line with Cooper's dictum (even if applied to Africa) to not look back into history; see: F. Cooper, *Decolonization and African Society: The Labour Question in French and British Africa* (Cambridge 1996) 6-7.

9 Remco Raben, 'De Dagen van de Grote Uittocht', *Indische Letteren* 32 (2017) 22; H.J.H. Alers, *Om een rode of groene merdeka. 10 jaren binnenlandse politiek Indonesië 1943-1953* (Eindhoven 1956).

10 T. Abdullah and S. Siddique, *Islam and Society in Southeast Asia* (Singapore 1986); T. Abdullah, *Indonesia: Towards Democracy* (Singapore 2009); Abdullah (ed.), *The Heartbeat*, 4.

11 T.N. Harper, 'A Long View on the Great Asian War', in: D. Koh Wee Hock (ed.), *Legacies of World War II in South and East Asia* (Singapore 2007); Arsip Nasional Republik Indonesia (hereafter ANRI), RA.3a. Alg. Secretarie Deel I/585, Nota Inzake het Indonesisch Binnenlandsch-Bestuur, 20 October 1948; R.B. Karels, 'Mijn Aardse Leven Vol Moeite en Strijd: Raden Mas Noto Soeroto, Javaan, Dichter, Politicus, 1888-1951' (PhD thesis in history, Universiteit van Amsterdam 2008) 223.

12 T. Harper, *Underground Asia: Global Revolutionaries and the Assault on Empire* (Bristol 2020); D. van Reybrouck, *Revolusi.*

13 See, for example: D. Péclard and D. Mechoulan, 'Rebel Governance and the Politics of Civil War' (working paper) *Swisspeace Publications* (Basel 2015) 5.

14 See, for example, R. Collins, *Violence: A Micro-sociological Theory* (Princeton, 2008); S.N. Kalyvas, *The Logic of Violence in Civil War* (Cambridge 2006).

15 P. Owen, *Economy of Force: Counterinsurgency and the Historical Rise of the Social* (Cambridge 2015)

16 R. Frakking, 'Independence or Death? Recruitment and Desertion during the Wars of Decolonization in Indonesia and Malaysia, ca. 1945-1960', in: G. Curless and M. Thomas (eds.), *Oxford Handbook Understanding Insurgencies* (forthcoming, Oxford); I. Thames, *Over grenzen: Liminaliteit en de ervaring van verzet* (oration, Utrecht University, 17 May 2016) 7.

17 Sartono Kartodirdjo, *Pemikiran Dan Perkembangan Historiografi Indonesia: Sebuah Alternatif* (Jakarta 1982); Sartono Kartodirdjo, *Elite Dalam Perspektif Sejarah* (Jakarta 1983); Sartono Kartodirdjo, *Pendekatan Ilmu Sosial Dalam Metodologi Sejarah* (Jakarta 1992).

18 *Reformasi* refers to the period of political reform following the collapse of the authoritarian New Order in May 1998.

19 This book will be published in Dutch to introduce Indonesian historiography about the revolution to the Dutch audience: *Onze Revolutie. Bloemlezing uit de Indonesische geschiedschrijving over de strijd voor de onafhankelijkheid, 1945-1949* (Forthcoming 2023, Amsterdam University Press).

20 Sri Margana, Julianto Ibrahim, Siti Utami Dewi Ningrum, Satrio Dwicahyo, and Ahmad Faisol, *Serangan Umum 1 Maret 1949 Sebagai Hari Nasional Penekakan Kedaulatan Negara* (Yogyakarta 2022).

21 For example, M. Heidhues, 'Anti-Chinese Violence in Java during the Indonesian Revolution, 1945-49', *Journal of Genocide Research* 14:3-4 (2012) 381-401.

22 P. Smith, 'Writing in the Rain: Erasure, Trauma, and Chinese Indonesian Identity in the Recent Work of FX Harsono', *Journal of Southeast Asian Studies* 46:1 (2015) 119-133.

23 One such example is Bart Luttikhuis and C.H.C. Harinck, 'Voorbij het koloniale perspectief: Indonesische bronnen en het onderzoek naar de oorlog in Indonesië, 1945-1949', *BMGN-Low Countries Historical Review* 132:2 (2017) 51-76.

24 Bambang Purwanto, 'Bersiap, kutukan kemerdekaan Indonesia yang menghantui Belanda', *Media Indonesia*, 23 August 2022, 7.

25 Remco Raben, 'Indonesische blik op de geschiedenis wordt als irrelevant weggezet', *NRC*, 19 January 2022.

26 There is a book within the larger project about Bersiap: Esther Captain and Onno Sinke. *Het geluid van geweld: Resonance of Violence. Bersiap and the Dynamics of Violence in the First Phase of the Indonesian Revolution, 1945-1946* (Amsterdam 2023).

2. The meaning of independence for women in Yogyakarta, 1945-1946

1 *Membonceng* or to ride along is a commonly used term in the Indonesian historiography of the revolution. In the Indonesian perspective, this term has a negative connotation as an illegal action of hiding behind legitimate authority.

2 Anthony Reid, *Indonesia, Revolusi, & Sejumlah Isu Penting* (Jakarta 2018) 131-151.

3 This is based on an analysis of digital textbooks available at *https://bsd.pendidikan.id* using the open-source, web-based application for text analysis *https://voyant-tools.org*.

4 Christine Dobbin, 'The Search for Women in Indonesian History' in: Ailsa Thomson Zainu'ddin (ed.), *Kartini Centenary: Indonesian Women Then and Now* (Melbourne 1996) 44-51; Kuntowijoyo, *Metologi Sejarah*. (Yogyakarta 2003) 113; Anton E. Lucas 'Wanita Dalam Revolusi: Pengalaman Selama Pendudukan Dan Revolusi, 1942-1950' *Prisma* 5 (1996) 17; Bambang Purwanto, *Gagalnya Historiografi Indonesiasentris?!* (Yogyakarta 2006) 29-31; Jean Gelman Taylor 'Images of the Indonesian Revolutions' in: Jane Drakard dan John Legge (eds.) *Indonesian Independence Fifty Years on 1945-1950* (Melbourne 1996) 13-16.

5 Department of Information Republic of Indonesia, *The Indonesian Women's Movement A Chronological Survey of the Women's Movement in Indonesia* (Jakarta 1968) 14-16; A. Eryono, *Wanita Indonesia* (Yogyakarta 1975.) 243-251; Ryadi Gunawan, 'Dimensi-Dimensi Perjuangan Kaum Perempuan Indonesia dalam Perspektif Sejarah', in: Fauzie Ridjal et al., (eds.), *Dinamika Gerakan Perempuan di Indonesia* (Yogyakarta 1993) 102-103; Lasmidjah Hardi et al. (eds.), *Sumbangsihku Bagi Ibu Pertiwi Kumpulan Pengalaman dan Pemikiran Buku V* (Jakarta 1985); Dharmono Hardjowijono et al. (eds.), *Replika Sejarah Perjuangan Rakyat Yogyakarta Jilid II* (Yogyakarta 1985); Tita Marlina and E. Kristi Poerwandari, 'Pergerakan Perempuan Indonesia 1928-1965', in: Elizabeth Kristi Poerwandari and Rahayu Surtiati Hidayat (eds.), *Perempuan Indonesia Dalam Masyarakat Yang Tengah Berubah* (Jakarta 2000) 88-91; Oemar Sanoesi, *Replika Sejarah Perjuangan Rakyat Yogyakarta* (Yogyakarta 1983); Galuh Ambar Sasi, 'Gerakan Perempuan Indonesia', Master's thesis, History, Universitas Negeri Yogyakarta (2010) 74-80; Galuh Ambar Sasi 'Di Tanah Kiblik: Perempuan Dalam Ge(Mer)Lap Revolusi', in: Sri Margana et al. (eds.), *Gelora di Tanah Raja: Yogyakarta Pada Masa Revolusi 1945-1949* (Yogyakarta 2017) 178; Irna H.N. Hadi Soewito, *Wanita Pejuang* (Jakarta 2005); Nani Soewondo and N. Surasno, *Kedudukan Wanita Indonesia Dalam Hukum dan Masjarakat* (Jakarta 1995) 236-141; Cora Vreede de Stuers, *Sejarah Perempuan Indonesia: Gerakan dan Pencapaian* (Depok 2008) 175-196; Sukanti Suryocondro, *Potret Pergerakan Wanita di Indonesia* (Jakarta 1984) 137.

6 Cindy Adams, *Bung Karno Penyambung Lidah Rakyat Indonesia* (Jakarta 1966) 363.

7 Rosihan Anwar, *Kisah-Kisah Zaman Revolusi Kemerdekaan* (Jakarta 2015) 119.

8 Inventaris Arsip Statis Pemerintahan Daerah Tingkat II Bone No. 175.

9 Mohammad Hatta, *Mendajung antara Dua Karang* (Jakarta 1979) 119.

10 Rosihan Anwar, *Kisah-Kisah Zaman*.

11 Susan Blackburn, *Kongres Perempuan Pertama* (Jakarta 2007) xxii.

12 Badan Musyawarah Museum, *Yogya Benteng Proklamasi* (Yogyakarta 1985); Suhartono W. Pranoto et al., *Yogyakarta Ibukota Republik Indonesia, 4 Januari 1946-27 Desember 1949* (Yogyakarta 2002); Galuh Ambar Sasi, 'Gelora Api (Ke)Merdeka(An) di Jawa Tengah', in: Jajat Burhanuddin and Amurwani Dwi Lestariningsih (eds.), *Sejarah Berita Proklamasi Kemerdekaan Indonesia* (Jakarta 2015); P.J. Suwarno, *Hamengku Buwono IX Dalam Sistem Birokrasi Pemerintahan Yogyakarta 1942-1974: Sebuah Tinjauan Historis* (Yogyakarta 1994); Tashadi et al. (eds.), *Sejarah Revolusi Kemerdekaan (1945-1949) di Daerah Istimewa Yogyakarta* (Jakarta 1991).

13 Galuh Ambar Sasi, Gelora Api (Ke)Merdeka(An), 80.

14 Galuh Ambar Sasi, 'Aisyiyah, Pionir Kesadaran Keindonesiaan' *https://alif.id/read/author/galuh-ambar/* (accessed 10 November 2020).

15 Lasmidjah Hardi et al., *Sumbangsihku Bagi Ibu*, 39-40, 174.

16 Anonymous, 'Hidoep Indonesia Merdeka.' *Sinar Baroe*, 2605 [1945]; Arsip Nasional Republik Indonesia (hereafter ANRI), Sekretariat Negara Republik Indonesia, *30 Tahun Indonesia Merdeka* (Jakarta 1981) 29.

17 PKO is now known as the PKU Muhammadiyah Hospital.

18 Lasmidjah Hardi et al. *Sumbangsihku Bagi Ibu*, 107.

19 Suratmi Iman Sudiyat 'Suratmi Iman Sudiyat', in: *50 Tahun Republik Indonesia di Yogyakarta: Sebuah Lintasan Sejarah* (Yogyakarta 1995)) 284.

20 Irna H.N. Hadi Soewito, *Wanita Pejuang* (Jakarta 2005) 356, 358; Anonymous 'Boekti Keboeasan Moesoeh', *Kedaulatan Rakjat* 1945; Suratmi Iman Sudiyat, 'Suratmi Iman Sudiyat', 286-287; Lasmidjah Hardi et al., *Sumbangsihku Bagi Ibu*, 40. Galuh Ambar Sasi, 'Gerakan Perempuan Indonesia, 135; De Stuers, *Sejarah Perempuan Indonesia*, 176.

21 Soekarsih, 'Boeroeh Wanita dan Perdjoangan Boeroeh' *Merdeka* (1946) 117; Saskia Wieringa, 'Aborted Feminism in Indonesia: A History of Indonesian Socialist Feminist' in: Saskia Wieringa (ed.), *Women Struggles and Strategies* (Sydney 1988) 76; *Verslag Konperensi Wanita Indonesia* (1946), Library of Perwari (Persatuan Wanita Republik Indonesia) Jakarta.

22 Pemimpin Poesat Perwari, 1946. 'Panggilan Perwari', *Merdeka*.

23 Triatmi Juliani, 'Suka Duka Di Masa Revolusi', in: Irna H.N. Hadi Soewito (ed.), *Seribu Wajah Wanita Pejuang Dalam Kancah Revolusi '45 Buku Pertama* (Jakarta 1995) 290; Uripah Sutikno 'Membantu PMI di Medan Laga', in: Irna H.N. Hadi Soewito (ed.), *Seribu Wajah Wanita*, 348.

24 Nationaal Archief, The Hague (hereinafter) NL-HaNA, Marine en Leger Inlichtingendienst, de Netherlands Forces Intelligence Service en de Centrale Militaire Inlichtingendienst in Nederlands-Indië (hereinafter NEFIS/CMI), 2.10.62 inv.no 4878.

25 This term is different from the term *bersiap* in Dutch historiography, which refers to the period of violence from September 1945 to mid-1946 against the Dutch, Indo-Europeans and those who were accused of being sympathetic to colonial rule.

26 Badan Musyawarah Museum, *Yogya Benteng Proklamasi*, 48; Tashadi et al. (eds.), *Sejarah Revolusi Kemerdekaan*, 57.

27 Suwarno, *Hamengku Buwono IX*, 174.

28 Senarai Arsip Paku Alam VIII No. 1347, Arsip Puro Pakualaman.

29 Selo Soemardjan, *Perubahan Sosial di Yogyakarta* (Depok 2009) 81.

30 Triatmi Juliani, 'Suka Duka di Masa Revolusi, 190.

31 Yayasan Indonesia Boekoe. 'Sejarah Kampung Patehan' (unpublished stencil) (Yogyakarta 2011).

32 Suwarno, *Hamengku Buwono IX*, 182.

33 Yayasan Indonesia Boekoe.

34 Umayi, 'Kenangan Manis Anggota WAPP', in: Irna H.N. Hadi Soewito (ed.), *Seribu Wajah Wanita*, 305.

35 Galuh Ambar Sasi, 'Gerakan Perempuan Indonesia', 180.

36 Widyati Soertinah A, 'Suara dari Front Ambarawa' in: Irna H.N. Hadi Soewito (ed.), *Seribu Wajah Wanita*, 354.

37 Galuh Ambar Sasi, 'Gerakan Perempuan Indonesia', 181.

38 Umayi, 'Kenangan Manis Anggota WAPP', 343.

39 Galuh Ambar Sasi, 'Gelora Api (Ke)Merdeka(An) di Jawa Tengah', 228.

40 Verslag Konperensi Wanita Indonesia 1946; Harry A. Poeze, *Tan Malaka, Gerakan Kiri, dan Revolusi Indonesia Jilid 2: Maret 1946-Maret 1947* (Jakarta 2009).

41 Sri Mangoensarkoro, *Pergerakan Wanita Indonesia* (Yogyakarta 1946) 24; NL-HaNA NEFIS/CMI, 2.10.62 inv.no 5595.

42 Sri Mangoensarkoro, *Pergerakan Wanita Indonesia*, 28-31.

43 Benedict R.O'G. Anderson, *Revoloesi Pemoeda: Pendudukan Jepang dan Perlawanan di Jawa 1944-1946* (Jakarta 1988); George McTurnan Kahin, *Nasionalisme & Revolusi Indonesia* (Depok 2013); Anton E. Lucas. *Peristiwa Tiga Daerah Revolusi dalam Revolusi* (Jakarta 1989); Harry A. Poeze, *Tan Malaka*; An-

thony Reid, *Sumatera: Revolusi dan Elite Tradisional* (Depok 2012); R. Smail, *Bandung Awal Revolusi 1945-1946* (Depok 2011); Wisesa, E. Dwi Aryo, 'Menghayati Sejarah Revolusi Kemerdekaan' *Prisma 7* (1988) 61, 67.

44 Soekarno, *Wanita Indonesia Selalu Ikut Bergerak dalam Barisan Revolusioner* (Jakarta 1964) 7-8.

45 Soekarno, *Wanita Indonesia,* 8.

46 S. Mangoensarkoro 'Pendidikan Nasional.', in: *30 Tahun Taman Siswa* (Yogyakarta 1956) 91-92.

47 S. Mangoensarkoro, 'Pendidikan Nasional', 92.

48 Soetan Sjahrir, 'Negara Jang Kita Dirikan Negara Kera'jatan: Revoloesi Kita Poen Revoloesi Kera'jatan.' *Kedaulatan Rakjat* (1946).

49 Verslag Konperensi Wanita Indonesia 1946.

50 H.R., 'Perempoean dalam Sejarah dan Masa', *Revolusioner,* 1946.

51 NL-HaNA NEFIS/CMI, 2.10.62 inv.no 04704.

52 Soekarsih, 'Boeroeh Wanita dan Perdjoangan Boeroeh.' *Merdeka* (1946) 117; NL-HaNA NEFIS/CMI, 2.10.62 inv.no 0632.

53 H.R., 'Perempoean Dalam Sejarah dan Masa', *Revolusioner,* 1946.

54 NL-HaNA NEFIS/CMI, 2.10.62 inv.no 05110.

55 Galuh Ambar Sasi, 'Di Tanah Kiblik', 188.

56 Sik Ien Tjoa, *Masa'alah Warganegara Indonesia* (Yogyakarta 1947); Min Pao, 'Masjarakat Tiongjoa di Djokja: Presiden Soekarno Akan Mengangkat Penasehat Tionghoa?', *Waspada* (1948); Tan Goan Po, 'Chineezen en de Nationale Beweging in Indonesia', in: Kementrian Penerangan, *Waarom Chineezen geen Vreemde Oosterlingen meer willen zijn in Indonesië* (Yogyakarta 1946) 7-10; Tjan Tjoe Som 'De Chineezen en het Indonesische burgerschap', in: *Waarom Chineezen geen,* 3-6.

57 Min Pao, 'Masjarakat Tiongjoa'.

58 Soe Hok Gie, 'Simpang kiri dari sebuah jalan; Kisah pemberontakan Madiun September 1948' (MA thesis University of Indonesia, Fakultas Sastra) (Jakarta 1969) 78-79.

59 Soe Hok Gie, 'Simpang kiri dari sebuah jalan', 89.

60 Raden Noerito Pringgoadisuryo, *Pikirans van een Javaanse Avonturier* (Amsterdam 2006) 66; Soe Hok Gie, 'Simpang kiri dari sebuah jalan', 89; Arsip Nasional Republik Indonesia (ANRI), Kepolisian/805; Kementrian Penerangan, 1946, NL-HaNA NEFIS/CMI, 2.10.62 inv.no 1097.

61 Hario Kecik, *Pemikiran Militer 2: Sepanjang Masa Bangsa Indonesia* (Jakarta 2009) 252.

62 Anonymous, 'No Title', *Revolusioner,* 9.

63 Pringgoadisuryo, *Pikirans van een Javaanse Avonturier,* 176.

64 De Stuers, *Sejarah Perempuan.*

3. The battle of the nation and pemuda subjectivity

1 For instance, Suhartono W. Pranoto. *Yogyakarta, Ibukota Republik Indonesia, 4 Januari 1946-27 Desember 1949: Yogyakarta Kota Revolusi* (Yogyakarta 2002); Eddy R. Soekamto and Lilih Prilian Ary Pranowo, *Yogyakarta Ibukota Perjuangan* (Yogyakarta 2009); Dwi Ratna Nurhajarini and Albiladiyah Al Ilmy (2012). *Yogyakarta, dari Hutan Beringin ke Ibukota Daerah Istimewa* (Yogyakarta 2012); Sri Margana, et al. *Tahta Tanah Raja* (Yogyakarta 2018).

2 *Kedaulatan Rakjat,* 2-6-1947.

3 Yinghong Cheng, *Creating the "New Man": From Enlightenment Ideals to Socialist Memories* (Honolulu 2009).

4 Judith Butler, *Gender Trouble: Feminism and the Subversion of Identity* (London 1990).

5 Judith Butler, 'Performative Acts and Gender Constitution: An Essay in Phenomenology and Feminist Theory' *Theatre Journal* 40:4 (1988) 519.

6 J. Butler, 'Performative Acts', 520.

7 Henri Lefebvre, *The Production of Space* (London 1991).

8 Reuben Rose-Redwood and Michael Glass, *Geographies of Performativities* (London 2014).

9 A perlocutionary act is the effect of an utterance on an interlocutor. For insights into perlucotionary and illocutionary acts, see Butler, 'Performative acts'.

10 n.a. *Pemuda Indonesia dalam Dimensi Sejarah Perjuangan Bangsa*, Jakarta: Yayasan Sumpah Pemuda. (Jakarta 1984).

11 Takashi Shiraishi, *An Age in Motion. Popular Radicalism in Java, 1912-1926* (Ithaca NY 1990).

12 Henk Schulte Nordholt, 'Modernity and Cultural Citizenship in the Netherlands Indies: An Illustrated Hypothesis', *Journal of Southeast Asian Studies* 42:3 (2011) 435-457.

13 Rudolf Mrázek , *Engineers of Happy Land: Technology and Nationalism in a Colony* (Princeton 2002) 157.

14 Ranajit Guha, *Dominance Without Hegemony: History and Power in Colonial India* (Cambridge 1997).

15 Benedict Anderson, *Java in a Time of Revolution: Occupation and Resistance. 1944-1946* (Ithaca, NY 1972).

16 Mrázek , *Engineers of Happy Land*, 159.

17 William Frederick, 'Appearance of Revolution: cloth, uniform and pemuda style in East Java, 1945-1949', in: Henk Schulte Nordholt (ed.), *Outward Appearances: Dressing State and Society in Indonesia* (Leiden 1997) 199-248.

18 David Wehl, *The Birth of Indonesia* (London 1948) 17.

19 Ali Sastroamidjojo, *Tonggak-tonggak di Perjalananku* (Jakarta 1974) 198.

20 I.N. Soebagijo, *Jusuf Wibisono: Karang Ditengah Gelombang* (Jakarta 1980) 46.

21 Bart Luttikhuis, 'Beyond Race: Constructions of 'Europeanness' in Late Colonial Legal Practice in the Netherlands Indies', *European Review of History* 20:4 (2013) 539-559.

22 Ann Laura Stoler, 'Rethinking Colonial Categories: European Communities and the Boundaries of Rule', *Comparative Studies in Society and History* 31:1 (1989) 134-161.

23 Partha Chaterjee, *The Nation and Its Fragments: Colonial and Postcolonial Histories* (Princeton 1974).

24 E. Locher-Scholten. *Women and the Colonial State: Essays on Gender and Modernity in the Netherlands Indies 1900-1942*. (Amsterdam 2000) 126-128.

25 Gayatri Spivak, 'Can the Subaltern Speak?', in: Cary Nelson and Lawrence Grossberg (eds.), *Marxism and the Interpretation of Culture* (London 1988) 80.

26 P.J. Soewarno, *Hamengkubuwono IX dan Sistem Birokrasi Pemerintahan Yogyakarta. 1942-1974: Sebuah Tinjauan Historis* (Yogyakarta 1994); see also Selo Soemardjan, *Social Changes in Jogjakarta* (Ithaca NY 1962).

27 *Kedaulatan Rakjat*, 6 January 1946; See also, Abidin Kusno, *Behind the Postcolonial: Architecture, Urban Space and Political Cultures in Indonesia* (London and New York, 2000).

28 *Kedaulatan Rakjat*, 6 January 1946.

29 Clifford Geertz, *Negara: The Theatre State in Nineteenth Century Bali* (Princeton 1980).

30 ORIDA (Oeang Republiek Indonesia Daerah or Regional Currency of the Republic of Indonesia).

31 Oey Beng To, *Sejarah Kebijakan Moneter Indonesia* (Jakarta 1991).

32 Suwandi Tjitrowarsito, 'Perdjalanan', in: H.B. Jassin (ed.), *Gema Tanah Air: Prosa dan Puisi 1942-1948* (Jakarta 1959).

33 *Kedaulatan Rakjat*, 17 May 1946.

34 *Friesch Dagblad*, 23 October 1947.

35 S. Sudjojono, *Cerita tentang Saya dan Orang-orang Sekitar Saya* (Jakarta 2017) 9. 'Tidak ada satu poster yang haus darah. Poster-poster kita harus memetik tali-tali harpa rasa kultur pemimpin dunia Barat yang paling halus. Kita ingatkan mereka pada Kilping, Rousseau, Shakespeare, dan Washington. Semboyan-semboyan Revolusi Perancis, Perang Kemerdekaan Amerika Serikat dan semangat Willem van Oranje kita tonjolkan. Kita dialog dengan mereka.'

36 Blanche D'Alpuget, *Mediator: A Biography of Richard Kirby* (Melbourne 1977) 74.

37 *Friesch Dagblad*, 17 October 1947.

38 *Friesch Dagblad*, 23 October 1947.

39 *Kedaulatan Rakjat*, 6 January 1946.

40 Sukarno, *Dibawah Bendera Revolusi. Jilid II*, (Jakarta 2015) 12.
41 Abrar Yusa, *Biografi: Komat-kamit Selo Soemardjan* (Jakarta 1995) 155.
42 John Coast, *Recruit to Revolution. Adventure and Politics in Indonesia* (London 1952) 96.
43 Mrázek , *Engineers of Happy Land* 157.
44 *Kedaulatan Rakjat*, 9 October 1946.
45 *Kedaulatan Rakjat*, 20 January 1947.
46 *Kedaulatan Rakjat*, 17 March 1947.
47 *Kedaulatan Rakjat*, 17 March 1947.
48 *Kedaulatan Rakjat*, 20 January 1947.
49 *Kedaulatan Rakjat*, 27 January 1947.
50 *Kedaulatan Rakjat*, 19 June 1947.
51 *Kedaulatan Rakjat*, 13 June 1947.
52 *Leeuwarder Courant*, 25 April 1947.
53 *Leeuwarder Courant*, 29 April 1947.
54 *Kedaulatan Rakjat*, 29 April 1947.
55 For how this analysis is used in another case, see Alexey Golubev, 'The Western Observers and the Western Gaze in the Affective Management of Soviet Subjectivity', *Russian Social Science Review* 61: 3-4 (2020) 251-280.
56 Nationaal Archief, The Hague (hereafter NL-HaNA), Netherlands Forces Intelligence Service and Centrale Inlichtingendienst in Nederlands-Indië, 2.10.62, inventaris nummer 6994; see also Hersri Setiawan, *Memoir Perempuan Revolusioner, Francisca C. Fanggidaej* (Yogyakarta 2006).
57 *Kedaulatan Rakjat*, 15 March 1947.
58 Siti Mahmudah Nur Fauziah, 'Malioboro Tempo Doeloe: Sejarah Kehidupan Sehari-hari 1890-1950', Bachelors' thesis, History, Universitas Gadjah Mada (2018) 242, 247.
59 *Kedaulatan Rakjat*, 15 March 1947.
60 Dimyati 'Djokdja Diduduki Chaos' in: H.B. Jassin (ed.), *Gema Tanah Air: Prosa dan Puisi 1942-1948* (Jakarta 1959) 7.
61 Quoted in Saksono Prijanto, 'Revolusi dari Perspektif Perempuan: Cerita Pendek Periode 1950an dan 1960an', in: Abdul Rozak Zaidan et al., *Revolusi, Nasionalisme dan Banjir Roman* (Jakarta 2005) 70.
62 Rusman Sutiasumarga, 'Gadis Bekasi', in: HB Jassin (ed.), *Gema Tanah Air: Prosa dan Puisi 1942-1948* (Jakarta 1959) 167.
63 Pieter t'Hoen, *Terug uit Djokja* (n.a.: 1946) 26.
64 Steven Farram, 'Wage War Against Beatle Music! Censorship and Music in Soekarno's Indonesia', *RIMA: Review of Indonesian and Malaysian Affairs* 41:2 (2007) 247.
65 Krishna Sen, 'What's Oppositional in Indonesian Cinema?', in: Anthony R. Guneratne & Wimal Dissanayake, *Rethinking Third Cinema* (London 2003) 149.
66 Homi K. Bhabha, H, 'Of Mimicry and Man: The Ambivalence of Colonial Discourse', in: Frederick Cooper and Ann Laura Stoler (eds.), *Tensions of Empire: Colonial Culture in a Bourgeois World* (Oakland 1997) 154.
67 *Kedaulatan Rakjat*, 24 June 1946.

4. Monsters and capitalists

1 I would like to express my gratitude to the Department of History, Faculty of Cultural Sciences, Universitas Gadjah Mada, for the research grant from the program 'Proclamation of Independence, Revolution, and War in Indonesia, 1945-1949'.
2 Muhammad Yuanda Zara, 'Voluntary Participation, State Involvement: Indonesian Propaganda in the Struggle for Maintaining Independence, 1945-1949' (Doctoral thesis in history, University of Amsterdam 2016); Muhammad Yuanda Zara, 'Indonesian Mockery of the Dutch during the Indonesian Struggle to Maintain Independence', *BMGN-Low Countries Historical Review* 136:3 (2021) 31-60.

3 Andi Suwirta, *Revolusi Indonesia dalam* News and Views: *Sebuah Antologi Sejarah* (Yogyakarta 2015).

4 A.D. Pirous, 'Sejarah poster sebagai alat propaganda perjuangan di Indonesia', *Jurnal Ilmu Desain* 1: 3 (2006) 139-158; Lasarus, *Perjuangan Seniman Lukis pada Masa Revolusi Fisik di Yogyakarta (1945-1949)* (Bachelor's thesis in history, Universitas Sanata Dharma 2009); Vincentia Marisa Prihatini, *Peranan Seniman dalam Perjuangan Mempertahankan Kemerdekaan Indonesia Tahun 1945-1949* (Bachelor's thesis in history, Universitas Negeri Yogyakarta 2015); Duta Fikra Abdu Hamid, *Poster Perjuangan pada Masa Revolusi Fisik di Indonesia Tahun 1945-1950* (Bachelor's thesis in history, Universitas Airlangga 2019).

5 Garth S. Jowett and Victoria O'Donnell, *Propaganda & Persuasion. Sixth Edition* (Los Angeles 2015) 1; Philip M. Taylor, *Munitions of the Minds: A History of Propaganda from the Ancient World to the Present Day. Third Edition* (Manchester and New York 2003) 6.

6 William Eckhardt, 'Making and Breaking Enemy Images', *Peace Research* 21:4 (1989) 11.

7 Marja Vuorinen, 'Introduction: Enemy Images as Inversions of the Self', in: Marja Vuorinen (ed.), *Enemy Images in War Propaganda* (Tyne 2012) 2.

8 Nicoletta F. Gullace, 'Barbaric Anti-Modernism: Representations of the "Hun" in Britain, North America, Australia and beyond', in: James Pearl (ed.), *Picture this: World War I Posters and Visual Culture* (Lincoln and London 2009) 68-69.

9 Kristen Williams Backer, 'Kultur-Terror: The Composite Monster in Nazi Visual Propaganda', in: Niall Scott (ed.), *Monsters and the Monstrous: Myths and Metaphors of Enduring Evil* (Amsterdam and New York 2007) 81.

10 David Welch, *World War II Propaganda: Analyzing the Art of Persuasion during Wartime* (Santa Barbara and Denver 2017) 179.

11 Suhatno, *Dr. H. Affandi: Karya dan Pengabdiannya* (Jakarta 1985) 61; Ray Rizal, *Affandi: Hari Sudah Tinggi* (Jakarta 1990) 29; Tashadi, et al., *Partisipasi Seniman dalam Perjuangan Kemerdekaan Daerah Istimewa Yogyakarta* (Jakarta 1996) 71-73.

12 This can be seen in several documents, most of which are Indonesian propaganda posters that were seized by the Dutch; see: Nationaal Archief, The Hague (hereinafter NL-HaNA) Algemene Secretarie van de Nederlands-Indische Regering (hereinafter AS), 2.10.14 inv.no 5465.

13 NL-HaNA AS, 2.10.14 inv.no 5465.

14 'Verzameling Republikeinse pamfletten en vlugschriften', 1947-1948 (KITLV, Special Collection/D Or. 663).

15 *Merdeka,* 12 October 1945, quoted in Andi Suwirta, *Revolusi Indonesia* 82.

16 Rosihan Anwar, *Sejarah Kecil, Petite Histoire Indonesia Jilid 2* (Jakarta 2009) 70; Rosihan Anwar, *Napak Tilas ke Belanda: 60 Tahun Perjalanan Wartawan KMB* (Jakarta 2010) 29.

17 *The Voice of Free Indonesia,* 1, without date, most probably the end of October 1945.

18 *Lasjkar,* 9 May 1946, quoted in Andi Suwirta, *Revolusi Indonesia dalam News and Views*, 95.

19 NL-HaNA, Marine en Leger Inlichtingendienst, de Netherlands Forces Intelligence Service en de Centrale Militaire Inlichtingendienst in Nederlands-Indië (hereinafter NEFIS/CMI), 2.10.62 inv.no 4690.

20 See Colin Moore, *Propaganda Prints: A History of Art in the Service of Social and Political Change* (London 2010) 158.

21 Mark Johnston, *Fighting the Enemy: Australian Soldiers and Their Adversaries in World War II* (Cambridge 2000) 87.

22 *Merdeka,* 25 September 1948.

23 Pramoedya Ananta Toer, et al., *Kronik Revolusi Indonesia Jilid V (1949)* (Jakarta 2014) 26-27.

24 *Merdeka,* 19 February 1949.

25 NL-HaNA NEFIS/CMI, 2.10.62 inv.no 5411. I would like to thank Sarkawi B. Husein who pointed out this propaganda poster to me.

26 NL-HaNA NEFIS/CMI, 2.10.62 inv.no 5411.

27 See the postcard entitled 'Geiten en Apenspel. Batavia. Ned-Indië', from circa 1900, in Olivier Johannes

Raap, *Soeka Doeka di Djawa Tempo Doeloe* (Jakarta 2015) 146.

28 'Verzameling Republikeinse pamfletten en vlugschriften', 1947-1948 (KITLV, Special Collection/D Or. 663).

29 'Verzameling Republikeinse pamfletten en vlugschriften', 1947-1948 (KITLV, Special Collection/D Or. 663).

30 Verzameling Republikeinse Pamfletten en Vlugschriften 1947-1948

31 Ibidem.

32 Ibidem.

33 Gert Oostindie, *Serdadu Belanda di Indonesia, 1945-1950: Kesaksian Perang Pada Sisi Sejarah yang Salah* (Jakarta 2016) 5.

34 *The Voice of Free Indonesia,* Edisi 12, 13 April 1946.

35 NL-HaNA AS, 2.10.14 inv.no 5465.

36 *'Indonesia didjadjah oleh Belanda. Dan hasil bumi Indonesia dibawa ke pasar doenia. Untuk kepentingan kapitalis Belanda. Hai kaum buruh!!! Djandjimoe pada tgl. 17-8-1945. Bahwa kamoe tak ingin bekerdja pada Belanda'.*

37 *'Saudara2!!! Akibat dari aksi Plosionil [sic] Belanda, jang maksudnja mengamankan dan mendjamin rakjat Indonesia, katanja. Tetapi bukti jang njata, kedjadian di Tjilewo dan lain2 tempat dalam Kewedanan Tjikampek. Petani2 jang sedang bekerdja di sawah, ditusuk dengan bajonet hingga mati. Saudara2!!! Djanganlah kedjadian jang tersebut itu kita biarkan sadja'.*

38 Ibidem. *'Selama masih ada Belanda pendjadjah di boemi kita, selama itu ada kekatjauan dan kesengsaraan! Karena itu maka dengan tjara apapun djuga, kita hantjurkan mereka'.*

39 H.M. Victor Matondang (ed.), *Percakapan dengan Dr. T.B. Simatupang* (Jakarta 1995) 14.

40 Caricature in *Merdeka,* republished in *The Voice of Free Indonesia* magazine, first edition, date and month unknown but presumably second half of October 1945.

41 Ibidem, 109.

42 Ooi Keat Gin, *Post-War Borneo, 1945-1950: Nationalism, Empire and State-Building* (Oxon 2013) 119.

43 Frank Palmos, *Surabaya 1945 Sakral Tanahku* (Jakarta 2016) 157.

44 Andi Suwirta, *Revolusi Indonesia,* 105.

45 Ibidem, 106.

46 Ibidem, 112.

47 *Merdeka,* 4 October 1948.

48 *Merdeka,* 4 October 1948.

49 NL-HaNA AS, 2.10.14 inv.no 5465.

50 The artist who created this poster appears to have deliberately changed the familiar phrase 'the man in the right place' to 'the man on the right please'. This may be a mockery of Van Mook, suggesting that he was not the right person to be a leader in postwar Indonesia. He is depicted as a feudal ruler who was in it for his own pleasure and at the expense of the native aristocrats who supported him.

51 Robert Cribb, *Gangsters and Revolutionaries: The Jakarta People's Militia and the Indonesian Revolution, 1945-1949* (Singapore 2009) 144-145.

52 NL-HaNA AS, 2.10.14 inv.no 5465.

53 NL-HaNA AS, 2.10.14 inv.no 5465.

54 Andi Suwirta, *Revolusi Indonesia,* 116.

55 *Merdeka,* 11 January 1947, quoted in Andi Suwirta, *Revolusi Indonesia* 115. See also another caricature that mocked the Federal Consultative Assembly (Bijeenkomst voor Federaal Overleg, BFO), a committee that was to determine what the federal United States of Indonesia would look like, in *Merdeka* on 31 March 1949, in which the Assembly was depicted as a bottle of liquor that intoxicates the Indonesian population.

5. The violence of Dutch public security

1 B.R.O'G. Anderson, *Java in a Time of Revolution: Occupation and Resistance, 1944-1946* (Jakarta 2006) 50-52; Soewarno, *Sejarah pertempuran 5 hari di Semarang / disusun oleh Panitia Penyusunan Sejarah Pertempuran Lima Hari di Semarang* (Semarang 1977) 87.

2 Gusti Asnan et al., *Menteri Pendidikan dan Kebudayaan Republik Indonesia 1945-2018* (Jakarta, Sheffield 2018) 147-158: Manus, MPB et al., *Tokoh-Tokoh Badan Penyelidikan Usaha-Usaha Persiapan Kemerdekaan Indonesia II* (Jakarta 1993) 108-112.

3 Soewarno, *Sejarah pertempuran 5 hari,* 22-23 and 40.

4 Soewarno, *Sejarah pertempuran 5 hari,* 34-37, 89-91 and 94-95; Soekirno, *Semarang* (Semarang 1956) 84; Osman Raliby, *Documenta Historica I* (Jakarta 1953) 33.

5 B. Brommer et al. (eds.), *Semarang. Beeld van een stad* (Purmerend 1995) 65.

6 NL-HaNA, Algemene Secretarie van de Nederlands-Indische Regering (hereinafter AS) 2.10.14 inv. no 2213, *Verslagen en overzichten van de Kenpeitai over de situatie in Semarang in de maand september 1945.*

7 This critical perspective was developed during two workshops on memory landscapes held in 2020 in Semarang and Yogyakarta. Students conducted micro-historical research on memory formation at various sites in and near Semarang (for the concept of memory landscapes, see: M. Eickhoff, D. Danardono, T. Rahardjo and H. Sidabalok, 'The Memory Landscapes of "1965" in Semarang', *Journal of Genocide Research* 19-4 (2017) 530-550, 531-532.

8 Anderson, *Java in a Time of Revolution,* 146-149; Kenichi Gotō, 'The Semarang Incident in the Context of Japanese-Indonesian Relations, in: Taufik Abdullah (ed.), *The Heartbeat of the Indonesian Revolution* (Jakarta 1997) 133-148; Han Bing Siong, 'The secret of major Kido; The battle of Semarang, 15-19 October 1945' in: *Bijdragen tot de Taal-, Land- en Volkenkunde* 152:3 (1996) 382-428, 398-399; Soewarno, *Sejarah pertempuran 5 hari.* For the number of casualties, see: P.M.H. Groen, '"Patience and bluff"; De bevrijding van de Nederlandse burgergeïnterneerden op Midden-Java (augustus-december 1945)', *Mededelingen van de Sectie Militaire Geschiedenis van de Landmachtstaf* 8 (1985) 91-154, 118.

9 B. Bouman, *Ieder voor zich en de Republiek voor ons allen: De logistiek achter de Indonesische Revolutie 1945-1950* (Amsterdam 2006) 72.

10 Brommer, *Semarang* 70-72; M. Scott, *Special Forces Commander. The Life and Wars of Peter Wand-Tetley OBE MC Commando, SAS, SOE and Paratrooper* (Barnsley 2011) 175-177. For more information on the key-area-strategy, see: P. Groen, *Marsroutes en dwaalsporen. Het Nederlands militair-strategisch beleid in Indonesië 1945-1950* (The Hague 1991) 28-29.

11 Suwarno, *Sejarah Pertempuran 5 Hari,* 224-227; Han Bing Siong, *Geschiedenis van de Vijfdaagse Strijd in Semarang, 14-19 October 1945* (Rijswijk 1995) 66-67. The stereotype can be found in the 1860s poem 'Vloekzang. De laatste dag der Hollanders op Java door Sentot' by Sicco Ernst Willem Roorda van Eysinga (https://socialhistory.org/bwsa/biografie/roorda-van-eysinga, accessed: 6-5-2021).

12 Groen, "Patience and bluff" 96-98, 105, 108.

13 Han Bing Siong, 'The Indonesian Need of Arms after the Proclamation of Independence', *Bijdragen tot de Taal-, Land- en Volkenkunde* 157-4 (2001) 799-830, 811-812.

14 R. McMillan, *The British Occupation of Indonesia. Britain, the Netherlands and the Indonesian revolution* (London/ New York 2005) 4, 13, 26-28; E. Touwen-Bouwsma, 'De opvang van burgergeïnterneerden op Java en Sumatra (15 augustus 1945- 15 april 1946), in: E. Touwen-Bouwsma and P. Groen (eds.), *Tussen Banzai en Bersiap. De afwikkeling van de Tweede Wereldoorlog in Nederlands-Indië* (The Hague 1996) 25-42, 28-29.

15 Groen, "Patience and bluff", 126-133.

16 Brommer, *Semarang* 73-74. Compare with: McMillan, *The British Occupation,* 29.

17 SAIP-dossier A. Visser; T. Sumarno et al., 'History of War "The Battles of Palagan Ambarawa" Reviewed From Universal War Strategy Perspective', *International Journal of Arts and Social Science* 4-3 (2021) 1-12, 2.

18 D.C.L. Schoonoord, *Nederlands-Indië onder Amerikaans, Australisch en Brits Geallieerd Militair Gezag (22 april 1944 tot 30 november 1946) en de Netherlands Indies Civil Administration (Nica)* (Amsterdam 2020) 831-832, 884-885, 947.

19 The National Archives, Kew (hereinafther TNA Kew) WO 203, Headquarters papers, Southeast Asia Command, 2. WO 203 inv.no 6011, 'Report on Activities of 5 Parachute Brigade Group in Semarang, January-May 1946', written by Brigadier Darling, 11 May 1946.

20 Ibidem, 14-15. Brommer, *Semarang.* 77-79; McMillan, *The British Occupation* 81, 89, 101; Schoonoord, *Nederlands-Indië,* 1007-1009.

21 M.F.A. Brok, 'Geschiedenis van een brigade', in: M. Brouwer et al. (eds.), *Tussen sawahs en bergen: het leven van de soldaat in de Tijger-brigade* (Semarang 1948) 1-38, 9.

22 Brommer, *Semarang,* 77-78.

23 For this strike, see: H. Burgers, *De Garoeda en de Ooievaar. Indonesie van kolonie tot nationale staat* (Leiden 2011) 475-477. For the letter, see: 'Open brief aan de heeren Gortzak, de Groot en de redactie van "De Waarheid"', *De Tijger. Weekblad van de Tijger-Brigade* 27 (2 November 1946).

24 Imam Soemardi et al., *Sedjarah TNI-AD Kodam VII/Diponegoro, Sirnaning Jakso katon Gapuraning Ratu,* (Semarang 1968) 68-71. Compare with A.H. Nasution, *The Indonesian National Army* (New York 1960) 138, 140-141 and 209.

25 Soemardi, *Sedjarah TNI-AD Kodam VII/Diponegoro,* 71.

26 Nasution, *The Indonesian National Army,* 215-220.

27 J.J.P. de Jong, *De Terugtocht. Nederland en de dekolonisatie van Indonesië* (Amsterdam 2015) 83-87.

28 'Republikeinsche Order "Staakt het Vuren"', *Nieuwe Courant* (15 February 1947).

29 Brommer, *Semarang,* 81.

30 R. Limpach and P. Groen, 'De oorlog met de Republiek Indonesië 1945-1950/1962', in: P. Groen et al. (eds.), *Krijgsgeweld en Kolonie. Opkomst en ondergang van Nederland als koloniale mogendheid 1916-2010* (Amsterdam 2021) 309-350, 322.

31 Brommer, *Semarang.* 82. Compare with: Lutvia Maharani. *Pegambilalihan Kota Salatiga dari Kekuasaan Belanda ke Pemerintah Republik Indonesia Tahun 1945-1950* (Unpublished thesis, Universitas Semarang, 2009) 89. For a discussion on Dutch culpability, see: M.S. Heidhues, 'Anti-Chinese violence in Java during the Indonesian Revolution', in: B. Luttikhuis and D.A. Moses (eds.), *Colonial Counterinsurgency and Mass Violence. The Dutch Empire in Indonesia* (London 2014) 155-175, 163, 167.

32 '4 Augustus, dag van Semarangs verlossing. Hoe de verbinding tussen West en Midden tot stand kwam', *Het Midden* (7 August 1947).

33 Groen, *Marsroutes* 117.

34 Limpach and Groen, 'De oorlog met de Republiek Indonesië, 325-336.

35 Groen, *Marsroutes* 122, 132; Bouman, *Ieder voor zich,* 174.

36 D.C. Anderson, 'The military aspects of the Madiun affair', *Indonesia* 21 (1976) 1-63, 1; Limpach and Groen, 'De oorlog met de Republiek Indonesië 320, 327, 336; Bouman, *Ieder voor zich,* 208, 213. Compare with: Burgers, *De Garoeda,* 519-520.

37 T. Bouma, *Naar een federaal Indonesië: De geschiedenis van de totstandkoming van de Republiek der Verenigde Staten van Indonesië en de bijdrage van federale Indonesische nationalisten aan de Indonesische onafhankelijkheid 1917-1949* (Hilversum 2020) 240-241, 269-272; De Jong, *De Terugtocht,* 155, 166.

38 H. Poeze, 'Walking the Tightrope: Internal Indonesian conflict', in: B. Luttikhuis and D.A. Moses (eds.), *Colonial Counterinsurgency and Mass Violence. The Dutch Empire in Indonesia* (London 2014) 176-197, 189-193.

39 Anderson, 'The military aspects of the Madiun affair', 44, 53; F. Gouda and T.W. Brocades Zaalberg, *American Visions of the Netherlands East Indies / Indonesia: U.S. Foreign Policy and Indonesian Nationalism, 1920-1949* (Amsterdam 2002) 35-36.

40 Groen, *Marsroutes* 127, 192-194; J. de Moor, *Generaal Spoor: Triomf en Tragiek van een Legercomman-*

dant (Amsterdam 2011) 336-342.

41 Limpach and Groen, 'De oorlog met de Republiek Indonesië', 336.

42 Brommer, *Semarang*, 83-85; Groen, *Marsroutes*, 180.

43 'Plechtige installatie Midden-Javaraad', *De Locomotief: Samarangsch handels- en advertentie-blad (hereinafter De Locomotief)*, 7 April 1949; 'Dr. R.V. Soedjito, *Kementerian Penerangan. Kami Perkenalkan* (1954) 124; 'Voorzitter dr. R.V. Soedjito residentarts van Tegal', *De Locomotief*, 25 February 1949. See also: http://www.konstituante.net/id/profile/KATHOLIK_valentinus_soedjito_dwidjoatmodjo (accessed 10 June 2021).

44 A.H. Nasution, *Sekitar Perang Kemerdekaan 10* (Bandung 1977) 467. 'Midden-Java. Erkenning van het Recomba-gebied van Midden-Java als een staatkundige eenheid, waarvan de status nader zal worden bepaald', *Staatsblad van Indonesië* 69 (1949); 'Midden-Java-Raad', *De Locomotief*, 25 March 1949. Compare with: A.A. Schiller, *The formation of Federal Indonesia, 1945-1949* (The Hague 1955) 134.

45 Groen, *Marsroutes* 226; De Jong, *De Terugtocht*, 258-259.

46 Bouman, *Ieder voor zich*, 302. For a descripton of this period (translated in Dutch, written in 1959), see: T.B. Simatupang, *Het laatste jaar van de Indonesische vrijheidsstrijd 1948-1949. Een authentiek verslag door de voormalig chef-staf van de Indonesische strijdkrachten* (Kampen 1985).

47 De Moor, *Generaal Spoor*, 337-338; Groen, *Marsroutes*, 175, 190, 226; Limpach and Groen, 'De oorlog met de Republiek Indonesië, 337.

48 Groen, *Marsroutes*, 210; Sri Margana et al., *Serangan Umum 1 Maret 1949* (Yogyakarta 2019).

49 Limpach and Groen, 'De oorlog met de Republiek Indonesië, 336-341.

50 Groen, *Marsroutes* 198, 200. Compare with: C. van Dijk, *Rebellion under the banner of Islam: The Darul Islam in Indonesia* (The Hague 1981) 142-143.

51 'Djokja overgedragen', *De Locomotief*, 30 June 1949.

52 Soemardi, *Sedjarah TNI-AD Kodam VII/Diponegoro*, 230-233; Soekirno, *Semarang*, 129.

53 NL-HaNA AS 2.10.14 inv.no 4992, 14 September 1949, J.M.J. Morsink, hoofd tijdelijke bestuursdienst Semarang to the Recomba voor Midden-Java; Compare with: G.C. Zijlmans, *Eindstrijd en ondergang van de Indische bestuursdienst. Het corps binnenlands bestuur op Java 1945-1950* (Amsterdam 1985) 111.

54 'Boediono, Raden', Kementerian Penerangan, *Kami Perkenalkan* (1954) 52.

55 Brommer, *Semarang*. 86. For a detailed description of the ceremony, see: 'Overdracht van Civiel Bestuur', *De Locomotief*, 29 December 1949.

56 'Kolonel Gatot Soebroto inspecteerde troepen', *De Locomotief*, 31 December 1949.

57 https://id.wikipedia.org/wiki/Taman_Makam_Pahlawan_Giri_Tunggal (accessed 20 July 2021); visit by the author on 1 February 2020. A plaque at the cemetery commemorates the inauguration.

58 C.L. Temminck Groll et al., *Dutch Overseas: Architectural Survey: Mutual Heritage of Four Centuries in Three Continents* (Zwolle 2002) 169-170.

59 Djawatan Penerangan Propinsi Jawa Tengah, *Propinsi Djawa-Tengah* (Semarang 1953) 48-55.

60 Kenichi Gotō, *Tensions of Empire: Japan and Southeast Asia in the Colonial and Postcolonial World* (Singapore 2003) 171-185.

61 H.T. Bussemaker, *Bersiap!: Opstand in het paradijs: de Bersiap-periode op Java en Sumatra 1945-1946* (Zutphen 2005) 173.

62 'de smadelijke, of moet ik zeggen "strategische" terugtocht van het Engels leger', J.F.M. Busselaar, *Belevenissen van een Landstorm-soldaat gedurende en na afloop van de Tweede Wereldoorlog* (Wateringen 1955) 28.

63 Sumarno 'History of War' 2. McMillan, *The British*, 29.

64 Examples can be found in Touwen-Bouwsma, 'De opvang van burgergeïnterneerden' 34. See also: TNA Kew, WO 203, Headquarters papers, Southeast Asia Command, 2, WO 203 inv.no 6011, 'Report on Activities of 5 Parachute Brigade Group in Semarang, January-May 1946', written by Brigadier Darling, 11 May 1946.

65 Busselaar, *Belevenissen van een Landstorm-soldaat* 27.

66 Bussemaker, *Bersiap!,* 153-193.

67 NL-HaNA Procureur-Generaal (hereinafter PG) 2.10.17 inv.no 65, Buitenkantoor Nefis Semarang, Onderwerp: verhoor Slamet-Depok. Opgemaakt op 12 mei 1946, door J. v. der Valk.

68 'Moord in de Bersiap-periode', *De Locomotief* (2 March 1948); 'Bersiap-moordenaars ter dood veroordeeld', *De Nieuwsgier* (28 August 1948).

69 NL-HaNA-AS 2.10.14 inv.no 3043, 2 February 1946, Nefis-Rapport on Semarang.

70 Brok, 'Geschiedenis van een brigade' 17.

71 'T-Brigade twee jaar op Java', *De Locomotief,* 6 March 1948.

72 Brommer, *Semarang.* The volumes on Surabaya (1994), Bandung (1996), Medan (1997), Yogyakarta and Solo (1998) followed the same format.

73 *De excessennota: Nota betreffende het archiefonderzoek naar de gegevens omtrent excessen in Indonesië begaan door Nederlandse militairen in de periode 1945-1950, ingeleid door Jan Bank* (The Hague 1996). This report refers to 19 cases from Central Java, all dating from the years 1947 to 1949.

74 See also M. Eickhoff, 'Weggestreept verleden? Nederlandse historici en het Rawagededebat', *Groniek Historisch Tijdschrift* 194 (2012) 53-67, 58.

75 Brommer, *Semarang.* 80. For Sutomo, see: Anderson, *Java in a Time of Revolution,* 451.

76 Nasution, *The Indonesian National Army,* 138.

77 Soemardi, *Sedjarah TNI-AD Kodam VII/Diponegoro,* 72-74.

78 Rosihan Anwar, *Sejarah Kecil Petite Histoire Indonesia Jilid 7, Kisah-Kisah Zaman Revolusi Kemerdekaan* (Jakarta 2015) 107-114.

79 Busselaar, *Belevenissen,* 29.

80 http://ilmiaindonesiaku.blogspot.com/2016/01/tradisi-haul-pahlawan-syuhada-di.html (accessed: 5 June 2022). The date of *Ahad,* 11 *Muharram* 1366 AH is problematic, as 11 *Muharram* 1366 AH was not a Sunday (*Ahad*). Dutch records indicate that the attack took place on 15 December 1946, which was indeed a Sunday, and which corresponds to 21 *Muharram* 1366 AH. It therefore seems likely that at some point 21 *Muharram* was misread or otherwise misidentified as 11 *Muharram.*

81 See: brief commemoration pamphlet titled 'Kisah Pahlawan Syuhada' dated 20 February 2003 of the committee of *syuhada* (martyr) commemoration in Bugen, Semarang.

82 The picture is taken by soldier G. Siebgens, see: Brommer *Semarang* 34.

83 NIMH 509, inv.nr. 1137, 15-12-1946, Action reports by 2-7 RI and 1 RS of *Actie Bestand.*

84 H. Supanto, *Hizbullah Surakarta, 1945-1950* (Surakarta 1992) 105-114.

85 NL-HaNA PG 2.10.17 inv.no. 745, Rapport over de republikeinse bestuursorganisatie in Semarang (undated).

86 'Icksan, Mr. Mohammad', *Kementerian Penerangan, Kami Perkenalkan* (Jakarta 1954) 62. See also: H. Poeze, *In het land van de overheerser; Indonesiërs in Nederland 1600-1950* (Dordrecht 1986) 178, 250.

87 Zijlmans, *Eindstrijd,* 37, 43.

88 In his letter, Icksan also referred to military problems, see: NL-HaNA PG 2.10.17, inv.no 1113, Icksan to Minister van Defensie (Dutch Translation), 26 May 1946.

89 Brommer, *Semarang,* 79.

90 For the establishment of the function of Recomba, see: Zijlmans, *Eindstrijd,* 54-56.

91 TNA Kew, WO 203, Headquarters papers, Southeast Asia Command, WO 203 inv.no 6011, 'Report on Activities of 5 Parachute Brigade Group in Semarang, January-May 1946', written by Brigadier Darling, 11 May 1946, 7.

92 P.H. Angenent, *De vorstenlandsche waterschapsordonnantie toegelicht,* (PhD thesis; Universiteit Leiden, 1933).

93 NL-HaNA AS 2.10.14 inv.no 3043, 18 May 1946, P.H. Angenent to D.R.A. van Langen; 24 May 1946, P.H. Angenent to AMACAB Batavia.

94 NL-HaNA AS 2.10.14 inv.no 3043, Telegram No. 2V163, Clg kab to CO AMACAB, 23-5-1946, (CO = Commanding officer; Clg kab = Kabinet van de Legercommandant); Telegram No. 105, CO AMACAB to Clg kab, 23 May 1946.

95 M. Bloembergen, *De geschiedenis van de politie in Nederlands-Indië: Uit zorg en angst* (Amsterdam 2009) 353, 359. Angenent collaborated with 4 police divisions, see: TNA Kew, WO 203, Headquarters papers, Southeast Asia Command WO 203 inv.no 6011, 'Report on Activities of 5 Parachute Brigade Group in Semarang, January-May 1946', written by Brigadier Darling, 11 May 1946, 10-11.

96 Nélia Dias, 'Exploring the senses and exploiting the land. Railroads, bodies and measurement in nineteenth-century French colonies', in: T. Bennett and P. Joyce (eds.), *Material Powers: Cultural Studies, History and the Material Turn* (London 2010) 171-198.

97 NL-HaNA PG 2.10.17 inv.no 131, 6 September 1946, Directeur van Verkeer en Waterstaat, het hoofd van de Post-, Telegraaf- en Telefoondienst L.A. Peletier to Procureur-Generaal.

98 NL-HaNA PG 2.10.17 inv.no 131, 31 July 1946, N.H. Postema, buitenkantoor Nefis Semarang aan hoofdkantoor Nefis in Batavia. See also: 31 July 1946, Verklaring van Oei Biauw Goen.

99 NL-HaNA PG 2.10.17 inv.no 131, 27 August 1946, Kolonel D.R.A. van Langen to the Procureur-Generaal in Batavia.

100 NL-HaNA PG 2.10.17 inv.no 131, 8 August 1946, Procureur-Generaal to Directeur van Verkeer en Waterstaat.

101 NL-HaNA PG 2.10.17 inv.no 131, 6 September 1946, Directeur van Verkeer en Waterstaat, het hoofd van de Post-, Telegraaf- en Telefoondienst L.A. Peletier to Procureur-Generaal.

102 NL-HaNA PG 2.10.17 inv.no 1111, 'Semarang' (undated). Compare with: NL-HaNA PG 2.10.17 inv.no 745, Rapport over de republikeinse bestuursorganisatie in Semarang (undated).

103 NL-HaNA PG 2.10.17 inv.no 1112, 'Semarang'.

104 See for example this Nefis overview of Central Javanese political activities: NL-HaNA PG 2.10.17 inv.no 647, N.E.F.I.S.-Buitenkantoor Semarang. Inlichtingen rapport t/m 7 Juli 1947.

105 Mochtar Hidajat, 'Menjingkap Tabir Perdjuangan Dibawah Tanah Dlm Kota Semg', *Suara Merdeka* (1964) 150.

106 See: NL-HaNA PG 2.10.17 inv.no 1112, 'Beknopt overzicht van de organisatie M.K.P.' For the MKP, see also: NL-HaNA PG 2.10.17 inv.no 1113, 26 May 1946, Icksan to Minster van Defensie (Dutch Translation), Verkorte Bijlage. NL-HaNA PG 2.10.17 inv.no 1113, Voorlopig verhoor Sariboen.

107 'De arrestatie van Mr. Icksan', *Nieuwe Courant* (1 July 1946).

108 Nasution, *The Indonesian National Army,* 216.

109 A.H. Nasution, *Sekitar Perang Kemerdekaan Indonesia 3* (Bandung 1977) 214-215.

110 R.I. see: NL-HaNA PG 2.10.17 inv.no 1113, 'Verdedigingsorganisatie Semarang'.

111 NL-HaNA PG 2.10.17 inv.no 1113, Verkort verslag van den strijd in de stad Semarang.

112 NL-HaNA Marine en Leger Inlichtingendienst, de Netherlands Forces Intelligence Service en de Centrale Militaire Inlichtingendienst in Nederlands-Indië (hereinafter NEFIS/CMI) 2.10.62 inv.no 2595 I-Igel (dossier Icksan), Aanvullende verklaring van Mr. Icksan naar aanleiding van het proces-verbaal van getuigenverhoor van Sariboen alias Soetjipto Dirahardjo. 25-9-1946, opgesteld door N.F.W. van den Arend'.

113 NL-HaNA NEFIS/CMI 2.10.62 inv.no 2595 I-Igel (dossier Icksan), 4 October 1946, N.F.W. van den Arend, hoofd buitenkantoor Nefis Semarang to Directeur Nefis Batavia. Betreft uitwijzing Icksan.

114 Abdul Salem, Sepangat, Ruslan, Sumargono.

115 Sukandar, Wirjono Kusumo, Emor Djajadinata, Himawan, Sutedjo, Sukamsi.

116 NL-HaNA PG 2.10.17 inv.no 1112, 3 July 1946, C.O.A.M.A.C.A.B. P.H. Angenent aan C.C.O.A.M.A.C.A.B., 'Voorziening in de Indonesische bestuursvoering te Semarang'.

117 NL-HaNA PG 2.10.17 inv.no 1112, 17 June 1946, Afschrift Verslag.

118 *Orang Terkemoeka di Djawa* (Jakarta 1944) 84.

119 NL-HaNA PG 2.10.17 inv.no 1112, 15 July 1946, Ch.W.A. Abbenhuis, C.C.O.A.M.A.C.A.B. to C.O.A.M.A.C.A.B.

120 'Hein Sassen op Midden-Java', in: G. van Pijkeren, *Loslaten, dat gaat niet meer. Oorlogsherinneringen van en aan meer dan 90 Ter Aarse Indiëgangers* (Nieuwkoop 2017) 13-30, 15.

121 Busselaar, *Belevenissen van een Landstorm-soldaat,* 28.

122 H.W. Horsten, *Saboteur, partizaan, stoottroeper* (Rotterdam 2004) 217.

123 'Ondanks de vreugde over de nieuwe overwinning konden velen een gevoel van mismoedigheid niet onderdrukken als ze de jonge knapen zagen, die zo maar de dood waren ingejaagd zonder een kans van slagen...'. [']. Brok, 'Geschiedenis van een brigade', 16.

124 NL-HaNA, Strijdkrachten in Nederlands-Indië (hereinafter SNI) 2.13.132 inv.no 294, D.R.A van Langen, 'Nota omtrent Semerang' (15 September 1946) 4.

125 Ibidem, 4-5.

126 Ibidem, 11 and 14.

127 NL-HaNA SNI 2.13.132 inv.no 2529, A.A.J.J. Thomson, 6-12-1946, 'Houding ten aanzien van Indonesische troepen'.

128 'De onderhandelingen te Semarang', *Het Midden* (25 February1947); 'De Militaire Situatie. Te Semarang werd op allen punten overeenstemming bereikt', *Algemeen Indisch Dagblad* (25 February 1947). See also: NL-HaNA SNI 2.13.132 inv.no 289, 22 February 1947, D.R.A. van Langen to Cgs.Leg., 'Bespreking met Indon.delegatie op 22.2.47 te Ngesrep'; 'Kort verslag van de bespreking tusschen de Ned en Indon delegatie gehouden in Kpg SRONDOL-WET AN 2 op woensdag 26 februari 1947.

129 NL-HaNA NEFIS/CMI 2.10.62 inv.no 2595 I-Igel (dossier Icksan), 2-4-1947, D.R.A. van Langen aan den Legercommandant.

130 NL-HaNA SNI 2.13.132 inv.no 3255, 2 Bataljon 7 Regiment Infanterie (2-7 RI). 1945-1948 Overzicht inzake verplaatsingen en gevoerde acties.

131 For this diary, see: A. Verhulst, *Zomaar wat Herinneringen aan mijn verblijf in Nederlands-Indie* editie III (Reüniecomité: Eindhoven, 1981 / 2017) 67, 71-72, 112.

132 Brok, 'Geschiedenis van een brigade' 23.

133 J.A.A. van Doorn, 'Een en ander over de grensfunctie van de status-quo-lijn in Midden-Java', *Mensch en Maatschappij* 24-2 (1949) 125-128.

134 W. Hulst, 'De lotgevallen van Poncke Princen, deel 1; Deserteur in Indië', *NRC* (14 September 1991).

135 Interview, 21 February 2020, Horison Hotel Yogyakarta.

136 NL-HaNA SNI 2.13.132 inv.no 294, D.R.A van Langen, 'Nota omtrent Semerang' (15-9-1946) 3.

137 NL-HaNA AS 2.10.14 inv.no 2559, 23 February 1948, Afschrift. Heroriëntatie van Bestuursvorm in Semarang'.

138 'Republikeinse Ambtenaren. B.A.P.R.I.S.-leden kunnen werkzaam blijven in federal verband', *De Locomotief* (16 February 1948). Compare with: NL-HaNA AS 2.10.14 inv.no 2559, 2 March 1948, Angenent to Luitenant Gouverneur-Generaal, 'onderwerp: nopens opheffing BAPRIS'; 7-4-1948, P.H, Angenent to Luitenant Gouverneur-Generaal, 'onderwerp: nopens opheffing BAPRIS',.

139 NL-HaNA PG 2.10.17 inv.no 1115, Nota over de politieke situatie in Midden-Java.

140 NL-HaNA PG 2.10.17 inv.no 1118, A.J.F van Weezel Errens, 'Tijdelijke bestuursdienst Semarang. Verslag over de maand februari 1948'.

141 Brouwer, *Tussen sawahs en bergen.*

142 NL-HaNA PG 2.10.17 inv.no 149, 20 July 1948, H.C. Bajetto, hoofd I.V.G. Ns. de Territoriaal ts Troepen Cdt. Midden-Java, 'Pro-Republikeinse propaganda'.

143 NL-HaNA PG 2.10.17 inv.no 149, 15 September 1948, L.G. Fokker, 'Geheim Rapport' to 'Chef der Recherche te Semarang'.

144 NL-HaNA PG 2.10.17 inv.no 149, 12 August 1948, L.G. Fokker, 'Geheim Rapport' to 'Chef der Recherche te Semarang'. Poernawi was later killed near Pati by the TNI for chosing the side of Muso. 8-6-1949, 'Aanvullend rapport', L.G. Fokker.

145 'Opgerolde organisatie', *De Locomotief,* 19 August 1948.

146 NL-HaNA PG 2.10.17 inv.no 911, Subversieve organisatie te Semarang Soedianto c.s.; 15-3-1949, Bambang Soemadi to Officier van Justitie Semarang.
147 NL-HaNA-PG 2.10.17 inv.no 911, 28 February 1949, Proces Verbaal Soedianto.
148 Ibidem, 9 March 1949, Proces Verbaal Bero.
149 Ibidem, 24 February 1949, Proces Verbaal Soewono.
150 Ibidem, 2 March 1949, Proces Verbaal Moertisoemarjo.
151 Ibidem, 4 March 1949, Proces Verbaal Kasimin.
152 Ibidem, 24 February 1949, Proces Verbaal Soengkowo.
153 Ibidem, 28 February 1949, Proces Verbaal Soedianto.
154 Ibidem, 21 February 1949, Proces Verbaal Benni.
155 Ibidem, 21 February 1949, Proces Verbaal Prawoto.
156 Ibidem, 7 March 1949, Proces Verbaal Giartisoemiati. Compare with: 8 March 1949, Proces Verbaal Sriati.
157 Visit Museum Mandala Bhakti 27 January 2020. A fifth frame is empty, but should probably be dedicated to the *Serangan Umum 1 Maret 1949* Yogyakarta.
158 https://www.npostart.nl/onze-jongens-op-java/28-11-2019/BV_101395137 (accessed: 6 August 2021)

6. East Java, 1949: the revolution that shaped Indonesia

1 For preliminary work on East Java, we are grateful to Hans Meijer.
2 Abdul Waid, *Bung Tomo: Hidup dan Mati Pengobar Semangat Tempur 10 November* (Yogyakarta 2019) 45-6. An audio recording of this excerpt is available at https://www.youtube.com/watch?v=nhc8YZifcCo&t=7s. The translation is our own. The speech went on for an hour.
3 Ari Sapto, *Republik dalam Pusaran Elite Sipil dan Militer*, Tim Mata Padi (ed.) (Yogyakarta 2018).
4 Christiaan Harinck, Nico van Horn and Bart Luttikhuis, 'Wie telt de Indonesische doden?', *De Groene Amsterdammer*, 26 July 2017.
5 Charles Tilly, *From Mobilization to Revolution* (New York 1978) 191.
6 J.J.P. de Jong, *De terugtocht: Nederland en de dekolonisatie van Indonesië* (Amsterdam 2015) 217-218.
7 Henri J.H. Alers, *Om een rode of groene merdeka: 10 jaren binnenlandse politiek: Indonesië, 1945-1953* (Eindhoven 1956) 13-16.
8 Ruth MVey, 'The Post-Revolutionary Transformation of the Indonesian Army', *Indonesia* 11 (1971) 131-176; Ruth McVey, 'The Post-Revolutionary Transformation of the Indonesian Army: Part II', *Indonesia* 13 (1972) 147-181; Benedict R. O'G. Anderson, *Java in a Time of Revolution: Occupation and Resistance 1944-1946* (Ithaca NY 1972).
9 Quoted in Anderson, *Java in a Time of Revolution*, 235-236.
10 Timothy Raeymaekers, Ken Menkhaus and Koen Vlassenroot, 'State and Non-State Regulation in African Protracted Crises: Governance without Government?', *Afrika Focus* 21:2 (2008) 7-21.
11 Herbert Feith and Lance Castles (eds.), *Indonesian Political Thinking 1945-1965* (Ithaca NY 1970) 96.
12 Irna H.N. Hadi Soewito, *Rakyat Jawa Timur Mempertahankan Kemerdekaan*, 3 vols. (Jakarta 1994) 265.
13 Hatta interview by American correspondent Daniel Schorr, reported in *Nieuwsgier*, 16 June 1948, cited in David Charles Anderson, 'The Military Aspects of the Madiun Affair', *Indonesia* 21 (1976) 39.
14 Ari Sapto, 'Dinamika Politik Masa Revolusi: Perbedaan Pandangan Elite Pusat dengan Elite Jawa Timur', *Sejarah dan Budaya* 7:2 (2013) 36.
15 Anderson, 'The Military Aspects of the Madiun Affair', 25.
16 'Towards the Republic of Indonesia' (*Menuju Republik Indonesia*), 1924; (https://www.marxists.org/indonesia/archive/malaka/1925-Menuju.htm, accessed 7 October 2021.
17 Harry A. Poeze, *Verguisd en vergeten: Tan Malaka, de linkse beweging en de Indonesische Revolutie, 1945-*

1949 (Leiden 2007) 1035-1050, 1394-1406.

18 George McTurnan Kahin, *Nationalism and Revolution in Indonesia* (Ithaca NY 1952) 382.

19 Sudarno et al., *Sejarah Pemerintahan Militer dan Peran Pamong Praja di Jawa Timur selama Perjuangan Fisik 1945-1950* (Jakarta 1993) 268-270.

20 J.A. de Moor, *Generaal Spoor: Triomf en Tragiek van een Legercommandant* (Amsterdam 2011) 341.

21 D.C.L. Schoonoord, *De Mariniersbrigade 1943-1949: Wording en Inzet in Indonesië* (The Hague 1988) 320.

22 De Moor, *Generaal Spoor*, 343.

23 P.M.H. Groen, *Marsroutes en Dwaalsporen: Het Nederlands Militair-strategisch Beleid in Indonesië 1945-1950* (The Hague 1991) 201.

24 Groen, *Marsroutes en dwaalsporen*, 219.

25 Schoonoord, *De Mariniersbrigade 1943-1949*, 273, 318.

26 Hadi Soewito, *Rakyat Jawa Timur*, 434-441.

27 Groen, *Marsroutes en Dwaalsporen*, 265.

28 T.B. Simatupang, *Report from Banaran: Experiences During the People's War* (Ithaca NY 1972 [1960]) 50, 137.

29 Sapto, *Republik dalam pusaran*, 4-6.

30 Esther Captain and Onno Sinke, *Het geluid van geweld: Bersiap en de dynamiek van geweld tijdens de eerste fase van de Indonesische revolutie, 1945-1946* (Amsterdam 2022) 169.

31 Dukut Imam Widodo, *Malang Tempo Doeloe*, 2 vols. (Tidar, Malang 2006) II, 128.

32 Mary Somers Heidhues, 'Anti-Chinese Violence in Java During the Indonesian Revolution, 1945-49', *Journal of Genocide Research* 14:3-4 (2012) 381-401.

33 Simatupang, *Report from Banaran*, 53.

34 Poeze, *Verguisd en Vergeten*, 126.

35 Sapto, *Republik dalam Pusaran*, 273-277.

36 Hadi Soewito, *Rakyat Jawa Timur*, 355-434 – including detailed incident reports.

37 Poeze, *Verguisd*, 1438-49.

38 Twang Peck Yang, *The Chinese Business Élite in Indonesia and the Transition to Independence, 1940-1950* (Kuala Lumpur 1998) 260-1; Sapto, *Republik dalam Pusaran*, 221-266.

39 Purnawan Basundoro, *Dua Kota Tiga Zaman: Surabaya dan Malang Sejak Kolonial sampai Kemerdeka-an* (Yogyakarta 2009) 194; Moeslim Dalidd et al., *Kotapradja Malang 50 Tahun* (Malang 1964) 17.

40 Rémy Limpach, *De Brandende Kampongs van Generaal Spoor* (Amsterdam 2016) 525, 440.

41 Hadi Soewito, *Rakyat Jawa Timur*, 378.

42 Ibidem, 460.

43 Roelf Spreeuwers, *De Lange Weg: Als Oorlogsvrijwilliger naar Ned. Indië* (Stadskanaal 1980) 182.

44 Helmi Wicaksono, 'Revolusi Fisik di kota Malang tahun 1945-1949' (Malang 2012) 59-78; Hadi Soewito, *Rakyat Jawa Timur*, 463-467.

45 J.A. de Moor, 'Het Korps Speciale Troepen: Tussen Marechaussee-formule en politionele actie', in: G. Teitler and P.M.H. Groen (eds.), *De Politionele Acties* (Amsterdam 1987) 125, 141.

46 Sudarno et al., *Sejarah Pemerintahan Militer dan Peran Pamong Praja di Jawa Timur Selama Perjuangan Fisik 1945-1950* (Jakarta 1993) 327-333.

47 J.A. de Moor, *Westerling's Oorlog: Indonesië 1945-1950 - De Geschiedenis van de Commando's en Parachutisten in Nederlands-Indië 1945-1950* (Amsterdam 1999) 536.

48 Nederlands Instituut voor Militaire Historie, The Hague (hereafter NIMH), toegang 509 Dekolonisatie van Nederlands-Indië (1945-1950) (hereafter 509), inv.nr. 1085.

49 Poeze, *Verguisd*, 1456.

50 Abdul Haris Nasution, *Sekitar Perang Kemerdekaan Indonesia*, 11 vols. (Bandung 1977-1979) X, 115; more details in De Moor, *Westerling's Oorlog*, 343f.

51 Limpach, *De Brandende Kampongs*, 398-399.

52 Bart Luttikhuis and C.H.C. Harinck, 'Voorbij het Koloniale Perspectief: Indonesische Bronnen en het Onderzoek naar de Oorlog in Indonesië, 1945-1949', *Low Countries Historical Review* 132:2 (2017) 74.

53 Simatupang, *Report from Banaran*, 72, 95, 129.

54 Mark Clodfelter, 'Aiming to Break Will: America's World War II Bombing of German Morale and Its Ramifications', *The Journal of Strategic Studies* 33:3 (2010) 401-435.

55 Roswita T. Djajadiningrat, *Pengalamanku di Daerah Pertempuran Malang Selatan* (Jakarta 1974) 36-38, 50.

56 NIMH, toegang 512 Antoniëtti/5 'Résumé van gevoerde acties (alleen voor gebruik in eigen compagnie)' door de 1e paracompagnie met betrekking tot de acties tussen 26 juli en 24 september 1947, and NIMH 509/ 1086, Verslag afkomstig van de 1e Parachutistencompagnie onder bevel van kapitein der Infanterie (KNIL) C. Sisselaar en eerste luitenant der Infanterie (KNIL) K.C. Hernaus; see also De Moor, *Het Korps Speciale Troepen*, 225.

57 Schoonoord, *De Mariniersbrigade*, 337-338; Limpach, *Brandende Kampongs*, 643-646; Anne-Lot Hoek, '"Jongens, laten we dit huis sparen"', *Vrij Nederland*, 10 July 2012.

58 Marjolein van Pagee and Stef Scagliola, 'Waar blijven de Indonesiërs in het debat over de Nederlandse oorlogsmisdaden in Indonesië?', *Historisch Tijdschrift Groniek* 206-207 (2015).

59 *De Locomotief*, 24 May 1949, 14 June 1949.

60 Groen, *Marsroutes*, 250.

61 Abdul Haris Nasution, *Fundamentals of Guerrilla Warfare* (Singapore 1965) 152.

62 Nationaal Archief, The Hague (hereafter NL-HaNA), 2.10.36.15 Indisch Archief, inv.no 13, Kort verslag door ondergetekende gebracht aan Indonesië 20-29 Juni 1949, Geheim, Mr J H van Maarseveen.

63 Irene V. Lessmeister, 'Between Colonialism and Cold War: The Indonesian War of Independence in World Politics, 1945-1949' (PhD dissertation in history, Cornell University, 2012) ii.

64 Kahin, *Nationalism and Revolution in Indonesia*, 235-8, 378-82.

65 De Moor, *Generaal Spoor: Triomf en tragiek van een legercommandant*, 13.

66 Hadi Soewito, *Rakyat Jawa Timur*, 637.

67 NL-HaNA, 2.21.036.02 Archief van D.C. Buurman van Vreeden inv.no 97, Buurman van Vreeden to Beel, Naleving van de order Staakt het Vuren, Zeer Geheim, Jakarta, 2 September 1949.

68 Sapto, *Republik dalam Pusaran*, 195-204.

69 Poeze, *Verguisd*, 1427-1429.

70 Sapto, *Republik dalam Pusaran*, 273-304.

71 Nanang S. Soetadji, *Sekelumit Pengalaman Semasa Revolusi, 1945-1950* (Jakarta 1998) 89-91. Copies of a storm of Indonesian correspondence about the incident ended up in Dutch archives (NIMH, Collectie Groen, inv.nrs. 364-370).

72 Tilly, *From Mobilization to Revolution*, 209.

73 Abdul Haris Nasution, *Tentara Nasional Indonesia*, 3 vols. (Bandung 1968) 217-226.

7. War logistics in revolutionary Central Java

1 Department of the Army, Field Manual FM 38-1, *Logistics Supply Management* (Washington DC 1958) 6-7.

2 D.M.O. Miller, 'A Handful of Rice?: Logistics in the Viet Minh Campaign', *The Army Quarterly and Defence Journal* 100:1 (1970) 105, quoted in Nazaruddin Zainun, *Logistik Tentara Nasional Indonesia dalam Perang Gerilya di Jawa Tengah, 1947-1948* (Pulau Pinang 2019) 2.

3 Nazaruddin Zainun, *Logistik Tentara Nasional Indonesia dalam Perang Gerilya di Jawa Tengah, 1947-1948* (Pulau Pinang 2019) 2.

4 The Royal Institution of Naval Architects, 'Poor State of Logistics Force Could be US Navy's Achilles Heel', *Warship Technology* (2019) 12.

5 Zainun, *Logistik Tentara Nasional*, 1-2.

6 Amrin Imran, et al., *Indonesia dalam Arus Sejarah Jilid 6: Perang dan Revolusi* (Jakarta 2012) 47.

7 Aiko Kurasawa, *Mobilisasi dan Kontrol: Studi tentang Perubahan Sosial di Pedesaan Jawa 1942-1945*, terj. Hermawan Sulystio (Jakarta 1993).

8 Soemitro Djojohadikoesomo, *Beberapa Soal Keoeangan* (Jakarta 1947) 27.

9 Noek Hartono, 'Bank Indonesia: Sejarah Lahir dan Pertumbuhannya', unpublished, no date. See also: Oey Beng To, *Sejarah Kebijakan Moneter, Jilid 1* (1945-1958) (Jakarta 1991) 21.

10 M.C. Ricklefs, *Sejarah Indonesia Modern, 1200-2004* (Jakarta 2005) 475.

11 M. Juflan, 'Blokade Belanda terhadap Kita Telah Diresmikan: Sikap Apakah Jang Seharoesnja Kita Ambil?', *Kedaulatan Rakjat,* 21 February 1946; Belanda tidak pernah mengakui telah melakukan Blokade ekonomi terhadap Indonesia. See: 'Geen Blokkade van Djogdja' *Trouw*, 28 July 1948.

12 Sunarto, 'Bagaimana Soal Blokade?' *Kedaulatan Rakjat,* 17 October 1948; M. Juflan, 'Blokade Belanda terhadap Kita Telah Diresmikan: Sikap Apakah Jang Seharoesnja Kita Ambil'?, *Kedaulatan Rakjat,* 21 February 1946.

13 'Moh Natsir: Nederland wil Republiek Ten Gronde Richten, Blokkade Oorzaak van Smokkelhandel', *Twentsche Courant*, 13 July 1948.

14 Brian Walsh, 'The Iraqi Economic Blockade: A Moral and Legal Analysis', *Peace Research* 27:1 (1995) 47-52, 47-48.

15 Nazaruddin Zainun, *Logistik Tentara Nasional,* 1-2.

16 *De Locomotief*, 11 September 1947

17 See: Ryadi Gunawan, 'Jagoan dalam Revolusi Kita', *Prisma* (1981) 42.

18 'De Situatie in Midden-Java', *De Locomotief*, 1 March 1948; See also: 'Semarang: Veilige Rust, Maar het Achterland is Small Soldaten doen er Hun Zware Plicht. Aanzienlijke Benden Onruststokers Trekken door Midden-Java', *Het Dagblad*, 16 October 1948.

19 Robert Cribb, *Gangsters and Revolutionaries : The Jakarta People's Militia and the Indonesian Revolution 1945-1949* (Honolulu 1991).

20 Henk Schulte Nordholt, *Kriminalitas, Modernitas, dan Identitas dalam Sejarah Indonesia* (Yogyakarta 2002) 22; Henk Schulte Nordholt. 'The Jago in the Shadow: Crime and 'Order' in the Colonial State in Java', *Review of Indonesian and Malaysian Affairs (RIMA)* 25:1 (1991) 82-83.

21 Tuong Vu, 'Of Rice and Revolution: The Politics of Provisioning and State-Society Relations in Java', *South East Asia Research* 11:3 (2003) 256.

22 'Marshall-hulp aan Indonesie Stopgezet', *Friesch dagblad*, 23 December 1948; 'Indonesie Kan Geen Voedsel Kopen: Door Stopzetting van de Marshall-hulp', *De Maasbode*, 7 March 1949; 'Afbraken Marshall-hulp voor Indonesië', *Het Parool*, 07 March 1949.

23 Tuong Vu, 'Of Rice and Revolution', 237.

24 Kementerian Pertahanan RI, 'Daftar Kerugian Harta Benda Rakyat Akibat Patroli Belanda', 1 August 1949. Arsip Dinas Sejarah Angkatan Darat (Disjarahad), Bandung.

25 Tuong Vu, 'Of Rice and Revolution', 237.

26 Ibidem.

27 The newly controlled Dutch areas in Central Java included Barokah (South Semarang), Tanggung (South Semarang), Mintareng (Southeast Semarang), Kedungjati (Southeast Semarang), Bajah (East Semarang), Wonokerjo (near Ambarawa), Ginggong (Southeast Semarang), Bumiayu, Mragondo (near Kudus), Bawang, Getasan, Sumowono, Bonomerto (near Salatiga), Banjarsari (near Salatiga), Kuncen (near Salatiga), Losari, Ngaglik (near Salatiga) and Sidomulyo (dekat Kudus). Areas in Central Java where great battles broke out but never fell under Dutch control were Cangkring (East Semarang), Godong (South Kudus), Pingit, Adimulyo (South Gombong), Karanganyar, Peji (near Gombong), Kenteng (near Gombong), Karanggayam, Puring (South Gombong), Waluyorejo (near Gombong), Pagaruyung and Sukorejo. Areas that were raided by the Dutch army but never fell under Dutch control were Jambu (near Ambarawa), Pingit, Puring, Bawalan and Ampel. Arsip Dinas Sejarah Angkatan Darat (Disjarahad) Bandung, Kementerian Pertahanan RI, 'Gerakan Kemajuan Belanda dan Daerah yang dikuasai'.

28 'Wij Moeten Weer Pioniers Worden', *De Locomotief*, 11 September 1947.

29 Tuong Vu, 'Of Rice and Revolution', 152.

30 Pierre van der Eng, 'Food for Growth: Trends in Indonesia's Food Supply, 1880-1995', *The Journal of Interdisciplinary History* 20:4 (2000) 601.

31 Arsip Dinas Sejarah, Markas Besar Angkatan Darat (Disjarahad) Bandung /82, Kementerian Pertahanan RI, 'Laporan Pelanggaran Belanda'. See also: Tuong Vu, 'Of Rice and Revolution', 137.

32 The number was not actually certain. It came from a report from the Russian News Agency TASS; also see: '138.000 Tentara Belanda di Indonesia', *Kedaulatan Rakjat,* 5 May 1947.

33 Gert Oostindie, *Serdadu Belanda di Indonesia, 1945-1950: Kesaksian Perang Pada Sisi Sejarah yang Salah* (Jakarta 2016) 8-9.

34 Sri Margana, et al.., *Gelora di Tanah Raja: Yogyakarta Pada Masa Revolusi 1945-1949* (Yogyakarta 2017) 103; A.H. Nasution, *Sekitar Perang Kemerdekaan Indonesia*, Jilid 1 (Jakarta 1977).

35 Ibidem, 109

36 Arsip Reksopustoko, Mangkunegaran Surakarta, no. S.2212, 'Berkas Tentang Laskar-Laskar Rakyat.

37 Wiyono, et al., *Sejarah Revolusi Kemerdekaan (1945-1949) Daerah Jawa Tengah* (Jakarta 1991) 81-83.

38 T.B. Simatupang, *Pelopor dalam Perang Pelopor dalam Damai* (Jakarta 1981), 88; Ferry Taufiq, *Akhirnya Sang Jenderal Mengalah: Jenderal Sudirman dalam Pusaran Konflik Politik* (Yogyakarta 2018) 86.

39 Nugroho Notosusanto, 'Angkatan Bersenjata Dalam percaturan Politik di Indonesia', *Prisma* (1979) 19-31.

40 A.H. Nasution, *Tentara Nasional Indonesia I* (Jakarta 1963) 295.

41 Han Bing Siong, 'The Indonesian Need of Arms after the Proclamation of Independence', *Bijdragen tot de Taal-, Land- en Volkenkunde* 157:4 (2001) 822-823.

42 W.G.J. Remmelink, 'The Emergence of the New Situation; The Japanese Army on Java after the Surrender', *Militaire Spectator* 147:2 (1978) 53.

43 Han Bing Siong, 'The Indonesian Need of Arms', 799.

44 Vice-Admiral the Earl of Mountbatten, *Post Surrender Tasks; Section E of the Report to the Combined Chiefs of Staff by the Supreme Allied Commander South East Asia, 1943-1945*, (London 1969) 290; Shizuo Miyamoto, 'Army Problems in Java after the Surrender', in: A. Reid and Oki Akira (eds.), *The Japanese Experience in Indonesia: Selected Memoirs of 1942-1945* (Athens 1986) 329.

45 *Warta Indonesia,* 10 October 1945.

46 Interview by *Suara merdeka* with Wongsonegoro; See *Suara Merdeka,* 18 October 1973.

47 Arsip Rekso Pustoko, no. S. 2747, 'Tjatatan Kronologi Awal Revoloesi'; see also: Karkono Kamajaya, '*Revolusi di Surakarta*', *Temu Ilmiah di Balai Kajian Sejarah dan Nilai Tradisional* (Yogyakarta 1993) 5-6; See also: Sajimin S., *'Peristiwa Revolusi Kemerdekaan di Surakarta'*, private manuscript, 25 June 1985, 3.

48 See: Kementerian Penerangan, *Republik Indonesia: Daerah Istimewa Yogyakarta* (Yogyakarta 1953) 39-40.

49 Student Army Cie Purwokerto, *Sejarah Perjuangan Tentara Pelajar Purwokerto* (Jakarta 1979) 31-33. See also: Nazaruddin Zainun, *Logistik Tentara Nasional*, 48.

50 Nasution, *Sekitar Perang kemerdekaan Indonesia: Proklamasi, Jilid* 1 (Bandung 1977) 225.

51 Nasution, *Sekitar Perang Kemerdekaan,* 358; Miyamoto reported 29,641 pieces, Wehl 30,250 pieces, and Woodburn Kirby, 31,190 pieces. See: Han Bing Siong, 'The Indonesian Need of Arms', 822.

52 See: Han Bing Siong, 'The Indonesian Need of Arms' 821-822.

53 Sartono Kartodirdjo, Marwati Djoened Poesponegoro, Nugroho Notosusanto (eds.), *Sejarah Nasional Indonesia VI: Jaman Jepang dan Jaman Republik Indonesia* (Jakarta 1975) 216.

54 Sartono Kartodirdjo et al. (eds), *Sejarah Nasional Indonesia VI,* 217.

55 Nazaruddin Zainun, *Logistik Tentara Nasional,* 33.

56 Arsip Dinas Sejarah Angkatan Darat (Disjarahad) in Bandung, Kementerian Pertahanan, 'Keadaan Daerah Pendudukan', 12 February 1948.

57 Tuong Vu, *Of Rice and Revolution,* 254-255.

58 A rice blockade was also implemented by the Indonesian youths in several other areas, including in Jakarta: Robert Cribb, 'Political Dimensions of the Currency Question 1945-1947', *Indonesia* 31 (April 1981), 115-116.

59 *Berjuang*, 12 January 1946.

60 Arsip Disjarahad Bandung, Kementerian Pertahanan RI, 'Kekejaman Belanda di beberapa Daerah', 8 May 1948.

61 'Tjara Belanda Berpropaganda', *Kedaulatan Rakjat*, 7 March 1947; *De Locomotief*, 3 September 1947.

62 *Arsip Pakualaman*, Senerai PA VIII No. 2016.

63 Tuong Vu, *Of Rice and Revolution*, 256.

64 'Indonesie Kan Geen Voedsel Kopen door Stopzetting van de Marshall-hulp', *De Maasbode*, 7 March 1949.

65 'Militairen in Indonesië Klagen over Voedsel', *De Waarheid*, 29 June 1948.

66 'Nederland Krijgt $599 Millioen Uit Marshall-Hulp', *Trouw*, 21 April 1948.

67 Nazaruddin Zainun, *Logistik Tentara Nasional*, 22.

68 'Crediet aan Nederland indië: Indonesië Deelt in de Marshall-Hulp van koningkrijk'', *Limburgsch Dagblad*, 9 July 1948.

69 A.H. Nasution, *Sekitar Perang Kemerdekaan Indonesia: Agresi Militer Belanda II, Jilid 9* (Jakarta 1979) 32-33.

70 'Marshall-hulp aan Indonesie Stopgezet', *Friesch Dagblad*, 23 December 1948

71 Nasution, ibidem, 33.

72 See: 'Pedoman Untuk Badan 'Pengawasan Makanan Ra'jat' *Arsip Rekso Pustoko Masa Mangkunegoro VIII No. 5040;* 'Dasar Peratoeran tentang melakoekan Pemilikan Padi' *Arsip rekso Pustoko Masa Mangkunegoro VIII No. 4952.*

73 Sayidiman Suryohadiprojo, 'Pemikiran Strategi Indonesia Masa Perang Kemerdekaan: Antara Konsep dan pelaksanaannya', *Histori* I (1992) 52.

74 'Instruksi Pimpinan Pertahanan Rakjat' Arsip Kementerian Penerangan no. 5516

75 Dwi Ratna Nurhajarini, 'Sleman Masa Revolusi Kemerdekaan, 1948-1949,' dalam, Julianto Ibrahim et al., *Masyarakat Pedesaan dan Revolusi Kemerdekaan di Daerah Istimewa Yogyakarta* (Yogyakarta 2020) 173.

76 Ibidem.

77 Nasution, *Sekitar Perang Kemerdekaan* (1979) 297-298.

78 Arsip Disjarahad Bandung, Kementerian Pertahanan RI/77, 'Pelaporan Sub Teritoriale Militaire Pekalongan', 26 June 1949.

79 See: Arsip Nasional Republik Indonesia, Jakarta (hereinafter ANRI), *Djogdja Documenten/120*, 'Surat dari Markas Besar Barisan Banteng Surakarta bagian Usaha (Soenandar) kepada Padoeka Jang Moelia Wakil Presiden tertanggal 3 Djoeni 1948; Requests could also be made directly to the Central Office in Surakarta upon approval from the Ministry of Finance or the Ministry of Defence: ANRI, Djogdja Documenten/216,Surat dari Komandan bataljon Genie Pionier Maj. R. Soebekti kepada Kantor Regi Candu dan Garam di Surakarta tertanggal 19 August 1948'; also see: Julianto Ibrahim, *Opium, dan Revolusi: Perdagangan Candu di Surakarta Pada Masa revolusi* (Yogyakarta 2013).

80 'Berita Daerah', *Kedaulatan Rakjat*, 5 November 1945.

81 *De Locomotief*, 11 September 1947.

82 'Optreden TNI Benden Wordt Steeds Brutaler: Indonesische Samenleving Geteisterd door Dagelijkse Overvallen', *Het Dagblad*, 13 September 1947.

83 Een Sprekende Lijst: De Dienst voor Legercontacten Geeft het Volgende Overzicht van Vijandelijke Activiteit Binnen Bezet Gebied op Java in het Tijdvak 29/9 t/m 26/10 1948, *De Locomotief*, 5 November 1948.

84 'Optreden TNI Benden Wordt Steeds Brutaler: Indonesische Samenleving Geteisterd door Dagelijkse

Overvallen', *Het Dagblad*, 13 September 1947.
85 Ibidem.
86 'De Algemene Situatie: Midden-Java', *Nieuwe Courant*, 11 August 1947.
87 'Terroristen Staan Terecht : Vele Strafzaken in Banjoemas', *De Locomotief*, 15 July 1948.
88 'Ibidem.
89 'Bende-Activiteit in Midden-Java', *De Nieuwsgier*, 13 November 1948.
90 'Geïnfiltreerde Benden in Midden-Java Rampok en Terreur' *Het Dagblad*, 13 November 1948.
91 'Salatiga: Rampok bij mantri verpleger', *De Locomotief*, 4 November 1948.
92 'Geïnfiltreerde Benden', *Het Dagblad*, 13 November 1948.
93 Nazarudin Zainun, *Logistik Tentara Nasional*, 60-61.
94 Ibidem, 61.
95 Arsip Disjarahad Bandung, Kementerian Pertahanan RI, 'Laporan Kekatjauan, 7 February 1948.
96 Arsip Disjarahad Bandung, Kementerian Pertahanan RI, 'Laporan Kekatjauan, 27 November 1947.
97 Arsip Disjarahad Bandung, Kementerian Pertahanan RI, 'pelaporan Garongan di Bandjarnegara', 21 September 1948.
98 Arsip Disjarahad Bandung, Kementerian Pertahanan RI, 'Laporan Garongan di Bandjarnegara', 23 July 1948.
99 Arsip Disjarahad Bandung, Kementerian Pertahanan RI/1891, 'Perlakoean Terhadap Orang Tionghoa di Salatiga', 23 June 1947.
100 Arsip Disjarahad Bandung, Kementerian Pertahanan RI/1146, 'Laporan Panitia Pembelaan Rakjat Daerah Keboemen', 10 September 1948.
101 'Rampok-Trein', *Het Nieuwsblad*, 18 September 1948.
102 Nasution, *Sekitar Perang Kemerdekaan Jilid 9* (1979), 386-387.
103 ANRI/5382, Jogja Documenten, 9 August 1947.
104 Nazaruddin Zainun, *Logistik Tentara Nasional*, 51.
105 Suryono Darusman, 'Arti Singapura Dalam Revolusi Indonesia', in: Kustiniyati Mochtar (ed.), *Memoar Pejuang Republik Indonesia Seputar 'Zaman Singapura' 1945-1950* (Jakarta 1992) 303-304.
106 Suryono Darusman, 'Operation Meriam Bee' Penyelundupan Senjata Terbesar' in: Kustiniyati Mochtar, (ed.), *Memoar Pejuang Republik Indonesia Seputar 'Zaman Singapura' 1945-1950* (Jakarta 1992) 78-80.
107 See: Julianto Ibrahim, *Perdagangan dan Penggunaan Candu di Surakarta pada Masa Revolusi, 1945-1950* (Yogyakarta 2013).
108 Ibidem. Also: Yong Mung Cheong, *The Indonesian Revolution and Singapore Connection 1945-1949* (Leiden 2003) 120-130.
109 'Sejarah Jawatan Regie Tjandu dan Garam (1945-1949), Jawatan Regie Garam (1949-1952), dan PGSN (1952-1961)', (Jakarta 1994) 8.
110 'Catalina in Riouw Archipel in Beslag Genomen: Wapens en Ammunitie van Philipijnen Bestemd voor de Republiek' *Het Dagblad*, 18 September 1948.
111 Nadere Bijzonderheden', *Het Dagblad*, 18 September 1948.
112 'Een Beeld van Batavia (bijzondere correspondentie)', *Nieuwe Apeldoornsche Courant*, 14 April 1948.
113 Tuong Vo, *Of Rice and Revolution*, 257.
114 'Sekitar Kesusahan Beras', *Min Pao*, 7 October 1948; 'Sekitar Harga Beras', *Keng Po*, 2 December 1948.
115 'Belanda Bertindak Leluasa', *Kedaulatan Rakjat*, 27 February 1948.
116 Ibidem.
117 'NICA telah Merampas 1.200.000 kwintal Padi' *Kedaulatan Rakjat*, 29 November 1948.
118 Arsip Disjarahad Bandung, *Kementerian Pertahanan RI*, 'Kekedjaman Belanda', 4 March 1948.
119 'Nica Mendarat dipoelau Karimoen Djawa: Pendoedoek Dirampoek dan Diperkosa, Kepala Daerah Ditjulik', *Kedaulatan Rakjat*, 23 May 1948. See also: Arsip Disjarahad Bandung, Kementerian Pertahanan RI, 3 April 1948.

120 'Indonesië Kan Geen Voedsel Kopen door Stopzetting van de Marshall-hulp', *De Maasbode*, 7 March 1949.
121 Arsip Disjarahad Bandung, Kementerian Pertahanan RI, 'Chronologisch Verslag bln. April 1949', May 1949.
122 Arsip Disjarahad Bandung, Kementerian Pertahanan RI, 'Laporan Kilat', 23 July 1949.
123 Arsip Disjarahad Bandung, Kementerian Pertahanan RI, 'Daftar Kerugian Harta Benda Rakyat Akibat Patroli Belanda', 1 August 1949.
124 Arsip Disjarahad Bandung, Kementerian Pertahanan RI, 24 September 1949.
125 Arsip Disjarahad Bandung, Kementerian Pertahanan, 'Laporan Kwartal II (19 March -19 June 1949) ', 10 July 1949.
126 Seskoad, *Serangan Umum 1 March 1949 di Yogyakarta: Latar Belakang dan Pengaruhnya* (Jakarta 1993) 232.
127 Pierre Heijboer, *Agresi Militer Belanda: Memperebutkan Pending Zambrut Sepanjang Katulistiwa, 1945-1949* (Jakarta 1998) 172; See also: S. Margana, et al. *Serangan Umum 1 March 1949 sebagai Hari Nasional Penegakan Kedaulatan Negara* (Yogyakarta 2022).
128 Nasution, *Sekitar Perang Kemerdekaan Jilid 9* (1979) 302.
129 Nasution, *Sekitar Perang Kemerdekaan Indonesia, Jilid 1* (Jakarta 1978) 57.
130 Nazarudin Zainun, *Logistik Tentara Nasional*, 75-76.
131 ANRI/5382, Jogja Documenten, 'Laporan dari staf Angkatan perang tanggal 9 August 1948 dan 9 Desember 1948 tentang uraian singkat kondisi di daerah.
132 Simatupang, *Laporan dari Banaran: Kisah Pengalaman Seorang Pradjurit Selama Perang Kemerdekaan* (Jakarta 1980) 66.
133 Nazarudin Zainun, *Logistik Tentara Nasional*, 77.
134 Arsip Disjarahad Bandung, Kementerian Pertahanan RI, 'Perampasan Beras di Tengah Perdjalanan', 16 February 1948.
135 Arsip Disjarahad Bandung, Kementerian Pertahanan RI, 'Verslag ', 13 February 1948.
136 Arsip Disjarahad Bandung, Kementerian Pertahanan RI, 'Pembeslahan bahan Makanan oleh Pihak Tentara', 10 September 1948.
137 Julianto Ibrahim, *Bandit dan Pejuang di Simpang Bengawan: kriminalitas dan Kekerasan Pada Masa revolusi di Surakarta, 1945-1950* (Surakarta 2004).
138 'Kondisi di Merapi-Merbabu', *Kedaulatan Rakjat*, 14 April 1951.

8. State-making is war-making

1 Y.M. Cheong, *H.J. van Mook and Indonesian Independence: A Study of His Role in Dutch-Indonesian Relations; 1945-48* (The Hague 1982) 58-59, 99; J.J.P. de Jong, *Diplomatie of strijd: Het Nederlandse beleid tegenover de Indonesische revolutie 1945-1947* (Amsterdam 1988) 173-174.
2 Private archive of G.B. Robinson, I.W. Kusuma, interview by G.B. Robinson, Sanur, 22 March 1986.
3 R. Susandi, interview by A. Hoek, translation by N.K. Sudiani, Denpasar, 29 April 2015.
4 T. Bouma, *Naar een federaal Indonesië: De geschiedenis van de totstandkoming van de Republiek der Verenigde Staten van Indonesië en de bijdrage van federale Indonesische nationalisten aan de Indonesische onafhankelijkheid 1917-1949* (Amsterdam 2019) 26.
5 See: A.H. Nasution, *Sekitar Perang Kemerdekaan Indonesia, jilid 4, Periode Linggarjati* (Bandung 1978) 395, 397; N.S. Pendit, *Bali Berjuang* (Denpasar 2008); R. Limpach, *De Brandende Kampongs van Generaal Spoor* (Amsterdam 2016) 737, 762-763; B.S. Harvey, 'South Sulawesi: Puppets and Patriots', in: A. Kahin (ed.), *Regional Dynamics of the Indonesian Revolution: Unity from Diversity* (Honolulu 1985) 207; H.J.H. Alers, *Om een rode of groene merdeka:10 jaren binnenlandse politiek Indonesië 1943-1953* (Eindhoven 1956) 146.
6 C. Tilly, 'War Making and State Making as Organized Crime', in: P. Evans, D. Rueschemeyer and T. Skocpol (eds.), *Bringing the State Back In* (Cambridge 1985) 171.

7 Political scientists Didier Péclard and Delphine Mechoulan argue correctly that Western research on the history of warfare has generally been too quick to view guerrilla movements as 'bandits' instead of analyzing the political motivation of the so-called rebels. D. Péclard and D. Mechoulan, 'Rebel Governance and the Politics of Civil War' (working paper) *Swisspeace Publications* (Basel 2015) 5.

8 M.R. Trouillot, *Silencing the past. Power and the Production of History* (Boston 1995) 27 and 96.

9 K.E.M. Bongenaar, *De ontwikkeling van het zelfbesturend landschap in Nederlandsch-Indië (1935-1999)* (Zutphen 2005) 527.

10 W. IJzereef, *De Zuid-Celebes affaire: Kapitein Westerling en de standrechtelijke executies* (Dieren 1984) 10.

11 See the contribution by Taufik Ahmad in this volume.

12 A.A.B. Wirawan, *Pusaran Revolusi Indonesia di Sunda Kecil 1945-1950* (Denpasar 2012) 115.

13 In the original book: I.G.N. Pindha, *Perang Bali* (Jakarta 2013) the word 'pemuda pejuang' is often used, which was translated as 'partisan' in the English version of the book (*Bali War*).

14 P. 't Hoen, 'Guerillastrijd woedt op Bali', *Het Parool*, 12 August 1946.

15 IJzereef, *De Zuid-Celebes affaire,* 69.

16 E. Pangalila-Ratulangi, interview by A. Hoek, Soest, 18 March 2018.

17 See Limpach, *De Brandende Kampongs*, 32; Bouma argues that the representatives for East Indonesia were not puppets: Bouma, *Naar een federaal Indonesië,* 22.

18 Nationaal Archief, The Hague (hereinafter NL-HaNA), Marine en Leger Inlichtingendienst, de Netherlands Forces Intelligence Service en de Centrale Militaire Inlichtingendienst in Nederlands-Indië (hereinafter NEFIS/CMI), 2.10.62 inv.no 1201, Buitenkantoor Bali/Lombok, Weekrapport 4 t/m 8 augustus 1946, 8 August 1946.

19 See: G.B. Robinson, *The Dark Side of Paradise: Political Violence in Bali* (Ithaca and London 1995) 19-51, and also: H.G.C. Schulte Nordholt, 'The Making of Traditional Bali: Colonial Ethnography and Bureaucratic Reproduction', in: P. Pels and O. Salemink (eds.) *Colonial Subjects: Essays on the Practical History of Anthropology* 8:1-4 (1999) 241-279.

20 NL-HaNA NEFIS/CMI 2.10.62 inv.no 1201 'Weekrapport 23 augustus 1946', 13 September 1946.

21 NL-HaNA NEFIS/CMI 2.10.62 inv.no 1201, 'Weekrapport 29 augustus 1946 t/m 5 september 1946', 19 September 1946.

22 NL-HaNA NEFIS/CMI 2.10.62 inv.no 1281, 'Zuiderafdeling van Borneo – overzicht over de periode van 16 t/m 31 juli 1946' and 'Politiek verslag over augustus 1946'.

23 Ibidem, 'Zuiderafdeling van Borneo – politiek verslag over augustus 1946' and 'Politiek verslag Zuiderafdeling van Borneo over de periode 16 t/m 31 oktober 1946'.

24 Universiteitsbibliotheek Leiden, Collectie Zijlmans, DH 1201, Interview Controleur De Vries.

25 Private Archive M. de Niet, 'Seven days of history', *The Voice of Free Indonesia*, Vol. II, 14 December 1946, III.

26 IJzereef, *De Zuid-Celebes affaire,* 86.

27 NL-HaNA NEFIS/CMI 2.10.62 inv.no 1312, Report by Mr. Th. J. van der Peijl, Makassar, 6 November 1946.

28 Private Archive M. de Niet, *The Voice of Free Indonesia*, 39, 19 October 1946, 16.

29 Private Archive M. de Niet, *The Voice of Free Indonesia*, 36, 28 September 1946, 15.

30 Field research on Bali even revealed a system of prison camps in which members of the opposition were systematically tortured and many were executed. For more details, see: A. Hoek, *De strijd om Bali: Imperialisme, Verzet en Onafhankelijkheid 1846-1950* (Amsterdam 2021)276-308 (chapter 9).

31 For more details on the Puputan Margarana, see: Hoek, *De strijd om Bali*, 342-376.

32 Lt. gouverneur-generaal (Van Mook) aan minister van overzeese gebiedsdelen (Jonkman), 11 dec. 1946, in: S. L. van der Wal, P.J. Drooglever and M.J.B. Schouten (eds.), *Officiële Bescheiden Nederlands-Indonesische Betrekkingen 1945-1950* (hereinafter *NIB*), 20 vols. (The Hague 1971-) VI, 540.

33 *De Volkskrant*, 19 December 1946.

34 Private archive of M. de Niet, 'Schrijven van Dr. L. Onvlee van 13 januari 1947 uit Melolo, Soemba,

behelsde indrukken van de door hem bijgewoonde conferentie te Denpasar'.

35 NL-HaNA, Archief F.M. van Asbeck, 2.21.183.03, inv.no 37, Brief aan F.M. van Asbeck en Kollewijn Hooggeleerde Heeren Van Asbeck en Kollewijn, 15 November 1947.

36 See for more details: IJzereef, *De Zuid-Celebes affaire*, 140-141.

37 Notulen van de 28ste vergadering van de commissie-generaal op 13 nov. 1946 *NIB* VI, 243.

38 Private archive of M. de Niet, Schrijven van Dr. Onvlee.

39 IJzereef, *De Zuid-Celebes affaire,* 159.

40 Private archive of G.B Robinson, Widja Kusuma interview by G.B. Robinson, Sanur, 22 March 1986.

41 For more details on the violence inflicted on Balinese opponents, see: Hoek, *De strijd om Bali,* 203-210.

42 NL-HaNA, Ministerie van Koloniën, 2.10.29, inv.no III.19, folder 728, 'Notities betreffende polsituatie (Bali V)', 13 December 1946.

43 NL-HaNA, Strijdkrachten in Nederlands-Indië (hereinafter SNI), 2.13.132 inv.no 185, Wekelijksch Inlichtingenrapport Nr. 33, v/m 12 Dec.'46 t/m 19 Dec. '46, A.J. Treffers, 2 januari 1947.

44 A.H. Nasution, *Sekitar Perang Kemerdekaan Indonesia*, Jilid 4, Periode Linggarjati (Bandung 1978) 133.

45 NL-HaNA SNI, 2.13.132 inv.no 185, Wekelijksch Inlichtingenrapport Nr. 33, v/m 12 Dec.'46 t/m 19 Dec. '46, A.J. Treffers, 2 January 1947

46 Harvey, 'South Sulawesi: Puppets and Patriots', 227-229; Wirawan, *Pusaran Revolusi Indonesia*, 3.

47 IJzereef, *De Zuid-Celebes affaire,* 13.

48 P.M.H. Groen, *Marsroutes en dwaalsporen: Het Nederlands militair-strategisch beleid in Indonesië 1945-1950* (The Hague 1991) 69-71.

49 Groen, *Marsroutes en Dwaalsporen*, 83.

50 J.J.P de Jong, *De terugtocht*: *Nederland en de dekolonisatie van Indonesië* (Amsterdam 2015) 101-102.

51 NL-HaNA NEFIS/CMI 2.10.62 inv.no 815, Co-Amacab H.J. Wijnmalen aan de directeur van het Binnenlands Bestuur W. Hoven, Palembang, 21 October 1946.

52 Notes of the 20th meeting of the Commission General on 1 November 1946 *NIB* VI, 61.

53 For an Indonesian history of this event, see: Nanda Julian Utama, *Pertempuran Palembang, Pertempuran Lima Hari Lima Malam 1947* (Yogyakarta 2021).

54 A. Hoek, 'De verzwegen moorden van Palembang', *Vrij Nederland*, 4 August 2017.

55 *Algemeen Handelsblad*, 7 January 1947.

56 A. Hoek, 'De verzwegen moorden'.

57 NL-HaNA, Ministerie van Koloniën, 2.10.29 inv.no 532, H.J. Wijnmaalen aan Van Mook, Geheim mailrapport 1947, 11 January 1947.

58 Nederlands Instituut voor Militaire Historie, The Hague (hereinafter NIMH), toegang 509 Dekolonisatie van Nederlands-Indië (1945-1950), inv.no 853, Continentenplan wordt uitgevoerd 1 t/m 5 jan. 1947.

59 A. Hoek, 'De verzwegen moorden'.

60 Notulen van de 38ste vergadering van de commissie-generaal op 15 jan. 1947, *NIB* VII76.

61 H.J. Van Mook, *The Stakes of Democracy in South-East Asia* (London 2015) 224.

62 'The Problems of Genocide', *NIOD Rewind Podcast*, Episode 14, Anne van Mourik and Thijs Bouwknegt with Dirk Moses, 2021.

63 I.N. Nita, interview by N.M.F. Aswarini, Marga, 25 June and 30 September 2017.

9. From the parliament to the streets

1 Ide Anak Agung Gde Agung, *From the Formation of the State of East Indonesia towards the Establishment of the United States of Indonesia* (Jakarta 1996).

2 J.R. Chaniago, *Menuju Negara Kesatuan Republik Indonesia: Peranan Pemimpin Lokal dalam Dinamika Politik di Sulawesi Selatan dan Sumatera Timur 1950* (PhD thesis in history, Universitas Gadjah Mada, 2002).

3 George McTurnan Kahin, *Nasionalisme & Revolusi Indonesia* (Depok 2013) 501-516; Taufik Abdullah

and A.B. Lapian (eds.), *Indonesia dalam Arus Sejarah. Jilid 7* (Jakarta 2012); Marwati Djoened Poesponegoro dan Nugroho Notosusanto (eds.), *Sejarah Nasional Indonesia, Jilid. 6* (Jakarta 1984); Barbara Hatley, 'Creating Culture for the New Nation South Sulawesi, 1950-1965', in: Jennifer Lindsay and Maya H.T. Liem (eds.), *Heirs to World Culture: Being Indonesian, 1950-1965* (Leiden 2012) 343-370.

4 Roel Frakking, 'Gathered on the Point of a Bayonet: The Negara Pasundan and the Colonial Defence of Indonesia, 1946-50', *The International History Review* 39:1 (2017) 33.

5 Frakking, 'Gathered', 33.

6 *Negara Soematera Timoer: Sepintas Laloe* (Badan Penerangan Negara Soematera Timoer); Karl J. Pelzer, *Planters against Peasants: The Agrarian Struggle in East Sumatra 1947-1958* (Leiden 1982) 1-16.

7 *Setahun Negara Djawa Timur* (Surabaya 1949).

8 Nationaal Archief, The Hague, (hereinafter NL-HaNA) Netherland Forces Intelligence Service (NEFIS) and Centrale Militaire Inlichtingendienst (CMI) (hereinafter NEFIS/CMI) 2.10.62, inv.no 4876; M. Sjamsoel Arieffin, *Negara Madoera* (Sampang 1948).

9 Frakking, 'Gathered', 33.

10 Willem IJzereef, *De Zuid-Celebes affaire: Kapitein Westerling en de standrechtelijke executies* (Dieren 1984) 13-15; Rémy Limpach, *Kekerasan Esktrem Belanda di Indonesia: Perang Kemerdekaan Indonesia 1945-1949* (Jakarta 2019) 67-68.

11 IJzereef, *De Zuid-Celebes Affaire*, 16-19.

12 Sarita Pawiloy, *Sejarah Perjuangan Angkatan 45 di Sulawesi Selatan* (Makassar 1987) 101; Badan Arsip dan Perpustakaan Daerah, Propinsi Sulawesi Selatan, *Arsip Regering van Oost Indonesie* (Ujung Pandang 2003) vii.

13 Anthony Reid, 'Australia's Hundred Days in South Sulawesi', in: D. Chandler and M.C. Rickleffs (eds.), *Nineteenth and Twentieth Century Indonesia: Essay in Honour of J.D. Legge* (Melbourne, 1986) 207.

14 Reid, 'Australia's Hundred Days', 215-216.

15 IJzereef, *De Zuid-Celebes affaire*, 45-49; Limpach, *Kekerasan Esktrem Belanda*, 69.

16 Ibidem, 70.

17 Kementerian Penerangan, *Presiden Kita P.J.M. Tjokorde Gde Rake Soekawati Melawat dari Poelau ke Poelau di N.I.T.* (Bandung 1948), 12; Sarkawi B. Husain, 'Gerakan Buruh di Makassar, 1946-1955', in: Dias Pradadimara, et al., *Negara dan Masyarakat Sulawesi Selatan di Tahun 1950-an* (Yogyakarta 2014) 106-107.

18 Sarkawi B. Husain, 'Gerakan Buruh di Makassar, 1942-1955' (Bachelor's thesis in history, Hasanuddin University Makassar, 1994) 107.

19 *Moe'tamar Denpasar Mentjiptakan Negara Indonesia Timoer* (Makassar nd) 3; *Den Pasar Pontianak. Lahirnja doea negara* (Komisariat Pemerintah Oemoem Borneo dan Timoer Besar, tanpa tahun) 8; NL-HaNA Algemene Secretarie van de Nederlands-Indische Regering (hereinafter AS), 2.10.14 inv.no 5016; Anthony Reid, *To Nation by Revolution: Indonesia in the 20th Century* (Singapore 2010). Unofficial talks in Denpasar among delegates of East Indonesia and representatives of the Dutch government led by General Commissioner (Alg. Regeerings Commisaris) W. Hoven had been conducted since 7 December 1946.

20 SUDARA (Sumber Darah Rakyat) was a political organization founded by Andi Mappanyukki, King of Bone, Sam Ratulangi, Najamuddin Daeng Malewa, Abdullah Bau Massepe, Mr. Binol and Mr. Pantow. See Radik Djarwadi cs, *Naskah Sedjarah 'CORPS HASANUDDIN' Pradjurit Tempur dan Pembangunan* (Ujung Pandang 1972) 2.

21 Barbara S. Harvey, 'South Sulawesi: Puppets and Patriots', in: Audrey R. Kahin (ed.), *Regional Dynamics of the Indonesian Revolution. Unity From Diversity* (Honolulu 1985) 220.

22 *Soeloeh Ambon*, 22 February 1947.

23 *Soeloeh Ambon*, 18 January 1947; original quote: '*...bahwa poetesan jang telah diambil di Den Pasar adalah hasil sebesar moengkin jang dapat tertjapai bagi Indonesia Timoer didalam keadaan politik pada dewasa ini*'.

24 Osman Raliby, *Documenta Historica: Sedjarah Dokumenter Dari Pertumbuhan dan Perdjuangan Negara*

Republik Indonesia I (Jakarta 1953) 477-478.

25 Kahin, *Nasionalisme & Revolusi Indonesia*, 502.

26 Ibidem.

27 Limpach, *Kekerasan Esktrem Belanda*, 67-102; Abdul Wahid, 'Berdamai dengan Masa Lalu yang Kelam', in: Gert Oost Indie (ed.), *Serdadu Belanda di Indonesia 1945-1950: Kesaksian Perang pada Sisi Sejarah yang Salah* (Jakarta 2016) vi-xiv.

28 W.A. van Goudoever, *Konperensi Malino 1946: Ke Arah Pembentukan Negara Indonesia Timur* (Makassar 2018) 63-64. Ida Anak Agung Gde Agung, *From the Formation*, 73.

29 Ide Anak Agung Gde Agung, *From the Formation*, 123-124.

30 Ibidem, 124.

31 Ibidem, 206.

32 Kementerian Penerangan, *Republik Indonesia Propinsi Sulawesi* (Jakarta 1953) 101.

33 Arsip Negara Indonesia Timur, Nomor Register 08, Dos 02 'Djawaban pemerintah terhadap pemendangan oemoem dari anggota-anggota parlement: Pidato P.J.M. Nadjamoeddin Dg. Malewa-Perdana Menteri'.

34 Goudoever, *Konperensi Malino 1946*, 64; 'Moektamar Den Pasar', *Pelita Rakjat*, 24 December 1946.

35 *Soeloeh Ambon*, 8 April 1947.

36 *Negara Baroe*, 19 March 1947, 1; 5 March 1947, 2; 8 February 1947, 2; Ilham, 'Ruang, Masyarakat, dan Kebudayaan: Modernitas di Kota Makassar pada Abad ke-20' (Dissertation in history, Universitas Gadjah Mada, 2019) 290.

37 Kementerian Penerangan, *Presiden Kita P.J.M. Tjokorde Gde Rake Soekawati Melawat Dari Poelau ke Poelau di Negara Indonesia Timoer* (Bandung 1948) 14-22; 59; *Soeloeh Ambon*, 24 April 1947.

38 Hanock Luhukay, 'Dari Makassar ke Ujung Pandang. Beberapa Catatan Perubahan Ketatanegaraan, Tata Pemerintahan dan Kehidupan Sosial Sebuah Kota Besar', manuscript, nd, 219.

39 'Moektamar Den Pasar', *Pelita Rakjat*, 24 December 1946.

40 'Sikap bidjaksana (Arungpone dan Merah putih)', *Pandji Negara*, 1 October 1949, 3; 'Proklamasi. Kepada para Zelfbestuur jg terhormat dari Daerah Selebes-Selatan', *Pandji Negara*, 1 October 1949, 11.

41 R.Z. Leirissa, *Kekuatan Ketiga Dalam Perjuangan Kemerdekaan Indonesia* (Jakarta 2006); Widhi Setyo Putro, 'Konferensi Inter-Indonesia Tahun 1949: Wujud Konsensus Nasional antara Republik Indonesia dengan Bijeenkomst Voor Federal Overleg', *Jurnal Sejarah Citra Lekha* 3:1 (2018) 41.

42 *Kedaulatan* (Makassar 1949), 5-11.

43 Kemenetrian Penerangan, *Propinsi Sulawesi* (Jakarta 1953) 161.

44 IJzereef, *De Zuid-Celebes affaire*, 63-68; Limpach, *Kekerasan Esktrem Belanda*, 70.

45 'Warta Politik Daerah Selebes Selatan Januari 1949-Pebruari 1950 dan Juni 1950', Arsip Pemerintahan Indonesia Timur 1946-1950, Register Number: 104, Box 23.; see also: Ide Anak Agung Gde Agung, *Dari Negara Indonesia Timur ke Negara Indonesia Serikat* (Yogyakarta 1985) 698-699.

46 Ide Anak Agung Gde Agung, *Dari Negara Indonesia Timur*, 700.

47 All of them can be read in: 'Laporan-laporan Mengenai Penyebaran Plakat-Plakat Anti NIT Januari-April 1950', Arsip Pemerintahan Indonesia Timur 1946-1950, Register Number: 153, Box 28. Besides pamphlets, mass demonstrations and large meetings were held in Gorontalo, Poso, Donggala, Takalar and Jeneponto.

48 H.A. Massiara Daeng Rapi, *Menyingkap Tabir Sejarah dan Budaya di Sulawesi Selatan* (Ujung Pandang, nd), 289-290.

49 *Propinsi Sulawesi*, 162; H.A. Massiara Daeng Rapi, *Menyingkap Tabir Sejarah* , 291-293.

50 'Laporan-laporan Mengenai Penyebaran Plakat-Plakat Anti NIT Januari-April 1950', Arsip Pemerintahan Indonesia Timur 1946-1950, Register Number: 153, Box 28..

51 Ricklefs, *Sejarah Indonesia Modern*, 351.

52 See: Archive: Arnas Perw. Sul-Sel. Warta Politi NIT Reg. 97; see also: Barbara Sillars Harvey, *Pemberon-*

takan Kahar Muzakkar Dari Tradisi ke DI/TII (Jakarta 1989) 163-168; For more on the dilemma faced by Andi Azis, see: Sritimuryati, *Peristiwa Andi Azis, Dilema Federalis dan Unitaris*, (Bachelor's thesis, Universitas Hasanuddin, 1986).

53 Mr. Dr. Ch. R.S. Soumil was the former minister of justice of the NIT in the second cabinet of Najamuddin Daeng Malewa, the Warrow Cabinet, the first and second cabinets of Anak Agung, and the Tatengkeng Cabinet. See: Ide Anak Agung Gde Agung, *Dari Negara Indonesia Timur*, 813-815.

54 Ibidem, 749; Ricklefs, *Sejarah Indonesia Modern*, 351-352.

55 Barbara Sillars Harvey, *Pemberontakan Kahar Muzakkar*, 171; H.A. Massiara Daeng Rapi, *Menyingkap Tabir Sejarah*, 295.

56 See: Ide Anak Agung Gde Agug, Dari Negara Indonesia Timur, 711, 745.

57 Daeng Rapi, *Menyingkap*, 296; Ide Anak Agung Gde Agug, *Dari Negara Indonesia Timur*, 752.

58 Ide Anak Agung Gde Agung, Dari Negara Indonesia Timur, 753-754, 796.

59 Daeng Rapi, *Menyingkap*, 296; Kementrian Penerangan, *Republik Indonesia*, 171. See: Harvey, *Pemberontakan*, 171.

60 Ide Anak Agung Gde Agung, *Dari Negara Indonesia Timur*, 756. For further information regarding the incident and its aftermath, see: Kementerian Peņerangan, *Propinsi Sulawesi*, 310-333.

61 Dias Pradadimara, 'Negara dan Masyarakat di Sulawesi Selatan di tahun-tahun 1950-an: Pengantar Historiografis', in: Dias Pradadimara, et al., *Negara dan Masyarakat*, 5.

62 Ide Anak Agung Gde Agung, *Dari Negara Indonesia Timur*, 765-771.

63 Ide Anak Agung Gde Agung, *Negara Kesatuan*, 18-19.

64 Daeng Rapi, *Menyingkap*, 302; Dias Pradadimara, 'Negara dan Masyarakat', 11; Ide Anak Agung Gde Agung, *Dari Negara Indonesia Timur*, 722.

10. The harsher they act, the more fuss there'll be

1 Nationaal Archief (NL-HaNA), Marine en Leger Inlichtingendienst, de Netherlands Forces Intelligence Service en de Centrale Militaire Inlichtingendienst in Nederlands-Indië (hereinafter NEFIS/CMI), 2.10.62 inv.no 4687, NEFIS Document No. 3358, nr. 21: Andi Djalanti to Patahoeddin, 6 November 1946.

2 T. Bouma, 'Naar een federaal Indonesië: De geschiedenis van de totstandkoming van de Republiek der Verenigde Staten van Indonesië en de bijdrage van federale Indonesische nationalisten aan de Indonesische onafhankelijkheid, 1917-1949', PhD Thesis, VU Amsterdam, 2020; J.J.P. de Jong, *De terugtocht: Nederland en de dekolonisatie van Indonesië* (Amsterdam 2015). P.M.H. Groen, 'Oprichting, functioneren en opeffing van de Deelstaat Oost-Indonesië 1946/1950', doctoral thesis, Utrecht University (1979); J.A. Jonkman, *Nederland en Indonesië beide vrij: Memoires van Mr. J.A. Jonkman* (Assen 1977), II, 135-36; W. A. van Goudoever, *Malino maakt historie: Een overzichtelijke bewerking van notulen en tekstuele redevoeringen ter conferentie van Malino 15-25 Juli 1946* (Batavia 1946) 8.

3 Shereen Ilahi, *Imperial Violence and the Path to Independence: India, Ireland and the Crisis of Empire* (London 2016); Rémy Limpach, *De brandende kampongs van Generaal Spoor* (Amsterdam 2016); Christopher Hale, *Massacre in Malaya: Exposing Britain's My Lai* (Gloucester 2013); C. Elkins, *Britain's Gulag: The Brutal End of Empire in Kenya* (London 2009).

4 H. Poeze and H. Schulte Nordholt, *Merdeka: De strijd om de Indonesische onafhankelijkheid en de ongewisse opkomst van de Republiek 1945-1950* (Amsterdam 2022) 155.

5 M. Brekel, *Massaexecuties op Sulawesi: Hoe Nederland wegkwam met moord in Indonesië* (Zutphen 2017); Limpach, *Brandende kampongs*, 247; Muhammad N. Said, *Korban 40,000 jiwa di Sulawesi Selatan* (Bandung 1985); W. IJzereef, *De Zuid-Celebes affaire: Kapitein Westerling en de standrechtelijke executies* (Dieren 1984) 141; 'Struggle organization' is a direct translation of '*badan perjuangan*', and refers to often paramilitary organizations that saw themselves as more than merely military units, and more as political entities as part of a larger peoples movement. Hence I have adopted struggle organization instead of 'resistance organization' as their activities were pointed more at local populations, and less against

Dutch troops.

6 R. Gunawan et al., *Sejarah Berita Proklamasi Kemerdekaan Indonesia* (Jakarta 2015); R. Djarwadi et al., *"'Corps" Hasanuddin': Pradjurit Tempur dan Pembangunan* (Draft Ke-II, Secretary General Corhas, 1972).

7 The term comes from genocide studies: A.D. Moses, *The Problems of Genocide: Permanent Security and the Language of Transgression* (Cambridge 2021) 35, 255, 258.

8 Moses, *The Problems*, 256-257.

9 Instruction on Non-Co-Operation, Java Command Headquarters No. 5/MBKD.1949, 5 January 1949, in A.H. Nasution, *Fundamentals in Guerrilla Warfare and The Indonesian Defence System Past and Future* (Information Service of the Indonesian Armed Forces, 1953) 157.

10 A. Appadurai, 'Dead Certainty: Ethnic Violence in the Era of Globalization', *Public Culture* 10:2 (1998) 242-243.

11 R. Desjarlais and A. Kleinman, 'Violence and Demoralization in the New World Disorder', *Anthropology Today* 10:5 (1994) 9.

12 Desjarlais and Kleinman, 'Violence and Demoralization', 11; Sutton, D.S. Sutton, 'Ritual and Culture of Cannibalism in Wuxuan, Guangxi, China, May to July 1968', *Comparative Studies in Society and History* 37:1 (1995) 153; A. Mbembe, *Necorpolitics*, S. Cochran, trans. (Durham 2019) 3.

13 S. Kalyvas, *The Logic of Violence in Civil War* (Cambridge 2005) chapter 5.

14 Kementerian Penerangan, *Politiek manifest der Indonesische regering* (Jakarta 1946) 2-3.

15 NL-HaNA NEFIS/CMI, 2.10.62 inv.no 3906, Notification Regarding the Measures Ensuing from the Proclamation of Admission of the Independence of the East-Indies, Osamu San Sei Ko No. 142, 7 September 1944.

16 NL-HaNA NEFIS/CMI, 2.10.62 inv.no 3985, Foto's Afkomstig van H. Aboe Bakar uit Makassar, No. 2656, 7 December 1946.

17 NL-HaNA NEFIS/CMI, 2.10.62 inv.no 4377, Inventarisstaat van Documenten, ontvangen van Buitenkantoor Makassar, behoorende bij Rapport Afd. VI, No. C111/314, No. 3048, 12 February 1947; See Romo Mangunwijaya's testimony in H. and T. Koetsier-Korvinus (eds.), *Vijftig Jaar 'Merdeka': In Gesprek met Indonesiërs en Nederlanders* (Kampen 1995) 100.

18 Kementerian Penerangan, *Politiek manifest*, 4-6.

19 IJzereef, *De Zuid-Celebes Affaire*, 54; NL-HaNA NEFIS/CMI, 2.10.62 inv.no 4704, Nefis Document 3374, Nr. 44a, Ministry of Foreign Affairs to Lt. General Sir Montagu Stapford, No. 442/38, 10 March 1946.

20 Gunawan et al., *Sejarah Berita Proklamasi*, 480; J.M. Pluvier, *Overzicht van de ontwikkeling der Nationalistische beweging in Indonesië in de jaren 1930 tot 1942* (The Hague 1953) 81; 'De Perserikatan Selebes', *Deli Courant*, 22 December 1930, 7.

21 G. McTurnan Kahin, *Nationalism and Revolution in Indonesia* (Ithaca NY 1963) 121-122; KITLV H1284/47, Interview IJzereef with Mr. N.C. Beudeker, 21 October 1981; B.S. Harvey, 'Tradition, Islam, and Rebellion: South Sulawesi 1950-1965', PhD thesis, Cornell University, Ithaca (1974) 120, 131; NL-HaNA AS, 2.10.14 inv.no 3212, Verslag i/z Japansche Activiteiten in Z. Celebes, 2 November 1945, annex to No.293/Aggo, 14 November 1945.

22 Harvey, 'Tradition', 131-132; Kementerian Penerangan, *Massacre in Macasser: It Happened This Time in South-Celebes Indonesia Anno Domini 1947* (Jakarta 1947) 1.

23 Gunawan et al., *Sejarah Berita Proklamasi*, 457; NL-HaNA NEFIS/CMI, 2.10.62 inv.no 1316, Rapport Nr. 101/III-2.d/G/S, 26 February 1946; NIOD, 400/4276, Lampiran II, Rapport over de Reis van Dr. Ratulangi in Augustus 1945, Inv.Nr. A.A. 29, 1945; Harvey, 'Tradition', 131-135.

24 IJzereef, *Zuid-Celebes*, 21-22; Harvey, *Tradition*, 138-139; NL-HaNA NEFIS/CMI, 2.10.62 inv.no 1315, Uittreksel uit Situatierapport op 10 Maart 1946 – No. 14, AD6/32400/G, 16 April 1946; Djawardi, *""Corps" Hasanuddin"*, 8.

25 KITLV H1284/10, Declaration to the Negara2 Serikat (dengan peranteraan Brigadier Generaal dari Ten-

tara Pendoedoekan Australia di Makassar), 17 November 1945.

26 NL-HaNA Algemene Secretarie van de Nederlands-Indische Regering (hereinafter AS), 2.10.14 inv.no 3212, Verslag i/z Japansche Activiteiten in Z.Celebes; KITLV H1039/25, H.J. Koerts to his parents, 26 December 1945. Curiously, Indonesian historiography to this day avers that the Japanese left a power vacuum (*kekosongan kekuasaan*) in South Sulawesi: R., Budiana, 'Perempuan di Balik Proklamasi: Kemederkaan Bukan Cuma Bilik Lelaki', https://tirto.id/perempuan-di-balik-proklamasi-kemerdekaan-bukan-cuma-milik-lelaki-fYmu (accessed 27 January 2021); O.R. Budiana, O.R., 'Cerita Penting di Tanggal 15 Agustus Bagi Indonesia, Ada Apa Ya?', https://www.beritabaik.id/teman-baik/pr-3782642905/cerita-penting-di-tanggal-15-agustus-bagi-indonesia-ada-apa-ya (accessed 27 January 2021); E.D., Sari, 'Sejarah Perjuangan Rakyat Dalam Mempertahankan Kemerdekaan Republik Indonesia di Muaradhua Ogan Komering Ulu Selatan Tahun 1945-1949, BA thesis, Universitas Muhammadiyah Palembang, 2019.

27 See, for example: KITLV H1284/29, Letter Koerts to IJzereef, 16 October 1981, 18.

28 IJzereef, *Zuid-Celebes*, 25; KITLV H1284/57, Manuscript J.J. Wesseling, *Wat deden Wij Nederlanders in Indonesië Periode 1936 – begin 1950 Zuid-Celebes en Soemba*, 27.

29 NL-HaNA AS, 2.10.14 inv.no 3212, Verslag i/z Japansche Activiteiten in Z.Celebes.

30 KITLV H1039/25, H.J. Koerts to his parents; KITLV H1284/29, Rapport NIGIS Makassar, November 1945.

31 KITLV H1284/54 Gesprek met M. Peddemors, 17 December 1981.

32 'Karaeng' is a Makassar title that can be translated as 'chief'. Arumpone is the special name for the King, the Aru of Bone.

33 H.J. Koerts, *De vrijheid wordt duur gekocht: Zuid-Celebes na de Japanse capitulatie* (Rolde 1991), 32.

34 KITLV H1039/25, Koerts to his parents.

35 KITLV H1284/57, Manuscript J.J. Wesseling; KITLV H1284/12, Verslag CONICA Makassar Force 25-11-45 to 3-1-46; for the declaration, see: KITLV H1039/25, Nio to Koerts, 19 January 1946; for nationalist organizing in Maros, see Gunawan et al, *Sejarah Berita Proklamasi Kemerdekaan Indonesia*, 464; like karaeng, 'datu' means 'ruler'.

36 Andi Widjajanto and Artanti Wardhani, *Hubungan Intelijen – Negara 1945-2004* (Jakarta 2008), 60; NL-HaNA NEFIS/CMI, 2.10.62 inv.no 4704, Nefis Document No. 3374, nr. 44f., Lapoer [sic] Ringkas, Tentang Keadaan di Soelawesi Selatan Sampai 26 November 1945.

37 Gunawan et al., *Sejarah Berita*, 477.

38 S. Daeng Mattata, *Luwu dalam Revolusi* (Ujung Pandang 1967) 217.

39 KITLV H1284/27, Memorie Betreffende het Troepencommando RES.Zuid.Celebes tot en met Juni 1947, 105-106; L. Patang, *Sulawesi dan Pahlawan2nya: Sejarah Perjuangan Kemerdekaan Republik Indonesia* (Jakarta 1975) 221; others name Kabasima Taico and Sukri as the founders of the Black Fan: S. Pawiloy, *et al.*, *Sejarah Perjuangan*, 466.

40 A. Reid, 'Australia's Hundred Days in South Sulawesi', in M.C. Chandler and D.P. Ricklefs (eds.), *Nineteenth and Twentieth Century Indonesia: Essays in Honour of Professor J.D. Legge* (Melbourne 1986), 206; KITLV H1284/142, Verslag Dr J. van Blom.

41 IJzereef, *Zuid-Celebes*, 26.

42 KITLV H1284/27, Memorie Betreffende het Troepencommando RES.Zuid.Celebes.

43 IJzereef, *Zuid-Celebes*, 22.

44 KITLV H1284/14, Ratulangi to CONICA Makassar, 26 December 1945; KITLV, H1284/17, Ratulangi to CONICA Makassar, 5 January 1946.

45 KITLV H973/10, Brieftelegram 11 April 1946; for the National Committees, see J. Drooglever, 'The *Komite Nasional Indonesia Pusat* and Internal Politics in the Republic of Indonesia', in T. Abdullah (ed.), *The Heartbeat of the Indonesian Revolution* (Jakarta 1997) 149-180.

46 S. Pawiloy et al., *Sejarah Perjuangan Angkatan 45 di Sulawesi Selatan 17 Agustus 1945-17 Agustus 1950*

(Ujung Pandang 1987) 124; KITLV, H1284/57, Manuscript Wesseling.

47 KITLV, H1284/27, Memorie Betreffende het Troepencommando RES.Zuid.Celebes.

48 KITLV, H973/13, De 'Poesat' en zijn Verbindingen, annex to Nr. 132, 14 Juni 1946.

49 Nationalist units were exhorted to continuously sound out how communities felt, see: NL-HaNA AS, 2.10.14 inv.no 3742, Vorm van Rapport (Vrije Nederlandse Vertaling), annex 2 to O.O.T. nr. 5.

50 KITLV H973/10, Brieftelegram Lion Cachet, 11 April 1946.

51 KITLV H1284/24, Overzicht van de Verzetsbeweging in de Afdeling "Mandar" (Periode Juli 1946-October 1947); Reid, 'Australia's Hundred', 214.

52 NL-HaNA, Strijdkrachten in Nederlands-Indië (hereinafter SNI), 2.13.132 inv.no 3363, Geschiedenis van het XVe Bataljon Infanterie 1946-1947.

53 NL-HaNA, 2.21.036.01 inv.no 71, Rapport-Enthoven, 16.

54 IJzereef, *Zuid-Celebes*, 73-74.

55 A.G. Martha, Ch. Wibisono and Y. Anwar, *Pemuda Indonesia dalam Dimensi Sejarah Perjuangan Bangsa* (Jakarta 1984) 153.

56 KITLV H1284/13, Ratulangi and Tadjoeddin Noor to W. Hoven, 20 October 1945.

57 H. Budiarti, 'Taking and Returning Objects in a Colonial Context: Tracing the Collections Acquired during the Bone-Gowa Military Expeditions', in P.J. ter Keurs (ed.), *Colonial Collections Revisited* (Leiden 2007) 127-130; in May 1948, the number of members nationalist parties had stood at 27,000: NL-HaNA AS, 2.10.14 inv.no 3204, Overzicht Politieke Ontwikkelingen Oost-Indonesië Mei 1948.

58 KITLV H1284/8, Kort Overzicht Betreffende de Indonesische Nationale Beweging in Indonesia, in het Bijzonder h.t.p. Gedurende het Japansche Tussenbestuur; H1284/52, Gesprek met Generaal b.d. C. Giebel, 28 October 1981; KITLV H1039/29, De Jong over Zuid Celebes, Artikel voor "Moesson".

59 Mao Tse Tung, *On Protracted Warfare*, Lecture Delivered at the Yenan Association for the Study of the War of Resistance Against Japan, May 1938.

60 D.E. Spencer, 'Reexamining the Relevance of Mao to Post-Modern Insurgency and Terrorism', *Intelligence Journal* 28:1 (2010) 148; S. Kalyvas, *The Logic of Violence in Civil War* (Cambridge 2005) chapter 5.

61 J.A.A. van Doorn and W.J. Hendrix, 'De planters belegerd. De positie van Europese planters tussen Nederlandse steun en Indonesisch verzet', in G. Teitler and P.M.H. Groen (eds.), *De Politionele Acties* (Amsterdam 1986) 49; T.B. Simatupang, *Het laatste Jaar van de Indonesische vrijheidsstrijd 1948-1949: Een authentiek verslag door de voormalig Chef-Staf van de Indonesische Strijdkrachten* (Kampen 1985) 108.

62 NL-HaNA Procureur-Generaal bij het Hooggerechtshof van Nederlands-Indië, 2.10.17 (hereinafter PG), inv.no 1324, Bevindingen inzake M.P. sld. Streiff; Bevindingen inzake Sgt. Kroos; Bevindingen inzake M.I.D. Sengkang, al in PG895-B6.

63 NL-HaNA NEFIS/CMI, 2.10.62 inv.no 4704, NEFIS Document 3375/2, Seroan Poetra Indonesia Sulawesi, Pidato Moh. Lahade Saleh ditjorong radio Jocjakarta, 14 March 1946; by chance or not, Lahade's words echo those of C. Anwar in his poem 'Dipo Negoro':

Punah di atas menghamba	Better destruction than slavery
Binasa di atas ditindas	Better extermination than oppression
Sesungguhnya jalan ajal baru tercapai	The hour of death can be an hour of new birth:
Jika hidup harus merasai	To be alive, you have to taste living.

From: C. Anwar, *The Voice of the Night: Complete Poetry and Prose of Chairil Anwar*, R. Burton, transl. (Athens 1993 [1970]) 6-7.

64 KITLV H1284/11, Rapport Wohlhoff-Koerts, 14-X-1945.

65 M.W. Poesponegoro and N. Notosusanto, *Sejarah Nasional Indonesia* 6 (Jakarta 1984) 104; KITLV H1284/11, Rapport Wohlhoff-Koerts, 14-X-1945; Reid, 'Australia's Hundred', 210-211.

66 Djawardi, *"Corps"*, 5-9; Poesponegoro and Notosusanto, *Sejarah Nasional*, 104; Reid, 'Australia's Hundred Days', 211, 215.

67 NL-HaNA, 2.21.036.01 inv.no 71, Rapport-Enthoven, 11; Reid, 'Australia's Hundred Days', 211.

68 KITLV H1284/11, Rapport Wohlhoff-Koerts, 14-X-1945.

69 Australian War Memorial (AWM) 52, 8/2/21/37, Summary of Events at Palopo, annex to Preliminary Report by Surveillance Party in the Area North of the Sadang River, Celebes – 19-27 Nov 1945; Gunawan *et al.*, *Sejarah Berita Proklamasi Kemerdekaan Indonesia*, 461.

70 KITLV H1039/25, J. L. Been to Van Hoogstraten, 20 October 1945; I. Anwar, *Perang Kota: Perlawan Rakyat Luwu 23 Januari 1946* (Makassar 2016) 64-65.

71 Masita, 'Eliminasi Orang-orang Pro NICA di Palopo dan Sekitarnya 1946-1950', BA thesis, Universitas Hasanuddin, Makassar, 2017, 44-48.

72 H. Chalik, A. Mekno, A. Galib and N. Lasang, *Sejarah Perlawanan Terhadap Imperialisme dan Kolonialisme di Daerah Sulawesi Tenggara* (Jakarta 1983) 111, 113; Djawardi, *"Corps"*, 24-25.

73 Djawardi, *"Corps"*, 24-25.

74 NL-HaNA, 2.40.62/1311, Rapport Dr J.W. de Klein, 16 August 1946, annex to DD2/313/G, 22 Augustus 1946; KITLV H1284/47, Interview Mr. N.C. Beudeker.

75 Pawiloy, et al., *Sejaran Perjuangan Angkatan 45*, 131; KITLV H1284/12, Verslag Conica Makassar Force 21-10-1945 to 30-10-1945.

76 Gunawan et al., *Sejarah Berita*, 479; KITLV, H1284/12, Verslag Conica Makassar Force 21-10-1945 to 30-10-1945; AWM52, 8/2/21/37, Preliminary Report by Surveillance Party in the Area North of the Sadang River, Celebes–19-27 Nov 1945; NL-HaNA NEFIS/CMI, 2.10.62 inv.no 1312, Uittreksel Situatie-rapport AROVJ No. 47, 22 October 46, annex I to DD2/73/ZG, 6 November 1946.

77 AWM52, 8/2/21/37, Notes on Discussion Between Comd Makassar Force and Dr Ratu Langie 2 Nov 45; NL-HaNA NEFIS/CMI, 2.10.62 inv.no 1311, Aanbieding 2e Rap; Ctr. De Klein, DD2/313/G, 22 Augustus 1946; NL-HaNA AS, 2.10.14 inv.no 3742, Positie van mr. Tadjoeddin Noor, Nota Inzake Mr. Tadjoeddin Noor, Parket PG 894/GS 25 March 1947; KITLV, 1284/12, Verslag 18/11-25/11.

78 Memorie Betreffende het Troepencommando RES.Zuid.Celebes, 77-78.

79 Memorie, 77, 46.

80 NL-HaNA, 2.14.14 inv.no 3742, Ma'loemat [sic] Tentara Lipan Badjeng, Annexes to Chapter III.

81 NL-HaNA NEFIS/CMI, 2.10.62 inv.no 4694, NEFIS Document No. 3365, Verslag Vergadering Voorbereidingscomité ter Oprichting der Regeering van de Republiek Indonesia op Celebes, 14 December 1946.

82 Memorie Betreffende het Troepencommando RES.Zuid.Celebes, 66-68, 79.

83 NL-HaNA, Ministerie van Justitie: Onderzoek naar excessen in Indonesië (hereinafter JUS), 2.09.95 inv.no 76, Nota van Overdracht van den Assistant Resident van Mandar, periode 13 Jan.1946-2 Juni 1947, annex to Assistant Resident Maurenbrecher to Hoog Militair Gerechtshof, No. 371, 1 July 1949.

84 Memorie Betreffende het Troepencommando RES.Zuid.Celebes, 60-61, 63-64, 76.

85 P. Staniland, *Networks of Rebellion: Explaining Insurgent Cohesion and Collapse* (Ithaca NY 2014).

86 Djawardi, *"Corps"*, 27-29. (The book places the meeting in June.); Memorie Betreffende het Troepencommando RES.Zuid.Celebes, 48-49.

87 Memorie, 60.

88 Memorie, 82-83.

89 NL-HaNA AS, 2.10.14 inv.no 3651, Sitrap Nr. 1, Nr. 218, 1 February 1946.

90 NL-HaNA NEFIS/CMI, 2.10.62 inv.no 1312, Annexes V, VI and VIII to DD2/73/ZG, 6 November 1946.

91 NL-HaNA, 2.21.036.01 inv.no 71, Rapport-Enthoven, 13.

92 NL-HaNA AS, 2.10.14 inv.no 3652, Sitrap Nr. 16, 31 July 1946.

93 Memorie Betreffende het Troepencommando RES.Zuid.Celebes, 69-70; NL-HaNA AS, 2.10.14 inv.no 3742, Afschrift van Verslag van de door de Laptoer Gehouden Zuivering van Vijandelijke Spionnen, 22 December 1946; Lijst van Spionnen van de Vijand die Opgeruimd Zijn, 20 January 1947; Laporan dari Hasil Pekedjaan "Laptoer", 2 March 1947, Ketoa Bagahian Oemoem to P.P.M.B.K; NL-HaNA JUS, 2.09.95 inv.no 150, Rapport Van Rij en Stam, 15 September 1954, 5.

94 NL-HaNA JUS, 2.09.95 inv.no 76, Nota van Overdracht van den Assistant Resident van Mandar, periode 13 Jan.1946-2 Juni 1947, annex to Assistant Resident Maurenbrecher to Hoog Militair Gerechtshof, No. 371, 1 July 1949; KITLV H1039/29, R. C. Kwantes to Koerts, 27 June 1991; KITLV H973/38.

95 NL-HaNA JUS, 2.09.95 inv.no 76, Nota van Overdracht van den Assistant Resident van Mandar; NL-HaNA, 2.40.62 inv.no 761311, Rapport Dr J.W. de Klein, 16 August 1946.

96 KITLV H1284/21, De Geschiedenis van het XIe Bat.Inf., 6; Memorie, 40. For a more comprehensive discussion, see IJzereef, Zuid-Celebes, 72-77.

97 See, for example: AWM52, 8/2/21/37, Conference with Rajah of Goa, HQ Makassar Force, 28 November 1945.

98 AWM52 8/2/21/37, War Diary HQ 21 Aust Inf Bde 1 Nov 45-10 Nov 45 Sheet 6; Ibidem, Notes on Discussion Comd Makassar Force and Dr Ratu Langie, 2 November 1945; KITLV H1284/14, Ratulangi to CONICA Makassar, 26 December 1945; AWM54 556/4/7 Removal of Dr. Ratulangi from Celebes; A. Reid, *The Indonesian National Revolution 1945-1950* (Westport 1974) 107; Ratulangi died in June 1949.

99 NL-HaNA, 2.9.95/76, Verklaring J. Biermans, Sergeant Beheerder Rustoord van het KNIL Malino, 12 September 1947.

100 KITLV H973/14, Excerpt uit de Nota, 17 October 1946.

101 NL-HaNA AS, 2.10.14 inv.no 3742, Aantekening E. Katoppo, Verklaring Abdul Moettalib dg. Tompo.

102 KITLV H1284/21, De Geschiedenis XIe Bat.Inf., 6; Memorie, 40.

103 NL-HaNA NEFIS/CMI, 2.10.62 inv.no 1312, DD2/73/ZG, 6 November 1946.

104 NL-HaNA SNI, 2.13.132 inv.no 1313, Colonel de Vries to General Spoor, 22 August 1947.

105 IJzereef, *Zuid-Celebes*, 74-75; Djawardi, *"Corps"*, 30.

106 AWM54 556/4/7, Free Indonesia Movement, AQ323-1, 1 November 1945; NL-HaNA SNI, 2.13.132 inv. no 1313, Proclamatie Brigadier F.O. Chilton, 29 October 1945; KITLV H1284/12, Verslag CONICA Makassar Force 21-10-45 to 30-10-1945.

107 IJzereef, *Zuid-Celebes*, 93; NL-HaNA SNI, 2.13.132 inv.no 1313, Kantoor Politieke Zaken to Spoor, 26 August 1947; Limpach, *Brandende Kampongs*, 284.

108 NL-HaNA NEFIS/CMI, 2.10.62 inv.no 4687, NEFIS Document No. 3358, nr. 21: Andi Djalanti to Patahoeddin, 6 November 1946.

109 NL-HaNA, Krijgsraden (te Velde) in Nederland, Europa, Canada, Australië, Nederlands-Indië, Nieuw-Guinea en het Verre Oosten (hereinafter KRV) 2.09.19, inv.no 182, Interview De Vries, Colonial General Staff KNIL, 31282 Zuid Celebes Affaire, 4 June 1949; NL-HaNA AS, 2.10.14 inv.no 3742, Spoor to Van Mook, No.Kab/1197/9245, 7 June 1948.

110 NL-HaNA KRV, 2.09.19 inv.no 182, Interview Jurgen Renke, MP Corporal in Pare-Pare, 2 May 1949; Getuigenverhoor JP Wiegeraad, 23 Juni 1949; D. Bultmann, 'S-21 as a Liminal Power Regime: Violently Othering Khmer Bodies into Vietnamese Minds', *Genocide Studies and Prevention: An International Journal* 14:3 (2020) 14-15; D.S. Sutton, 'Ritual and Culture', 142.

111 NL-HaNA AS, 2.10.14 inv.no 3742, Rapport Betreffende de Verdiensten van den Controleur 1ste klasse W.G. van der Wolk, 28 April 1947.

112 NL-HaNA KRV, 2.09.19 inv.no 182, Interview La Itjin, 45 year, Pabitjara van het District Maewa, 12 May 1949.

113 Limpach, *Brandende kampongs*, 247.

114 'Stadsnieuws. Bevolking van Makassar Huldigt de Speciale Troepen', *Makassaarsche Courant*, 14 March 1947.

115 Rapport-Enthoven, 102-103, 106.

116 Djawardi, *"Corps"*, 29.

117 Eyewitness' Statement One, Kementerian Penerangan, *Massacre in Macassar: It Happened in This Time in South Celebes Indonesia Anno Domini 1947* (Yogyakarta 1947) 2.

118 NL-HaNA AS, 2.10.14 inv.no 3742, Barendrecht to Enthoven, 25 August 1947; NL-HaNA KRV, 2.09.19 inv.no 182, Interview Mahoeseng, 5 May 1949.

119 NL-HaNA KRV, 2.09.19 inv.no 182, Interview La Side te Amparita, 13 May 1949; Interview with Ahmad

Ba Madhan te Amparita, 13 May 1949; NL-HaNA AS, 2.10.14 inv.no 3742, Verklaring M. Mantjoer and Letter to Territoriaal Commandant, Resident Zuid-Celebes, Hoofd Plaatselijk Bestuur, de Burgemeester Makassar en anderen; both in Annex I to 'Een Stukje Geschiedenis', Nederlandse Perscommentaren, Paleisrapport RVD Bijlage I, 21 July 1947.

120 NL-HaNA AS, 2.10.14 inv.no 3202, Verslag van het Bezoek aan Makassar van 17-20 April 1947 van Drs. M. Weisglas.

121 'Geen Voedseltekort in Indonesië: Rijstpositie Bevredigend', *Het Nieuwsblad voor Sumatra*, 9 July 1948, 1; NL-HaNA AS, 2.10.14 inv.no 3437, Departement van Economische Zaken, *De Economische Toestand van Indonesië: Voorjaar 1949* (Batavia 1949) 21, 26; Ibidem, 2.

122 *De Economische Toestand van Indonesië: Voorjaar 1949*, 3.

123 For early, small-scale beginnings, see: NL-HaNA NEFIS/CMI, 2.10.62 inv.no 4704, NEFIS Document 3375/35, M. P. La Wawo andi Makkasaoe and A. Baso Massepe to Hadji Abd. Kamrim, 24 November 1945 and 3375/44e, Oesoel Oesoel Kepada Pemerintah, "Penundjang Repoeblik Indonesia" Pare2 Soelawesi, M. Amin and La Nakka, 25 January 1946.

124 Djawardi, *"Corps"*, 32-33.

125 NL-HaNA NEFIS/CMI, 2.10.62 inv.no 4704, NEFIS Document 3375/10, Soerat-Koeasa, M.B.O. Bahagian Organisasi Oeroesan T.R.I. Soelawesi, Nr. 108/Ig-2/2A, 24 March 1946.

126 NL-HaNA NEFIS/CMI, 2.10.62 inv.no 4704, NEFIS Document 3375/30, F. J. Mohede to Governor Sulawesi, No. 12, 19 March 1946; Document 3375/15, Bevel Markas Tertinggi Tentara, No. 427/IG.e/2, 16 August 1946; Djawardi, *"Corps"*, 33.

127 Memorie, 62, 83.

128 Memorie, 84-85; instead of November (Dutch sources), R. Darwas, *Sejarah Perjuangan Kemerdekaan di Daerah TK II Kabupaten Barru* (Ujung Pandang 1990) 141, mentions early December.

129 M. Firman, 'Konferensie Paccekke di Barru Tahun 1947', Ba thesis, Makassar State University (2019) 9-11; Djawardi, *"Corps"*, 35-37; Memorie, 97-99.

130 NL-HaNA NEFIS/CMI, 2.10.62 inv.no 4704, NEFIS Document 3375/25, Lahade to Saad, 20 February 1947 and 3375/36, Tjontoh Sembejan2 dan Banjaknja Lembar yang Diperloekan.

131 Suriadi Mappangara, et al, *Pergolakan di Sulawesi Selatan: Studi Kasus Konferensi Paccekke 1945-1947* (Barru 2007) 130; Djawardi, *"Corps"*, 37-38.

132 Memorie, 74.

133 NL-HaNA NEFIS/CMI, 2.10.62 inv.no 4060, K.R.I.S. Ma'loemat 1, annex to Agno: 26/1629, 13 December 1946.

134 M. Saelan, *Dari Revolusi '45 Sampai Kudeta '66: Kesaksian Wakil Komandan Tjakrabirawa* (Jakarta 2001), 79-81.

135 Memorie, 86.

136 Djawardi, *"Corps"*, 34-35; Memorie, 41.

137 Firman, 'Konferensie Paccekke', 10; Djawardi, *"Corps"*, 34-35; NL-HaNA AS, 2.10.14 inv.no 2674, Overzicht de Infiltraties of Pogingen daartoe van Republikeinsche Strijdkrachten in de Malino-gebieden na 25 Maart 1947, annex to No. Kab/631/P.Z., 29 May 1947.

138 Djawardi, *"Corps"*, 36, 38; Jupri, 'Abu Bakar Lambogo Gerakan Perjuangan Rakyat Enrang (1945-1947)', BA thesis, Makassar State University (2019) 13; M. van Pagee, 'Malik Wil Excuses voor de Onthoofding van zijn Vader', *NRC* 21 May 2016.

139 NL-HaNA NEFIS/CMI, 2.10.62 inv.no 6953, CMI Document 5646/1, Enkele Gegevens, waarvan de Regering op de Hoogte Dient te Zijn, Chef Staf I Resimen Hasanuddin, Andi Mattalatta, 15 February 1948.

140 Daeng Romo and his bodyguard, for example, died defending LAPRIS headquarters in Lengkese, see: Djawardi, *"Corps"*, 29.

141 KITLV H1039/29, Koerts to Kwantes, 13 July 1991; KITLV H1284/57, Manuscript Wesseling, 49.

142 NL-HaNA NEFIS/CMI, 2.10.62 inv.no 6953, CMI Document 5646/2, Valse Beschuldigingen, No.

145/K.R./48, 15 February 1948; S. Abidin, 'Andi Selle dalam Pergolakan Bersenjata di Sulawesi Selatan (1950-1964)', *Yupa* 1:1 (2017) 31.

143 NL-HaNA JUS, 2.09.95 inv.no 76, Nota van Overdracht van den Assistant Resident van Mandar.

144 Djawardi, *"Corps"*, 29; NL-HaNA NEFIS/CMI, 2.10.62 inv.no 4682, Bekentenis van Andi Mandatjingi, 24 February 1947, annex to Ago.: 1/167/Z.G., 24 April 1947.

145 Memorie, 94-95.

146 Memorie, 74-75, 99.

147 Memorie, 108-109.

148 Chalik et al., *Sejarah Perlawanan*, 133-135.

149 A. Reid, *The Indonesian National Revolution 1945-1950* (Westport 1974) 107; Reid, 'Australia's Hundred', 220.

150 G. Kamandoko, *Kisah 124 Pahlawan dan Pejuang Nusantara* (Yogyakarta 2006) 279-280.

151 NL-HaNA JUS, 2.09.95 inv.no 76, Verklaring van de Olt. Vermeulen, J.B; NL-HaNA AS, 2.10.14 inv.no 3742, Former Assistant-Resident M. Peddemors to Minister Overzeese Gebiedsdelen, 16 Juli 1947, annex to R.45/No. 206, 25 July 1947.

152 KITLV H973/14, Excerpt uit Rapport van Kofman en Krol van begin Feb (uit Archief P.G.); NL-HaNA AS, 2.10.14 inv.no 3742, Bespreking van de Heeren Hoven, Felderhof, Gen. Buurman van Vreede, Idenburg, Koets en Veldhuis, 31 January 1947.

153 KITLV H1284/50, Interview Mr. J.J. Wesseling, 14 December 1981; KITLV H1039/29, De Jong over Zuid Celebes, artikel voor "Moesson".

154 NL-HaNA AS, 2.10.14 inv.no 3204, Overzicht Politieke Ontwikkelingen Oost-Indonesië Mei 1948.

155 NL-HaNA NEFIS/CMI, 2.10.62 inv.no 1328, Baris Besar Perjandjian Penjerahan, annex to Ultimatum aan Zelfbestuurders, Agno.617/DD2/G, 16 September 1946.

156 See, for example NL-HaNA NEFIS/CMI, 2.10.62 inv.no 1322, Politiek Verslag van den Controleur van Gowa over de Maand Juli 1946, Agno: 418/G, 9 Augustus 1946.

157 NL-HaNA AS, 2.10.14 inv.no 3204, Overzicht Politieke Ontwikkeling Oost-Indonesië, Augustus 1948.

158 NL-HaNA NEFIS/CMI, 2.10.62 inv.no 1332, Afschrift, 13 Augustus 1946, annex to Aanbieding verslag v.d. Ctr.B.B. de Klein, Agno. ZG/13, 17 August 1946.

159 NL-HaNA AS, 2.10.14 inv.no 3204, Overzicht Politieke Ontwikkeling Oost-Indonesië, Mei 1948.

160 NL-HaNA AS, 2.10.14 inv.no 3204, Politiek Verslag betreffende de Staat Oost -Indonesië. Periode: maanden October en November 1948; Overzicht Politieke Ontwikkeling Oost-Indonesië Mei 1948.

161 KITLV H1284/51, Gesprek met Mr. H.B. Eldering, 15 December 1981; Memorie, 73.

162 NL-HaNA AS, 2.10.14 inv.no 3204, Overzicht Politieke Ontwikkeling Oost-Indonesië, Mei 1948.

163 Memorie, 55.

164 Memorie, 45-46.

165 Sarita Pawiloy, *Sejarah Perjuangan Angkatan 45 di Sulawesi Selatan 17 Agustus 1945-17 Agustus 1950* (Ujung Pandang: Dewan Harian Daerah Angkatan 45 Propinsi Sulawesi Selatan, 1987), 179-180.

166 Djawardi, *"Corps"*, 38-39, Memorie, 96, 64.

167 R. Frakking, '"Collaboration is a Delicate Concept": Alliance-formation and the Colonial Defense of Indonesia and Malaysia, 1945-1957', PhD Thesis, European University Institute, Florence, 2017; J. W. M. Schulten, 'De Tweede Politionele Actie: Politieke en militaire achtergronden', *Militaire Spectator* 167 (1998), 624-630.

168 NL-HaNA AS, 2.10.14 inv.no 2479, Memorandum, Waarnemend Algemeen Secretaris to HVK, 25 July 1949.

169 NL-HaNA AS, 2.10.14 inv.no 3208, Interne Informatie – Nota, No: 3, 15 April 1949.

170 NL-HaNA AS, 2.10.14 inv.no 3210, Vice-Admiral A.S. Pinke to The High Representative of the Crown, 15 September 1949.

171 NL-HaNA AS, 2.10.14 inv.no 3203, Bijlage VII, Oost Indonesië, annex to Politiek Rapport aan Hoofd

RVD betreffende dienstreis naar Makassar 25 – 30.1.'48; Richard Chauvel, 'Republik Maluku Selatan and Social Change in Ambonese Society During the Late Colonial Period', *Cakalele*, 1, 1-2 (1990), 21.

172 NL-HaNA AS, 2.10.14 inv.no 2479, Memorandum, Waarnemend Algemeen Secretaris, 25 July 1949; NL-HaNA SNI, 2.13.132 inv.no 839, Annexes B and C to Nr. 257 A/GS15, 11 March 1950.

173 NL-HaNA SNI, 2.13.132 inv.no 866, Undated Concept Note, 1950, annex to Kab/433, 30 May1950; NL-HaNA SNI, 2.13.132 inv.no 4663, Nr. 18501/GS 01, Afwikkeling Reorganisatie KNIL, 26 June 1950; NL-HaNA SNI, 2.13.132 inv.no 866, Memorandum Betreffende de Beëindiging van de Reorganisatie van het KNIL, annex to Kab 500 A, 15 July 1950; NL-HaNA SNI, 2.13.132 inv.no 839, Planningsvergadering Ddo. 1 June 1950; *ibid*, Nr. 257 A/GS15, Nota, 11 Maart 1950.

174 NL-HaNA AS, 2.10.14 inv.no 2703, Het Programma, annex to Oesman Djafar to Hatta, 14 April 1947, No. 12a/M/GP/47-S, 14 April 1947, CMI Document No. 5415, 27 December 1948.

175 NL-HaNA AS, 2.10.14 inv.no 3208, Interne Informatie Nota No. 7, 28 October 1949; NL-HaNA AS, 2.10.14 inv.no 2680, J. A. Gulden to Commandant van het Leger, Kab/DCMI/1258, 7 March 1949; NL-HaNA SNI, 2.13.132 inv.no 531, Door Djocja geïnspireerde Republikeinse Activiteit in de Negara Oost Indonesië, 29 November 1948; 'Evacuatie KNIL naar N.I.T.', *Het Nieuwsblad voor Sumatra* 25 March 1950, 3.

176 NL-HaNA AS, 2.10.14 inv.no 2674, Uit Politiek Dagrapport CMI No. 103, 13 August 1949; Uit Politiek Dagrapport CMI No. 108, 20 August 1949.

177 NL-HaNA SNI, 2.13.132 inv.no 531, Door Djocja geïnspireerde Republikeinse Activiteit.

178 NL-HaNA SNI, 2.13.132 inv.no 4692, Telegram NR 10186, 07-2000 Augustus; Telegram Overste Tymann to CNRI, undated; Telegram NR 100, 070800 Aug; Telegram 061030; NL-HaNA SNI, 2.13.132 inv. no 4693, Telegram 060700 Aug; Bijlage II, III and XIV, annexed to Makassar-incidenten, 1-20 August 1950; NL-HaNA SNI, 2.13.132 inv.no 834, Nr. 423/VS/TI, 24 Mei 1950.

179 Djawardi, *"Corps"*, 55; NL-HaNA SNI, 2.13.132 inv.no 851, NR TC 1680; Beknopt Resumé, 10 April 1950; Beknopt Resumé, 11 April 1950; Beknopt Resumé, 12 April 1950; Beknopt Resumé, 15 April 1950; Beknopt Resumé, 22 April 1950.

180 '"Vrijheids-proclamatie" van de Raad der Molukken', *Het Nieuwsblad voor Sumatra*, 27 April 1950, 1; M. C. Ricklefs, *A History of Modern Indonesia Since ca. 1200* (Hampshire 2001) 285.

181 NL-HaNA, 2.21.036.01 inv.no 71, Rapport-Enthoven, 9.

11. Polombangkeng, South Sulawesi

1 Mangulung's letter addressed to P.J.M. Prime Minister of Eastern Indonesia, 31 March 1948 in the Archives of South and Southeast Sulawesi Province Reg. 182

2 William Cummings, *Making Blood White: Historical Transformations in Early Modern Makassar* (Honolulu 2002) 131.

3 J. Tideman, 'De Batara Gowa op Zuid Celebes', *BKI* 61 (1908) 379-80.

4 Henk Schulte Nordholt, 'The jago in the shadow: crime and "order" in the colonial state in Java', *Review of Indonesian and Malaysian affairs* 25:1 (1991) 74-91.

5 Margreet Van Till, *Banditry in West Java, 1869-1942* (Singapore 2011) 84; Bondan Kanumoyoso, 'Beyond the City Wall: Society and Economic Development in the Ommelanden of Batavia, 1684-1740', PhD dissertation, Universiteit (Leiden 2011) 96; Ong Hok Ham, *From Priyayi sampai Nyi Blorong Historis Nusantara Reflection* (Jakarta 2002) 101-106.

6 Eric J. Hobsbawm, *Bandits* (Harmondsworth 1972) 98.

7 Anton Blok, 'The Peasant and the Brigand: Social Banditry Reconsidered', *Comparative Studies in Society and History* 14:4 (1972) 494-503.

8 Studies on banditry in Latin America include Billy Jaynes Chandler, *The Bandit King: Lampiao of Brazil* (College Station1978); Linda Lewin, 'Oral Tradition and Elite Myth: The Legend of Antonio Silvino in

Brazilian Popular Culture', *Journal of American Lore* 2 (1979); Paul Vanderwood, *Disorder and Progress: Bandits, Police, and Mexican Development* (Lincoln 1981); Rosalie Schwartz, *Lawless Liberators: Political Banditry and Cuban Independence* (Durham, NC 1989); Richard W. Slatta, 'Rural Criminality and Social Conflict in Nineteenth-Century Buenos Aires Province', *The Hispanic American Historical Review* 60:3 (1980) 450-72.

9 Schwartz, *Lawless Liberators*.

10 Sartono Kartodirdjo, *The Peasants' Revolt of Banten in 1888: Its Conditions, Course and Sequel; A Case Study of Social Movements in Indonesia* (The Hague 1966), 110-11, 34–39.

11 Sartono Kartodirdjo, *Modern Indonesia: Tradition and Transformation* (Yogyakarta 1988); For more about changes in colonial politics and the emergence of social movement in Banten, see Sartono Kartodirjo, *Pemberontakan Petani Banten* (Jakarta 2015)

12 Suhartono W. Pranoto, *Apanage dan Bekel: Perubahan Sosial di Pedesaan Surakarta 1830-1920* (Yogyakarta 1991) 139-166.

13 Suhartono W. Pranoto, *Jawa: Bandit-Bandit Pedesaan: Studi Historis 1850-1945* (Yogyakarta 2000) 2.

14 Anton Lucas, *One Soul One Struggle: Peristiwa Tiga Daerah dalam Revolusi Indonesia* (Yogyakarta 2004).

15 Robert Cribb, *Gangsters and Revolutionaries: The Jakarta People's Militia and the Indonesian Revolution, 1945-1949* (Jakarta-Kuala Lumpur 2008) 171-179.

16 Edward L. Poelinggomang, *Perubahan Politik dan Hubungan Kekuasaan Makassar 1906-1942* (Yogyakarta 2004).

17 M. Nafsar Palallo, *Bandit sosial di Makassar: jejak perlawanan I Tolok Dg. Magassing* (Makassar 2008).

18 Mustari Bosra, *Laskar Lipan Bajeng: Perjumpaan Agama dan Nasionalisme dalam Perjuangan Bangsa Indonesia* (Makassar 2009).

19 W.T. IJzereef, 'De wind en de bladeren: Hierarchie en autonomie in Bone en Polombangkeng, 1850-1950' , PhD thesis Rijksuniversiteit Groningen, 1994.

20 See Leonard Y. Andaya, *The Heritage of Arung Palakka: A History of South Sulawesi (Celebes) in the Seventeenth Century* (Dordrecht 2013) 263.

21 Regarding the conquest of Polombangkeng by Gowa, see William Cummings, *A Chain of Kings: the Makassarese Chronicles of Gowa and Talloq* (Leiden 2007) 33.

22 IJzereef, 'De wind en de bladeren', 152.

23 P.J. Kooreman, 'De feitelijke toestand in het gouvernementsgebied van Celebes en Onderhoorigheden ' in *De Indische Gids I* (Amsterdam 1883), 494.

24 IJzereef, 'De wind en de bladeren'

25 Departement van Economische Zaken, *Volkstelling 1930 Deel V: Inheemsche Bevolking van Borneo, Celebes, De Kleine Soenda Eilanden en De Molukken* (Batavia 1936) 129.

26 IJzereef, 'De wind en de bladeren'.

27 Staatsblad 1824, no. 31a. Regeringsalmanak voor Nederlands-Indië 1860, 130-131; Arsip Nasional Republik Indonesia, (ANRI), *Ikhtisar keadaan politik Hindia-Belanda tahun 1839-1848* (Jakarta 1973) 263; Dias Pradadimara, 'Dibentuknya Negara Kolonial di Sulawesi Bagian Selatan di Abad ke-19', *Lensa Budaya* 12:2 (2017) 56-60.

28 'Regerings-Almanak 1860', 130-131; Regerings-Almanak voor Nederlands-Indië 1874, 208-210.

29 Harry J. Benda, 'The Pattern of Administrative Reforms in the Closing Years of Dutch Rule in Indonesia', *The Journal of Asian Studies* 25:4 (1966) 589-605.

30 Daud Limbugau, 'Terbentuknya Wilayah Administrasi Pemerintah Hindia Belanda di Sulawesi Selatan 1924-1874', Thesis: Universitas Gadjah Mada (1982) 75.

31 See Vervolg geschiedkundig overzicht van het Gouvernement Celebes en Onderhoorigheden van 1846 tot en met 186, (ANRI, bundle Makassar Nomor 354); J. Tideman, 'Het Landschap Laikang', *Bijdragen tot de Taal-, Land- en Volkenkunde* 59:1 (1906) 648-49.

32 Kooreman, 'De feitelijke toestand', 203.

33 Ijzereef, 'De wind en de bladeren', 161.

34 Henk Schulte Nordholt, *Kriminalitas, Modernitas dan Identitas dalam Sejarah Indonesia* (Yogyakarta 2002) 10-11.

35 H.J. Koerts, 'Amtenar BB di Sulawesi Selatan', in: S.L. van der Wal (ed.), *Kenang-Kenangan Pangrehpraja Belanda 1920-1942* (Jakarta 2001) 47.

36 Heather Sutherland, 'Political Structure and Colonial Control in South Sulawesi', in: R. Schefold, J.W. Schoorl, and J. Tennekes (eds.), *Man, Meaning, and History* (The Hague 1980) 235.

37 H.N. Swart, 'Memorie van Overgave (September 1906-April 1908)', *Koloniaal Verslag* (1916) 9.

38 *Bataviaasch Nieuwsblad*, 24 November 1908.

39 Taufik Ahmad, 'Genealogi Konflik Agraria di Polongbangkeng, Takalar', *Masyarakat Indonesia* 40:2 (2014); Ridwan Effendy, *I Tolok: Studi Hubungan Antar Teks* (Makassar 2005).

40 Crime statistics; April, May, June and July 1915; in Takalar 76 cases of robbery, Gowa 8 cases, Jeneponton, 45 cases and Bonthain 7 cases. Until August 1915, there were 140 cases of robbery, see *Koloniaal Verslag*, 1916, 44; Another report by Th.A.L. Heyting shows different numbers: in June 39 cases, July 46 cases, August 8 cases, September 2 cases; October and November each 1 case, see Th.A.L. Heyting, Memorie van Overgave, 1915, 46-55.

41 Swart, 'Memorie van Overgave', 44.

42 *Het Nieuws van den Dag voor Nederlandsch-Indië*, 27 November 1916.

43 Poelinggomang, *Perubahan Politik*, 171.

44 'Uit de Indische Bladen, Tolo neergelegd', *Het Nieuws van den Dag voor Nederlandsch-Indië*, 25 November 1915

45 *Bataviaasch Nieuwsblad*, 8 July 1915, *Het Nieuws van den Dag voor Nederlandsch-Indië*, 26 August 1915

46 Poelinggomang, *Perubahan Politik*, 167.

47 'Uit de Indische Bladen, Tolo neergelegd', *Het Nieuws van den Dag voor Nederlandsch-Indië*, 25 November 1915.

48 Muhammad Abduh et al., *Sejarah Perlawanan Terhadap Imperialisme dan Kolonialisme di Sulawesi Selatan* (Jakarta 1985).

49 'Het Rooverwezen op Celebes', *Nieuwe Rotterdamsche Courant*, 25 August 1924.

50 Tajudding Karaeng Lewa, *Polongbangkeng Dalam Lintasan Sejarah Perjuangan Kemerdekaan Republik Indonesia* (Jakarta 2007) 68.

51 IJzereef, 'De wind en de bladeren', 169; Goedhart, 'De Inlandsche Rechtsgemeenschappen', 249.

52 NL-HaNA, Marine en Leger Inlichtingendienst, de Netherlands Forces Intelligence Service en de Centrale Militaire Inlichtingendienst in Nederlands-Indië (hereinafter NEFIS/CMI), 2.10.62 inv.no 1325, 'Familie-Verhoudingen Karaeng Polombangkeng; IJzereef, 'De wind en de bladeren', 165.

53 Military training had been thoroughly thought through by the Japanese military rulers. They were fully aware of the potential of the youths who could be mobilized for Japan's war purposes. See Aiko Kurasawa, *Kuasa Jepang di Jawa: Perubahan Sosial di Pedesaan 1942-1945* (Depok 2015) 373-398.

54 Haji Sultan Daeng Mile, *Sejarah Perjuangan Rakyat Limbung (Bajeng)* (1968) 8.

55 IJzereef, 'De wind en de bladeren', 219.

56 Anthony Reid, *Indonesia, Revolusi dan Sejumlah Isu Penting* (Jakarta 2018) 228.

57 H. Mualwi Saelan, *Dari Revolusi 45 Sampai Kudeta 65: Kesaksian Wakil Komandan Tjakrabirawa* (Jakarta 2001) 39-41.

58 Makkattang Daeng Sibali, *Lipan Bajeng* (1985) 37.

59 IIzereef, 'De wind en de bladeren', 179-80.

60 Edward L. Poelinggomang and Suriadi Mappangara (eds.), *Sejarah Sulawesi Selatan* Jilid 2 (Makassar 2005) 147.

61 Sibali, *Lipan Bajeng*, 46.

62 IJzereef, 'De wind en de bladeren', 216.
63 Ibidem.
64 Mile, *Sejarah Perjuangan,* 13.
65 Sibali, *Lipan Bajeng,* 44.
66 IJzereef, 'De wind en de bladeren', 218.
67 H. Jamallong Daeng Tappa, interview, 9 December 2018.
68 IJzereef, 'De wind en de bladeren', 218.
69 Ibidem, 222. Daeng Nuhung, interview, 20 December 2018 in Polombangkeng.
70 NL-HaNA, NEFIS/CMI, 2.10.62 inv.no 1326, 'Verslag tentang keadaan politiek dalam onderafdeling Makassar selama bahagian jang ke doea dari boelan September 1946, 3-4.
71 IJzereef, 'De wind en de bladeren', 157.
72 Harvey, 'Tradition, Islam, and rebellion', 155.
73 Daeng Bani dan Muhtar Daeng Rau, interview 10 December 2018
74 Muhtar Daeng Rau, interview in Polombangkeng, 10 December 2018.
75 H. Jamallong daeng Tappa, interview 12 May 2018.
76 IJzereef, 'De wind en de bladeren', 220.
77 Sibali, *Lipan Bajeng,* 21.
78 See IJzereef, 'De wind en de bladeren', 222.
79 Mile, *Sejarah Perjuangan Rakyat Limbung (Bajeng).*
80 *De Locomotief,* 10 January 1948 reported the capture of the 'pembunuh Massal', Basullu Daeng Lawa.
81 *Het Dagblad,* 16 October 1946.
82 Maarten Hidskes, *Di Belanda tak Seorang pun Mempercayai Saya: Korban Metode Westerling di Sulawesi Selatan, 1946-1947* (Jakarta 2018) 90.
83 IJzereef, 'De wind en de bladeren', 222.
84 Mauluddin Aidid Sikki, *Sejarah Perjuangan Kelaskaran Lipan Bajeng* (Takalar 1987) 34.
85 H.H. Riri Amin Daud, *Biografi Pahlawan Ranggong Dg. Romo* (Ujung Pandang 1971) 17.
86 Muhammad Arfah, Muhammad Amir and Faisal, *Biografi pahlawan Ranggong Dg. Romo, Panglima LA-PRIS: Sebuah Biografi Perjuangan di Sulawesi Selatan* (Ujung Pandang 1991) 76.
87 Arsip Kabinet Perdana Menteri RI Jogjakarta No. 90.
88 Arsip Kabinet Perdana Menteri RI Jogjakarta No. 90.
89 Daeng Ngatu, interviewed by the author in Polombangkeng, 12 December 2018.
90 IJzereef, 'De wind en de bladeren'225.
91 Ibidem, 224.
92 Sarita Pawiloy, *Sejarah Revolusi Kemerdekaan 1945-1949 Daerah Sulawesi Selatan* (Ujung Pandang 1979) 126.
93 *Het Dagblad,* 11 May 1946.
94 *Het Dagblad,* 12 October 1946.
95 *Het Dagblad,* 16 October 1946.
96 Badan Arsip dan Perpustakaan Daerah Provinsi Sulawesi Selatan (hereafter BAPDPSS), Private archive of A.M. Rahman Tamma, No. 184.
97 Tajuddin M. Kr Lewa, *Polongbangkeng dalam Lintasan Sejarah Perjuangan Kemerdekaan Republik Indonesia* (Makassar 2007) 32.
98 *Negara Baroe,* 6 February 1947.
99 Harvey, 'Tradition, Islam, and rebellion', 152.
100 IJzereef, 'De wind en de bladeren', 226.
101 *Limburgsch Dagblad,* 21 May 1947.
102 *Het Dagblad,* 29 July 1947.
103 *Provinciale Drentsche en Asser Courant,* 11 August 1947.

104 Daud, *Biografi Pahlawan Ranggong Dg. Romo*, 90.
105 IJzereef, 'De wind en de bladeren', 227.
106 *De Locomotief*, 10 January 1948.
107 Private archive of A.R. Tamma, Reg. 188.
108 The BPPRI had been established in Polombangkeng the previous day, 6 February 1950. Arsip Kabinet Perdana Menteri RI Yogyakarta, No. 89
109 BAPDPSS, Arsip Provinsi Sulawesi Selatan dan Tenggara (hereinafter APSST) Reg. 182, 'Laporan Perampokan di Cikoang-Topejawa'.
110 APSST, Reg. 182, 'Laporan Perampokan di Kampung Lengkese'.
111 APSST, Reg. 182, 'Laporan Penembakan-Penembakan di Jalan raya Takalar'.

12. Association with the people must be friendly

1 I would like to extend my gratitude to Muhammad Aprianto for his translations of some documents and articles that were needed for writing this chapter.
2 Kementerian Penerangan, *Republik Indonesia: Propinsi Djawa Barat* (Djakarta 1953) 189-190; 'Struggle organization' is a direct translation of '*badan perjuangan*', and refers to often paramilitary organizations that saw themselves as more than merely military units, and more as political entities as part of a larger peoples movement. Hence I have adopted struggle organization instead of 'resistance organization' as their activities were pointed more at local populations, and less against Dutch troops.
3 Kementerian Penerangan, *Republik Indonesia*, 190.
4 Nationaal Archief (hereinafter NL-HaNA), Strijdkrachten in Nederlands-Indië (hereinafter SNI), 2.13.132 inv.no 3356, Verslag over het 1e Kwartaal 1949, Nr. 40/Co/IV-Geheim.
5 'UNCI-rapport over Militaire Toestand op Java en Sumatra', *Het Nieuwsblad voor Sumatra*, 2 May 1949, 2.
6 Kementerian Penerangan, *Republik Indonesia*, 190.
7 M. Gordon, *Extreme Violence and the 'British Way': Colonial Warfare in Perak, Sierra Leone and Sudan* (London 2020); K. Wagner, 'Savage Warfare: Violence and the Rule of Colonial Difference in Early British Counterinsurgency', *History Workshop Journal* 85 (2018) 218-237; R. Limpach, *De Brandende kampongs van Generaal Spoor* (Amsterdam 2016).
8 J.R.W. Smail, *Bandung in the Early Revolution 1945-1950: A Study in the Social History of the Indonesian Revolution* (Jakarta 2009) chapter 6; A. Husein, 'H. R. Soekardi Komandan Resimen III/TKR Pejuang "The Convoy Battle"', *Majalah Veteran* 1:6 (2011) 40-43; for TNI's primacy see: K. E. McGregor, *History in Uniform: Military Ideology and the Construction of Indonesia's Past* (Singapore 2007).
9 C. Formichi, *Islam and the Making of the Nation: Kartosuwiryo and the Political Islam in 20th Century Indonesia* (Leiden 2012); C. van Dijk, *Rebellion Under the Banner of Islam: The Darul Islam in Indonesia* (The Hague 1981); R. Frakking, 'Gathered on the Point of a Bayonet': The Negara Pasundan and the Colonial Defence of Indonesia, 1946-50', *International Historical Review* 39:1 (2017) 30-47.
10 Typically, E.P. Pambudi, E. Kurniawan, A. Yuliarto et al., *Soedirman: Seorang Panglima, Seorang Martir* (Jakarta 2012); T. van den Berge, *H. J. van Mook, 1894-1965: Een vrij en gelukkig Indonesië* (Bussum 2014); I. Bachtiar (ed.), *Catatan Jendral Pranoto Reksosamodra: Dari Boedo Oetomo Sampai Nirbaya* (Jakarta 2014); R. Cribb, 'Military Strategy in the Indonesian Revolution: Nasution's Concept of "Total People's War" in Theory and Practice', *War & Society* 19:2 (2001) 143-154.
11 For more on the *pemuda*, see W. Frederick, *Visions and Heat: The Making of the Indonesian Revolution* (Athens 1989).
12 See: R. Frakking and M. Thomas, 'Windows on the Microdynamics of Insurgent and Counterinsurgent Violence: Evidence from Late Colonial Southeast Asia and Africa Compared' in T. Brocades Zaalberg and B. Luttikhuis (eds.), *Empire's Violent End: Comparing Dutch, British, and French Wars of Decolonization, 1945-1962* (Ithaca NY 2022), 62-63, 65.

13 For an analysis in which violence is merely 'present', see, for example, Gordon, *Extreme Violence and the 'British Way'*.

14 For this 'interiority' of colonial violence, see: R.N. Price, 'The Psychology of Colonial Violence', in: Ph. Dwyer and A. Nettelbeck (eds.), *Violence, Colonialism and Empire in the Modern World* (London 2018) 25-51; V. Houben, 'Repertoires of European Panic and Indigenous Recaptures in Late Colonial Indonesia', in: H. Ficher-Tiné (ed.), *Anxieties, Fear and Panic in Colonial Settings: Empires on the Verge of a Nervous Breakdown* (London 2016) 259-278.

15 Hilmar Farid, 'Dealing with the Legacies of a Violent Past', in: G. Oostindie, B. Schoenmaker and F. van Vree (eds), *Beyond the Pale: Dutch Extreme Violence in the Indonesian War of Independence, 1945-1949* (Amsterdam 2022) 476.

16 For a remark on Republican-nationalist versus Dutch violence, see R. Frakking, 'The Harsher They Act, The More Fuss There'll be: The Dynamics of Violence in South Sulawesi, 1945-1950', 4 in this volume.

17 Farid, 'Dealing with the Legacies of a Violent Past', 475.

18 Three years earlier, the USS Renville had seen action in Okinawa, only to turn up again during the Second Indochina War: J. Mooney (ed.), *Dictionary of American Naval Fighting Ships* VI (Washington, 1976) 76.

19 General Assembly Official Records, Supplement No. 1 (A/565), *Annual Report of the Secretary-General on the Work of the Organization 1 July 1947- 30 June* (New York 1948) 23.

20 G. Mct. Kahin, *Nationalism and Revolution* (Ithaca NY 1963) 227-228.

21 G. Kahin, *Nationalism*, 224-225.

22 *Annual Report of the Secretary-General*, 23.

23 Article Four of the Six Additional Principles from the Negotiations Toward a Political Settlement Submitted by the Committee of Good Offices at the Fourth Meeting on January 17, 1948, in: C. Wolf, Jr., *The Indonesian Story: The Birth, Growth and Structure of the Indonesian Republic* (New York 1948) 188-189.

24 A.E. Kawilarang, *Officier in dienst van de Republiek Indonesië (ervaringen 1942-1961)* (Breda 1994) 86, 97; Radio Address of Queen Wilhelmina of the Netherlands, Delivered from The Hague, 3 February, 1948, to the People of the United States and Great Britain, in C. Wolf, Jr., *The Indonesian Story*, 190.

25 The Consul General at Batavia (Livengood) to the Secretary of State, 501.BC-Indonesia/1-548: Telegram, 5 January 1948, in: J.G. Reid and D.H. Stauffer (eds.), *Foreign Relations of the United States of America, 1948, The Far East and Australasia*, VI (Washington 1974), document 39.

26 Collection KITLV/Arsip Indonesia/Arsip Bandung2 – Markas Besar Angkatan Darat Dinas Sejarah/Divisi III Jateng 1949 s/d 1951 [hereafter MBAD], untitled, Markas Murba Terpendam, 5 February 1949.

27 Smail, *Bandung*, 109-110; A. Razak Rasyid, 'Episode Dramatis Penyiaran Proklamasi di Studio Radio Bandung', in: Dewan Harian Nasional Angkatan 45, *Terbukalah Jalanku: Seri Pengalaman dan Pandangan Tentang Perjoangan 45* (Jakarta 1984) 130; A. Nasution, *The Indonesian National Army, Book I* (Jakarta 1956) 84.

28 Willard H. Elsbree, *Japan's Role in Southeast Asian Nationalist Movements, 1940 to 1945* (Cambridge, Mass. 1953); Urip Sumoharjo was ex-KNIL; so were Nasution and Kawilarang, for example: Smail, *Bandung*, 109, note 72; Kawilarang, *Officier in dienst*, 15-16; Nasution, *Indonesian National Army*, 110, 138-139, 156-157.

29 Nasution, *Indonesian National Army*, 140; A. R. Rasyid, 'Episode Dramatis Penyiaran Proklamasi di Studio Bandung' in Dewan Harian Nasional Angkatan 45 (ed.), *Buku Terbukalah Jalanku Seri Pengalaman dan Pandangan Tentang Perdjoeangan 45* (Jakarta 1984) 130.

30 Nasution, *Indonesian National Army*, 139, 155; R. Cribb, *Gangsters and Revolutionaries: The Jakarta People's Militia and the Indonesian Revolution 1945-1949* (Honolulu 1991) chapter 1, 52, 75-76; 60-61; Smail, *Bandung*, 119-121; Anderson, *Java*, 1, 16, the quote can be found on page 33.

31 Collection KITLV/Arsip Indonesia/Arsip Bandung2 – MBAD, untitled, Markas Murba Terpendam, 5

February 1949.

32 Arsip Nasional Republik Indonesia (hereafter ANRI), RA.26 inv.no 47, Beberapa Anggota Poelisi Negara daerah Jogjakarta to P. Toean Poetjoek Pimpinan Polisi Tentara dan Polisi Negara, undated; Cowboy-isme, Nasuputra in *Patriot* No: 14 61.Th.II, 14 October 1947; Cribb, *Gangsters*, 71, 76; Nasution, *Indonesian National Army*, 155.

33 Cribb, *Gangsters*, 6-63, 65, 71-76; Nasution, *National Army*, 140; Anderson, *Java*; 47, 126-127, 297; Heryanto, 'Peristiwa Meladakmya Gudang Mesiu Dayeuh Kolot 1946', Bachelor's thesis in history, Universitas Pedidikan Indonesia (2010) 86; Smail, *Bandung*, 172-173; I.N. Raditya, 'Sejarah Pindahnya Ibu Kota RI dari Jakarta ke Yogyakarta pada 1946', https://tirto.id/sejarah-pindahnya-ibu-kota-ri-dari-jakarta-ke-yogyakarta-pada-1946-efr4, accessed 31 August 2021.

34 Husein, 'H.R. Soekardi', 40-43.

35 NL-HaNA SNI, 2.13.132 inv.no 223, Operatief Weekrapport, Nr: 36/C-II-n, 10 January 1947; Overzicht en ontwikkeling van de Toestand, No. 35/III-C, 28 January 1947; NL-HaNA, Marine en Leger Inlichtingendienst, de Netherlands Forces Intelligence Service en de Centrale Militaire Inlichtingendienst in Nederlands-Indië (hereinafter NEFIS/CMI), 2.10.62 inv.no 1081, Indon. politie, No. 432/C.P., 17 August 1946; NL-HaNA SNI, 2.13.132 inv.no 223, Overzicht en ontwikkeling van de Toestand, No. 35/III-C, 28 January 1947.

36 ANRI, RA.24 inv.no1688, Keadaan Kaboepaten Tangerang dari Moelai Pampflet ditoeroenkan Hingga Djatoehnya Tangerang, May 1946.

37 Collection KITLV, Arsip Indonesia, Arsip Disjarahad/Buku Sejarah Dokumenter Buku Induk Ke-I Jilid I Bab III (hereinafter Buku)/No. 47, Ganggioean NIC terhadap Kereta Api, *Antara*, 23 December 1946.

38 Collection KITLV, Arsip Indonesia, Arsip Disjarahad/Buku/No. 10, 'Nica memcoba Memperluas Daerahnhya di Bogor Selatan', *Antara*, 2 December 1946; No. 25, 'Sekitar Pertempoeran Maseng', *Antara*, 7 January 1947.

39 Collection KITLV, Arsip Indonesia, Arsip Disjarahad, Buku/No. 48, 'Aktiviteit Tentara Belanda sedjak Tentara Inggeris pergi', *Antara*, 24 December 1946.

40 NL-HaNA, Nederlandsche Handels-Maatschappij (hereinafter NHM) 2.20.01 inv.no 9811, No. 23 in *Correspondentie van Jhr. Mr. W.J. de Jonge*, 3 May 1947; NL-HaNA, Federatie van Verenigingen van Bergcultuurondernemingen in Indonesië (hereinafter FVB) 2.20.50, inv.no 68, VVO/Privé No.28, Van 't Oever to P.A. Verhulst, 6 May 1947.

41 J.A. Jonkman, *Nederland en Indonesië beide vrij: Memoires van mr. J.A. Jonkman* (Assen, 1977) 2, 117.

42 Collection KITLV, Arsip Indonesia, Arsip Disjarahad, Buku/No. 193, Djoemlah Pelanggaran Cease Fire Order oleh Belanda', *Kedaulatan Rakyat*, 23 August 1947; Cribb, *Gangsters*, 148.

43 Ahmad, 'Pembuntukan', 18-19.

44 ANRI, RA.24 inv.no 1290, Laporan Keadaan Djawa Barat; A. A. Ahmad, 'Pembuntukan Wilayah Pertahanan Priangan Timur dan Perpindahan Ibukota Propinsi Jawa Barat ke Lebaksiuh Tahun 1947-1948', *JASMERAH* 1:2 (2019) 17.

45 ANRI, RA.24 inv.no 1290, Laporan Keadaan Djawa Barat, 26 July 1947.

46 Collection KITLV, Arsip Indonesia, Arsip Disjarahad, Buku/No. 215, Mesjid Mendjadi Sasaran Belanda, *Kedaulatan Rakjat*, 29 September 1947.

47 NL-HaNA, FVB 2.20.50 inv.no 60, Maandverslag Poerwakarta over de maand november 1947, annex to No. Pr. 2324, 22 December 1947; R. Frakking, 'Het Middel Erger dan de Kwaal: De Opkomst en Ondergang van het Instituut der Ondernemingswachten, 1945-1950', Master's thesis in history, Utrecht University (2011) 43-44.

48 Frakking, 'Middel', 11-13; I Anak Agung Gde Agung, *'Renville' als keerpunt in de Nederlands-Indonesische Onderhandelingen* (Alphen aan de Rijn 1980) 82-84, 87-94.

49 For the roots of the Pasundan, see: E. Ekajadi, 'Paguyuban Pasundan: A Sundanese Revival (1913-1918)', *Journal of Asian and African Studies* 66 (2003) 21-55.

50 NL-HaNA Algemene Secretarie van de Nederlands-Indische Regering (hereinafter AS), 2.10.14 inv.no 2417, A. K. Widjojoatmodjo to Director of the Cabinet of the Lt. Governor-General, undated and Aan de Commissie-Generaal te Batavia, Raden Sadikin and Mas Machmoed, Partai Ra'jat Pasoendan petition, 23 November 1946.

51 R. Frakking, '"Collaboration is A Delicate Concept": Alliance-formation and the Colonial Defence of Indonesia and Malaysia, 1945-1957', PhD thesis in history, European University Institute (2017) 22, 226.

52 NL-HaNA AS, 2.10.14 inv.no 2426, Proclamatie van de Territoriaal ts. Troepencommandant van West-Java, January 1949, Frakking, 'Collaboration', 91-93, 226; Suyoso, 'Pasundan en de Republiek', *Het Dagblad*, 13 January 1949, 1.

53 'Batavia Begint in Effectief "Cease Fire" te Geloven', *Algemeen Handelsblad*, 30 January 1948, 1.

54 'Uitvoering van Wapenstilstand', *Nieuwe Courant*, 9 February 1948, 1.

55 ANRI, RA6 inv.no988, Suara Djawa Barat, annex to Atas Nama Masyarakat Keresidenan Cirebon/Djawa Barat, Bunawi to the President, 4 August 1949.

56 NL-HaNA NEFIS/CMI 2.10.62 inv.no 1719, De Negara Islam Indonesia: De Staat op Islamietische Grondslag voor Geheel Indonesië. 28 September 1949; Formichi, *Islam and the Making*, chapter 2; H.H. Dengel, *Darul Islam – NII dan Kartosuwirjo: "Angan-Angan yang Gagal"* (Jakarta 2011) 21-23.

57 NL-HaNA NEFIS/CMI 2.10.62 inv.no 1719, De Negara Islam Indonesia.

58 Ibidem.

59 S.M. Kartosuwirjo, 'Memboeta Toeli', *Fadjar Asia*, 29 January 1929, quoted in: Dengel, *Darul Islam*, 14-15.

60 Panggilan, Madjelis Islam Pusat, No. 60/P./48, 8 July 1948, in Dengel, *Darul Islam*, 230.

61 NL-HaNA NEFIS/CMI 2.10.62 inv.no 1719, Bekendmaking no. 3, Imam H.I.M. Tjorko, 2 November 1948, annex to No. G/355/29, 24 January 1949.

62 S. Soebardi, 'Kartosuwiryo and the Darul Islam Rebellion in Indonesia', *Journal of Southeast Asian Studies* 14:1 (1983) 1-17; NL-HaNA NEFIS/CMI 2.10.62 inv.no 1719, De Negara Islam Indonesia.

63 Frakking, 'Collaboration', 255.

64 NL-HaNA SNI, 2.13.132 inv.no 416, CMI Document No. 5014, Ons Gemeenschappelijk Standpunt (Strijdorganizaties van West-Java), 18 August 1948, annex to Signalement No. 17; NL-HaNA Procureur-Generaal bij het Hooggerechtshof van Nederlands-Indië (hereinafter PG) 2.10.17, inv.no 1002, Versl. Recomba West-Java April 1948, 532/Rec.Pol, 5 May 1948; Collection KITLV/Arsip Indonesia/Arsip Disjarahad/Operasi Jawa Barat Tahun1949/11, No.9/1949, Politiek-politioneel Verslag van de Residentie Buitenzorg over de Periode van 26 Augustus tot en met 25 September 1949.

65 NL-HaNA PG 2.10.17, inv.no 1002, Rap.Recomba West-Java, March 1948.

66 NL-HaNA SNI, 2.13.132 inv.no 418, Oorlogsbevel Cdt. Div Slw/Cdt. Def.West-Java No.III, 19 December 1947, annex to No. G/291/24, 15 January 1948; NL-HaNA PG 2.10.17, inv.no 1001, Daroel Islam, XPO 305, 17 July 1948, annex to CMI No. 5494.

67 Frakking, 'Collaboration', 244.

68 ANRI, RA18 inv.no 135, Siaran Kilat, Kedudukan Pegawai-pegawai Republik Indonesia Didaerah Pendudukan Belanda; NL-HaNA SNI, 2.13.132 inv.no 412, Statuten en Strijdprogramma "Patimah", annex to No.: G/276/222, 3 March 1948; O. Djamhoer, Chef Staf FPBH 88 to Loerah Bachram, No. 12/b, 24 January 1948; O. Djamhoe to Cdt 5e Troep, undated, unnumbered, both annex to Docn. FPBH88, No. G/276/340, 15 April 1948.

69 ANRI, RA24 inv.no 1399, Tindjauan Di-Tempat-2 Peradjurit Hidjrah, 4 March 1948.

70 NL-HaNA, Collection 216 S.H. Spoor, 2.21.036.01, inv.no 77, De Staatssecretaris voor de Binnenlandse Veiligheid deelt het Volgende Mede, 10 July 1948; Collection KITLV/Arsip Indonesia/Arsip Disjarahad/MKBD 1949, Panglima Komando Djawa, Kol. AH Nasution, No. 11/MBKD/49, Instruksi Pasukan Gerilja Desa, 25 January 1949; Collection KITLV/Markas Besar Angkatan Darat Dinas Sejarah/Intel Priangan (Jawa Barat) Tahun 1946-1949, No. 32/Sub DKII B/I/'49, 15 November 1949.

71 NL-HaNA NEFIS/CMI 2.10.62 inv.no 2992, Zeer Geheim Rapport Inzake de "Field Preparation"-organizatie, 18 Juni 1948.

72 Collection KITLV/Markas Besar Angkatan Darat Dinas Sejarah/Intel Priangan (Jawa Barat) Tahun 1946-1949, No. 32/Sub DKII B/I/'49, 15 November 1949.

73 NL-HaNA NEFIS/CMI 2.10.62 inv.no 2994, Rapport IV Cie V Bat.Regt."Bogor" Brig. "Tjitaroem", 28 Juni 1949, annex to No.: II/3282A2r, 6 August 1949.

74 NL-HaNA AS, 2.10.14 inv.no 3752, Kampung Banen, Desa Tjidjurai to the Wali Negara Pasundan, 3 February 1949.

75 Frakking, 'Collaboration', 228-229.

76 M. Lohanda, *Growing Pains: The Chinese and the Dutch in Colonial Java, 1890-1942* (Jakarta 2002).

77 NL-HaNA AS, 2.10.14 inv.no 5526, 5526, Lot der Chinezen uit Madja, No. GI/US/160, 9 March 1949 and Massagraf van Chinezen, Kab./458/PZ, 5 March 1948; ANRI, RA.24 inv.no 1290, Lapuran Keadaan Djawa Barat, No. R/749/1947, 26 July 1947.

78 NL-HaNA NEFIS/CMI 2.10.62 inv.no 1719, Rapport betr. rechtspraak in N.I.I., annex to No.; G/355/91, 24 February 1949; Collection KITLV/Markas Besar Angkatan Darat Dinas Sejarah Himpunan Dokumen Intel Divisi – IV Siliwangi 1949, Situatie D/I Daerah Selatan, 18 December 1949.

79 NL-HaNA AS, 2.10.14 inv.no 4987, F.129, 13 October 1949; 'Ontstellende Terreur van Darul Islam', *Java-Bode* 10 October 1949.

80 NL-HaNA NEFIS/CMI 2.10.62 inv.no 1719, Rapport betr. rechtspraak in N.I.I.

81 NL-HaNA SNI, 2.13.132 inv.no 393, VVD Weekrapport van 26 Jan. t/m 2 Feb.'48, No.: G/WR/12/48, 10 February 1948.

82 NL-HaNA AS, 2.10.14 inv.no 3463, Uittreksel uit het Maandverslag over September 1948 van de Ressort-leider van het ALS Tasikmalaya.

83 NL-HaNA PG 2.10.17, inv.no 1001, Dienst der Staatspolitie Afd. PAM Jogjakarta, 9 June 1948, annex to CMI Document No. 5494, 27 December 1948.

84 Collection KITLV/Arsip Indonesia/Arsip Disjarahad/Himpunan Dokumen MKBD Tahun 1949/46, Keadaan Djawa Barat, Markas Besar Komando DJawa, No. 3/50 II/rdg/50, 26 May 1949.

85 ANRI, RA3a inv.no149, Bestuur Persatoean Tionghoa Tjoe Kiat Koen aan Kabinet Luitenant Gouverneur Generaal, 10 July 1948; 'Aanklacht van Chinese Consul-Generaal', *Algemeen Handelsblad*, 9 August 1947.

86 NL-HaNA AS, 2.10.14 inv.no 4988, Oprichting Buurtgenootschappen ter Bestrijding Darul-Islam, annex to Reg.No. H.C. Jav.III/24 49, 7 November 1949.

87 NL-HaNA PG 2.10.17 inv.no 1002, D.I. Daroel Islam, PG/NP, No. 388/26, 1 February 1949.

88 NL-HaNA PG 2.10.17 inv.no 1002, Tentara Islam Indonesia, rap. Verbrugh 17/8-48; Collection KITLV/Markas Besar Angkatan Darat Dinas Sejarah Himpunan Dokumen Intel Divisi – IV Siliwangi 1949, Daftar: Kampung-Kampung, Orang-orang yang harus membajar biaja kepada D.I.

89 NL-HaNA NEFIS/CMI 2.10.62 inv.no 2994, Bekendmaking no. 5/S.T./49, 17 June 1949, annex to No, 38/P.P./R.I./'49, 23 June 1949.

90 Frakking, 'Middel Erger', 207-208; NL-HaNA, FVB 2.20.50 inv.no 60, Uit Mailoverzicht Nr. 20, Nr. F. 1513/L.28, 5 July 1948.

91 ANRI RA4 inv.no 9, Verslag Dr R.W. van Diffelen, F.130, 3 October 1949.

92 ANRI RA10 inv.no 83, Vertaling I: Vergunning voor Vergadering en Demonstratie ns. De Commissie "Anti Daerah Pasundan" 13 March 1948 and Vertaling II: Dagorder No.32/PB/48/III, 14 March 1948, annex to CMI Document No.: 5325, 27 December 1948; for 1947 local anti-pasundan 'resolutions', see ANRI, RA6 inv.no 956.

93 ANRI, AlgSec inv.no133, Oprichting van de "Gerakan Plebisit Repoeblik Indonesia" met Batavia als Centrum, Geh.ag.965/APO3/48.

94 Collection KITLV/Arsip Indonesia/Disjarahad/Intel Jawa Barat 1949, Laporan Umum Luar Rayon, 1

August 1949 to 21 August 1949.

95 ANRI, RA24 inv.no 1291, Laporan Harian, 23 December 1947.

96 'Aanklacht van Chinese Consul-Generaal', *Algemeen Handelsblad*, 9 August 1947; 'De Chinezen', *De Heerenveensche Koerier*, 28 August 1947; Collection KITLV/Arsip Disjarahad/Himpunan Dokumen MBKD Tahun 1949/47, Bangsa Tionghoa, No. 0141/MKBD/HCGT/49, 25 May 1949.

97 NL-HaNA NEFIS/CMI 2.10.62 inv.no 927, Screening ex-TNI-militairen te Bdg, No. 575, 3 June 1948.

98 ANRI, RA3a, No. 1842/B23III, 21 September 1948, Consul General for China to Mr. T. Elink Schuurman, Head Far Eastern Office.

99 NL-HaNA SNI, 2.13.132 inv.no 416, Joint Weekly Report, 29 Augustus – 5 September, Team No. 7 Milobs, Signalement No. 13, annex to No. 5867/JD2, 13 September 1948; NL-HaNA SNI, 2.13.132 inv.no 414, Vorming der Totale Kracht en Voorlopige Comm. Raad, No. 3/DPC/KT-48, 28 Juni 1948, annex to No.: G/276/556, 28 July 1948.

100 NL-HaNA AS, 2.10.14 inv.no 3463, Uittreksel uit het Maandverslag over September 1948, annex to No.Kab./2487/21340/PZ, 22 October 1948; Uittreksel uit het Maandverslag over Augustus 1948, annex to No. Kab./2291/21151/PZ, 30 September 1948; NL-HaNa, 2.21.249/102, De Bamboe Roentjing-Beweging in West-Java, Bulletin No. 9, 23 Augustus 1948; ANRI, RA24 inv.no 906, Memorandum Div. Siliwangi, No. W3.2072/[?] III-48, 24 April 1948; Perihal Brigade Tjitarum, 22 April 1948.

101 S.M. Jalhay, *Allen zwijgen: Van merdeka en andjing – Nica tot Apra* (Purmerend 1983) 136-140.

102 NL-HaNA SNI, 2.13.132 inv.no 1314, Optreden der "Roode Baretten" te Soekaboemi, No.: 412/R, 12 April 1949 and Ernstige misdragingen militairen, Nr. T.C.544/A14, 29 September 1949.

103 ANRI, Alg.Sekr inv.no 922, A Survey of Post-War Social Conditions in the Netherlands-Indies, anonymous, 1948; NL-HaNA SNI, 2.13.132 inv.no 1396, Telegram to General Spoor, No. 86, undated.

104 NL-HaNA AS, 2.10.14 inv.no 3027, Verslag 1e halfjaar 1948; Frakking, 'Middel', 122-123.

105 Ibidem, Verslag West Java over het eerste halfjaar 1948.

106 Ibidem, Verslag van den Recomba West-Java over het 4e kwartaal 1947.

107 Ibidem, Verslag West Java over het Eerste halfjaar 1948.

108 Collection KITLV/ARSIP Indonesia/ARSIP Disjarahad/Operasi Jawa Barat Tahun 1949, Annex I to No. 10, Overzicht van Extremistische Activiteit in de Residentie Buitenzorg gedurende de Periode 25 Augustus 1949 tot en met 25 September 1949.

109 NL-HaNA AS, 2.10.14 inv.no 3027, Verslag 1e halfjaar 1948; also see R. Raben, 'De Tweede Wereldoorlog in Indonesië als een geschiedenis van beweging en begrenzing', *Tijdschrift voor Geschiedenis* 122:4 (2009) 476-491.

110 ANRI, RA.4 inv.no 43, '100 Dagen Plan' Darul Islam, November 1948.

111 See, for example ANRI, RA3a inv.no 1014, Recomba Midden Java Angenent to Director Department Social Affairs, No.320/44/48, 9 January 1948.

112 NL-HaNA AS, 2.10.14 inv.no 3027, Verslag Tweede Kwartaal 1948.

113 Ibidem, Verslag 1e halfjaar 1948.

114 Ibidem, Verslag tweede kwartaal 1948.

115 Ibidem, Verslag tweede kwartaal 1948.

116 NL-HaNA SNI, 2.13.132 inv.no 411, Lt.Kol.Tri Sulung to all TRI cdt. Brig. VI Malabar Div SP88, No. 70/AA/8/Mtb/48, 1 November 1948.

117 ANRI, RA3a inv.no 1014, Onderhoud met Akkerman van Sociale Zaken, No.136/IZ, 6 April 1949.

118 Collection KITLV/Arsip Indonesia Arsip Disjarahad/Intel Jawa Barat 1949, Annex to Commandant Bat. "E" to Local Joint Committeee VI in Bandung, No. 64/BIV/IX/49, 11 April 1949.

119 NL-HaNA AS, 2.10.14 inv.no 3027, Verslag tweede kwartaal 1948.

120 Frakking, 'Gathered', 37.

121 NL-HaNA SNI, 2.13.132 inv.no 1250, Oprichten KNIL batn, 25 June 1948; Inpassing van de TNI in de federale strijdkrachten, No. Kab./2243/2169, 25 September 1948; 18,000 man plan, 18 March 1949.

122 Frakking, 'Gathered', 38.

123 NL-HaNA, Collectie H.L. s' Jacob, 2.21.361, inv.no 4, Lovink to Van Maarseveen, Ref. nr. 10510, 13 November 1949; Beginselen Nopens de Ontruiming van Gebieden en de daarmede gepaard gaande concentratie in verband met de a.s. Souvereiniteitsoverdracht, No.Kab./3839, 14 November 1949; 'Plan s' Jacob geen Uitweg uit Moeilijkheden?', *Indische Courant voor Nederland*, 26 October 1949; 'De Patrouillezones op Midden-Java', *Arnhemse Courant*, 27 October 1949; 'Republiek aanvaardt het Plan s' Jacob', *De Vrije Pers*, 30 September 1949; 'Plan-s' Jacob: Niet Aanvaardbaar?', *De Locomotief*, 27 December 1949.

124 Nederland betaalt Voedsel en Kleding Republikeins Leger', *Het Parool*, 24 October 1949.

125 Frakking, 'Gathered', 36-37; NL-HaNA AS, 2.10.14 inv.no 3620, F.129, 13 October 1949; F.131, 17 October 1949.

126 C. van Dijk, *Rebellion*, 99-100.

127 Collection KITLV/Arsip Disjarahad/Himpunan Dokumen MBKD Tahun 1949/58B, Maklumat No. 20, Markas Besar Komando Djawa Panglima Kolonel A.H. Nasution, 5 June 1949.

128 Collection KITLV/Arsip Disjarahad/Himpunan Dokumen MBKD Tahun 1949/60, Maklumat No. 21, Markas Besar Komando Djawa, Agn. No.247/30/49 5-9-49.

129 See note 2; Kementerian Penerangan, *Republik Indonesia*, 190.

130 Collectie KITLV/Markas Besar Angkatan Darat Dinas Sejarah. Intel Priangan (Jawa Barat) Tahun 1946-1949, Pengumaman/Seruan KKK Garut, Kmd. KKK Garut, Letnan I, A. Kunaeffie, No. 2/49, 19 December 1949.

131 Collection KITLV/Markas Besar Angkatan Darat Dinas Sejarah. Intel Prigangan (Jawa Barat) Tahun 1949, Kantor Kabupaten Garut, Hiburan TNI, 22 December 1949.

132 Collection KITLV/Markas Besar Angkatan Darat Dinas Sejarah. Intel Priangan (Jawa Barat) Tahun 1946-1949, Kmd. KMD III to KMD2. Bn E.G.F., 25 December 1949.

133 NL-HaNA, 2.20.01 inv.no 8910, Resumé Vergadering Dagelijkse Besturen ALS, ZWSS en CPV met de Onder-voorzitters der Bonden, No. 19, 16 November 1949, annex to VV/No. 105; Collectie KITLV/Markas Besar Angkatan Darat Dinas Sejarah. Intel Priangan (Jawa Barat) Tahun 1946-1949, Laporan, TNI Div IV.SLW. Bri. XIIIp[?] Bat. [?], undated; Luit. U Suarta, No.: 32/Sub D.K.II/B/I/49, 18 November 1949.

134 NL-HaNA AS, 2.10.14 inv.no 3369, Memorandum Secretary of State for Internal Affairs Van der Wal, 17 September 1947.

135 Peraturan Panglima Tentara dan Territorium III Djawa-Barat No. 25, 8 December 1950, in Kementerian Penerangan, *Republik Indonesia: Propinsi Djawa Barat*, 211-212; for the SP88, see Cribb, Gangsters, 170-173.

136 Collection KITLV/Markas Besar Angkatan Darat Dinas Sejarah. Intel Priangan (Jawa Barat) Tahun 1946-1949, Luit. U Suarta, No.: 32/Sub D.K.II/B/I/49, 18 November 1949; Tentara Nasional Indonesia, Bag. I/Bat.B/12ᵃ Slw to Cdt. Bag.I/KMDI, 226/020/I/a-'49, undated; Collection KITLV/ARSIP Indonesia/Arsip Disjarahad.Operasi Jawa Barat Tahun 1949, No. 11. No. 9 [sic]/1949, Politiek-politioneel Verslag van de Residentie Buitenzorg over de Periode van 25 Augustus tot en met 25 September 1949.

137 Collection KITLV/ARSIP Indonesia/Arsip Disjarahad. Operasi Jawa Barat Tahun 1949, No. 10, Overzicht van Extremistische Activiteit in de Residentie Buitenzorg gedurende de Periode 26 Augustus 1949 tot en met 25 September 1949; No. 11. No. 9 [sic]/1949, Politiek-politioneel Verslag van de Residentie Buitenzorg over de Periode van 25 Augustus tot en met 25 September 1949.

138 'Minister Djuanda opent Textielcongres', *Indische Courant voor Nederland*, 7 June 1950.

139 'De Ontvangst', *De Vrije Pers*, 26 May 1949; 'Merkwaardige Belevenissen bij Evacuatie uit Djokja', *Het Nieuwsblad voor Sumatra*, 7 June 1949.

140 In Sukoharjo, Central Java, for example: 'Niet Welkom', *Het Nieuwsblad voor Sumatra*, 26 May 1950.

141 'Zes Millioen [sic] voor Steun aan Evacue's', *Java-Bode*, 25 May 1950; 'Duizenden Évacué's in West-Java', *Het Nieuwsblad voor Sumatra*, 22 April 1950; 'Chaos op West-Java drijft Duizenden naar Steden', *De*

Volkskrant, 1 April 1950.

142 'Darul Islam Actief', *Java-Bode*, 25 May 1950.

143 NL-HaNA, 2.20.10 inv.no 8911, Afschrift van Enkele Passages uit Resumé Nr. 4 van de Vergadering van de Dagelijkse Besturen van ALS, ZWSS en CPV met de Ondervoorzitters der Bonden, 7 March 1950.

144 'Arrestaties in Buitenzorg', *Het Dagblad*, 4 August 1948; 'Rampok-Partij op Java', *De Telegraaf*, 8 October 1949; 'Demak', *De Locomotief*, 14 November 1949; 'Rampok in Bogorse', *Java-Bode*, 14 December 1950; 'Zevenhonderd Rampokgevallen Laagterecord in Batavia', *De Zaanlander*, 22 December 1950; Rampok in Dessa', *Algemeen Indisch Dagblad*, 13 October 1951.

145 'Moorden en Ontvoeringen in Indramajoese', *Algemeen Indisch Dagblad*, 31 August 1951.

146 NL-HaNA, 2.20.10 inv.no 8911, Afschrift van Enkele Passages uit Resumé Nr. 4 van de Vergadering van de Dagelijkse Besturen van ALS, ZWSS en CPV met de Ondervoorzitters der Bonden, 7 March 1950.

13. Fighting over Depok

1 See The Liang Djie, *Sedjarah Pemerintahan Kota Djakarta* (Jakarta 1958) 129; See also Lampiran 1, Naskah Rekomendasi Penetapan Tiang Telepon Pancoran Mas sebagai Struktur Cagar Budaya, Depok, 2020; J. de Vries, 'De Depokkers: Geschiedenis, sociale structuur en taalgebruik van een geïsoleerde gemeenschap', *Bijdragen tot de Taal-, Land- en Volkenkunde* 132:2/3 (1976) 228-248.

2 Amri Marzali, 'Krisis Identitas Pada Orang Depok Asli', *Berita Antropologi* 22 (1975) 5; See also Asep Suryana, 'Transformasi Sosial Pribumi Depok Tahun 1930-1960', *Jurnal Masyarakat dan Budaya* 6:2 (2004) 29-48.

3 H.Th. Bussemaker, *Na de oorlog: van Bersiap to Linggarjati 1945-1946*, http://www.tongtong.nl/indische-school/contentdownloads/bussemaker_bersiap.pdf, accessed 3 January 2020; Th.H. Bussemaker, *Bersiap! Opstand in het paradijs: De Bersiap-periode op Java en Sumatra 1945-1946* (Zutphen 2005) 14; Remco Raben, 'Het geweld van de bersiap', *Historisch Nieuwsblad* 7 (2011) https://web.archive.org/web/20220409134602/https://www.historischnieuwsblad.nl/het-geweld-van-de-bersiap/ (accessed 12 October 2022).

4 Quoted in Harry A. Poeze's review of Jan-Karel Kwisthout's 'De Mardijkers van Tugu en Depok. Vrijmaking, bevrijding, en merdeka', *Bijdragen tot de Taal-, Land- en Volkenkunde* 17:2/3 (2019) 411; For a comparison, see a contemporary standardized Dutch narrative of the event, 'Het Drama van Depok', *NRC Handelsblad*, 5 December 1986; Stichting Oorlogsverhalen, interview by *Pia van der Molen* of Rita Young *https://oorlogsverhalen.com/oorlogsverhalen/rita-young/* (accessed 12 October 2022).

5 There are several works written by Indonesian scholars about this event, including Wenri Wanhar, *Gedoran Depok. Revolusi Sosial Di Tepi Jakarta* (Depok 2011); Wisnu Rega Aditya, 'Revolusi Sosial di Kota Depok 1945-1955', (Master's thesis; Universitas Negeri Semarang 2017) ; Mumuh Muhsin Z. (ed.), *Depok 1942-1967; Masa Pendudukan Jepang Hingga Masa Orde Lama* (Depok 2013).

6 Rémy Limpach, *Kekerasan Ekstrem Belanda di Indonesia. Perang kemerdekaan Indonesia 1945-1949* (Jakarta 2019) 34.

7 Bernard H.M. Vlekke, 'Progress Toward Self-Government', *Far Eastern Survey* 14:24 (1945) 349.

8 Limpach, *Kekerasan Ekstrem Belanda,* 34.

9 P. Bleeker, 'Nieuwe bijdragen tot de kennis der bevolkingstatistiek van Java', *Bijdragen tot de Taal-, Land- en Volkenkunde van Nederlandsch-Indië*, 16:3-4 (1869) 477.

10 Heru Erwantoro, 'Etnis Betawi: Kajian Historis', *Patanjala* 6:1 (2014) 1-16; Yasmine Shaki Shahab, *The Creation of Ethnic Tradition: The Betawi of Jakarta* (PhD thesis; School of Oriental and African Studies, London 1994; Lance Castles, *Profil Etnik Jakarta* (Jakarta 2007); See Remco Raben, 'Round about Batavia: Ethnicity and Authority in the Ommelanden, 1650-1800', in: Kees Grijns and Peter J.M. Nas, *Jakarta – Batavia: Socio-cultural Essays* (Leiden 2000); Mona Lohanda, *The Kapitan Cina of Batavia, 1837-1942: A History of Chinese Establishment in Colonial Society* (Jakarta 1996).

11 See the detailed history of his land purchases in Tri Wahyuning M. Irsyam, *Berkembang dalam Bayang-Bayang Jakarta: Sejarah Depok 1950-1990-an* (Jakarta 2017) 40; see also De Vries, 'De Depokkers', 230-235.

12 B. Ter Haar and W. Moll, *Geschiedenis der Christelijke kerk in Nederlandsch-Indië, deel II* (Amsterdam 1869) 552.

13 Bobby Fernandes, *Perkembangan Gereja-gereja Wilayah Layanan Depok dan Cimanggis, 1948-1981* (Master's thesis; Universitas Indonesia, Jakarta 2008); see also De Vries, 'De Depokkers', 233.

14 For further information on the memorial see Alqiz Lukman, 'Desonansi Memori Monumen Kolonial: Studi Kasus Tugu Cornelis Chastelein, Depok, Jawa Barat', *Amerta. Jurnal Penelitian dan Pengembangan Arkeologi* 38:1 (2020) 77-92. This fact seems to have been used to build a myth about the name Depok, which is said to be the acronym for *De Eerste Protestantse Organisatie van Kristenen*. But the name Depok had already existed before Christianity was proselytized in this area.

15 See Tri Wahyuning M. Irsyam, *Berkembang*, 48-50.

16 Marzali, 'Krisis Identitas', 8-9.

17 See Tri Wahyuning M. Irsyam, *Berkembang*.

18 For a comparison of the conceptual discussion of the patronage, see H. ten Dam, 'Kerja Sama dan Struktur Masyarakat di Desa Cibodas', in: Sajogyo and Pujiwati Sajogyo (eds.) *Sosiologi Pedesaan. Kumpulan Bacaan Jilid 1* (Yogyakarta 1999) 108-128.

19 Suryana, 'Transformasi Sosial Pribumi', 33.

20 Ibidem, 36.

21 Marzali, 'Krisis Identitas', 12.

22 Ibidem, 10.

23 See correspondence of Robert Kiek about the event, *Provinciale Drentsche en Asser Courant*, 17 October 1945.

24 Amri Marzali, 'Krisis Identitas', 13.

25 W.F. Wertheim, *Indonesian Society in Transition: A Study of Social Change* (Bandung 1956) 132.

26 Jan Pluvier, *South-East Asia from Colonialism to Independence* (Kuala Lumpur 1974) 179.

27 H.J. Benda, *The Crescent and Rising Sun: Indonesian Islam under Japanese Occupation, 1942-1945* (The Hague/ Bandung 1958).

28 Laszlo Sluimers, 'The Japanese Military and Indonesian Independence', *Journal of Southeast Asian Studies* 27:1 (1996) 27.

29 *Friesch Dagblad*, 18 October 1945.

30 Elly Touwen-Bouwsma, 'Japanese Minority Policy. The Eurasian on Java and the Dilemma of Ethnic Loyalty', *Bijdragen tot de Taal-, Land- en Volkenkunde* 152:4 (1996) 554.

31 Ibidem, 559

32 Stichting Oorlogsverhalen, interview *Pia van der Molen* with Rita Young, *https://oorlogsverhalen.com/oorlogsverhalen/rita-young/* (accessed 12 October 2022).

33 Touwen-Bouwsma, 'Japanese Minority Policy', 559.

34 Nio Joe Lan, *Dalem Tawanan Djepang* (Jakarta 2008).

35 *Soerabajasch Handelsblad*, 24 February 1942.

36 Mariska Heijmans-Van Bruggen, *De Japanse bezetting in Dagboeken: Buiten de Kampen* (Amsterdam 2001) 152

37 J.F. van Dulm, *Geïllustreerde Atlas van de Japanse Kampen in Nederlands-Indië 1942-1945, deel 1* (Viella 2000) 104.

38 Marzali, 'Krisis Identitas', 11.

39 Robert Cribb, *Gangsters and revolutionaries: The Jakarta People's Militia and the Indonesian revolution 1945-1949* (Jakarta/Kuala Lumpur 2008).

40 Remco Raben, 'Anti-Chinese Violence in the Indonesian Revolution', a rough draft paper presented to Konferensi Dekolonisasi dan Posisi Etnis Tionghoa di Indonesia 1930-an s/d 1960-an, Padang (18-21 June 2006) 3.

41 Interview with Boy Loen, 13 June 2018.

42 See the interview by Wenri Wanhar with Cornelis Josef Jonathans, 'Peristiwa Gedoran Depok (3): Revolusi Oktober di Kampung Belanda Depok', *JPNN.COM*, 11 October 2015; see also the testimony of J. Dolf Jonathans, 'Riwayat Kaum Depok', *KOMPAS TV*, 4 April 2017.

43 Interview by Wenri Wanhar with Jeanette Tholense, 'Peristiwa Gedoran Depok (2): Saya Saksikan Peristiwa Gedoran Depok dari Awal sampai Akhir', *JPNN.COM*, 11 October 2015.

44 *De Volkskrant,* 16 October 1945.

45 See Arsip National Republik Indonesia (hereafter ANRI), Algemene Secretarie Tempelaars, 1942-1950, No. 153, annex III.

46 Interview by Wenri Wanhar with Jeanette Tholense, 'Peristiwa Gedoran Depok (2): Saya Saksikan Peristiwa Gedoran Depok dari Awal sampai Akhir', *JPNN.COM*, 11 October 2015.

47 See the testimony of Joshua Dolf Jonathan, 'Indonesia Dalam Peristiwa-Gedoran Depok: Catatan Kelam Belanda Depok', *TV One*, 6 April 2019; 'Riwayat Kaum Depok', *KOMPAS TV*, 4 April 2017. For comparison see the interview by Wenri Wanhar with Jeanette Tholense, 'Peristiwa Gedoran Depok (2): Saya Saksikan Peristiwa Gedoran Depok dari Awal sampai Akhir', *JPNN.COM*, 11 October 2015; Wanhar, *Gedoran Depok* (2011).

48 *De Tijd*, 18 October 1945.

49 *De Volkskrant*, 16 October 1945; *Provinciale Drentsche en Asser Courant*, 17 October 1945; *De Heerenveensche Koerier*, 19 October 1945; *Penjoeloeh*, 25 October 1945; *Telex*, 22 October 1945.

50 National Archives of the Republic of Indonesia, Arsip Nasional Republik Indonesia, (hereinafter ANRI), Algemene Secretarie Tempelaars, 1942-1950, No. 153. Annex III.

51 ANRI, Algemene Secretarie Tempelaars, *1942-1950,* No. 153. Annex III.

52 See ANRI, Algemene Secretarie Tempelaars, 1942-*1950,* No. 153. Annex III.

53 Interview by Wenri Wanhar with Adung Sakam and Misar Daeran, 'Peristiwa Gedoran Depok (3): Revolusi Oktober di Kampung Belanda Depok', *JPNN.COM*, 11 October 2015.

54 Wisnu Prasetyo, 'Margonda, Belanda Depok, dan Peristiwa Gedoran', *detikNews*, 9 November 2015.

55 A.H. Nasution, *Sekitar Perang Kemerdekaan Indonesia Jilid 2: Diplomasi atau Bertempur.* (Bandung 1977) 530-531.

56 *Het Parool,* 18 October 1945

57 *Penjoeloeh*, 25 October 1945.

58 ANRI, Algemene Secretarie Tempelaars, *1942-1950,* No. 153. Annex I Depok Report; De *Heerenveensche Koerier*, 19 October 1945; *Helmondsch Dagblad,* 18 October 1945; *Algemeen Handelsblad*, 18 October 1945; *Friesch Dagblad,* 18 October 1945. An eyewitness stated that at least 30 people were killed. See Stichting Oorlogsverhalen, *https://oorlogsverhalen.com/oorlogsverhalen/rita-young/,* interview by *Pia van der Molen* with Rita Young.

59 *Helmondsch Dagblad,* 16 October 1945; *Nieuwe Courant*, 29 August 1947.

60 Stichting Oorlogsverhalen, *https://oorlogsverhalen.com/oorlogsverhalen/rita-young/,* interview *Pia van der Molen* with Rita Young. Testimony of J. Dolf Jonathan in 'Riwayat Kaum Depok', *KOMPASTV* , 4 April 2017; 'Indonesia Dalam Peristiwa–Gedoran Depok: Catatan Kelam Belanda Depok', *TV One*, 6 April 2019.

61 Stichting Oorlogsverhalen, interview by *Pia van der Molen* with Rita Young, *https://oorlogsverhalen.com/oorlogsverhalen/rita-young/.*

62 See Bussemaker, *Bersiap!,* 146; Bussemaker, 'Na de oorlog'; Stichting Oorlogsverhalen, interview by *Pia van der Molen* with Rita Young, *https://oorlogsverhalen.com/oorlogsverhalen/rita-young/*; See ANRI, Algemene Secretarie Tempelaars, 1942-1950, No. 153. Annex III.

63 See interview by Wenri Wanhar with Jeanette Tholense, 'Peristiwa Gedoran Depok (2): Saya Saksikan Peristiwa Gedoran Depok dari Awal sampai Akhir', *JPNN.COM*, 11 October 2015.

64 *Het Dagblad*, 6 March 1948.

65 Wanhar, *Gedoran Depok*, 103; See also Pemerintah Kota Depok, *Peraturan Daerah Kota Depok No. 1/1999 tentang Sejarah Singkat Kota Depok* (Depok 1999) appendix 1.

66 ANRI, Algemene Secretarie Tempelaars, 1942-1950, No. 153. Annex 1 Depok Report.

67 See interview by Wenri Wanhar of Cornelis Josef Jonathans, 'Peristiwa Gedoran Depok (3): Revolusi Oktober di Kampung Belanda Depok', *JPNN.COM*, 11 October 2015; *Algemeen Handelsblad*, 18 October 1945; See *Leeuwarder Koerier*, 19 October 1945.

68 Testimony of J. Dolf Jonathan in "Riwayat Kaum Depok", *KOMPAS TV* , 4 April 2017; 'Indonesia Dalam Peristiwa-Gedoran Depok: Catatan Kelam Belanda Depok', *TV One*, 6 April 2019.

69 *Friesch Dagblad*, 18 October 1945.

70 *De Waarheid*, 16 October 1945.

71 *NRC Handelsblad*, 5 December 1986; see interview by Wenri Wanhar of Jeanette Tholense, 'Peristiwa Gedoran Depok (2): Saya Saksikan Peristiwa Gedoran Depok dari Awal sampai Akhir', *JPNN.COM*, 11 October 2015.

72 *Leeuwarder Courant,* 19 October 1945; See also interview by Wenri Wanhar of Jeanette Tholense, 'Peristiwa Gedoran Depok (2): Saya Saksikan Peristiwa Gedoran Depok dari Awal sampai Akhir', *JPNN.COM*, 11 October 2015.

73 *Provinciale Drentsche en Asser Courant*, 17 October 1945.

74 *Trouw*, 15 July 1947.

75 Wim van den Doel, 'The Dutch Empire. An Essential Part of World History', *Bijdragen en Mededelingen Betreffende de Geschiedenis der Nederlanden* 125:2/3 (2010), 203.

76 Hendi Johari, 'Gejolak Revolusi di Selatan Jakarta', *Historia*, 13 April 2012.

77 Wenri Wanhar, 'Margonda Sang Legenda Revolusi', *Historia*, 21 January 2014.

78 Pemerintah Kota Depok (1999) Lampiran 1; *Het Dagblad*, 25 March 1946.

79 *Merdeka*, 25 March 1946; *Het Dagblad*, 25 March 1946.

80 *Merdeka*, 25 March 1946; *Het Dagblad*, 25 March 1946

81 *Merdeka*, 25 March 1946; *Merdeka*, 27 March 1946.

82 *Het Dagblad*, 29 March 1946.

83 *Het Dagblad*, 3 October 1946.

84 *Amigoe di Curacao*, 17 April 1946; *Amigoe di Curacao*, 8 April 1946; *Amigoe di Curacao,* 23 April 1946.

85 *Trouw*, 15 July 1947.

86 *Het Dagblad*, 22 February 1947.

87 *Trouw*, 15 July 1947.

88 *Trouw*, 15 July 1947.

89 *De Tijd*, 18 December 1947; *Provinciale Drentsche en Asser Courant*, 19 December 1947.

90 *Nieuwe Courant*, 4 January 1950.

91 See interview by Wenri Wanhar of Jeanette Tholense, 'Peristiwa Gedoran Depok (2): Saya Saksikan Peristiwa Gedoran Depok dari Awal sampai Akhir', *JPNN.COM*, 11 October 2015.

92 *Het Dagblad*, 21 April 1949.

93 The new provisions regarding the abolition of *particuliere landerij* were confirmed by Law No. 1 of 1958 concerning the Elimination of Private Estate; Government Regulation (PP) No.18 of 1958 concerning the Implementation of the Law on the Elimination of Private Estate (Law No. 1 of 1958, State Gazette No. 2 of 1958); Government Regulation (PP) No. 37 of 1963 concerning Amendments to Government Regulation No. 18 of 1958.

14. A successful transition

1 Taomo Zhou, *Revolusi, Diplomasi, Diaspora: Indonesia, Tiongkok, dan Etnik Tionghoa, 1945-1967* (Jakarta 2019) 35.

2 Zhou, *Revolusi, Diplomasi, Diaspora*, 8.

3 Shabri et al., *Kedudukan dan Peran Dayah di Aceh pada Masa Revolusi Kemerdekaan (1945-1949)* (Banda Aceh 2005); Inawati, Zainal Abidin A.W, and Rusdi Sufi, 'Peranan Husein Yusuf Dalam Memperjuangkan Aceh Masa Revolusi Kemerdekan Tahun 1945-1949', *Jurnal Mahasiswa Pendidikan Sejarah* 1 (2016) 110-119; Muhamad Rizal, 'Persatuan Ulama Seluruh Aceh Pada Masa Revolusi Kemerdekaan Indonesia 1945-1949', (Bachelor's thesis in history, Universitas Indonesia, 2008); Bambang Satriya, Suwirta, and Ayi Budi Santosa, 'Teungku Muhammad Daud Beureueh dan Revolusi di Aceh (1945-1950)', *Factum: Jurnal Sejarah dan Pendidikan Sejarah* 7:1 (2018) 27-42; Halimah, Suprayitno and Warjio, 'Revolusi di Tanah Alas: Peranan Masyarakat dalam Mempertahankan Kemerdekaan Indonesia Tahun 1945-1950', *Yupa: Historical Studies Journal* 4:2 (2020) 62-72; Kurniawati, 'Perang Cumbok dan Gerakan Tentara Perjuangan Rakyat (TPR) di Aceh (Desember 1945-Maret 1946)', *Jurnal Sejarah Lontar* 5:2 (2008) 20-35; S.M. Amin, *Sekitar Peristiwa Berdarah di Atjeh* (Jakarta 1956).

4 Daniel S. Lev, 'Yap Tiam Hien and Aceh', *Indonesia* 82 (2006) 97-133.

5 Arif Zulkifli et al., *Yap Tiam Hien, Sang Pendekar Keadilan* (Seri Buku Saku Tempo) (Jakarta 2014).

6 Emilyus E. Ismail, *Pedagang Cina dan Kegiatan Jengek di Pelabuhan Bebas Sabang* (Banda Aceh 1979).

7 Irchamni Sulaiman, *Pengusaha Aceh dan Pengusaha Cina di Kotamadya Banda Aceh Sabang* (Banda Aceh 1983).

8 A. Rani Usman, *Etnis Cina Perantauan di Aceh.*

9 Wildan et al., 'Repertoar Bahasa Masyarakat Cina di Aceh', *Jurnal Bahasa dan Seni* 38:2 (2010) 131-141.

10 Deni Sutrisna, 'Peunayong: Kampung Lama Etnis Cina di Kota Banda Aceh', *BAS* 21 (2008) 30-40.

11 Fahriza Murti and Triyanto, 'Adaptasi Budaya Etnis Tionghoa di Meulaboh Aceh Barat (Studi: Masyarakat Tionghoa Non-Muslim)', *Community* 4:1 (2018) 123-139.

12 Wildan et al., 'Repertoar'.

13 Irchamni Sulaiman, *Pengusaha Aceh dan Pengusaha Cina di Kotamadya Banda Aceh*, 14.

14 A. Rani Usman, *Etnis Cina Perantauan di Aceh* (Jakarta 2009) 326-327.

15 Wildan et al., 'Repertoar', 140.

16 Irchamni Sulaiman, *Pengusaha Aceh*, 26-27.

17 Kong Yuanzhi, *Muslim Tionghoa, Cheng Ho* (Jakarta 2000) 97.

18 Paul van 't Veer, *Perang Belanda di Aceh*, transl.: Aboebakar (Banda Aceh 1977) 201-202.

19 Leo Suryadinata, *Negara dan Etnis Tionghoa: Kasus Indonesia* (Jakarta 2002) 8.

20 Departement van Landbouw, Nijverheid en Handel, *Volkstelling 1930, Voorlopige Uitkomsten 2e Gedeelte*, (Batavia 1931).

21 Lev, 'Yap Tiam Hien and Aceh', 97-133.

22 Ismail, *Pedagang Cina*, 24.

23 J. Thomas Lindblad, 'The Outer Islands in the 19th Century: Contest for Periphery', in Howard Dick et al. (eds.), *The Emergence of A National Economy: An Economic History of Indonesia, 1800-2000* (New South Wales and Honolulu 2002) 103.

24 J. Langhout, *Vijftig Jaren Economische Staatkunde in Atjeh.* (The Hague 1923) 146, 162, 169.

25 See Pusat Dokumentasi dan Informasi Aceh, Seri Informasi Aceh Th VI, No. 1, 1982, Laporan Politik Gubernemen Aceh dan Daerah Takluknya Selama Pertengahan Pertama Tahun 1928 (Alih Bahasa: Aboe Bakar) 66.

26 https://www.kompasiana.com/andi.irawan/pecinan-tua-peunayong-romantisme-sejarah-tionghoa-di-aceh

27 https://news.detik.com/berita/d-3854423/peunayong-kampung-china-di-aceh-yang-ada-sejak-sultan-iskandar-muda

28 Leo Suryadinata, *Negara dan Etnis Tionghoa: Kasus Indonesia* (Jakarta 2002) 8.

29 Charles A. Coppel, *Indonesian Chinese in Crisis* (Kuala Kumpur 1983) 27-28.

30 Lev, 'Yap Tiam Hien', 97-133.

31 Coppel, *Indonesian Chinese* 29.

32 Coppel, *Indonesian Chinese*, 5-29.
33 Leo Suryadinata, *Politik Tionghoa Peranakan di Jawa 1917-1942* (Jakarta 1981); Donald E. Wilmott, *The National Status of the Chinese in Indonesia 1900-1958* (Jakarta 2009).
34 Mary Somers Heidhues, 'Anti-Chinese violence in Java during the Indonesian Revolution, 1945-49', *Journal of Genocide Research* 14:3-4 (2012) 381-401.
35 A.J. Piekaar, *Aceh dan Peperangan dengan Jepang*, Buku II, transl.: Aboe Bakar (Banda Aceh 1981) 150.
36 S.M. Amin, *Kenang-Kenangan dari Masa Lampau* (Jakarta 1978) 125.
37 There were eight internment camps during Japanese occupation in Aceh: in Sabang, Sigli, Bireun, Lhokseumawe, Takengon, Meulaboh, Langsa and Kualasimpang. See H. Bos, *Nederlanders in Japanse kampen* (Amstelveen 1975).
38 Arsip Nasional Republik Indonesia (hereafter ANRI), Algemene Secretarie, inv.no 190.
39 M. Nur El Ibrahimy, *Mata Rantai yang Hilang: Dari Sejarah Perjuangan Kemerdekaan Indonesia di Aceh* (Jakarta 1996) 15.
40 S.M. Amin, *Kenang-Kenangan dari Masa Lampau,* 21.
41 Nazaruddin Sjamsuddin, *Revolusi di Serambi Mekkah: Perjuangan Kemerdekaan dan Pertarungan Politik di Aceh 1945-1949* (Jakarta 1999) 77.
42 Anthony Reid, *Perjuangan Rakyat, Revolusi dan Hancurnya Kerajaan di Sumatra* (Jakarta 1987) 312.
43 Sjamaun Gaharu, 'Perebutan Kekuasaan dari Tangan Djepang', in: Komite musjawarah Angkatan 45 Daerah Istimewa Atjeh (eds.), *Modal Revolusi 45* (Kutaraja 1960) 28.
44 Ismuha, *Ulama Aceh Dalam Perspektif Sejarah* (Jakarta 1976).
45 Ismuha, *Ulama Aceh*, 14.
46 T. Ibrahim Alfian et al., *Revolusi Kemerdekaan Indonesia di Aceh 1945-1949* (Banda Aceh 1982) 40-41.
47 Dinas Perpustakaan dan Kearsiapan Aceh, Arsip nomor inventaris: 21100-24-AC01-AC01-217/12.
48 Abdullah Ali et al., *Sejarah Perjuangan Rakyat Aceh dalam Perang Kemerdekaan 1945-1949* (Banda Aceh 1984) 209.
49 S.M. Amin, *Kenang-kenangan,* 95.
50 A.K. Jakobi, *Aceh Daerah Modal Long March Ke Medan Area* (Jakarta 1992) 219.
51 https://www.cia.gov/index.html, CA-RDP82-00457R002400470009-9, report dated 12 January 1949.
52 https://www.cia.gov/index.html, CA-RDP82-00457R001800500006-5, report dated 26 August 1948.
53 A.K. Jakobi, *Aceh Daerah Modal,* 93.
54 ANRI, Collection NEFIS-ARA, inv.no 22.
55 Taomo Zhou, *Revolusi, Diplomasi, Diaspora* 35.
56 Pusat Dokumentasi dan Informasi Aceh, Seri Informasi Aceh Thn. V No. 1, 1981. Laporan Politik Gubernemen Aceh dan Daerah Takluknya Selama Tahun 1939, transl.: Aboebakar (Banda Aceh) 8-9.
57 Taomo Zhou, *Revolusi, Diplomasi, Diaspora,* 35.
58 Nazaruddin Sjamsuddin, *Revolusi di Serambi Mekah* 91-92; see also Anthony Reid, *The Blood of the People: Revolution and the End of Traditional Rule in Northern Sumatra* (Kuala Lumpur 1979); El Ibrahimy, *Mata Rantai.*
59 Abdullah Hussain, *Peristiwa Kemerdekaan di Aceh* (Jakarta 1990) 20, 27, 30.
60 T.A. Talsya, *Batu Karang di Tengan Lautan: Perjuangan Kemerdekaan di Aceh 1945-1946* (Banda Aceh 1990) 84.
61 El Ibrahimy, *Mata Rantai*, 15.
62 Anthony Reid, *Perjuangan Rakyat* 319-320.
63 El Ibrahimy, *Mata Rantai* 16.
64 Pusat Dokumentasi dan Informasi Aceh, Seri Informasi Aceh Th. V No. 5, 1981, *Aceh dan Peperangan dengan Jepang*, Buku II, karya A.J. Piekaar, transl.: Aboe Bakar (Banda Aceh) 101-102.
65 Talsya, *Batu Karang*, 39.
66 Talsya, *Batu Karang*, 107.

67 Efendi Setiawan, *Tionghoa Medan: Komunitas Paling Kontroversial di Indonesia* (Jakarta 2018) 148.
68 Talsya, *Batu Karang*, 117.
69 Ibidem, 215.
70 Ibidem, 235.
71 Ibidem, 346-347.
72 Ibidem, 19.
73 T.A. Talsya, *Modal Perjuangan Kemerdekaan (Perjuangan Kemerdekaan di Aceh) 1947-1948*), book II (Banda Aceh 1990) 146-152.
74 Amin, *Kenang-Kenangan*, 125.
75 Charles A. Coppel, *Tionghoa Indonesia*, 27-28
76 Seri Informasi Aceh Th. V No. 5, 1981, *Aceh dan Peperangan dengan Jepang*, Buku II, karya A.J. Piekaar (Alih Bahasa: Aboe Bakar) (Banda Aceh) 150.
77 Amin, *Kenang-Kenangan*, 125.
78 https://www.cia.gov/index.html, CA-RDP82-00457R002500650008-9, report dated 24 March 1949.
79 T.A. Talsya, *Batu Karang*, 95.
80 Arsip Perhubungan dengan Bangsa Tionghoa, Dinas Perpustakaan dan Kearsipan Aceh, inv.no 21100-24-AC01-AC01-184/11.
81 https://serambiwiki.tribunnews.com/2020/01/21/sejarah-singkat-vihara-dharma-bhakti-di-aceh-bukti-keberagaman-agama-ada-di-kota-syariat-islam.
82 https://news.detik.com/berita/d-3854423/peunayong-kampung-china-di-aceh-yang-ada-sejak-sultan-iskandar-muda.
83 Arsip Pendaftaran Kelahiran/Kematian Bangsa Tinghoa dan Eropa di Aceh Tahun 1947, Dinas Perpustakaan dan Kearsipan Aceh, inv.no 21100-24-AC01-AC01-162/10.
84 Ibidem, inv.no 21100-24-AC01-AC01-162/10.
85 Arsip Pemberitahuan Perkawinan/Kematian Keturunan Tionghoa dalam Keresidenan Aceh Tahun 1948-1949, Dinas Perpustakaan dan Kearsipan Aceh, inv.no 21100-24-AC01-AC01-163/10.
86 Ibidem, inv.no 21100-24-AC01-AC01-163/10.
87 Talsya, *Modal Perjuangan*, 264, 307-308.
88 Ibidem, 87-8.
89 Ibidem, 169.
90 Abdullah Hussain, *Peristiwa Kemerdekaan*, 33-35.

15. Navigating contested middle ground

1 Nationaal Archief, The Hague (hereinafter NL-HaNA), Marine en Leger Inlichtingendienst, de Netherlands Forces Intelligence Service en de Centrale Militaire Inlichtingendienst in Nederlands-Indië (hereinafter NEFIS/CMI) 2.10.62 inv.no 3950, Manifesto of the First General Meeting of the 'Hua Chiao Chung Hui, Medan', 9 December 1945.
2 NL-HaNA NEFIS/CMI 2.10.62 inv.no 3950, Outlines of organization of the of the 'Hua Chiao Chung Hui, Medan', 9 December 1945.
3 Anthony Reid, *The Blood of the People: Revolution and the End of Traditional Rule in Northern Sumatra* (Kuala Lumpur 1979).
4 *Tempo*, 19-25 August 2019 (Special issue on independence: 'Aktivis Cina di awal Republic [Chinese activists at the beginning of the Republic]); Leo Suryadinata and Didi Kwartanada (eds.), *Tionghoa dalam Keindonesiaan: Peran dan Kontribusi bagi Pembangunan Bangsa* III (Jakarta 2016); especially part 7 vol. 3, 315-420.
5 Huang Hanqing, 'Mianlan Shi Huaqiao Bao'andui Wenti Shuping', in: North Sumatra Overseas Chinese Historical Association (ed.), *Yinni Subei Huaqiao Huaren Cangsang Suiyue / Seratus Tahun Pancaroba Etnis Tionghoa Sumatera Utara* (Hong Kong 2015) 747-759, 747.
6 Cui Yisheng, 'Duli Chuqi de Bao'andui Shijian', *Guo Ji Ri Bao*, 27 June 2011 (Serial, 27 June-6 July

2011), taking as an example an article on the CSC by Teguh Setiawan (published in *Republika*, on 12 April).

7 Cui Yisheng, 'Duli Chuqi de bao'andui Shijian', 9 July 2011.

8 Reid, *The Blood of the People*, 148; Anthony Reid, 'The birth of the Republic in Sumatra', *Indonesia* 12 (1971) 21-46.

9 Biro Sejarah PRIMA, *Medan Area Mengisi Proklamasi* (Medan 1976) 721.

10 Ibidem. See also Mohammad Said, *Empat Belas Boelan Pendoedoekan Inggris di Indonesia* (Medan 1946) 121.

11 Hamka, *Kenang-kenangan Hidup* (Kuala Lumpur 1966) 273-274.

12 Biro Sejarah PRIMA, *Medan Area*, 721.

13 Said, *Pendoedoekan Inggeris*, 121.

14 NL-HaNA NEFIS/CMI 2.10.62 inv.no 5404, *Menoedjoe persatoean Tionghoa-Indonesia: Seroean Pihak Bangsa Tionghoa* Medan, 17 September 1945.

15 *Kerakjatan*, 18 December 1945.

16 NL-HaNA NEFIS/CMI 2.10.62 inv.no 3950, Outlines of organization of the Hua Chiao Chung Hui, Medan", 9 December 1945.

17 NL-HaNA NEFIS/CMI 2.10.62 inv.no 3950, List of members and representatives of the First General Meeting of the Members of the 'Hua Chiao Chung Hui, Medan', 9 December 1945; For a discussion of the pre-war Chinese elite in Medan, see Dirk Aedsge Buiskool, *Prominent Chinese During the Rise of a Colonial City: Medan 1890-1942* (PhD thesis in history, University of Utrecht, 2019).

18 *Kerakjatan*, 11 December 1945.

19 NL-HaNA NEFIS/CMI 2.10.62 inv.no 3950, Manifesto of the First General Meeting of the 'Hua Chiao Chung Hui, Medan', 9 December 1945.

20 NL-HaNA, Ministerie van Koloniën: Supplement, 2.10.03 inv.no 86 and 87; *Kerakjatan*, 13 December 1945. Overviews of the Indonesian and Chinese press in Medan.

21 NL-HaNA Algemene Secretarie van de Nederlands-Indische Regering (hereinafter AS), 2.10.14 inv.no 3100, HQ 26th Indian Division Weekly Intelligence Summary No. 11, Medan, 1 January 1946, attachment to Rapport van Sumatra No. 2, C.A.M. Brondgeest, Medan, 6 January 1946.

22 NL-HaNA Procureur-Generaal bij het Hooggerechtshof van Nederlands-Indië (hereinafter PG) 2.10.17, inv.no 679, Rapport over het Chinese Security Corps (PAO AN TUI), (verbindingsofficier) J. Hoogland, Medan, 25 October 1946.

23 'Barisan Pengawal Tionghoa', *Soeloeh Merdeka*, 3 January 1946.

24 'Pengawal Tionghoa hendak ke Mana?' *Soeloeh Merdeka*, 4 January 1946.

25 NL-HaNA NEFIS/CMI 2.10.62 inv.no 3950, Bimonthly political and economic overviews for North Sumatra by CO-AMACAB for the East Coast of Sumatra (Spits), December 1945-January 1946.

26 Ibidem.

27 'Soerat terboeka', *Soeloeh Merdeka*, 7 January 1946.

28 'Pertemoean Pembesar2 Pemerintah N.R.I dengan Wakil2 Bangsa Tionghoa', *Soeloeh Merdeka*, 10 January 1946.

29 For more on Pesindo, its roots in the Badan Pemuda Indonesia (BPI) and its relation to Pesindo in Java, see Reid, *The Blood of the People*, 164.

30 Biro Sejarah PRIMA, *Medan Area Mengisi Proklamasi*, 206-207.

31 Ibidem, 223-224.

32 Ibidem, 278-281.

33 Reid, *The Blood of the People*, 230-245. Mohammad Said, 'Apa itu "Revolusi Sosial Tahun 1946" di Sumatera Timur', *Merdeka*, 17 February-1 March 1972; translated by Benedict Anderson and Toenggoel Siagian as 'What was the "social revolution of 1946" in East Sumatra', *Indonesia* 15 (1973) 145-168, 174.

34 NL-HaNA NEFIS/CMI 2.10.62 inv.no 751, Report HQ 26th Indian Division, Bureau CI Medan, 11 April 1946.

35 NL-HaNA, (Supplement) 2.10.03 inv.no 86 and 87, *Sinar Deli*, 13 December 1945; *Kerakjatan*, 18 December 1945.

36 NL-HaNA PG 2.10.17, inv.no 679, Rapport over het Chinese Security Corps (PAO AN TUI), (verbindingsofficier) J. Hoogland, Medan, 25 October 1946.

37 See Nationaal Archief (NL-HaNA), Strijdkrachten in Nederlands-Indië (hereinafter SNI), 2.13.132 inv. no 1340, Instructions issued by Brigadier Morrison on 23 April 1946, attachment to the Report on the origins and development of the Chinese Security Corps in East Sumatra, Chief Constable of Police, W.G. Eybergen, 30 October 1947.

38 M.A. Loderichs et al., *Medan: Beeld van een stad* (Purmerend 1997); Freek Colombijn, *Under Construction: The Politics of Urban Space and Housing During the Decolonization of Indonesia, 1930-1950* (Leiden 2010); Usman Pelly, *Urban Migration and Adaptation in Indonesia: A Case Study of Minangkabau and Mandailing Batak Migrants in Medan, North Sumatra* (PhD dissertation in history, University of Illinois, 1983).

39 Said, *Pendoedoekan Inggeris di Indonesia*, 98.

40 NL-HaNA NEFIS/CMI 2.10.62 inv.no 1566, General report on the Medan Chinese General Association, 9/12-1945 to 31/1-1947.

41 NL-HaNA PG 2.10.17, inv.no 679, H.Q. 26th Indian Division Weekly Intelligence Summary No. 29, (Medan) 4 May 1946; NL-HaNA SNI, 2.13.132 inv.no 25; Rapport over het Chinese Security Corps (PAO AN TUI), (verbindingsofficier) J. Hoogland, Medan, 25 October 1946.

42 Cui Yisheng, 'Duli Chuqi de Bao'andui Shijian', 2 July 2011.

43 NL-HaNA NEFIS/CMI 2.10.62 inv.no 1566, General report on the Medan Chinese General Association, 9/12-1945 to 31/1-1947.

44 NL-HaNA NEFIS/CMI 2.10.62 inv.no 5318, Welcoming speech for the visit of Vice President Hatta, by the Chairman of the Chinese General Association East Sumatra, July 1947, confiscated document.

45 NL-HaNA, Commandant der Zeemacht in Nederlands-Indië, 2.13.72, inv.no 12, Report of a visit to the Chinese Security Corps in Medan, unsigned, Batavia, 7 October 1946; NL-HaNA SNI, 2.13.132 inv.no 1340, Report on the origins and development of the Chinese Security Corps in East Sumatra, Chief Constable of Police, W.G. Eybergen, 30 October 1947 (including attachments).

46 See especially NL-HaNA SNI, 2.13.132 inv.no 1340, The report on the CSC by Chief Constable Eybergen; in this period (April-June 1947), the CSC actually established ties with various Indonesian insurgent groups: see the group picture taken at a meeting of the leaders of the CSC and Indonesian army units, Amran Zamzami, *Jihad Akbar di Medan Area* (Jakarta 1990), 111; NL-HaNA NEFIS/CMI 2.10.62 inv. no 4732, Letters Napindo to Pao An Tui, Batang Kuis, May 1947; NL-HaNA NEFIS/CMI 2.10.62 inv.no 4734, Letter Resimen Istimewa Medan Area (RIMA) to Pao An Tui, Binjai, 19 May 1947.

47 Politiek verslag Sumatra van regeringsadviseur voor politieke zaken Sumatra (Van de Velde) over juni 1947, in: S.L. van der Wal, P.J. Drooglever and M.J.B. Schouten (eds.), *Officiële Bescheiden Nederlands-Indonesische Betrekkingen 1945-1950* (hereafter *NIB*), 20 vols. (The Hague 1971-) IX 547-565, 555; NL-HaNA NEFIS/CMI 2.10.62 inv.no 4867 and 5064, Confiscated documents on evacuation orders and negotiations.

48 NL-HaNA SNI, 2.13.132 inv.no 352, Daily overviews Commander Z-Brigade, 20 July-18 August 1947; NL-HaNA, Inventaris van het fotoarchief van de Dienst Legercontacten Indonesië (DLC), 1946-1950 – negatieven, entry number 2.24.04.02, inventory number 11 (7471-7483, Photographs taken by the Dutch army communication service (Dienst Legercontacten), for example Rapportage Deli Toea (Photo series Deli Toea), July 1947 (by army photographers Sergeant Ben Huisman and A.J.M. Loomans.

49 Overzicht van de toestand bij Medan van regeringscommissaris voor bestuursaangelegenheden [Recomba] Noord-Sumatra (Van de Velde), 26 juli 1947, NIB X, 68-70, 70; NL-HaNA SNI, 2.13.132 inv.no 352, Daily overviews Commander Z-Brigade, 20 July-18 August 1947.

50 Hans Post (pseud. Hubert Paas), *Banjir over Noord-Sumatra: Politionele Actie*, vol. 2 (Medan 1947).

51 Verslag van de regeringscommissaris voor bestuursaangelegenheden van Noord-Sumatra (Van de Velde), August 1947, *NIB* X, 605-612; NL-HaNA SNI, 2.13.132 inv.no 1340, Overview of the formation, organization, distribution of tasks, dislocation, etc of the Chinese Security Corps, Police Inspector C. den Haan, Medan, 10 October 1947.

52 NL-HaNA, Nederlands Gezantschap in China (Peking, Chunking, Nanking), 2.05.90, inv.no 851, On the arrest of leftist Chinese leaders and reactions from members of the Chinese General Association.

53 Xin Zhonghua Bao (New China Times), 14 August 1947. See also Star Weekly, 16 November 1947.

16. The everyday life of the Chinese community in Padang

1 Novianti Mariyatul Hakim, 'Bertahan Hidup Dalam Masa Yang Sulit: Kehidupan Sehari-Hari Masyarakat Tionghoa Pada Masa Revolusi di Surabaya', *Jurnal Al- Qalam* 25:3 (2019) 549-560.

2 Jumhari, 'Rakit Yang Terombang-Ambing: Ambivalensi Sikap Politik dan Orientasi Ekonomi Orang China Palembang Pada Masa Revolusi', *Analisis Sejarah* 9:2 (2020) 30-40.

3 Mary Somers Heidhues, 'Anti-Chinese Violence in Java During the Indonesian Revolution, 1945-49', *Journal of Genocide Research* 14:3-4 (2012) 381-401.

4 Ravando, 'Now is the time to Kill All Chinese: Social Revolution and Massacre of Chinese in Tangerang, 1945- 1946', Master's Thesis, Leiden University, 2017.

5 To name but a few: Fatimah Enar, et al., *Sumatera Barat 1945-1949* (Padang 1978); A. Nasrun, *Butir-butir Berceceran: Sepanjang Jalan Revolusi* (Padang 1979); Audrey Kahin et al., *Perjuangan Kemerdekaan Sumatera Barat dalam Revolusi Nasional Indonesia 1945-1950* (Padang 1989); Ismael Lengah, *Cerita Untuk Anak Cucu: Keikutsertaan dalam Perang Kemerdekaan* (DHD 45 Sumatera Barat 1995); Mestika Zed et al., *Sumatera Barat di Panggung Sejarah 1945-1995* (Jakarta 1998); Idrian Idroes, 'Peranan BPPI di Padang Kota Perjuangan', *Memorial* (unpublished, 1997) 31-34; Etmi Hardi et al., 'Gurita Revolusi: Peranan Kurir, Mata-Mata dan Tentara Semut dalam Revolusi di Sumatera Barat 1945-1949', *Monograph* (Padang 2001) 17-18.

6 Erniwati, *140 Tahun Heng Beng Tong: Sejarah Perkumpulan Tionghoa 1876-2016* (Depok 2016).

7 Laila Kholid Alfirdaus et al., 'The Position of Minang-Chinese Relationship in The History of Inter-Ethnic Group Relations in Padang, West Sumatra', *Humaniora* (2016) 83-84.

8 Ibidem.

9 Alf Lüdtke, 'Introduction: What Is the History of Everyday Life and Who are Its Practitioners?' in Alf Lüdtke (ed.), *The History of Everyday Life: Reconstructing Historical Experience and Ways of Life* (New Jersey 1995) 4. See also Brad S. Gregory, 'Review: Is Small Beautiful? Microhistory and the History of Everyday Life, History and Theory', *History And Theory* 38:1 (1999) 100-110; Harald Dehne, 'Have We Come Any Closer to Alltag? Everyday Reality and Workers' Lives as an Object of Historical Research in the German Democratic Republic', in: Alf Lüdtke, *The History of Everyday Life*, 116-148; Richard R. Beeman, 'Small Things Remembered: Writing the History of Everyday Life in Early America', Reviewed by Richard R. Beeman, *American Quarterly* 42:1 (1990) 108-115; Paul Steege, Andrew Stuart Bergeson, Maureen Healy and Pamela E. Swett, 'The History of Everyday Life: A Second Chapter', *The Journal of Modern History* 80:2 (2008) 358-378.

10 Bambang Purwanto, 'Menulis Kehidupan Sehari-hari Jakarta: Memikirkan Kembali Sejarah Sosial Indonesia', in: Henk Schulte Nordholt, Bambang Purwanto, Ratna Saptari (eds.), *Perspektif Baru Penulisan Sejarah Indonesia* (Jakarta 2008) 17, 269.

11 Jang A. Muttalib and Sudjarwo, 'Gelandangan dalam kancah Revolusi', in: Aswab Mahasin (ed.), *Gelandangan Pandangan Ilmuwan Sosial* (Jakarta 1984) 15-34.

12 Erniwati, *Asap Hio di Ranah Minang: Komunitas Tionghoa di Sumatera Barat* (Yogyakarta 2007) 43.

13 Sativa Sutan Aswar, *Antakesuma Suji Dalam Adat Minangkabau*, (Jakarta 1999) 41-42.

14 Ibidem.

15 Ibidem, 45.

16 Ibidem, 44.

17 Elizabeth E. Grave, *The Minangkabau Response to Dutch Colonial Role in the Nineteenth Century* (Singapore 2010) 83-84.

18 Freek Colombijn, *Poco-Poco (Kota) Padang: Sejarah Sebuah Kota di Indonesia Pada Abad ke-20 dan Penggunaan Ruang* (Yogyakarta 2006) 293-295.

19 Christine Dobbin, *Kebangkitan Islam dalam Ekonomi Petani yang Sedang Berubah: Sumatera Tengah 1784-1847* (Jakarta 1992) 92-93.

20 Mestika Zed, 'Kota Padang Tempo Doeloe (Zaman Kolonial)', *Monograf* (Padang 2009) 6.

21 Erniwati, 'Pariaman (Saat) Tionghoa Pariaman' in: Budi Susanto (ed.), *Masih (Kah) Indonesia* (Jakarta 2007) 269-283.

22 Mestika Zed, Emizal Amri and Etmihardi, *Sejarah Perjuangan Kemerdekaan: 1945-1949 di Kota Padang dan Sekitarnya* (Padang 2002) 104-107.

23 Amura, *Sejarah Revolusi Kemerdekaan di Minangkabau 1945-1950* (Jakarta 1979) 30-43; Ahmad Husein, *Sejarah Perjuangan Kemerdekaan di Minangkabau/Riau 1945-1950 Jilid 1* (Jakarta 1978) 223-224.

24 Mestika Zed et al., *Sejarah Perjuangan*, 98; Ahmad Husein, *Sejarah Perjuangan Kemerdekaan,* 84.

25 Staf Umum Angkatan Darat-I, *Masalah China di Indonesia* (Jakarta 1961)14.

26 Erniwati, 'Cina Padang dalam Dinamika Masyarakat Minangkabau: Dari Revolusi sampai Reformasi', Dissertation, Universitas Indonesia, Jakarta 2011, 74.

27 *Masjarakat*, 16 April 1946.

28 NL-HaNA, Marine en Leger Inlichtingendienst, de Netherlands Forces Intelligence Service en de Centrale Militaire Inlichtingendienst in Nederlands-Indië (hereinafter NEFIS/CMI), 2.10.62 inv.no 1690.

29 See Mestika Zed et al., *Sejarah Perjuangan*, 98.

30 NL-HaNA NEFIS/CMI, 2.10.62 inv.no 780.

31 Idrian Idroes, 'Riwayat Hidup Drs. H. Idrian Idroes M.S', *Memorial* (DHD 45 Provinsi Sumatera Barat, no date) 55.

32 See Etmi Hardi et al., 'Gurita Revolusi', 10; *Haluan,* 10 August 1976.

33 Maryetti, et al., *Peranan Kaum Wanita Dalam Perjuangan Kemerdekaan di Front Timur Kota Padang 1945-1950* (Padang 1993) 7; NL-HaNA NEFIS/CMI, 2.10.62 inv.no 1332.

34 Idran Idroes was among the 150 child soldiers based in Palinggam Village from September to October 1945; Idrian Idroes SM. Sulaiman, 'Peranan BPPI di Padang Kota Perjuangan', *Memorial,* (unpublished, 1997) 31-34.

35 Ibidem, 41.

36 Idrian Idroes, 'Riwayat Hidup', 31.

37 Ismael Lengah, *Cerita Untuk Anak,* 35-36; Ahmad Husein, *Sejarah Perjuangan Kemerdekaan,* 230-260.

38 Ibidem, 259.

39 S.L. van der Wal, *Officiële Bescheiden betreffende de Nederlands-Indonesische Betrekkingen 1945-1950, elfde deel, 1 September-25 November 1947* (The Hague 1983).

40 Mestika Zed et al., *Sejarah Perjuangan*, 295.

41 A.S. Nasrun, *Butir-butir Berceceran: Sepanjang Jalan Revolusi* (Padang) 19.

42 S.L. van der Wal, *Officiële Bescheiden betreffende de Nederlands-Indonesische Betrekkingen 1945-1950, vierde deel 31 Maart 1946 – 16 Juli 1946* (The Hague 1974) 22; Idrian Idroes, 'Peranan BPPI di Padang Kota', 66.

43 NL-HaNA NEFIS/CMI, 2.10.62 inv.no 5372.

44 NL-HaNA NEFIS/CMI, 2.10.62 inv.no 0793.

45 *Sin Po*, 'Hoakiaw Di Sumatera' (22 April 1946).

46 Arsip Nasional Republik Indonesia (hereinafter ANRI), Nefis BK Padang ddo 23/7/1946 (EC6/51546); ANRI, Inventaris Nefis No 95.

47 Idrian Idroes, 'Peranan BPPI di Padang Kota', 31-34.

48 Ibidem, 56, 70-71.

49 Letter from Chung Hua Chung Hui Pondok Padang to the Allied forces dated 18 July 1946. NL-HaNA Procureur- Generaal bij het Hooggerechtshof van Nederlands-Indië (hereinafter PG) 2.10.17, inv.no 1167.

50 NL-HaNA PG 2.10.17, inv.no 03128.

51 NL-HaNA NEFIS/CMI, 2.10.62 inv.no 00782.

52 Ibidem.

53 NL-HaNA NEFIS/CMI, 2.10.62 inv.no 00785.

54 NL-HaNA NEFIS/CMI, 2.10.62 inv.no 00780.

55 NL-HaNA NEFIS/CMI, 2.10.62 inv.no 5372.

56 Idrian Idroes, 'Riwayat Hidup', 55.

57 NL-HaNA NEFIS/CMI, 2.10.62 inv.no 5372.

58 Idrian Idroes, 'Peranan BPPI di Padang Kota', 70-71.

59 NL-HaNA NEFIS/CMI, 2.10.62 inv.no 793.

60 NL-HaNA NEFIS/CMI, 2.10.62 inv.no 01866.

61 Marah Joenoes, *Mr.H.ST.Moh.Rasjid Perintis Kemerdekaan, Pejuang Tangguh, Berani dan Jujur* (Jakarta 2003) 81.

62 See *Anggaran Dasar dan Anggaran Rumah Tangga Himpunan Tjinta Teman Padang* (Padang 1987). The name of three organizers and the years of their administration were obtained from photographs found in the Hok Tek Tong secretariat in Padang.

63 See *Reglement Peratoeran dari Kongsi Heng Beng Tong* (1894).

64 Meeting Minutes Hok Tek Tong (Padang, 23 August 1945).

65 Ledger of Heng Beng Tong (Padang 1878-1958) Erniwati, *140 Tahun Heng Beng Tong,* 36.

66 Meeting Minutes Hok Tek Tong (Padang, 3 November 1946).

67 Meeting Minutes Hok Tek Tong (Padang, 15 June 1946).

68 Meeting Minutes Hok Tek Tong (Padang, 25 August 1946).

69 Meeting Minutes Hok Tek Tong (Padang, 8 February 1946).

70 Ahmad Husein et al., *Sejarah Perjuangan Kemerdekaan RI di Minangkabau/Riau 1945-1950* (Jakarta 1991) 394-395.

71 'Laporan Politik atas Sumatra dari Gubernur Amacab Sumatra Spits selama bulan Mei 1946', in S.L. van der Wal, *Officiële Bescheiden betreffende de Nederlands-Indonesische Betrekkingen 1945-1950, vierde deel 31 Maart 1946 – 16 Juli 1946* (The Hague 1974) 398.

72 Etmi Hardi, et al., 'Gurita Revolusi', 17-18.

73 'Oetjapan Selamat Pendoedoek Padang', *Waspada*, 31 March 1947.

74 'Protes Pendoedoek', *Waspada*, 31 March 1947.

75 Etmi Hardi, et al., 'Gurita Revolusi', 17-18; Ahmad Husein et al., Loc Cit. (1991) 395; 401-411.

76 Kementerian Penerangan, *Republik Indonesia: Propinsi Sumatera Tengah* (Jakarta 1953) 161.

77 Fatimah Enar et al., *Sumatera Barat,* 113-117.

78 See Hamka, *Kenangan-Kenangan Hidup* (Jakarta 1974) 134; also Audrey Kahin, 'Some Preliminary Observations on West Sumatra during the Revolution', *Indonesia* 18 (1974) 89-90.

79 Abrar Yusra, *Azwar Anas: Teladan dari Ranah Minang* (Jakarta 2011) 21-22.

80 S.L. van der Wal, *Officiële Bescheiden betreffende de Nederlands-Indonesische Betrekkingen 1945-1950, vierde deel 31 Maart 1946 – 16 Juli 1946* (The Hague 1974).

81 'Politiek Verslag van Sumatra van de chief Commanding over Juni en Juli 1946', in S.L. van der Wal, *Officiële Bescheiden betreffende de Nederlands-Indonesische Betrekkingen 1945-1950, vierde deel, 31 Maart 1946 – 16 Juli 1946* (The Hague 1974) 149.

82 NL-HaNA NEFIS/CMI, 2.10.62 inv.no 799a.

83 *Bila bahan makan habis, kita akan mati membawa sejarah hidup dalam persamaan dan mati di atas persamaan, terutama untuk orang kaya harus insyaf.*

84 NL-HaNA NEFIS/CMI, 2.10.62 inv.no 74.
85 NL-HaNA NEFIS/CMI, 2.10.62 inv.no 102.
86 Geheim Politiek Dag Rapport no 152.
87 NL-HaNA Strijdkrachten in Nederlands-Indië (hereinafter SNI) 2.13.132, inv.no 160.
88 Sulardi, *Pao An Tui 1947-1949 Tentara Cina*, Jakarta, (Jakarta 2015) 5.
89 NL-HaNA NEFIS/CMI, 2.10.62 inv.no 780.
90 S.L. van der Wal, Ibidem.
91 NL-HaNA NEFIS/CMI, 2.10.62 inv.no 2590.
92 NL-HaNA SNI 2.13.132, inv.no 1690.
93 Shipping pass/permit for Oei Ho Tjeng dated 20 September 1948. NL-HaNA NEFIS/CMI, 2.10.62 inv.no 2590.
94 NL-HaNA SNI 2.13.132, inv.no 1703.
95 NL-HaNA NEFIS/CMI, 2.10.62 inv.no 3128.
96 Meeting Minutes HokTek Tong (Padang, 12 September 1948).
97 Ledger of Heng Beng Tong Padang 1878-1958.
98 See the invitation letter from Heng Beng Tong dated 29 December 1946 to Hok Tek Tong on meeting to be held on 12 January 1947 (Heng Beng Tong Secretariat in Padang).
99 Meeting Minutes Hok Tek Tong (Padang, 21 September 1947).
100 Meeting Minutes Rapat Hok Tek Tong (Padang, 13 February 1948).
101 Meeting Minutes Hok Tek Tong (Padang, 12 May 1948); Meeting Minutes Hok Tek Tong (Padang, 13 July 1948).
102 Meeting Minutes Hok Tek Tong (Padang, 13 July 1948); Meeting Minutes Hok Tek Tong (Padang, 29 August 1948).

17. Playing it safe

1 Sartono Kartodirdjo, 'Wajah Revolusi Indonesia Dipandang dari Perspektivisme Struktural', *Prisma* 8 (1981) 3.
2 Anthony Reid, 'Revolusi Sosial: Revolusi Nasional', *Prisma* 8 (1981) 37-38; Mohammed Sahid, 'What Was the "Social Revolution of 1946" in East Sumatra?', *Indonesia* 15 (1973).
3 Richard McMillan, *The British Occupation of Indonesia 1945-1946: Britain, the Netherlands and the Indonesian Revolution* (London 2005).
4 Karl J. Pelzer, *Planter and Peasant: Colonial Policy and the Agrarian Struggle in East Sumatra, 1863-1947* (The Hague 1978) 63.
5 Ibidem, 35.
6 A. Mani, 'Indians in North Sumatra', in: K.S. Sandhu and A. Mani (eds.), *Indian Communities in Southeast Asia* (Singapore 1993) 57.
7 Jan Breman, *Menjinakkan sang Kuli: Politik Kolonial, Tuan Kebun dan Kuli di Sumatra Timur pada Awal Abad ke-20* (Jakarta 1997) 56-57.
8 Mani, 'Indians', 57.
9 Rubber and oil palm plantation owners preferred to use contract workers from Java because they were cheaper. Ann Laura Stoler, *Capitalism and Confrontation in Sumatra's Plantation Belt, 1870-1979* (Michigan 1995) 30.
10 Thee Kian-Wie, *Plantation Agriculture and Export Growth: An Economic History of East Sumatra, 1863-1942* (Jakarta 1977) 38-39.
11 Mani, 'Indians', 58.
12 *Volkstelling 1930, Deel VII: Chineezen en andere Vreemde Oosterlingen in Nederlandsch-Indië* (Batavia 1935) 298, 309.
13 Ibidem, 28; NL-HaNA Inventaris van de Memories van Overgave, 1852-1962 (1963), (herinafter MvO) 2.10.39, inv.no 676, 'Ruychaver, M.J. (controleur); Memorie van Overgave van de onderafdeling Bened-

en-Deli', 1926.

14 Mani, 'Indians', 51.

15 *De Sumatra Post,* 16 November 1927.

16 L.C. Westenenk, 'De Chetti', *Koloniale Studiën* 6:2 (1922) 4.

17 NL-HaNA MvO, 2.10.39 inv.no 676; *Tjinpo*, 22 May 1928.

18 Saifuddin Mayudin, *Anna Amartya Dharma D. Kumarasamy (D.K): Biografi* (Medan 2014) 9-10; Apriani Harahap, *Voor Indiërs: Sejarah Kehidupan Sehari-hari Orang India di Kota Medan pada Abad ke-20,* Master's thesis, History, Universitas Gadjah Mada, Yogyakarta (2014) 108-113.

19 Jayati Bhattacharya, *Beyond the Myth: Indian Business Communities in Singapore* (Singapore 2011) 48-49; lihat juga *Tjinpo,* 22 May 1928.

20 Mani, 'Indians', 85, 87.

21 Idem, 'Sikhs in Multi-ethnic Indonesia', in: Shamsul A.B. and Arunajeet Kaur (eds.), *Sikhs in Southeast Asia: Negotiating an Identity* (Singapore 2011) 150.

22 Dirk A. Buiskool, 'Medan, A Plantation City on the East Coast of Sumatra 1870-1942', in: Freek Colombijn et al. (eds.), *Kota Lama, Kota Baru: Sejarah Kota-Kota di Indonesia sebelum dan setelah Kemerdekaan* (Yogyakarta 2005) 288.

23 Westenenk, 'De Chetti', 7.

24 R. Supomo, *Sistim Hukum di Indonesia sebelum Perang Dunia II* (Jakarta 1958) 12-17, 88-96; Gouw Giok Siong, *Warga Negara dan Orang Asing: Berikut Peraturan-peraturan dan Tjontoh-tjontoh* (Jakarta 1958) 28-33.

25 *Staatsblad van Nederlandsche-Indië 1886* No. 57 (Batavia 1867) 1-2.

26 Johan Hasselgren, *Rural Batak, Kings in Medan; The Development of Toba Batak Ethno-religious Identity in Medan, Indonesia, 1912-1965* (Uppsala 2000) 55-56.

27 Dirk A. Buiskool, *Prominent Chinese during the Rise of a Colonial City Medan 1890-1942*, PhD thesis in history, Universiteit Utrecht (2019) 62-63.

28 *De Sumatra Post,* 9 November 1927.

29 *De Sumatra Post,* 4 January 1928.

30 Harahap, *Voor Indiërs,* 148; NL-HaNA MvO, 2.10.39 inv.no 676.

31 *Pewarta Deli,* 7 August 1917.

32 *Pewarta Deli,* 22 October 1920.

33 *Tjinpo,* 8 May 1924.

34 M.J. Lusink, *Kroniek 1924* (The Hague 1925) 10.

35 Bambang Purwanto, *Praktik Kewarganegaraan di Indonesia dalam Perspektif Historiografi* (Yogyakarta 2019) 23, 26-27.

36 Tengku Luckman Sinar, *Orang India di Sumatera Utara* (Medan 2008) 24.

37 *De Sumatra Post*, 4 Maret 1932; *Bintang Oemoem*, 9 Agustus 1941.

38 *De Indische Courant,* 14 May 1930; Ornit Shani, 'Gandhi's Salt March: Paradoxes and Tensions in the Memory of Nonviolent Struggle in India', in: Anna Reading and Tamar Katriel (eds.), *Cultural Memories of Nonviolent Struggles: Powerful Times* (Basingstoke 2015) 32-34.

39 *Algemeen Handelsblad,* 6 May 1930.

40 A.J.S. Reid, *The Blood of the People: Revolution and the End of Traditional Rule in Northern Sumatra* (Kuala Lumpur 1979) 108-109, 122-124.

41 NL-HaNA Netherlands Forces Intelligence Service [NEFIS] and Centrale Militaire Inlichtingendienst [CMI] in The Netherlands East Indies (hereinafter NEFIS/CMI), 2.10.62, inv.no 712, ' Section CSDIC (I) Singapore District SEAC Raport No. 1512', 12 February 1946.

42 Willard H. Elsbree, *Japan's Role in Southeast Asian Nationalist Movements, 1940 to 1945* (Cambridge 1953) 32-36.

43 NL-HaNA NEFIS/CMI 2.10.62, inv.no 712.

44 *Sumatra Sinbun,* 14 October 1943.
45 NL-HaNA NEFIS/CMI 2.10.62, inv.no 712.
46 Ibidem; Tan Kia Lih, *The Indian National Army: A Force for Nationalism?* Master's thesis in history, National University of Singapore (2011) 84-98.
47 *Waspada,* 11 January 1948.
48 NL-HaNA NEFIS/CMI 2.10.62, inv.no 712; *Kita Sumatora Sinbun,* 28 October 1943.
49 Mani, 'Indians', 61.
50 NL-HaNA NEFIS/CMI 2.10.62, inv.no 712.
51 *Sumatra Sinbun,* 2 April 1943.
52 E. Touwen-Bouwsma, 'Japanese Minority Policy: The Eurasians on Java and the Dilemma of Ethnic Loyalty', *Bijdragen tot de Taal-, Land- en Volkenkunde* 152:4 (1996) 559.
53 Aiko Kurasawa and Mitsuko Nanke, *Bibliografi Beranotasi Sumber Sejarah Masa Pendudukan Jepang di Indonesia* (Jakarta 2018) 26, 28.
54 George McTurnan Kahin, *Nationalism and Revolution in Indonesia* (Ithaca NY 1952) 138-140.
55 Anthony Reid, 'Revolusi Sosial: Revolusi Nasional', *Prisma* 8 (1981) 37.
56 Tengku Luckman Sinar, 'Sumatera Timur menjelang Proklamasi dan setelah Proklamasi Kemerdekaan Indonesia', in: Taufik Abdullah et al. (eds.), *Denyut Nadi Revolusi Indonesia* (Jakarta 1997) 141.
57 M. van Langenberg, *National Revolution in North Sumatra: Sumatera Timur and Tapanuli 1942-1950* (n.p. 1976) 273.
58 Sinar, 'Sumatera Timur menjelang Proklamasi', 142; Anthony Reid, 'The Birth of the Republic in Sumatra', *Indonesia* 12 (1971) 34, 38.
59 Suprayitno, *Mencoba (Lagi) menjadi Indonesia, dari Federalisme ke Unitarisme: Studi tentang Negara Sumatera Timur 1947-1950* (Yogyakarta 2001) 54-55.
60 Reid, *The Blood of the People,* 157; M. van Langenberg, *National Revolution,* 290-292.
61 Rémy Limpach, *Kekerasan Ekstrem Belanda di Indonesia: Perang Kemerdekaan Indonesia 1945-1949* (Jakarta 2019) 31.
62 McMillan, *The British Occupation of Indonesia,* 116-117, 123-124.
63 Reid, *The Blood of the People,* 161-168.
64 Mcmillan, *The British Occupation of Indonesia,* 147.
65 *The Straits Times,* 17 October 1945.
66 *Mimbar Oemoem,* 14 November 1945.
67 NL-HaNA Inventaris van het archief van het Ministerie van Koloniën (hereinafter MvK) 2.10.03, inv.no 87, 'Uittreksels van artikelen uit de Maleise en Chinese pers te Medan voor zover van belang voor de plaatselijke situatie', November 1945.
68 McMillan, *The British Occupation of Indonesia,* 155.
69 Interview with Kuna Serangan, 20 May 2018. Kuna Serangan (1928) is an Indian born in Medan.
70 *Waspada,* 2 December 2014.
71 McMillan, *The British Occupation of Indonesia,* 156-163.
72 Ibidem, 162; *Waspada,* 27 August 2010.
73 *Semangat Merdeka,* 19 September 1946.
74 *Merdeka,* 24 May 1946.
75 NL-HaNA NEFIS/CMI 2.10.62, inv.no 1876, 'Dagelijks overzicht van de Indonesische pers', 27 June 1946.
76 *Soeloeh Merdeka,* 23 November 1945.
77 *Waspada,* 11 January 1948.
78 Interview with Kuna Serangan, 20 May 2018.
79 Mani, 'Indians', 66; Mayudin, *Anna Amartya Dharma,* 79.
80 Ann Laura Stoler, 'Working the Revolution: Plantation Laborers and the People's Militia in North Sumatra', *Journal of Asian Studies* 47:2 (1988) 232.

81 Anthony Reid, *The Blood of the People,* 163.
82 J.J. van de Velde, *Surat-surat dari Sumatra, 1928-1949* (Jakarta 1987) 135.
83 *Pelita Rakjat*, 1 August 1946.
84 *Het Dagblad*, 6 February 1946.
85 Sinar, *Orang India,* 14.
86 *Het Dagblad*, 23 July 1946.
87 *Nieuwe Courant*, 13 November 1946.
88 A. Mani, 'Indians', 59.
89 Hakimuddin, *Role of the Muslim League in Indian Politics from 1940-47*, Doctoral dissertation in political science, Aligarh Muslim University (1990) 170-218.
90 Sinar, *Orang India,* 14.
91 *Het Dagblad*, 6 February 1946.
92 *Morning Tribune*, 16 July 1946.
93 *Semangat Merdeka,* 23 July 1946.
94 Ibidem.
95 Ibidem.
96 *Indian Daily Mail*, 1 August 1946; 2 November 1946.
97 *Free Press of India,* 29 October 1946, see: https://opus.lib.uts.edu.au/handle/10453/28098, accessed 1 December 2020.
98 Ibidem.
99 NIOD Archief van de Indische Afdeling van het Rijksinstituut voor Oorlogsdocumentatie, inv.no 2276, 'Report on the activities from September to November 1945 of delegation of the international Committee of the Red Cross in Medan (Sumatra's Oostkust)'.
100 *Mimbar Oemoen,* 27 June 1946.
101 *Kedaulatan Rakjat,* 23 July 1946.
102 *Indian Daily Mail*, 2 November 1946.
103 *Merdeka,* 20 October 1946.
104 *Malaya Tribune*, 2 November 1946.

Abbreviations

ALRI	Angkatan Laut Republik Indonesia (Navy of the Republic of Indonesia)
AMACAB	Allied Military Administration Civil Affairs Branch
AMAI	Angkatan Muda Arab Indonesia (Arab Indonesia Young Generation)
AMKA	Angkatan Muda Kereta Api (Young Railroad Workers)
AMRI	Angkatan Muda Republik Indonesia (Youth Forces of the Republic of Indonesia)
AMT	Angkatan Muda Tentara (Young Generation Army)
Angkatan Muda PTT	Young Post and Telegraph Workers
API	Angkatan Pemuda Indonesia (Indonesian Youth Force)
APRIS	Angkatan Perang Republik Indonesia Serikat (National Military Forces of the Republic of the United States of Indonesia)
APS	Askar Perang Sabil (Army of the Holy War)
BAPRIS	Badan Perwakilan Rakyat Indonesia Semarang (Representative Body of the Indonesian People of Semarang)
BB	Binnenlands Bestuur (Colonial Civil Administration)
BFO	Bijeenkomst voor Federaal Overleg (Federal Consultative Assembly)

BKOW	Badan Kontak Organisasi Wanita (Women's Organization Contact Agency)
BKR	Badan Keamanan Rakyat (People's Security Agency)
BOMPA	Badan oentoek Membantoe Pertahanan Asia (Body for Assisting the Defence of Asia)
BPGD	Badan Pembantu Garis Depan (Frontline Supporting Forces)
BPI	Barisan Pemuda Indonesia (Indonesian Youth Front)
BPKKP	Badan Penolong Korban Keluarga Perjuangan (Agency to Support War Victims and Family)
BPKR	Badan Pusat Keselamatan Rakyat (Centre for People's Security)
BPPI	Badan Penerangan Pemuda Indonesia (Indonesian Youth Information Agency)
BPPRI	Biro Pejuang Pengikut Republik Indonesia (Bureau of Supporters of the Republic of Indonesia)
BPR	Badan Perwakilan Rakyat (House of Representatives)
BPRI	Barisan Pemberontak Rakyat Indonesia (Indonesian People's Rebel Front)
BPRI	Barisan Pemberontak Republik Indonesia (Indonesian People's Revolutionary Front)
Brigade SS	Brigade Semarang Stoottroep
CGA	Chinese General Association
CONICA	Commanding Officer of NICA
CSC	Chinese Security Corps
DPRS	Dewan Perwakilan Rakyat Sementara (Provisional House of Representatives)
DST	Depot Speciale Troepen (Special Forces)
FDR	Front Demokrasi Rakyat (People's Democratic Front)
GAMI	Gerakan Anti Merdeka Indonesia (Movement Against Indonesian Independence)
GAPKI	Gabungan Perjuangan Kemerdekaan Indonesia (Association of the Struggle for Indonesian Independence)
GASEMPA	Gabungan Sekolah Menengah Pati (Union of Pati High Schools)
GERDAK	Gerakan Rakyat Daerah Pendudukan (People's Movement in Occupied Areas)
GOC	Good Offices Committee
GPP	Gabungan Pembela Proklamasi (Group in Defence of the Proclamation)

GPTP Gabungan Perkumpulan Tionghoa Perantauan (Association of Overseas Chinese)
HTT Himpunan Tjinta Teman or Hok Tek Tong (Society of Affectionate Friends)
IFTU International Federation of Trade Unions camp
ILL Indian Independence League
INA Indian National Army
IPI Ikatan Pelajar Indonesia (Indonesian Students Association)
IVG Inlichtingen en Veiligheidsgroep (Intelligence and Security Group)
Jawatan PPBM Jawatan Persediaan dan Pembagian Bahan Makanan (Service for Food Provision and Distribution)
KL Koninklijke Landmacht (Royal Netherlands Army)
KMB Konferensi Meja Bundar (Round Table Conference)
KNI Komite Nasional Indonesia (Indonesian National Committee)
KNIL Koninklijk Nederlands-Indisch Leger (Royal Netherlands East Indies Army)
KNIP Komite Nasional Indonesia Pusat (Central Indonesian National Committee
KODM Komando Onderdistrik Militair (Military Sub-district Command)
KRIS Kebaktian Rakyat Indonesia Sulawesi (Loyalty of the Indonesian People of Sulawesi)
KRIS-M Kebaktian Rahasia Islam Muda (Secret Islamic Youth Service)
KST Korps Speciale Troepen (Special Forces Corps)
KUKB Yayasan Komite Utang Kehormatan Belanda (Committee of Dutch Debts of Honour)
LAPRIS Laskar Pemberontak Rakyat Indonesia Sulawesi (Indonesian People's Rebel Army in Sulawesi)
LAPTUR Laskar Pemberontak Turatea (Rebel Militia Turatea)
LASWI Laskar Wanita Indonesia (Indonesian Women's Militia)
LBI Laskar Buruh Indonesia (Indonesian Labour Militia)
LEGITIA Lembaga Gabungan Indonesia Tionghoa dan Arab (Indonesian Chinese and Arab Joint Institute)
LEO Laskar Ekstremis Oembaran (Oembaran Extremist Militia)
LOC Leger Organisatie Centrum (Army Organization Centre)
Masyumi Majelis Syuro Muslimin Indonesia (Council of Indonesian Muslim Associations)
MPK Markas Perjuangan Kota (City Struggle Headquarters)

MPP	Markas Pusat Pertempuran (Central Battle Headquarters)
MTD	Motor Transportdienst Semarang (Motor Transport Service Semarang)
Napindo	Nasional Pelopor Indonesia (Indonesian National Pioneers)
NEFIS	Netherlands Forces Intelligence Service
NICA	Netherlands Indies Civil Administration
NII	Negara Islam Indonesia (Indonesian Islamic State)
NIT	Negara Indonesia Timur (State of East Indonesia)
NRI	Negara Republik Indonesia (State of the Republic of Indonesia)
OCYMA	Overseas Chinese Young Men's Association
OSVIA	Opleidingsschool voor Inlandsche Ambtenaren (Training School for Native Civil Servants)
OVW'ers	Oorlogsvrijwilligers (war volunteers)
PDRI	Pemerintah Darurat Republik Indonesia (Emergency Government of the Republic of Indonesia)
Pepolit	Pendidikan Politik Tentara (Political Education of the Armed Forces)
Perwani	Persatuan Wanita Indonesia (Indonesian Women's Federation)
Perwari	Persatuan Wanita Republik Indonesia (Indonesian Women's Federation of the Republic of Indonesia)
Pesindo	Pemuda Sosialis Indonesia (Socialist Youth of Indonesia)
Peta	Pembela Tanah Air (Fatherland Defence Corps)
PI	Perhimpunan Indonesia (Indonesian Society)
PKI	Partai Komunis Indonesia (Indonesian Communist Party)
PKO	Pertolongan Kesehatan Oemoem (General Health Aid)
PKR	Partai Kedaulatan Rakyat (Party of Popular Sovereignty)
PKRI	Partai Katolik Republik Indonesia (Catholic Party of the Republic of Indonesia)
PKRS	Pusat Keselamatan Rakyat Sulawesi (Sulawesi People's Welfare Centre)
PMI	Palang Merah Indonesia (Indonesian Red Cross)
PMR	Pengawasan Makanan Rakyat (Supervision of People's Food)
PNI	Partai Nasional Indonesia (Indonesian National Party)
PORI	Persatuan Olah Raga Republik Indonesia (Republic of Indonesia Sports Union)
PPKI	Panitia Persiapan Kemerdekaan Indonesia (Preparatory Committee for Indonesian Independence)

PPNI	Pusat Pemuda Nasional Indonesia (Indonesian National Youth Centre)
PPRI	Pengikut Pejuang Republik Indonesia (Supporters of Indonesian Freedom Fighters)
PRI	Pemuda Republik Indonesia (Youth of the Republic of Indonesia)
PRI	Penunjang Republik Indonesia (Support for the Republic of Indonesia)
PRP	Partai Rakyat Pasundan (Pasundan People's Party)
PUSA	Persatuan Ulama Seluruh Aceh (All-Aceh Ulama Association)
PWR	Partai Wanita Rakyat (Women's Party for the People)
RAPWI	Recovery of Allied Prisoners of War and Internees
Recomba	Regeringscommissaris voor Bestuursaangelegenheden (government commissioner for administrative affairs)
RIS	Republik Indonesia Serikat (United States of Indonesia)
RMS	Republik Maluku Selatan (Republic of South Maluku)
RTC	Round Table Conference
RVD	Regerings Voorlichtingsdienst (Netherlands Information Service)
SEAC	South-East Asia Command
SMP	Sekolah Menengah Pertama (Junior high school)
SP88	Satuan Pemberontakan 88 (Rebellion Unit 88)
SUDARA	Sumber Darah Rakyat (Source of the People's Blood)
THHK	Tiong Hoa Hwee Koan (local Chinese office)
TII	Tentara Islam Indonesia (Indonesian Islamic Army)
TKR	Tentara Keamanan Rakyat (People's Security Army, TNI predecessor)
TKR	Tentara Keselamatan Rakyat (People's Safety Army)
TNI	Tentara Nasional Indonesia (Indonesian National Armed Forces)
TP	Tentara Pelajar (Student Army)
TRI	Tentara Republik Indonesia (Army of the Republic of Indonesia, TNI predecessor)
TRIPS	Tentara Republik Indonesia Persiapan Sulawesi (Preparatory Army of the Republic of Indonesia, Sulawesi)
TRM	Tentara Rakyat Mataram (Mataram People's Army)
UN	United Nations
WKI	Wanita Kristen Indonesia (The Indonesian Christian [Protestant] Women)

Glossary

algojo	executioner
alun-alun	city square
Angkatan Muda PTT	Young Post and Telegraph Workers
Badan Kontak Organisasi Wanita	Women's Organization Contact Agency
Badan Perhimpunan Masyarakat Indonesia	Agency of Indonesian Social Associations
badan perjuangan	struggle body
badik	Buginese kris
balai kota	town hall
Balai Penyelidikan Kimia	Chemical Research Institute
Bandung Lautan Api	Bandung Fire Sea
bapak	literally 'father', a charismatic older leader
Barisan Banteng	Buffalo Front
Barisan Banteng Hitam	Black Bull Front
Barisan Kelima	The Fifth Column
Barisan Maling-Maling	Thieves' Front
Barisan Pelopor Pertahanan Negara	National Defence Pioneers Front
Barisan Pemberontak Ganggawa	Ganggawa Rebel Front

Barisan Pendem	Underground Corps
Barisan Pengawal Tionghoa	Chinese Security Battalion
Barisan Srobot	seizing unit
Belanda Depok	the Dutch of Depok
bendewezen	banditry
bersiap	get ready, be ready
bezettingsleger	occupying army
bugot	traitor
bumi hangus	scorched earth
bumiputra	indigenous
Bundo Kanduang	local noblewoman
buruh	labourer
Christengemeente te Depok	Christian Municipality of Depok
controleur	colonial inspector
daerah	area
dapur umum	communal kitchen
Depok Lama	Old Depok
desa	village
Dewan Keamanan	Security Council
Dewan Perwakilan Rakyat Jawa-Tengah Sementara	Temporary Representative Council of the People of Central Java
Divisie Materieel Park	Equipment Division
Djamaat Mesehi Depok	Depok Christian Congregation
djongos	house boy
eigendom verponding	absolute property rights
Fonds Perjuangan	Fighting Fund
gallarang	territorial unity, traditional functionary
gaplek	cassava
garis demarkasi	demarcation line
gedor	batter down a door, looting
gemeente	municipality
Gerakan Muda Bajeng	Young Bajeng Movement
Hadat Tinggi	High Council
Hari Sumpah Pemuda	Youth Pledge Day
Harimau Indonesia	Indonesian Tigers
heiho	(Indonesian) auxiliary soldiers (for Japan)
Hua Chiau Chung Hui	Overseas Chinese Association

jago	strong leader, bandit
Jantung Kiblik	Heart of the Republic
Kadipaten	princely state
kambuik	little baskets made of dried leaves
kampong	urban village
karaeng	king, aristocrats
kaum plesiran	place of pleasure
kawedanan	district
kebaya	Javanese blouse
kekosongan kekuasaan	power vacuum
Kelompok Kulon	West Group
Kelompok Wetan	South Group
Kementerian Pertahanan	Ministry of Defence
Kenpeitai	Japanese military police
klemak-klemek	soft movements
Komando Ketentaraan Kota	City Army Command
Komite Gabungan Indonesia-Tionghoa-India	Committee of Indonesian-Chinese-Indian Union
Komite Nasional Indonesia Daerah Sulawesi	South Sulawesi branch of the Republic's Indonesian National Committee
Komite Pengurus Bahan Makanan	Staple Food Committee
koo	head
kooti	province
Kota harapan	city of hope
Kota Hijrah	city of Islamic Restoration
Kota impian	city of dreams
Kota kongres	congress city
Kota masa depan Indonesia	city of the future of Indonesia
landerijen	estates
landschappen	administrative territories
laskar	militia
Laskar Gajah Mada	Gajah Mada Militia
Laskar Lipan Bajeng	Lipan Bajeng Militia
Laskar Merah	Red Militia
Laskar Puteri Indonesia	Indonesian Girls Militia
laskar rakyat	people's militia
Lembaga Demokrasi Baru Pemuda Sumatera	Sumatran Youth Institute for New Democracy

Lembaga Gabungan Bangsa India	Institute of Indian Union
lenggoang	bandits
Lipan Bajeng	Bajeng Centipede
Majelis Harian Hadat Tinggi	traditional rulers council
mandoer (mandor)	supervisor
mangsa siap-siapan	time to get ready
Mardijkers van Depok	freemen of Depok
Markas Agung	Supreme Headquarters
merdeka	freedom, independence
Milik Republik Indonesia (RI)	property of the Republic of Indonesia
negara	state
niemandsland	no man's land
onderdistrict	sub-district
Orang Depok Asli	Original Citizens of Depok
pabicara	customary office-bearer
paccalaya	leader of a union of villages
paduka	Your Highness
paduka yang mulia	Your Excellency
pahlawan	hero
pajonga	administer of a territory
palagan	battles
Panca Koa	Five Tasks
Panitia Persiapan Kemerdekaan Indonesia	Indonesian Independence Preparatory Committee
Partai Kebangsaan	National Party
particuliere landerij	private estate
Pasukan Alap-Alap	Falcon Force
pasukan maling	units of thieves
patih	regent
pekan olahraga nasional	national sports games week
pemuda	youth
pemudi	youth (girls)
penggedoran	robbery
peranakan	Indonesian-born
perang sabil	holy war
Peristiwa Tiga Daerah	Three Regions Affair
Perkumpulan Naga Kuning	Association of Yellow Dragon
Persatuan Golongan Indonesia	Indonesian Union of Groups

Persatuan India-Indonesia	India-Indonesia Union
Persatuan Tionghoa Cu Kiat Kun	Chinese Unitary Front
Pertempuran Lima Hari Lima Malam	Battle of Five Days and Five Nights
priyayi	Javanese royalty
Pusat Kebudayaan	Cultural Centre
rampokan	robbery
rampokkers	bandits
Regimen Tentara Pelajar Islam Indonesia	Indonesian Islamic Student Army Regiment
romusha	forced labourers (under Japanese occupation)
ruko (rumah toko)	shop-houses
Sekolah Guru Putri	Girls Teachers College
semi-officieele vertegenwoordiging	semi-official representatives
serangan kilat	lightning attack
serangan umum	general attack
sholat ghaib	commemoration
surat pas	special permit to pass
syuhada	martyr
Taman Makam Pahlawan	Heroes Cemetery
tani	farmer
Temporaire Krijgsraad	temporary court martial
Tentara Cilik	Child Soldiers
Tentara Kambuik	Kambuik Army
Tentara Samuik	Child Soldiers
Tijdelijke Bestuursdienst	Temporary Administrative Service
toloq	social banditry (Sulawesi)
Tugu Muda	Monument for the Youngsters
tukang kayu	carpenter
ulama	Islamic cleric
uleebalang	nobility (North Sumatra)
Vreemde Oosterlingen	Foreign Easterners
Wanita Pembantu Perjuangan	Women's Assistance for Struggle
wedana	head of district
wijkenstelsel	zoning system
wijkmeester	quarter leader
zelfbesturen	autonomous regions
zelfbestuur	self-governing territory
zuiveren	to clear, to purge

Bibliography

Archival institutions, organizations and libraries

Arsip Dinas Sejarah Angkatan Darat (Disjarahad, Army Historical Service), Bandung
Arsip Nasional Republik Indonesia (ANRI, National Archive of the Republic of Indonesia), Jakarta
Arsip Puro Pakualaman (Archive of Puro Pakualaman), Yogyakarta
Australian War Memorial (AWM), Canberra
Badan Arsip dan Perpustakaan Daerah Provinsi Sulawesi Selatan (The Library and Archive Agency of South Sulawesi Province), Makassar
Dinas Perpustakaan dan Kearsipan Aceh (The Library and Archive Agency of Aceh), Banda Aceh
Heng Beng Tong (HBT, Himpunan Bersatu Teguh, The Society of Firm Unity) secretariat, Padang
Hok Tek Tong (HTT, Himpunan Tjinta Teman, The Society of Affectionate Friends) secretariat, Padang
Koninklijk Instituut voor Taal-, Land-, en Volkenkunde (KITLV, Royal Netherlands Institute of Southeast Asian and Caribbean Studies), Leiden
Leiden University Libraries (Special Collections KITLV), Leiden
Museum dan Perpustakaan Gedung Joang 1945 Sumatera Barat (The Museum and Library of Gedung Joang 1945 in West Sumatra), Padang
Nationaal Archief (NL-HaNA, National Archives), The Hague
Nederlands Instituut voor Militaire Historie (NIMH, the Netherlands Institute for Military History), The Hague
NIOD Institute for War, Holocaust and Genocide Studies, Amsterdam
Perpustakaan Rekso Pustoko (Rekso Pustoko Library), Surakarta
Pusat Dokumentasi dan Informasi Aceh (Centre for Documentation and Information of Aceh), Banda Aceh
Pusat Dokumentasi dan Informasi Kebudayaan Minangkabau (Centre for Cultural Information and Documentation of Minangkabau), Padang Panjang
The National Archives, Kew, London

Newspapers and periodicals

Algemeen Handelsblad
Algemeen Indisch Dagblad
Amigoe di Curacao
Amsterdamsch Dagblad
Arnhemse Courant
Berjuang
Bintang Oemoem
De Heerenveensche Koerier
De Indische Courant
Deli Courant
De Locomotief
De Maasbode
De Nieuwe Nederlander
De Nieuwsgier
De Sumatra Post
De Telegraaf
De Tijd
De Tijger. Weekblad van de Tijger-Brigade
De Volkskrant
De Vrije Pers
De Waarheid
De Zaanlander
Djawa Baroe
Free Press of India
Friesch Dagblad
Haluan
Helmondsch Dagblad
Het Dagblad
Het Midden
Het Nieuwsblad
Het Nieuwsblad voor Sumatra
Het Nieuws van den Dag voor Nederlandsch-Indië
Het Parool
Indian Daily Mail
Indische Courant voor Nederland
Istri Maandblad
Java-Bode
Kedaulatan Rakjat
Keng Po
Kita Sumatora Sinbun
Kerakjatan
Leeuwarder Courant
Leeuwarder Koerier
Limburgsch Dagblad
Makassaarsche Courant
Malaya Tribune
Masyarakat
Merdeka
Mimbar Oemoem
Minggu Pagi
Min Pao
Morning Tribune
Negara Baroe
Nieuwe Apeldoornsche Courant
Nieuwe Courant
Nieuwe Rotterdamsche Courant
NRC Handelsblad
Pandji Negara
Pantja Raja
Pelita Rakjat
Penjoeloeh
Pewarta Deli
Provinciale Drentsche en Asser Courant
Revolusioner
Semangat Merdeka
Sinar Baroe
Sinar Deli
Sin Po
Soeloeh Ambon
Soeloeh Merdeka
Soerabajasch Handelsblad
Suara Merdeka
Sumatra Sinbun
Telex
The Guardian
The Straits Times
The Voice of Free Indonesia
Tjinpo
Trouw
Twentsche Courant
Vrij Nederland
Warta Indonesia
Waspada

Websites

detikNews
JPNN.com
Kompas TV
TV One

References

Abduh, Muhammad et al., *Sejarah Perlawanan Terhadap Imperialisme dan Kolonialisme di Sulawesi Selatan* (Jakarta 1985).

Abdullah, T. (ed.), *The Heartbeat of the Indonesian Revolution* (Jakarta 1997).

Abdullah, T., *Indonesia: Towards Democracy* (Singapore 2009).

Abdullah, Taufik and A.B. Lapian (eds.), *Indonesia dalam Arus Sejarah. Jilid 7* (Jakarta 2012).

Abdullah, T. and S. Siddique, *Islam and Society in Southeast Asia* (Singapore 1986).

Adams, Cindy, *Bung Karno: Penyambung Lidah Rakyat Indonesia* (Jakarta 1966).

Aditya, Wisnu Rega, 'Revolusi Sosial di Kota Depok 1945-1955' (Master's thesis; Universitas Negeri Semarang 2017).

Agung, Ide Anak Agung Gde, *"Renville" als keerpunt in de Nederlands-Indonesische onderhandelingen* (Alphen aan de Rijn 1980).

Agung, Ide Anak Agung Gde, *Dari Negara Indonesia Timur ke Republik Indonesia Serikat* (Yogyakarta 1985).

Agung, Ide Anak Agung Gde, *From the Formation of the State of East Indonesia towards the Establishment of the United States of Indonesia* (Jakarta 1996).

Ahmad, Taufik, 'Genealogi Konflik Agraria di Polongbangkeng, Takalar', *Masyarakat Indonesia* 40:2 (2014) 145-158.

Alers, H.J.H., *Om een rode of groene merdeka. 10 jaren binnenlandse politiek Indonesië 1943-1953* (Eindhoven 1956).

Alfian, T. Ibrahim et al., *Revolusi Kemerdekaan Indonesia di Aceh 1945-1949* (Banda Aceh 1982).

Alfirdaus, Laila Kholid, Eric Hiariej, and Farsiajana Adeney-Risakotta, 'The Position of Minang-Chinese Relationship in the History of Inter-Ethnic Group Relations in Padang, West Sumatra', *Humaniora* (2016) 83-84.

Ali, Abdullah et al., *Sejarah Perjuangan Rakyat Aceh dalam Perang Kemerdekaan 1945-1949* (Banda Aceh 1984).

Amin, S.M., *Sekitar Peristiwa Berdarah di Atjeh* (Jakarta 1956).

Amin, S.M., *Kenang-Kenangan dari Masa Lampau* (Jakarta 1978).

Amura, *Sejarah Revolusi Kemerdekaan di Minangkabau 1945-1950* (Jakarta 1979).

Andaya, Leonard Y., *The Heritage of Arung Palakka: A History of South Sulawesi (Celebes) in the Seventeenth Century* (Dordrecht 2013).

Anderson, Benedict R.O'G., 'Cultural Factors in the Indonesian Revolution', *Asia* 20 (1971) 48-65.

Anderson, Benedict R.O'G., *Java in a Time of Revolution: Occupation and Resistance 1944-1946* (Ithaca NY 1972).

Anderson, Benedict R.O'G., *Revoloesi Pemoeda: Pendudukan Jepang dan Perlawanan di Jawa 1944-1946* (Jakarta 1988).

Anderson, B.R.O'G., *Java in a Time of Revolution: Occupation and Resistance, 1944-1946* (Jakarta, Sheffield 2006).

Anderson, David Charles, 'The Military Aspects of the Madiun Affair', *Indonesia* 21 (1976) 1-63. http://dx.doi.org/https://doi.org/10.2307/3350956.

Angenent, P.H., *De vorstenlandsche waterschapsordonnantie toegelicht* (PhD thesis; Universiteit Leiden 1933).

Anggaran Dasar dan Anggaran Rumah Tangga Himpunan Tjinta Teman Padang (Padang 1987).

Annual Report of the Secretary-General on the Work of the Organization 1 July 1947-30 June, Supplement No. 1 (A/565) (New York 1948).

Anwar, C., 'Dipo Negoro', *The Voice of the Night: Complete Poetry and Prose of Chairil Anwar*, transl. by Burton Raffel (Athens 1993 [1970]).

Anwar, Rosihan, *Sejarah Kecil, Petite Histoire Indonesia. Jilid 2* (Jakarta 2009).

Anwar, Rosihan, *Napak Tilas ke Belanda: 60 Tahun Perjalanan Wartawan KMB* (Jakarta 2010).

Anwar, Rosihan, *Sejarah Kecil, Petite Histoire Indonesia. Jilid 7: Kisah-Kisah Zaman Revolusi Kemerdekaan* (Jakarta 2015).

Appadurai, A., 'Dead Certainty: Ethnic Violence in the Era of Globalization', *Public Culture* 10:2 (1998) 225-247.

Arfah, Muhammad, Muhammad Amir, and Faisal, *Biografi Pahlawan Ranggong Dg. Romo, Panglima Lapris: Sebuah Biografi Perjuangan di Sulawesi Selatan* (Ujung Pandang 1991).

Arieffin, M. Sjamsoel, *Negara Madoera* (Sampang 1948).

Aritonang, Jan Sihar, *Sejarah Perjumpaan Kristen dan Islam di Indonesia* (Jakarta 2004).

Aritonang, J.S. and Karel Steenbrink, *A History of Christianity in Indonesia* (Leiden 2008).

Asnan, Gusti, et al., *Menteri Pendidikan dan Kebudayaan Republik Indonesia 1945-2018* (Jakarta 2018).

Astuti, Meta Sekar Puji, *Apakah Mereka Mata-Mata?: Orang-Orang Jepang di Indonesia (1868-1942)* (Yogyakarta 2008).

Aswar, Sativa Sutan, *Antakesuma Suji dalam Adat Minangkabau* (Jakarta 1999).

Azis, Muhammad Abdul, *Japan's Colonialism in Indonesia* (The Hague 1955).

Bachtiar, I. (ed.), *Catatan Jendral Pranoto Reksosamodra: Dari Boedo Oetomo sampai Nirbaya* (Jakarta 2014).

Backer, Kristen Williams, 'Kultur-Terror: The Composite Monster in Nazi Visual Propaganda', in: Niall Scott (ed.), *Monsters and the Monstrous: Myths and Metaphors of Enduring Evil* (Amsterdam, New York 2007).

Badan Musyawarah Museum, *Yogya Benteng Proklamasi* (Yogyakarta 1985).

Bambang Purwanto, *Praktik Kewarganegaraan di Indonesia dalam Perspektif Historiografi* (Yogyakarta 2019).

Bank, Jan (ed.) *De excessennota: Nota betreffende het archiefonderzoek naar de gegevens omtrent excessen in Indonesië begaan door Nederlandse militairen in de periode 1945-1950* (The Hague 1996).

Basset, D.K., 'The "Amboyna Massacre" of 1623', *Journal of Southeast Asian History* 1:2 (1960) 1-19.

Basundoro, Purnawan, *Dua Kota Tiga Zaman: Surabaya dan Malang sejak Kolonial sampai Kemerdekaan* (Yogyakarta 2009).

Beckett, Paul A., 'Algeria vs. Fanon: The Theory of Revolutionary Decolonization, and the Algerian Experience', *The Western Political Quarterly* 26:1 (1973) 5-27.

Beeman, Richard R., 'Review: Small Things Remembered: Writing the History of Everyday Life in Early America', *American Quaterly* 42:1 (1990) 108-115.

Benda, H.J., *The Crescent and Rising Sun: Indonesian Islam under Japanese Occupation, 1942-1945* (The Hague, Bandung 1958).

Benda, Harry J., 'The Pattern of Administrative Reforms in the Closing Years of Dutch Rule in Indonesia', *The Journal of Asian Studies* 25:4 (1966) 589-605.

Berge, T. van den, *H.J. van Mook, 1894-1965: Een vrij en gelukkig Indonesië* (Bussum 2014).

Bhabha, Homi K., 'Of Mimicry and Man: The Ambivalence of Colonial Discourse', in: Frederick Cooper and Ann Laura Stoler (eds.), *Tensions of Empire: Colonial Culture in a Bourgeois World* (Oakland 1997) 152-60.

Bhattacharya, Jayati, *Beyond the Myth: Indian Business Communities in Singapore* (Singapore 2011).

Biro Sejarah PRIMA, *Medan Area Mengisi Proklamasi* (Medan 1976).

Blackburn, Susan, *Kongres Perempuan Pertama* (Jakarta 2007).

Bleeker, P., 'Nieuwe bijdragen tot de kennis der bevolkingstatistiek van Java', *Bijdragen tot de Taal-, Land- en Volkenkunde van Nederlandsch-Indië* 16:3-4 (1869) 447-637.

Bloembergen, M., *De geschiedenis van de politie in Nederlands-Indië: Uit zorg en angst* (Amsterdam 2009).

Blok, Anton, 'The Peasant and the Brigand: Social Banditry Reconsidered', *Comparative Studies in Society and History* 14:4 (1972) 494-503.

Bongenaar, K.E.M., *De ontwikkeling van het zelfbesturend landschap in Nederlandsch-Indië (1935-1999)* (Zutphen 2005).

H. Bos and Stichting Cultuurgeschiedenis van de Nederlanders Overzee, Nederlanders in Japanse kampen: tekeningen en voorwerpen gemaakt in burgerinternerings- en krijgsgevangenenkampen 1942-1945: een tentoonstelling (Amstelveen 1975).

Bosra, Mustari, *Laskar Lipan Bajeng: Perjumpaan Agama dan Nasionalisme dalam Perjuangan Bangsa Indonesia* (Makassar 2009).

Bouma, Tjalling, *Naar een federaal Indonesië: De geschiedenis van de totstandkoming van de Republiek der Verenigde Staten van Indonesië en de bijdrage van federale Indonesische nationalisten aan de Indonesische onafhankelijkheid, 1917-1949* (PhD thesis; VU Amsterdam 2020).

Bouma, Tjalling, *Naar een federaal Indonesië: De geschiedenis van de totstandkoming van de Republiek der Verenigde Staten van Indonesië en de bijdrage van federale Indonesische nationalisten aan de Indonesische onafhankelijkheid 1917-1949* (Hilversum 2020).

Bouman, B., *Ieder voor zich en de Republiek voor ons allen: De logistiek achter de Indonesische revolutie 1945-1950* (Amsterdam 2006).

Brekel, M., *Massaexecuties op Sulawesi: Hoe Nederland wegkwam met moord in Indonesië* (Zutphen 2017).

Breman, Jan, *Menjinakkan Sang Kuli: Politik Kolonial, Tuan Kebun dan Kuli di Sumatra Timur pada Awal Abad Ke-20* (Jakarta 1997).

Brok, M.F.A., 'Geschiedenis van een brigade', in: M. Brouwer et al. (eds.), *Tussen sawahs en bergen: Het leven van de soldaat in de Tijger-brigade* (Semarang 1948) 1-38.

Brommer, B. et al. (eds.), *Semarang. Beeld van een stad* (Purmerend 1995).

Budi, Langgeng Sulistyono, 'Permasalahan Sosial Perkotaan pada Periode Revolusi: Kriminalitas di Yogyakarta 1947-1948', *Lembaran Sejarah* 1:2 (1998).

Budiana, O.R., 'Cerita Penting di Tanggal 15 Agustus bagi Indonesia, Ada Apa Ya?', https://www.beritabaik.id/teman-baik/pr-3782642905/cerita-penting-di-tanggal-15-agustus-bagi-indonesia-ada-apa-ya (accessed 27 January 2021).

Budiana, R., 'Perempuan di Balik Proklamasi: Kemerdekaan Bukan Cuma Bilik Lelaki'. https://tirto.id/perempuan-di-balik-proklamasi-kemerdekaan-bukan-cuma-milik-lelaki-fYmu (accessed 27 January 2021).

Budiarti, H., 'Taking and Returning Objects in a Colonial Context: Tracing the Collections Acquired during the Bone-Gowa Military Expeditions', in: P.J. ter Keurs (ed.), *Colonial Collections Revisited* (Leiden 2007) 125-144.

Buiskool, Dirk A., 'Medan, A Plantation City on the East Coast of Sumatra 1870-1942', in: Dirk A. Buiskool, *Prominent Chinese during the Rise of a Colonial City Medan 1890-1942* (PhD thesis in history; Universiteit Utrecht 2019).

Buiskool, Dirk Aedsge, *Prominent Chinese during the Rise of a Colonial City: Medan 1890-1942* (PhD thesis in history; Universiteit Utrecht 2019).

Bultmann, D., 'S-21 as a Liminal Power Regime: Violently Othering Khmer Bodies into Vietnamese Minds', *Genocide Studies and Prevention: An International Journal* 14:3 (2020) 11-26.

Burgers, H., *De garoeda en de ooievaar. Indonesië van kolonie tot nationale staat* (Leiden 2011).

Busselaar, J.F.M., *Belevenissen van een Landstorm-soldaat gedurende en na afloop van de Tweede Wereldoorlog* (Wateringen 1955).

Bussemaker, H.T., *Bersiap! Opstand in het paradijs: De Bersiap-periode op Java en Sumatra 1945-1946* (Zutphen 2005).

Bussemaker, H.Th., *Na de oorlog: Van Bersiap tot Linggarjati* (The Hague 2008).

Butler, Judith, 'Performative Acts and Gender Constitution: An Essay in Phenomenology and Feminist Theory', *Theatre Journal* 40:4 (1988) 519-531.

Butler, Judith, *Gender Trouble. Feminism and the Subversion of Identity* (London 1990).

Captain, Esther and Onno Sinke, *Het geluid van geweld: Bersiap en de dynamiek van geweld tijdens de eerste fase van de Indonesische revolutie, 1945-1946* (Amsterdam 2022).

Castles, Lance, *Profil Etnik Jakarta* (Jakarta 1972).

Chalik, H. et al., *Sejarah Perlawanan terhadap Imperialisme dan Kolonialisme di Daerah Sulawesi Tenggara* (Jakarta 1983).

Chandler, Billy Jaynes, *The Bandit King: Lampiao of Brazil* (College Station 1978).

Chaniago, J.R., *Menuju Negara Kesatuan Republik Indonesia: Peranan Pemimpin Lokal dalam Dinamika Politik di Sulawesi Selatan dan Sumatera Timur 1950* (PhD thesis; Universitas Gadjah Mada, Yogyakarta 2002).

Chaterjee, Partha, *The Nation and its Fragments: Colonial and Postcolonial Histories* (Princeton 1974).

Cheng, Yinghong, *Creating the "New Man": From Enlightenment Ideals to Socialist Memories* (Honolulu 2009).

Cheong, Y.M., *H.J. van Mook and Indonesian Independence: A Study of His Role in Dutch-Indonesian Relations, 1945-48* (The Hague 1982).

Cheong, Yong Mung, *The Indonesian Revolution and Singapore Connection 1945-1949* (Leiden 2003).

Clodfelter, Mark, 'Aiming to Break Will: America's World War II Bombing of German Morale and Its Ramifications', *The Journal of Strategic Studies* 33:3 (2010) 401-435. http://dx.doi.org/10.1080/01402390903189436.

Clulow, Adam, '"Great Help from Japan": The Dutch East India Company's Experiment with Japanese Soldiers', in: Adam Clulow and Tristan Mostert (eds.), *The Dutch and English East India Companies: Diplomacy, Trade and Violence in Early Modern Asia* (Amsterdam 2018) 179-210.

Coast, John, *Recruit to Revolution. Adventure and Politics in Indonesia* (London 1952).

Collins, R., *Violence: A Micro-Sociological Theory* (Princeton 2008).

Colombijn, Freek, *Poco-Poco (Kota) Padang: Sejarah Sebuah Kota di Indonesia pada Abad Ke-20 dan Penggunaan Ruang* (Yogyakarta 2006).

Colombijn, Freek, *Under Construction: The Politics of Urban Space and Housing during the Decolonization of Indonesia, 1930-1950* (Leiden 2010).

Colombijn, Freek et al. (eds.), *Kota Lama, Kota Baru: Sejarah Kota-Kota di Indonesia sebelum dan setelah Kemerdekaan* (Yogyakarta 2005).

Cooper, F., *Decolonization and African Society: The Labour Question in French and British Africa* (Cambridge 1996).

Coppel, Charles A., *Indonesian Chinese in Crisis* (Kuala Lumpur 1983).

Cribb, Robert, 'Political Dimensions of the Currency Question 1945-1947', *Indonesia* 31 (1981) 113-136.

Cribb, R., *Gangsters and Revolutionaries: The Jakarta People's Militia and the Indonesian Revolution 1945-1949* (Honolulu 1991).

Cribb, R., 'Military Strategy in the Indonesian Revolution: Nasution's Concept of "Total People's War" in Theory and Practice', *War & Society* 19:2 (2001) 143-154.

Cribb, Robert, *Gangsters and Revolutionaries: The Jakarta People's Militia and the Indonesian Revolution, 1945-1949* (Jakarta 2008).

Cribb, Robert, *Gangsters and Revolutionaries: The Jakarta People's Militia and the Indonesian Revolution, 1945-1949* (Singapore 2009).

Cribb, Robert, *Para Jago dan Kaum Revolusioner Jakarta, 1945-1949* (Jakarta 2010).

Cui Yisheng, 'Duli Chuqi de Bao'andui Shijian', *Guo Ji Ri Bao*, 27 June 2011 (serial, 27 June-6 July 2011).

Cummings, William, *Making Blood White: Historical Transformations in Early Modern Makassar* (Honolulu 2002).

Cummings, William, *A Chain of Kings: The Makassarese Chronicles of Gowa and Talloq* (Leiden, Boston 2007).

Daeng Rapi, H.A. Massiara, *Menyingkap Tabir Sejarah dan Budaya di Sulawesi Selatan* (Ujung Pandang, no year).

Dalidd, Moeslim et al., *Kotapradja Malang 50 Tahun* (Malang 1964).

D'Alpuget, Blanche, *Mediator: A Biography of Richard Kirby* (Melbourne 1977).

Dam, H. ten, 'Kerja Sama dan Struktur Masyarakat di Desa Cibodas', in: Sajogyo and Pujiwati Sajogyo (eds.), *Sosiologi Pedesaan. Kumpulan Bacaan Jilid 1* (Yogyakarta 1999) 108-128.

Darusman, Suryono, 'Arti Singapura dalam Revolusi Indonesia', in: Kustiniyati Mochtar (ed.), *Memoar Pejuang Republik Indonesia Seputar "Zaman Singapura" 1945-1950* (Jakarta 1992).

Darusman, Suryono, '"Operation Meriam Bee" Penyelundupan Senjata Terbesar', in: Kustiniyati Mochtar (ed.), *Memoar Pejuang Republik Indonesia Seputar "Zaman Singapura" 1945-1950* (Jakarta 1992).

Darwas, R., *Sejarah Perjuangan Kemerdekaan di Daerah TK II Kabupaten Barru* (Ujung Pandang 1990).

Daud, H.H. Riri Amin, *Biografi Pahlawan Ranggong Dg. Romo* (Ujung Pandang 1971).

Dehne, Harald, 'Have We Come Any Closer to Alltag? Everyday Reality and Workers' Lives as an Object of Historical Research in the German Democratic Republic', in: Alf Lüdtke (ed.), *The History of Everyday Life: Reconstructing Historical Experiences and Ways of Life* (Princeton NJ 1995) 116-148.
Dengel, Holk H., *Darul Islam – NII dan Kartosuwirjo: "Angan-Angan yang Gagal"* (Jakarta 2011).
Departement van Economische Zaken, *De economische toestand van Indonesië: Medio 1949* (Batavia 1949).
Departement van Economische Zaken, *De economische toestand van Indonesië: Voorjaar 1949* (Batavia 1949).
Departement van Landbouw, Nijverheid en Handel, *Volkstelling 1930. Voorlopige uitkomsten 2e gedeelte* (Batavia 1931).
Department of Information Republic of Indonesia, *The Indonesian Women's Movement: A Chronological Survey of the Women's Movement in Indonesia* (Jakarta 1968).
Department of the Army, *Logistics Supply and Management* (Washington DC 1958).
Desjarlais, R., and A. Kleinman, 'Violence and Demoralization in the New World Disorder', *Anthropology Today* 10:5 (1994) 9-12.
Dias, Nélia, 'Exploring the Senses and Exploiting the Land. Railroads, Bodies and Measurement in Nineteenth-Century French Colonies', in: T. Bennett and P. Joyce (eds.), *Material Powers. Cultural Studies, History and the Material Turn* (London 2010) 171-198.
Dijk, C. van, *Rebellion under the Banner of Islam: The Darul Islam in Indonesia* (The Hague 1981).
Dimyati, 'Djokdja Diduduki Chaos', in: H.B. Jassin (ed.), *Gema Tanah Air: Prosa dan Puisi 1942-1948* (Jakarta 1959).
Djajadiningrat, Roswita T., *Pengalamanku di Daerah Pertempuran Malang Selatan* (Jakarta 1974).
Djarwadi, Radik, *Naskah Sedjarah "CORPS HASANUDDIN" Pradjurit Tempur dan Pembangunan* (Ujung Pandang, no year).
Djarwadi, R. et al., *"Corps Hasanuddin": Pradjurit Tempur dan Pembangunan* (no place 1972).
Djawatan Penerangan Propinsi Jawa Tengah, *Propinsi Djawa-Tengah* (Semarang 1953) 48-55.
Djojohadikoesomo, Soemitro, *Beberapa Soal Keoeangan* (Jakarta 1947).
Dobbin, Christine, *Kebangkitan Islam dalam Ekonomi Petani yang sedang Berubah: Sumatera Tengah 1784-1847* (Jakarta 1992).
Dobbin, Christine, 'The Search for Women in Indonesian History', in: Ailsa Thomson Zainuddin (ed.), *Kartini Centenary: Indonesian Women Then and Now* (Melbourne 1996).
Doel, Wim van den,'The Dutch Empire. An Essential Part of World History', *Bijdragen en Mededelingen Betreffende de Geschiedenis der Nederlanden* 125:2/3 (2010) 179-209.
Doorn, J.A.A. van, 'Een en ander over de grensfunctie van de status-quo-lijn in Midden-Java', *Mensch en Maatschappij* 24:2 (1949) 125-128.
Doorn, J.A.A. van and W.J. Hendrix, 'De planters belegerd. De positie van Europese planters tussen Nederlandse steun en Indonesisch verzet', in: G. Teitler and P.M.H. Groen (eds.), *De Politionele Acties* (Amsterdam 1986) 44-72.
Drooglever, J., 'The *Komite Nasional Indonesia Pusat* and Internal Politics in the Republic of Indonesia', in: T. Abdullah (ed.), *The Heartbeat of the Indonesian Revolution* (Jakarta 1997) 149-180.
Dulm, J.F. van, *Geïllustreerde atlas van de Japanse kampen in Nederlands Indië, 1942-1945. Deel I* (Viella 2000).
Dulm, J. van et al., *Geïllustreerde atlas van de Japanse kampen in Nederlands-Indië 1942-1945. Deel II (supplement)* (Purmerend 2002).
Eckhardt, William, 'Making and Breaking Enemy Images', *Peace Research* 21:4 (1989) 87-95.
Effendy, Ridwan, *I Tolok: Studi Hubungan Antar Teks* (Makassar 2005).
Eickhoff, M., 'Weggestreept verleden? Nederlandse historici en het Rawagededebat', *Groniek Historisch Tijdschrift* 194 (2012) 53-67.
Eickhoff, M. et al., 'The Memory Landscapes of "1965" in Semarang', *Journal of Genocide Research* 19:4 (2017) 530-550.
Ekajadi, E., 'Paguyuban Pasundan: A Sundanese Revival (1913-1918), *Journal of Asian and African Studies*

66 (2003) 21-55.
Elkins, C., *Britain's Gulag: The Brutal End of Empire in Kenya* (London 2009).
Elsbree, Willard H., *Japan's Role in Southeast Asian Nationalist Movements, 1940 to 1945* (Cambridge MA 1953).
Enar, Fatimah et al., *Sumatera Barat 1945-1949* (Padang 1978).
Eng, P. van der, 'Food for Growth: Trends in Indonesia's Food Supply, 1880-1995', *The Journal of Interdisciplinary History* 30:4 (2000) 591-616.
Erniwati, *Asap Hio di Ranah Minang: Komunitas Tionghoa di Sumatera Barat* (Yogyakarta 2007).
Erniwati, 'Pariaman (Saat) Tionghoa Pariaman', in: Budi Susanto (ed.), *Masih (Kah) Indonesia* (Yogyakarta 2007) 269-283.
Erniwati, *Cina Padang dalam Dinamika Masyarakat Minangkabau: Dari Revolusi sampai Reformasi* (PhD thesis; Jakarta 2011).
Erniwati, *140 Tahun Heng Beng Tong: Sejarah Perkumpulan Tionghoa 1876-2016* (Depok 2016).
Erwantoro, Heru, 'Etnis Betawi: Kajian Historis', *Patanjala* 6:1 (2014) 1-16.
Eryono, A., *Wanita Indonesia* (Yogyakarta 1975).
Farid, Hilmar, 'Dealing with the Legacies of a Violent Past', in: G. Oostindie, B. Schoenmaker and F. van Vree (eds.), *Beyond the Pale: Dutch Extreme Violence in the Indonesian War of Independence, 1945-1949* (Amsterdam 2022) 472-485.
Farram, Steven, 'Wage War Against Beatle Music! Censorship and Music in Soekarno's Indonesia', *RIMA: Review of Indonesian and Malaysian Affairs* 41:2 (2007) 247-277.
Fashina, Oladipo, 'Frantz Fanon and the Ethical Justification of Anti-Colonial Violence', *Social Theory and Practice* 15:2 (1989) 179-212.
Fauziah, Siti Mahmudah Nur, 'Malioboro Tempo Doeloe: Sejarah Kehidupan Sehari-Hari 1890-1950' (Bachelor's thesis; 2018).
Feith, Herbert and Lance Castles (eds.), *Indonesian Political Thinking 1945-1965* (Ithaca NY 1970).
Fernandes, Bobby, 'Perkembangan Gereja-Gereja Wilayah Layanan Depok dan Cimanggis, 1948-1981 (Master's thesis; Universitas Indonesia, Jakarta 2008).
Firman, M., 'Konferensie Paccekke di Barru Tahun 1947' (Bachelor's thesis; Makassar State University 2019).
Formichi, C., *Islam and the Making of the Nation: Kartosuwiryo and Political Islam in 20th Century Indonesia* (Leiden 2012).
Frakking, R., 'Het middel erger dan de kwaal: De opkomst en ondergang van het Instituut der Ondernemingswachten, 1945-1950' (Master's thesis in history; Universiteit Utrecht 2011).
Frakking, R., *"Collaboration is a Delicate Concept": Alliance-Formation and the Colonial Defense of Indonesia and Malaysia, 1945-1957* (PhD thesis; European University Institute, Florence 2017).
Frakking, R., "Gathered on the Point of a Bayonet": The Negara Pasundan and the Colonial Defence of Indonesia, 1946-50', *International Historical Review* 39:1 (2017) 30-47.
Frakking, R., 'Independence or Death? Recruitment and Desertion during the Wars of Decolonization in Indonesia and Malaysia, ca. 1945-1960', in: G. Curless and M. Thomas (eds.), *Oxford Handbook Understanding Insurgencies* (Oxford 2022).
Frederick, William H., *Indonesian Urban Society in Transition: Surabaya 1926-1946* (PhD thesis; University of Hawaii, Honolulu/Ann Arbor, Michigan 1981).
Frederick, W., *Visions and Heat: The Making of the Indonesian Revolution* (Athens 1989).
Frederick, William, 'The Appearance of Revolution: Cloth, Uniform and Pemuda Style in East Java, 1945-1949', in: Henk Schulte Nordholt (ed.), *Outward Appearances: Dressing State and Society in Indonesia* (Leiden 1997) 199-248.
Gaharu, Sjamaun, 'Perebutan Kekuasaan dari Tangan Djepang', in: Komite Musjawarah Angkatan 45 Daerah Istimewa Atjeh (ed.), *Modal Revolusi 45* (Kutaraja 1960).
Games, Alison, 'Violence on the Fringes: Virginia (1622) and Amboyna (1623) Massacres', *History* 99:3 (2014) 505-529.

Geertz, Clifford, *Negara: The Theatre State in Nineteenth Century Bali* (Princeton 1980).
Goedhart, O.M., 'De inlandsche rechtsgemeenschappen in de onderafdeeling Takalar (1920)', in: *Adatrechtbundel XXXI* (The Hague 1928) 311-352.
Golubev, Alexey, 'The Western Observers and the Western Gaze in the Affective Management of Soviet Subjectivity', *Russian Social Science Review* 61:3-4 (2020) 251-280.
Gordon, M., *Extreme Violence and the "British Way": Colonial Warfare in Perak, Sierra Leone and Sudan* (London 2020).
Gouda, F. and T.W. Brocades Zaalberg, *American Visions of the Netherlands East Indies / Indonesia: U.S. Foreign Policy and Indonesian Nationalism, 1920-1949* (Amsterdam 2002).
Goudoever, W.A. van, *Malino maakt historie: Een overzichtelijke bewerking van notulen en tekstuele redevoeringen ter Conferentie van Malino 15-25 Juli 1946* (Batavia 1946).
Goudoever, W.A. van, *Konperensi Malino 1946. Ke Arah Pembentukan Negara Indonesia* Timur (Makassar 2018).
Gouw Giok Siong, *Warga Negara dan Orang Asing: Berikut Peraturan-Peraturan dan Tjontoh-Tjontoh* (Jakarta 1958).
Grave, Elizabeth E., *The Minangkabau Response to Dutch Colonial Role in the Nineteenth Century* (Singapore 2010) 83-84.
Gregory, Brad S., Review: 'Is Small Beautiful? Microhistory and the History of Everyday Life, History and Theory', *History and Theory* 38:1 (1999) 100-110.
Groen, P.M.H., 'Oprichting, functioneren en opheffing van de deelstaat Oost-Indonesië, 1946-1950' (doctoraalscriptie; Universiteit Utrecht 1979).
Groen, P.M.H., '"Patience and bluff": De bevrijding van de Nederlandse burgergeïnterneerden op Midden-Java (augustus-december 1945)', *Mededelingen van de Sectie Militaire Geschiedenis van de Landmachtstaf* 8 (1985) 91-154.
Groen, P.M.H., *Marsroutes en dwaalsporen: Het Nederlands militair-strategisch beleid in Indonesië 1945-1950* (The Hague 1991).
Guha, Ranajit, *Dominance without Hegemony: History and Power in Colonial India* (Cambridge 1997).
Gullace, Nicoletta F., 'Barbaric Anti-Modernism: Representations of the "Hun" in Britain, North America, Australia and Beyond', in: James Pearl (ed.), *Picture This: World War I Posters and Visual Culture* (Lincoln, London 2009) 61-78.
Gunawan, Ryadi, 'Jagoan dalam Revolusi Kita', *Prisma* 8 (1981) 41-51.
Gunawan, Ryadi, 'Dimensi-Dimensi Perjuangan Kaum Perempuan Indonesia dalam Perspektif Sejarah', in: Fauzie Ridjal et al. (eds.), *Dinamika Gerakan Perempuan di Indonesia* (Yogyakarta 1993) 99-106.
Gunawan, R. et al., *Sejarah Berita Proklamasi Kemerdekaan Indonesia* (Jakarta 2015).
Haar, B. ter and W. Moll, *Geschiedenis der Christelijke kerk in Nederlandsch Indië, deel II* (Amsterdam 1869).
Hadi, Syaiful et al., *70 Th Histori Masa Depan* (Jakarta 2015).
Hakim, Novianti Mariyatul, 'Bertahan Hidup dalam Masa yang Sulit: Kehidupan Sehari-Hari Masyarakat Tionghoa pada Masa Revolusi di Surabaya', *Jurnal Al-Qalam* 25:3 (2019) 549-560.
Hakimuddin, *Role of the Muslim League in Indian Politics from 1940-47* (doctoral dissertation in political science; Aligarh Muslim University 1990).
Hale, Chr., *Massacre in Malaya: Exposing Britain's My Lai* (Gloucester 2013).
Halimah, Suprayitno and Warjio, 'Revolusi di Tanah Alas: Peranan Masyarakat dalam Mempertahankan Kemerdekaan Indonesia Tahun 1945-1950', *Yupa: Historical Studies Journal* 4:2 (2020) 62-72.
Hamid, Duta Fikra Abdu, 'Poster Perjuangan pada Masa Revolusi Fisik di Indonesia Tahun 1945-1950' (Bachelor's thesis in history; Universitas Airlangga, Surabaya 2019).
Hamka, *Kenang-Kenangan Hidup* (Kuala Lumpur 1966).
Hamka, *Kenangan-Kenangan Hidup* (Jakarta 1974).
Han Bing Siong, *Geschiedenis van de vijfdaagse strijd in Semarang, 14-19 October 1945* (Rijswijk 1995).

Han Bing Siong, 'The Secret of Major Kido: The Battle of Semarang, 15-19 October 1945', *Bijdragen tot de Taal-, Land- en Volkenkunde* 152:3 (1996) 382-428.
Han Bing Siong, 'The Indonesian Need of Arms after the Proclamation of Independence', *Bijdragen tot de Taal-, Land- en Volkenkunde* 157:4 (2001) 799-830.
Harahap, Apriani, 'Voor Indiërs: Sejarah Kehidupan Sehari-Hari Orang India di Kota Medan pada Abad Ke-20' (Master's thesis in history; Universitas Gadjah Mada, Yogyakarta 2014).
Hardi, Etmi et al., *Gurita Revolusi: Peranan Tentara Semut dalam Revolusi di Sumatera Barat 1945-1949* (Padang 2001).
Hardi, Lasmidjah et al., *Sumbangsihku bagi Ibu Pertiwi: Kumpulan Pengalaman dan Pemikiran, Buku V* (Jakarta 1985).
Hardjowijono, Dharmono et al., *Replika Sejarah Perjuangan Rakyat Yogyakarta Jilid II* (Yogyakarta 1985).
Harinck, Christiaan, Nico van Horn, and Bart Luttikhuis, 'Wie telt de Indonesische doden?', *De Groene Amsterdammer* (2017) 12-15.
Harper, T.N., 'A Long View on the Great Asian War', in: D. Koh Wee Hock (ed.), *Legacies of World War II in South and East Asia* (Singapore 2007).
Harper, T., *Underground Asia: Global Revolutionaries and the Assault on Empire* (Bristol 2020).
Hartono, Noek, 'Bank Indonesia: Sejarah Lahir dan Pertumbuhannya' (no place no year).
Harvey, Barbara Sillars, *Tradition, Islam, and Rebellion: South Sulawesi 1950-1965* (PhD thesis; Cornell University, Ithaca NY 1974).
Harvey, Barbara S., 'South Sulawesi: Puppets and Patriots', in: Audrey R. Kahin (ed.), *Regional Dynamics of the Indonesian Revolution. Unity From Diversity* (Honolulu 1985) 207-325.
Hasselgren, Johan, *Rural Batak, Kings in Medan: The Development of Toba Batak Ethno-Religious Identity in Medan, Indonesia, 1912-1965* (Uppsala 2000).
Hatley, Barbara, 'Creating Culture for the New Nation South Sulawesi, 1950-1965', in: Jennifer Lindsay and Maya H.T Liem (eds.), *Heirs to World Culture: Being Indonesian, 1950-1965* (Leiden 2012).
Hatta, M., *Mendajung antara Dua Karang: Keterangan Pemerintah dimuka Sidang B.P.K.N.P. di Djokja pada Tahun 1948* (Yogyakarta 1951).
Hatta, Mohammad, *Kumpulan Karangan* (Djakarta 1953).
Hatta, Mohammad, *Mendajung antara Dua Karang* (Jakarta 1979).
Hatta, R. Mohammad, 'Uang Belanja Pemberian Sri Sultan Masih Tersimpan Sebagai Kenangan', in: Atmakusumah (ed.), *Tahta untuk Rakyat: Celah-Celah Kehidupan Sultan Hamengku Buwono IX* (Jakarta 1982).
Heidhues, M., 'Anti-Chinese Violence in Java during the Indonesian Revolution, 1945-49', *Journal of Genocide Research* 14:3-4 (2012) 381-401. http://dx.doi.org/10.1080/14623528.2012.719371.
Heidhues, M.S., 'Anti-Chinese Violence in Java during the Indonesian Revolution', in: B. Luttikhuis and D.A. Moses (eds.), *Colonial Counterinsurgency and Mass Violence. The Dutch Empire in Indonesia* (London 2014) 155-175.
Heijboer, Pierre, *Agresi Militer Belanda: Memperebutkan Pending Zambrut Sepanjang Katulistiwa, 1945-1949* (Jakarta 1998).
Heijmans-van Bruggen, Mariska, *De Japanse bezetting in dagboek: Buiten de kampen* (Amsterdam 2001).
Hidajat, Mochtar, 'Menjingkap Tabir Perdjuangan Dibawah Tanah dlm Kota Semarang', *Suara Merdeka* (1964).
Hidskes, Maarten, *Di Belanda Tak Seorang Pun Mempercayai Saya: Korban Metode Westerling di Sulawesi Selatan, 1946-1947* (Jakarta 2018).
Hobsbawm, Eric J., *Bandits* (Harmondsworth 1972).
Hoek, Anne-Lot, 'Jongens, laten we dit huis sparen', *Vrij Nederland*, 10 July 2012.
Hoek, A., 'De verzwegen moorden van Palembang', *Vrij Nederland*, 4 August 2017.
Hoek, A., *De strijd om Bali: Imperialisme, verzet en onafhankelijkheid 1846-1950* (Amsterdam 2021).
Hoen, P. 't, 'Guerillastrijd woedt op Bali', *Het Parool*, 12 August 1946.

Hoen, Pieter 't, *Terug uit Djogja* (no place 1946).
Horsten, H.W., *Saboteur, partizaan, stoottroeper* (Rotterdam 2004).
Houben, V., 'Repertoires of European Panic and Indigenous Recaptures in Late Colonial Indonesia', in: H. Ficher-Tiné (ed.), *Anxieties, Fear and Panic in Colonial Settings: Empires on the Verge of a Nervous Breakdown* (London 2016) 259-278.
Huang Hanqing, 'Mianlan Shi Huaqiao Bao'andui Wenti Shuping', in: North Sumatra Overseas Chinese Historical Association (ed.), *Yinni Subei Huaqiao Huaren Cangsang Suiyue / Seratus Tahun Pancaroba Etnis Tionghoa Sumatera Utara* (Hong Kong 2015) 747-759.
Hulst, W. 'De lotgevallen van Poncke Princen, deel 1: Deserteur in Indië', *NRC Handelsblad*, 14 September 1991.
Husain, Sarkawi B., 'Gerakan Buruh di Makassar, 1946-1955', in: Dias Pradadimara et al., (eds.), *Negara dan Masyarakat Sulawesi Selatan di Tahun 1950-an* (Yogyakarta 2014) 101-113.
Husein, Abu, 'H.R. Soekardi Komandan Resimen III/TKR Pejuang "The Convoy Battle"', *Majalah Veteran* 1:6 (2011) 40-43.
Husein, Ahmad, *Sejarah Perjuangan Kemerdekaan di Minangkabau/Riau 1945-1950 Jilid 1* (Jakarta 1978).
Husein, Ahmad et al., *Sejarah Perjuangan Kemerdekaan RI di Minangkabau/Riau 1945-1950* (Jakarta 1991).
Hussain, Abdullah, *Peristiwa Kemerdekaan di Aceh* (Jakarta 1990).
Ibrahim, Julianto, *Bandit dan Pejuang di Simpang Bengawan: Kriminalitas dan Kekerasan pada Masa Revolusi di Surakarta, 1945-1950* (Surakarta 2004).
Ibrahim, Julianto, *Opium dan Revolusi: Perdagangan Candu di Surakarta pada Masa Revolusi* (Yogyakarta 2013).
Ibrahimy, M. Nur El, *Mata Rantai yang Hilang: Dari Sejarah Perjuangan Kemerdekaan Indonesia di Aceh* (Jakarta 1996).
Idroes, Idrian, 'Riwayat Hidup Drs. H. Idrian Idroes M.S', *Memorial* (Provinsi Sumatera Barat no year).
Idroes, Idrian, 'Peranan BPPI di Padang Kota Perjuangan', *Memorial* (unpublished manuscript; no place 1997).
IJzereef, W., *De Zuid-Celebes affaire: Kapitein Westerling en de standrechtelijke executies* (Dieren 1984).
IJzereef, Wilhelmus Theodorus, *De wind en de bladeren: Hierarchie en autonomie in Bone en Polombangkeng, 1850-1950* (PhD thesis; Rijksuniversiteit Groningen 1994).
Ilahi, S., *Imperial Violence and the Path to Independence: India, Ireland and the Crisis of Empire* (London 2016).
Ilham, *Ruang, Masyarakat, dan Kebudayaan: Modernitas di Kota Makassar pada Abad Ke-20* (PhD thesis; Universitas Gadjah Mada, Yogyakarta 2019).
Imran, Amrin et al., *Perang dan Revolusi, Volume 6* (Jakarta 2012).
Inawati, Zainal Abidin A.W. and Rusdi Sufi, 'Peranan Husein Yusuf dalam Memperjuangkan Aceh Masa Revolusi Kemerdekaan Tahun 1945-1949', *Jurnal Mahasiswa Pendidikan Sejarah* 1 (2016) 110-119.
Irsyam, Tri Wahyuning M., *Berkembang dalam Bayang-Bayang Jakarta: Sejarah Depok 1950-1990-an* (Jakarta 2017).
Ismail, Emilyus E., *Pedagang Cina dan Kegiatan Jengek di Pelabuhan Bebas Sabang* (Banda Aceh 1979).
Ismuha, *Ulama Aceh dalam Perspektif Sejarah* (Jakarta 1976).
Jakobi, A.K., *Aceh Daerah Modal: Long March ke Medan Area* (Jakarta 1992).
Jalhay, S.M., *Allen zwijgen: Van merdeka en andjing-Nica tot APRA* (Purmerend 1983).
Joenoes, Marah, *Mr. H. ST. Moh. Rasjid: Perintis Kemerdekaan, Pejuang Tangguh, Berani dan Jujur* (Jakarta 2003).
Johari, Hendi, 'Gejolak Revolusi di Selatan Jakarta', *Historia* (2012).
Johnston, Mark, *Fighting the Enemy: Australian Soldiers and Their Adversaries in World War II* (Cambridge 2000).
Jong, J.J.P. de, *Diplomatie of strijd: Het Nederlandse beleid tegenover de Indonesische revolutie 1945-1947* (Amsterdam 1988).
Jong, J.J.P. de, *De terugtocht: Nederland en de dekolonisatie van Indonesië* (Amsterdam 2015).

Jonkman, J.A., *Nederland en Indonesië beide vrij: Memoires van mr. J.A. Jonkman* (Assen 1977).
Jowett, Garth S. and Victoria O'Donnell, *Propaganda & Persuasion. Sixth Edition* (Los Angeles 2015).
Juliani, Triatmi, 'Suka Duka di Masa Revolusi', in: Irna H.N. Hadi Soewito (ed.), *Seribu Wajah Wanita Pejuang dalam Kancah Revolusi '45, Buku Pertama* (Jakarta 1995).
Jumhari, 'Rakit yang Terombang-Ambing: Ambivalensi Sikap Politik dan Orientasi Ekonomi Orang China Palembang pada Masa Revolusi', *Analisis Sejarah* 9:2 (2020) 30-40.
Kahin, Audrey, 'Some Preliminary Observations on West Sumatra during the Revolution', *Indonesia* 18 (1974) 77-117.
Kahin, A. (ed.), *Regional Dynamics of the Indonesian Revolution* (Honolulu 1985).
Kahin, Audrey et al., *Perjuangan Kemerdekaan Sumatera Barat dalam Revolusi Nasional Indonesia 1945-1950* (Padang 1989).
Kahin, George McTurnan, *Nationalism and Revolution in Indonesia* (Ithaca NY 1952).
Kahin, George McTurnan, *Nationalism and Revolution* (Ithaca NY 1963).
Kahin, George McTurnan, *Nasionalisme & Revolusi Indonesia* (Depok 2013).
Kalyvas, S.N., *The Logic of Violence in Civil War* (Cambridge 2006).
Kamandoko, G., *Kisah 124 Pahlawan dan Pejuang Nusantara* (Yogyakarta 2006).
Karels, R.B., *Mijn aardse leven vol moeite en strijd: Raden Mas Noto Soeroto, Javaan, dichter, politicus, 1888-1951* (PhD thesis; Universiteit van Amsterdam 2008).
Kartodirdjo, Sartono, *The Peasants' Revolt of Banten in 1888: Its Conditions, Course and Sequel: A Case Study of Social Movements in Indonesia* (The Hague 1966).
Kartodirdjo, Sartono, 'Wajah Revolusi Indonesia Dipandang dari Perspektivisme Struktural', *Prisma* 10:8 (1981) 3-13.
Kartodirdjo, Sartono, *Pemikiran dan Perkembangan Historiografi Indonesia: Sebuah Alternatif* (Jakarta 1982).
Kartodirdjo, Sartono, *Elite dalam Perspektif Sejarah* (Jakarta 1983).
Kartodirdjo, Sartono, *Pendekatan Ilmu Sosial dalam Metodologi Sejarah* (Jakarta 1992).
Kartodirdjo, Sartono, 'Kisah Dua Kota Fragmen yang Teringat', in: Taufik Abdullah (ed.), *Denyut Nadi Revolusi* (Jakarta 1997).
Kartodirdjo, Sartono, *Pemikiran dan Perkembangan Historiografi Indonesia* (Yogyakarta 2014).
Kartodirdjo, Sartono et al. (eds.), *Sejarah Nasional Indonesia V* (Jakarta 1975).
Kartodirdjo, Sartono, Nugroho Notosusanto, dan Marwati Djoened Poesponegoro (eds.), *Sejarah Nasional Indonesia VI: Jaman Jepang dan Jaman Republik Indonesia* (Jakarta 1975).
Kawilarang, A.E., *Officier in dienst van de Republiek Indonesië (ervaringen 1942-1961)* (Breda 1994).
Kecik, Hario, *Pemikiran Militer 2* (Jakarta 2009).
Kementerian Penerangan, *Politiek manifest der Indonesische regering* (Djakarta 1946).
Kementerian Penerangan, *Presiden Kita P.J.M. Tjokorde Gde Rake Soekawati Melawat Dari Poelau ke Poelau di Negara Indonesia Timoer* (Bandung 1948).
Kementerian Penerangan, *Massacre in Macasser: It Happened This Time in South-Celebes Indonesia Anno Domini 1947* (Djakarta 1947).
Kementerian Penerangan, *Republik Indonesia: Daerah Istimewa Jogjakarta* (Djakarta 1953).
Kementerian Penerangan, *Republik Indonesia: Propinsi Djawa Barat* (Djakarta 1953).
Kementerian Penerangan, *Republik Indonesia: Propinsi Djawa Tengah* (Djakarta 1953).
Kementerian Penerangan, *Republik Indonesia: Propinsi Sulawesi* (Djakarta 1953).
Kementerian Penerangan, *Republik Indonesia: Propinsi Sumatera Tengah* (Djakarta 1953).
Kenichi Gotō, 'The Semarang Incident in the Context of Japanese-Indonesian Relations', in: Taufik Abdullah (ed.), *The Heartbeat of the Indonesian Revolution* (Jakarta 1997) 133-148.
Kenichi Gotō, *Tensions of Empire: Japan and Southeast Asia in the Colonial and Postcolonial World* (Singapore 2003).

Koerts, H.J., 'Amtenar BB di Sulawesi Selatan', in: S.L. van der Wal (ed.), *Kenang-Kenangan Pangrehpraja Belanda 1920-1942* (Jakarta 2001) 41-71.
Koerts, H.J., *De Vrijheid wordt duur gekocht: Zuid-Celebes na de Japanse capitulatie* (Rolde 1991).
Koetsier, H. and T. Koetsier-Korvinus (eds.), *Vijftig jaar "merdeka": In gesprek met Indonesiërs en Nederlanders* (Kampen 1995).
Komisariat Pemerintah Oemoem Borneo dan Timoer Besar, *Den Pasar Pontianak. Lahirnja Doea Negara* (no place no year).
Kong Yuanzhi, *Muslim Tionghoa, Cheng Ho* (Jakarta 2000).
Kooreman, P.J. 'De fei[telij]ke toestand in het go[uver]nemementsgebied van Celebes en onderhoorigheden', *De Indische Gids* (1883) 1, 171-204; 2, 358-385; 3, 637-656 (Amsterdam 1883).
Kuntowijoyo, *Metodologi Sejarah* (Yogyakarta 2003).
Kurasawa, Aiko, *Kuasa Jepang di Jawa: Perubahan Sosial di Pedesaan 1942-1945* (Depok 2015).
Kurasawa, Aiko, *Mobilisasi dan Kontrol: Studi Tentang Perubahan Sosial di Pedesaan Jawa, 1942-1945* (Jakarta 1993).
Kurasawa, Aiko and Nanke Mitsuko, *Bibliografi Beranotasi Sumber Sejarah Masa Pendudukan Jepang di Indonesia* (Jakarta 2018).
Kurniawati, 'Perang Cumbok dan Gerakan Tentara Perjuangan Rakyat (TPR) di Aceh (Desember 1945-Maret 1946)', *Jurnal Sejarah Lontar* 5:2 (2008) 20-35.
Kusno, Abidin, *Behind the Postcolonial: Architecture, Urban Space and Political Cultures in Indonesia* (London, New York 2000).
Kwisthout, Jan-Karel, *De Mardijkers van Tugu en Depok: Vrijmaking, bevrijding, en merdeka* (Zoetermeer 2018).
Langenberg, M. van, *National Revolution in North Sumatra: Sumatera Timur and Tapanuli 1942-1950* (no place 1976) 290-292.
Langhout, J., *Vijftig jaren economische staatkunde in Atjeh* (The Hague 1923).
Lasarus, 'Perjuangan Seniman Lukis pada Masa Revolusi Fisik di Yogyakarta (1945-1949)' (Bachelor's thesis in history; Universitas Sanata Dharma, Yogyakarta 2009).
Lefebvre, Henri, *The Production of Space* (London 1991).
Leirissa, R.Z., *Kekuatan Ketiga dalam Perjuangan Kemerdekaan Indonesia* (Jakarta 2006).
Lengah, Ismael, *Cerita untuk Anak Cucu: Keikutsertaan dalam Perang Kemerdekaan* (Sumatera Barat 1995)
Lessmeister, Irene V., *Between Colonialism and Cold War: The Indonesian War of Independence in World Politics, 1945-1949* (PhD thesis; Cornell University, Ithaca NY 2012).
Lev, Daniel S., 'Yap Tiam Hien and Aceh', *Indonesia* 82 (2006) 97-133.
Lewa, Tajudding Karaeng, *Polongbangkeng dalam Lintasan Sejarah Perjuangan Kemerdekaan Republik Indonesia* (Makassar 2007).
Lewin, Linda, 'Oral Tradition and Elite Myth: The Legend of Antonio Silvino in Brazilian Popular Culture', *Journal of American Lore* 2 (1979) 157-204.
Limbugau, Daud, 'Terbentuknya Wilayah Administrasi Pemerintah Hindia Belanda di Sulawesi Selatan 1924-1874' (thesis; Universitas Gadjah Mada, Yogyakarta 1982).
Limpach, Rémy, *De brandende kampongs van Generaal Spoor* (Amsterdam 2016).
Limpach, Rémy, *Kekerasan Ekstrem Belanda di Indonesia: Perang Kemerdekaan Indonesia 1945-1949* (Jakarta 2019).
Limpach, R. and P. Groen, 'De oorlog met de Republiek Indonesië 1945-1950/1962', in: P. Groen et al. (eds.), *Krijgsgeweld en kolonie. Opkomst en ondergang van Nederland als koloniale mogendheid 1916-2010* (Amsterdam 2021) 309-350.
Lindblad J., Thomas, 'The Outer Islands in the 19th Century: Contest for Periphery', in: Howard Dick et al. (eds.), *The Emergence of a National Economy: An Economic History of Indonesia, 1800-2000* (New South Wales, Honolulu 2002).

Locher-Scholten, E., *Women and the Colonial State: Essays on Gender and Modernity in the Netherlands Indies 1900-1942* (Amsterdam 2000).
Loderichs, M.A. et al., *Medan: Beeld van een stad* (Purmerend 1997).
Logemann, J.H.A., 'The Indonesian Problem', *Pacific Affairs* 20:1 (1947) 30-41.
Lohanda, M., *Growing Pains: The Chinese and the Dutch in Colonial Java, 1890-1942* (Jakarta 2002).
Lucas, Anton E., *Peristiwa Tiga Daerah Revolusi dalam Revolusi* (Jakarta 1989).
Lucas, Anton E., 'Wanita dalam Revolusi: Pengalaman selama Pendudukan dan Revolusi, 1942-1950', *Prisma* 5 (1996).
Lucas, Anton, *One Soul One Struggle: Peristiwa Tiga Daerah dalam Revolusi Indonesia* (Yogyakarta 2004).
Lüdtke, Alf, 'Introduction: What Is the History of Everyday Life and Who are Its Practitioners?', in: Alf Lüdtke (ed.), *The History of Everyday Life: Reconstructing Historical Experience and Ways of Life* (New Jersey 1995).
Luhukay, Hanock, 'Dari Makassar ke Ujung Pandang. Beberapa Catatan Perubahan Ketatanegaraan, Tata Pemerintahan dan Kehidupan Sosial Sebuah Kota Besar' (unpublished manuscript).
Lukisan Revolusi Rakjat Indonesia, 1945-1949 (Yogyakarta 1949).
Lukman, Alqis, 'Desonansi Memori Monumen Kolonial: Studi Kasus Tugu Cornelis Chastelein, Depok, Jawa Barat', *Amerta. Jurnal Penelitian dan Pengembangan Arkeologi* 38:1 (2020) 77-92.
Lusink, M.J., *Kroniek 1924* (The Hague 1925).
Luttikhuis, Bart, 'Beyond Race: Construction of "Europeanness" in Late Colonial Legal Practice in the Netherlands Indies', *European Review of History* 20:4 (2013) 539-559.
Luttikhuis, Bart and C.H.C. Harinck, 'Voorbij het koloniale perspectief: Indonesische bronnen en het onderzoek naar de oorlog in Indonesië, 1945-1949', *Low Countries Historical Review* 132:2 (2017) 51-76. http://dx.doi.org/https://doi.org/10.18352/bmgn-lchr.10340.
Maharani, Lutvia, 'Pegambilalihan Kota Salatiga dari Kekuasaan Belanda ke Pemerintah Republik Indonesia Tahun 1945-1950' (unpublished thesis; Universitas Semarang 2009).
Mangoensarkoro, Sri, *Pergerakan Wanita Indonesia* (Yogyakarta 1946).
Mangoensarkoro, S., 'Pendidikan Nasional', *30 Tahun Taman Siswa* (Yogyakarta 1956).
Mani, A., 'Indian in North Sumatra', in: K.S. Sandhu and A. Mani (eds.), *Indian Communities in Southeast Asia* (Singapore 1993) 57.
Mani, A., 'Sikhs in Multi-Ethnic Indonesia', in: Shamsul A.B. and Arunajeet Kaur (eds.), *Sikhs in Southeast Asia: Negotiating an Identity* (Singapore 2011).
Manus, MPB et al., *Tokoh-Tokoh Badan Penyelidikan Usaha-Usaha Persiapan Kemerdekaan Indonesia II* (Jakarta 1993).
Mao Tse-tung, *On Protracted Warfare*, lecture delivered at the Yenan Association for the Study of the War of Resistance against Japan, May 1938.
Mappangara, Suriadi et al., *Pergolakan di Sulawesi Selatan: Studi Kasus Konferensi Paccekke 1945-1947* (Barru 2007).
Margana, Sri et al., *Gelora di Tanah Raja: Yogyakarta pada Masa Revolusi 1945-1949* (Yogyakarta 2017).
Margana, Sri et al. *Tahta Tanah Raja* (Yogyakarta 2018).
Margana, Sri et al., *Serangan Umum 1 Maret 1949* (Yogyakarta 2019).
Margana, Sri et al., *Serangan Umum 1 Maret 1949 sebagai Hari Nasional Penegakan Kedaulatan Negara* (Yogyakarta 2022).
Marlita, Tita and E. Kristi Poerwandari, 'Pergerakan Perempuan Indonesia 1928-1965', in: Elizabeth Kristi Poerwandari and Rahayu Surtiati Hidayat (eds.), *Perempuan Indonesia dalam Masyarakat yang Tengah Berubah* (Jakarta 2000).
Martha, A.G., Ch. Wibisono, and Y. Anwar, *Pemuda Indonesia dalam Dimensi Sejarah Perjuangan Bangsa* (Jakarta 1984).
Maryetti et al., *Peranan Kaum Wanita dalam Perjuangan Kemerdekaan di Front Timur Kota Padang 1945-*

1950 (Padang 1993).
Marzali, Amri, 'Krisis Identitas pada Orang Depok Asli', *Berita Antropologi* 22 (1975) 55-74.
Masita, 'Eliminasi Orang-Orang Pro NICA di Palopo dan Sekitarnya 1946-1950' (Bachelor's thesis; Universitas Hasanuddin, Makassar 2017).
Matondang, H.M. Victor (ed.), *Percakapan dengan Dr. T.B. Simatupang* (Jakarta 1995).
Mattata, S. Daeng, *Luwu dalam Revolusi* (Ujung Pandang 1967).
Mayudin, Saifuddin, *Anna Amartya Dharma D. Kumarasamy (D.K): Biografi* (Medan 2014).
Mbembe, A., *Necropolitics*, transl. by S. Cochran (Durham 2019).
McGregor, K., *History in Uniform: Military Ideology and the Construction of Indonesia's Past* (Honolulu, Singapore 2007).
McMillan, R., *The British Occupation of Indonesia 1945-1946. Britain, the Netherlands and the Indonesian Revolution* (London, New York 2005).
McVey, Ruth, 'The Post-Revolutionary Transformation of the Indonesian Army', *Indonesia* 11 (April 1971) 131-176. http://dx.doi.org/https://doi.org/10.2307/3350748.
McVey, Ruth, 'The Post-Revolutionary Transformation of the Indonesian Army: Part II', *Indonesia* 13 (April-1972) 147-181. https://doi.org/10.2307/3350685.
Meteray, Bernarda, 'Berita Proklamasi di Maluku', in: Jajat Burhanuddin and Amurwani Dwi Lestariningsih (eds.), *Sejarah Berita Proklamasi di Indonesia* (Jakarta 2015).
Miller, D.M.O., 'A Handful of Rice, Logistic in the Viet Minh Campaign', *The Army Quarterly and Defence Journal* 100:1 (1970) 105-115.
Miyamoto, Shizuo, 'Army Problems in Java after the Surrender', in: A. Reid and Oki Akira (eds.), *The Japanese Experience in Indonesia: Selected Memoirs of 1942-1945* (Athens 1986) 325-340.
Moeljati, 'Dari Cakra hingga Membantu Tentara', in: Irna H.N. Hadi Soewito (ed.), *Seribu Wajah Wanita Pejuang dalam Kancah Revolusi '45, Buku Kedua* (Jakarta 1998).
Moe'tamar Denpasar Mentjiptakan Negara Indonesia Timoer (Makassar no year).
Mook, H.J. van, *The Stakes of Democracy in South-East Asia* (London 2015).
Mooney, J. (ed.), *Dictionary of American Naval Fighting Ships* VI (Washington 1976).
Moor, J.A. de, 'Het Korps Speciale Troepen: Tussen marechaussee-formule en politionele actie', in: G. Teitler and P.M.H. Groen (eds.), *De Politionele Acties* (Amsterdam 1987).
Moor, J.A. de, *Westerling's oorlog: Indonesië 1945-1950; De geschiedenis van de commando's en parachutisten in Nederlands-Indië 1945-1950* (Amsterdam 1999).
Moor, J. de, *Generaal Spoor: Triomf en tragiek van een legercommandant* (Amsterdam 2011).
Moore, Colin, *Propaganda Prints: A History of Art in the Service of Social and Political Change* (London 2010).
Moses, A.D., *The Problems of Genocide: Permanent Security and the Language of Transgression* (Cambridge 2021).
Mountbatten, Earl Louis, *Post Surrender Tasks: Section E of the Report to the Combined Chiefs of Staff by the Supreme Allied Commander South East Asia, 1943-1945* (London 1969).
Mourik, Anne van and Thijs Bouwknegt, 'The Problems of Genocide', *NIOD Rewind Podcast*, Episode 14, with Dirk Moses (2021).
Mrázek, Rudolf, *Engineers of Happyland: Technology and Nationalism in a Colony* (Princeton 2002).
Muhsin Z., Mumuh (ed.), *Masa Pendudukan Jepang hingga Masa Orde Lama* (Depok 2013).
Murakami, N., 'The Japanese at Batavia in the XVIIth Century', *Monumenta Nipponica* 2:2 (1939) 355-373.
Murti, Fahriza and Triyanto, 'Adaptasi Budaya Etnis Tionghoa di Meulaboh Aceh Barat (Studi: Masyarakat Tionghoa Non-Muslim)', *Community* 4:1 (2018) 123-139.
Muttalib, Jang A. and Sudjarwo, 'Gelandangan dalam Kancah Revolusi', in: Aswab Mahasin (ed.), *Gelandangan Pandangan Ilmuwan Sosial* (Jakarta 1984) 15-34.
Nasrun, A., *Butir-Butir Berceceran: Sepanjang Jalan Revolusi* (Padang 1979).

Nasution, A.H., *Fundamentals in Guerilla Warfare and the Indonesian Defence System Past and Future* (no place 1953).
Nasution, A.H., *The Indonesian National Army, Book 1* (Jakarta 1956).
Nasution, A.H., *The Indonesian National Army* (New York 1960).
Nasution, A.H., *Tentara Nasional Indonesia 1* (Jakarta 1963).
Nasution, Abdul Haris, *Fundamentals of Guerrilla Warfare* (Singapore 1965).
Nasution, Abdul Haris, *Tentara Nasional Indonesia.* 3 vols. (Bandung 1968).
Nasution, Abdul Haris, *Sekitar Perang Kemerdekaan Indonesia.* 11 vols. (Bandung 1977-1979).
Nasution, A.H., *Sekitar Perang Kemerdekaan Indonesia. Jilid 1: Proklamasi* (Jakarta 1977).
Nasution, A.H., *Sekitar Perang Kemerdekaan Indonesia. Jilid 2: Diplomasi atau Bertempur* (Bandung 1977).
Nasution, A.H., *Sekitar Perang Kemerdekaan Indonesia. Jilid 3* (Bandung 1977).
Nasution, A.H., *Sekitar Perang Kemerdekaan Indonesia. Jilid 4: Periode Linggarjati* (Bandung 1978).
Nasution, A.H., *Sekitar Perang Kemerdekaan Indonesia. Jilid 9: Agresi Militer Belanda II* (Jakarta 1979).
Nasution, A.H., *Sekitar Perang Kemerdekaan Indonesia. Jilid 10: Perang Gerilya Semesta II* (Bandung 1979).
Newsinger, John, 'A Forgotten War: British Intervention in Indonesia 1945-1946', *Race & Class* 30:4 (1989) 51-66.
Nio Joe Lan, *Dalem Tawanan Djepang* (Jakarta 2008).
Notosusanto, Nugroho, 'Angkatan Bersenjata dalam Percaturan Politik di Indonesia', *Prisma* 8 (1979) 19-31.
Nurhajarini, Dwi Ratna and Albiladiyah Al Ilmy, *Yogyakarta, dari Hutan Beringin ke Ibukota Daerah Istimewa* (Yogyakarta 2012).
Nurhajarini, Dwi Ratna, 'Sleman Masa Revolusi Kemerdekaan, 1948-1949', in: Julianto Ibrahim et al. (eds.), *Masyarakat Pedesaan dan Revolusi Kemerdekaan di Daerah Istimewa Yogyakarta* (Yogyakarta 2020).
Oey Beng To, *Sejarah Kebijakan Moneter. Jilid 1 (1945-1958)* (Jakarta 1991).
Ong Hok Ham, *Dari Soal Priyayi sampai Nyi Blorong: Refleksi Historis Nusantara* (Jakarta 2002).
Ooi Keat Gin, *Post-War Borneo, 1945-1950: Nationalism, Empire and State-Building* (Oxon 2013).
Oostindie, Gert, *Serdadu Belanda di Indonesia 1945-1950. Kesaksian Perang pada Sisi Sejarah yang Salah* (Jakarta 2016).
Oostindie, G., B. Schoenmaker and F. van Vree (eds), *Beyond the Pale: Dutch Extreme Violence in the Indonesian War of Independence, 1945-1949* (Amsterdam 2022).
Orang Terkemoeka di Djawa (Jakarta 1944).
Ornit Shani, 'Gandhi's Salt March: Paradoxes and Tensions in the Memory of Nonviolent Struggle in India', in: Anna Reading and Tamar Katriel (eds.), *Cultural Memories of Nonviolent Struggles: Powerful Times* (Basingstoke 2015) 32-51.
Owen, P., *Economy of Force: Counterinsurgency and the Historical Rise of the Social* (Cambridge 2015).
Pagee, Marjolein van and Stef Scagliola, 'Waar blijven de Indonesiërs in het debat over de Nederlandse oorlogsmisdaden in Indonesië?', *Historisch Tijdschrift Groniek* 206-207 (2015) 131-143.
Palallo, M. Nafsar, *Bandit Sosial di Makassar: Jejak Perlawanan I Tolok Dg. Magassing* (Makassar 2008).
Palmos, Frank, *Surabaya 1945 Sakral Tanahku* (Jakarta 2016).
Pambudi, E.P. et al., *Soedirman: Seorang Panglima, Seorang Martir* (Jakarta 2012).
Panitya Pembangunan Monumen Perjoangan '45 Klaten, *Sejarah Perjuangan Rakyat Kabupaten Klaten* (Klaten 1976).
Pao Min, 'Masjarakat Tiongjoa di Djokja: Presiden Soekarno Akan Mengangkat Penasehat Tionghoa?', *Waspada* (1948).
Partokusumo, Karkono Kamajaya, 'Revolusi di Surakarta' (workshop paper; Yogyakarta 1993).
Patang, L., *Sulawesi dan Pahlawan2nya: Sejarah Perjuangan Kemerdekaan Republik Indonesia* (Jakarta 1975).
Pawiloy, Sarita, *Sejarah Revolusi Kemerdekaan 1945-1949 Daerah Sulawesi Selatan* (Ujung Pandang 1979).
Pawiloy, Sarita, *Sejarah Perjuangan Angkatan 45 di Sulawesi Selatan* (Ujung Pandang 1987).
Péclard, D. and D. Mechoulan, 'Rebel Governance and the Politics of Civil War', *Swisspeace Publications*

(working paper; Basel 2015).

Pedoman Kota Besar Makassar (Makassar 1954).

Pelly, Usman, *Urban Migration and Adaptation in Indonesia: A Case Study of Minangkabau and Mandailing Batak Migrants in Medan, North Sumatra* (PhD thesis in history; University of Illinois 1983).

Pelras, Christian, 'Patron-Client Ties among the Bugis and Makassarese of South Sulawesi', in: Roger Tol, Kees van Dijk and Greg Acciaoli (eds.), *Authority and Enterprise among the People of South Sulawesi* (Leiden 2000) 15-54.

Pelzer, Karl J., *Planter and Peasant: Colonial Policy and the Agrarian Struggle in East Sumatra, 1863-1947* (The Hague 1978).

Pelzer, Karl J., *Planters against Peasants: The Agrarian Struggle in East Sumatra 1947-1958* (The Hague 1982).

Pemerintah Kota Depok, *Peraturan Daerah Kota Depok No. 1/1999 tentang Sejarah Singkat Kota Depok* (Depok 1999).

Pemuda Indonesia dalam Dimensi Sejarah Perjuangan Bangsa (Jakarta 1984).

Pendit, N.S., *Bali Berjuang* (Denpasar 2008).

Peters, Robbie, *Surabaya 1945-2010. Neighbourhood, State, and Economy in Indonesia's City of Struggle* (Singapore 2013).

Piekaar, A.J., *Aceh dan Peperangan dengan Jepang, Buku II*, transl. by Aboe Bakar (Banda Aceh 1981).

Pijkeren, G. van, *Loslaten, dat gaat niet meer. Oorlogsherinneringen van en aan meer dan 90 Ter Aarse Indiëgangers* (Nieuwkoop 2017).

Pirous, A.D., 'Sejarah Poster sebagai Alat Propaganda Perjuangan di Indonesia', *Jurnal Ilmu Desain* 1:3 (2006).

Pluvier, J.M., *Overzicht van de ontwikkeling der nationalistische beweging in Indonesië in de jaren 1930 tot 1942* (The Hague 1953).

Pluvier, Jan, *South-East Asia from Colonialism to Independence* (Kuala Lumpur 1974).

Poelinggomang, Edward L., *Perubahan Politik dan Hubungan Kekuasaan Makassar 1906- 1942* (Yogyakarta 2004).

Poelinggomang, Edward L. and Suriadi Mappangara (eds.), *Sejarah Sulawesi Selatan Jilid 2* (Makassar 2005).

Poesponegoro, Marwati Djoened and Nugroho Notosusanto (eds.), *Sejarah Nasional Indonesia* Jilid 6 (Jakarta 1984).

Poesponegoro, Marwati Djoened and Nugroho Notosusanto (eds.), *Sejarah Nasional Indonesia 1-6* (Jakarta 2010).

Poeze, H., *In het land van de overheerser: Indonesiërs in Nederland 1600-1950* (Dordrecht 1986).

Poeze, Harry A., *Verguisd en vergeten: Tan Malaka, de linkse beweging en de Indonesische revolutie, 1945-1949* (Leiden 2007).

Poeze, Harry A., *Tan Malaka, Gerakan Kiri dan Revolusi Indonesia Jilid 2: Maret 1946-Maret 1947* (Jakarta 2009).

Poeze, H., 'Walking the Tightrope: Internal Indonesian Conflict', in: B. Luttikhuis and D.A. Moses (eds.), *Colonial Counterinsurgency and Mass Violence. The Dutch Empire in Indonesia* (London 2014) 176-197.

Poeze, Harry A., 'Jan-Karel Kwisthout. De Mardijkers van Tugu en Depok: Vrijmaking, bevrijding, en merdeka', *Bijdragen tot de Taal-, Land- en Volkenkunde van Nederlandsch-Indië* 17:2/3 (2019) 411.

Poeze, H. and H. Schulte Nordholt, *Merdeka: De strijd om de Indonesische onafhankelijkheid en de ongewisse opkomst van de republiek 1945-1950* (Amsterdam 2022).

Post, Hans (pseud. Hubert Paas), *Banjir over Noord-Sumatra: Politionele Actie, vol. 2* (Medan 1947).

Po Tan Goan, 'Chineezen en de nationale beweging in Indonesië', in: Kementrian Penerangan (ed.), *Waarom Chineezen geen Vreemde Oosterlingen meer willen zijn in Indonesië* (Yogyakarta 1946).

Pradadimara, Dias, 'Dibentuknya Negara Kolonial di Sulawesi Bagian Selatan di Abad Ke-19', *Lensa Budaya* 12:2 (2017) 56-60.

Pranoto, Suhartono W., *Apanage dan Bekel: Perubahan Sosial di Pedesaan Surakarta 1830-1920* (Yogyakarta

1991).
Pranoto, Suhartono W., *Jawa: Bandit-Bandit Pedesaan: Studi Historis 1850-1945* (Yogyakarta 2000).
Pranoto, Suhartono W. et al., *Yogyakarta, Ibukota Republik Indonesia, 4 Januari 1946-27 Desember 1949: Yogyakarta Kota Revolusi* (Yogyakarta 2002).
Price, R.N., 'The Psychology of Colonial Violence', in: Ph. Dwyer and A. Nettelbeck (eds.), *Violence, Colonialism and Empire in the Modern World* (London 2018) 25-51.
Prihatini, Vincentia Marisa, 'Peranan Seniman dalam Perjuangan Mempertahankan Kemerdekaan Indonesia Tahun 1945-1949' (Bachelor's thesis in history; Universitas Negeri Yogyakarta 2015).
Prijanto, Saksono, 'Revolusi dari Perspektif Perempuan: Cerita Pendek Periode 1950an dan 1960an', in: Abdul Rozak Zaidan et al., *Revolusi, Nasionalisme dan Banjir Roman* (Jakarta 2005).
Pringgoadisuryo, Raden Noerito, *Pikirans van een Javaanse avonturier* (Arnhem 2006).
Probowinoto, B., 'Djoega Golongan Kristen Berdjoang', *Merdeka* (1946).
Purwanto, Bambang, *Gagalnya Historiografi Indonesiasentris?!* (Yogyakarta 2006).
Purwanto, Bambang, 'Menulis Kehidupan Sehari-Hari Jakarta: Memikirkan Kembali Sejarah Sosial Indonesia', in: Henk Schulte Nordholt, Bambang Purwanto, and Ratna Saptari (eds.), *Perspektif Baru Penulisan Sejarah Indonesia* (Jakarta 2008).
Purwanto, Bambang, 'Proklamasi Kemerdekaan, Revolusi, dan Perang di Indonesia, 1945-1949: Sebuah Pengantar', in: Rémy Limpach, *Kekerasan Ekstrem Belanda di Indonesia. Perang Kemerdekaan Indonesia 1945-1949* (Jakarta 2019) xi-xxiv.
Purwanto, Bambang, 'Bersiap, Kutukan Kemerdekaan Indonesia yang Menghantui Belanda', *Media Indonesia*, 23 August 2022.
Putro, Widhi Setyo, 'Konferensi Inter-Indonesia Tahun 1949: Wujud Konsensus Nasional antara Republik Indonesia dengan Bijeenkomst voor Federaal Overleg', *Jurnal Sejarah Citra Lekha* 3:1 (2018) 34-42.
Raap, Olivier Johannes, *Soeka Doeka di Djawa Tempo Doeloe* (Jakarta 2015).
Raben, Remco, 'Round About Batavia: Ethnicity and Authority in the Ommelanden, 1650-1800', in: Kees Grijns and Peter J.M. Nas (eds.), *Jakarta-Batavia: Socio-Cultural Essays* (Leiden 2000).
Raben, Remco, 'Anti-Chinese Violence in the Indonesian Revolution' (rough draft paper presented to the Konferensi Dekolonisasi dan Posisi Etnis Tionghoa di Indonesia 1930-an s/d 1960-an; Padang 2006).
Raben, Remco, 'Het geweld van de Bersiap', *Historisch Nieuwsblad* 7 (2011) 41-46.
Raben, Remco, 'De dagen van de Grote Uittocht', *Indische Letteren* 32 (2017) 20-32.
Raben, Remco, 'Indonesische blik op de geschiedenis wordt als irrelevant weggezet', *NRC*, 19 January 2022.
Raditya, 'Sejarah Pindahnya Ibu Kota RI dari Jakarta ke Yogyakarta pada 1946', https://tirto.id/sejarah-pindahnya-ibu-kota-ri-dari-jakarta-ke-yogyakarta-pada-1946-efr4 (accessed 31 August 2021).
Raeymaekers, Timothy, Ken Menkhaus, and Koen Vlassenroot, 'State and Non-State Regulation in African Protracted Crises: Governance without Government?', *Afrika Focus* 21:2 (2008) 7-21. http://dx.doi.org/https://doi.org/10.1163/2031356X-02102003.
Raliby, Osman, *Documenta Historica. Sedjarah Dokumenter dari Pertumbuhan dan Perdjuangan Negara Republik Indonesia I* (Jakarta 1953).
Ravando, '"Now is the Time to Kill All Chinese": Social Revolution and Massacre of Chinese in Tangerang, 1945-1946' (Master's thesis; Universiteit Leiden 2017).
Razak Rasyid, A., 'Episode Dramatis Penyiaran Proklamasi di Studio Radio Bandung', in: Dewan Harian Nasional Angkatan 45 (ed.), *Terbukalah Jalanku: Seri Pengalaman dan Pandangan Tentang Perjoangan 45* (Jakarta 1984).
Reid, Anthony, 'The Birth of the Republic in Sumatra', *Indonesia* 12 (1971) 21-46.
Reid, A., *The Indonesian National Revolution 1945-1950* (Westport 1974).
Reid, A., *The Blood of the People: Revolution and the End of Traditional Rule in Northern Sumatra* (Kuala Lumpur 1979).
Reid, A., 'Australia's Hundred Days in South Sulawesi', in D.P. Chandler and M.C. Ricklefs (eds.), *Nineteenth*

and Twentieth Century Indonesia: Essays in Honour of Professor J.D. Legge (Melbourne 1986) 201-223.
Reid, Anthony, 'Revolusi Sosial: Revolusi Nasional', *Prisma* 9:8 (1981) 37-38.
Reid, Anthony, *Perjuangan Rakyat, Revolusi dan Hancurnya Kerajaan di Sumatra* (Jakarta 1987).
Reid, Anthony, *To Nation by Revolution. Indonesia in the 20th Century* (Singapore 2010).
Reid, Anthony, *Sumatera: Revolusi dan Elite Tradisional* (Depok 2012).
Reid, Anthony, *Indonesia, Revolusi, dan Sejumlah Isu Penting* (Jakarta 2018).
Reid, J.G. and D.H. Stauffer (eds.), *Foreign Relations of the United States of America, 1948. The Far East and Australasia VI* (Washington 1974).
Remmelink, W.G.J., 'The Emergence of the New Situation: The Japanese Army on Java after the Surrender', *De Militaire Spectator* 147:2 (1978) 49-66.
Republik Indonesia, *Daerah Istimewa Yogyakarta* (Jakarta 1953).
Reybrouck, D. van, *Revolusi: Indonesië en het ontstaan van de moderne wereld* (Amsterdam 2020).
Ricklefs, M.C., *Sejarah Indonesia Modern* (Yogyakarta 1991).
Ricklefs, M.C., *A History of Modern Indonesia Since ca. 1200* (Hampshire 2001).
Ricklefs, M.C., *Sejarah Indonesia Modern, 1200-2004* (Jakarta 2005).
Rizal, Muhamad, 'Persatuan Ulama Seluruh Aceh pada Masa Revolusi Kemerdekaan Indonesia 1945-1949' (Bachelor's thesis in history; Universitas Indonesia, Jakarta 2008).
Rizal, Ray, *Affandi: Hari Sudah Tinggi* (Jakarta 1990).
Roadnight, Andrew, 'Sleeping with the Enemy: Britain, Japanese Troops and the Netherlands East Indies', *History* 87:286 (2002) 245-268.
Robinson, G.B., *The Dark Side of Paradise: Political Violence in Bali* (Ithaca NY, London 1995).
Roendingan Badan Perwakilan Sementara Negara Indonesia Timoer: Sidang Pertama (1947).
Roeslan, Abdulgani, 'Melacak Jejak Revolusi Nasional', *Prisma* 8 (1981) 62-72.
Rose-Redwood, Reuben and Michael Glass, *Geographies of Performativities* (London 2014).
Royal Institution of Naval Architects, 'Poor State of Logistics Force Could be US Navy's Achilles Heel', *Warship Technology* (July/August 2019) 12-15.
Saelan, H. Mualwi, *Dari Revolusi 45 sampai Kudeta 65: Kesaksian Wakil Komandan Tjakrabirawa* (Jakarta 2001).
Said, Mohammad, *Empat Belas Boelan Pendoedoekan Inggris di Indonesia* (Medan 1946).
Said, Mohammad, 'Apa itu "Revolusi Sosial Tahun 1946" di Sumatera Timur', *Merdeka*, 17 February-1 March 1972.
Said, Mohammad, 'What Was the "Social Revolution of 1946" in East Sumatra', transl. by Benedict Anderson and Toenggoel Siagian, *Indonesia* 15 (1973) 145-168.
Said, Muhammad N., *Korban 40,000 Jiwa di Sulawesi Selatan* (Bandung 1985).
Sajimin, S. Sajimi, 'Peristiwa Revolusi Kemerdekaan di Surakarta' (private manuscript; no place 1985).
Salam, Aprianus et al., *G.P. Hadinegoro dan B.R. Ay Ismusiratun: Dua Bangsawan Laskar Kesultanan Yogyakarta* (Yogyakarta 2012).
Sanoesi, Oemar, *Replika Sejarah Perjuangan Rakyat Yogyakarta* (Yogyakarta 1983).
Sapto, Ari, 'Dinamika Politik Masa Revolusi: Perbedaan Pandangan Elite Pusat dengan Elite Jawa Timur', *Sejarah dan Budaya* 7:2 (2013) 31-46. http://dx.doi.org/10.17977/sb.v7i2.4745.
Sapto, Ari, *Republik dalam Pusaran Elite Sipil dan Militer*, ed. by Tim Mata Padi (Yogyakarta 2018).
Sari, E.D., 'Sejarah Perjuangan Rakyat dalam Mempertahankan Kemerdekaan Republik Indonesia di Muaradhua Ogan Komering Ulu Selatan Tahun 1945-1949' (Bachelor's thesis; Universitas Muhammadiyah, Palembang 2019).
Sasi, Galuh Ambar, 'Gerakan Perempuan Indonesia' (Master's thesis in history; Universitas Negeri Yogyakarta 2010).
Sasi, Galuh Ambar, 'Gelora Api (Ke)Merdeka(An) di Jawa Tengah', in: Jajat Burhanuddin and Amurwani Dwi Lestariningsih (eds.), *Sejarah Berita Proklamasi di Indonesia* (Jakarta 2015).

Sasi, Galuh Ambar, *Konstruksi Perempuan Indonesia Masa Jepang* (2015). http://archive.ivaa-online.org/khazanahs/artist/4126.

Sasi, Galuh Ambar, 'Di Tanah Kiblik: Perempuan dalam Ge(mer)lap Revolusi', in: *Gelora di Tanah Raja: Yogyakarta pada Masa Revolusi 1945-1949* (Yogyakarta 2017).

Sasi, Galuh Ambar, 'Aisyiyah, Pionir Kesadaran Keindonesiaan' (2018). https://alif.id/read/galuh-ambar/aisyiyah-pionir-kesadaran-keindonesiaan-b211424p/ (accessed 10 November 2020).

Sastroamidjojo, Ali, *Tonggak-Tonggak di Perjalananku* (Jakarta 1974).

Satriya, Bambang, Suwirta, and Ayi Budi Santosa, 'Teungku Muhammad Daud Beureueh dan Revolusi di Aceh (1945-1950)', *Factum: Jurnal Sejarah dan Pendidikan Sejarah* 7:1 (2018) 27-42.

Schiller, A.A., *The Formation of Federal Indonesia, 1945-1949* (The Hague 1955).

Schoonoord, D.C.L., *De mariniersbrigade 1943-1949: Wording en inzet in Indonesië*, ed. by Hans Meijer (The Hague 1988).

Schoonoord, D.C.L., *Nederlands-Indië onder Amerikaans, Australisch en Brits geallieerd militair gezag (22 april 1944 tot 30 november 1946) en de Netherlands Indies Civil Administration (Nica)* (Amsterdam 2020).

Schulte Nordholt, Henk, 'The Jago in the Shadow: Crime and "Order" in the Colonial State in Java', *Review of Indonesian and Malaysian Affairs (RIMA)* 25:1 (1991) 74-91.

Schulte Nordholt, H.G.C., 'The Making of Traditional Bali: Colonial Ethnography and Bureaucratic Reproduction', in: P. Pels and O. Salemink (eds.), *Colonial Subjects: Essays on the Practical History of Anthropology* 8:1-4 (1999) 241-279.

Schulte Nordholt, Henk, *Kriminalitas, Modernitas, dan Identitas dalam Sejarah Indonesia* (Yogyakarta 2002).

Schulte-Nordholt, Henk, 'Modernity and Cultural Citizenship in the Netherlands Indies: An Illustrated Hypothesis', *Journal of Southeast Asian Studies* 42:3 (2011) 435-457.

Schwartz, Rosalie, *Lawless Liberators: Political Banditry and Cuban Independence* (Durham NC 1989).

Scott, M., *Special Forces Commander. The Life and Wars of Peter Wand-Tetley OBE MC Commando, SAS, SOE and Paratrooper* (Barnsley 2011).

Sekretariat Negara Republik Indonesia, *30 Tahun Indonesia Merdeka* (Jakarta 1981).

Sen, Krishna, 'What's Oppositional in Indonesian Cinema?', in: Anthony R. Guneratne and Wimal Dissanayake (eds.), *Rethinking Third Cinema* (London 2003) 159-77.

Seskoad, *Serangan Umum 1 Maret 1949 di Yogyakarta: Latar Belakang dan Pengaruhnya* (Jakarta 1993).

Setahun Negara Djawa Timur (Surabaya 1949).

Setiawan, Efendi, *Tionghoa Medan: Komunitas Paling Kontroversial di Indonesia* (Jakarta 2018).

Setiawan, Hersri, *Memoir Perempuan Revolusioner, Francisca C. Fanggidaej* (Yogyakarta 2006).

Setyorini, 'Bangsawan versus Raja: Sekitar Peristiwa Konflik Tanah Gedung DPRD DIY 1960-1966' (Yogyakarta 2008).

Shabri et al., *Kedudukan dan Peran Dayah di Aceh pada Masa Revolusi Kemerdekaan (1945-1949)* (Banda Aceh 2005).

Shahab, Yasmine Shaki, *The Creation of Ethnic Tradition: The Betawi of Jakarta* (PhD thesis; School of Oriental and African Studies, London 1994).

Shiraishi, Takashi, *An Age in Motion. Popular Radicalism in Java, 1912-1926* (Ithaca NY 1990).

Sikki, Mauluddin Aidid, *Sejarah Perjuangan Kelaskaran Lipan Bajeng* (Takalar 1987).

Simatupang, T.B., *Report from Banaran: Experiences during the People's War* (Ithaca NY 1972 [1960]).

Simatupang, T.B., *Laporan dari Banaran* (Jakarta 1980).

Simatupang, T.B., *Pelopor dalam Perang Pelopor dalam Damai* (Jakarta 1981).

Simatupang, T.B., *Het laatste jaar van de Indonesische vrijheidsstrijd 1948-1949: Een authentiek verslag door de voormalig chef-staf van de Indonesische strijdkrachten* (Kampen 1985).

Sinar, Tengku Luckman, 'Sumatera Timur menjelang Proklamasi dan setelah Proklamasi Kemerdekaan Indonesia', in: Taufik Abdullah et al. (eds.), *Denyut Nadi Revolusi Indonesia* (Jakarta 1997).

Sinar, Tengku Luckman, *Orang India di Sumatera Utara* (Medan 2008).

Sjahrir, Soetan, 'Negara jang Kita Dirikan Negara Kera'jatan: Revoloesi Kita Poen Revoloesi Kera'jatan', *Kedaulatan Rakjat* (1946).

Sjamsuddin, Nazaruddin, *Revolusi di Serambi Mekkah: Perjuangan Kemerdekaan dan Pertarungan Politik di Aceh 1945-1949* (Jakarta 1999).

Slatta, Richard W., 'Rural Criminality and Social Conflict in Nineteenth-Century Buenos Aires Province', *The Hispanic American Historical Review* 60:3 (1980) 450-472.

Sluimers, Laszlo, 'The Japanese Military and Indonesian Independence', *Journal of Southeast Asian Studies* 27:1 (1996) 19-36.

Smail, J.R.W., *Bandung in the Early Revolution 1945-1950: A Study in the Social History of the Indonesian Revolution* (Jakarta 2009).

Smail, R., *Bandung Awal Revolusi 1945-1946* (Depok 2011).

Smith, P., 'Writing in the Rain: Erasure, Trauma, and Chinese Indonesian Identity in the Recent Work of FX Harsono', *Journal of Southeast Asian Studies* 46:1 (2015) 119-133.

Soebardi, S., 'Kartosuwiryo and the Darul Islam Rebellion in Indonesia', *Journal of Southeast Asian Studies* 14:1 (1983) 1-17.

Soebroto, Rohmah Soemohardjo, *Oerip Soemohardjo Letnan Jenderal TNI (22 Februari 1893-17 November 1948)* (Jakarta 1973).

Soedibyo, Fatimah, 'Andil Perjuangan: Perjalanan Hidupku Melintasi Kancah Revolusi Kemerdekaan', in: Irna H.N. Hadi Soewito (ed.), *Seribu Wajah Wanita Pejuang dalam Kancah Revolusi '45, Buku Kedua* (Jakarta 1998).

Soe Hok Gie, 'Simpang Kiri dari Sebuah Jalan: Kisah Pemberontakan Madiun September 1948' (Master's thesis; Universitas Indonesia, Jakarta 1969).

Soekamto, Eddy R. and Lilih Prilian Ary Pranowo, *Yogyakarta Ibukota Perjuangan* (Yogyakarta 2009).

Soekarno, *Wanita Indonesia Selalu Ikut Bergerak dalam Barisan Revolusioner* (Jakarta 1964).

Soekarno, *Dibawah Bendera Revolusi. Jilid II* (Jakarta 2015).

Soekarsih, 'Boeroeh Wanita dan Perdjoangan Boeroeh', *Merdeka* (1946).

Soekirno, *Semarang* (Semarang 1956).

Soemardi, Imam et al., *Sedjarah TNI-AD Kodam VII/Diponegoro, Sirnaning Jakso Katon Gapuraning Ratu* (Semarang 1968).

Soemardjan, Selo, *Social Changes in Jogjakarta* (Ithaca NY 1962).

Soemardjan, Selo, *Perubahan Sosial di Yogyakarta* (Depok 2009).

Soepanto, H., *Hizbullah Surakarta, 1945-1950* (Surakarta 1992).

Soeripto, Dartiyah, 'Serba-Serbi Perjuangan', in: Irna H.N. Hadi Soewito (ed.), *Seribu Wajah Wanita Pejuang dalam Kancah Revolusi '45, Buku Pertama* (Jakarta 1995).

Soetadji, Nanang S., *Sekelumit Pengalaman semasa Revolusi, 1945-1950* (Jakarta 1998).

Soewarno, *Sejarah Pertempuran 5 Hari di Semarang / Disusun oleh Panitia Penyusunan Sejarah Pertempuran Lima Hari di Semarang* (Semarang 1977).

Soewarno, P.J., *Hamengkubuwono IX dan Sistem Birokrasi Pemerintahan Yogyakarta. 1942-1974: Sebuah Tinjauan Historis* (Yogyakarta 1994).

Soewito, Irna H.N. Hadi, *Rakyat Jawa Timur Mempertahankan Kemerdekaan*. 3 vols. (Jakarta 1994).

Soewito, Irna H.N. Hadi, *Wanita Pejuang* (Jakarta 2005).

Soewondo, Nani and N. Surasno, *Kedudukan Wanita Indonesia dalam Hukum dan Masjarakat* (Jakarta 1995).

Somers Heidhues, Mary, 'Anti-Chinese Violence in Java during the Indonesian Revolution, 1945-49', *Journal of Genocide Research* 14:3-4 (2012) 381-401.

Som Tjan Tjoe, 'De Chineezen en het Indonesische burgerschap', in: Kementrian Penerangan (ed.), *Waarom Chineezen geen Vreemde Oosterlingen meer willen zijn in Indonesië* (Yogyakarta 1946).

Spencer, D.E., 'Reexamining the Relevance of Mao to Post-Modern Insurgency and Terrorism', *Intelligence*

Journal 28:1 (2010) 146-152.
Spivak, Gayatri, 'Can the Subaltern Speak?', in: Cary Nelson and Lawrence Grossberg (eds.), *Marxism and the Interpretation of Culture* (London 1988) 271-313.
Spreeuwers, Roelf, *De lange weg: Als oorlogsvrijwilliger naar Ned. Indië* (Stadskanaal 1980).
Staatsblad van Nederlandsche-Indië 1886 57 (Batavia 1867) 1-2.
Staf Umum Angkatan Darat-I, *Masalah China di Indonesia* (Jakarta 1961).
Staniland, P., *Networks of Rebellion: Explaining Insurgent Cohesion and Collapse* (Ithaca NY 2014).
Steege, Paul et al., 'The History of Everyday Life: A Second Chapter', *The Journal of Modern History* 80:2 (2008) 358-378.
Stoler, Ann Laura, 'Working the Revolution: Plantation Laborers and the People's Militia in North Sumatra', *Journal of Asia Studies* 47:2 (1988) 227-247.
Stoler, Ann Laura, 'Rethinking Colonial Categories: European Communities and the Boundaries of Rule', *Comparative Studies in Society and History* 31:1 (1989) 134-161.
Stoler, Ann Laura, *Capitalism and Confrontation in Sumatra's Plantation Belt, 1870-1979* (Michigan 1995).
Subagijo, I.N., *Jusuf Wibisono: Karang ditengah Gelombang* (Jakarta 1980).
Subanar, G. Budi, *Kesaksian Revolusioner Seorang Uskup di Masa Perang: Catatan Harian MGR. A. Soegijapranata, SJ 13 Februari 1947-17 Agustus 1949* (Yogyakarta 2003).
Sudarno et al., *Sejarah Pemerintahan Militer dan Peran Pamong Praja di Jawa Timur selama Perjuangan Fisik 1945-1950* (Jakarta 1993).
Sudiyat, Suratmi Iman, 'Soeratmi Iman Soedijat', in: *50 Tahun Republik Indonesia di Yogyakarta: Sebuah Lintasan Sejarah* (Yogyakarta 1995).
Sudjojono, R., *Cerita tentang Saya dan Orang-Orang Sekitar Saya* (Jakarta 2017).
Suhatno, *Dr. H. Affandi: Karya dan Pengabdiannya* (Jakarta 1985).
Sukarno, *Dibawah Bendera Revolusi. Djilid Pertama* (Djakarta 1964).
Sulaiman, Idrian Idroes SM., 'Peranan BPPI di Padang Kota Perjuangan', *Memorial* (unpublished manuscript; no place 1997) 31-34.
Sulaiman, Irchamni, *Pengusaha Aceh dan Pengusaha Cina di Kotamadya Banda Aceh Sabang* (Banda Aceh 1983).
Sulardi, *Pao An Tui 1947-1949: Tentara Cina* (Jakarta 2015).
Sumarno, T. et al., 'History of War "The Battles of Palagan Ambarawa" Reviewed From Universal War Strategy Perspective', *International Journal of Arts and Social Science* 4-3 (2021) 1-12.
Supomo, R. *Sistim Hukum di Indonesia sebelum Perang Dunia II* (Jakarta 1958).
Suprayitno, *Mencoba (Lagi) Menjadi Indonesia, dari Federalisme ke Unitarisme: Studi tentang Negara Sumatera Timur 1947-1950* (Yogyakarta 2001).
Suryadinata, Leo, *Politik Tionghoa Peranakan di Jawa 1917-1942* (Jakarta 1981)
Suryadinata, Leo, *Negara dan Etnis Tionghoa: Kasus Indonesia* (Jakarta 2002).
Suryadinata, Leo and Didi Kwartanada (eds.), *Tionghoa dalam Keindonesiaan: Peran dan Kontribusi bagi Pembangunan Bangsa* III (Jakarta 2016).
Suryana, Asep, 'Transformasi Sosial Pribumi Depok Tahun 1930-1960', *Jurnal Masyarakat dan Budaya* 6:2 (2004) 29-48.
Suryocondro, Sukanti, *Potret Pergerakan Wanita di Indonesia* (Jakarta 1984).
Suryohadiprojo, Sayidiman, 'Pemikiran Strategi Indonesia Masa Perang Kemerdekaan: Antara Konsep dan Pelaksanaannya', *Histori* 1 (1992) 40-57.
Sutherland, Heather, 'Political Structure and Colonial Control in South Sulawesi', in: R. Schefold, J.W. Schoorl, and J. Tennekes (eds.), *Man, Meaning, and History* (The Hague 1980) 235-245.
Sutiasumarga, Rusman, 'Gadis Bekasi', in: HB Jassin, *Gema Tanah Air: Prosa dan Puisi 1942-1948* (Jakarta 1959).
Sutikno, Uripah, 'Membantu PMI di Medan Laga', in: Irna H.N. Hadi Soewito (ed.), *Seribu Wajah Wanita*

Pejuang dalam Kancah Revolusi '45, Buku Pertama (Jakarta 1995).

Sutrisna, Deni, 'Peunayong: Kampung Lama Etnis Cina di Kota Banda Aceh', *BAS* 21 (2008) 30-40.

Sutton, D. S., 'Ritual and Culture of Cannibalism in Wuxuan, Guangxi, China, May to July 1968', *Comparative Studies in Society and History* 37:1 (1995) 136-172.

Suwarno, P.J., *Hamengku Buwono IX dalam Sistem Birokrasi Pemerintahan Yogyakarta 1942-1974: Sebuah Tinjauan Historis* (Yogyakarta 1994).

Suwirta, Andi, *Revolusi Indonesia dalam* News and Views: *Sebuah Antologi Sejarah* (Yogyakarta 2015).

Talsya, T.A., *Batu Karang di Tengan Lautan: Perjuangan Kemerdekaan di Aceh 1945-1946* (Banda Aceh 1990).

Talsya, T.A., *Modal Perjuangan Kemerdekaan (Perjuangan Kemerdekaan di Aceh) 1947-1948), book II* (Banda Aceh 1990).

Tan Kia Lih, 'The Indian National Army: A Force for Nationalism?' (Master's thesis in history; National University of Singapore 2011).

Taomo Zhou, *Revolusi, Diplomasi, Diaspora: Indonesia, Tiongkok, dan Etnik Tionghoa, 1945-1967* (Jakarta 2019).

Tashadi et al., *Sejarah Revolusi Kemerdekaan (1945-1949) di Daerah Istimewa Yogyakarta* (Jakarta 1991).

Tashadi et al., *Partisipasi Seniman dalam Perjuangan Kemerdekaan Daerah Istimewa Yogyakarta* (Jakarta 1996).

Tauchid, Moh. 'Renungan Taman Siswa', in: *30 Tahun Taman Siswa* (Yogyakarta 1956).

Taufiq, Ferry, *Akhirnya Sang Jenderal Mengalah: Jenderal Sudirman dalam Pusaran Konflik Politik* (Yogyakarta 2018).

Taylor, Jean Gelman, 'Images of the Indonesian Revolution', in: Jane Drakard and John Legge (eds.), *Indonesian Independence Fifty Years On 1945-1995* (Melbourne 1996) 13-36.

Taylor, Philip M., *Munitions of the Minds: A History of Propaganda from the Ancient World to the Present Day.* Third edition (Manchester, New York 2003).

Temminck Groll, C.L. et al., *Dutch Overseas: Architectural Survey: Mutual Heritage of Four Centuries in Three Continents* (Zwolle 2002).

Tentara Pelajar Cie Purwokerto, *Sejarah Perjuangan Tentara Pelajar Purwokerto* (Jakarta 1979).

Thames, I., 'Over grenzen: Liminaliteit en de ervaring van verzet' (inaugural lecture; Universiteit Utrecht, 17 May 2016).

Thee Kian-wie, *Plantation Agriculture and Export Growth: An Economic History of East Sumatra, 1863-1942* (Jakarta 1977).

The Liang Djie, *Sedjarah Pemerintahan Kota Djakarta* (Djakarta 1958).

Tideman, J., 'Het landschap Laikang', *Bijdragen tot de Taal-, Land- en Volkenkunde* 59:1 (1906): 648-656.

Tideman, J., 'De Batara Gowa op Zuid Celebes', *BKI* 61 (1908) 350-390.

Tideman, J., 'De Toe Badjeng en de legende omtrent hun oorsprong', *BKI* 61 (1908) 488-500.

Tideman, J., 'Zuid-Celebes voorheen en thans', Indisch Genootschap, Algemeene vergadering van 18 Januari (1910) 72-91.

Tilly, Charles, *From Mobilization to Revolution* (New York 1978).

Tilly, C., 'War Making and State Making as Organized Crime', in: P. Evans, D. Rueschemeyer and T. Skocpol (eds.), *Bringing the State Back In* (Cambridge 1985).

Tjitrowarsito, Suwandi, 'Perdjalanan', in: H.B. Jassin (ed.), *Gema Tanah Air: Prosa dan Puisi 1942-1948* (Jakarta 1959).

Tjoa Sein Ien, *Masa'alah Warganegara Indonesia* (Yogyakarta 1946).

Toer, Pramoedya Ananta et al., *Kronik Revolusi Indonesia Jilid V (1949)* (Jakarta 2014).

To Oey Beng, *Sejarah Kebijakan Moneter Indonesia* (Jakarta 1991).

Touwen-Bouwsma, E., 'De opvang van burgergeïnterneerden op Java en Sumatra (15 augustus 1945- 15 april 1946), in: E. Touwen-Bouwsma and P. Groen (eds.), *Tussen Banzai en Bersiap. De afwikkeling van de Tweede Wereldoorlog in Nederlands-Indië* (The Hague 1996) 25-42.

Touwen-Bouwsma, Elly 'Japanese Minority Policy. The Eurasian on Java and the Dilemma of Ethnic Loyalty', *Bijdragen tot de Taal-, Land- en Volkenkunde van Nederlandsch-Indië* 152:4 (1996) 553-572.
Tull, T.S., 'RAPWI-report', in: *Geschiedenis van de vijfdaagse strijd in Semarang* (Gouda 1995).
Twang Peck Yang, *The Chinese Business Elite in Indonesia and the Transition to Independence, 1940-1950* (Kuala Lumpur 1998).
Umayi, 'Kenangan Manis Anggota WAPP', in: Irna H.N. Hadi Soewito (ed.), *Seribu Wajah Wanita Pejuang dalam Kancah Revolusi '45, Buku Pertama* (Jakarta 1995).
Usman, A. Rani, *Etnis Cina Perantauan di Aceh* (Jakarta 2009).
Utama, Nanda Julian, *Pertempuran Palembang, Pertempuran Lima Hari Lima Malam 1947* (Yogyakarta 2021).
Vanderwood, Paul, *Disorder and Progress: Bandits, Police, and Mexican Development* (Lincoln 1981).
Veer, Paul van 't, *Perang Belanda di Aceh*, transl. by Aboe Bakar (Banda Aceh 1977).
Velde, J.J. van de, *Surat-Surat dari Sumatra, 1928-1949* (Jakarta 1987).
Verhulst, A., *Zomaar wat herinneringen aan mijn verblijf in Nederlands-Indië editie III* (Eindhoven 2017 [1981]).
Vickers, Adrian. *A History of Modern Indonesia* (Cambridge 2005).
Vlekke, Bernard H.M., 'Progress Toward Self-Government', *Far Eastern Survey* 14:24 (1945) 348-350.
*Volkstelling 1930, Deel VII: Chineezeen en andere Vreemde Oosterlingen in Nederlandsch-Indi*ë (Batavia 1935).
Vreede-De Stuers, Cora, *Sejarah Perempuan Indonesia: Gerakan dan Pencapaian* (Depok 2008).
Vries, J. de, 'De Depokkers: Geschiedenis, sociale structuur en taalgebruik van een geïsoleerde gemeenschap', *Bijdragen tot de Taal-, Land- en Volkenkunde van Nederlandsch-Indië* 132:2-3 (1976) 228-248.
Vuorinen, Marja, 'Introduction: Enemy Images as Inversions of the Self', in: Marja Vuorinen (ed.), *Enemy Images in War Propaganda* (Newcastle upon Tyne 2012).
Vu Tuong, 'Of Rice and Revolution: The Politics of Provisioning and State-Society Relations in Java', *South East Asia Research* 11:3 (2003) 237-268.
Wagner, K., '"Calculated to Strike Terror": The Amritsar Massacre and the Spectacle of Colonial Violence', *Past and Present* 233 (2016) 185-225.
Wagner, K., 'Savage Warfare: Violence and the Rule of Colonial Difference in Early British Counterinsurgency', *History Workshop Journal* 85 (2018) 218-237.
Wahid, Abdul, 'Berdamai dengan Masa Lalu yang "Kelam"', in: Gert Oostindie, *Serdadu Belanda di Indonesia 1945-1950. Kesaksian Perang pada Sisi Sejarah yang Salah* (Jakarta 2016).
Wahid, Abdul and Yulianti (eds.), *Onze revolutie. Bloemlezing uit de Indonesische geschiedschrijving over de strijd voor de onafhankelijkheid, 1945-1949* (Amsterdam 2023).
Waid, Abdul, *Bung Tomo: Hidup dan Mati Pengobar Semangat Tempur 10 November* (Yogyakarta 2019).
Wal, S.L. van der, P.J. Drooglever, and M.J.B. Schouten (eds.), *Officiële bescheiden Nederlands-Indonesische betrekkingen 1945-1950*. 20 vols. (The Hague 1971-).
Wal, S.L. van der, *Officiële bescheiden betreffende de Nederlands-Indonesische betrekkingen 1945-1950, vierde deel, 31 maart-16 juli 1946* (The Hague 1974).
Wal, S.L. van der, *Officiële bescheiden betreffende de Nederlands-Indonesische betrekkingen 1945-1950, elfde deel, 1 September-25 November 1947* (The Hague 1983).
Walsh, Brian, 'The Iraqi Economic Blockade: A Moral and Legal Analysis', *Peace Research* 27:1 (1995) 47-52.
Wanhar, Wenri, *Gedoran Depok Revolusi Sosial di Tepi Jakarta* (Depok 2011).
Wanhar, Wenri, 'Margonda Sang Legenda Revolusi', *Historia* (2014).
Warouw, Jozef A., *KRIS 45 Berjuang Membela Negara: Sebuah Refleksi Perjuangan Revolusi KRIS (Kebaktian Rakyat Indonesia Sulawesi)* (Jakarta 1995).
Wehl, David, *The Birth of Indonesia* (Crows Nest 1948).
Welch, David, *World War II Propaganda: Analyzing the Art of Persuasion during Wartime* (Santa Barbara, Denver 2017).

Wertheim, W.F., *Indonesian Society in Transition: A Study of Social Change* (Bandung 1956).
Westenenk, L.C., 'De Chetti', *Koloniale Studiën* 6:2 (1922) 4.
Wicaksono, Helmi, 'Revolusi Fisik di Kota Malang Tahun 1945-1949' (thesis; Universitas Negeri Malang 2012).
Widjajanto, Andi and Artanti Wardhani, *Hubungan Intelijen – Negara 1945-2004* (Jakarta 2008).
Widodo, Dukut Imam, *Malang Tempo Doeloe*. 2 vols. (Malang 2006).
Widyati Soertinah, A., 'Suara dari Front Ambarawa', in: Irna H.N. Hadi Soewito (ed.), *Seribu Wajah Wanita Pejuang dalam Kancah Revolusi '45, Buku Pertama* (Jakarta 1995).
Wieringa, Saskia, 'Aborted Feminism in Indonesia: A History of Indonesian Socialist Feminism', in: Saskia Wieringa (ed.), *Women Struggles and Strategies* (Sydney 1988).
Wightwick, A., 'Welsh Historian Reveals Key Role in Securing £20m Payout for Mau Mau Torture Victims', *Wales Online*, June 2013. https://www.walesonline.co.uk/news/wales-news/mau-mau-torture-welsh-historians-4073034 (accessed 15 April 2022).
Wildan et al., 'Repertoar Bahasa Masyarakat Cina di Aceh', *Jurnal Bahasa dan Seni* 38:2 (2010) 131-141.
Wilmott, Donald E., *The National Status of the Chinese in Indonesia 1900-1958* (Jakarta 2009).
Wirawan, A.A.B., *Pusaran Revolusi Indonesia di Sunda Kecil 1945-1950* (Denpasar 2012).
Wisesa, E. Dwi Aryo, 'Menghayati Sejarah Revolusi Kemerdekaan', *Prisma* 7 (1988).
Wiyono et al., *Sejarah Revolusi Kemerdekaan (1945-1949) Daerah Jawa Tengah* (Jakarta 1991).
Wolf Jr., C., *The Indonesian Story: The Birth, Growth and Structure of the Indonesian Republic* (New York 1948).
Yayasan Indonesia Boekoe, 'Sejarah Kampung Patehan' (unpublished stencil; Yogyakarta 2011).
Yusa, Abrar, *Biografi: Komat-Kamit Selo Soemardjan* (Jakarta 1995).
Yusra, Abrar, *Azwar Anas: Teladan dari Ranah Minang* (Jakarta 2011).
Zainun, Nazaruddin, *Logistik Tentara Nasional Indonesia dalam Perang Gerila di Jawa Tengah, 1947-1948* (Pulau Pinang 2019).
Zara, Muhammad Yuanda, *Voluntary Participation, State Involvement: Indonesian Propaganda in the Struggle for Maintaining Independence, 1945-1949* (PhD thesis in history; Universiteit van Amsterdam 2016).
Zara, Muhammad Yuanda, 'Indonesian Mockery of the Dutch during the Indonesian Struggle to Maintain Independence', *BMGN-Low Countries Historical Review* 136:3 (2021) 31-60.
Zed, Mestika et al., *Sumatera Barat di Panggung Sejarah 1945-1995* (Jakarta 1998).
Zed, Mestika, Emizal Amri, and Etmihardi, *Sejarah Perjuangan Kemerdekaan: 1945-1949 di Kota Padang dan Sekitarnya* (Padang 2002).
Zed, Mestika, 'Kota Padang Tempo Doeloe (Zaman Kolonial)', *Monograf* (Padang 2009).
Zijlmans, G.C., *Eindstrijd en ondergang van de Indische bestuursdienst. Het corps binnenlands bestuur op Java 1945-1950* (Amsterdam 1985).
Zulkifli, Arif et al., *Yap Tiam Hien, Sang Pendekar Keadilan* (Seri Buku Saku Tempo) (Jakarta 2014).

Acknowledgements

Revolutionary Worlds is the result of a collaboration between the Indonesian research group of the project 'Proclamation of Independence, Revolution and War in Indonesia, 1945-1949' at Universitas Gadjah Mada (UGM) in Yogyakarta and the Dutch research group of the 'Regional Studies' project carried out under the umbrella of the research programme *Independence, Decolonization, Violence and War in Indonesia, 1945-1950*.

We started our collaboration in 2017 with a workshop in Yogyakarta, and from that moment onwards, we exchanged and shared sources and literature; discussed perspectives, concepts and approaches; read and discussed each other's work; and conducted research in both countries. It was not always an easy process. Across vast distances, we had to find ways to make the project work while navigating within the public debate on decolonization and its related political sensitivities that took different forms in both countries. However, through yearly conferences in Indonesia and mutual research visits, the project developed and we became a dynamic Indonesian-Dutch research group. When the collaboration was severely disrupted in 2020 by the Covid pandemic, which made traveling impossible and hampered archival research, we managed to proceed with online workshops, which were fortunately able to build on relationships that had already been established. We succeeded in completing this book thanks to the commitment and perseverance of all the researchers as well as the support of the programme management of the UGM, the Royal Netherlands Institute of Southeast Asian and Caribbean Studies (Koninklijk Instituut voor Taal-, Land- en Volkenkunde, KITLV), the NIOD Institute for War, Holocaust and Genocide Studies, and the Netherlands Institute for Military History (Nederlands Instituut voor Militaire Historie, NIMH).

Naturally, a project of this size and length has depended on and is indebted to many different people who in one way or another have contributed to this edited volume. In our acknowledgements we have chosen to mention those who were most directly involved.

We would like to express our special gratitude to Bambang Purwanto and Henk Schulte Nordholt, who together delivered an essential contribution at the start of the collaboration by connecting the two groups and helping to bring the researchers together at the intersection of the two historiographies.

As a research group we are very grateful to Gerry van Klinken, who joined the project and the editorial team in a later stage and whose editorial skills and suggestions in terms of content were instrumental in making this book.

We would also like to extend our gratitude to our colleagues at the *Independence, Decolonization, Violence and War in Indonesia, 1945-1950* research programme as well as the Scientific Advisory Commission for their valuable feedback during our discussions.

We thank Taufiq Hanafi for his Indonesian-to-English translations of nine chapters and his crucial advice on many matters; Gioia Marini, our editor who has made our texts better; Alex Berndsen-Rietdijk for the Dutch-to-English translation of one chapter; Klarijn Loven for editing the references, Erik van Oosten for producing the maps; Ellen Klinkers, Harco Gijsbers and Rene Kok for the image editing; Femke Jacobs, who created the index; Paul Bakkum for his assistance and Tom van den Berge, Eveline Buchheim, Gert Oostindie, Fridus Steijlen and Frank van Vree for their final comments.

PHOTO CREDITS

The selection of photographs in this book is the result of careful consideration that took into account the fact that there are differing views on the display of explicit and upsetting images. The final selection reflects our attempt to achieve a balance in relation to respect for the victims and their families, visual evidence, parity and diversity.

Organization

Proclamation of Independence, Revolution and War in Indonesia, 1945-1949

Bambang Purwanto	project leader, editor
Abdul Wahid	project leader, editor
Yulianti	coordinator, editor
Satrio (Ody) Dwicahyo	coordinator
Wildan Sena Utama	coordinator
Uji Nugroho Winardi	coordinator
Rika Sri Sayekti	supporting staff
Taufik Ahmad	researcher
Galuh Ambar Sasi	researcher
Maiza Elvira	researcher
Farabi Fakih	researcher
Apriani Harahap	researcher
Sarkawi B. Husain	researcher
Julianto Ibrahim	researcher
Tri Wahyuning M. Irsyam	researcher
Gayung Kasuma	researcher
Erniwati	researcher
Mawardi Umar	researcher
Muhammad Yuanda Zara	researcher

Regional Studies

Martijn Eickhoff	researcher, project leader, editor
Roel Frakking	researcher, project leader, editor
Ireen Hoogenboom	coordinator, editor
Gerry van Klinken	researcher, editor
Maarten van der Bent	researcher
Anne-Lot Hoek	researcher
Hans Meijer	researcher
Anne van der Veer	researcher
Muhammad Alif Ichsan	research assistant
Muhammad Aprianto	research assistant
Fynn Franke	research assistant
Mia Intentilia	research assistant
Emma Keizer	research assistant
Dhia Oktoriza Sativa	research assistant

About the authors

Taufik Ahmad is a researcher at the Research Center for Society and Culture, part of Indonesia's National Research and Innovation Agency. He received his PhD in history from the Universitas Indonesia in 2022. His dissertation was titled *Toloq dan Kontestasi Otoritas: Perbanditan di Polombangkeng, Sulawesi Selatan, 1905-1950*. His research interest lies in the history of Communist political prisoners in South Sulawesi and in the local history of South Sulawesi. His publications on these topics include 'South Sulawesi: The Military, Prison Camps and Forced Labour' in *The Contours of Mass Violence in Indonesia, 1965-1968* (2012) and *Kamp Pengasingan Moncongloe* (2009).

Maarten van der Bent studied political science at the Vrije Universiteit Amsterdam and cultural anthropology at Uppsala University. From 2018 to 2021, he was involved as a researcher in the research programme *Independence, Decolonization, Violence and War in Indonesia 1945-1950*, first as part of the Royal Netherlands Institute of Southeast Asian and Caribbean Studies (KITLV) and later under the NIOD Institute for War, Holocaust and Genocide Studies. He is currently associated as a researcher with the Expert Centre Restitution, the knowledge centre for issues related to looted art and restitution, which is housed at the NIOD Institute.

Martijn Eickhoff (editor) is director of the NIOD Institute for War, Holocaust and Genocide Studies and is also Endowed Professor of Archaeology and Heritage of War and Mass Violence at the University of Groningen. He researches the history, cultural dimensions and after-effects of large-scale violence and regime change in Europe and Asia in the nineteenth and twentieth centuries, with a particular emphasis on their spatial, material and transnational aspects. He obtained his doctorate from the University of Amsterdam (2003) with research on Dutch pre- and protohistorical archaeology and its confrontation with National Socialism. A recent research topic is the 'memory landscapes' of mass anti-Communist violence in Indonesia in the period 1965-1968. He has also published, often in collaboration with Marieke Bloembergen, on the relationship between archaeology, politics, colonialism, heritage and violence in Indonesia.

Erniwati is a lecturer in the Department of History at the Universitas Negeri Padang. She is also director of the Center for Ethnicity and Conflict Studies (CETCOS) at the same university, a post she has held since 2006. She finished her Master's degree in history at the Universitas Gadjah Mada with her thesis titled *Asap Hio di Ranah Minang: Komunitas Tionghoa di Sumatera Barat*. In 2007, she obtained her PhD from the Universitas Indonesia. Her dissertation was titled *Cina Padang dalam Dinamika Masyarakat Minangkabau: Dari Revolusi hingga Reformasi*. Her publications include *Samaun Bakri: Berjuang Untuk Republik Hingga Akhir Hayat* (2020); *Kota Solok Menuju Masa* Depan (2019); *Hasan Basri: Perjalanan Birokrat Sejati* (2017); and *140 Tahun Heng Beng Tong: Sejarah Perkumpulan Tionghoa 1876-2016* (2016).

Farabi Fakih is head of the Department of History Master's programme at the Universitas Gadjah Mada. He finished his PhD at the Institute for History in Leiden University on the topic of Indonesian state decolonization. His main research interests include the Indonesian decolonization of state institutions, business and knowledge history. He has also conducted research on Indonesian urban history, including Yogyakarta during the revolutionary and early post-colonial period, particularly its position as a 'revolutionary capital' and how decolonization changed the spatial patterns of European housing. He recently published a book titled *Authoritarian Modernization in Indonesia's Early Independence Period. The Foundation of the New Order State (1950-1965)* (2020 Brill).

Roel Frakking (editor) is a lecturer in political history in the Department of History and Art History at the University of Utrecht. He was the coordinator and co-editor of the *Revolutionary Worlds* project that was part of the research programme titled *Independence, Decolonization, Violence and War in Indonesia 1945-1950*. He obtained his PhD from the European University Institute in Florence, Italy.

Apriani Harahap is a lecturer in the Department of History Education, Faculty of Social Sciences at the State University of Medan. She obtained her Master's degree in history from the Universitas Gadjah Mada with her thesis titled *Voor Indiers: Sejarah Kehidupan Sehari-Hari Orang India Di Kota Medan Abad Ke-20*. She has published several articles, including 'Current Activities and Conditions of Merdeka Square in Medan' (2022); 'Tamils Identity in Early Twentieth Century Medan' (2021), 'Esplanade (Merdeka Square) of Medan City as a Symbol of Colonial City Civilization' (2021); 'Bandar Dagang Kuno Kota Cina: Kajian Historis dan Penerapannya' in *Pembelajaran Sejarah Abad* 21 (2021); and 'Orang India di Perkebunan Tembakau Deli: Narasi Foto, 1872-1900' (2019). She has also collaborated on an animation video called Eight National Heroes from North Sumatra: Digital Learning Media to Enhance Student Nationality Character (2019).

Ireen Hoogenboom (editor) is a coordinator of joint research on Indonesia at the Royal Netherlands Institute of Southeast Asian and Caribbean Studies (KITLV) in Leiden. She obtained her Master's degree in languages and cultures of Southeast Asia and Oceania from Leiden University in 2002. She has been a project manager for Asian Studies in Amsterdam (ASIA, part of the International Institute of Asian Studies) and an editor for the KITLV Press and the *Journal of the Humanities and Social Sciences of Southeast Asia and Oceania*. Since 2012, she has been working on several research projects on the Indonesian war of independence. She contributed to both the Dutch and the Indonesian versions of *Soldaat in Indonesië 1945-1950: Getuigenissen van een oorlog aan de verkeerde kant van de geschiedenis* (Gert Oostindie, 2015 and 2016). Within the research programme *Independence, Decolonization, Violence and War in Indonesia 1945-1950*, she has been coordinator of the collaboration with the Indonesian researchers and is co-editor of *Revolutionary Worlds*.

Anne-Lot Hoek is an independent researcher, historian and author of *De strijd om Bali. Imperialisme, verzet en onafhankelijkheid 1846–1950* (De Bezige Bij 2021), which was shortlisted for the 2022 Dutch Libris History Prize. She is also a PhD candidate at the Amsterdam School for Humanities at the University of Amsterdam. She has been writing about the Indonesian war of independence since 2012 for the *NRC Handelsblad*, *De Groene Amsterdammer*, *Vrij Nederland* and *de lage landen*. In the past, she researched on human rights violations during the Namibian independence war (1966–1989) and worked as a researcher at the African Studies Centre in Leiden on two book publications about the history of Dutch development aid in Africa.

Sarkawi B. Husain is head of the Department of History, Faculty of Humanities at the Universitas Airlangga Indonesia. His research interests include environmental history, social and political history, urban history and the study of borders. His publications include a book chapter titled 'Chinese Cemeteries as a Symbol of Sacred Space. Control, Conflict, and Negotiation in Surabaya, Indonesia' in *Cars, Conduits, and Kampongs*; 'The Modernization of the Indonesian City, 1920-1960' (2015 Brill); and 'History, Education, and Border Area: An Introduction Study on Education at the Indonesia-Malaysia border, Sebatik Island, North Kalimantan' in *Kasetsart Journal of Social Sciences* (2021).

Julianto Ibrahim is a lecturer in the Department of History and the Vocation School at the Universitas Gadjah Mada. He earned his Bachelor's and Master's degrees in history from the Universitas Gadjah Mada. He is currently working on his PhD at the same university on the topic of the funding of the Indonesian revolution. His publications include *Dinamika Sosial dan politik Masa Revolusi Indonesia, 1945-1950* (2014); *Opium dan Revolusi: Perdagangan dan Penggunaan Candu di Surakarta Pada Masa Revolusi* (2013); *Kraton Surakarta dan Gerakan Anti Swapraja* (2008); and *Bandit dan pejuang di Simpang Bengawan: Kriminalitas dan kekerasan masa Revolusi di Surakarta* (2004).

Tri Wahyuning M. Irsyam is Lecturer Emeritus in the Department of History at the Universitas Indonesia. She currently works as an independent historian. She received her PhD in history from the Universitas Gadjah Mada in 2015 with her dissertation titled *Berkembang dalam Bayang-Bayang Jakarta: Sejarah Depok 1950an-1990an*, which was published by Yayasan Obor Indonesia. She is currently active as chairperson of the advisory board for the heritage society of Depok City.

Gerry van Klinken (editor) is honorary professor of Southeast Asian history at the University of Queensland (Historical and Philosophical Inquiry), the University of Amsterdam (Anthropology), and the Royal Netherlands Institute of Southeast Asian and Caribbean Studies (KITLV) in Leiden. His monographs include *Postcolonial Citizenship in Provincial Indonesia* (Singapore 2019) and *The Making of Middle Indonesia: Middle Classes in Kupang Town, 1930s-1980s* (Leiden 2014). He is currently researching the history of the disaster politics of storms in Asia.

Bambang Purwanto (editor) is a professor of history in the Department of History, Faculty of Cultural Sciences at the Universitas Gadjah Mada in Yogyakarta, Indonesia. He obtained his PhD in history from SOAS University of London (the School of Oriental and African Studies) in 1992. Since then, he has contributed to the development of research on Indonesian and Southeast Asian history. In 2008, he was appointed to the position of Leiden University Chair in the History of Dutch-Indonesian Relations at the Universitas Gadjah Mada, which he held until 2017. His publications include *Gagalnya Historiografi Indonesiasentris?!* (2006); *Perspektif Baru dalam Penulisan Sejarah Indonesia* (2008, 2nd edition 2013), edited with Henk Schulte Nordholt and Ratna Saptari; and *Sites, Bodies, and Stories: Imagining Indonesian History* (2015), edited with Susan Legêne and Henk Schulte Nordholt. His latest publication is *Praktik Kewarganegaraan di Indonesia dalam Perspektif Historiografis* (2019). He has published a number of articles in national and international journals.

Galuh Ambar Sasi is an assistant professor in the Education of History study programme at the Universitas Kristen Satya Wacana (UKSW) in Salatiga, Indonesia. She obtained her Bachelor's degree in the education of history from the Universitas Negeri Yogyakarta in 2005 and her Master's degree in history from the Universitas Gadjah Mada. She is mainly interested in collective memory and women's engagement in the Indonesian revolution.

Mawardi Umar is a lecturer in history at the Universitas Syiah Kuala in Banda Aceh, Indonesia. He received his Master's degree in history from the Universitas Gadjah Mada and Leiden University. His main research interest lies in Aceh. He has published several works, including *Mendukung Pertumbuhan Ekonomi di Daerah Modal: Bank Indonesia dalam Dinamika Perekonomian Aceh* (2021); *Menuju Universitas yang Mandiri dan Modern:*

60 Tahun Universitas Syiah Kuala (2021); *Menghadapi Gelombang Pasang di Serambi: Kontribusi Bersama untuk Aceh Setelah Tsunami 2004* (2018); *Mengadu Nasib di Kebun Karet: Nasib Buruh Perkebunan Karet di Aceh Timur, 1900-1939* (2016); and *Darul Islam Aceh: Pemberontak atau Pahlawan?* (2006).

Anne van der Veer is a former PhD candidate at the Leiden University Institute for History. She has examined the ways in which Chinese Indonesians navigated the Japanese occupation and the National Revolution in East Sumatra, Indonesia during the years 1942 to 1949. She currently works as a software engineer.

Abdul Wahid (editor) is chairperson of the Department of History, Faculty of Cultural Sciences at the Universitas Gadjah Mada. In 2009, he completed the Advanced Master's programme at Leiden University. He received his PhD in history from the University of Utrecht with the dissertation titled *From Revenue Farming to State Monopoly: The Political Economy of Taxation in Colonial Indonesia, Java c. 1816-1942*. He was a visiting lecturer at the School of Historical and Philosophical Studies of the University of Melbourne and was a research fellow at the Royal Netherlands Institute of Southeast Asian and Caribbean Studies (Koninklijk Instituut voor Taal, Land- en Volkenkunde, KITLV) in Leiden from June 2017 to April 2021. His main research interests lie in the socio-economic history of Indonesia and Southeast Asia, including colonialism, decolonization, violence and the formation of nation-states. His works have been published in a number of national and international journals. Recently, his PhD dissertation was translated into Bahasa Indonesia and published by UGM Press with the title *Politik Perpajakan Kolonial di Indonesia: Antara Eksploitasi dan Resistensi* (2021).

Yulianti (editor) is a lecturer in the Department of History, Faculty of Cultural Sciences at the Universitas Gadjah Mada. She is currently also teaching at the Center for Religions and Cross-Cultural Studies at the graduate school of the same university. She obtained her PhD in history in 2020 as part of a joint PhD project between the Institute for History at Leiden University and the Universitas Gadjah Mada. Her dissertation was titled *The Making of Buddhism in Modern Indonesia: South and Southeast Asian Networks and Agencies, 1900-1959*. Her research interests lie in Buddhism in maritime Southeast Asia, transnational history, women's history, and heritage and material culture studies.

Muhammad Yuanda Zara is a lecturer in the History Study Programme at the Universitas Negeri Yogyakarta (UNY). He obtained his Bachelor's degree from the Universitas Gadjah Mada in 2007 and his Master's degree from Leiden University (2010). With a dissertation titled *Voluntary Participation, State Involvement: Indonesian Propaganda in the Struggle for Maintaining Independence, 1945-1949*, he received his PhD from the University of Amsterdam in 2016. Recently his research interests have focused on colonialism and the Japanese occupation in Indonesia, the Indonesian revolution, media and propaganda, and Islam in twentieth-century Indonesia. His works have been published in such journals as *Media History, Southeast Asian Studies, BMGN-Low Countries Historical Review, Tijdschrift voor Geschiedenis, Bijdragen tot de Taal-, Land- en Volkenkunde, Wacana, Journal of Indonesian Islam, Al-Jami'ah: Journal of Islamic Studies, Advances in Southeast Asian Studies,* and *Studia Islamika.*

Index

Overview of publications resulting from the research programme Independence, Decolonization, Violence and War in Indonesia, 1945,-1950

Publications Amsterdam University Press

Gert Oostindie, Thijs Brocades Zaalberg, Eveline Buchheim, Esther Captain, Martijn Eickhoff, Roel Frakking, Azarja Harmanny, Meindert van der Kaaij, Jeroen Kemperman, Rémy Limpach, Bart Luttikhuis, Remco Raben, Peter Romijn, Onno Sinke, Fridus Steijlen, Stephanie Welvaart, Esther Zwinkels, *Over de grens. Nederlands extreem geweld in de Indonesische onafhankelijkheidsoorlog, 1945-1949*

Gert Oostindie, Thijs Brocades Zaalberg, Eveline Buchheim, Esther Captain, Martijn Eickhoff, Roel Frakking, Azarja Harmanny, Meindert van der Kaaij, Jeroen Kemperman, Rémy Limpach, Bart Luttikhuis, Remco Raben, Peter Romijn, Onno Sinke, Fridus Steijlen, Stephanie Welvaart, Esther Zwinkels, *Beyond the Pale. Dutch Extreme Violence in the Indonesian War of Independence*, 1945-1949

Abdul Wahid en Yulianti (red), *Onze Revolutie. Bloemlezing uit de Indonesische geschiedschrijving over de strijd voor de onafhankelijkheid, 1945-1949*

Esther Captain en Onno Sinke, *Het geluid van geweld. Bersiap en de dynamiek van geweld tijdens de eerste fase van de Indonesische revolutie, 1945-1946*

Esther Captain and Onno Sinke, *Resonance of Violence. Bersiap and the Dynamics of Violence in the First Phase of the Indonesian Revolution, 1945-1946*

Remco Raben en Peter Romijn, mmv Maarten van der Bent en Anne van Mourik, *Talen van geweld. Stilte, informatie en misleiding in de Indonesische onafhankelijkheidsoorlog, 1945-1949*

Remco Raben and Peter Romijn, with Maarten van der Bent and Anne van Mourik, *Tales of Violence. Dutch Management of Information in the Indonesian War of Independence, 1945-1949*

Jeroen Kemperman, Emma Keizer en Tom van den Berge, *Diplomatie en geweld. De internationale context van de Indonesische onafhankelijkheidsoorlog, 1945-1949*

Rémy Limpach, *Tasten in het duister. Inlichtingenstrijd tijdens de Indonesische onafhankelijkheidsoorlog, 1945-1949*

Rémy Limpach, *Stumbling in the Dark. The Battle for Intelligence in the Indonesian War of Independence, 1945-1949*

Azarja Harmanny, *Grof geschut. Artillerie en luchtstrijdkrachten in de Indonesische onafhankelijkheidsoorlog, 1945-1949*

Esther Zwinkels, *De klewang van Vrouwe Justitia. Recht en onrecht in de Indonesische onafhankelijkheidsoorlog, 1945-1949*

Esther Zwinkels, *The Harsh Sword of Lady Justice. Law and Impunity in the Indonesian War of Independence, 1945-1949*

Bambang Purwanto, Roel Frakking, Abdul Wahid, Gerry van Klinken, Martijn Eickhoff, Yulianti and Ireen Hoogenboom (eds), *Revolutionary worlds. Local perspectives and dynamics during the Indonesian independence war, 1945-1949*

Meindert van der Kaaij, *Een kwaad geweten. De worsteling met de Indonesische onafhankelijkheidsoorlog vanaf 1950*

Eveline Buchheim, Satrio Dwicahyo, Fridus Steijlen en Stephanie Welvaart, *Sporen vol betekenis. In gesprek met 'Getuigen & Tijdgenoten' over de Indonesische onafhankelijkheidsoorlog / Meniti Arti. Bertukar Makna bersama 'Saksi & Rekan Sezaman' tentang Perang Kemerdekaan Indonesia*

Van Rij en Stam. Rapporten van de Commissie van onderzoek naar beweerde excessen gepleegd door Nederlandse militairen in Indonesië, 1949-1954 (Bronnenpublicatie), ingeleid en bezorgd door Maarten van der Bent

Other publications

Thijs Brocades Zaalberg, Bart Luttikhuis en anderen, 'Extreem geweld tijdens dekolonisatieoorlogen in vergelijkend perspectief, 1945-1962' in: *BMGN – Low Countries Historical Review*, Volume 135 nr.2

Thijs Brocades Zaalberg en Bart Luttikhuis (eds), *Empire's Violent End. Comparing Dutch, British, and French Wars of Decolonization, 1945–1962*. Cornell University Press